Scott Hempling

Regulating Public Utility Performance

The Law of Market Structure, Pricing and Jurisdiction

Section of
Environment,
Energy, and Resources
AMERICAN BAR ASSOCIATION

Cover design by Amanda Fry/ABA Publishing.

The materials contained herein represent the views of the author in his individual capacity and should not be construed to be the views of the author's clients, or of the American Bar Association or the Section of Environment, Energy, and Resources, unless adopted pursuant to the bylaws of the Association.

Nothing contained in this book is to be considered as the rendering of legal advice for specific cases, and readers are responsible for obtaining such advice from their own legal counsel. This book is intended for educational and informational purposes only.

Printed in the United States of America.

17 16 15   5 4

Library of Congress Cataloging-in-Publication Data

Hempling, Scott, author.
   Regulating public utility performance : the law of market structure, pricing and jurisdiction / by Scott Hempling ; Section of Environment, Energy, and Resources, American Bar Association.
       pages cm
   Includes bibliographical references and index.
   ISBN 978-1-62722-292-1 (alk. paper)
1. Public utilities—Law and legislation—United States. 2. Public utilities—Rates—Law and legislation—United States. I. American Bar Association. Section of Environment, Energy, and Resources, sponsoring body. II. Title.
   KF2094.H46 2013
   343.7309—dc23

                                                                     2013030298

Discounts are available for books ordered in bulk. Special consideration is given to state bars, CLE programs, and other bar-related organizations. Inquire at ABA Publishing, American Bar Association, 321 N. Clark Street, Chicago, Illinois 60654-7598.

www.ShopABA.org

To my parents, Claire Hernick Hempling and Harold George Hempling, who taught me values and discipline.

SUMMARY OF CONTENTS

CONTENTS

xii   Contents

FIGURES

PREFACE

For over a century, the law of public utility regulation has supported and disciplined the nation's infrastructural industries: rail, trucking, electricity, gas, telecommunications and water. Regardless of industry or era, utility law has shared five features: its *mission* (to align private utility behavior with the public interest); its *diversity* (from state grants of exclusive franchises to federal constitutional protection of shareholder investment); its integration of *multiple professional fields* (accounting, economics, engineering and finance); its *sources* (constitutions, statutes, rules, adjudications, judicial review); and its *flexibility* (accommodating multiple market structures and public purposes). Using these features, utility law helps make trillions of dollars flow annually from consumers to utilities.

New political challenges are causing policymakers and practitioners to stretch regulation's principles and processes. Facing climate change, they ask: Should utilities and their customers become responsible for "greening" energy production and consumption? Debating universal service, they ask: Should we bring broadband to every home, and at what cost and whose cost? Concerned about privacy, they ask: Should consumers' private consumption of data be available to profit-seekers? These questions, and many others, expose two tensions: ideological (e.g., private vs. public ownership, government intervention vs. "free market"); and federal–state (e.g., Which aspects of utility service are "national," requiring uniform regulation, and which are "local," warranting state experimentation?).

With so many dollars and values at stake, this work seeks to provide readers with a common grasp of the powers, responsibilities and rights of all those who make or live with these trillion-dollar decisions: legislators and regulators, utilities and competitors, investors and consumers, workers and environmentalists, states and localities. To serve this educational purpose, I have organized the polyglot of legal sources from regulatory statutes, constitutional law, antitrust law, contract law and tort law, into four major areas:

- *Market structure:* Which entities are authorized to sell what products? What is the appropriate mix of monopoly and competitive markets?

- *Pricing:* What standards ensure that sellers are fairly compensated and customers not exploited?
- *Jurisdiction:* Given the multistate makeup of today's infrastructures, markets and providers, how do federal and state commissions interact when regulating the same utilities and the same transactions? How do commissions apply their 1930s-era statutes to modern challenges?
- *Corporate structure, mergers and acquisitions:* What business activities, conducted through what types of transactions, should exist within a utility's corporate family? How do mergers and acquisitions affect a utility's accountability to the public?

The present book addresses the first three areas: market structure, pricing and jurisdiction. A companion volume will address corporate structure, mergers and acquisitions.[1]

With the mastery made possible by this material, I hope the work can achieve three other goals.

Enable practitioners and decisionmakers to act effectively in all regulated industries. The physical, transactional and statutory specifics of a single utility industry can take years to master. As a result, many regulatory practitioners, both lawyers and non-lawyers, burrow into a single industry, even into sub-specialties like gas purchasing, electric transmission pricing or telecommunications mergers. But policymakers—legislators, commissioners and their staff—must address all industries and all specialties. While this work is not a substitute for in-depth works on specific industries (examples of which are cited throughout), its illustrations from multiple industries can help readers spread the successes and quarantine the failures.

Help non-lawyers become conversant with law. Every regulatory decision is a legal decision. It establishes powers, responsibilities or rights. It must account for precedents—the statutory and constitutional boundaries established by our predecessors—especially when seeking to stretch or change those boundaries. It must be built on facts and logic, arranged to satisfy the standards imposed by law. Anyone intending to make, influence, explain or defend a regulatory decision—any expert witness, advocate, commissioner, legislator—needs to know the law. For forty years, Alfred Kahn's great treatise, *The Economics of Regulation: Principles and Institutions,* has made lawyers literate in that foundational field. While the present work cannot claim to achieve Kahn's quality, it aspires to replicate its purpose: to bring legal literacy to non-lawyers.

Help prepare policymakers to adjust the law to accommodate technological change. By mastering regulatory law, we can spot its mismatches with our economic and social goals. A monopoly held for a century casts a long shadow into the next. Those working

---

1. Utilities can be owned by private investors; by government bodies at the local, state or federal level; or by consumer cooperatives. While many of the legal principles in this book can apply to all three categories, the focus is on the regulation of investor-owned utilities.

to introduce competition for broadband and smart grid, in electricity storage and energy conservation, in markets where the incumbent still controls the bottlenecks, need to understand the legal basis for that control and the appropriate ways to loosen it. Those who want to head the other way, toward a to return to traditional monopoly regulation and away from the risks of competition, also need to know which principles to retain and which to amend.

In short, my purpose is to present the legal fundamentals that practitioners need to make public-spirited proposals and utility regulators need to make public-spirited decisions. The purpose here is neither to support nor to critique those decisions, but instead to describe breadth of and boundaries on regulators' discretion to make them. While the book aims for neutrality, it is shaped by this perspective: The purpose of regulation is to regulate—to (a) define standards of performance, (b) hold utilities accountable for their performance, and (c) compensate them consistent with their performance. And because law both authorizes and restricts, this book describes both the legal means by which regulators can act and the legal limits on their actions.

My book of essays, *Preside or Lead: The Attributes and Actions of Effective Regulators*, describes the personal qualities, institutional structures and political forces that support, and undermine, regulation's public interest mission. That book's premise is clear from its title: the public interest is best served by those who lead. For readers who accept that role, I hope the present work supports their leadership with substantive muscle.

ACKNOWLEDGMENTS

Three decades of immersion in public utility law have exposed me to countless individuals, from court of appeals judges to law students, all of whom have helped me learn the body of law presented here. I wish I could thank each one personally, but there are too many.

I learned much of the foundation of regulatory law as a new lawyer nearly thirty years ago at Spiegel & McDiarmid, especially from Cindy Bogorad, Dan Davidson, Dan Guttman, Frances Francis, Jim Horwood, Robert Jablon, Robert McDiarmid and the late George Spiegel and David Straus. Having spent most of my career in electricity, I needed a tutor in telecommunications. Tillman Lay performed that role admirably, offering case examples, critiquing my drafts and contributing substance to several subchapters. His mastery of his field, both microscopic and telescopic, was indispensable.

Special thanks go to those professional colleagues who provided peer review, insights and background resources: Alan Barak, Christopher Barr, Peter Bradford, Nancy Brockway, Sarah Bronin, Nick Brown, Miguel Campo, Ron Cerniglia, Judge Richard Cudahy (U.S. Court of Appeals for the Seventh Circuit), Erin Cullum, Jennifer Dickman, Dianne Dusman, Michael Dworkin, Carolyn Elefant, Natara Feller, Eric Filipink, Bob Finkelstein, Matthew Freedman, Craig Glazer, Hayley Goodson, Billy Jack Gregg, Marcel Hawiger, Lucas Head, Stephen Hill, Seth Hollander, Richard Hitt, Peter Hopkins, Bill Julian, John Kwoka, Kurt Janson, Larry Landis, David Lapp, Stephen Littlechild, Thomas Long, Sam Loudenslager, Brandon Pierce, Sonny Popowsky, Jason Rauch, Cheryl Roberto, Dina Sarbanes, Shawn Shurden, Thomas Stanton, Scott Strauss, Robert Stumberg, Ingrid White, Myung Yi and George Young. The students in my public utility law seminar at Georgetown University Law Center were always perceptive contributors to my thinking.

Jessica Austin de Vides, my long-time administrator, organized our internal team of reviewers and law clerks with uncompromising commitment to quality and to the cause of effective regulation. Margaret Austin brought her eagle eye to the copyediting. Leah Goodwin added her unmatched skill in document preparation with patience and poise. Elizabeth Watson was a dream of a diagram-maker. Colin Beckman, Conrad Bolston,

Dylan Borchers, Raffi Melanson, Jessica Nyman and Bruce Strong checked sources and cites expertly. Of course, any errors are mine only.

The American Bar Association has been a welcoming and committed partner. Megan McCulloch and Peter Wright, leaders of the Book Publishing Board within the ABA's Section of Environment, Energy and Resources, supported this project from the beginning and led the peer-review process, which included anonymous reviewers whom I thank as well. Leslie Keros, Executive Editor at the ABA, provided patient, professional guidance throughout, while the ABA's Amelia Stone added her experienced eye on dissemination.

For whatever clarity and succinctness the reader finds in my writing, much responsibility lies with my high school English teacher, W. Benjamin Hutto; my college thesis advisor, Edward Pauley; and Neil Larson, the creator of the near-magical software program Maxthink. José Guadalupe Gómez Argueta, Cristiann Vides López, Debra Knopman, Jane Stewart and Ann Turpin were constant reminders of what creativity, craftsmanship and sweat can produce.

Carlito Caliboso, David Hadley, Larry Landis, Brandon Presley and Judy Sheldrew, five of the most dedicated commissioners I have worked with, were powerful reminders of what public actors can do with legal knowledge. Irving Like, David Penn and Harry Trebing pressed me to make public service the core of my career. My wife, Margaret Flaherty, the most honest communicator I know, has persuaded juries with her prosecutorial integrity and now enchants collectors with her ceramics. Her confidence in and support for my work are gifts from some sacred place.

ABOUT THE AUTHOR

Scott Hempling has taught the law of public utilities to a generation of regulators and practitioners. As an attorney, he has assisted clients from all industry sectors—regulators, utilities, consumer interests, regional transmission organizations, independent competitors and environmental organizations. As an expert witness, he has testified numerous times before state commissions and before committees of the United States Congress and the legislatures of Arkansas, California, Maryland, Minnesota, Nevada, North Carolina, South Carolina, Vermont and Virginia. As a seminar presenter and conference speaker, he has appeared throughout the United States and in Canada, Central America, Germany, Italy, India, Jamaica, Mexico, New Zealand and Nigeria.

His articles have appeared in *The Electricity Journal*, *Public Utilities Fortnightly*, *ElectricityPolicy.com* and other professional publications, covering such topics as mergers and acquisitions, the introduction of competition into formerly monopolistic markets, corporate restructuring, ratemaking, utility investments in nonutility businesses, transmission planning, renewable energy and state–federal jurisdictional issues. From 2006 to 2011, he was the Executive Director of the National Regulatory Research Institute.

Hempling is an adjunct professor at Georgetown University Law Center, where he teaches courses on public utility law and on regulatory litigation. He is the author of *Preside or Lead? The Attributes and Actions of Effective Regulators* (2013).

Hempling received a B.A. *cum laude* in (1) Economics and Political Science and (2) Music from Yale University, where he was awarded a Continental Grain Fellowship and a Patterson research grant. He received a J.D. *magna cum laude* from Georgetown University Law Center, where he was the recipient of an *American Jurisprudence* award for Constitutional Law. More detail is available at www.scotthemplinglaw.com.

ABBREVIATIONS

AFOR	alternative forms of regulation
AFUDC	allowance for funds used during construction
AMI	advanced metering infrastructure
ARPU	average revenue per user
BOC	Bell Operating Company
CEI	comparably efficient interconnection
CLEC	competitive local exchange carrier
CMRS	commercial mobile radio service
COLR	carrier of last resort
CPE	customer premises equipment
CWIP	construction work in progress
DPT	delivered price test
DSL	digital subscriber line
DSM	demand side management
EAS	extended area service
ERO	electric reliability organization
EWG	exempt wholesale generator
FCC	Federal Communications Commission
FERC	Federal Energy Regulatory Commission
FPA	Federal Power Act
FPC	Federal Power Commission
FTC	Federal Trade Commission
HHI	Herfindahl-Hirschman Index
ICC	Interstate Commerce Commission
ILEC	incumbent local exchange carrier

ISO	independent system operator
ISP	Internet service provider
LD	long distance
LDC	local distribution company
LEC	local exchange carrier
MFJ	Modification of Final Judgment
MOPR	minimum offer price rule
NEPA	National Environmental Protection Act
NERC	North American Electric Reliability Council
NGA	Natural Gas Act of 1938
NGPA	Natural Gas Policy Act of 1978
NIST	National Institute of Standards and Technology
O&M	operations and maintenance
OMS	outage management system
ONA	open network architecture
OSS	operations support system
PCA	protective connecting arrangement
PANS	pretty amazing new stuff
PGA	purchased gas adjustment
POTS	plain old telephone service
PUHCA	Public Utility Holding Company Act of 1935
PURPA	Public Utility Regulatory Policies Act of 1978
QF	qualifying facility
RBOC	Regional Bell Operating Company
ROE	return on equity
RTO	regional transmission organization
SAIDI	system average interruption duration index
SAIFI	system average interruption frequency index
SEC	Securities and Exchange Commission
SLC	subscriber line charge
SQI	service quality index
TDUs	transmission dependent utilities
TELRIC	total element long-run incremental cost
UNE	unbundled network element
USF	universal service fund
VoIP	voice over Internet protocol

CHAPTER ONE

Regulatory Law

Purposes, Powers, Rights and Responsibilities

The law of regulation serves the purpose of regulation. This chapter begins by explaining that purpose, as viewed from varied perspectives. It then describes the specific purpose of utility regulatory law: to define the powers, responsibilities, rights and procedures that direct, guide and constrain the actors and agencies with a stake in utility regulation. The chapter closes by describing the subjects and sources of regulatory law and relating those topics to the organization of this work.

1.A. Purposes of regulation

Regulation's purpose varies with one's perspective. Economists see regulation as a means to exploit economies of scale from natural monopolies while reducing economic loss in markets with imperfections; imperfections such as high entry barriers, unique products and insufficient information. Absent regulation, those imperfections can lead to destructive competition, unanticipated scarcity, insufficient innovation, negative or positive "externalities" arising from "public goods," and the "deadweight" economic loss that results when demand and supply curves intersect suboptimally.[1]

Then there are perspectives of interest groups: consumers ("Protect us from abuse of monopoly power"), shareholders ("Set rates that allow us to earn a fair return on investment"), lenders ("Ensure cash flow sufficient to pay down debt"), competitors of the incumbent utility ("Create conditions allowing new entrants to compete and win on the merits"), low-income advocates ("Make essential services affordable"), environmental advocates ("Minimize environmental damage associated with production and consumption"), rural residents ("Ensure universal service") and large industrial customers ("Set rates that allow us to compete globally"). Each of these perspectives occupies a narrow band on the private interest spectrum. Some are conflicting. A regulator will find it hard to honor them all.

Overlapping with interest group perspectives are political perspectives. Depending on one's views, regulation reduces inequities in wealth; protects the vulnerable from deceptive sales practices and price-gouging; "eliminat[es] price as the basis of exchange" in resources that have special societal value (such as worker safety, cultural treasures and endangered species);[2] or responds when people "demand more for society than any individual will seek for herself as a consumer."[3] These purposes too can come into conflict—with each

1. *See* Frederick M. Scherer & David Ross, Industrial Market Structure and Economic Performance 21–23 (1990); Richard Pierce & Ernest Gellhorn, Regulated Industries 38–62 (1999); Joseph P. Tomain & Richard D. Cudahy, Energy Law in a nutshell 26–32 (2004).
2. *See* Sidney A. Shapiro & Joseph P. Tomain, Regulatory law and Policy: Cases and Materials 58–62 (2003). This citation is not meant to imply that the authors have that perspective or exclude other perspectives; it is one among many they identify.
3. Lisa Bressman, Edward Rubin & Kevin Stack, The Regulatory State 62, 79–87 (2010). Again, this perspective is only one among many identified by the authors.

other and with a view that regulation is less able to solve these problems than are unregulated markets.

Given these possibilities of conflict, some describe the role of regulation as "balancing" the interests of shareholders and consumers. A balance presumes opposition of interests. But customers' and shareholders' legitimate interests—reasonable prices, reasonable returns, satisfied customers and satisfied shareholders—are consistent and mutually reinforcing. High-quality performance and efficient consumption benefit multiple interests: consumers, shareholders, bondholders, employees, the environment and the nation's infrastructure. What regulation must balance is not competing private interests but competing components of the public interest—e.g., long-term versus short-term needs, affordable rates versus efficient price signals, environmental values versus global competitiveness.[4]

For the practitioner and decisionmaker seeking clarity of purpose, the best single lodestar is the statutory language. Regulatory statutes commonly direct regulators to act "in the public interest." This command necessarily presumes that private interests, absent regulation's constraints and inducements, will diverge from the public interest.[5] Universal, reliable, safe service at reasonable rates doesn't happen by itself. In short, regulation is necessary to align private behavior with the public interest. Regulation defines standards for performance, then assigns consequences, positive and negative, for that performance. The purpose of regulation is performance.

1.B. Purposes of regulatory law

Regulatory law establishes the powers, responsibilities and rights that achieve regulation's purpose. How does law distribute these powers, responsibilities and rights among those with a stake in regulatory outcomes?[6]

1.B.1. Powers

Legislatures receive their powers from constitutions. Using those powers, they establish the responsibilities and rights of citizens and businesses. Legislatures also delegate a portion of their powers to commissions by enacting statutes spelling out duties, procedures, conditions and instructions. Some state commissions also receive powers directly from

---

4. *Cf.* Columbia Gas Transmission Corp. v. FERC, 750 F.2d 105, 112 (D.C. Cir. 1984) (interpreting statute to mean that "Commission is vested with wide discretion to balance competing equities against the backdrop of the public interest").

5. The premise is neither universally shared nor permanently held. Policymakers revisit regulatory statutes when they perceive changes in the facts supporting the original enactment. That has been the case with each of the federal statutes discussed in this book, and many state statutes. The wisdom of regulatory statutes, and their changes, is a subject of continuous debate. The point here is that when a regulatory statute does exist, it exists because its enactors concluded that constraints and inducements were necessary to align private actions with the public interest.

6. Experienced lawyers are welcome to skip this short section, but non-lawyers and new lawyers will benefit from understanding how law organizes its multiple components to produce public interest results.

their state constitutions.[7] Regulated entities can receive powers, too, such as when statutes grant utilities the power to take private land by eminent domain[8] or to cut off customers who violate tariff provisions.

A commission's regulatory power has substantive scope, also called "jurisdiction." A commission's jurisdiction, whether established by statute or constitution, specifies the actors and actions to be regulated. A statute can either order or authorize. It can order a commission to take specified actions under specified circumstances, such as issuing by a specified date a rule on transmission pricing or area-code renumbering, or acting on a merger application or rate increase request. Or the statute can merely empower the commission to act, implicitly leaving the commission with discretion not to act. The commission's discretionary power can be exercised affirmatively, such as by issuing rules on corporate structure or instituting enforcement proceedings on service quality, or reactively, such as by processing a utility's merger application or a customer's complaint seeking a rate decrease.

1.B.2. Responsibilities

A commission's responsibilities are those mandated by its statute: its specified duties to act affirmatively or to react expediently. But a commission's responsibilities are not limited by these mandates. It has an obligation to use its discretionary powers actively, to pursue the statute's public interest purposes. Failure to exercise this discretion brings, in the rare case, a writ of mandamus;[9] in the more common case, legislative pressure through oversight hearings and budget amendments.

Utilities have responsibilities also: to provide the obligatory services defined by their franchise agreements and statutes, to maintain quality levels defined by commission rule, and to comply with tariffs ordered or approved by commissions. Utilities have discretion in how they carry out their responsibilities;[10] but their failure to exercise that discretion timely and prudently can bring investigations, penalties and cost disallowances.[11] And

---

7. *See, e.g.,* Ariz. Corp. Comm'n v. Arizona, 830 P.2d 807 (Ariz. 1992) (finding that state commission could limit interaffiliate transactions although no statute granted that power; authority came from the state constitutional provision authorizing commission to set retail rates).
8. *See infra* Chapter 2.E on eminent domain.
9. A writ of mandamus is an extraordinary order from a court to a public official or agency to take specified action. *See, e.g.,* Cnty. of Santa Fe v. Pub. Serv. Co. of N.M., 311 F.3d 1031 (10th Cir. 2002) (reversing lower court's denial of mandamus sought by landowners against county; county had a "non-discretionary" duty to stop utility's unlawful construction of power line); N. States Power Co. v. U.S. Dep't of Energy, 128 F.3d 754, 758–59 (D.C. Cir. 1997) (granting writ of mandamus precluding DOE from excusing its failure to accept nuclear waste timely; the "remedy of mandamus is a drastic one, to be invoked only in extraordinary situations; . . . only if (1) the plaintiff has a clear right to relief; (2) the defendant has a clear duty to act; and (3) there is no other adequate remedy available to plaintiff") (quoting other sources).
10. *See infra* the discussion of "management prerogative" at Chapter 2.D.3.d.
11. *See, e.g.,* Investigation into the Reliability and Quality of the Electric Distribution Service of Potomac Electric Power Company, Order No. 84564; Case No. 9240, 295 P.U.R.4th 373 (Md. Pub. Serv. Comm'n, Dec. 21, 2011) (imposing $1 million fine for utility's poor outage performance, including "inconsistent and sometimes contradictory tree trimming practices over a decade," and "failure to conduct periodic

customers have responsibilities: to pay for service timely, to refrain from actions that endanger or disrupt service and to cooperate with the utility in solving service problems.[12]

1.B.3. Rights

Statutes and constitutions create rights in both regulated entities and those whom regulation protects.

Customers have the substantive right to receive service at commission-set quality levels, at a "just and reasonable" rate authorized by the commission.[13] They also have the procedural rights to intervene in commission proceedings and to petition courts for judicial review of commission decisions.

Utilities have the substantive right to charge rates that provide a reasonable opportunity to earn a fair return[14] and to receive commission approval of corporate structures, mergers, acquisitions and reorganizations that satisfy statutory standards.[15] They also have the procedural rights to present facts that support their substantive rights and to confront opposing witnesses, along with the right to judicial review.

Landowners have rights—to protest when the utility proposes to lay pipes and powerlines on their property and to be paid the constitutionally required "just compensation" if they lose.[16]

Where statutes or commissions have authorized competition in previously monopoly markets, the *new competitors* have rights, such as electric generators' right to non-discriminatory transmission access and competitive local exchange carriers' right to buy or rent "unbundled network elements."[17]

1.B.4. Procedures

Policymakers act in multiple ways. They gather information, pass statutes, promulgate rules, issue orders that adjudicate disputes, and bring enforcement actions. These actions must conform to procedural law, as established by statutes, the Constitution and a commission's

---

inspections of sub-transmission and distribution lines or to direct after-storm inspections or patrols"). *See also infra* the discussion of service quality at Chapter 2.D.

12. *See, e.g.,* Weber v. Union Light, Heat and Power Co., Case No. 2000-066, 2000 Ky. PUC LEXIS 1342 (Ky. Pub. Serv. Comm'n, Aug. 4, 2000) (utility's commission-approved tariff makes customer responsible for "maintenance and upkeep of service line on the customer's side from the point of delivery"); Peoples Natural Gas Company's Request to Establish a Tariff for Repairing and Replacing Farm-Tap Lines, Dkt. No. G-011/M-91-989, 1993 Minn. PUC LEXIS 92 (Minn. Pub. Serv. Comm'n May 25, 1993) (describing customer's obligation to allow utility to inspect taps for leaks).

13. *See infra* Chapter 2.D on service quality; Chapters 6 and 7 on cost-based and market-based rates, respectively; and Chapter 9 on the filed rate doctrine.

14. *See infra* Chapter 6.B on the statutory and constitutional mandates for rates that compensate utilities commensurate with their performance and risk.

15. Corporate structure will be covered in the companion volume.

16. *See infra* Chapter 2.E on eminent domain and Chapter 6.B on the Fifth Amendment's guarantee of "just compensation."

17. *See infra* Chapter 4.B on "unbundling."

own rules. Procedural law induces accountability, by empowering the public to observe and influence agency decisionmaking, and by authorizing courts to review the results. Procedures protect against arbitrariness—actions lacking in fact, logic or legal authority—whether those actions are by regulators setting rates, imposing penalties or passing on mergers; or by utilities taking private land or cutting off service. When a commission sets rates, for example, it is exercising a legislative function, because the legislature could set rates directly. While the ratesetting function is legislative, the procedures are often adjudicatory, requiring expert testimony under oath, cross-examination, orders based on substantive evidence and prohibitions on *ex parte* contacts. This work does not cover procedural law. Its focus is regulators' statutory powers, what they do with those powers, and the constitutional limits on those powers.[18]

1.C. Subjects and sources of regulatory law
1.C.1. Subjects
Regulatory jurisdiction is defined by nouns and verbs: actors and actions, regulated companies performing regulated activities. Examples of *regulated actors*—the nouns—include: for electricity, generating companies, transmission owners, local distribution companies, vertically integrated companies that combine some or all of those functions, regional transmission organizations, and holding companies; for gas, producers, pipelines, local distribution companies, marketers and storage providers; and for telecommunications, local exchange companies (incumbent and competitive, national and rural), wireless providers, equipment sellers and Internet service providers. Examples of *regulated actions*—the verbs—include: selling at wholesale or retail; merging, acquiring, consolidating or disposing of companies or assets; issuing equity and debt securities; and acquiring and building on land.

To deal with these actors and actions, to perform the regulatory function of aligning private actions with the public interest, legislatures and commissions have created substantive legal principles in four areas.

Market structure: Who has a right to sell which products and own which facilities? How easy is entry and exit? Are customers served best—in terms of efficiency, innovation and accountability—by a competitive market or a monopoly market? These are questions of market structure, addressed in Part 1. Its four chapters discuss the responsibilities and rights of the traditional regulated monopoly, including the obligation to serve, quality of service, the power of eminent domain and limits on liability for negligence (Chapter 2); the process of authorizing competition to allow entry by newcomers (Chapter 3); the distinct step of ensuring that authorized competition becomes effective competition, by

---

18.   There are, of course, numerous texts on administrative law, including the law of procedure. *See, e.g.*, STEPHEN G. BREYER & RICHARD B. STEWART, ADMINISTRATIVE LAW AND REGULATORY POLICY (1979); SIDNEY A. SHAPIRO & JOSEPH P. TOMAIN, REGULATORY POLICY: CASES AND MATERIALS (2003); LISA BRESSMAN, EDWARD RUBIN & KEVIN STACK, THE REGULATORY STATE (2010).

"unbundling" competitive from noncompetitive services and by reducing entry barriers (Chapter 4); and then monitoring the new markets to prevent anti-competitive behavior, such as price squeeze, predatory pricing, tying and market manipulation (Chapter 5).

Pricing: Prices, set properly—that is, consistent with the statutory "just and reasonable" standard and the Constitution's "just compensation" mandate—both compensate the seller for its performance and induce customers to consume efficiently. Part 2 addresses pricing's many facets. In noncompetitive markets, regulators set the prices based on some version of cost (Chapter 6). In markets that allow competitors but that are still subject to a "just and reasonable" statute, some commissions allow sellers to set prices on their own—so-called "market pricing"—subject to regulatory screening and monitoring (Chapter 7). Then there are three longstanding restrictions on sellers' pricing discretion: the ban on undue discrimination (Chapter 8), the requirement to charge only the "filed rate" (Chapter 9), and the ban on retroactive ratemaking (Chapter 10). A fourth feature of regulated rates is the *Mobile-Sierra* doctrine, an interpretation of federal regulatory statutes that defines when regulators may let parties out of their contracts (Chapter 11).

Jurisdiction—Federal, state and future: Our nation's founders gave us two levels of government. Each level makes law through legislatures, agencies and courts. As a result, regulators and utilities are accountable to six fora simultaneously: state legislatures (which might also delegate franchising powers to municipalities), Congress, state agencies, federal agencies, state courts, and federal courts. With technological advances, utility–customer transactions that once were mostly intrastate have become interstate, complicating the relationship between federal and state regulation. How federal and state decisionmakers share the same regulatory road, without burning brakes, grinding gears or colliding, is the subject of Chapter 12. The present book concludes with Chapter 13, which identifies regulation's current uncertainties—uncertainties arising when statutes drafted under one set of industry facts must address new industry facts.

Corporate structure, mergers and acquisitions: Mergers, acquisitions, divestitures, product diversification, territorial expansion, holding company structures, interaffiliate transactions, and issuances of debt and equity—these actions affect everything else: market structure, pricing, service quality, financial strength and competitive viability. They will be the subject of a separate volume.

1.C.2. Sources
Decisions affecting market structure, pricing, corporate structure, control changes and financial structure are made by government and private actors. Their actions are authorized, directed, guided and confined by substantive statutory law and constitutional law.

Substantive statutory law establishes (1) the regulator's duties and powers; (2) the sellers' and buyers' obligations, rights and powers; and (3) each player's remedies against the others. The range of substantive law looks like an entire law school curriculum: specific substantive statutes like the Interstate Commerce Act, Federal Power Act, Natural Gas Act and Communications Act and their state-level counterparts; and more general legal subjects like antitrust law, torts, contracts and property law.

Constitutional law protects parties by defining and limiting the government's powers. The Commerce Clause authorizes Congress to act, but confines those actions to matters involving or affecting interstate commerce. The "dormant" Commerce Clause restricts states' powers to regulate, and discriminate against, interstate commerce. The Contract Clause restricts states' powers to impair existing contracts. The Takings Clause prohibits government from "taking" private property without paying the owner "just compensation." The Supremacy Clause allows Congress to preempt states from enacting or applying state laws inconsistently with congressional intent. The Due Process Clause requires fair hearing procedures and applies the Takings Clause to the states. State constitutional law makes an occasional appearance also—especially in the minority of states whose regulatory commission was created by state constitution rather than statute.

Procedural law also plays a role, establishing procedures for making decisions and resolving grievances.

The relationship among subjects, sources, decisionmakers, decisions, regulated actors and regulated actions is displayed in Figure 1. The citizenry's desire to involve regulators in market structure, sales and other matters leads to statutes, which combine with pre-existing general law and constitutional boundaries to create a body of law—the body discussed in this work. That body of law is expressed by the various regulatory decision-makers through statutes, orders, rules and other means. Those decisions apply to the actions of regulated actors, as those actions and actors are specified by the regulatory decisions.

Figure 1
Decisionmakers Use Law to Regulate Actors and Their Actions

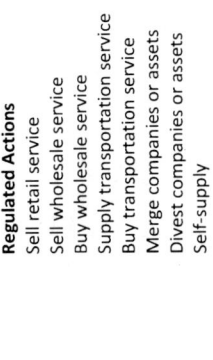

Legal Sources

Industry-Specific Statutes
Natural Gas Act
Natural Gas Policy Act
Public Utility Regulatory Policies Act
Federal Power Act
Communications Act
State counterparts

General Law
Antitrust
Bankruptcy
Consumer protection
Contracts
Eminent domain
Property
Tort
Administrative procedure

Constitutional Provisions
Commerce Clause
Takings Clause
Due Process Clause
Supremacy Clause
Contract Clause
Compact Clause
First Amendment
Tenth Amendment

Regulatory Subjects
Market structure
Sales of service
Corporate structure
Financial structure
Quality of service
Eminent domain

Regulatory Decisionmakers
Congress
State legislatures
FERC
FCC
State commissions
Federal courts
State courts

Regulatory Decisions
Legislation
Agency adjudication
Agency rulemaking
Agency enforcement
Judicial review

Regulated Actors
Vertically integrated utility
Distribution-only utility
Generation-only company
Transmission-only utility
Independent marketer
Incumbent local exchange carrier
Competitive local exchange carrier
Holding company
Regional transmission organization
Pipeline

Regulated Actions
Sell retail service
Sell wholesale service
Buy wholesale service
Supply transportation service
Buy transportation service
Merge companies or assets
Divest companies or assets
Self-supply

PART ONE

Market Structure
From Monopolies to Competition—
Who Can Sell What to Whom?

A market is a place where sellers and buyers meet to exchange goods or services for value. A market is defined by geography and product, viewed from the customer's perspective: vegetarian restaurants in downtown Baltimore, non-firm wholesale electricity in New England, firm transportation of wholesale gas in the Midwest, wireless service in Wisconsin. A market can also have a time element, when time is essential to the consumer: restaurants serving Sunday brunch, taxi service available after extra-inning baseball, firm gas transportation needed for winter weekdays.

Market structure, in turn, describes (a) the geographic area in which transactions occur; (b) the products and services being sold in that geographic area; (c) the identities, characteristics and market shares of the sellers and buyers of those products and services in that geographic area; and (d) the entry costs and entry barriers, including any "bottleneck facilities"—assets essential for competition, controlled by one competitor but not economically duplicable by other competitors.

In the abstract, there are three types of market structures: perfect competition (many sellers, with none able to influence price or supply because customers can freely shop); monopoly (single seller able to control price and supply); and oligopoly (small number of sellers able to influence price and supply). The same concepts exist from the buyer side: Monopsony and oligopsony are markets with a single buyer or few buyers, respectively. In reality, the spectrum from perfect competition to monopoly or monopsony has many possible points. A given market's location on that spectrum depends on facts: the number of buyers and sellers, their relative shares of the sales made, their control of resources essential to competitive viability (such as raw materials and transportation), buyers' access to alternatives, and the ease with which sellers can enter and exit.

Given this range of possibilities, policymakers use law to shape market structures to their preferences. If they prefer a monopoly structure, they enact laws and rules that determine its features: the process for granting the franchise; the franchisee's powers, responsibilities and rights; the factors, if any, allowing entry by alternative suppliers; and the criteria for revoking and transferring the franchise. If policymakers prefer competition, they use law to specify who is eligible to compete in which product markets, what quality and safety standards competitors must meet, what actions constitute unfair competition or consumer abuse, and what penalties will follow.

These policy preferences can change. For most of the 20th century, utility service was dominated by monopolies—often vertically integrated entities that controlled the final sale to the consumer and the inputs to that sale. To convert these monopoly markets into potentially competitive markets requires legal change: removing statutory barriers to competition, allocating and pricing access to "bottleneck facilities," defining unfair competition and creating the enforcement tools necessary to prevent it.

Part 1 describes the law that supports these markets' structures and policymakers' efforts to convert them. Chapter 2 describes the traditional monopoly model. That model comprises the seven legal dimensions that define the powers, responsibilities and rights of the utility and its consumers: exclusive service territory, obligation to serve, consent to regulation, quality of service, the power of eminent domain, limited liability for negligence, and the right to charge "just and reasonable" rates.

The ensuing chapters then describe the three legal steps necessary to convert a traditional monopoly market into a competitive market. The first step, discussed in Chapter 3, is to authorize competition: by amending the statutes that prohibited competition and by determining the right competition analog for each of the traditional monopoly's seven dimensions. But authorizing competition does not guarantee effective competition. Chapter 4 therefore discusses the actions regulators take—"unbundling" competitive from noncompetitive services and reducing entry barriers in the markets for competitive services—to prevent the incumbent from blocking the new competitors. And because every zealous competitor aspires to be a monopoly, successful conversion requires a third step: monitoring markets to prevent the behaviors that weaken competition. That is the subject of Chapter 5.

Together, these four chapters reflect not only the legal developments of the past half century, but also today's world: a layering of traditional monopolies, effective competition, potential competition, and competitors striving to dominate competition, all made continuously unpredictable by changes in technology, customer preferences and political directions.

CHAPTER TWO
The Traditional Utility Monopoly

[F]ar from affecting the public injuriously, [the government-granted franchise] has become one of the most important agencies of civilization for the promotion of the public convenience and the public safety.[1]

For most of the twentieth century, the market structure faced by most retail consumers of electricity, gas, telecommunications and water was a monopoly. The incumbent provider was a vertically integrated company, government-selected, providing prescribed services within a defined territory at approved prices. Supporting this market infrastructure was a legal infrastructure, called a franchise: a "special privilege," granted by the state government to the utility, to provide defined services subject to defined obligations.[2]

The franchise relationship comprises rights, obligations, powers and protections, all designed to align the incumbent's self-interest with the public interest. It typically has seven distinct dimensions:

1. *Exclusive retail franchise*: The utility's right to be the sole provider of a government-prescribed service within a state-defined service territory.
2. *Obligation to serve*: The utility's obligation to serve all customers in that service territory, without undue discrimination.
3. *Consent to regulation*: The utility's consent to all reasonable regulation.
4. *Quality of service*: The utility's obligation to meet service quality standards established by the regulator.
5. *Power of eminent domain*: The utility's power to take private property when necessary to satisfy its public service obligation.
6. *Limit on liability*: The utility's protection from lawsuits for ordinary negligence.

---

1. New Orleans Gas Co. v. La. Light Co., 115 U.S. 650, 669 (1885).
2. *See id.* at 669 (describing a franchise as "belonging to the government, to be granted, for the accomplishment of public objects, to whomsoever, and upon what terms it pleases"); Bank of Augusta v. Earle, 38 U.S. (13 Pet.) 519, 595 (1839) (describing franchises as "special privileges conferred by government upon individuals, and which do not belong to the citizens of the country generally of common right"). Courts also have distinguished a "franchise" from a "license." In *McPhee & McGinnity Co. v. Union Pac. R.R. Co.*, 158 F. 5, 10 (8th Cir. 1907), the Court explained that while a franchise is

    [a] right or privilege which is essential to the performance of the general function or purpose of the grantee, and which is and can be granted by the sovereignty alone, such as the right or privilege of a corporation to operate an ordinary or commercial railroad, a street railroad, city waterworks or gasworks, and to collect tolls therefor, . . . [a license is a] right or privilege not essential to the general function or purpose of the grantee, and of such a nature that a private party might grant a like right or privilege upon his property, such as a temporary or revocable permission to occupy or use a portion of some public ground, highway, or street. . . .

7. *Just and reasonable rates*: The utility's right to charge rates set by the regulator, designed to provide a reasonable opportunity to earn a fair return on equity investment.

This Chapter discusses the first six dimensions of the monopoly franchise and their many variations. Chapters 3, 4 and 5 address policymakers' efforts to introduce competition into these historically monopoly markets. Just and reasonable ratemaking will occupy Chapters 6–11.

2.A. Exclusive retail franchise

A retail franchise is exclusive when the state (a) defines a geographic area, (b) prohibits retail competition for a particular set of services within that area, and (c) appoints a company to be the sole seller of those services. While the term "exclusive" sounds absolute, it is a theme with variations. After illustrating exclusivity granted expressly by statute, we discuss seven variations. Each variation injects uncertainty or impermanence. The ultimate in impermanence is the state's power to revoke a franchise and transfer it to a better performer.

2.A.1. Exclusivity express in statute

South Dakota's statute grants an electric utility company the sole right to serve in its assigned territory, permanently:

> Each electric utility has the exclusive right to provide electric service at retail at each and every location where it is serving a customer as of March 21, 1975, and to each and every present and future customer in its assigned service area.[3]

For existing and new customers, the incumbent utility is the only option.

Until when? Legislatures have three options and a variation on them. First, where the statute grants exclusivity with no express term limit (the South Dakota situation), exclusivity lasts until the Legislature changes the statute. Second, the statute could fix the term; Nevada's statute prescribes 50 years.[4] Third, rather than fixing the term, the statute could authorize the Commission to set the term, thus implicitly or explicitly allowing rivals to compete periodically to be the next franchisee. (*See* the discussion of franchise competition at Chapter 2.A.2.f below.) Finally, each of these approaches could authorize the

---

3.   S.D. CODIFIED LAWS § 49-34A-42.
4.   *See* NEV. REV. STAT. § 709.210 ("If, upon the hearing of the application, it appears to the satisfaction of the board of county commissioners that the applicant is engaged in the business of furnishing electric light, heat or power within two or more counties of this state and that the granting of the franchise is in the best interests of the residents of the county, the board of county commissioners shall thereupon grant the franchise for a term not exceeding 50 years.").

Commission to revoke the franchise, or eliminate exclusivity, for inadequate performance, as discussed in Chapter 2.A.3 below.

Why do statutes grant exclusivity? Most frequently, policymakers grant an exclusive franchise to serve a particular product market when they determine, or assume, that the product market is a "natural monopoly." Judge Posner provides a useful definition of "natural monopoly":

> The term does not refer to the actual number of sellers in a market but to the relationship between demand and the technology of supply. If the entire demand within a relevant market can be satisfied at lowest cost by one firm rather than by two or more, the market is a natural monopoly, whatever the actual number of firms in it.[5]

A "natural monopoly" is not a utility company with a monopoly; it is a market with particular demand and supply characteristics. Those characteristics cause policymakers to seek ways to avoid wasteful competition. As the U.S. Supreme Court explained, discussing local distribution of natural gas:

> [B]y the time natural gas became a widely marketable commodity, the States had learned from chastening experience that public streets could not be continually torn up to lay competitors' pipes, that investments in parallel delivery systems for different fractions of a local market would limit the value to consumers of any price competition, and that competition would simply give over to monopoly in due course. It seemed virtually an economic necessity for States to provide a single, local franchise with a business opportunity free of competition from any source, within or without the State, so long as the creation of exclusive franchises under state law could be balanced by regulation and the imposition of obligations to the consuming public upon the franchised retailers.[6]

Whether a particular market is a natural monopoly market, justifying the grant of an exclusive franchise, has occupied regulators for a century. Their recent and current struggles will occupy us in Chapters 3, 4 and 5. To provide the foundation for that discussion, we turn now to exclusivity's seven variations.

---

5. Richard A. Posner, *Natural Monopoly & Its Regulation*, 21 STAN. L. REV. 548 (1999). Judge Posner's definition of "natural monopoly" helps avoid confusion arising from the multiple ways speakers and writers use the term "monopoly." In each of the following four sentences, the word means something different: "This utility is a monopoly." "This utility has a monopoly." "This market is a monopoly market." "This market is a natural monopoly market."
6. Gen. Motors Corp. v. Tracy, 519 U.S. 278, 290 (1997).

2.A.2. Seven variations on exclusivity

South Dakota-style exclusivity, express and permanent, is not the regulator's only choice because natural monopoly is not the only possibility. What if a non-incumbent can offer a lower-quality alternative to the incumbent's service at a lower price? What if some customers can serve themselves, alone or in groups, more economically than the incumbent can? What happens when adjacent incumbent monopolies compete to attract new or expanding industrial customers? What if, within the range of the monopoly services historically provided by the incumbent, there are one or more services better provided by a specialty company? What if the state, dissatisfied with the incumbent, wants to replace it? What if the state never promised exclusivity, but exclusivity just "happened," and now a newcomer wants a shot? The following seven examples illustrate that exclusivity need be neither certain nor permanent.

2.A.2.a. New service offered by non-incumbent

Whereas South Dakota's statute shuts the door on competitors, Maine's statute leaves an opening:

> [N]o public utility may furnish any of the services set out in section 2101 [including gas, electricity, water, ferries and public heating] in or to any municipality in or to which another public utility is furnishing service or is authorized to furnish a similar service *without the approval of the commission.*[7]

This statute permits a second utility to provide service within a municipality already served by another utility, if the Commission approves. What facts might justify an approval?

In a 1985 case, Saco River Communications proposed to offer Maine citizens discounted intrastate long-distance telephone service, purchased wholesale from other telephone companies. Saco's customers would have to dial extra numbers and sometimes wait for a line, but Saco would charge less than the incumbent charged for higher-quality service. The incumbent telephone company opposed the invasion. The Commission approved it, based on a three-part test: (1) Is there a "public need" for the proposed service? (2) Does the applicant have the necessary technical ability? (3) Does the applicant have adequate financial resources? On appeal, the Maine Supreme Judicial Court focused on "public need":

> To find that a public need for a particular type of service exists means that such particular service *is not presently being provided.* (Were it provided, the need would not exist, having been satisfied). . . . [I]n the evaluation of whether another public utility should be granted a certificate of public convenience and necessity, *existing service that fails*

---

7.   ME. REV. STAT. tit. 35-A, § 2102(1) (emphasis added).

to provide a particular type of service for which a public need exists is, for that reason alone, inadequate. . . . [W]e believe it fair to assume that the public always desires (and, therefore, there is a public need for) comparable service at lower costs.[8]

Does the incumbent, when criticized for inadequacy, have an opportunity to cure? In Maine, the incumbent telephone company had no chance to head off Saco by curing the inadequacy, that is, by offering the service Saco proposed.[9] Wisconsin, in contrast, gives the incumbent a chance to cure. One utility may serve another utility's customers by extending a line to them, but only if "the service rendered or to be rendered by the [invaded utility] is inadequate and *is not likely to be made adequate . . . .*"[10] And in Kentucky, to justify a newcomer's invasion of the incumbent's territory,

the inadequacy must be due either to a substantial deficiency of service facilities, beyond what could be supplied by normal improvements in the ordinary course of business; or to indifference, poor management or disregard of the rights of consumers, persisting over such a period of time as to establish an inability or unwillingness to render adequate service.[11]

Comment on regulatory technique: The examples from South Dakota, Maine, Wisconsin, and Kentucky show that whether to authorize new entry into an exclusive service territory depends on four variables:

1.   Is the incumbent's service inadequate?
2.   Does inadequacy mean merely poor service, or does it include failure to provide a service offered by a prospective new entrant?
3.   Does the incumbent have a chance to cure its inadequacy?
4.   Does poor service reflect (a) inadequate facilities that the incumbent is able to cure; or (b) indifferent or poor management, indicating that the incumbent is unable or unwilling to serve?

How policymakers use these variables affects how accountable the utility is for its performance. Compare two incumbents: one facing multiple risks of entry, with no opportunity to cure; the other utility enjoying a statutory promise of exclusivity, permanently, with opportunity to cure. Which one will be more likely to keep its facilities reliable, its service

---

8.   Standish Tel. Co. v. Public Util. Comm'n, 499 A.2d 458, 459–63 (Me. 1985) (emphasis added). This 1985 case refers to Section 2302, whose language today appears in Me. Rev. Stat. § 2102.
9.   *Id.* at 464.
10.   Wis. Stat. § 196.495(1m)(b) (emphasis added).
11.   Ky. Utils. Co. v. Pub. Serv. Comm'n, 252 S.W.2d 885, 890 (Ky. Ct. App. 1952).

high-quality and innovative, its menu of customer choices diverse and dynamic, and its prices reasonable?

2.A.2.b. Customer self-service

Some large electric customers—say, automotive and chemical plants—want to produce their own electricity by building, owning, and operating their own generating units. Because this "self-generation" (also called "inside-the-fence generation") breaches the exclusive franchise wall, it sometimes is regulated by the state. The type of regulation depends on the regulator's judgment about benefits and risks. Here are two contrasting approaches.

Benefits: Self-generation can give the customer (a) back-up power during utility outages, (b) peak demand power for high-demand periods when the utility has shortages, (c) economic power for when the self-generator's cost is less than the utility's rate, (d) pollution reduction when the self-generator's emissions are less than the utility's and (e) power-quality enhancement where the customer's special equipment requires uninterrupted flow.[12] These benefits led California to enact legislation requiring the Commission to "adopt energy conservation demand-side management and other initiatives in order to reduce demand for electricity and reduce load during peak demand periods."[13] The initiatives include "[d]ifferential incentives for renewable or super-clean distributed generation resources pursuant to Section 379.6."[14] Section 379.6, in turn, authorizes the Commission to collect funds from ratepayers to assist self-generation, so as to "improve efficiency and reliability of the distribution and transmission system, and reduce emissions of greenhouse gases, peak demand, and ratepayer costs."[15]

Risks: A self-generating customer reduces its purchases from the utility. That reduction means the customer no longer pays its pro rata share of fixed costs previously incurred by the utility to serve the customer (to the extent those fixed costs were recovered through

---

12. The term "power quality" has varying definitions. The Institute of Electrical and Electronics Engineers (IEEE) *Standard Dictionary of Electrical and Electronics Terms* defines power quality as "the concept of powering and grounding sensitive electronic equipment in a manner that is suitable to the operation of that equipment." Here is a more technical definition:

    Perhaps the best definition of power quality is the provision of voltages and system design so that the user of electric power can utilize electric energy from the distribution system successfully, without interference or interruption. A broad definition of power quality borders on system reliability, dielectric selection on equipment and conductors, long-term outages, voltage unbalance in three-phase systems, power electronics and their interface with the electric power supply, and many other areas. A narrower definition focuses on issues of waveform distortion.

    MASOUD ALIAKBAR GOLKAR, POWER QUALITY IN ELECTRIC NETWORKS: MONITORING, AND STANDARDS, http://www.icrepq.com/icrepq07/273_aliakbar.pdf (last visited Aug. 29, 2012).
13. CAL. PUB. UTIL. CODE § 379.5(b).
14. *Id.*
15. For details on California's Self-Generation Incentive Program, *see About the Self-Generation Incentive Program*, CAL. PUB. UTILS COMM'N, http://www.cpuc.ca.gov/PUC/energy/DistGen/sgip/aboutsgip.htm (last visited Dec. 29, 2011).

variable customer charges). Someone then—either the utility's shareholders or its non-self-generating customers—must absorb those unrecovered costs. As the Massachusetts Department of Public Utilities explained: "[T]o a large extent," a utility's "common costs . . . operate as a closed system. . . . [I]f self-generating customers consume fewer kilowatt-hours from the electric company, transition costs are shifted from self-generating customers to non-self-generating customers."[16]

The regulatory concern with cost-shifting involves not only equity but efficiency. If the new capacity created through self-generation idles efficient existing utility capacity, we have what economists call "uneconomic bypass."[17] To prevent cost-shifting and uneconomic bypass, the regulator can require the self-generator to bear the costs it otherwise would leave behind. This requirement causes the customer to rethink its math: on departure, its total cost will include its own construction and operating costs, plus its pro rata share of the utility's previously incurred fixed costs. Only if this total is less than the utility's rate to the customer will the self-generation be economical for both the customer *and* the utility (and its customers). A policy requiring the customer to pay its pro rata share of the utility's fixed costs, sometimes called an "exit charge," aims to align the customer's interest with the utility's interest. That is the Massachusetts solution. The Department has authority to assess all self-generating customers an amount equal to what they would have paid had they stayed; the fee is triggered if "self-generation decreases an electric company's gross revenues by ten percent."[18]

2.A.2.c. Group self-service

Recall that the Maine statute prohibits one "public utility" from *selling* to the customers of another, without Commission approval. What if the service provider is a group of consumers serving themselves? Is the provider a "public utility," obligated to obtain Commission approval to invade the utility's territory? Or is the group a non-utility, free to act without approval? The Maine Commission addressed these questions in two contrasting cases.

---

16. Letter from Ann G. Berwick et al., Chair, Massachusetts Department of Public Utilities, to William F. Welch, Clerk of the Massachusetts Senate, and Steven James, Clerk of the Massachusetts House of Representatives, Annual Report Concerning Self-Generation, at 2 (July 1, 2011), *available at* http://www.env. state.ma.us/dpu/docs/electric/11-11/91311dpuordb.pdf (last visited June 25, 2012) ("Mass. Department Letter").

17. Uneconomic bypass occurs when the self-generating customer's total incremental cost (the one-time cost of building the plant, plus the operating costs) is (a) less than the total rate it pays the utility, making it a positive move for the customer; but (b) greater than the utility's marginal costs (i.e., the cost of producing one more unit of energy), making it a negative result for society. Uneconomic bypass wastes society's resources by increasing "the total industry costs of providing a given level of service." J. GREGORY SIDAK & DANIEL F. SPULBER, DEREGULATORY TAKINGS AND THE REGULATORY CONTRACT 78 (1998); *see also id.* at 30–31 (discussing uneconomic bypass).

18. *Mass. Department Letter, supra* note 16, at 2. The authority for the exit charge is MASS. GEN. LAWS ch. 164, § 1G(g).

Kimball Lake Shores: Kimball Lake Shores was a residential development owned by a real estate trust. The sole trustee was Douglas Forbes, who lived in the development. On learning that the development's well water was undrinkable, he constructed a water system. He ran the system with "extreme informality." He did most of the maintenance himself, billed the development's residents to cover the system's costs, covered yearly deficits with his personal funds, and reported the system's income and expenses on his personal taxes. He called the system a "co-op." The board of directors of the development's association, on a vote of all the residents receiving water from the system, had the power to approve Forbes' proposed water rates, although no formal documents required this procedure. As the Commission described things:

> This "Co-op" has no officers, no by-laws or regulations and no document exists governing its nature or control. All persons in Kimball Lake Shores who use water from the water system become members of the "Co-op" without formal agreement and in no other manner than by merely paying their bills. Participation in the water system is open to anyone purchasing property in the development, but not to anyone outside the development. There is no evidence that the "Co-op" has an exclusive franchise within the development, but there is no other water system in the development, although some owners get water from private wells. . . . Mr. Forbes constructed the water system as a practical adjunct to his interest in the property it serves in order to enhance its value to potential buyers. . . . At this time, nothing in the laws of this State prevents any group of property owners in Kimball Lake Shores who are dissatisfied with Mr. Forbes' "Co-op" from constructing an alternative water system.

Admitting it was a "close case," the Commission found that the provider was not a "public utility." The test was

> whether or not [the entity] holds himself expressly or implicitly as engaged in the business of supplying his product or services to the *public as a class* or to any limited portion of it, as contradistinguished as holding himself out as serving or ready to serve only particular individuals. The public or private character is not dependent upon the number of persons by whom used, but whether open to use and service of all members of the public to the extent of its capacity.[19]

---

19. Kimball Lake Shores Association & Douglas P. Forbes, Order M. #221, 1980 Me. PUC LEXIS 1, at *12–13 (Jan. 30, 1980) (emphasis added) (quoting other sources).

To determine whether the provider is supplying to "the public as a class," rather than "only particular individuals," the Commission considers seven factors, no one of which controls:

1.   The size of the undertaking (a "relatively unimportant" factor)
2.   Whether the enterprise is operated for profit (absence of profit "suggests an identity of interest between the agency supplying the service and the persons served")
3.   Whether the system is owned by the users (important because "it establishes a substantial identity of interest between the enterprise and its customers," as distinct from a purpose of serving the general public)
4.   Whether the terms of the service are under the control of its users ("If the users overcharge themselves they have harmed none of the public and may return their money to themselves if they wish. If they undercharge themselves on a rate that is less than just and reasonable they must make up the deficit if they wish the system to continue to operate effectively. The intervention of a public agency is unnecessary.")
5.   The manner in which the service is offered to prospective users (a factor not worth a "great deal of weight . . . because it is clearly possible to purchase membership in a system owned and controlled by the residents of a particular subdivision or area, and which would not be devoted to the public use").
6.   Limitation of service to organization members or other readily identifiable individuals.
7.   Whether membership in the group is mandatory.[20]

These seven factors "tend to focus on the relative degree of identity of interest between those taking utility service and the owners of the utility and whether the utility has undertaken to serve the general public."[21]

Central Monhegan: The seven-part test produced the opposite result in *Central Monhegan* because the provider failed most of the seven tests. The provider served:

---

20.   *Id.* at *29–37.
21.   Central Monhegan Power, Docket No. 96-481, 1996 WL 677622, at *4 (Me. Pub. Util. Comm'n Oct. 17, 1996) (citing *Kimball*). The Maine Commission reached the same result in *New England Telephone Co.*, Request for Advisory Ruling, Docket No. 84-208, Advisory Ruling (Me. Pub. Util. Comm'n June 20, 1985). Kimball's counterpart there was a Robert Burton, who:

supplied electricity to his own residence, the Island Inn and store (both owned by him), and fifteen friends and relatives. Individuals arranged for the service with him, and there was no indication that he would supply power on demand. Fees were collected only to cover costs and for a reserve for improvements. The Commission found the restrictive nature and limited scope of his offerings precluded a decision that he served the public at large. The Commission also noted that Mr. Burton did not have a monopoly on the service he provided and that if customers were unhappy with his service or rates, they were free to find another supplier.

Central Monhegan Power, 1996 WL 677622 at *4.

over 79 accounts (some customers have more than one account). This includes the school, library, stores, restaurants, hotels and NYNEX, as well as residential customers. . . . Although it is unclear whether Central [Monhegan Power] currently operates profitably [(Factor 2)], Messrs. Remick and Lord stated in 1987 that they intended to operate Central as a profit-making venture and there is no indication that it operates as a not-for-profit organization. If a system is owned by its users (Factor 3), this class of users is distinct from the public. Although Central is owned by at least two of its users, none of the other users has a financial interest in the business. Likewise, customers (except Messrs. Lord and Remick) do not exercise any control (Factor 4) over the rates charged or the services they receive.

Service appears to be offered to any prospective user (Factor 5) where Central is physically capable of providing service. Service is not restricted to certain members or relatives and family only (Factors 6 and 7). Central has held itself out to anyone who wants service to which it can economically and physically provide service.

Due to limited space on the island for more large generators and safety concerns about customer-owned generators, "for all practical purposes, residents are limited to taking their primary service from Central." Based on these factors, the Commission declared Central Monhegan a "public utility," but given the "small size of . . . [the company's] operation, the Commission left open "the extent to which our rules will apply . . . ."[22]

Modern application: Group self-supply is an old question with modern applications. Neighborhoods and industrial parks are considering "micro-grids" for electric service and gas-buying cooperatives for gas service.[23] They will have to confront questions of exclusivity and bypass.

2.A.2.d. Adjacent monopolies as rivals: Locational and fringe competition
Just as municipalities and states compete to attract tax base, utilities compete to attract customers. When factories and corporate headquarters look for a home, they consider energy costs (along with labor availability, proximity to highways and rail lines, taxes, school systems, and cultural life).[24] In this respect, Southern California Edison and San Diego Gas & Electric, each a monopoly in its own service territory, were rivals. They

---

22. *Id.*
23. *See, e.g.*, Sara C. Bronin, *Curbing Energy Sprawl with Microgrids*, 43 CONN. L. REV. 547 (2010); Kari Twaite, Note, *Monopoly Money: Reaping the Economic and Environmental Benefits of Microgrids in Exclusive Utility Service Territories*, 34 VT. L. REV. 975 (2010).
24. *See* City of Groton v. Conn. Light & Power, 662 F.2d 921, 934 (2d Cir. 1981) ("Competition exists if the monopoly utility and the [wholesale customer] municipalities are in geographic proximity and are generally each seeking to have retail businesses locate within their respective franchise areas."); Conway Corp. v. Fed. Power Comm'n, 510 F.2d 1264, 1268 (D.C. Cir. 1975) (wholesale competitors "seek to maintain customer satisfaction with the quality and price of their service in order to attract new industries and to retain existing customers"), *aff'd*, 426 U.S. 271 (1976).

knew that "locational decisions by new customers may be predicated upon comparative performance." In Orange County, their "rivalry . . . focused primarily on rate disparities between the two utilities." Indeed, "SDG&E expended at least $400,000 to retain its service territory and offered a 5 percent rate reduction along with other financial incentives to the City of South Laguna," hoping it would leave SCE.[25]

Can a large customer reach across the service territory boundary, to take service from the adjacent utility? Some states say "yes," producing "fringe-area competition." It includes (a) "competition to serve new developments in nonfranchised areas located between existing franchise areas," and (b) "competition to serve previously undeveloped areas near the boundary between franchise areas."[26] An example is Wisconsin's "500-foot rule": if two utilities can both reach a new, currently unserved premises with a line measuring 500 feet or less and no such line is currently available, they can compete to serve the customer.[27]

---

25.   Southern Cal. Edison and San Diego Gas & Elec., Decision No. 91-05-028, 1991 Cal. PUC LEXIS 253, at *236–37, *236 n.68, *238, *240 n.70, *262, 122 P.U.R.4th 225 (finding "across-the-fence" rivalry between two utilities). This case will reappear in the companion book on corporate structure, mergers and acquisitions, because the California Commission cited the loss of this rivalry as a reason to reject the companies' proposed merger. The Commission also looked askance at the 5 percent rate reduction to South Laguna, remarking that "such tactics may be illegal given the well understood duty of monopoly providers to treat all customers within the service territory in a non-discriminatory manner." *Id.* at *240 n.70.

26.   Mark Frankena & Bruce Owen, Electric Utility Mergers: Principles of Antitrust Analysis 123 (1994).

27.   See Wis. Stat. § 196.495(1m)(b) (discussed in Adams-Marquette Elec. Coop., Inc. v. Pub. Serv. Comm'n, 188 N.W.2d 515, 522 (Wis. 1971)). Professor James Meeks, author of a seminal article on competition in the electric industry, has taken a dim view of fringe-area competition. He argues that "any extensive competition in another's service area is so wasteful as to be undesirable, and even on the margins such competition is probably not worth promoting." He focused his skepticism on a particular scenario:

> Assume Company A and Company B are serving adjoining areas. Their present lines are 1,000 yards apart. A new plant is built 100 yards from A's lines and 900 yards from B's lines. Obviously it would be most economical for A to build the line to the plant and furnish the service. But suppose that B offers a lower rate because of more economical operation or a willingness to accept lower profit rate. Company A might meet the competition by underwriting a lower price to the plant from higher prices in its protected areas, resulting in discriminatory pricing, which benefits only the customers for which competition exists. Such discrimination is the most likely short-term response if permitted by the local regulatory commission. It would seem to be undesirable in its own right and useless in terms of the goals of competition. Another response might be an attempt by A to produce and distribute cheaper power, but this is a long-term proposition. The plant cannot wait for A to build more economical generation, and once B has commenced service, A is effectively prevented from gaining the customer back when and if A does economize. Thus, competition has led to a relatively permanent less-than-economically-optimum service pattern. Moreover, once B has built the line, it is in its best interest to make further incursions into the area, perhaps even duplicating A's lines and equipment, since the cost of spreading out from the lines serving the plant is nominal compared to the return represented by adding nearby customers.
> It should be recognized, however, that even in this kind of situation, there is incentive for A to economize over the long run, so that it can compete in future, similar competitive situations. This may justify the loss of real economies in some cases in order to provide incentive to take advantage of such economies in the future. Whether the less efficient system will so respond is uncertain, and probably depends substantially on the individual circumstances, especially the likelihood of future opportunities for competition. In most instances, the cost paid in unnecessary distribution lines is probably not worth the possibility that competition will still be possible at some future

2.A.2.e. Exclusive franchisee for a specific service

What if the state wants a special service to be provided on a monopoly franchise basis, but decides the incumbent lacks the necessary expertise or commitment? Some states have assigned the new service, or reassigned an existing one, to a specialist—a separate, exclusive franchisee.

Hawaii, Vermont, Oregon and Maine are the prominent examples. Each has appointed a non-incumbent to provide energy efficiency services formerly provided by the utility.[28] And the Maine Commission is investigating whether to appoint a "smart grid coordinator." The coordinator would have the exclusive responsibility, within the incumbent utility's service territory, to "manage[] access to smart grid functions and associated infrastructure, technology, and applications within the service territory of a transmission and distribution utility."[29]

---

date. Moreover, the fact that the system will continue to be guaranteed at least a minimum profit no matter how the competitive battle ends reduces the incentive to innovate, although it does not destroy it since higher profits may be possible.

James E. Meeks, *Concentration in the Electric Power Industry: The Impact of Antitrust Policy*, 72 COLUM. L. REV. 64, 94–95 (1972). Despite the article's 1972 vintage, it is worth re-applying its reasoning to current facts, as new technologies make possible new forms of entry. The full article is a landmark deserving every reader's attention.

28. *See How Efficiency Vermont Works*, EFFICIENCYVERMONT.COM, http://efficiencyvermont.com/about_us/information_reports/how_we_work.aspx (last visited Jan. 21, 2012) (describing Efficiency Vermont's responsibility to provide "technical assistance and financial incentives to help Vermont households and businesses reduce their energy costs with energy-efficient equipment and lighting" and "energy-efficient approaches to construction and renovation"); *About Us*, HAWAII ENERGY.COM, http://www.hawaiienergy.com/4/our-team (last visited Jan. 21, 2012) (describing Hawaii Energy's ratepayer-funded conservation and efficiency programs); *About Us*, ENERGYTRUST OF OREGON, http://energytrust.org/about (last visited Jan. 21, 2012) (describing Energy Trust of Oregon's responsibility to invest in cost-effective energy efficiency and assist with the above-market costs of renewable energy); *About Efficiency Maine*, EFFICIENCYMAINE.COM, http://www.efficiencymaine.com/about (last visited Jan. 21, 2012) (describing Efficiency Maine's technical assistance, cost-sharing, training, and education programs to reduce the use of electricity and heating fuels through energy-efficiency improvements and the use of cost-effective alternative energy).

29. *See* ME. REV. STAT. tit. 35-A §§ 3143(1)(B), (5) (noting that "the commission may authorize no more than one smart grid coordinator within each transmission and distribution utility service territory." The Maine Commission in 2010 opened a proceeding entitled Investigation into Need for Smart Grid Coordinator and Smart Grid Coordinator Standards, Docket Number 2010-267. As of spring 2013, the Commission had suspended the proceeding in order to conduct a pilot program in which a contractor is hosting a competitive bidding process to select "non-transmission alternatives" (to transmission) in a defined subregion within the state. *See* RICHARD SILKMAN & MARK ISAACSON, GRIDSOLAR, LLC, INVESTIGATION INTO NEED FOR SMART GRID COORDINATOR AND SMART GRID COORDINATOR STANDARDS (Dec. 16, 2010), http://www.gridsolarme.com/smartgrid/docket2010-267/GridSolar_Direct_Case_as_filed.pdf (last visited Jan. 29, 2013). For an analysis of rationales for shifting grid coordination responsibility from the incumbent utility to an independent entity, see Chapter 4.B.5.d and especially JOHANN J. KRANZ & ARNOLD PICOT, TOWARD AN END-TO-END SMART GRID: OVERCOMING BOTTLENECKS TO FACILITATE COMPETITION AND INNOVATION IN SMART GRIDS (National Regulatory Research Institute June 2011), http://www.energycollection.us/Energy-Regulators/Toward-End-End.pdf.

2.A.2.f. Competition for the exclusive franchise

"[T]he public has an obvious interest in competition, 'even though that competition be an elimination bout.'"[30] Consider a municipally-owned power system located within an investor-owned utility's boundaries. The two entities "compete, at least theoretically and on a long-term basis, for service areas. If plaintiffs [municipalities] were to become unable to serve their customers profitably, Penn Power [the investor-owned utility] would logically be in the best position to assume plaintiffs' present service."[31]

We call this type of competition "franchise competition": competition for the exclusive franchise, for "the right to serve all of the customers in a given territory, usually for a specific period of time."[32] Retail franchise competition provides consumers "with their most meaningful opportunity to compare alternate price, quality, and service. Indeed, at the retail service level, it is this very potential that provides an incentive for [wholesale competitors] to control costs and improve their performance in the areas that they serve."[33]

Evidence of the high stakes in franchise competition is a leading case on anti-competitive behavior, *Otter Tail Power Co. v. United States*.[34] Otter Tail was the exclusive incumbent utility, serving residents of towns in Minnesota, North Dakota, and South Dakota. Hoping to perpetuate its monopoly, Otter Tail sought to prevent the towns from establishing their own power systems once Otter Tail's franchises expired. The utility (a) refused to sell the towns wholesale power, (b) refused to transmit to them wholesale power produced by third parties, and (c) used litigation tactics to impede the towns' efforts to form their own systems. The U.S. District Court found that Otter Tail was attempting to "monopolize," and had monopolized, the retail distribution of electricity, in violation of Section 2 of the Sherman Antitrust Act. The U.S. Supreme Court upheld the lower court's decision.[35]

2.A.2.g. No statutory exclusivity

On August 1, 1994, the three members of the New Hampshire Public Utilities Commission found on their desks a "Petition for Permission and Approval to do Business on a Limited Basis as a Public Utility in New Hampshire."[36] Submitted by the confidently named Freedom

---

30. Hecht v. Pro-Football, Inc., 570 F.2d 982, 991 (D.C. Cir. 1977) (quoting Union Leader Corp. v. Newspapers of New England, Inc., 284 F.2d 582, 584 n.4 (1st Cir. 1960)).
31. Borough of Ellwood City v. Pa. Power Co., 462 F. Supp. 1343, 1346 (W.D. Pa. 1979).
32. Groton v. Conn. Light & Power Co., 662 F.2d 921, 930 (2d Cir. 1981).
33. Town of Massena v. Niagara Mohawk Power Corp., No. 79-CV-163, 1980 U.S. Dist. LEXIS 9382, at *28 (N.D.N.Y. 1980).
34.   410 U.S. 366 (1973).
35. *Otter Tail* will reappear in this work several times. *See infra* Chapter 4.B.2 (relating to a legal monopoly's exposure to antitrust liability) and Chapter 4.B.3 (relating to "essential facilities doctrine"). For a municipalization dispute that produced a different outcome, *see Town of Massena*, 1980 U.S. Dist. LEXIS 9382 (N.D.N.Y. 1980) (finding that the investor-owned utility did not violate the Sherman Act because it did not refuse unconditionally to transmit third-party power to Massena and because the requested transmission involved unresolved engineering and technical concerns).
36. Freedom Elec. Co, 161 P.U.R.4th 491 (N.H. Pub. Util. Comm'n June 19, 1995).

Electric Company, the petition sought permission to sell retail power competitively to customers of the incumbent utility, Public Service Company of New Hampshire (PSNH).

For decades, PSNH had enjoyed what it thought was an exclusive service territory. Here is the Commission's summary of PSNH's main argument, joined by the state's other utilities:

> [F]ranchise territories [in New Hampshire] are exclusive as a matter of law. PSNH asserted that by issuance of the electric service territory franchise map, the Commission has implicitly recognized the exclusivity of franchise territories. It argued that because a franchise constitutes a property right, it must be fairly compensated for any loss of that property right. PSNH also asserted that pursuant to N.H. REV. STAT. § 374:28, the Commission may only take away a franchise if there has been inadequate service or failure to serve, neither of which are alleged here.[37]

The Commission rejected these arguments on statutory, constitutional, and policy grounds.

Statute: The Commission conceded that "historically, utility franchises have been considered exclusive in nature and that our orders granting franchises have referred to 'exclusive service territories.'" But such orders granting exclusivity "cannot be viewed as permanent given the Commission's express authority to 'alter, amend, suspend, annul, set aside or otherwise modify any order made by it.'" Moreover, the Commission may grant a franchise only if it "would be for the public good, and not otherwise." Further, there was "no statute that provides that the authorization of a public utility to serve a particular area automatically confers an exclusive right to serve that area," or that "prohibits authorization of competition in the provision of electric utility services." Given these factors, there was no statutory right to permanent exclusivity.[38] The New Hampshire Supreme Court upheld the Commission: "[U]nder the plain language of RSA 374:26 the PUC is both authorized *and obligated* to grant a competing electric utility franchise when it determines that such grant would serve the public good."[39]

Constitution: The Commission and state supreme court also relied on New Hampshire's Constitution:

> Free and fair competition in the trades and industries is an inherent and essential right of the people and should be protected against all monopolies and conspiracies which tend to hinder or destroy it.[40]

---

37. *Id.* at 318–19.
38. *Id.* at 323–24 (citing N.H. REV. STAT. §§ 365:26, :28).
39. Appeal of Pub. Serv. Co. of N.H., 676 A.2d 101, 103 (N.H. 1996) (emphasis added).
40. N.H. CONSTITUTION OF 1784 art. 83.

Citing this sentence, the court found that "[l]imitations on the right of the people to 'free and fair competition' must be construed narrowly, with all doubt resolved against the establishment or perpetuation of monopolies. [The New Hampshire statutes] thus should not be interpreted as creating monopolies capable of outliving their usefulness."[41]

Policy: Its legal discretion established, the Commission turned to policy, declaring its "belief that regulation should not be regarded as an unadaptable structure. Utility regulation should exist in its present form only as long as the need for a natural monopoly exists . . . . As the electric industry changes, we should not artificially maintain what was put in place to accomplish far different goals." The court agreed. "That the commission may have historically interpreted the public good as requiring monopolies in the provision of retail electric service does not preclude it from adopting a new paradigm based on changing concepts of what the public good requires."[42]

The *Freedom Electric* decisions, both the Commission's and the court's, provide several insights into exclusivity, statutory interpretation, and commission powers:

1.   Unless a statute explicitly grants a utility irrevocable exclusivity, there is statutory room for the commission to authorize entry by competitors.
2.   A long history of exclusivity in fact does not create a right of exclusivity in law.
3.   State constitutional hostility toward monopolies is relevant to interpreting state franchise statutes.
4.   Given statutory flexibility, an exclusive franchise is exclusive only as long as the Commission makes it so.[43]

* * *

We have just discussed seven variations on the theme of exclusivity, ranging from South Dakota's permanence to New Hampshire's impermanence. Many of these options appear in Figure 2. The hypothetical American Power & Light has a lot to worry about: eight consumer efforts to reduce their dependency on the incumbent, and a relocating manufacturer comparing AP&L's rates with those of the neighboring utility. "Exclusive" does not always mean "certain."

In these variations on exclusivity, the common theme is policymaking discretion: Has the statute granted the regulator discretion to invite competitors? What standards should apply to these invitations? How do regulators use these standards to induce appropriate

---

41.   *Appeal of Pub. Serv. Co.*, 676 A.2d at 105 (internal citations omitted).
42.   *Id.* at 107.
43.   Neither the Commission nor the state Supreme Court opinions dealt with the merits of introducing competition; they addressed only the Commission's authority to allow a competitor to enter. Following the *Freedom* decision, the Commission held a detailed proceeding culminating in an order authorizing retail competition. In that proceeding, the author served as outside counsel to the Commission.

Figure 2
How Exclusive Is the Exclusive Franchise?

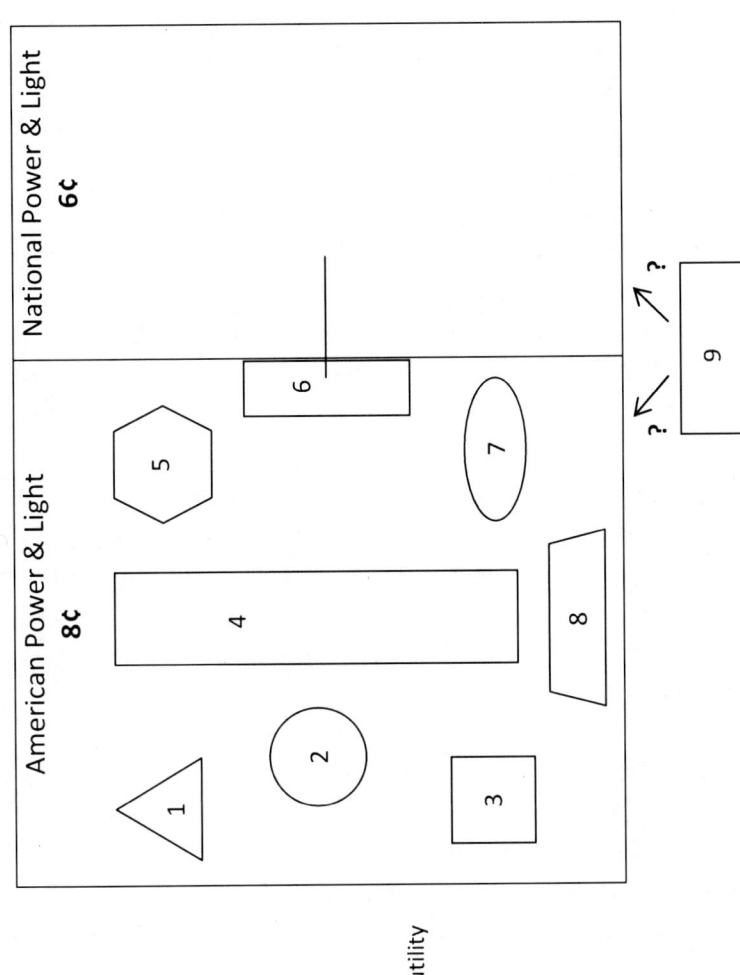

1. Industrial self-generator
2. Neighborhood microgrid
3. Community water well for summer homes
4. State-franchised energy efficiency utility
5. City council meetings on municipalization
6. Industrial park's interconnection with lower-cost utility
7. Homeowner's solar panel
8. Demand response aggregator
9. Manufacturing plant considering relocation

performance from service providers, whether incumbent or new? We turn now to the ultimate form of performance accountability—the commission's power to revoke a utility's
franchise and grant it to someone else.

2.A.3. Franchise revocation

"[I]n every grant of franchise is the implied condition that it may be lost by misuse."[44] No
exclusive franchise is permanent—even South Dakota's grant of the right to serve "each
and every future customer." What a statute grants, it can take away.[45]

But states do not revoke franchises frequently or lightly. Whether revocation is legal,
practical, and wise depends on answers to these questions: Who has the power to revoke?
What are the lawful reasons to revoke? What are the necessary procedures? Does the
government owe compensation to the departing franchisee? Is there a new franchisee
willing, ready, and able to serve, one that will perform better than its predecessor? As
discussed next, the answers to the legal questions depend on the franchise's terms, the
statutes creating the regulatory apparatus, and principles of contract law, property law,
and constitutional law.[46]

2.A.3.a. Revocation authority

Granting and revoking a franchise is a legislative function.[47] Some legislatures have delegated both these powers to their commissions: "Implicit in the [commission's] power to
grant a franchise is the power to revoke it for breach of the franchise's conditions."[48] In
contrast, Maryland distinguishes between revoking the franchise (which only the Legislature may do, because the Legislature granted the franchise), and revoking the utility's
right to exercise the franchise (which the Commission may do, because the Commission
polices quality of service). As a Maryland appellate court explained: "Although the economic effect of an order revoking a utility's right to exercise a franchise could, in some
instances, be tantamount to revocation of the franchise itself, it is not necessarily so. The

---

44. Redfield Tel. Co. v. Ark. Pub. Serv. Comm'n, 621 S.W.2d 470, 471–72 (Ark. 1981) (citing Pub. Serv. Comm'n v. Havemeyer, 296 U.S. 506 (1936) (upholding Puerto Rico's power to revoke a utility's franchise)).
45. *See* City of Worcester v. Worcester Consol. St. Ry. Co., 196 U.S. 539, 552 (1905) (holding that "the legislature had the right to modify or abrogate the conditions on which the locations in the streets and public ways had been granted, after such conditions had been originally imposed by it"); Kan. Gas and Elec. Co. v. Pub. Serv. Comm'n of Kan., 261 P. 592, 594 (Kan. 1927) (emphasizing that the police power "can neither be abdicated nor bargained away, and is inalienable even by express grant; and that all con-tract and property rights are held subject to its fair exercise").
46. For some of the research on this subsection, I am indebted to Tim Mastrogiacomo, a student in my 2011 class on public utility regulation at Georgetown University Law Center.
47. *Redfield Tel. Co.*, 621 S.W.2d at 501.
48. Valley Rd. Sewerage Co., 712 A.2d 653, 659 (N.J. 1998) (quoting N.J. STAT. § 48:2-14 for the propo-sition that no franchise granted to a public utility by a political subdivision is valid until approved by the Board of Public Utilities); *see also* VT. STAT. tit. 30, § 231(a) (granting to the Board both powers to grant and revoke).

franchise remains as a valuable asset which, under certain conditions, may be sold and which, in other hands, may again be exercisable."[49]

2.A.3.b. Revocation justifications

An exclusive utility franchise can take different legal forms: a contract between utility and municipality, a state statute or local ordinance, a state commission order or a state statute. One or more of those documents will determine, implicitly or explicitly, the permissible bases for revocation.

If the franchise is "revocable-at-will," the government grantor can revoke it for any reason or no reason.[50] Revocable-at-will does not mean revocable-without-due-process, however. If the revoking entity is a state administrative agency, it must follow state administrative procedure law: the agency must act on a public record, give affected parties an opportunity to be heard, base decisions on substantial evidence and not act arbitrarily or capriciously. If the revoking entity is the legislature, these administrative law requirements do not apply.

If a franchise is not revocable-at-will, the revoking agency must have reasons to revoke—namely, violations of franchise conditions, including obeying all regulatory rules. Connecticut statutes authorize the commission to revoke the franchise right if the utility fails to "provide service which is adequate to serve the public convenience and necessity" or if its rates "are so excessive in comparison to the rates charged by other public service companies providing the same or similar service as to inhibit the economic development of the area . . . or impose an unreasonable cost on the costumers."[51] Utilities have lost their franchise rights when they—

- had an "'abysmal' history of violating legal and environmental requirements" and "a history of making and breaking promises to regulatory agencies";[52]
- continued violating the franchise grant's prohibition against providing electricity for lighting;[53]
- failed to resolve problems of water quality and inadequate infrastructure, and lacked sufficient financing to correct the problems;[54]

---

49. *See* Highfield Water Co. v. Pub. Serv. Comm'n, 416 A.2d 1357, 1365 (Md. Ct. Spec. App. 1980) (upholding the Commission's authority to revoke the right to exercise the franchise), *cert. denied*, 421 A.2d 957 (Md. 1980).

50. *See* S. Bell Tel. & Tel. Co. v. City of Richmond, 98 F. 671, 673 (Va. Cir. Ct. 1899) ("[T]he power of repeal [of the grant] does not depend on either the necessity for it, or on the soundness of the reasons assigned for it.").

51. Conn. Gen. Stat. § 16-10a.

52. *Valley Rd. Sewerage Co.*, 712 A.2d at 660 (upholding Board's decision).

53. Old Colony Trust Co. v. City of Tacoma, 230 F. 389, 394 (9th Cir. 1916) (upholding revocation decision).

54. *Highfield Water Co.*, 416 A.2d at 136–66 (rejecting utility's statutory argument that "once the PSC authorizes the exercise of a franchise it loses all control over that exercise"; the effect of such loss of

- failed to resolve numerous customer-service complaints; the failure "could not be attributed to lack of operating funds but rather to the philosophy and ability of the present management and, therefore, customer difficulties with service would persist as long as the present management was associated with the Company;"[55] and
- "operated with a disregard for good business practices and its statutory obligations as a public utility. . . ."[56]

Not all poor performance leads to franchise revocation. In a multi-year investigation, the Vermont Public Service Board found that executives of Citizens Utility Company had persistently mismanaged the company, violated laws, and disobeyed Board directives. Management was "seriously flawed," accounting practices were "seriously deficient," and rates were excessive. Although the Board believed the situation justified franchise revocation, it decided that a forced sale would cause uncertainty and transaction costs as a new company corrected Citizens' mistakes. The Board instead imposed $60,000 in fines, ordered a refund, and halved the authorized return on equity, finding that investors should earn no more than ratepayers earn on their passbook accounts. The Board also placed Citizens on "'a multi-year period of strict regulatory probation,' during which the Company will be required to reform its accounting procedures, managerial structure, and processes for regulatory compliance."[57]

What if the poor performance stems from insufficient finances? In Montana, the utility got no break:

> No utility should be heard to argue . . . that it cannot and/or will not make the necessary improvements because it does not have the financial resources. If the current management and/or owners . . . are unable or unwilling to discharge their obligations in the operation of the public utility then they should arrange for some other entity to conduct those services.[58]

---

authority "would be to remove [the PSC's] ultimate ability to enforce its orders and thus to emasculate its ability to regulate, to perform its legislative duties"), *cert. denied*, 288 Md. 736 (Md. 1980).

55. *Redfield Tel. Co.*, 621 S.W.2d at 471–72 (upholding Commission's finding that public necessity required revocation of the certificate to serve, or transfer of the plant and certificate to an "able third party").

56. Lone Mountain Springs Water Co., Utility Div. Dkt. No. 92.9.55, Order No. 5660f, 1994 Mont. PUC LEXIS 4, at ¶ 73 (Mont. Pub. Util. Comm'n Aug. 22, 1994) (warning that if the utility "continues to operate as it has historically, ignoring public utility obligations and good business practices," the Commission will order it put up for sale).

57. *See* Investigation of Citizens Util. Co., Docket Nos. 5841/5849, 2004 Vt. PUC LEXIS 63, at *1 (Vt. Pub. Util. Comm'n Apr. 7, 2004). Citizens Utilities Co. later changed its name to Citizens Communications Co. The Board eventually approved the transfer of most of Citizens' distribution assets to the Vermont Electric Cooperative, and its transmission and generation assets to others. *Id.*

58. La Casa Grande Water Co., Utility Div. Dkt. No. 91.2.3, Order No. 5610d, 1994 Mont. PUC LEXIS 2, at *13 (Mont. Pub. Util. Comm'n Aug. 22, 1994) (quoting previous order).

2.A.4. Regulatory options for franchise accountability

Exclusivity has gradations. From South Dakota's shut door to New Hampshire's open door, policymakers can choose ways to encourage or discourage non-incumbents to compete with or replace the incumbent. Each option is an opportunity to induce performance—the very purpose of regulation. To review, the options include:

1. Rely, exclusively and permanently, on a single franchisee (with the possibility of revoking the incumbent's franchise due to poor service). (South Dakota)
2. Maintain the incumbent's right to serve, but authorize entry by non-incumbents to provide useful services not provided by the incumbent. (Maine: *Saco River Communications*)
3. Allow self-generation, assisted with ratepayer dollars (California) or conditioned on exit fees. (Massachusetts)
4. Authorize self-service and private provision to a self-contained group. (Maine: *Kimball Lake Shores*)
5. Allow fringe-area competition, such as by authorizing adjacent utilities to compete for unserved new load located within a specified distance from service-territory boundaries. (Wisconsin)
6. Grant exclusive franchises to non-incumbents for specified services, such as energy efficiency or smart-grid coordination. (Hawaii, Vermont, Oregon, Maine)
7. Rely exclusively on a single franchisee, but limited to a stated term of years followed by a competition for the right to be the new franchisee. (Nevada)
8. Interpret the statute as providing no promise of exclusivity. (New Hampshire)
9. Combinations of the foregoing.

Each of these choices involves tradeoffs, between stability and predictability on the one hand, and innovation and competitive pressure on the other. If the purpose of regulation is performance, regulators must ask: "What combination of these approaches most likely assures the desired performance?" Professor Alfred Kahn famously wrote that the "central, continuing responsibility of legislatures and regulatory commissions [is] finding the best possible mix of inevitably imperfect regulation and inevitably imperfect competition."[59]

---

59. 2 Alfred E. Kahn, The Economics of Regulation: Principles and Institutions 114 (1988); 1 Alfred E. Kahn, The Economics of Regulation: Principles & Institutions, at xxxiv (1988).

Regulators can apply this statement to the franchise context by continuously re-examining the role of exclusivity and its variations, with these questions:

1. When the commission identifies the possibility of new services, should the incumbent have the first shot at providing new services, or should the commission invite competitors?

2. Should the commission wait for the incumbent or others to propose new services, or should the commission itself continuously identify new service needs and call for applications?

3. Which regulatory context leads to better performance: one where the utility is at no risk of losing business opportunities by failing to offer new services, or one where any applicant who shows "need," defined as a new service not presently provided, can enter to provide that service?

My recommendation: Given the chronic differential in expertise and person-power between a utility and its regulators, regulators can literally use all the help they can get.[60] This view argues for the Commission opening the door to new entrants who offer new services, rather than relying exclusively on the incumbent. This approach does not necessarily sacrifice the static efficiency associated with the incumbent's economies of scale. The Commission can and should take those economies into account to avoid inefficiently splintering service components among multiple sellers. But the continuous inquiry will be worth the effort.

2.B. Obligation to serve

A utility's obligation to serve is defined by statute. Washington State's provision is typical:

> Every telecommunications company shall, upon reasonable notice, furnish to all persons and corporations who may apply therefor and be reasonably entitled thereto suitable and proper facilities and connections for telephonic communication and furnish telephone service as demanded.[61]

This short passage achieves three things. It establishes (a) the universe of customers falling within the obligation, (b) the definition of the service to be provided, and (c) the utility's obligation to maintain infrastructure sufficient to provide the service to the customers. This subchapter elaborates on these concepts. It begins by describing three objectives typical

---

60. I have written critically about this differential in two essays: Scott Hempling, *Regulatory Resources: Does the Differential Make a Difference? (Part I)*, SCOTTHEMPLINGLAW.COM (Oct. 1, 2008), http://www.scotthemplinglaw.com/regresources1; Scott Hempling, *Regulatory Resources: Does the Differential Make a Difference? (Part II)*, SCOTTHEMPLINGLAW.COM (Sept. 30, 2008), http://www.scotthemplinglaw.com/regresources2.

61. WASH. REV. CODE § 80.36.090.

of the obligation to serve: preventing monopolistic discrimination, ensuring citizen access to essential services, and developing the community's economy. It then explains the obligation's limits. There is no obligation to serve customers who violate tariff provisions; further, customers whose service causes unusual costs must pay up before service starts. This section closes by explaining that the obligation to serve is the *utility's* obligation: It cannot be contracted away.

2.B.1. The anti-discrimination objective

Douglaston, New York, was a remote community, located within the gas utility's franchise territory but 1.5 miles beyond the utility's existing distribution lines. The utility resisted serving the community, arguing that doing so would "require an expenditure of money upon which the prospective earnings would not provide an adequate return." The New York Commission ordered service, and the U.S. Supreme Court upheld the order. A utility's obligation to serve does not vary with its profit potential:

> Corporations which devote their property to a public use may not pick and choose, serving only the portions of the territory covered by their franchises which it is presently profitable for them to serve and restricting the development of the remaining portions by leaving their inhabitants in discomfort without the service which they alone can render. To correct this disposition to serve where it is profitable and to neglect where it is not, is one of the important purposes for which these administrative commissions, with large powers, were called into existence . . . .

Even if the utility's return on its Douglaston investment was low, there was "every prospect of its soon becoming ample" due to expected load growth. Further, "no claim was made by the company that the comparatively small loss . . . would render its business as a whole unprofitable."[62]

The obligation to serve prevents a utility from discriminating against the desperate—extorting higher rates by threatening to withhold service: "[A utility] may not use its privileged position, in conjunction with the demand which it has created, as a weapon to control rates by threatening to discontinue that part of its service if it does not receive the

---

62. New York *ex rel.* N.Y. & Queens Gas Co. v. McCall, 245 U.S. 345, 350–51 (1917). Technically, the *McCall* Court's decision did not affirm the utility's state law obligation to serve. The Court assumed there was an obligation, as a basis for finding that the Commission's order compelling service did not violate the utility's constitutional right to just compensation. That right is protected by the Fifth Amendment's Takings Clause, as applied to the states through the Fourteenth Amendment's Due Process Clause. Note also that the Court assessed the rate's constitutionality by examining the return for the entire company rather than only the return on the disputed investment. In doing so, the Court anticipated the landmark "end result" test of *Hope Natural Gas v. Fed. Power Comm'n*, 320 U.S. 591 (1944). We will discuss this concept in detail in Chapter 6.B, concerning constitutional limits on ratemaking.

rate demanded."[63] A utility dissatisfied with its commission-approved rates can challenge commission decisions in court. It can even request release from its franchise obligations. But while it enjoys the franchise, it must honor its obligation to serve.

2.B.2. The citizen access objective

When imposing an obligation to serve, policymakers must answer the question, "Serve what products?" The traditional answer was straightforward: electric current at a specified voltage, natural gas and water at specified pressures, a telephone dial tone enabling local and long-distance calls. With advances in technology and the entry of new providers, policymakers have expanded the obligatory services, reflecting new political judgments about the services citizens need. Consider these examples:

Telecommunications: As described by Bluhm and Bernt, telephone companies with "carrier of last resort" obligations under state law have had to provide these "basic services":

(1) Voice service, defined as two-way switched voice-quality connections to the rest of the public switched network.

(2) Single-line service (as opposed to party-line service).

(3) Switching capabilities that include: (a) "Touch-tone" (dual tone multi-frequency) dialing. (b) Call waiting, call forwarding, and three-way calling. (c) "Equal access," . . . allow[ing] a customer to make a toll call using the network of its preferred interexchange carrier by dialing a "1" and a ten-digit telephone number. (d) Toll limitation, [which] blocks or limits the toll calls made by certain customers. (e) Out-of-channel signaling (such as Signaling System Number Seven).

(4) A rate design that: (a) Offers a residential local exchange rate and a single-line business rate. (b) Permits unlimited calling within a local exchange area (and often 'extended' local service areas or "EAS" areas) without additional charges.

(5) Interconnection to or direct provision of certain ancillary telecommunications services: (a) Interconnection to interexchange companies of the customer's choice for toll calling. (b) Directory assistance. (c) Operator services allowing customers to make specialized requests, such as for "collect" calls. (d) Emergency services such as "911" and "enhanced 911". (e) "Relay" (sometimes called "711") services providing special services for the hearing impaired. (f) "Toll blocking" that allows low-income customers to prevent their line from originating direct-dialed toll calls.

(6) The opportunity to be listed in a written directory, with an option for non-listed and non-published service, and annual distribution of a local telephone directory.

(7) The ability to transmit computer data using a modem at a specified rate."[64]

---

63.   United Fuel Gas Co. v. R.R. Comm'n of Ky., 278 U.S. 300, 309 (1929).
64.   Peter Bluhm & Phyllis Bernt, National Regulatory Research Institute Carriers of Last Resort:

This obligatory list could grow to include broadband. The Federal Communications Commission has declared that "[e]veryone in the United States today should have access to broadband services supporting a basic set of applications that include sending and receiving e-mail, downloading Web pages, photos and video, and using simple video conferencing."[65]

Electricity: Some states, concerned with both climate change and local economic development, have required utilities to offer "green power," "smart meters," customer education, and "demand response."[66]

2.B.3. The economic development objective

The obligation to serve includes an obligation to plan and prepare to serve. The utility is responsible for its service territory's entire needs, now and in the future. As the New Jersey Supreme Court declared:

> The burden assumed [by accepting a franchise] . . . was a community service; it was not limited to the establishment of a system suitable only to the then current needs. Included

---

UPDATING A TRADITIONAL DOCTRINE 6 (July 2009), http://www.nrri.org/pubs/telecommunications/COLR_july09-10.pdf.

65. FEDERAL COMMUNICATIONS COMMISSION, CONNECTING AMERICA: NATIONAL BROADBAND PLAN 135 (2010), http://download.broadband.gov/plan/national-broadband-plan.pdf. The FCC has even specified download speeds and quality:

> Every household and business location in America should have access to affordable broadband service with the following characteristics:
>
> > Actual download speeds of at least 4 Mbps and actual upload speeds of at least 1 Mbps. An acceptable quality of service for the most common interactive applications.
>
> The FCC should review and reset this target every four years.

Bluhm and Bernt caution state regulatory agencies against adding broadband to the obligation to serve, absent either "a broad consensus that includes the state legislature" or an FCC ruling making broadband a component of federal universal-service programs. *Id.* at 52, 135.

66. *See, e.g.,* MO. REV. STAT. § 393.1030(1) (requiring the Commission, "in consultation with the [Department of Natural Resources], [to] prescribe by rule a portfolio requirement for all electric utilities to generate or purchase electricity generated from renewable energy resources"); MD. PUB. UTIL. CODE § 7-211(g)(2) (directing the Commission to "require each electric company to implement a cost-effective demand-response program in the electric company's service territory that is designed to achieve a targeted reduction of at least 5 percent by the end of 2011, 10 percent by the end of 2013, and 15 percent by the end of 2015, in per capita peak demand of electricity consumed in the electric company's service territory during 2007"); PA. STAT. § 2807(f)(1) (requiring electric distribution companies to file with the Commission a smart-meter-technology procurement and installation plan with the Commission for approval). "Demand response," as defined by the Federal Energy Regulatory Commission, means a "reduction in the consumption of electric energy by customers from their expected consumption in response to an increase in the price of electric energy or to incentive payments designed to induce lower consumption of electric energy." 18 C.F.R. § 35.28(b)(4) (2010). *See generally* ERIC FILIPINK, NATIONAL REGULATORY RESEARCH INSTITUTE, SERVING THE "PUBLIC INTEREST": TRADITIONAL VS. EXPANSIVE UTILITY REGULATION (2009), *available at* http://www.nrri.org/pubs/multiutility/NRRI_filipink_public_interest_jan10-02.pdf (describing expanding regulatory roles).

also was the utility's duty to keep in view the *probable growth* of the township, both in population and in structural development, and to make gradual extensions of its *mains to meet the reasonable demands that would inevitably result.*[67]

A utility does not just serve customers; it creates infrastructure to support a population and its economy. This purpose supports the regulatory trend of redefining the service obligation to include providing the infrastructure that supports such products as smart grid, broadband and green power.

2.B.4. Limits on the obligation to serve

The obligation to serve is not unlimited. It extends only to eligible customers, as defined by the utility's tariffs. As Bluhm and Bernt explain:

> The duty to serve does not require a COLR (carrier of last resort) to serve every person who might apply for service from its service area. A COLR can decline to serve a financially disqualified customer, such as one who still owes money from a prior period. . . . [A] carrier may decline to serve a customer whose equipment is hazardous or who interferes with service to others.[68]

Common exceptions to the obligation to serve include:

1. Non-paying customers. (For impoverished customers, states usually prohibit winter shutoffs, while providing the utility with taxpayer or ratepayer funding to cover the service costs.)[69]
2. Customers who violate the tariff's safety provisions.
3. Customers who reside remotely from the central population. (The utility's obligation to serve is usually conditioned on the customer paying a special tariff charge to cover the cost of connecting.)

---

67. Bd. of Fire Comm'rs of Fire Dist. No. 3, Township of Piscataway v. Bd. of Pub. Util. Comm'rs, 142 A.2d 85, 87 (N.J. 1958) (emphasis added).
68. Bluhm & Bernt, *supra* note 64, at 7 (citing N.Y. Comp. Codes R. & Regs. tit. 16, § 609.3(a)(2); 16 Tex. Admin. Code tit. § 26.23; Wash. Admin. Code § 480-120-061(f)).
69. *See, e.g.,* Minn. Stat. § 216B.096, subdivision 5(a):

> During the cold weather period, a utility may not disconnect and must reconnect [the] utility heating service of a customer whose household income is at or below 50 percent of the state median income if the customer enters into and makes reasonably timely payments under a mutually acceptable payment agreement with the utility that is based on the financial resources and circumstances of the household; provided that, a utility may not require a customer to pay more than ten percent of the household income toward current and past utility bills for utility heating service.

2.B.5. Contracts that undermine the obligation

A utility cannot comply with its obligation to serve if it contracts away its managerial powers or its essential assets. Courts and commissions forbid such transactions. Here are four examples, three old, one modern.

a. Pennsylvania Water & Power (a Pennsylvania utility) had a wholesale electric contract with Consolidated Gas (a Maryland utility). The contract gave Consolidated "the power to control (1) the prices at which [Penn Water] may sell its product; (2) the extent to which [Penn Water] may extend its plant; (3) the territory in which [Penn Water] may sell its product; and (4) the amount of back feed energy which [Penn Water] must purchase from Consolidated." The agreement also required Penn Water to get Consolidated's approval before agreeing to buy or sell electric power with any third party, or to invest in or dispose of any property exceeding $50,000. The court invalidated the agreement. Besides violating antitrust law, it "disable[d] [Penn Power] from performing its proper function as a public utility under the public utility laws of Pennsylvania":

> Penn Water's power to propose prices and improvements and extend its services has been surrendered to Consolidated, and there can be no doubt that this surrender amounts to a transfer *pro tanto* [i.e., to that extent] of its powers and franchises to [Consolidated] without approval of the Pennsylvania Commission in violation of the Pennsylvania statute.[70]

b. A contract between two competing gas companies, in which one agreed to forgo installing more gas pipes, met the same fate: "It is also too well settled to admit of doubt that a corporation cannot disable itself by contract from performing the public duties which it has undertaken, and by agreement compel itself to make public accommodation or convenience subservient to its private interests."[71]

c. The New Jersey Legislature granted Millville and Glassboro Railroad Company a franchise to serve. The railroad company then leased its roads, buildings, and rolling stock to Thomas and his partners. Thomas, a non-franchisee, now controlled all the assets necessary to provide Railroad's franchised service. The lower court invalidated the lease, and the U.S. Supreme Court upheld the lower court:

> Where a corporation, like a railroad company, has granted to it by charter a franchise intended in large measure to be exercised for the public good, the due performance of those functions being the consideration of the public grant, any contract which disables the corporation from performing those functions[,] which undertakes, without the consent of the State, to transfer to others the rights and powers conferred by the charter,

---

70. Pa. Water & Power Co. v. Consol. Gas, Elec. Light & Power Co. of Baltimore, 184 F.2d 552, 567 (4th Cir. 1950).
71. Gibbs v. Baltimore Gas Co., 130 U.S. 396, 410 (1889).

and to relieve the grantees of the burden which it imposes, is a violation of the contract with the State, and is void as against public policy.[72]

Although Railroad's state-granted charter had a standard clause allowing it to enter into contracts with others, the clause did not authorize the utility to contract away its ability to satisfy its obligation to serve.

d. Modern question: What happens when a merger limits a utility's powers? Since the mid-1980s, U.S. utilities have been parties to dozens of mergers and acquisitions. (The companion book on corporate structure, mergers and acquisitions will address this subject in detail.) A common transaction is acquisition of the state-regulated utility by a holding company. The holding company's stock is publicly traded, its debt publicly rated. Because the holding company's financial performance will depend on the utility's financial performance, the holding company needs to control the utility's expenditures. That control necessarily diminishes the utility's pre-merger freedom to act. At what point does this diminution disable, unlawfully, the utility from carrying out its obligation to serve?

The Maryland Commission addressed this question in the merger of Exelon and Constellation Energy Group. Exelon Corp. (Exelon) was a holding company owning the utilities Commonwealth Edison Co. and PECO Energy Co., serving customers in Illinois and Pennsylvania, respectively. Constellation was (and is) a holding company owning the utility Baltimore Gas & Electric (BGE). (Both holding companies had other holdings.) The parties to the merger agreement were the two holding companies; BGE was not a contracting party. The holding companies' agreement contained the following limits on BGE's independent spending for a particular project: BGE's CEO could spend up to $25 million (equal to the CEO's pre-merger arrangement with Constellation); BGE's Board could approve up to $75 million (up from its current Constellation-granted authority of $50 million). Any BGE expenditures exceeding $75 million would require Exelon approval.

These constraints triggered opposition from intervenors. By limiting BGE's independent spending authority, they argued, Exelon could allocate to its non-utility activities scarce capital that BGE needed to carry out its obligation to serve. In its Order approving the merger, the Maryland Commission accepted the expenditure limits without change. The Commission imposed other conditions, however, that limited dividend payments from BGE to the holding company. The Commission also reserved its pre-existing authority to order BGE's divestiture from Exelon, or to revoke BGE's franchise, should Exelon's ownership harm BGE.[73]

---

72. Thomas v. R.R. Co., 101 U.S. 71, 83 (1879).
73. Merger of Exelon Corp. & Constellation Energy Group, Order No. 84,698, Case No. 9271, 295 P.U.R.4th 183 (Md. Pub. Serv. Comm'n Feb. 17, 2012). In this proceeding, the author was a witness for the State of Maryland. The spending limits discussed above are located in the Commission order at text accompanying notes 298 and 299. We will return to this "contracting away" topic in Chapter 6.C.2.c, concerning

* * *

The obligation to serve is a state law concept with three purposes: prevent discrimination, ensure citizen access to essential services and plan and provide the infrastructure required by the local economy. The obligation is not unlimited; the utility need not serve tariff-violators, non-payers and remote residents who fail to cover special costs. Whatever the obligation is, the utility cannot lawfully contract it away, disabling itself from carrying out the duties it accepted along with the franchise.

Now a century old, the obligation to serve has modern applications, with forces moving in opposite directions. New technologies and new policy goals have caused some jurisdictions to expand the list of obligatory services. On the other hand, acquisitions by holding companies have produced limits on local utilities' spending authority, leading to possible future tensions between holding company objectives and utility obligations.

2.C. Consent to regulation

Utilities can challenge in court a regulatory decision's rationality, the quality of its factual support, its consistency with statutes and the procedures by which it was issued. But they cannot otherwise challenge regulation's existence. When utilities accept the obligation to serve, they consent to regulation. Centuries old, this principle entered American legal precedent in *Munn v. Illinois*.[74]

An Illinois statute capped the prices charged by grain elevators and warehouses. Their owners argued that the cap violated the Constitution's Fifth and Fourteenth amendments by "taking" their property—their profits associated with the higher prices—without "just compensation."[75] Upholding the statute, the U.S. Supreme Court found two justifications for the state's regulation: the facilities' dominant market position, and their "public interest" status. Chicago occupied a strategic location between (a) the grain-producing regions of the Midwest, and (b) the water ports that moved the grain to the East Coast and Europe. The elevators were controlled by only nine firms, a number small enough to make price-fixing possible. These facts led the court to declare that the grain elevators "may be a 'virtual' monopoly":

> [The elevators] stand . . . in the very "gateway of commerce," and take toll from all who pass. Their business most certainly "tends to a common charge, and is become a thing

---

"prudent" cost as a component of "just and reasonable" rates. We will see there that a utility cannot escape an imprudence disallowance by saying "it was my subcontractor's fault."

74.   94 U.S. 113 (1877).
75.   The Fifth Amendment to the U.S. Constitution states, in relevant part: "[N]or shall private property be taken for public use, without just compensation." It is applied to the states through the Fourteenth Amendment. Chicago, B. & Q.R. Co. v. Chicago, 166 U.S. 226 (1897). See Chapter 6.B.2 for a detailed discussion of how these constitutional provisions protect utility investments.

of public interest and use." Every bushel of grain for its passage "pays a toll, which is a common charge . . . ."[76]

While this "virtual monopoly" was a justification for regulation, it was not a necessary justification. The court's list of long-regulated businesses included non-monopolies: "[I]t has been customary in England from time immemorial, and in this country from its first colonization, to regulate ferries, . . . hackmen, bakers, millers, wharfingers, innkeepers . . . ." (also mentioned were chimney-sweeping, hackney carriages, hauling by cartmen, wagoners, carmen, draymen, and auctioneers). The real justification for regulation, therefore, was that the grain-storage business affected the public. When someone—

devotes his property to a use in which the public has an interest, he, in effect, grants to the public an interest in that use, and must submit to be controlled by the public for the common good, to the extent of the interest he has thus created. He may withdraw his grant by discontinuing the use; but, so long as he maintains the use, he must submit to the control.[77]

That the price cap decreased the businesses' market value did not make it unlawful:

It matters not in this case that [the owners] had built their warehouses and established their business before the regulations complained of were adopted. What they did was from the beginning subject to the power of the body politic to require them to conform to such regulations as might be established by the proper authorities for the common good. They entered upon their business and provided themselves with the means to carry it on subject to this condition. If they did not wish to submit themselves to such inter-ference, they should not have clothed the public with an interest in their concerns. The same principle applies to them that does to the proprietor of a hackney-carriage, and as to him it has never been supposed that he was exempt from regulating statutes or ordi-nances because he had purchased his horses and carriage and established his business before the statute or the ordinance was adopted.[78]

---

76. *Munn*, 94 U.S. at 132.
77. *Id.* at 125–32 (quoting cases from England); *see also* Baltimore Gas & Elec. v. Heintz, 760 F.2d 1408, 1424 n.14 (4th Cir. 1985) ("[T]he very notion of a public service company presupposes 'distinctive public constraints . . . administered by a government agency that supervises the availability and quality of the firm's services, the price to be charged for such services, and a number of ancillary matters, including the firm's financial practices, its relations with other public service companies, and mergers and other corporate changes.'") (quoting G. E. Jones, *Origins of the Certificate of Public Convenience and Neces-sity: Developments in the States, 1870–1920*, 79 COLUM. LAW REV. 426, 426 (1979)).
78. *Munn*, 94 U.S. at 133–34.

Can a business escape regulation if it is not "affected with the public interest"? Not since *Nebbia v. New York*.[79] Erasing *Munn*'s public–private distinction, the U.S. Supreme Court there declared that all economic actors consent to regulation implicitly. With milk producers threatened by price-cutting, New York established minimum and maximum retail prices. Nebbia, a grocer, was convicted (it was a crime) of pricing below the legal minimum. Attacking the regulation, he sought to distinguish *Munn* on the grounds that his was not an "an enterprise of a sort which the public itself might appropriately undertake, or one whose owner relies on a public grant or franchise for the right to conduct the business, or in which he is bound to serve all who apply; in short, such as is commonly called a public utility; or a business in its nature a monopoly." Upholding New York's price minimums, the court abandoned *Munn*'s public–private distinction. "'[A]ffected with a public interest' is the equivalent of 'subject to the exercise of the police power.'" Put another way, "there is no closed class or category of business affected with a public interest." Violation of the Fourteenth Amendment would exist only if the regulation was "arbitrary in [its] operation and effect," or "demonstrably irrelevant to the policy the legislature is free to adopt, and hence an unnecessary and unwarranted interference with individual liberty." Absent these defects, all economic regulation is constitutionally valid.[80]

Before we apply the "consent" concept to modern regulation, consider three more examples.

1. The City of Portland granted a railroad the right to use city streets, but later prohibited the company from transporting particular types of cars. The U.S. Supreme Court upheld the City's power to restrict, reasonably, the franchise's exercise. The "power to regulate" was available even if it "could defeat the franchise granted by the state" or "impair the contract" under which the franchise was formed. The City was free to "legislate in the light of facts and conditions which would make the restrictions reasonable."[81]

2. New Hampshire imposed a special tax on utility franchise-holders. The state Supreme Court rejected the franchisee's challenge: "The exercise of a utility franchise is not a 'common right' but rather a special right which the State may and does grant or withhold at pleasure, to perform acts which are monopolistic and therefore subject to public regulation in the public interest."[82]

3. New Hampshire authorized a railroad to build a bridge, but limited the bridge's profits to 10 percent of their capital stock, so as to "secure to the public the enjoyment

---

79.   291 U.S. 502 (1934)

80.   *Id.* at 531–37; *see also* New Orleans Waterworks Co. v. Rivers, 115 U.S. 674, 681 (1885) ("[N]otwithstanding the exclusive privileges granted to the plaintiff, the power remains with the state, or with the municipal government of New Orleans, acting under legislative authority, to make such regulations as will secure to the public the uninterrupted use of the streets as well as prevent the distribution of water unfit for use, and provide for such a continuous supply in quantity as protection to property, public and private, may require.").

81.   S. Pac. Co. v. City of Portland, 227 U.S. 559, 573–74 (1912).

82.   Opinion of the Justices, 137 A.2d 726, 732 (N.H. 1958).

of the property devoted to public use at reasonable rates." Rejecting the railroad's legal challenge to the profit cap, the state Supreme Court declared:

> The grantee need not accept the grant unless he chooses to do so. It is for him to say whether the benefits conferred outweigh the burdens imposed. He may reject the gift; but if he accepts it, he must take it with all the qualifications and burdens that are thereto annexed.
>
> The [company] by accepting their charter and acting under it bound themselves to do all things therein required of them.[83]

Modern applications: Despite its medieval origins, *Munn* remains strong precedent. In upholding the Federal Communications Commission's rates for pole attachments, the Supreme Court cited *Munn* in finding that "[i]t is of course settled beyond dispute that regulation of rates chargeable from the employment of private property devoted to public uses is constitutionally permissible."[84] Why should practitioners today be concerned with legal principles settled a century ago? *Munn* and *Nebbia*, along with the Oregon and New Hampshire examples, distill to this principle: governments that regulate economic activity reasonably do not violate the Constitution. Disappointment alone does not make a legal case. By entering the utility sector (actually, any economic sector), a business consents to reasonable regulation. One can challenge in court a regulation's rationality, its consistency with statutes, and the procedures used to promulgate it, but one cannot challenge a regulation's existence.

2.D. Quality of service
2.D.1. Statutory bases
A restaurant faces pressures both daily and long term. Daily, it has to make the menu distinct, serve fresh food hot and timely, keep the ovens working and heed all health rules. Long term, it needs to anticipate changes in customer tastes, recruit the next top chefs and arrange financing to replace equipment. Within a single square mile, a dozen competing restaurants are doing the same. A utility blessed with an exclusive franchise doesn't have a dozen competitors. The pressure for excellence must come from somewhere else. That somewhere else is the regulator's power, granted by statute, to establish and enforce quality standards. Here are three examples:

- *New York*: The Commission has the power to investigate the "methods employed" by utilities in producing and delivering gas and electricity, and to order "such

---

83. New Hampshire v. Manchester & Lawrence R.R., 38 A. 736, 738, 740 (N.H. 1896).
84. *See* Fed. Commc'ns Comm'n. v. Fla. Power Corp., 480 U.S. 245, 253 (1987).

reasonable improvements as will best promote the public interest, preserve the public health and protect those using such gas or electric and those employed."[85]

- *District of Columbia*: The Commission has the power "to order reasonable improvements as will reasonably promote the public interest" and the power "to prescribe from time to time the efficiency of the electric transmission and distribution system."[86]

- *Kansas*: The Kansas Commission has "the full power, authority and jurisdiction to supervise and control the electric public utilities . . . [and] to do all things necessary and convenient for the exercise of such power, authority and jurisdiction." Each utility, in turn, "shall be required to furnish reasonably efficient and sufficient service and facilities for the use of any and all products or services rendered, furnished, supplied or produced by such electric public utility."[87]

And while commissions set quality standards, utilities must do more than merely obey:

> One of the most important duties of a public utility, inherent in its franchise to serve the public, is the duty *to take the initiative* in proposing reasonable rates and rendering adequate services, taking into account changing conditions; and the utility is not relieved from this duty because its activities are subject to governmental regulation, for a regulatory commission is not clothed with the responsibility or qualified to manage the utility's business.[88]

What do commissions do with their statutory authority over quality of service? After describing the components of quality, both old and new, this subchapter describes how regulators act to establish and enforce quality standards.

2.D.2. Components of quality: Traditional and new

Quality of service has many dimensions. Traditional ones include technical quality, reliability, meter accuracy, safety and customer relations. Here are typical examples in each category:

Technical quality: Electric utilities must "adopt a set of normal standard voltages" for different service categories, and "maintain the adopted standard secondary voltages so the same shall not normally vary more than plus or minus 5 percent of the standard at the service entrance."[89] Gas utilities must ensure that their product's impurities do not

---

85. N.Y. Pub. Serv. Law § 66(2).
86. D.C. Code § 34-301.
87. Kan. Stat. §§ 66-101, -101b.
88. Pa. Water & Power Co. v. Consol. Gas, Elec. Light & Power Co. of Baltimore, 184 F.2d 552, 567 (4th Cir. 1950) (emphasis added).
89. Or. Admin. R. § 860-023-0020.

exceed stated caps for hydrogen sulfide, sulphur, grains of sulphur and ammonia; further, "[n]o gas shall contain impurities which may cause excessive corrosion of mains or piping or form corrosive or harmful fumes when burned in a properly designed and adjusted burner."[90] Water must be (a) "potable, and, insofar as practicable, free from objectionable odors, taste, color, and turbidity"; and (b) available to each customer at pressure levels between 25 and 125 pounds per square inch.[91]

Reliability: State-level regulations often define reliability in terms of outage duration and frequency. Standard indices are "system average interruption duration index" or "SAIDI" (the sum of the customer interruption hours divided by the total number of customers served); and "system average interruption frequency index" or "SAIFI" (the sum of the number of customer interruptions divided by the total number of customers served).[92]

Meter accuracy: Oregon utilities must test meters before installing, ensure that meters do not have "an error in registration in excess of two percent under conditions of normal operation," adopt schedules for periodic testing and repair of meters, and keep records of all tests.[93]

Safety: Concerning downed electricity wires, Maryland utilities must respond "within four hours after notification by a fire department, police department, or 911 emergency dispatcher at least 90 percent of the time." Gas utilities must ensure that "[t]he odorant level throughout the entire company distribution system [is] sufficient so that gas is detectable at 1/10 of the lower explosive limit."[94]

Customer relations: A Maryland utility must "answer within 30 seconds, on an annual basis, at least 75 percent of all calls offered to the utility for customer-service or outage-reporting purposes." Further, "[e]ach utility shall achieve an annual average abandoned-call percentage rate of 5 percent or less, calculated by dividing the total number of abandoned calls by the total number of calls offered to the utility for customer service or outage reporting purposes."[95]

While the traditional quality dimensions remain relevant, new quality standards are emerging. Driving these standards are technology, competition, and customers' desire for control. In telephony, for example,

> [c]hanges in technology have made some traditional service-quality standards irrelevant, while introducing the need for new ones. For example, past service-quality standards routinely measured the average "off-hook" time delay before a customer received a dial

---

90. *Id.* § 860-023-0025.
91. Md. Code Regs. §§ 20.70.07.01–.02.
92. Md. Code Pub. Util. Cos. § 7-213; *see also* Md. Code Regs. § 20.50.12.02(D) (setting standards for SAIDI and SAIFI for each electric utility for the years 2012–2015).
93. Or. Admin. R. 860-023-0015.
94. Md. Code Regs. §§ 20.50.12.07, 20.55.09.06.
95. Md. Code Regs. § 20.50.12.08(A)–(B).

tone. Newer switching technologies have largely eliminated this concern. Conversely, new technologies also sometimes prompt new standards. For example, some states have standards relating to the frequency and length of signaling system failures, while others have considered adding measurements for the speed of porting numbers between carriers.[96]

In electricity, climate change concerns and customers' desire to control their costs have led policymakers to establish new service quality expectations. Most prominent are regulatory initiatives to (a) design programs that pay customers for reducing demand; (b) approve utility investments in so-called "advanced metering infrastructure" (including "smart grid" and smart meters") which, when combined with time-of-use pricing, help utilities and customers reduce power costs; and (c) require utilities to purchase and offer renewable resources.[97]

---

96. PETER BLUHM & SHERRY LICHTENBERG, FUNDAMENTALS OF TELECOMMUNICATIONS REGULATION: MARKETS, JURISDICTION, AND CHALLENGES 35 (National Regulatory Research Institute 2011), http://www.nrriknowledgecommunities.org/documents/83467/7bb0d474-4d21-479d-bf84-58eac5ef87a7.

97. "Demand response," as defined by the Federal Energy Regulatory Commission, means a "reduction in the consumption of electric energy by customers from their expected consumption in response to an increase in the price of electric energy or to incentive payments designed to induce lower consumption of electric energy." 18 C.F.R. § 35.28(b)(4) (2010). FERC has ordered regional transmission organizations to offer to bidders of demand response access and pricing comparable to that offered to generators. This treatment includes paying compensation equal to the "locational marginal price" applicable at the place and time demand response is bid (provided the demand response offer satisfies FERC's "cost-effectiveness" test). Demand Response Compensation in Organized Wholesale Energy Markets, Order No. 745, 134 FERC ¶ 61,187, *on reh'g*, Order No. 745-A, 134 FERC ¶ 61,187 (2011), *denying reh'g*, Order No. 745-B, 134 FERC ¶ 61,187 (2012), *appeal docketed*, Elec. Power Supply Ass'n v. FERC, No. 11-1486, et al (D.C. Cir. 2011).
   For advanced metering infrastructure, the Federal Energy Regulatory Commission has provided these definitions:

   Advanced Metering Infrastructure (AMI): AMI is defined as the communications hardware and software and associated system software that creates a network between advanced meters and utility business systems and which allows collection and distribution of information to customers and other parties, such as competitive retail providers, in addition to providing information to the utility itself.

   Advanced or Smart Metering: A system including measurement devices and a communication network, public and/or private, that records customer consumption [and possibly other parameters] hourly or more frequently and that provides for daily or more frequent transmittal of measurements to a central collection point.

   AMI Network: A system including measurement devices and a communication network, public and/or private, that records customer consumption [and possibly other parameters] hourly or more frequently and that provides for daily or more frequent transmittal of measurements to a central collection point.

   FED. ENERGY REGULATORY COMM'N, SURVEY ON DEMAND RESPONSE, TIME-BASED RATE PROGRAMS/TARIFFS AND ADVANCED METERING INFRASTRUCTURE (GLOSSARY), *available at* http://www.ferc.gov/industries/electric/indus-act/demand-response/2008/survey/glossary.pdf. *See generally* NANCY BROCKWAY, ADVANCED METERING INFRASTRUCTURE: WHAT REGULATORS NEED TO KNOW ABOUT ITS VALUE TO RESIDENTIAL CUSTOMERS, *available at* http://nrri.org/pubs/multiutility/advanced_metering_08-03.pdf . For a compilation of state renewable purchase requirements, see the Database of State Initiatives for Renewables and Efficiency, a site funded by the U.S. Department of Energy, available at http://www.dsireusa.org/ and, in particular, Justin Barnes, *Renewable Portfolio Standards Update: 2012's Compliance*

2.D.3. Regulatory requirements

Regulatory requirements vary across three dimensions: legal source (rules, statutes and orders); type of requirement (standards and actions); and remedy (financial penalties and directives). These dimensions allow regulators to induce service quality in multiple ways—subject to the "management prerogative" constraint.

2.D.3.a. Legal sources: Rules, statutes and orders

Quality of service requirements appear in multiple legal sources.

Regulations: Most frequently, quality standards appear in regulations or tariffs approved by the Commission, as in the Oregon and Maryland examples quoted above.

Statutes: Less frequently, standards are specified by statute. A 2011 Illinois statute required the utility to "develop and file with the Commission multi-year metrics designed to achieve, ratably over a ten-year period, improvement over baseline performance values" in these areas, among others:

> "Twenty percent improvement in the System Average Interruption Frequency Index," compared to the prior ten years' average.
>
> "Fifteen percent improvement in the system Customer Average Interruption Duration Index," and "twenty percent improvement in the System Average Interruption Frequency Index for its Southern Region," compared to the prior ten years' average.
>
> "Seventy-five percent improvement in the total number of customers who exceed the service-reliability targets" set forth in Commission regulations.

The statute also required specific percentage reductions in the number of estimated bills and in the dollars of uncollectible expense.[98]

A middle ground is a statute directing a commission to promulgate specific standards. Responding to citizen anger over electricity outages, the Maryland Legislature directed the state commission to issue new rules on SAIFI, SAIDI, downed wire response, customer communications, vegetation management, periodic equipment inspections, annual reliability reporting, and "any other performance measurement that the Commission determines to be reasonable."[99]

Merger orders: Commissions also create quality standards in orders approving mergers. In one proposed transaction, the New York Commission found that that the acquirer's "corporate structure and financial condition . . . are detriments which . . . in turn, lead to increased risks of service quality degradation." The Commission therefore conditioned

---

Modifications, Progress and Prognostications, THE RENEWABLE ENERGY MARKETS ASSOCIATION (Mar. 6, 2012), http://www.renewablemarketers.org/pdf/REMA_RPS_webinar_final.3.6.2012.pdf.
98.   *See* 220 ILL. COMP. STAT. 5/16-108.5(f)(1)–(3).
99.   MD. CODE PUB. UTIL. COS. § 7-2131.

its merger approval on a prospective scheme of negative revenue adjustments for service interruptions, gas pipeline leaks, late responses to gas leak calls and excavation damages.[100] In contrast, the Massachusetts Department declined to impose special service quality conditions on a merger, preferring to address the subject in a separate proceeding on service quality or rates. The Department found that existing rules on customer interruptions, line losses, spare inventory practices, emergency response times, unaccounted-for gas, and other factors were sufficient.[101]

Telecommunications mergers also feature quality of service conditions. Approving the merger of U.S. West and Qwest, the Arizona Corporation Commission adopted conditions establishing penalties equal to twice the cost of compliance. The penalties would apply for violations relating to (a) hiring of service quality technicians, and (b) replacing troubled cross boxes and pedestals, with penalties increasing for each year of non-compliance. The company also had to invest $402 million in modernization and maintenance, with a portion designated for upgrading services in rural areas, and convert all remaining central office switches to digital.[102]

Bankruptcy orders: The Hawaii Public Utilities Commission established quality conditions in its approval of Hawaiian Telcom's bankruptcy reorganization. The utility's proposed reorganization plan had acknowledged that financial recovery depended on penetrating the market for "next-generation television services." The Consumer Advocate raised concerns that, under pressure to succeed in these new markets, the utility would fail to improve the quality of its traditional services. The Commission accepted the Consumer Advocate's proposed condition, requiring the Company to

> provide quarterly status reports identifying service-improvement action plans that include milestones and a time schedule to improve the % Out of Service Troubles Cleared in 24 Hours service measurement to meet the commission's objective level. These reports shall include, but not be limited to, all the improvement plans that Applicants believe are required to meet the service objective, the implementation dates of those plans,

100. Iberdola, Case 07-M-0906, 2008 N.Y. PUC LEXIS 448, at *36–39 (N.Y. Pub. Serv. Comm'n Sept. 9, 2008); *see also* PacifiCorp & Scottish Power, Docket No. UE-981627, 1999 Wash. UTC LEXIS 594, *48 (Wash. Util. & Transp. Comm'n Oct. 14, 1999) (requiring corrective measures to five worst-performing circuits under Condition 20); Enron Corp. & Portland Gen. Elec., Dkt. No. UM-814, Order No. 97-196, 1997 Ore. PUC LEXIS 15, at *15–16 (Or. Public Util. Comm'n June 4, 1997) (establishing Service Quality Measures under Condition 11).

101. Nat'l Grid plc & KeySpan Corp. Merger, D.P.U. 07-30, 2010 Mass. PUC LEXIS 28, at *31–41, 283 P.U.R.4th 144 (Mass. Dep't Telecomm. & Energy June 9, 2010).

102. Merger of Qwest Commc'ns Corp. & U.S. West Commc'ns, Inc., Dkt. No. T-01051B-99-0497, Decision No. 62672, 2000 Ariz. PUC LEXIS 1 (Ariz. Corp. Comm'n June 30, 2000). The author's companion volume on corporate structure, mergers and acquisitions will discuss mergers in detail, including a section focusing on quality standards contained in merger orders.

the progress achieved relative to the identified milestones and time schedule, problems encountered and corrective actions being taken.[103]

Alternative Forms of Regulation: Incumbent local exchange carriers have sought state commission approval of so-called "AFORs." These plans replaced traditional, cost-based review of pricing and tariff terms with pricing discretion, thereby separating the utility's revenue from its costs.[104] This feature created a risk: "[U]nder an AFOR a utility could focus on profit enhancement through cost cutting to such an extent that it would allow its service quality to deteriorate."[105] Commissions approving AFORs therefore required detailed quality standards, often coupled with penalties in the form of compensation to consumers.[106]

AFORs did spawn disputes over service quality. In Vermont, the incumbent Verizon acknowledged its failure to meet the performance benchmark for "Average Speed of Answer-Repair Center." Verizon then sought a waiver of penalty because it experienced (among other things) an "unanticipated increase in call volumes during a time of increased employee absenteeism [due to a labor dispute] and that it took reasonable measures in response to the crisis" (Vermont Board's paraphrasing of Verizon's statements). The utility also argued that summer call volumes had exceeded its predictions. These factors, it argued, made its failure excusable. The Board disagreed. The factors were "not exceptional"; they were within the realm of risks the company had accepted in return for the AFOR flexibility. "More fundamentally, Verizon is clearly in a better position than ratepayers to appraise and manage the relevant labor risks (and its management is being compensated for the duty) and a fundamental purpose of the Service Quality Plan is to place such risks with Verizon rather than ratepayers."[107]

2.D.3.b. Types of regulatory requirements: Inputs and outcomes

A service quality regulation can require *actions*—verbs like "installing meters" or "trimming trees." Or it can prescribe *results*—nouns like "limits on outages," "reductions in estimated (as opposed to meter-read) bills," and "the time customers wait for repairs." In the latter case, the utility then chooses the actions that produce the required results. The distinction is between inputs and outcomes.

---

103. Hawaiian Telcom, Inc., Docket No. 2010-0001, 2010 Haw. PUC LEXIS 475, at *84–89 (Haw. Pub. Util. Comm'n Sept. 22, 2010) (Ordering ¶ 3(M)).
104. Cost-based ratemaking is the subject of Chapter 6.
105. Investigation into Bell Atl. Maine's Alternate Form of Regulation, Dkt. No. 99-851, 1999 Me. PUC LEXIS 315, at *5 (Me. Pub. Util. Comm'n Dec. 27, 1999).
106. *See* BLUHM & LICHTENBERG, *supra* note 96, at 34. The rate aspects of these plans are discussed below, at Chapter 6.E.2 and 6.E.3, concerning "just and reasonable" ratemaking.
107. Verizon New England Inc., 2004 Vt. PUC LEXIS 161 (Vt. Pub. Serv. Bd. Sept. 20, 2004).

The Illinois statute's "metrics," discussed in Chapter 2.D.3.a, exemplify the standards approach: reductions in the frequency and duration of interruptions, increases in the percent of customers exceeding service reliability targets, percentage reductions in estimated bills. Standards are common in wireline telephone service:

> The most common areas for carrier performance monitoring are the speed of wireline service installation, mean time to restore service, mean time to repair troubles, and service availability (often expressed as the percentage of outages longer in duration than 24 hours). A common metric measures the percentage of new service requests that are completed within a fixed number of days. Most states also have metrics for service reliability, typically measuring trouble report rates and the timeliness and percentage of success in clearing reported troubles that affect service. Many states also measure carrier responsiveness, such as the average time taken by a carrier to answer customer calls for assistance from an operator, directory assistance, business office assistance, or repair calls.[108]

Maryland prescribes both inputs and outcomes. The SAIFI and SAIDI requirements are outcomes, but the "vegetation management" requirement requires some frequency of tree trimming. And the Illinois statute, in addition to the standards discussed above, commands the utility to spend an "estimated" $1.1 billion on electric-system upgrades, modernization projects and training facilities, and an estimated $1.5 billion on transmission and distribution infrastructure and smart-grid electric system upgrades, over and above the 2008–2010 annual average.[109]

2.D.3.c. Remedies: Financial penalties and directed actions

Financial penalties can take the form of return-on-equity reductions, fines and cost disallowances.

Return-on-equity reductions: In traditional "cost-based" ratemaking, commissions include a "return on equity" to compensate shareholders for their investment. "Courts have held consistently that a utility commission is free to award a higher rate of return for superior service or lower a rate of return for inferior service."[110] The Vermont Board, in a 150-page decision detailing Citizens Utilities' multiple quality problems, reduced the

---

108. *See* BLUHM & LICHTENBERG, *supra* note 96, at 35 (citing 170 IND. ADMIN. CODE § 7-1.2-9 (requiring company to complete 92 percent of installation requests in five business days); CONN. AGENCIES REGS. § 16-247g-2 (requiring company to clear 90 percent of all service repair requests in any given 24-hour period within 24 hours); 170 IND. ADMIN. CODE § 7-1.2-13(c) (requiring company to clear 90 percent of troubles within two business days); 170 IND. ADMIN. CODE § 7-1.2-16(a) (requiring company to answer calls to repair service within an average of 60 seconds)).

109. 220 ILL. COMP. STAT. 5/16-108.5(b)(1).

110. Missouri *ex rel.* Pub. Counsel v. Pub. Serv. Comm'n, 274 S.W.3d 569, 576 (Mo. Ct. App. 2009) (upholding Missouri Commission's decision not to lower utility's return due to storm outage performance). Chapter

utility's ROE to the level of a "passbook account."[111] The Illinois statute just discussed requires the Commission to reduce the authorized return on equity by five to ten basis points, depending on the type of utility, for each year that each metric is not achieved.[112]

Fines: Some statutes authorize the commission to assess a daily fine for performance shortfalls.[113] After investigating Potomac Electric Power Company's outage problems in 2010–11, the Maryland Commission imposed a fine of $1 million. The Commission's blunt words could hardly have pleased the company's executives and shareholders:

> We conclude that Pepco indeed failed to provide an acceptable level of service during 2010 and for at least the preceding few years. Pepco's failure to maintain its system properly over a period of years subjected its customers to excessively high frequencies and long durations of electric outages, during storm events and on fair weather days, and Pepco compounded those reliability problems through poor customer communication.
>
> Pepco offers myriad excuses for its performance, but we are not buying. We reject, for example, Pepco's claim that it has been providing "stable" electric service. The Company's electric service has been stable only in the sense that in the years prior to and including 2010, it remained stagnated in fourth quartile or bottom half performance, as measured by applicable reliability indices. We also dismiss Pepco's claim that common reliability indices are not useful measures of the Company's performance because of Pepco's "substantial canopy of very mature trees." We recognize each Maryland utility must respond appropriately to its unique geographical and environmental challenges to provide reliable service. But to the extent Pepco faces higher vegetative management obstacles than other utilities, it must dedicate appropriate resources to address those obstacles. We also reject Pepco's argument that its new Outage Management System ("OMS") is making the Company look bad by reporting higher numbers of outages, as well as the Company's argument that its customers developed unexpectedly high expectations concerning electric reliability. To the contrary, we find that the Company's OMS reported data accurately, and that the expectations of Pepco's customers are neither unreasonably high nor unexpected.[114]

---

6 will explain that "just and reasonable rates" allow the utility a reasonable opportunity to recover its prudent costs and earn a fair return on equity investment.

111.   Citizens Utilities Co., Docket Nos. 5841/5849 (Vt. Pub. Serv. Bd. June 16, 1997), *available at* http://www.state.vt.us/psb/orders/1997/files/5841FNL_1.pdf.

112.   *See* 220 ILL. COMP. STAT. 5/16-108.5(f-5)(1)–(2). A basis point is 1/100 of a percentage point.

113.   *See, e.g.*, MD. CODE PUB. UTIL. COS. § 13-201(b)(1) (authorizing the Commission to levy a civil penalty of up to $25,000 per day per violation against "a person who violates a provision of this division, or an effective and outstanding direction, ruling, order, rule or regulation of the Commission").

114.   Investigation into the Reliability and Quality of the Electric Distribution Service of Potomac Electric Power Company, 295 P.U.R.4th 373, 2011 Md. PSC LEXIS 37, at *101–02 (Md. Pub. Serv. Comm'n 2011) (footnotes omitted) (adding that "[s]hould the Company be unable to raise the quality of its electric service to an acceptable level in the near term, it will face the risk of additional, heavier fines").

Cost disallowance: A financial consequence distinct from lowering the return on equity reductions and imposing fines is cost disallowance: removing from the utility's revenue requirement specific expenses associated with the service quality problem. In the Pepco order discussed above, the Commission reserved for the next rate case whether the reliability-enhancing expenditures Pepco will need to make will be larger than necessary due to Pepco's prior imprudence.

Directed actions: Some commissions address quality problems by directing remedial responses. After investigating a utility's inadequate response to a storm, the Massachusetts Department of Public Utilities issued twenty-one directives, including requiring a new equipment repair process (eleven of fifty-four trucks had been out of service), improving communications processes (patrols were ineffective and telephone lines inadequate), revising safety standards and creating contingency plans for outages that occur during labor disputes. (Due to a strike, inadequately trained management personnel were handling hot distribution lines. The company also had declined the strikers' offer to assist in service restoration, causing unionized workers from other utilities to decline to help, thus lengthening the outage.) The Department also ordered the utility to reconsider its decision to close a customer-service center.[115]

Compensation to customers: Absent an express statutory provision, there is no regulatory power to compel payment to a customer. While "[n]othing precludes customers from asking the Company to reimburse them for damages as a gesture of good will, . . . tariffed electric service is not a contract relationship, . . . and claims sounding in tort . . . lie within the jurisdiction of the courts, not the Department."[116] Nor is compensation available from the courts, in most states, except in cases of gross negligence. Chapter 2.F will explain why.

2.D.3.d. The "management prerogative" constraint

A commission that orders actions instead of setting standards risks a run-in with the "management defense." Also called "management prerogative," "invasion of management" or, more colloquially, "regulators don't run companies," this doctrine limits the regulator's discretion to direct. Early courts blocked regulators' directives because they "infringed on" or "usurped" owners' rights.[117] Commissions defend their decisions by arguing that

---

115. W. Mass. Elec. Co., D.P.U. 95-86, 165 P.U.R.4th 70 (Mass. Dep't Pub. Util. 1995).

116. *Id.* at text accompanying n.8 (citing Band v. Mass. Elec. Co., D.P.U. 87-AD-27 (Mass. Dep't Pub. Util. May 12, 1993); Abizaid v. Bos. Gas Co., D.P.U. 1941 (Mass. Dep't Pub. Util. 1980) (hard copy on file with department).

117. Other judicial rationales for invalidating commission directives included "the now discredited doctrine of substantive due process" and an "overly robust" view of the Takings Clause. Robert Stumberg, Management Prerogatives in Utility Regulation: Guidance for State Regulators (unpublished paper) (on file with author) (citing Note, *"Management Invaded"—A Real or False Defense?*, 5 STAN. L. REV. 110, 116–17 (1952)); *see also* Thomas R. Dowling, *Attacks on Executives: Revival of the Invasion of Management Defense and Public Utility Autonomy*, 50 ST. LOUIS L.J. 629, 636–37 (2006). The Takings Clause, as Chapter 6.B will detail, obligates regulators to provide "just compensation" for shareholder investments where such compensation is consistent with the shareholders' legitimate expectations.

the authority to regulate necessarily includes the authority to oversee and supervise utility actions, which is not equivalent to acting as management.[118] Today, courts resolve these disputes using statutory interpretation: Did the legislature grant the commission the power to prescribe?[119] Illustrating this approach are three examples of management prerogative disputes in the service quality space.

1. General Telephone's quality problems were due to its outdated central office switching equipment, which the utility purchased from its manufacturing subsidiary. The Commission ordered the utility to use competitive bidding. The utility claimed "management prerogative" but lost. The "major purpose . . . was better service for the consumer, rather than an officious desire to run General's business. . . . [O]nly through competitive bidding could General be pried away from its dependence on the antiquated equipment being manufactured by . . . its affiliate."[120]

2. The Conlin-Strawberry Water Company "suffer[ed] pump failures, water supply deficiency, lack of system alarms, inaccurate monthly water quality reporting, questionable daily monitoring, and non-use of an automated control system." The California Commission ordered that the company "immediately replace" its system manager. The Commission rejected the management prerogative defense as "long outdated." The Commission declared that it had "the power to order a utility to hire qualified personnel, and to order the replacement of nominally qualified personnel who are not performing adequately, even where such actions essentially substitute for the judgment of utility management."[121]

3. When the West Virginia-American Water Company announced in 2011 that it would terminate thirty-one workers, the union filed a complaint, asserting that the layoffs threatened the utility's ability to provide safe and adequate water. The West Virginia Public Service Commission stayed the layoffs pending an investigation of their effect on service quality. The Commission acknowledged that the utility "has the management flexibility to determine proper staffing levels." But the Commission had an

> overriding statutory obligation to assure that all utilities under its jurisdiction maintain reasonable services and practices in furnishing their products. If a utility engages in

---

118. *See* Judy Sheldrew, *Shutting the Barn Door Before the Horse is Stolen: How and Why State Public Utility Commissions Should Regulate Transactions Between a Public Utility and Its Affiliates*, 4 Nᴇᴠ. L.J. 164, 167 (2003).

119. *See* Mountain States Tel. & Tel. Co. v. Pub. Serv. Comm'n of Wyo., 745 P.2d 563, 568–70 (Wyo. 1987) (commission ordered utility to publish a directory itself or bid the service out, rather than contract the job to its affiliate; court found that statute granting commission authority over utility services "to or for the public" was sufficient to overcome management defense). Management prerogative disputes also have arisen when commissions disallow imprudent costs and rearrange corporate structure and finance. We will address these two separate areas in Chapter 6.C.4 and the companion volume, respectively.

120. Gen. Tel. v. Pub. Utils. Comm'n, 670 P.2d 349, 355–56 (Cal. 1983).

121. Strawberry Prop. Owners Ass'n, v. Conlin-Strawberry Water Co., Inc., Decision No. 97-10-032, Case No. 95-01-038, 1997 Cal. PUC LEXIS 954, at *12–15 (Cal. Pub. Util. Comm'n Oct. 9, 1997) (citing *General Telephone*, 670 P.2d 349).

unreasonable practices, acts or services, such as placing itself in a position where it cannot carry out its utility service obligations the Commission may by order fix reasonable measurements, regulations, acts, practices or services.[122]

The company criticized the order as "equivalent to the Commission acting as a super board of directors" (Commission's paraphrasing). The Commission nonetheless proceeded with its investigation, emphasizing its authority to anticipate problems:

> The Commission does not want deterioration of the quality of service of [West Virginia-American Water Company (WVAWC)] in this situation, and it does not believe that the Commission is required to wait for that to happen before we investigate the significant changes announced by WVAWC.[123]

The Commission also relied on its statutory authority to "fix" a utility's "practices, acts or service" that are "insufficient." The Commission described its actions as "not acting outside of its jurisdiction or acting as a 'super board of directors,' it is instead complying with the statutory mandate and authority of the Commission as part of its supervision of public utilities." The Commission emphasized that it

> takes these steps only because this situation requires an extraordinary remedy. The Commission has no intention of becoming, and will not become, an appellate authority for adjudications of disputes regarding day-to-day, ordinary management or staffing decisions of any utility.[124]

After an investigation and subsequent orders,[125] the Commission (a) lifted the injunction as to 21 of the 31 workers, requiring ten to remain on the job; and (b) directed the

---

122. Util. Workers Union of Am. v. W. Va.-Am. Water Co., Case No. 11-0740-W-C, 289 P.U.R.4th 507, 2011 W. Va. PUC LEXIS 1258, at *3–4 (W. Va. Pub. Serv. Comm'n May 31, 2011) (citing W. Va. Code R. § 24-2-7).

123. *W. Va.-Am. Water Co.*, Case No. 11-0740-W-GI, 2011 W. Va. PUC LEXIS 1351, at *7–8 (W. Va. Pub. Serv. Comm'n June 9, 2011). It did not help the utility's case (as the Commission pointed out in its June 9, 2011 order) that in a rate case only months earlier, its President had testified: "I have carefully evaluated the needs of the Company and firmly believe we need the 316 employees requested to maintain adequate service to our customers." The Commission had accepted that testimony and authorized rates reflecting the full cost of those employee positions. *W. Va.-Am. Water Co.*, Case No. 10-0920-W-42T, at 64 (W. Va. Pub. Serv. Comm'n Apr. 18, 2011).

124. *W. Va.-Am. Water Co.*, Case No. 10-0920-W-42T, 293 P.U.R.4th 107, 2011 W. Va. PUC LEXIS 2425, at *7–8 (W. Va. Pub. Serv. Comm'n Oct. 13, 2011) (citing W. Va. Code R. § 24-3-7).

125. With the Spring 2011 injunction in place, the Commission held an investigation. That investigation resulted in an order lifting the injunction for twenty-one of the thirty-one workers, but requiring the utility to keep the remaining ten employees. The Commission found they were needed for essential services including valve maintenance (to limit the risk of and damage from leaks), meter reading and shutoff work. The company must keep these individuals on the job until the utility's next rate case. As for the twenty-one workers to be laid off, the Commission said it was not "endors[ing] the utility's decisions,

company to "refrain, at this time, from reducing its employee level below 289 positions." The Commission also required that the utility "not proceed with reductions in budgeted positions unless it can attest to a continuation of service quality to customers, including the quality and availability of water supply and responsiveness to customers."[126] In its final order in the dispute, the Commission described how it weighed the values at stake:

> The Commission is not charged with resolving collective bargaining disputes, and we are uncomfortable with either side reducing what we view as quality of service issues to pro-union/pro-management arguments. Likewise, we are equally concerned with arguments that seem to confer on management some unrestricted right to direct the operations of WVAWC as they deem appropriate. Management's right to conduct the affairs of a utility is neither unrestricted nor absolute. As a public utility, that right is limited by and conditioned by the requirements of case and statutory law.[127]

While these three cases all involve rejections of the management defense, there are certainly cases that uphold it. An Alabama court found that a commission rule prohibiting "collector's calls on delinquent accounts prior to termination notice . . . improperly interferes with management prerogatives and the efficient operation of the company."[128] And an Oklahoma court held that the Commission lacks power to order a railroad to provide lockers for road crews, absent a request from the interested parties.[129]

---

but merely allowing WVAWC management the freedom to operate its business and assume full responsibility for the outcomes." *Id.* at *52–53.

126. *W. Va.-Am. Water Co.*, Case No. 10-0920-W-42T, at *8 (W. Va. Pub. Serv. Comm'n Feb. 2, 2012). The Commission later modified the 289 employee minimum to require that the utility "explain any future reductions in staffing levels below 288 employees as part of the quarterly monitoring report following any future termination."

127. *Id.* at 4. For another commission decision addressing employee layoff, see *S. Cal. Edison Co.*, 2001 Cal. PUC LEXIS 1024 (Cal. Pub. Util. Comm'n Nov. 8, 2001). The Commission ordered two utilities to rescind certain layoffs "to the extent that the positions . . . *adversely affect* the . . . utility's ability to: fully staff . . . customer call centers; read meters on a monthly basis for all customers; timely respond to service calls and outages; and to connect new customers." Southern California Edison had admitted that as a result of the layoffs, "there would be serious degradations of service, including the risk of customer overcharges if meters were read every other month, instead of monthly." Rejecting the utilities' "management defense" arguments, the Commission asserted that it "unavoidably engages, to some extent, in some functions of management. . . . Those functions flow out of the state's exercise of the police power in the regulation of public utilities." Here, it was "implementing its statutory duty to ensure that SCE and PG&E provide adequate, efficient, just and reasonable service." The Commission also rejected arguments that its actions were preempted by federal labor laws.

128. *Ala. Power Co. v. Ala. Pub. Serv. Comm'n*, 421 So. 2d 1260, 1262, (Ala. 1982) (citing utility's statutory right to collect "just and reasonable rates . . . under honest, efficient and economical management").

129. *Mo. Pac. R.R. v. Corp. Comm'n of Okla.*, 672 P.2d 44, 52 (Okla. 1983) ("The Commission may regulate functions of corporations falling within its jurisdiction, only if the activity is impressed with a public interest. The power does not extend to adjudication of private labor disputes.").

2.E. Eminent domain

Eminent domain is the "power inherent in a sovereign state of taking or of authorizing the taking of any property within its jurisdiction for a public use or benefit."[130] Most states grant this power to public utilities, subject to regulatory guidelines and review. After describing the power's purposes and limits, this subchapter addresses the tension that arises when a utility seeking to use it has both public service and private entrepreneurial purposes. We close with examples of federal authority in what is primarily a state law concept.

2.E.1. Power, purposes and limits

Rhode Island's statute states the typical criteria for exercising the eminent domain power:

> If the commission shall determine that the proposed taking is for the benefit of the people of the state, and that it is necessary in order that the petitioner may render adequate service to the public, and that the use to which the property taken will be put will not unduly interfere with the orderly development of the region and scenic development, it shall issue a certificate authorizing the company to proceed with condemnation.[131]

This language includes three distinct standards. Each was at issue when the Rhode Island Public Utilities Commission addressed Narragansett Electric's request to condemn private property for a 345 kV transmission line.

- *Benefit to the public*: The eminent domain power is available only for the utility to serve its obligatory customers, not to advance its private business interests. "[P]romotion of the production, supply, and reliability of electric power," the Commission found, is an appropriate public purpose. Here, the proposed transmission line was "the most viable means of meeting the company's future growth needs."
- *Necessary for adequate service*: There must be a "clear necessity" to acquire the specific property. While the need must be clear, however, it need not be immediate. It must, however, "materialize in the reasonably foreseeable future" or be "fairly anticipated." The issue is not timing, but relative certainty. In Narragansett's case, consumer demand was reaching the utility system's physical limits, causing a risk to reliability. This evidence was not speculative, even though the utility had twice revised the projected need date. Further, the line's status as a backup rather than primary supply line did not make it less necessary. What mattered was that the line "will contribute" to reliability in Rhode Island.

---

130. Oregon v. Lundberg, 825 P.2d 641, 642–43 n.1 (Or. 1992) (internal quotation marks omitted) (citation omitted).
131. R.I. GEN. LAWS § 39-1-31.

- *No undue interference*: The utility action may not unduly interfere with the region's "orderly development and the scenic development." The utility therefore must select "a route designed to best develop the natural area intruded upon and to minimize the harm which might come to the scenic beauty of such area."

If the proposal meets these three criteria, the Commission will defer to the utility's routing decision unless the decision is arbitrary, capricious, an abuse of discretion or in bad faith. Here, the unavoidable private inconvenience was outweighed by the public benefits, so the Commission approved the line.[132]

2.E.2. Public–private overlap

Consumers Power, a franchised utility serving in Michigan, wanted to build a long-distance, high-voltage transmission line. The line would interconnect Consumers Power's Michigan transmission system with Public Service Company of Indiana's system, at the Michigan-Indiana border. The new line, in conjunction with one to be built by PSI in Indiana, would "form a 116-mile pathway over which Consumers and PSI could exchange up to 500 megawatts (mw) of electricity."[133]

Embedded in the public benefit was a private motive. Consumers Power was owned by a holding company, CMS Energy, that was looking to grow through acquisitions. CMS Energy also had a wholesale generation affiliate, MCV. MCV had no retail franchise obligation to serve, but owned large amounts of surplus generation capacity—a large gas plant converted from the utility's half-built nuclear plant. The wholesale generation affiliate hoped to sell the surplus capacity on a "merchant" basis in wholesale markets, including Indiana. ("Merchant" sales are sales made for entrepreneurial purposes, rather than sales made to carry out a franchise obligation.) The utility was also a partial owner of MCV.

As required by the Michigan statute, Consumers Power sought court permission to use the power of eminent domain. The court sought the Michigan Commission's advice on the question of "public necessity." The Commission found that the line would (1) help CMS Energy (the holding company) acquire or "pool with" an Indiana utility[134] and (2) allow

---

132. Narragansett Elec. Co., Dkt. No. 1440, 65 P.U.R.4th 198, 222–30 (R.I. Pub. Utils. Comm'n Feb. 28, 1985), *aff'd*, 97 P.U.R.4th 527 (R.I. 1988).
133.   Consumers Power Co., Case Nos. U-10059, U-10061, 140 P.U.R.4th 332, 1993 Mich. PSC LEXIS 19, at *1 (Mich. Pub. Serv. Comm'n Jan. 28, 1993).
134. Opponents presented internal company documents showing that CMS intended to use the line as the first stage in a strategy of acquiring other utilities. "Pooling" is a category of power sales transactions in which two or more utilities exchange power to suit their individual needs. Exchanges of capacity between a winter-peaking utility and a summer-peaking utility, for example, allow each utility to avoid owning extra capacity to serve its peak. Other forms of pooling include "economy exchanges" (sometimes called "split-savings exchanges," where for a specific hour, the utility with lower operating costs sells its power to a utility with higher operating costs, with the two utilities splitting the savings) and "maintenance exchanges," where the two utilities stagger their maintenance outages so that each can rely on the other's surplus.

the MCV affiliate to transmit merchant power to the Indiana utility (private purposes). Applying a "heightened scrutiny" test because of the affiliate relationships,[135] the Commissioners overlapped and split. Two of the three members held that the line was *useful* for a public purpose, including additional capacity to serve obligatory load, the ability to sell excess power to new markets, and enhanced competition. Two found, however, that the line was *not necessary* for a public purpose. One commissioner found that it was neither useful nor necessary. The effect of the decision was to allow the line costs to be recovered in retail rates (because the line was useful), but to advise the court that Consumers Power's request did not satisfy the public need standard because the line was not "necessary." The Commission also warned (noting that "Consumers has, on occasion, misinformed the Commission and attempted to circumvent its orders") that

> if the assertions in the record regarding the intended use of the line or the magnitude of its expected public benefits later prove to be untrue, the Commission will take appropriate action. This includes, but is not limited to, denying recovery of the . . . line's costs in future rate cases and compensating ratepayers through the power supply cost recovery process for any failure to use the line in a manner that produces the lowest possible costs for Consumers' customers.[136]

2.E.3. Federal roles

While the typical eminent domain case involves a state-jurisdictional utility acting under state law, certain eminent domain powers emanate from federal law. Section 7(h) of the Natural Gas Act grants the right of eminent domain to an entity that has received from the Federal Energy Regulatory Commission a certificate of public convenience and necessity under Section 7(c). This eminent domain power is available when the certificate holder "cannot acquire by contract, or is unable to agree with the owner of property to the compensation to be paid for, the necessary right-of-way . . . and the necessary land or other property."[137]

For electric transmission lines, the law is more complicated. Section 216 of the Federal Power Act[138] authorizes FERC to grant a "construction permit," preemptive of state law, to an applicant for the "construction or modification of electric transmission facilities

---

135. A detailed discussion of interaffiliate relationships and regulatory responses will appear in the companion volume on corporate structure, mergers and acquisitions.

136. *Consumers Power Co.*, 140 P.U.R.4th 332, 1993 Mich. PSC LEXIS 19 at *31–32. Three weeks after receiving the Commission's views, the state court ruled against Consumers (not based on the opponents' claims that the line was merely a private undertaking, but on the grounds that the line was not necessary for a public purpose). Condemnation was, therefore, not available as a tool to acquire the needed right of way. Consumers dropped its plans to build the line.

137. 15 U.S.C. § 717f(h).

138. 16 U.S.C. § 824p.

in a national interest electric transmission corridor." The applicant must work through a multi-step process. The first step occurs at the U.S. Department of Energy, which must have designated the area crossed by the transmission facilities as a "national interest electric transmission corridor." To designate a corridor, DOE must find that the area is "experiencing electric energy transmission capacity constraints or congestion that adversely affects consumers," based on a consideration of five factors set forth in Section 216(a)(4).[139]

If the facility is located within a DOE-designated corridor, FERC can grant the permit if it makes all of the five findings set forth in Section 216(b)(2)–(6).[140] But FERC does not have jurisdiction to make these findings unless the applicant first satisfies the criteria in Section 216(b)(1): FERC must find that the state in which the facility will be built has not approved, or cannot approve, the siting of the facility because of one of three reasons: (a) the state commission lacks authority to approve or to consider interstate benefits; (b) the applicant does not qualify, under state law, as an entity eligible to site a project because it does not serve end-use customers; or (c) the state has "withheld approval for more than a year" or conditioned its approval "in such a manner that the proposed construction or modification will not significantly reduce transmission congestion in interstate commerce or is not economically feasible."[141] If FERC's jurisdiction is triggered for one of these rea-

---

139.   The five factors that the Department of Energy "may consider" are:

> (A) the economic vitality and development of the corridor, or the end markets served by the corridor, may be constrained by lack of adequate or reasonably priced electricity;
> (B)(i) economic growth in the corridor, or the end markets served by the corridor, may be jeopardized by reliance on limited sources of energy; and
> (ii) a diversification of supply is warranted;
> (C) the energy independence of the United States would be served by the designation;
> (D) the designation would be in the interest of national energy policy; and
> (E) the designation would enhance national defense and homeland security.

16 U.S.C. § 824p(a)(4). In *California Wilderness Coalition v. U.S. Department of Energy*, 631 F.3d 1072 (9th Cir. 2011), the Ninth Circuit vacated the Congestion Study required of DOE by Section 216(a)(1), for failure to "consult" with states sufficiently. The Court also vacated DOE's designation of particular corridors because it did not consider properly the environmental consequences under the National Environmental Protection Act ("NEPA").

140.   Those five findings, listed in Section 216(b)(2)–(6), are:

> (2) the facilities to be authorized by the permit will be used for the transmission of electric energy in interstate commerce;
> (3) the proposed construction or modification is consistent with the public interest;
> (4) the proposed construction or modification will significantly reduce transmission congestion in interstate commerce and protects or benefits consumers;
> (5) the proposed construction or modification is consistent with sound national energy policy and will enhance energy independence; and
> (6) the proposed modification will maximize, to the extent reasonable and economical, the transmission capabilities of existing towers or structures.

141.   The meaning of the phrase "withheld approval" was addressed by the Court of Appeals in *Piedmont Environmental Council v. FERC*, 558 F.3d 304 (4th Cir. 2009). FERC had interpreted the phrase to include a state saying "no," i.e., rejecting an application. The Court disagreed: "withheld" means inaction;

sons and if the applicant satisfies the five criteria, its rights are similar to those stated in the Natural Gas Act. Section 216(e) of the Federal Power Act grants a permit holder the right of eminent domain if the permit holder "cannot acquire by contract, or is unable to agree with the owner of the property to the compensation to be paid for, the necessary right-of-way to construct or modify the transmission facilities . . . ."

This brief mention of federal eminent domain powers raises a larger question: In utility regulation, how well do our federal and state statutes mesh? We will address this question in detail in Part 3, relating to jurisdiction.

2.F. Limited liability for negligence

A fire destroys a warehouse because the water company failed to maintain enough water supply and water pressure to douse the flames. Lawsuit dismissed. "The failure in such circumstances to furnish an adequate supply of water is at most the denial of a benefit. It is not the commission of a wrong."[142]

A college employee is hit by a car because the utility failed to maintain the traffic lights. Lawsuit dismissed. "[O]rdinarily an electric company under contract to make repairs and maintain street lights has no common law duty to third persons who are injured . . . ."[143]

Citizens hurt by a utility's carelessness are often surprised, and disappointed, to learn they have no recourse. This subsection explains the majority rule in the states: utilities cannot be sued for ordinary negligence, only gross negligence. After explaining the rule and its policy bases, we describe how different parties and their defenses can produce different outcomes. We then discuss exceptions to the rule, and close with a comment on its role in federal regulation.

2.F.1. General limitation and its justifications

"Courts are virtually unanimous that provisions limiting a public utility's liability are valid so long as they do not purport to grant immunity or limit liability for gross negligence."[144]

---

it does not mean acting negatively. A state's rejection therefore ousts FERC's jurisdiction to issue a construction permit. *Piedmont Envtl. Council*, 558 F.3d at 315.

142. H.R. Moch Co. v. Rensselaer Water Co., 159 N.E. 896, 899 (N.Y. 1928) (Cardozo, Ch. J.) (holding that water company's conduct was "mere negligent omission, unaccompanied by malice or other aggravating elements"). *But see* Long v. District of Columbia, 820 F.2d 409, 418–19 (D.C. Cir. 1986) (upholding jury award to widow of traffic accident victim; utility company, in contracting with city to maintain traffic lights, "thereby acquired a duty to foreseeable plaintiffs (in this case, members of the travelling public) to perform these services with reasonable care"); CF Indus., Inc. v. Transcon. Gas Pipe Line Corp., 448 F. Supp. 475, 481–82 (W.D.N.C. 1978) (noting that North Carolina is "one of a handful of states which has rejected the reasoning of Judge Hand in *Moch*").

143. Vaugran v. E. Edison Co., 719 N.E.2d 520 (Mass. App. Ct. 1999) (dismissing claim for traffic injuries because the fact that visibility was diminished did not mean that the utility should assume that plaintiff would "forgo [sic] other protective measures"); *see also* Arenado v. Fla. Power & Light Co., 523 So. 2d 628 (Fla. Dist. Ct. App. 1988) (holding that a utility owes no duty to a driver killed in an accident because of service disruption to a traffic light), *review dismissed*, 541 So. 2d 612 (Fla. 1989).

144. Garrison v. Pac. Nw. Bell, 608 P.2d 1206, 1211 (Or. Ct. App. 1980).

The lawsuit-blocking provisions appear in statutes, commission-approved tariffs and case law. Why? As one court explained:

> Courts upheld these limitations on the public policy grounds that they balanced lower rates for all customers against the burden of limited recovery for some, and that the technological complexity of modern utility systems and resulting potential for service failures unrelated to human errors justified liability limitations.[145]

A typical utility serves millions of customers, employs thousands of workers, owns hundreds of trucks, handles tons of fuel and tends to an untold number of pipes, pumps and wires. Every day, every hour, something could go wrong. What if every error could generate a lawsuit for negligence? Consider the fire at a telephone switching station serving Chicago suburbs, disrupting over 100 million telephone calls. The utility's commission-approved tariff limited its liability. The Illinois Supreme Court dismissed the class action lawsuit and upheld the tariff:

> Given the imagination and resourcefulness of today's litigants, it is easy to speculate that [the utility's liability] might run into the tens or even hundreds of millions of dollars. In short, the plaintiffs could well end up owning the telephone company . . . [or] phone rates would have to be increased astronomically to recoup such liability payments.[146]

---

145. Transmission Access Policy Study Grp. v. FERC, 225 F.3d 667, 727 (D.C. Cir. 2000). For other cases upholding limited-liability provisions, see *Central Power and Light*, 1981 Tex. PUC LEXIS 247, at *7 (Pub. Util. Comm'n Tex. 1981) (finding that at least forty-five states have approved electric tariffs containing limited-liability provisions); Olson v. Mountain States Tel. Co., 580 P.2d 782, 784 (Ariz. App. 1978); Waters v. Pac. Tel. Co., 523 P.2d 1161, 1164 (Cal. 1974); Professional Answering Serv., Inc. v. Chesapeake & Potomac Tel. Co., 565 A.2d 55, 60 (D.C. App. 1989); Landrum v. Fla. Power & Light, 505 So. 2d 552, 554 (Fla. Dist. Ct. App. 1987), *review denied*, 513 So. 2d 1061 (Fla. 1987); S. Bell Tel. & Tel. Co. v. Invenhek, Inc., 204 S.E.2d 457, 460 (Ga. Ct. App. 1974); Ill. Bell Switching Station Litigation, 641 N.E.2d 440, 445 (Ill. 1994); Singer Co. v. Balt. Gas & Elec., 558 A.2d 419, 427 (Md. Ct. Spec. App. 1989); Wilkinson v. New England Tel. and Tel. Co., 97 N.E.2d 413, 416 (Mass. 1951); Valentine v. Mich. Bell Tel., 199 N.W.2d 182, 185 (Mich. 1972); Computer Tool & Eng'g Co. v. N. States Power Co., 453 N.W.2d 569, 572 (Minn. Ct. App. 1990); Warner v. Sw. Bell Tel. Co., 428 S.W.2d 596, 601 (Mo. 1968) (for interruption of service); Bulbman Inc. v. Nev. Bell, 825 P.2d 588, 590 (Nev. 1992); Lee v. Consol. Edison, 413 N.Y.S.2d 826, 828 (N.Y. App. Div. 1978); Investigation into Limitation of Liab. Clauses Contained in Util. Tariffs, 1987 Ohio PUC Lexis 825, ¶ 4 (Pub. Utils. Comm'n Ohio 1987) (permitting tariff limitation of liability but requiring disclaimer); Garrison v. Pac. Nw. Bell, 608 P.2d 1206, 1211 (Or. 1980); Behrend v. Bell Tel. Co., 363 A.2d 1152, 1165 (Pa. 1976), *vacated and remanded*, 374 A.2d 536 (Pa. 1978), *reinstated*, 390 A.2d 233 (Pa. 1978); Pilot Indus. v. S. Bell Tel., 495 F. Supp. 356, 361 (D.S.C. 1979); Sw. Bell Tel. Co. v. Rucker, 537 S.W.2d 326, 332 (Tex. Civ. App. 1976); Liab. Limitations, Disclaimers or Indem. Provisions in Telecomms. Tariff Filings, 137 P.U.R.4th 436 (W.Va. Pub. Serv. Comm'n 1992); Schaafs v. W. Union Tel. Co., 215 F. Supp. 419, 420 (E.D. Wis. 1963) (based on statute and tariff); Strauss v. Belle Realty Co., 482 N.E.2d 34, 38 (N.Y. 1985) (holding ConEd not liable for damages incurred by third parties due to blackout); Ky. Agric. Energy Corp. v. Bowling Green Mun. Utils. Bd., 735 F. Supp. 226, 230 (W.D. Ky. 1989) (wholesaler of electric power not liable to retail customer to whom power was resold).

146. *Illinois Bell*, 641 N.E.2d at 446; *see also* Strauss v. Belle Realty Co., 482 N.E.2d 34, 36 (N.Y. 1985) (observing that "the liability of utilities for consequential damages for failure to provide service . . . [can]

And the bicyclist who collided with a motorist because the street light failed lost because the court

> consider[ed] the cost of imposing this liability on public utilities, the current public utility rate structures, the large numbers of streetlights, the likelihood that streetlights will become periodically inoperable, the fact that motor vehicles operate at night with headlights, the slight chance that a single inoperative streetlight will be the cause of a motor vehicle collision, and the availability of automobile insurance to pay for damages.[147]

Defending this treatment, tort scholars Prosser and Keeton stress the difference between a conventional company and a utility. The conventional company can reject customers who bring a higher risk of damage from service interruptions. Because they can screen their customers, they are liable to the customers they accept. But a utility has an obligation to serve all (*see* Chapter 2.B)—including, for example, hospitals, where loss of service would mean loss of lives:

> [T]he imposition of tort liability on those who must render continuous service . . . to all who apply for it under all kinds of circumstances could be ruinous and the expense of litigating and settling claims over the issue of whether or not there was negligence could be a greater burden to the rate payer than can be socially justified.[148]

The answer to this cold reality? Buy insurance—and when crossing the street, look both ways.[149]

---

be enormous”); *Bulbman*, 825 P.2d at 590 (“absent liability limitations such as that contained in [the tariff], the broad liability exposure faced by utilities would create tremendous upward pressure on utility service rates); *Waters*, 523 P.2d at 1164; *Landrum*, 505 So. 2d at 554 (“[A] limitation of liability contained in a tariff is an essential part of the rate” and thus “[a] broadened liability exposure must inevitably raise the cost and thereby the rates, of electric service.”); Abraham v. N.Y. Tel. Co., 380 N.Y.S.2d 969, 972 (N.Y. Civ. Ct. 1976) (finding that if not properly limited, liability can have “a catastrophic impact on the rates to be charged the public at large”).

147. White v. S. Cal. Edison Co., 30 Cal. Rptr. 2d 431, 437 (Cal. Ct. App. 1994). The Maryland Commission has used similar logic, finding that limited liability provisions “are a reasonable protective measure to reduce the possibilities of widespread utility liability and thus keep rates lower for all customers, whereas those customers needing protection from variations in electric service are able to do so without imposing such costs upon the vast body of ratepayers.” Liability of Electric Power Companies for Injury or Damages Resulting from Problems in the Delivery of Electric Power, 1991 Md. PSC Lexis 60, at *31–32 (Md. Pub. Serv. Comm’n 1991).

148. W. Page Keeton, Prosser & Keeton on Torts § 93, at 671 (5th ed. 1984).

149. *See* Keeton, *supra* note 148, § 92, at 663 (“Substantial losses of this kind are normally incurred by industrial and commercial customers who can insure against losses”).

2.F.2. Parties and defenses

The liability cases distinguish between two types of plaintiffs. One is the utility customer who is harmed by the outage; say, a meatpacking plant whose meat spoils because the freezers fail. The other is a "third party," a non-customer like an accident victim. Then there are two types of utility defenses. Most common is the one already discussed: holding utilities liable would make electric service too expensive. This defense arises in both the customer cases and the third-party cases. The other defense arises specifically in the third-party cases: that there is no "privity" between the utility and the third party; put another way, the utility owes no duty to the third party because they have no legal relationship.[150]

2.F.3. Exceptions to the general rule

Negligence immunity is the majority rule, but it is not the universal rule. Here are three examples of exceptions.

1. The Virginia Supreme Court has held that "[p]ublic policy forbids . . . common carriers and other public service companies, including power companies, [from] contract[ing] against liability for the breach of public duties." Nor may the utility shift responsibility, for negligence committed in its public duties, to its private contractor.[151]

2. The Utah Commission directed its utility to eliminate tariff language granting immunity from liability for negligence, citing its existing policy that such provisions are "seldom just and reasonable" and will be approved only where the record has established that "(1) it is in the public interest to provide the particular utility service and to encourage the provision of the service, and (2) there is a substantial likelihood that the service would not be provided in the absence of limitations of liability."[152]

3. The New Jersey Supreme Court imposed liability on a water company, where insufficient water pressure left firemen unable to save an apartment building. Describing its prior holdings (insulating the utility from liability) as "like a dinosaur from the past," the court overruled itself: "The immunity of private water companies from liability for negligently failing to maintain adequate water pressure for fire extinguishing is an anomaly in New Jersey tort law, but it is an anomaly of our own creation. We must take responsibility for its elimination."[153]

---

150. *See, e.g.,* White v. S. Ca. Edison Co., 30 Cal. Rptr. 2d at 437 ("There is no contractual relation between the utility and the injured party, and the injured party is not a third party beneficiary of the utility's contract with the public entity. The public utility owes no general duty to the public to provide streetlights."); *see also* Grosshans v. Rochester Gas & Elec. Corp., 478 N.Y.S.2d 402, 403 (N.Y. App. Div. 1984) ("[A] public utility may not be held liable for negligent failure to supply service absent a contractual relationship between plaintiff and the utility.").

151. Richardson-Wayland Elec. Corp. v. Va. Elec. Power Co., 247 S.E.2d 465, 467–68 (Va. 1978) (striking clause that made contractor the indemnifier of the utility's negligence).

152. Bradley v. Utah Power and Light, Case No. UPL-E-89-9, Order No. 23287, 1990 Ida. PUC LEXIS 137, at *10 (Ida. Pub. Utils. Comm'n Sept. 1990) (internal quotation marks omitted).

153. Weinberg v. Dinger, 524 A.2d 366 (N.J. 1985).

2.F.4. No immunity: Gross negligence

In 1977, Consolidated Edison's storm-caused blackout left 3 million customers without power. One was a grocery store chain whose food spoiled and whose customers stayed home. Recognizing that ConEd's tariff insulated it from liability for ordinary negligence, Food Pageant alleged gross negligence. The jury heard evidence that, at the time of the key lightning strike, (1) a major tie line and generating plant had been out of service; (2) gas turbines maintained for peak hours were unavailable because their operators had been sent home early; (3) the utility had failed to maintain, inspect and/or protect certain relays, circuit breakers, towers and transmission lines; and (4) the employee in charge of the system lacked sufficient experience, knowledge and expertise (among other errors, he failed to follow the pool operator's instructions to "shed load"). This evidence persuaded the jury members to find gross negligence and award damages.[154]

But a phone company's directory error, listing a child psychiatrist as an "osteopath," was not gross negligence. The grossly negligent are reckless; they act with an "I don't care" attitude. The utility's error did not sink to that level: "So long as defendant trains its employees to recognize that there is a difference between the categories of physicians which is significant for directory classification purposes, defendant's failure to train its employes [sic] in the details of physicians' training and job functions is not gross negligence."[155]

2.F.5. Federal–state relations

What if a company is a "public utility" under federal law, providing "unbundled" transmission service subject to Federal Power Act jurisdiction but providing no service subject to state jurisdiction?[156] With no state-jurisdictional service there is no state-approved tariff; and with no state-approved tariff there is no state-approved tariff provision limiting its negligence liability. Is the company vulnerable to negligence suits in state court?

In 1996, FERC issued its landmark Order No. 888, requiring transmission owners to file tariffs offering transmission service on a non-discriminatory basis.[157] Transmission owners wanted the federal tariffs to include a provision limiting their state law negligence liability. FERC declined, not wanting to "use the tariff . . . as an instrument for defining exclusive and preemptive federal laws for liability for all damages that might arise from

---

154.   Food Pageant v. Consol. Edison, 429 N.E.2d 738 (N.Y. 1981).
155.   Garrison v. Pac. Nw. Bell, 608 P.2d 1206, 1211–12 (Or. Ct. App. 1980).
156.   We discuss this concept of "unbundled" service in Chapter 4.
157.   Promoting Wholesale Competition Through Open Access Non-Discriminatory Transmission Services by Public Utilities, Recovery of Stranded Costs by Public Utilities and Transmitting Utilities, Order No. 888, 75 FERC ¶ 61,080 (1996), *order on reh'g*, Order No. 888-A, 78 FERC ¶ 61,220, *order on reh'g*, Order No. 888-B, 81 FERC ¶ 61,248 (1997), *order on reh'g*, Order No. 888-C, 82 FERC ¶ 61,046 (1998), *aff'd in relevant part sub nom.* Transmission Access Policy Study Group v. FERC, 225 F.3d 667 (D.C. Cir. 2000), *aff'd sub nom.* New York v. FERC, 535 U.S. 1 (2002). Chapter 3.A will discuss this event as well as related ones in the gas and telecommunications industries.

the operation of the transmission system."[158] FERC later modified its view, in the special situation of "regional transmission organizations" (RTOs). An RTO is a corporation that has received by contract, from transmission owners, the authority and obligation to operate and provide transmission service over the owners' facilities.[159] FERC has approved tariff provisions that do provide liability protection for certain RTOs and for the transmission owners who have transferred their transmission facilities to the RTOs. These provisions preempt state tort law that otherwise could subject the providers to negligence suits. As FERC explained:

> Midwest ISO [one of eight RTOs] and stand-alone transmission companies are solely regulated by the Commission for their provision of transmission services [under FERC's Order No. 888], so the Commission is the only regulator with the ability to ensure that they are protected from potentially excessive damage awards by adequate limitation of liability provisions. Many state commissions in the Midwest ISO footprint have traditionally allowed, and continue to allow, utilities to limit their liability to gross negligence. We believe that Midwest ISO and its Transmission Owners should be afforded similar protection. Otherwise, disparate treatment is a disincentive to participate in Midwest ISO.[160]

FERC has declined, however, to extend the RTOs' liability protection to entities that provide FERC-jurisdictional transmission service but are not RTO members. Southern Company is a holding company whose five utility subsidiaries own transmission facilities. They use these transmission facilities not only to carry power to their retail customers, but also to provide FERC-mandated transmission service under Order No. 888. Southern sought a tariff provision protecting it from lawsuits for ordinary negligence that might occur when providing FERC-jurisdictional service. The provision would limit its liability to "Transmission Customers and/or third parties for damages (whether direct, indirect or punitive) resulting from service interruptions, except in instances of gross negligence or intentional misconduct." FERC denied the request. Southern had only asserted, but not proved, that its utilities remained unprotected from state law negligence suits. The RTOs, in contrast, "were created by and solely regulated by the Commission, and otherwise would be without limitations on liability."[161]

* * *

---

158. Order No. 888-B, 81 FERC ¶ 61,248, at p. 62,080 (1997).
159. Regional Transmission Organizations, 89 FERC ¶ 61,285 (1999) (discussed in more detail in Chapters 3.A.1 and 4.B.5.d).
160. Midwest Indep. Transmission Sys. Operator, Inc., 110 FERC ¶ 61,164, at P 29 (2005).
161. S. Co. Servs., Inc., 113 FERC ¶ 61,239, at P 7 (2005).

For most of the last century, public utility service was provided by companies with monopoly franchises: the exclusive right, granted by state government, to provide specified services within specified territories. In return for this right (whose exclusivity was and is not always absolute), the utility consented to continuous regulation. That regulation established an obligation to serve all customers, without undue discrimination, consistent with quality of service standards established by the regulator. To acquire land needed for physical infrastructure, most states granted the utility power of eminent domain; and to protect the utility from lawsuits arising from inevitable errors, most states limited the utility's liability for ordinary negligence. For retail electricity, retail natural gas, water and even some aspects of telephone service, some version of the franchised monopoly market structure remains in place today.

The next three chapters describe how policymakers have changed this market structure by making some geographic and product markets available to competitors. The first step is authorizing competition by modifying the statutes that make the incumbent's role exclusive. And because authorizing competition is not the same as making competition effective, the second step involves reducing the incumbent's market power by "unbundling" its monopoly services from its competitive services and lowering other entry barriers. The third step is monitoring the new market to detect and punish anti-competitive behavior, such as price squeezes, predatory pricing, tying and market manipulation.

CHAPTER THREE
Authorizing Competition

The "central, continuing responsibility of legislatures and regulatory commissions" is "finding the best possible mix of inevitably imperfect regulation and inevitably imperfect competition."[1]

Long-distance and local telephone service, wholesale natural gas supply, wholesale electric generation, retail electric and gas service, energy efficiency and demand management: All are services, historically provided by franchised monopolies, that some jurisdiction has subjected to competition. These competition experiments continue, for those services and new ones. Federal and state policymakers today are debating appropriate market structures for broadband, gas and electricity storage, distributed generation, energy conservation, "smart grid," and other new services.

A forty-year flow of statutory change, agency action and court review reveals several common steps. Each competition experiment starts with questions: For each candidate product or service, will competition be physically feasible and economically efficient? Will investors risk their dollars on the new competitors? Will competition lower prices, while increasing quality and inducing innovation? How will those benefits compare to potential losses in economies of scale and scope? How will we manage the risk that effective competition does not develop, leaving incumbents with market power in unregulated markets? These are the non-legal questions, requiring the expertise of engineers, economists, accountants, financial analysts, technologists, marketing specialists, investors, consumers and the market players themselves.

Once policymakers identify the products and services appropriate for competition, they face three main legal steps, addressed in the three chapters that follow.

Authorizing competition: The six legal features of the traditional franchised monopoly, discussed in Chapter 2, require revision for a market served by competitors. The *exclusive franchise* protected the franchisee from competition. Utilities' *consent to regulation* allowed the government to constrain the franchisee's actions without facing constitutional challenges. The *obligation to serve* and *quality of service standards* ensured that all eligible customers received satisfactory service. *Eminent domain powers* allowed the utility to take private property when necessary to serve the public. *Limited liability* protected the utility from lawsuits for ordinary negligence. Adapting these concepts to competition requires legal changes. Those changes are the subject of this Chapter.

Making competition effective: Authorizing competition does not ensure effective competition. It makes entry legal but not necessarily feasible. The policymaker still must

---

1. 2 Alfred E. Kahn, The Economics of Regulation: Principles and Institutions, at xxxvii, 114 (1970, 1988).

address "entry barriers"—the difference in entry cost between incumbent and newcomer. If new entrants are deterred by high entry costs, merely authorizing competition will not protect consumers from excess prices and inadequate service. (Even with effective competition, consumers still need protections against deceptive advertising, unsafe practices and indecipherable contract terms.) One type of entry barrier is a physical facility that is necessary for competition but owned or controlled by the incumbent. Examples are electric transmission and distribution facilities, gas pipelines and distribution systems, the telephone company's "last mile," and radio-frequency spectrum. Known as "bottleneck facilities" or "essential facilities," these assets cannot be economically duplicated by the new entrant, yet are necessary for market entry. Then there are non-physical entry barriers derived from the incumbent's first-mover advantage: economies of scale and scope, and customer characteristics like loyalty, inertia and shopping inexperience. The legal steps to mitigate these factors are discussed in Chapter 4.

Monitoring competition: The preceding steps change market structure by identifying products and services appropriate for competition, authorizing competitive access and reducing entry barriers. The final step, once competition has been authorized and made effective, is to monitor the market. Optimism about "competition" stimulates policy but it does not guarantee results. Not every competitor plays fair—the rational incumbent resists competition, while the new competitors can cut corners. These tendencies undermine the competitive forces freed by the prior two steps. Descriptions of these behaviors and the regulatory responses are the subject of Chapter 5.

Experience being the best teacher, we begin our three-chapter tour with brief histories of structural change in the electricity, gas and telecommunications industries.[2] We then turn to the main subject of this chapter: how policymakers have adjusted the incumbent's six legal characteristics to make room for newcomers.

3.A. Historical summary

Policymakers considering competition have wrestled with these questions: For which products and services will competition likely help the consumer? How must we revise the

---

2. "Brief" and "tour" are the key words. These discussions are not substitutes for in-depth study of the industries, for those who seek to specialize. Readers wishing more historic detail should consult works specific to the industries of interest. *See, e.g.*, TELECOMMUNICATIONS REGULATION TODAY AND TOMORROW (Eli Noam ed., 1983); Warren Lavey, *The Public Policies That Changed the Telephone Industry into Regulated Monopolies: Lessons from Around 1915*, 39 FED. COM. L.J. 171 (1987); William Byrnes, *Telecommunications Regulation: Something Old and Something New, in* THE COMMUNICATIONS ACT: A LEGISLATIVE HISTORY OF THE MAJOR AMENDMENTS, at 31, 90–99 (Max Paglin ed., 1999); RICHARD PIERCE & ERNEST GELLHORN, REGULATED INDUSTRIES IN A NUTSHELL (1999); JOSEPH TOMAIN & RICHARD CUDAHY, ENERGY LAW IN A NUTSHELL (2011); STUART BROTMAN, COMMUNICATIONS LAW AND PRACTICE § 5.01[4] (2012); STUART MINOR BENJAMIN, HOWARD A. SHELANSKI, JAMES B. SPETA & PHILLIP J. WEISER, TELECOMMUNICATIONS LAW AND POLICY, chs. 4–5, 8–12 (3d ed. 2012); ENERGY LAW AND TRANSACTIONS (William A. Mogel & David J. Muchow eds., 2012); WILLIAM A. MOGEL, REGULATION OF THE GAS INDUSTRY (2012).

incumbent's legal status? Who should own or control which assets? Are there bottleneck facilities? If so, should the government guarantee access, and on what terms? What roles should regulators (as opposed to, or in addition to, "market forces") play in sorting all this out? The following summaries of industry transitions focus on these questions, to provide context for the subsequent discussion of the legal principles common to these regulatory efforts.

3.A.1. Electricity

The electricity industry consists of four major activities. Generation is the conversion of energy from fossil, nuclear, renewable, hydroelectric or other sources into electric current. Transmission is the long-distance transportation of electric current, from the generation source to substations close to load centers. Distribution is the physical delivery of electricity over a network of wires and equipment from the transmission system (usually from a substation) to the consumer.[3] Aggregation is the service of planning for the customers' total needs (called "load" or "demand") and procuring sufficient resources to meet those needs. Aggregation includes all the activities necessary to serve customers reliably: forecasting customers' demand; acquiring (through construction or purchase) sufficient generation, transmission and distribution resources to serve that demand; installing and maintaining meters to measure customer consumption; and billing customers and processing payments.

Before the 1980s: Most customers were served by vertically integrated utilities—entities that performed all four activities. Each utility owned and operated generation, transmission, and distribution facilities, and carried out the aggregation functions. By performing all of these activities, the utility provided to retail customers a single "bundled" product—electric service—within an exclusive local territory whose boundaries were defined by the state.[4] Many vertically integrated utilities also had wholesale customers, such as cities, towns and cooperatives, who would buy "bulk power" (generation and transmission) from the utilities and then handle the final two stages (physical distribution and aggregation) themselves.[5] While these utilities had a state law obligation to serve at retail,[6] a small subset had a distinct federal law obligation to transmit power for competitors.[7]

---

3.   *See Electric Glossary,* MADISONGASANDELECTRIC.COM, http://www.mge.com/about/electric/glossary. htm (last visited Jan. 29, 2013).

4.   See Chapter 2.A.1 for a discussion of exclusive service territories.

5.   This common market structure—a local vertically integrated utility serving as a monopoly within a state-defined service territory—was a result of the "single integrated public-utility system" requirement of the Public Utility Holding Company Act of 1935, which broke up thirteen geographically spread holding companies, each of which controlled many utility companies and non-utility businesses. 49 Stat. 821, § 11(b) (codified at 15 U.S.C. § 79k(b)) (repealed in 2005) ("PUHCA"). The role of holding companies in modern regulation will be detailed in the companion volume on corporate structure, mergers and acquisitions.

6.   See Chapter 2.B for a discussion of obligation to serve.

7.   This federal law transmission obligation existed due to court orders under antitrust law, *see, e.g.,* Otter Tail Power Co. v. United States, 410 U.S. 366 (1973); or orders of the Nuclear Regulatory Commission

1978: During the second Arab oil embargo of the 1970s, Congress sought to (a) reduce the demand for fossil fuels, and (b) overcome utilities' traditional "reluctan[ce] to purchase power from, and to sell power to, the nontraditional facilities."[8] Among the new statutes was the Public Utility Regulatory Policies Act of 1978 (PURPA).[9] PURPA modified the pre-1978 vertically integrated, monopoly market structure by introducing wholesale sellers. Investors could form and acquire specialized generators, called "qualifying facilities" (QFs). To become a qualifying facility, a generator had to be either a "cogenerator" or a "small power producer."[10] PURPA granted a QF the right to compel its "host utility" (the utility in whose service territory the QF was located) to buy the QF's capacity and energy, at a price equal to the utility's "avoided cost." Avoided cost, in turn, is "the incremental costs to an electric utility of electric energy or capacity or both which, but for the purchase from the qualifying facility or qualifying facilities, such utility would generate itself or purchase from another source."[11] A host utility that declined to buy had to transmit the QF's output to an adjacent utility, which then had to purchase the output at *its* avoided

---

(NRC), *see, e.g.,* Ala. Power Co., 13 N.R.C. 1027, 1061 (1981); Toledo Edison Co. & Cleveland Elec. Illuminating Co., 10 N.R.C. 265, 327–34 (1979); Consumers Power Co., 6 N.R.C. 887, 1036–44 (1977). *See generally* James E. Meeks, *Concentration in the Electric Power Industry: The Impact of Antitrust Policy,* 72 Colum. L. Rev. 64 (1972).

The NRC's role in transmission access will come as a surprise to practitioners recently entering regulation. Section 105(c) of the Atomic Energy Act of 1954, as amended, required the NRC to conduct antitrust reviews of applications to construct or operate nuclear facilities, submitted under section 103 of that Act. *See* Pub. L. 91–560, 84 Stat. 1472 (1970). In some cases (such as those cited in this footnote), those reviews led to NRC conditions requiring the licensee to offer transmission service to its competitors. Congress added this provision on the premise that nuclear power would be inexpensive relative to other sources; if traditional utilities controlled that source they would have an unfair competitive advantage over others. The NRC's antitrust review powers were repealed by the Energy Policy Act of 2005. Despite this repeal, the NRC asserts that it maintains certain antitrust review authority, in the following circumstances:

1. violation of existing license conditions, in which the NRC can revoke or suspend the license and/or impose financial penalties;
2. transfer of a license containing antitrust conditions;
3. changes in law or facts affecting existing antitrust conditions (in which case Staff should would pay "[p]articular attention . . . to whether there have been regulatory developments to promote competition in the relevant market since the antitrust conditions were first imposed");
4. a court has found that a licensee has violated the antitrust laws, in which case the NRC "may suspend or revoke the license or take other action"; and
5. any use of "special nuclear material or atomic energy" violates the antitrust laws (in which case the NRC must report the violation to the Attorney General).

See S. Hom and C. Pittiglio, U.S. Nuclear Regulatory Commission, NUREG-1574, Rev. 2, Standard Review Plan on Transfer and Amendment of Antitrust License Conditions and Antitrust Enforcement 7–9 (2007), *available at* http://pbadupws.nrc.gov/docs/ML0722/ML072260035.pdf.
8. FERC v. Mississippi, 456 U.S. 742, 750 (1982).
9. 16 U.S.C. §§ 2601 *et seq.*
10. The terms "cogenerator" and "small power producer" are defined in 16 U.S.C. § 796(18)(A) and 18 C.F.R. § 292.203. A "cogenerator" uses fossil fuels efficiently by producing both heat and electricity; a "small power producer" makes specified types of renewable energy within specified size limits.
11. 18 C.F.R. § 292.101(b)(6).

cost.[12] A QF was exempt from the "integrated public-utility system" requirement of the Public Utility Holding Company Act (PUHCA).[13] As a result, a QF's owner could be any type of company, located anywhere, and could own unlimited numbers of QFs located anywhere, except that a public utility or its holding company could own no more than 50 percent of the equity interest in a QF.[14]

1992: Aiming to inject competition into wholesale generation markets, Congress passed the Energy Policy Act of 1992. One provision amended PUHCA to allow investors to create and acquire "exempt wholesale generators" (EWGs). An EWG, like a QF, was exempt from PUHCA's "integrated public-utility system" restriction. The effect was to allow generating companies to enter wholesale markets anywhere, thus increasing the number and types of potential wholesale generation competitors. Unlike a QF, an EWG could use any type of fuel, but also unlike a QF, it had no right to compel a purchase by a retail utility.

The 1992 Act also authorized FERC, upon complaint, to order transmission-owning utilities to provide transmission service to others on FERC-set terms. FERC later found that its 1992 transmission authority did little to encourage wholesale competition: few prospective customers filed complaints, and the complaint process itself was unwieldy.[15] This weakness in FERC's 1992 transmission authority led, in 1996, to Order No. 888.

1996: Recognizing that transmission facilities were bottleneck facilities—essential for competition, controlled by the incumbent and not economically duplicable by competitors—FERC issued its landmark Order No. 888.[16] Order No. 888 required all transmission-owning public utilities[17] to file tariffs committing the utility to provide

---

12. 18 C.F.R. § 292(d).
13. 18 C.F.R. § 292.602(b). PUHCA's "integrated public-utility system" requirement will be discussed in the companion volume on corporate structure, mergers and acquisitions.
14. 18 C.F.R. § 292.206(b). The 2005 amendments to PURPA authorized utilities to seek from FERC an exemption from its obligation to buy capacity and energy from a QF, if the utility makes one of three showings demonstrating that QFs in its region have access to multiple buyers in a competitive market. 16 U.S.C. § 824a-3(m)(1)(A)–(C).
15. *See* Promoting Wholesale Competition Through Open Access Non-discriminatory Transmission Services by Public Utilities, Recovery of Stranded Costs by Public Utilities and Transmitting Utilities, Order No. 888, 75 FERC ¶ 61,080, at text accompanying n.67 (1996) ("[T]he ability to spend time and resources litigating the rates, terms and conditions of transmission access is not equivalent to an enforceable voluntary offer to provide comparable service under known rates, terms and conditions.") (quoting Hermiston Generating Co., 69 FERC ¶ 61,035, at p. 61,165 (1994), *reh'g denied*, 72 FERC ¶ 61,071 (1995)), *order on reh'g*, Order No. 888-A, 78 FERC ¶ 61,220, *order on reh'g*, Order No. 888-B, 81 FERC ¶ 61,248 (1997), *order on reh'g*, Order No. 888-C, 82 FERC ¶ 61,046 (1998), *aff'd in relevant part sub nom.* Transmission Access Policy Study Group v. FERC, 225 F.3d 667 (D.C. Cir. 2000), *aff'd sub nom.* New York v. FERC, 535 U.S. 1 (2002).
16. Named for FERC's then-new headquarters building, 888 North Capitol St. NE.
17. That is, "public utilities" as defined by the Federal Power Act. Section 201(f) exempts from this category government-owned utilities and, as interpreted by the courts and FERC, rural electricity cooperatives that still have loans outstanding to the Rural Utilities Service. These exempt entities, if they own transmission facilities, do not have a direct obligation to provide transmission service. But FERC has ruled, under the so-called reciprocity requirement, that they must provide that service if they want to take service from the public utilities that do have the Order No. 888 obligation. *See* Order No. 888, 75 FERC ¶ 61,080 at text accompanying nn.297–99.

transmission service to eligible customers. The tariffs must offer transmission customers access "on the same or comparable basis, and under the same or comparable terms and conditions, as the transmission provider's uses of its system."[18] Eligible customers include (a) buyers and sellers of wholesale power, and (b) buyers and sellers of retail power within states that have authorized retail competition.[19]

1996–present: Nearly half the states investigated whether to introduce competition for retail electricity service into historically exclusive service territories. A subset of these states enacted statutes or issued rules to do so. Within a few years, several of these states repealed their competition statutes. As of 2012, seventeen states and the District of Columbia allowed retail electricity competition.[20]

1999: FERC issued Order No. 2000,[21] encouraging (but not requiring) transmission-owning utilities to form and join "regional transmission organizations" (RTOs). An RTO has received from its member utilities the contractual authority and obligation to control the utilities' transmission systems. That control makes the RTO a "public utility"—the legal provider, under the Federal Power Act, of transmission service over a large, multi-utility, multi-state region (except in the cases of California, New York and Texas, where the RTO operates only within the state). The RTO's transmission service must comply with Order No. 888.

2005: Congress repealed the Public Utility Holding Company Act of 1935. As a result, any type of entity can own any type of utility asset and perform any type of electric service function, in any location.[22]

Today: Competition in wholesale generation markets is legally possible anywhere in the mainland United States. Competition in retail transmission markets is legally possible in certain states. Physical distribution, due to its natural monopoly characteristics, remains a monopoly service provided by traditional utilities. Transmission service also remains largely a monopoly service, provided in RTO regions by the RTO and in non-RTO regions by traditional utilities.[23] Some states that already have authorized competition for

---

18. Order No. 888, 75 FERC ¶ 61,080 at text accompanying n.72.
19. *Id.* at n.194, text accompanying nn.284, 289–90.
20. These states are California, Connecticut, Delaware, District of Columbia, Illinois, Maine, Maryland, Massachusetts, Michigan, Montana, New Hampshire, New Jersey, New York, Ohio, Oregon, Pennsylvania, Rhode Island and Texas. *See* PHILLIP R. O'CONNOR, RETAIL ELECTRIC CHOICE: PROVEN, GROWING, SUSTAINABLE (Apr. 2012), http://www.competecoalition.com/files/COMPETE_Coalition_2012_Report. pdf. Arkansas and Nevada repealed their statutes soon after the California difficulties of 1999–2000.
21. 18 C.F.R. Part 35, Regional Transmission Organizations, Order No. 2000, 89 FERC ¶ 61,285 (1999).
22. The companion volume on corporate structure, mergers and acquisitions will discuss PUHCA repeal in detail, along with provisions added to the Federal Power Act Section 203 to increase FERC's authority to regulate certain acquisitions by and of utilities and their assets.
23. "Largely," because possibilities are emerging for storage as a competitor to transmission; it is also feasible, and permissible, for transmission entrepreneurs to compete either to (a) construct new lines or (b) buy and resell capacity on existing lines. *See, e.g.*, Transmission Planning and Cost Allocation by Transmission Owning and Operating Public Utilities, Order No. 1000, 136 FERC ¶ 61,051, at PP 256–57 (2011) (discussing benefits of non-incumbent transmission developers proposing transmission

retail electric services are asking whether some features of "physical distribution," such as metering, should also be subject to competition. If so, sellers could compete to provide different types of meters, allowing for pricing which varies with actual costs, such as hourly pricing or seasonal pricing.

3.A.2. Gas

The natural gas industry traditionally had six main categories of activity: (1) exploration and production, (2) pipeline transportation from gas fields to local markets, (3) sale of gas at wholesale to local distribution companies, (4) local physical distribution of gas from pipelines to consumers, (5) retail sales of gas to consumers and (6) storage (which can occur at any of the previous stages).[24]

Before the 1980s: Exploration and production companies found and produced the gas, then sold it to large interstate pipelines. These pipelines performed three functions: transporting over multi-state distances to local markets, reselling it at wholesale to local distribution companies (LDCs), and storing the gas for future sales. (The wholesale sales function is sometimes called the "merchant" function.) In their dealings with LDCs, the pipelines usually sold their transportation service and wholesale gas as a single "bundled" product. An LDC therefore had to buy its gas from the pipeline that transported it, at the interconnection between the LDC and the pipeline (known as the "city gate"). And because an LDC often had access to only one pipeline, the LDC was a captive gas purchaser; it could not shop for gas among multiple suppliers. There was competition among producers to sell gas to pipelines, but from a typical LDC's perspective there was little competition among pipelines to sell or transport the gas. (Even LDCs with multiple suppliers often had limited competitive supply options, if separations in distribution segments or internal transportation limits prevented them from substituting one pipeline's supply for another's.) The LDCs, in turn, operating as state-franchised monopolies within state-defined service territories, physically distributed and re-sold the gas to retail customers, subject to state commission regulation.

The pipelines' two activities—transporting and wholesaling natural gas—were regulated by the Federal Power Commission (FPC) under the Natural Gas Act of 1938 (NGA), 15 U.S.C. § 717 *et seq.* The NGA also gave the FPC power to certify the construction of new pipelines. Until 1954, the FPC did not regulate producers' wellhead prices because the NGA did not grant the FPC express jurisdiction to do so.

---

solutions in competition with incumbents), *order on reh'g*, Order No. 1000-A, 139 FERC ¶ 61,132, *order on reh'g*, Order No. 1000-B, 141 FERC ¶ 61,044 (2012).

24. Some gas companies are vertically integrated; i.e., they engage in one or more production, pipeline, storage and distribution businesses. From 1935 to 2005, the business activities and geographic scope of gas companies were restricted by the "integrated public-utility system" requirement of the Public Utility Holding Company Act of 1935.

In 1954, the Supreme Court issued its landmark *Phillips* decision, interpreting the NGA to require the FPC to regulate wellhead prices. The Court reasoned that producers selling gas to interstate pipelines were "natural gas companies" subject to the Act.[25] The *Phillips* decision led the FPC to experiment with various pricing methods, including producer-by-producer pricing based on each producer's cost, "area" prices based on average contract prices for five distinct gas production areas, and national price ceilings. These pricing methods made interstate markets less attractive to gas sellers than intrastate markets, contributing to actual and anticipated natural gas shortages during the 1970s. Congressional dissatisfaction with these pricing methods and results led Congress to the Natural Gas Policy Act of 1978, 15 U.S.C. § 3301 *et seq.* ("NGPA"). The NGPA replaced the FPC's wellhead price-setting with statute-specified price ceilings for so-called "new gas" while leaving controls in place for gas produced before 1978. The NGPA phased out some of those gas ceilings by 1985. In 1989, Congress passed the Natural Gas Wellhead Decontrol Act, amending the NGPA to eliminate all wellhead price controls as of January 1, 1993.

1985: In Order No. 436, FERC provided incentives to interstate pipelines to "unbundle" their transportation function from their wholesale sales function.[26] (To "unbundle" services is to offer them for sale separately, leaving the buyer free to buy some but not all.)[27] Pipelines could offer customers unbundled transportation service on a first-come, first-served basis. This unbundling freed a customer from having to buy the gas from the pipeline; the customer could buy gas directly from a producer or marketer, then hire the pipeline to transport it. Under Order No. 436, the pipeline still could sell gas bundled with its transportation, in competition with the unbundled gas sold by producers. To prevent the pipelines-as-transporters from favoring their own gas over competing sources, Order No. 436 required pipelines to offer the transportation on a non-discriminatory basis. The Commission later imposed, in Order No. 497, "Standards of Conduct" to ensure that pipelines could not provide superior information or access to their affiliates.[28]

1992: Whereas Order No. 436 was voluntary, Order No. 636 was mandatory.[29] It required pipelines to unbundle transportation service from merchant service. All customers

---

25. Phillips Petrol. Co. v. Wisconsin, 347 U.S. 672 (1954).

26. Regulation of Natural Gas Pipelines After Partial Wellhead Decontrol, Order No. 436, 125 FERC ¶ 61,190, *order on reh'g*, Order No. 436-A, 33 FERC ¶ 61,448 (1985), *order on reh'g*, Order No. 436-B, 34 FERC ¶ 61,204, *order on reh'g*, Order No. 436-C, 34 FERC ¶ 61,404, *order on reh'g*, Order No. 436-D, 34 FERC ¶ 61,405, *order on reh'g*, Order No. 436-E, 34 FERC ¶ 61,403 (1986), *vacated and remanded sub nom.* Associated Gas Distributors v. FERC, 824 F.2d 981 (D.C. Cir. 1987), *cert. denied*, 485 U.S. 1006 (1988).

27. Chapter 4.B discusses unbundling in detail.

28. Inquiry Into Alleged Anti-Competitive Practices Related to Marketing Affiliates of Interstate Pipelines, Order No. 497, 43 FERC ¶ 61,420 (1988), *order on reh'g*, Order No. 497-A, 49 FERC ¶ 61,334 (1989), *order extending sunset date*, Order No. 497-B, 53 FERC ¶ 61,367 (1990), *order extending sunset date*, Order No. 497-C, 57 FERC ¶ 61,356 (1991), *reh'g denied*, 58 FERC ¶ 61,139 (1992), *aff'd in part and remanded in part sub nom.* Tenneco Gas v. FERC, 969 F.2d 1187 (D.C. Cir. 1992).

29. Pipeline Service Obligations and Revisions to Regulations Governing Self-Implementing Transportation; and Regulation of Natural Gas Pipelines After Partial Wellhead Decontrol, Order No. 636, 59 FERC

then could shop separately for transportation service, gas commodity and storage service. Order No. 636 also barred pipelines from selling gas, either unbundled or bundled, except at points upstream of their transportation system. Pipeline companies wishing to sell gas had to create "marketing affiliates" that operated at arm's length from the pipeline business. Pipelines also had to offer customers "no-notice" transportation service, storage access, "capacity release," and flexibility in choosing receipt and delivery points—four actions aimed at helping customers match deliveries to their needs.[30]

Today: There is no federal price regulation of wellhead gas. Interstate pipelines continue to transport gas, but do not buy and resell it (though their marketing affiliates do). FERC continues to regulate the price of pipeline transportation under the Natural Gas Act. The industry also has marketers and brokers. Marketers buy gas from producers (or other marketers), then resell it to LDCs or to retail customers (if the state allows retail competition in gas sales). Marketers can be independent of or affiliated with producers, pipelines, or LDCs. Marketers can also re-bundle transportation service and storage (purchased from pipelines or released by LDCs) with the gas commodity. Brokers play a similar re-bundling role, except they do not take ownership of the gas or pipeline capacity. LDCs still sell the bundled product of physical distribution and the gas commodity to retail customers. Finally, a number of states allow entry by retail competitors in gas sales. In these states, consumers can buy gas from marketers, and the LDC is obligated by state law to deliver it.[31]

¶ 61,030, *order on reh'g*, Order No. 636-A, 60 FERC ¶ 61,102, *on reh'g*, Order No. 636-B, 61 FERC ¶ 61,272 (1992), *reh'g denied*, Notice of Denial of Rehearing, 62 FERC ¶ 61,007 (1993), *aff'd in part and remanded in part sub nom.* United Distribution Co. v. FERC, 88 F.3d 1105 (D.C. Cir. 1996), *cert. denied sub nom.* Associated Gas Distribs. v. FERC, 520 U.S. 1224 (1997).

30.   One industry history of these services explains:

> No-notice[] transportation services allow LDCs and utilities to receive natural gas from pipelines on demand to meet peak service needs for its customers, without incurring any penalties. These services were provided based on LDC and utility concerns that the restructuring of the industry may decrease the reliability needed to meet their own customers' needs. The capacity release programs allow the resale of unwanted pipeline capacity between pipeline customers. Order 636 requires interstate pipelines to set up electronic bulletin boards, accessible by all customers on an equal basis, which show the available and released capacity on any particular pipeline. A customer requiring pipeline transportation can refer to these bulletin boards, and find out if there is any available capacity on the pipeline, or if there is any released capacity available for purchase or lease from one who has already purchased capacity but does not need it.

History of Regulation, NATURALGAS.ORG, http://www.naturalgas.org/regulation/history.asp (last visited Jan. 27, 2013).

31.   For more detailed history and description of the gas industry's structure, see Richard J. Pierce, Jr., *The State of the Transition to Competitive Markets in Natural Gas and Electricity*, 15 ENERGY L.J. 323 (1994); Richard J. Pierce, Jr., *Reconstituting the Natural Gas Industry from Wellhead to Burnertip*, 25 ENERGY L.J. 57 (2004); and JOSEPH P. TOMAIN & RICHARD D. CUDAHY, ENERGY LAW IN A NUTSHELL (2d ed. 2011).

3.A.3. Telecommunications

The physical components of telephone service include customer premises equipment (CPE), the local loop, switches and long-distance lines. As the D.C. Circuit described it: "[The] equipment starts at every subscriber's wall plug; it includes the line, or 'loop,' between each subscriber's premises and the local telephone company central office. Switching equipment at the office routes each incoming call out onto the local loop of the subscriber receiving the call, or out to another local office where the call may be switched onto the long-distance lines of AT&T or another long-distance carrier."[32] Another term often used is the "local exchange network," usually owned entirely by the incumbent local exchange carrier (ILEC). The local exchange network includes "the local loops (wires connecting telephones to switches), the switches (equipment directing calls to their destinations), and the transport trunks (wires carrying calls between switches) that constitute a local exchange network."[33]

Before the mid-1970s: Most U.S. telephone service, both local and long-distance, was provided to the nation's residents and businesses on a regulated, monopoly basis by subsidiaries of American Telephone and Telegraph (AT&T). For local telephone service, each AT&T subsidiary received a state-granted, exclusive franchise within a state-defined service territory. (In a minority of situations, non-AT&T companies had similar exclusive franchises.) Most of the nation's long-distance service was provided by a separate AT&T subsidiary, while yet another subsidiary (Western Electric) dominated the manufacture of telephones and related customer premises equipment ("CPE").[34] Western Electric had no government-granted franchise; its dominant position stemmed from carrier tariffs (both AT&T and non-AT&T), approved by state and federal regulators, restricting the use of non-carrier-provided CPE.[35]

Late 1960s through early 1980s: As a result of "technological advances [that] reduced the entry costs" for AT&T's long-distance competitors, the Federal Communications Commission issued a series of decisions opening long-distance and CPE markets to competition.[36] "By 1979, competition in the provision of long-distance service was well established . . . ."[37]

---

32. Nat'l Ass'n of Regulatory Util. Comm'rs v. FCC, 737 F.2d 1095, 1103–04 (D.C. Cir. 1984).
33. AT&T Corp. v. Iowa Utils. Bd., 525 U.S. 366, 371 (1999).
34. Customer premises equipment includes "the basic telephone, answering machines, key systems, and PBX switchboards." Computer and Commc'ns Indus. Ass'n v. FCC, 693 F.2d 198, 204 n.14 (D.C. Cir. 1982).
35. *See, e.g.,* STUART BROTMAN, COMMUNICATIONS LAW AND PRACTICE (2012), § 5.02[2][a], at 5-29.
36. MCI Telecomms. Corp. v. AT&T, 512 U.S. 218, 220 (1994).
37. *Id.; see generally* Lincoln Tel. &. Tel. Co. v. FCC, 659 F.2d 1092, 1105, 1109, 1104 n.62 (D.C. Cir. 1981) (applying FCC's broad policy favoring competitive entry in the "specialized communications field"; and clarifying that (a) the policy was not restricted to private line services and (b) the long-distance interconnection obligations also applied to non-RBOC-affiliated ILECs); Bell Tel. Co. of Pa. v. FCC, 503 F.2d 1250 (3d Cir. 1974) (upholding an FCC decision requiring AT&T's incumbent local telephone company (ILEC) affiliates to permit competitive long-distance service providers to interconnect with local exchange networks on reasonable terms and conditions); MCI Telecomms. Corp. v. FCC, 580 F.2d 590 (D.C. Cir. 1978) (reaffirming AT&T ILEC affiliates' interconnection obligation); Specialized Common

The transition to a competitive CPE market began earlier,[38] but did not gain traction until 1975, when the FCC set standards for CPE interconnection with the network, supplanting incumbent local exchange carriers' tariff-based limitations.[39]

During this same time period, the FCC grappled with two related issues: (1) whether and how to define and separate (a) the growing and unregulated field of computer, or data, processing, from (b) the regulated world of telecommunications service; and (2) how to regulate telecommunications carriers' participation in data-processing markets.[40] The FCC's efforts yielded three decisions between 1966 and 1990: *Computer I,*[41] *Computer II*[42] and *Computer III.*[43] The FCC drew a line between "basic transmission services" (pure transport of customer-supplied information without change in form or content) and "enhanced services" (services that combine basic transmission services with computer processing applications to enable the generation, manipulation or storage of customer-supplied information).[44] The FCC continued regulation of "basic services" as "common carrier" services under Title II of the Communications Act of 1934 while discontinuing regulation of "enhanced services" because their markets were "truly competitive." The FCC also discontinued rate regulation of CPE, and required that it be "unbundled" from

---

Carrier Servs., 29 F.C.C.2d 870, 940 (1971), *aff'd sub nom.* Washington Utils. & Transp. Comm'n v. FCC, 513 F.2d 1142, 1164 (9th Cir. 1975).

38. *See* Chapter 4.B.6.c (discussing the *Hush-a-Phone* and *Carterphone* cases).

39. *See* N.C. Utils. Comm'n v. FCC, 552 F.2d 1036 (4th Cir. 1977) (upholding the FCC's registration program implementing its policy authorizing customer-provided equipment); Proposals for New or Revised Classes of Interstate and Foreign Message Toll Service (MTS) and Wide Area Telephone Service (WATS), First Report and Order, 56 F.C.C.2d 593 (1975), *on recon.,* Memorandum Opinion and Order, 58 F.C.C.2d 716 (1976). The FCC's CPE interconnection standards, as amended over time, can be found at 47 C.F.R. §§ 68.1 *et seq.*

40. *See* 1 Peter W. Huber, Michael K. Kellog, & John Thorne, Federal Telecommunications Law § 12.4.1, at 12–30 (2d ed. 2012 Supp.).

41. Regulatory and Policy Problems Presented by the Interdependence of Computer and Communications Services and Facilities ("*Computer I*"), Tentative Decision, 28 F.C.C.2d 291 (1970), *amended by* Final Decision and Order, 28 F.C.C.2d 267 (1971), *aff'd,* Memorandum Opinion and Order, 34 F.C.C.2d 557 (1972), *aff'd in part and rev'd in part sub nom.* GTE Service Corp. v. FCC, 474 F.2d 724 (2d Cir. 1973), *on remand,* Order, 40 F.C.C.2d 293 (1973).

42. Amendment of Section 64.702 of the Commission's Rules and Regulations ("*Computer II*"), Tentative Decision, 72 F.C.C.2d 358 (1979), *amended by* Final Decision, 77 F.C.C.2d 384, *on recon.,* Memorandum Opinion and Order on Reconsideration, 84 F.C.C.2d 50 (1980), *on further recon.,* Memorandum Opinion and Order on Further Reconsideration, 88 F.C.C.2d 512 (1981), *aff'd sub nom.* Computer & Commc'ns Indus. Ass'n v. FCC, 693 F.2d 198 (D.C. Cir. 1982), *cert. denied,* 461 U.S. 938 (1983).

43. Amendment of Section 64.702 of the Commission's Rules and Regulations ("*Computer III*"), Report & Order, 104 F.C.C.2d 958, (1986), *on recon.,* Memorandum Opinion and Order on Reconsideration, 2 FCC Rcd. 3035 (1987), *on further recon.,* Memorandum Opinion and Order on Further Reconsideration, 3 FCC Rcd. 1135 (1988), *on supplemental notice,* Report and Order, 2 FCC Rcd. 3072 (1987), *on recon.,* Memorandum Opinion and Order on Reconsideration, 3 FCC Rcd. 1150 (1988), *vacated sub nom.* California v. FCC, 905 F.2d 1217 (9th Cir. 1990), *on remand,* Report and Order, 5 FCC Rcd. 7719 (1990).

44. *Computer II,* 77 F.C.C.2d at 420–21. The boundary between "basic" and "enhanced" service is, for most practical purposes, equivalent to the boundary drawn between "telecommunications services" and "information services" in the 1984 Modification of Final Judgment breaking up AT&T (discussed in the next subsection), and later codified in the Telecommunications Act of 1996. *See* 47 U.S.C. §§ 153 (20), (43), (46) (defining information service, telecommunications, and telecommunications service).

basic transmission service so that competitors could sell it separately. These various decisions preempted state laws that either precluded independents from providing CPE or regulated enhanced services.[45] The FCC originally required AT&T to use separate subsidiaries for basic and enhanced services (so-called "structural separation") to prevent cross-subsidization; but later, in *Computer III*, permitted AT&T and other local exchange carriers (LECs) to offer enhanced services subject to non-structural safeguards.[46]

1984: While the FCC was adopting new policies and rules to promote competition in the long-distance-service and CPE markets, others were pursuing antitrust actions against AT&T. These actions asserted that AT&T was monopolizing long-distance and CPE markets by refusing to provide competitors with non-discriminatory interconnection to AT&T's local telephone networks. Some actions were private lawsuits by new entrants such as MCI.[47] Most relevant was the lawsuit filed by the U.S. Department of Justice in the mid-1970s, culminating in a 1982 settlement (effective January 1, 1984) to break up the Bell system.[48]

Known as the Modification of Final Judgment (MFJ),[49] the settlement divested AT&T's monopoly functions from its competitive activities. All twenty-two LEC Bell Operating Companies ("BOCs"), holders of state-franchised monopolies, were combined into seven Regional Bell Operating Companies ("RBOCs," or "Baby Bells"), each independent of the other and of AT&T. The RBOCs would provide local exchange services only; they were prohibited from providing long-distance service or information services and from manufacturing CPE. The MFJ also required the RBOCs to provide all long-distance providers with "equal access" to the RBOCs' LEC networks. The remainder of AT&T could continue to provide long-distance service, to manufacture and sell CPE, to provide information services and to provide any other products and services.[50]

---

45. *See* Commc'ns Indus. Ass'n v. FCC, 693 F.2d at 205, 207(describing FCC preemption of CPE and enhanced services); N.C. Utils. Comm'n v. FCC, 552 F.2d 1036 (4th Cir. 1977) (affirming FCC order permitting interconnection of all FCC-registered CPE to the network, notwithstanding contrary state rules); N.C. Utils. Comm'n v. FCC, 532 F.2d 787 (4th Cir. 1976) (upholding FCC decision preempting NCUC from prohibiting connection of privately-owned terminal equipment to the network unless used exclusively for interstate communications); *Computer II*, 77 F.C.C.2d at 387–89, 384 ¶ 12, 428, 433 (preempting all tariffing of CPE and requiring CPE to be unbundled from carriers' regulated services); *see also* Brotman, *supra* note 35, §§ 4.02[2][d], 5.02[2][b]-[c].
46. *See Computer III*, 104 F.C.C.2d at 1125. We will discuss the various forms of structural separation in Chapter 4.B.5.
47. *See, e.g.*, MCI Commc'ns Corp. v. AT&T, 708 F.2d 1081 (7th Cir. 1983); MCI Commc'ns v. AT&T, 462 F. Supp. 1072 (N.D. Ill. 1978).
48. United States v. AT&T Co., 552 F. Supp. 131 (D.D.C. 1982), *aff'd sub. nom.*, Maryland v. United States, 460 U.S. 1001 (1983).
49. The MFJ was ostensibly a "modification" of an earlier 1956 consent decree between AT&T and the Department of Justice, although the MFJ was largely a rewrite of the original consent decree.
50. *See* United States v. W. Elec. Co., 46 F.3d 1198, 1200 (D.C. Cir. 1995) (describing the MFJ); *see also* William J. Byrnes, *Telecommunications Regulation: Something Old and Something New, in* The Communications Act: A Legislative History of the Major Amendments 1934–1996, at 31, 48–49 (1999); Huber, *supra* note 40, § 4.5.7.

1993: Advances in cellular technology had allowed wireless mobile service to penetrate local and long-distance telephone markets.[51] This development led policymakers to re-examine how the FCC used its exclusive jurisdiction under the Communications Act of 1934 to regulate wireless and other radio services. In 1993, Congress amended Section 332(c) of the Communications Act. The amendments preempted state regulation of wireless service entry and rates and gave the FCC authority to exempt wireless carriers from some of the common carrier obligations rooted in Title II of the Communications Act.[52]

1996: The Telecommunications Act of 1996 revised the MFJ's industry structure.[53] Congress "sought to 'uproo[t]' the incumbent [local exchange carriers'] monopoly and to introduce competition in its place."[54] Among the Act's many features, four are most relevant to this discussion. First, the Act authorized competition in local telephone service (sometimes called "local exchange service") by preempting state laws that had granted exclusive monopoly franchises.[55] The RBOCs (also called "incumbent local exchange carriers" or "ILECs") could continue to provide local telephone service; but so could newcomers (called "competitive local exchange carriers" or "CLECs").

Second, to ensure that the newly authorized competition became effective competition, the Act addressed the ILECs' market power, in several ways. As of 1996, the ILECs controlled "bottleneck facilities"—facilities that were not economically duplicable, yet were essential to compete in the local exchange market. The Act therefore required ILECs to offer the CLECs access to those facilities. This required offer took two forms: (1) the right to purchase and resell the ILECs' retail telephone services, and (2) the right to buy access to components of the ILECs' bottleneck facilities at wholesale prices, enabling the CLECs to re-bundle these components to create their own retail products. These components were called "unbundled network elements" ("UNEs").[56] Examples of these UNEs were "loops, switches, operational support systems and databases."[57] Other aids to competitive entry included "number portability" (requiring the ILECs to allow customers to keep their existing phone numbers when switching to a new supplier),[58] and "dialing parity" (prohibiting ILECs from requiring a competitor's customers to dial more numbers than ILEC customers to reach the same place).[59] Further, LECs were required to

---

51. *See* John W. Berresford, *Amendments to Section 332-Mobile Radio, in* THE COMMUNICATIONS ACT: A LEGISLATIVE HISTORY OF THE MAJOR AMENDMENTS 1934–1996, at 105, 106 (Max D. Pagin ed., 1999).
52. 47 U.S.C. §§ 332(c)(1)–(3).
53. Pub. L. No. 104-104, 110 Stat. 56 (1996). The 1996 Act also dealt with broadcasting and cable television.
54. Verizon Commc'ns, Inc. v. Law Offices of Curtis V. Trinko, LLP, 540 U.S. 398, 402 (2004) (quoting Verizon Commc'ns, Inc. v. FCC, 535 U.S. 467, 488 (2002)).
55. 47 U.S.C. § 253(a).
56. *See* 47 U.S.C. § 251(c).
57. PETER BLUHM & SHERRY LICHTENBERG, FUNDAMENTALS OF TELECOMMUNICATIONS REGULATION: MARKETS, JURISDICTION, AND CHALLENGES 18 (National Regulatory Research Institute Jan. 2011), *available at* http://www.nrri.org/pubs/telecommunications/NRRI_telecomm_overview_jan11-03.pdf.
58. 47 U.S.C. § 251(b)(2).
59. 47 U.S.C. § 251(b)(3).

interconnect with competing carriers, so that customers of different carriers could communicate with each other.[60]

Third, the 1996 Act removed the MFJ's restrictions on the RBOCs' entry into other markets. It allowed the RBOCs to enter the long-distance market if they proved, on a state-by-state basis, that they satisfied a "competitive checklist" intended to remove their market power over local markets.[61] The 1996 Act also lifted the MFJ's bar on the RBOCs' entry into the information service and cable television markets.

Fourth, the 1996 Act added a new provision requiring the FCC to "forbear" from applying any provision of the 1934 Act or FCC rule to telecommunications carriers or services, where the FCC determines that the provision or rule is (a) "not necessary to ensure" that the "charges, practices, classifications, or regulations" concerning that carrier or service are "just and reasonable and are not unjustly or unreasonably discriminatory" and (b) "not necessary for the protection of consumers"; and where the forbearance is "consistent with the public interest." An FCC decision to forbear preempts states from enforcing or applying any provision that was subject to the forbearance.[62]

Today: By eliminating the MFJ's structural restrictions, the 1996 Act has led to the following features of today's industry structure: (a) entry by the RBOCs into long-distance markets; (b) entry by post-1984 AT&T into local telephone markets (AT&T thus joining other long-distance companies that already had that right); (c) the mergers of RBOCs, reducing their numbers from seven to three;[63] (d) mergers of RBOCs and long-distance telephone companies;[64] (e) RBOC acquisitions and other mergers resulting in companies that provide long-distance service, local wireline telephone service and cellular service;[65] and (f) the repeal by some states of state commission authority to set rates for local telephone service.[66]

---

60. 47 U.S.C. §§ 251(a)(1),(c).
61. *See* 47 U.S.C. §§ 271(c)(2)(B)–(d)(3)(A); *see also Verizon v. Trinko*, 540 U.S. at 402 (2003). In addition to satisfying the checklist, the RBOC seeking entry into the long-distance market had to show either "(1) the introduction of competition into local markets, *or* (2) the failure of a competing carrier to request access to or interconnection with the local service supplier (or the competing carrier's failure to engage in 'good faith' negotiations)." AT&T v. Iowa Utils. Bd., 525 U.S. 366, 415 (1999) (Breyer, J., concurring in part and dissenting in part) (citing 47 U.S.C. §§ 271(c)(1)(A)–(B)).
62. 47 U.S.C. § 160.
63. *See, e.g.*, Ameritech Corp., Memorandum Opinion and Order, 14 FCC Rcd. 14,712 (1999), *vacated sub nom.* Ass'n. of Commc'ns Enterprises v. FCC, 235 F.3d 662 (D.C. Cir. 2001), *modified*, 16 FCC Rcd. 5714 (2001) (merger of SBC and Ameritech); NYNEX Corp., Memorandum Opinion and Order, 12 FCC Rcd. 19,985 (1997) (merger of Bell Atlantic and NYNEX); Pacific Telesis Group, Memorandum Opinion and Order, 12 FCC Rcd. 2624 (1997) (merger of SBC and Pacific Telesis).
64. *See, e.g.*, SBC Communications, Inc., Memorandum Opinion and Order, 20 FCC Rcd. 18,290 (2005) (SBC acquisition of AT&T); Verizon Communications, Inc., Memorandum Opinion and Order, 20 FCC Rcd. 18433 (2005) (Verizon acquisition of MCI).
65. *E.g.*, GTE Corp., Memorandum Opinion and Order, 15 FCC Rcd. 14,032 (2000) (merger of Bell Atlantic and GTE to form Verizon); AT&T Inc., Memorandum Opinion and Order, 22 FCC Rcd. 5662, *on recon.*, 22 FCC Rcd. 6285 (2007) (merger of AT&T (f/k/a SBC) with BellSouth).
66. *See, e.g.*, Neb. Rev. Stat. §§ 86-141 to 86-148; Tex. Util. Code § 52.007.

* * *

The seminal actions to authorize competition are displayed in Figure 3. It shows the body issuing the authorization, the action (i.e., the law or order) containing the authorization, and the year. For electric and gas, the key distinction is between wholesale service and retail service, because the federal statutes (Federal Power Act and Natural Gas Act) leave retail service to the states. For telecommunications, the key distinction is between long-distance service and local exchange service.

Each of these structural transitions raised the problem of "stranded investment." This phrase refers to certain investments made by utilities, during the decades preceding these industry transitions, to carry out their obligations to serve then-captive customers. Once policymakers authorized competition, the incumbent no longer had guaranteed customers to pay for the costs of these historic investments. "Stranded investment" refers to that portion of this historic, obligatory investment that (a) has not been recovered from customers as of the time they become free to shop and (b) is less than the market value of the investment. We will discuss this issue in Chapter 3.C.1.

3.A.4. Three variables

These brief histories display three important variables affecting the introduction of competition:

1. The level of government introducing competition can be federal or state.
2. The initiating entity can be the legislature or the regulator.
3. The injection point for competition can be retail or wholesale.

To recap: In electricity, the federal government introduced competition at wholesale. In the Public Utility Regulatory Policies Act of 1978, Congress required utilities to purchase wholesale capacity and energy from "qualifying facilities." Congress acted again in 1992 to expand the universe of wholesale generation entrants by exempting them from PUHCA while authorizing FERC to grant transmission access to wholesale sellers on complaint. FERC then followed with Order No. 888, which made the transmission of wholesale power an obligation of all public utility transmission owners (and transmission of retail power, in states which authorized retail competition). Retail competition in electricity was a state decision—usually authorized by state legislatures, but in some states by the regulator.

In gas, the federal government introduced competition in gas sales at wholesale. Acting without new statutory authority (relying instead on the 1938 Natural Gas Act), FERC required pipelines to unbundle transportation service from wholesale sales. Decisions to introduce gas competition at retail were state decisions.

Figure 3
Authorizing Competitive Entry: Who Did What, When?

	Wholesale			Retail		
	Body	Action	Date	Body	Action	Date
Electricity	Congress	PURPA	1978	State legislatures	Various statutes	app. 1996–2000
	Congress	EPAct	1992	NY PSC, NH PUC	Orders	1996
	FERC	Orders 888, 889	1996			
Gas	FERC	Order 436	1985	State legislatures	Various statutes	app. 1996–2000
	FERC	Order 636	1992			

	Long Distance			Local Exchange Service		
	Body	Action	Date	Body	Action	Date
Telecommunications	FCC	*Specialized Carrier* decisions (interstate long distance)	1970s	FCC	Decisions in *IBM*, 59 Rad. Reg. 2d (P&F) 964 (1986) and *Shared Tenant Services*, 3 FCC Rcd. 6931 (1988) (requiring ILECs to permit interconnection of non-ILEC-owned shared switches to the local network	mid-1980s
	States	Some legislatures and commissions authorized entry for intrastate service. *See, e.g.,* Saco River Communications, 499 A.2d 458 (Me. 1985)	late 1970s–early 1980s	States	Some legislatures and commissions authorized local competition.	pre-1996
	U.S. DoJ/ U.S. Dist. Ct.	Antitrust breakup of AT&T	1984			
	Congress	Telecommunications Act (e.g., 47 U.S.C. § 251)	1996	Congress	Telecommunications Act (e.g., 47 U.S.C. § 253)	1996

In telecommunications, the federal government took the lead, with the FCC starting the process, the Department of Justice following up through the MFJ, and then Congress stepping in by passing the 1996 Act. The Act was aimed at introducing competition at both retail (by preempting state monopoly laws) and wholesale (by requiring ILECs to share their facilities with CLECs).

With these summaries of industry transitions in mind, we turn now to the legal principles policymakers used to effect them. This chapter's focus is the legal actions unique to retail competition—specifically, the changes in the six legal features of the retail utility monopoly. Legal issues associated with introducing wholesale competition will appear in Chapters 4 and 5.

3.B. Eliminating the legal monopoly at retail

Recall from Chapter 2 the six main legal features of a traditional retail monopoly: exclusive franchise, obligation to serve all customers, consent to regulation, quality of service, power of eminent domain, and limit on liability for negligence. When the government seeks to introduce competition at retail, it must adjust these legal features. This subchapter describes how.

3.B.1. Exclusive franchise

Recall the statutes from South Dakota and Maine. South Dakota's law barred all retail competitors, forever. Maine's law allowed entry if the applicant convinced the Commission that its proposed new service was not offered by the incumbent and would benefit the public. Other states required entrants to prove the incumbent's inadequacy, but even then allowed entry only if the incumbent failed to cure.

Retail competition statutes remove these barriers. Maine's statute did the deed with one sentence: "Beginning on March 1, 2000, all consumers of electricity have the right to purchase generation services directly from competitive electricity providers . . . ."[67] Less concisely but no less clearly, Pennsylvania's statute provides:

Consistent with the time line set forth in section 2806 (relating to implementation, pilot programs and performance-based rates), the commission shall allow customers to choose among electric generation suppliers in a competitive generation market through direct access. Customers should be able to choose among alternatives such as firm and interruptible service, flexible pricing and alternate generation sources, including reasonable

---

67.   ME. REV. STAT. tit. 35-A, § 3202. Exempted from retail competition in Maine were customers of municipal or cooperative systems. Some states distinguished these systems from those owned by investor-owned utilities on the grounds that the citizen-owners of municipal systems and the customer-owners of cooperative systems have the power, through their votes, to decide whether to introduce competition. Customers of investor-owned companies, in contrast, can influence the companies only through commission proceedings or by urging their legislators to amend statutes.

and fair opportunities to self-generate and interconnect. These alternatives may be provided by different electric generation suppliers.[68]

Both statutes specify the service for which competition is authorized: electric generation service, and only that service. In Pennsylvania, other retail-oriented services remained the utility's exclusive responsibility: "The electric distribution company shall continue to provide customer service functions consistent with the regulations of the commission, including meter reading, complaint resolution and collections."[69] Other states took a different path. Texas, for example, removed the customer service and billing functions from the incumbent utility, allowing the new retail competitors to differentiate themselves by offering those services.[70]

3.B.2. Obligation to serve

In a regulated monopoly market, the franchised public utility must serve all customers in its assigned territory.[71] In an unregulated competitive market, suppliers have no statutory service obligation. They can pick and choose their customers, provided they use no impermissible criteria to exclude.[72]

For the new retail competition in electricity and gas, most legislatures imposed no obligation to serve. But if no one had an obligation to serve, who would serve the unlucky—customers who missed the deadline for selecting suppliers, or who were rejected by suppliers for financial, geographic, racial, ethnic or other reasons?[73] Or customers whose suppliers later quit the market without warning? For these situations, legislatures mandated "last resort" service (sometimes called "default" or "standard offer" service, or in telecommunications, "carrier of last resort" service). Most states assigned this service obligation to the incumbent utility; other states hosted a competition for the opportunity to provide the service. "Last resort" service in the retail competition model is thus a political "descendant" of the obligation to serve in the traditional retail monopoly model.

But there is tension between (a) maintaining an obligation to serve and (b) promoting a competitive market. An assured supply source invites customer inertia—a tendency to stay with the government-sponsored default provider rather than shop the competitive

---

68. 66 PA. CONS. STAT. § 2804(2).
69. *Id.* § 2807(d).
70. *See* SUSAN F. TIERNEY, ERCOT TEXAS'S COMPETITIVE POWER EXPERIENCE: A VIEW FROM THE OUTSIDE LOOKING IN 4 (Oct. 2008), http://www.analysisgroup.com/uploadedFiles/Publishing/Articles/Tierney_ERCOT_Texas_study_11-08.pdf.
71. *See supra* Chapter 2.B. The obligation to serve is, of course, subject to conditions discussed there.
72. *See, e.g.,* Heart of Atlanta Motel v. United States, 379 U.S. 241 (1964) (upholding provision in Civil Rights Act of 1964 prohibiting racial discrimination in places of public accommodation).
73. *But see* CONN. GEN. STAT. § 16-245(g) (stating that the regulator "shall prohibit each licensee from declining to provide service to customers for the reason that the customers are located in economically distressed areas.").

market. Customer inertia is an entry barrier because new competitors must spend more money to attract the indecisive than the incumbent has to spend to retain them.[74] To address this tension, policymakers have considered five questions:[75]

1. *Who should provide retail default service?* Most state statutes assigned default customers to the incumbent. Doing so raises the entry barrier to non-incumbents. A few states took a different path, either (a) assigning the default service obligation to the new competitors in proportion to their market share, or (b) allowing competitors to bid for the default supplier role.[76]

2. *Who should provide the wholesale supply that serves default customers?* Some states required the retail default provider to procure wholesale supply using competitive procurement, that is, issuing requests for proposals and accepting bids. This approach created entry opportunities at wholesale. Other states allowed the incumbent to use its own supply, thereby reducing entry at wholesale. As for the competitive procurement processes, some were run by the incumbent default provider (creating a risk that incumbent would select an affiliated supplier); others were run (or observed) by a state-appointed independent party (reducing the risk of affiliate self-dealing).

3. *What is the appropriate contract term for the wholesale supply?* The choices include long-term contracts, short-term spot purchases, portfolios of multiple-length contracts, or "laddered" arrangements (such as buying annually a three-year contract covering one-third of the needed supply). Each arrangement type varies in volatility, predictability and actual rate levels, and therefore in attractiveness to the default customer. Attractiveness affects inertia. The less attractive default service is, the more likely customers will shop, and thus the lower the entry barrier to new competitors.

4. *What price should the default customer pay?* Where the default provider is the incumbent, the state can control the price. Some states kept that price low and stable, even capping it below market prices. Such actions pleased the public at the expense of competitive entry, but produced an inevitable price spike when the caps came off.[77] Texas

74. See Chapter 4.C.3 for a discussion of inertia as entry barrier.
75. I am grateful to Jumoke Fajemirokun, a student in my 2011 public utility law class at Georgetown University Law Center, for allowing me to use ideas from her semester paper discussing these options.
76. The Pennsylvania statute introducing retail gas competition allowed "any party [to] petition the commission to become the supplier of last resort to some or all customers except for those customers identified in subsection (a)(2)(i)." 66 PA. CONS. STAT. § 2207(h). The customers identified in subsection (a)(2)(i) were "customers who have not chosen an alternative natural gas supplier or who choose to be served by their supplier of last resort." *Id.* The remaining customers—those whom "any party" could petition to serve as the "supplier of last resort"—were therefore "customers who are refused supply service from a natural gas supplier" and "customers whose natural gas supplier has failed to deliver its requirements." *Id.* §§ 2207(a)(2)(ii)–(iii).
77. The Pennsylvania Public Utility Commission explained the problem on its website. Referring to the 1997 statute that introduced retail competition, the Commission stated: "In exchange for the recovery of stranded costs, generation, transmission and distribution rates were capped at 1996 levels . . . . While Pennsylvania consumers' rates have been capped, the market prices for electricity have risen. The magnitude of those increases will depend upon market prices when the EDC acquires its power . . . . [A]ll utility

took the opposite approach: it made default service unattractive by pricing it to reflect rising power costs.[78]

5. *Should there be restrictions on customer switching?* Facing volatile prices for competitive service and stable prices for default service, the rational customer will switch back and forth—if permitted. But customer convenience conflicts with economic efficiency. The default provider's service obligation requires it to maintain sufficient supply for all possible customers, both switchers and non-switchers. Knowing this, switchers face no risk of insufficient supply. But switchers leave behind costs that non-switchers must bear—the default supplier's costs to stand ready to serve. This mismatch between cost-causing behavior and cost-bearing responsibility creates economic inefficiency. The solutions include "minimum stay requirements" for default service and special charges for switching. These solutions bring their own tension: by making switching unattractive, they make it harder for new suppliers to build a customer base.[79]

In the telecommunications sector, the last-resort service issue is more complex. Prior to the 1980s, AT&T's tariffs, approved by state commissions and the FCC, shifted costs from local phone service to long-distance service to keep local rates low.[80] This cost-shifting became impractical when policymakers introduced competition into long-distance, CPE and local service markets, because not all competitors bore comparable shares of the shifted costs. The FCC therefore instituted a series of intercarrier compensation (ICC) programs and universal service fund (USF) programs. Some states added their own USF programs. These programs were designed in varying ways to make inter-service cost allocations explicit and, in the case of USF programs, to require carriers to contribute into a common fund. That fund, in return, is redistributed to LECs in high-cost areas, or to low-income customers, to defray the cost of local service. In addition, most states had historically imposed "carrier of last resort" (COLR) obligations, almost always on the ILEC.[81]

---

rate caps have expired as of Jan. 1, 2011." PENNSYLVANIA PUBLIC UTILITY COMMISSION, THE EXPIRA-
TION OF ELECTRIC GENERATION RATE CAPS (2011), http://www.puc.state.pa.us/general/consumer_ed/
pdf/Rate_Caps.pdf.

78. "Texas designed its five-year transition in a way that assisted the state and its electricity customers in actually moving to full competition, rather than temporarily preventing customers from seeing price signals reflecting the realities of today's energy market conditions. The transition allowed for periodic price adjustments to its default price (the "Price to Beat," or "PTB") when underlying fuel and purchased power prices changed." TIERNEY, *supra* note 70, at 4.

79. For additional readings on default service, see Taff Tschamler, *Designing Competitive Electric Markets: The Importance of Default Service and its Pricing*, 13 ELEC. J. 75 (Mar. 2000); TIERNEY, *supra* note 70, at 4; and Lynne Kiesling, *Retail Restructuring and Market Design in Texas, in* ELECTRICITY RESTRUC-TURING: THE TEXAS STORY 154, 157 (Lynne Kiesling & Andrew N. Kleit eds., 2009).

80. As two authors explained: "[B]efore the widespread introduction of long-distance competition, AT&T's long-distance revenues helped defray LEC expenses. This arrangement allowed many LECs to reduce local rates (particularly residential rates) while still recovering all of their costs, including the costs of providing local service in high-cost areas." PETER BLUHM & PHYLLIS BERNT, NATIONAL REGULATORY RESEARCH INSTITUTE, CARRIERS OF LAST RESORT: UPDATING A TRADITIONAL DOCTRINE 20 (2009).

81. *See id.* at 20–23 and sources cited therein.

More recently, a few states have passed laws eliminating ILECs' COLR obligations, on the theory that the competitive marketplace, especially the availability of wireless service, has rendered them unnecessary.[82] The challenges of administering ICC and USF remain, including whether to make these funds available for broadband service.[83]

3.B.3. Consent to regulation

By accepting the obligation to serve, a utility consents to regulation. The law infers that consent not merely because of the utility's monopoly statute but also because of the public's need for protection. That need does not disappear when new competitors arrive, because the public still has a stake in the new sellers' competence and creditworthiness.[84] State competition statutes therefore regulate both (1) the physical relationship between competitive seller and the distribution utility (e.g., interconnections, notification about load size, scheduling of deliveries, resource location and availability, outage reporting); and (2) the commercial relationship between the competitive seller and the consumer (quality of service, billing arrangements, fraud). This regulation occurs through licensing.[85]

---

82. *See, e.g.,* Mo. Rev. Stat § 392.460; Mich. Comp. Laws § 484.2313; Kan. Stat. § 50-6,103; Ala. Code § 37-2A-8.

83. *See* Connect America Fund, Report and Order and Further Notice of Proposed Rulemaking, 26 FCC Rcd. 17,663 (2011) ("*CAF Order*") (petitions for reconsideration pending).

84. *See supra* Chapter 2.C (discussing *Nebbia v. New York*, 291 U.S. 502 (1934), which erased the public–private distinction in *Munn v. Illinois* and declared that all economic actors impliedly consent to regulation).

85. Licensing conditions can be extensive. Consider this provision from Connecticut's retail competition statute:

> As conditions of continued licensure, in addition to the requirements of subsection (c) of this section: (1) The licensee shall comply with the National Labor Relations Act and regulations, if applicable; (2) the licensee shall comply with the Connecticut Unfair Trade Practices Act and applicable regulations; (3) each generating facility operated by or under long-term contract to the licensee shall comply with regulations adopted by the Commissioner of Energy and Environmental Protection . . . ; (4) the licensee shall comply with the [renewable energy] portfolio standards . . . ; (5) the licensee shall be a member of the New England Power Pool or its successor or have a contractual relationship with one or more entities who are members of the New England Power Pool or its successor and the licensee shall comply with the rules of the regional independent system operator and standards and any other reliability guidelines of the regional independent systems operator; (6) the licensee shall agree to cooperate with the [department] and other electric suppliers in the event of an emergency condition that may jeopardize the safety and reliability of electric service; (7) the licensee shall comply with the code of conduct established pursuant to section 16-244h; (8) for a license to a participating municipal electric utility, the licensee shall provide open and non-discriminatory access to its distribution facilities to other licensed electric suppliers; (9) the licensee or the entity or entities with whom the licensee has a contractual relationship to purchase power shall be in compliance with all applicable licensing requirements of the Federal Energy Regulatory Commission; (10) each generating facility operated by or under long-term contract to the licensee shall be in compliance with . . . state environmental laws and regulations; (11) the licensee shall comply with the renewable portfolio standards . . . ; (12) the licensee shall offer a time-of-use price option to customers. Such option shall include a two-part price that is designed to achieve an overall minimization of customer bills by encouraging the reduction of consumption during the most energy intense hours of the day. The licensee shall file its time-of-use rates with the Public Utilities Regulatory Authority. . . . The [department] may

Consent to regulation means consent not only to regulation as it exists at time of entry, but to all future regulation, as this Colorado telephone provision makes clear:

> A person holding a certificate of public convenience and necessity to provide basic service shall be subject to the evolving definition of basic service developed by the commission under subsection (2) of this section and the system of financial support for universal service established by the commission under subsection (5) of this section.[86]

3.B.4. Quality of service

Quality of service regulation, discussed in Chapter 2.D, is not confined to monopoly utilities. Competitive suppliers face quality of service regulation in numerous markets: restaurants, hospitals, pharmaceuticals, taxis, trucking, bars and butchers. The new competitors in formerly monopoly markets are no different.

State examples: Under Connecticut's retail electricity competition statute, each license applicant must demonstrate "technical, managerial and financial capability" to provide electric generation service.[87] Colorado's statute on retail telecommunications competition requires that basic service be available at "high quality," and authorizes the Commission to "delay or deny a price increase" if a provider breaches the commission's quality of service rules.[88]

Federal example: Electricity, gas and telecommunications are network industries. Across all boundaries—corporate, state and service territory—physical assets are interconnected. Interconnectedness means interdependence. A single seller's quality error can affect customers throughout the interconnected network. Physical interconnectedness leads to commercial interconnectedness. When introducing competition, regulators seek to expand the geographic areas in which trades occur. Expanding trading areas means more interconnectedness, which increases the likelihood that each entity's error affects others.

This line of reasoning has led federal electricity regulators to enter the quality of service space. The prominent example is reliability. For most of the last century, actions affecting reliability were regulated by states exclusively; there was no federal jurisdiction.[89] State quality of service regulation consisted primarily of ensuring that each utility (a) had

---

establish additional reasonable conditions to assure that all retail customers will continue to have access to electric generation services.

Conn. Gen. Stat. § 16-245(g).
86. Colo. Rev. Stat. § 40-15-502(6)(b).
87. Conn. Gen Stat. § 16-245(c).
88. Colo. Rev. Stat. § 40-15-502(3)(b)(II); *see also* 66 Pa. Cons. Stat. § 2807(d) (retaining quality of service regulation of the incumbent utility, whose default service "shall, at a minimum, be maintained at the same level of quality under retail competition").
89. Parties to wholesale contracts, which were subject to FERC's jurisdiction, could include quality of service provisions, but FERC had no authority outside of its contract approval role to create and enforce quality standards.

sufficient reserve capacity to meet its own customers' demands under most contingencies (such as outage of a generating plant or transmission line); (b) operated and maintained its plants prudently; and (c) minimized the duration and frequency of intra-service territory outages, through proper attention to distribution facilities and vegetation. Utilities also cooperated to create reliability standards through then-named North American Electric Reliability Council, but membership and cooperation was voluntary.[90]

This exclusive reliance on state-level review and utility voluntarism was not well-matched with the introduction of wholesale electricity competition. New sellers interconnected to the existing transmission system, often distant from their contractual loads, then engaged in numerous long-distance transactions. This meant more traffic on transmission highways originally designed for local transactions involving fewer sellers. Growing competition among formerly cooperating utilities made data-sharing and mutual outage assistance less likely. After several multistate outages produced headlines (and constituent complaints), Congress responded in 2005 by creating a federal regulatory role in reliability, set forth in Section 215 of the Federal Power Act.[91] Section 215 required FERC to certify a single "electric reliability organization" (ERO) to establish and enforce, subject to FERC review, reliability standards for 'owners, users and operators' of the "bulk power system."[92] As the new ERO, FERC selected the North American Electric Reliability Corporation, the successor to the North American Electric Reliability Council.[93] The new NERC then established a series of Reliability Standards enforceable against a growing universe of entities participating in power supply markets.[94]

---

90. The North American Electric Reliability Council's predecessor, the National Electric Reliability Council, was formed in 1968 in response to the blackout of 1965, which left 30 million people without power in the northeastern United States and southeastern Ontario, Canada. The Council's name was changed from "National" to "North American" in 1981 in recognition of Canada's participation. For more information on the history of NERC, see *Company Overview: History*, NERC.COM, http://www.nerc.com/page.php?cid=1|7|11 (last visited Jan. 27, 2013).

91. 16 U.S.C. § 824o.

92. FERC's regulations implementing Section 215 of the Federal Power Act are contained in 18 C.F.R. Part 39 and 18 C.F.R. Part 40. FERC has established a definition for the "bulk power system"—all facilities operated at or above 100 kV, along with a process for case-by-case exceptions. Revisions to Electric Reliability Organization Definition of Bulk Electric System and Rules of Procedure, Order No. 773, 141 FERC ¶ 61,236, at P 95 (2012). Further discussion appears in Chapter 12.C.1, concerning "bright lines" in the federal–state relationship.

93. FERC issued an order certifying NERC as the Electric Reliability Organization for the United States on July 20, 2006. *See* Order Certifying North American Electricity Reliability Corp. as the Electricity Reliability Organization and Ordering Compliance Filing, 116 FERC ¶ 61,062 (2006).

94. Compliance with NERC's approved Reliability Standards, rules and procedures are required of all entities whose activity affects the "bulk-power system," as defined in Section 215(a)(1). These entities are listed in NERC's Compliance Registry. For a current list of all organizations registered with NERC, see *Compliance: Registration and Certification*, NERC.COM, http://www.nerc.com/page.php?cid=3|25 (last visited Jan. 27, 2012).

   The specific standards applicable to a particular entity depended on which of 14 functions it performed. NERC's Reliability Standards are characterized according to the following functional categories: Resource and Demand Balancing; Communications; Critical Infrastructure Protection; Emergency Preparedness and Operations; Facilities Design, Connections, and Maintenance; Interchange Scheduling and

The new federal role overlaps with the state role. Section 215(i) preserves states' reliability regulation, to the extent "not inconsistent with" the federal scheme.[95]

3.B.5. Power of eminent domain

State law grants utilities eminent domain power, but only for "public," not private, uses.[96] Before the competition era, this public–private boundary was readily drawn. The land condemnor was the franchised utility, using eminent domain power for infrastructure projects necessary to carry out its obligation to serve. In electricity, wholesale generation competition changed this picture. The new generation entrant needing land could be an entrepreneur with no franchise obligation. (And under FERC's Order No. 1000, there now can be "merchant" transmission companies with no obligation to serve.[97]) From this fact difference, a problem has emerged: if eminent domain power is available to some competitors but not to others, competition is distorted. This problem has emerged in two forms: seller differences and technology differences.

3.B.5.a. Type of seller

Suppose a traditional utility and a non-utility are competing to serve retail or wholesale customers. Assume that each needs to build generation to serve the sought-for load. If the state statute grants eminent domain power only to the utility, the non-utility is

---

Coordination; Interconnection Reliability Operations and Coordination; Modeling, Data, and Analysis; Nuclear, Personnel Performance, Training, and Qualifications; Protection and Control, Transmission Operations; Transmission Planning; and Voltage and Reactive. *See Reliability Standards*, NERC.COM, http://www.nerc.com/page.php?cid=2|20 (last visited Jan. 27, 2013).

Major FERC orders approving NERC rules are available on FERC's webpage. *See Electric Reliability*, FERC.GOV, http://www.ferc.gov/industries/electric/indus-act/reliability.asp. These major orders include: 18 C.F.R. Part 40 Mandatory Reliability Standards for the Bulk-Power System, Order No. 693, 118 FERC ¶ 61,218, *order on reh'g denied*, Order No. 693-A, 120 FERC ¶ 61,053 (2007) (approving 83 of 107 Reliability Standards proposed by NERC as well as NERC Glossary of Terms); Mandatory Reliability Standards for Critical Infrastructure Protection, Order No. 706, 122 FERC ¶ 61,040, *order on reh'g denied*, Order No 706-A, 123 FERC ¶ 61,174 (2008), *order on clarification*, Order No. 706-B, 126 FERC ¶ 61,229, *order on clarification denied*, Order No. 706-C, 127 FERC ¶ 61,273 (2009); and Version 4 Critical Infrastructure Prot. Reliability Standards, Order No. 761, 139 FERC ¶ 61,058 (2012).

95. 16 U.S.C. § 824o(i). Chapter 12 will discuss the federal–state regulatory relationship in more detail. For additional background on the federal reliability role, see John S. Moot, *A Modest Proposal For Reforms of the FERC's Reliability and Enforcement Programs*, 33 ENERGY L.J. 475 (2012) (making recommendations for reforming the electric reliability program and the assessment of civil penalties in enforcement proceedings); Enforcement of Statutes, Orders, Rules, and Regulations; Revised Policy Statement on Penalty Guidelines, 132 FERC ¶ 61,216 (2010); 18 C.F.R. Part 40 Revision to Electric Reliability Organization Definition of Bulk Electric System, Order No. 743, 133 FERC ¶ 61,150 (2010); Revisions to Electric Reliability Organization Definition of Bulk Electric System and Rules of Procedure, Notice of Proposed Rulemaking, 139 FERC ¶ 61,247 (2012); *Report of the System Reliability, Planning, and Compliance Meeting*, 32 ENERGY L.J. 759 (2011); *Report of the System Reliability, Planning, and Compliance Meeting*, 30 ENERGY L.J. 831 (2009).

96. *See supra* Chapter 2.E.

97. *See* Transmission Planning and Cost Allocation by Transmission Owning and Operating Public Utilities, Order No. 1000, 136 FERC ¶ 61,051, at PP 256–57 (2011), *order on reh'g*, Order No. 1000-A, 139 FERC ¶ 61,132, *order on reh'g*, Order No. 1000-B, 141 FERC ¶ 61,044 (2012).

disadvantaged. Massachusetts solved this problem by revising its statute, expanding the class of entities authorized to use eminent domain:

> Any electric or gas company, generation company, or wholesale generation company may petition the department for the right to exercise the power of eminent domain with respect to the facility or facilities specified and contained in a petition . . . or a bulk power supply substation if such [electric or gas] company is unable to reach agreement with the owners of land for the acquisition of any necessary estate or interest in land.[98]

What if the existing statute limits the eminent domain power to "public utilities"? A commission might interpret the term to include the new competitors. In Pennsylvania's Marcellus region, shale gas discoveries have attracted companies hoping to build pipelines to move the product to market. Some have sought "public utility" status, so as to gain the eminent domain power available traditional incumbent utilities. Granting one such request, the Pennsylvania Public Utility Commission applied a four-part test, requiring the applicant to show that it

- "will be transporting or conveying natural or artificial gas by pipeline or conduit for compensation";
- "will serve any and all potential customers needing to move gas through the pipeline system";
- "intends to utilize negotiated contracts to secure customers; contracts are not meant to be exclusionary, but rather to establish technical requirements, delivery points, and other terms and conditions of service"; and
- "has made a commitment to expand its capacity, as needed, to meet increased customer demand."[99]

The Massachusetts and Pennsylvania examples illustrate one type of tension: limits on eminent domain powers conflicted with state competition goals. What if the conflict is between state and federal policies; specifically, between state eminent domain limits and federal competition goals? This problem arises in FERC's orders on transmission "interconnection." As explained in Chapter 3.A.1, FERC's Order No. 888, issued in 1996, prohibited undue discrimination by providers of transmission service. Each investor-owned, transmission-owning utility must offer transmission service to others, including generation competitors, on terms comparable to how the utility uses its facilities for its

---

98.   Mass. Gen. Laws ch. 164 § 69R.
99.   Laser Ne. Gathering Co., Docket No. A-2010-2153371, 2011 Pa. PUC LEXIS 1303, at *30 (Pa. Pub. Util. Comm'n Aug. 25, 2011).

own customers.[100] FERC subsequently issued Order No. 2003, making "interconnection service" a distinct utility obligation requiring the same non-discriminatory treatment.[101]

An interconnection facility is the line connecting a generator to the utility's main transmission system. Interconnection service involves designing, constructing and connecting the interconnection facility, sometimes over long distances. If the interconnection facility crosses private land, the interconnecting generator might need eminent domain power. What if the state makes eminent domain power available only to traditional utilities, and not to the new, non-utility "merchant" generators needing the new interconnection service? FERC recognized the problem: if a utility was competing with the new merchant companies to build generation, it could exercise its eminent domain power discriminatorily, favoring its own interconnection over its competitors'. FERC's rule forbade favoritism: the utility must either offer to use its eminent domain power for its competitors, or not use it for itself.

Utilities and state commissions challenged FERC's requirement as "commandeering states' eminent domain authority." The court of appeals disagreed:

> We recognize that a state's authority to exercise the eminent domain power, and to license public utilities to do so, is an important state power. But FERC has done nothing more than impose a non-discrimination provision on public utilities. The orders explicitly leave state law untouched, specifying that any exercise of eminent domain by a public utility pursuant to the orders' non-discrimination mandate be "consistent with state law." [Citation omitted.] Thus the states remain completely free to continue licensing public utilities to exercise eminent domain, or to discontinue that practice. To be sure, if hitherto a utility would not have exercised eminent domain to enable interconnection with an independent generator, the orders, conditionally, compel the utility either to broaden its use of the state-provided authority for the benefit of independents, or to drop the use for its own and its affiliates' power. But the modifier conditionally is critical. Nothing in the federal rule compels either continued state retention of the license, or public utilities' continued employment of eminent domain . . . . [T]he orders here leave state law completely undisturbed and bind only utilities—not state officials.[102]

In short: Under the Federal Power Act, where state law eminent domain power is available to the utilities but not to the non-utilities, the result must be evenhanded. Utilities don't have to use the power for their own interconnections; but if they do, they must use it for their competitors' too.

---

100. Order No. 888 will reappear in Chapter 4.B.3, concerning "unbundling."
101. 18 C.F.R. Part 35; Standardization of Generator Interconnection Agreements and Procedures, Order No. 2003, 104 FERC ¶ 61,103 (2003).
102. Nat'l Ass'n of Regulatory Util. Comm'rs v. FERC, 475 F.3d 1277, 1283 (D.C. Cir. 2007).

3.B.5.b. Type of technology

What if the utility's eminent domain power is available only for some technologies but not others? Since 1917, Section 27-7 of the Oklahoma statutes had this language:

> Except as otherwise provided in this section, any person, firm or corporation organized under the laws of this state, or authorized to do business in this state, to furnish light, heat or power by electricity or gas, or any other person, association or firm engaged in furnishing lights, heat or power by electricity or gas shall have and exercise the right of eminent domain in the same manner and by like proceedings as provided for railroad corporations by laws of this state.[103]

Concerned about a wind developers' "land rush," the 2011 General Assembly added this sentence: "The power of eminent domain shall not be used for the siting or building of wind turbines on private property." Wyoming's statute fine-tunes things further, banning eminent domain use for wind collector systems, unless the condemnor is the utility:

> No person qualified to exercise the condemnation authority granted by this section, except a public utility that has been granted a certificate of public convenience and necessity pursuant to W.S. 37–2-205, shall exercise the authority for the erection, placement or expansion of collector systems associated with commercial facilities generating electricity from wind.[104]

Both statutes can have legitimate purposes, yet disadvantage certain energy investments relative to others.

3.B.6. Limited liability for negligence

Chapter 2.F described how most states limit the incumbent utility's liability for ordinary negligence. A franchised utility providing default service to gas or electric customers will enjoy its pre-competition protection from liability. Its new competitors will not. If this difference yields a cost difference, competition will not be evenhanded. As of this writing the author is unaware of any state addressing this difference.

3.C. Constitutional questions

3.C.1. Definitions: "Sunk costs" and "future profits"

When the government authorizes competition in a historically monopoly market, the incumbent's shareholders are disappointed. Their company's market position, and the

---

103.   Okla. Stat. tit. 27, § 7.
104.   Wyo. Stat. § 1-26-815.

associated profit expectations, are no longer secure. Has the government violated the shareholders' constitutional rights? The Fifth Amendment to the U.S. Constitution states, in part: "[N]or shall private property be taken for public use, without just compensation."[105] Has the government taken private property without just compensation? The question requires one to distinguish between two possible disappointments: foregoing recovery of sunk costs, and foregoing future profits. After describing these distinct concepts, we present a constitutional analysis that addresses each one.

A utility's obligation to serve includes the obligation to invest in the infrastructure necessary to serve: generation, transmission, pipelines, switching equipment, wires, poles and pumping stations. Investors in an exclusive franchise have a reasonable expectation that their utility's obligation to serve will be matched by the customers' obligation to pay. That obligation to pay provides for a stable revenue flow that covers the incumbent's expenses, debt, recovery of the shareholders' investment and a return on that investment.[106]

When government allows customers to seek new suppliers, the utility's revenue flow is stable no longer. The incumbent then faces two possible disappointments: it might not recover its prior investment (what economists call "sunk costs"), and it will no longer earn the relatively secure return associated with the monopoly service.[107] These two disappointments are sometimes conflated into the single term "stranded investment." The conflation is inaccurate, because the two concepts—sunk costs and future profits—differ in their legal and practical treatment.

The utility has a sunk cost problem if, at the time the formerly captive customers gain the freedom to shop, (a) the utility's unrecovered book cost associated with resources built or acquired to serve its formerly obligatory load exceeds (b) the market value of those resources.[108] The problem arises from five factors, acting in combination:

1. The production of electricity is capital intensive.
2. Load growth is incremental, while major infrastructure additions are lumpy. These additions come on line in large chunks because economies of scale reduce their per-unit cost. It is therefore often efficient, in the long run, to add a plant ahead of demand, and then have load "grow into" the new capacity. These factors mean that at any point in time, the utility will likely have surplus capacity.

---

105. U.S. Const. amend. V.
106. These components of the utility's revenue flow will be discussed in Chapter 6.A, concerning cost-based ratemaking.
107. I use the term "relatively secure" because, as will be discussed in Chapter 6.B, traditional cost-based ratemaking does not guarantee a profit; it provides only a reasonable opportunity to earn a fair profit.
108. Book cost is original cost less accumulated depreciation. Accumulated depreciation is the amount already recovered from customers through depreciation expense included in the utility's revenue requirement. In traditional ratemaking, the customers would already have paid the utility for the part of its original investment that was recovered in rates through the depreciation expense (along with a return on the undepreciated amount). See Chapters 6.A and 6.B for more explanation of traditional ratemaking.

3.   Under traditional ratemaking, the investment cost of infrastructure capital additions is amortized, that is, allocated to ratepayers over the plant's useful life. If regulators expect a plant to last 30 years, they set rates to recover 1/30 of its original cost in each of those years. This annual fraction, multiplied by the original cost, is the depreciation expense. (The rates also are designed to recover a return on the as-yet-unrecovered cost.)[109]

4.   If the government introduces competition prior to the 30th year (as will always be the case for at least some of the utility's infrastructure), part of the utility's original investment will not yet have been recovered from ratepayers. If all of the utility's customers then find new sellers, the utility would have unrecovered book cost.

5.   The utility will be able to recover its unrecovered book cost only if it can find buyers for the infrastructure (or the output from that infrastructure), at a market price that equals or exceeds the unrecovered book value. If the anticipated recovery is below the unrecovered book cost, the difference is called "stranded costs."

Each of the transitions discussed in Chapter 3.A—for electricity, gas and telecommunications—had to confront the stranded investment problem.

Wholesale electricity: While investor-owned utilities make most of their sales to retail customers, they also have wholesale customers, often small companies owned by municipalities or cooperatives. Those wholesale customers that were distribution-only entities depended on their local investor-owned utility for power supply (which the utility would provide from its own generation or through purchases from third parties). Then came FERC's Order No. 888, enabling these wholesale customers to use their utilities' transmission systems to find other suppliers and import their purchases. These customer actions could leave the incumbents with unrecovered generation costs, incurred by the incumbents historically on the expectation that the customers would remain dependent.

Retail electricity: Retail presented a parallel to wholesale. Retail utilities that historically had invested in power supply (again, either by building and owning capacity or by contracting to purchase from third parties, or both) no longer would have dependent customers whose monthly payments assured recovery of the sunk costs.

Wholesale gas: Recall that prior to the 1980s, LDCs depended on pipelines for supply, because (a) the pipelines bundled gas supply with transportation service, and (b) LDCs did not have physical and economic access to alternative pipelines. To serve these dependent LDCs, pipelines bought gas from producers under long-term contracts. When FERC, in Order Nos. 436 and 636, encouraged and then ordered pipelines to unbundle

---

109.   In some situations, regulators set rates based on accelerated depreciation, i.e., allowing the utility to recover a disproportionate share of a plant's costs in the early years of its life. Even in jurisdictions with accelerated depreciation, however, competition could have been introduced prior to cost recovery having occurred in full.

transportation service from wholesale sales, LDCs became free to buy gas directly from producers. This change in market structure left the pipelines with long-term purchase obligations to gas producers but no assured customers.

Telecommunications: For reasons explained in Chapter 3.C.3.c.iv below, the telecommunications industry has faced less of a stranded investment problem than other utilities.

That was a summary of the sunk cost problem. The future profits problem exists because a utility that loses its exclusive franchise forgoes the relatively secure profit flow that came with it. Does the Constitution protect shareholders from these disappointments over sunk cost and future profit? We address the case law on these two subjects next, in reverse order.

3.C.2. Shareholder expectations of future profits

Does the Constitution protect utilities' expectations of future profits? Courts have taken two paths to the answer, depending on the pre-competition relationship between utility and government. Where there has been a contract promising a competition-free franchise, the courts have viewed the government's introduction of competition as a breach of contract, violating the U.S. Constitution's Contract Clause and triggering an obligation to pay just compensation. Where there has been no contract, the courts have shown the utility no sympathy.

3.C.2.a. Contract precluding competition

When a legislature grants to a company a charter to create a public utility, here is what it says, in effect:

> If you will embark with your time, money, and skill in an enterprise which will accommodate the public necessities, we will grant to you, for a limited period, or in perpetuity, privileges that will justify the expenditure of your money, and the employment of your time and skill . . . . Such a grant is a contract, with mutual considerations, and justice and good policy alike require that the protection of the law should be assured to it.[110]

A contract is how the U.S. Supreme Court viewed the government-utility relationship in *New Orleans Waterworks Co. v. Rivers*.[111] An 1877 state statute authorized the City of New Orleans to establish a private corporation, New Orleans Waterworks Company, and to grant the company a fifty-year "exclusive privilege of supplying the City of New Orleans and its inhabitants with water from the Mississippi, or any other stream or river, by mains or conduits, and for erecting and constructing any necessary works or engines or machines for that purpose." The grant included an obligation to serve: the company

---

110.   The Binghamton Bridge, 70 U.S. 51, 74 (1865) (describing what a legislature says to its "public-spirited" citizens when it grants a utility charter).

111.   115 U.S. 674 (1885).

had to lay sufficient pipes and procure sufficient water "as the wants of the population required." After fifty years, the city could buy the physical plant; if the city did not do so, the grant would extend for another fifty years, "but without any exclusive privilege or right to supply water." The statute also allowed the company to set its own rates, provided "the net profits should not exceed [10 percent] per annum."[112]

The city granted the franchise authorized by the statute, and New Orleans Waterworks Company commenced service. Two years later, Louisiana changed its mind. A new state constitution, adopted in 1879, contained this provision: "[T]he monopoly features in the charter of any corporation now existing in the state, save such as may be contained in the charters of railroad companies, are hereby repealed."[113] Acting under this "no more monopolies" provision, the City Council eliminated Waterworks's monopoly. It passed an ordinance authorizing Robert C. Rivers[114] to lay pipes under City streets to provide water to his hotel.

Waterworks sued to stop Rivers and won. The City's exclusive grant to Waterworks was a contract, which even a state constitution could not impair:

> The permission given to [Rivers] by the city council to lay pipes in the streets for the purpose of conveying water to his hotel is plainly in derogation of the state's grant to [Waterworks], for, if that body can accord such a use of the public ways to [Rivers], it may grant a like use to all other citizens and to corporations of every kind; thereby materially diminishing, if not destroying, the value of [Waterworks'] contract, upon the faith of which it has expended large sums of money, and rendered services to the public which might otherwise have been performed by the state or the city at the public expense.

The U.S. Supreme Court gave Waterworks what it sought: "a decree perpetually restraining [Rivers] from laying pipes, conduits, or mains in the public ways of New Orleans for the purpose of conveying water from the Mississippi River to his hotel."[115] New Orleans still could break Waterworks's monopoly, but it would have to pay:

> The rights and franchises which have become vested upon the faith of such contracts can be taken by the public, upon just compensation to the company, under the state's power of eminent domain . . . . In that way the plighted faith of the public will be kept with those who have made large investments upon the assurance by the state that the contract with them will be performed.[116]

---

112.   Id. at 677–78.
113.   Id. at 680.
114.   Nice name for a fellow whose business depended on the Mississippi River.
115.   Id. at 682–83.
116.   New Orleans Gas Co. v. La. Light Co., 115 U.S. 650, 673 (1885).

Appropriate compensation is the subject of Chapter 3.C.3 below. The point here is that the Supreme Court viewed (a) a statutory promise of monopoly status as a contract, (b) the expectation created by the contract as a property right, and (c) the state constitution's breach of that monopoly as a breach of contract, requiring compensation because of the damage to the property right.

3.C.2.b. No contract precluding competition

During the New Deal, the federal government loaned money to municipalities to construct electric distribution systems within areas already served by an investor-owned utility. The loans would be secured by the municipalities' revenues from retail power sales. Alabama Power, an investor-owned utility, sued the U.S. Government, arguing that the new municipals would invade its service territory. The U.S. Supreme Court found no constitutional injury: "[T]he mere fact that petitioner [Alabama Power] will sustain financial loss by reason of the lawful competition" does not equal a constitutional violation. Since the utility had no exclusive franchise, "[i]f its business be curtailed or destroyed by the operations of the municipalities, it will be by lawful competition from which no legal wrong results . . . . What [the utility] anticipates, we emphasize, is damage to something it does not possess—namely, a right to be immune from lawful municipal competition."[117]

Underlying *Alabama Power* is a tension that continues today: the tension between the private investor's desire for certainty and the government's desire for "creative destruction."[118] The famous example of this tension is the U.S. Supreme Court opinion in *Proprietors of Charles River Bridge v. Proprietors of Warren Bridge*.[119] There the parties fought over the best ways to cross the Charles River. The opinion's 50 pages and 180-year shadow (or spotlight, depending on one's point of view) warrant a detailed summary. First the facts, then the court's reasoning.

Ferry: The Massachusetts Legislature allowed Harvard College to run a ferry service over the Charles River between Charlestown and Boston and to keep the profits from the operation.

Bridge #1 (Charles River Bridge): To make river crossing more convenient, the Legislature subsequently granted Thomas Russell a charter to build a bridge at the ferry's location. The forty-year charter allowed the new company, "The Proprietors of the Charles River Bridge," to charge tolls. During the forty years, the bridge owner had to pay Harvard

---

117. Ala. Power Co. v. Ickes, 302 U.S. 464, 478–80 (1938); *see also* Tenn. Elec. Power Co. v. Tenn. Valley Auth., 306 U.S. 118, 139 (1939) (rejecting utility's claim that TVA's entry into their territory violated the Fifth Amendment's Takings Clause; absent express language granting perpetual exclusivity, the utility's existing franchises "confer[red] no contractual or property right to be free of competition either from individuals, other public utility corporations, or the state or municipality granting the franchise.").

118. FRED BOSSELMAN ET AL., ENERGY, ECONOMICS AND THE ENVIRONMENT 134–36 (2000) (quoting S. I. KUTLER, PRIVILEGE AND CREATIVE DESTRUCTION: THE CHARLES RIVER BRIDGE CASE (1971)).

119. 36 U.S. 420 (1837).

"reasonable annual compensation" for the income Harvard would have received from the ferry had the bridge not been built. After forty years the bridge would belong to the Commonwealth of Massachusetts. The bridge opened in 1786; its charter was later extended to seventy years.

Bridge #2 (Warren Bridge): In 1828, midway through the Charles River Bridge's charter term, the Legislature chartered a second company, "The Proprietors of the Warren Bridge," to build a second bridge nearby ("about fifty rods apart"). This charter required the builders to turn the bridge over to the state after it recovered its costs, but no later than 6 years after beginning operation. Once the state received ownership, it ended the tolls, making passage free.

The Charles River Bridge owners sued the state. Their charter was exclusive and perpetual, they argued. Chartering the second bridge destroyed the value of their bridge, and therefore "impaired the obligation of [their] contract" with the Commonwealth.

The Court's reasoning: The Supreme Court found that plaintiff Charles River Bridge could prevail only by showing that the State had breached a contract. "It is well settled, by the decisions of this court, that a state law may be retrospective in its character, and may divest vested rights; and yet not violate the constitution of the United States, unless it also impairs the obligation of a contract." Here, there was no breach because the Charles Bridge charter never surrendered the Legislature's continual power to do what is necessary to "promote the happiness and prosperity of the community by which it [i.e., the government] is established." Chartering a second bridge, even if doing so destroyed the value of the first one, was the government's way of promoting the public good:

> [I]n a country like ours, free, active and enterprising, continually advancing in numbers and wealth, new channels of communication are daily found necessary both for travel and trade; and are essential to the comfort, convenience and prosperity of the people.

Absent an explicit statement, the government will not be deemed to have abandoned its powers to meet the public's needs. Moreover, the government's decision to force competition among infrastructure options was not new:

> Turnpike roads have been made in succession, on the same line of travel; the later ones interfering materially with the profits of the first. These corporations have, in some instances, been utterly ruined by the introduction of newer and better modes of transportation and travelling. In some cases, railroads have rendered the turnpike roads on the same line of travel so entirely useless, that the franchise of the turnpike corporation is not worth preserving.

If plaintiffs like Charles River Bridge could block legislative decisions like this one, public improvements would be impossible, with dire consequences:

> [Y]ou will soon find the old turnpike corporations awakening from their sleep, and calling upon this court to put down the improvements which have taken their place. The millions of [dollars] which have been invested in railroads and canals, upon lines of travel which had been before occupied by turnpike corporations, will be put in jeopardy. We shall be thrown back to the improvements of the last century, and obliged to stand still, until the claims of the old turnpike corporations shall be satisfied; and they shall consent to permit these states to avail themselves of the lights of modern science, and to partake of the benefit of those improvements which are now adding to the wealth and prosperity, and the convenience and comfort, of every other part of the civilized world.[120]

Scholar Stanley Kutler sums up the implications:

> The Charles River Bridge case had much more at stake than a relatively petty local dispute over a new, free bridge. The Warren Bridge was a symbol for the rapid technological developments competing for public acceptance against existing, privileged property forms. The destruction of the vested interest in favor of beneficial change reflected a creative process vital to ongoing development and progress . . . . The competing principles of the parties in the bridge case fundamentally involved the state's role and power of encouraging or implementing innovations for the advantage of the community . . . .[121]

* * *

The bottom line: A government can grant monopoly status, and it can remove that status. Whether compensation is owed the monopoly holder for its foregone profit depends on what commitment the government made. If there was a contractual commitment to prevent competition, some compensation is owed. If there was no commitment, the investors took their chances. This next subchapter applies this longstanding, straightforward principle to the modern question of "stranded investment": When government decides to inject competition into an exclusive franchised territory, does the U.S. Constitution entitle the incumbent to receive sunk costs—unrecovered book costs—incurred to carry out its obligation to serve?

---

120. *Charles River Bridge*, 36 U.S. at 551–53.
121. Bosselman, *supra* note 118, at 134–36.

3.C.3. Shareholder expectation of sunk cost recovery

To understand the Constitution's treatment of sunk cost recovery, we first must clarify what is a "taking." We then review the court decisions on takings in the utility regulation context. While the courts have focused on the Constitution's Fifth Amendment, we close with some comments on the Constitution's Contract Clause.

3.C.3.a. Takings Clause

Recall the language of the Fifth Amendment: "[N]or shall private property be taken for public use, without just compensation."[122] In public utility regulation, what "property" is "taken," for which "just compensation" is due? Courts and commissions today use Justice Brandeis's approach in *Missouri ex rel. Southwestern Bell Telephone Co. v. Public Service Commission*:

> The thing devoted by the investor to the public use is not specific property, tangible and intangible, but capital embarked in the enterprise. Upon the capital so invested the Federal Constitution guarantees to the utility the opportunity to earn a fair return.[123]

The property "taken" is the shareholder investment spent by the utility to fulfill its public service obligations. The "just compensation" is the recovery of and return on that investment, authorized by the regulator when it sets the utility's rates.

Suppose a utility with an exclusive franchise prudently invests $90 million to build a 30-year asset needed to fulfill its public service obligations. After ten years (one-third of the asset's useful life), the government frees those customers to buy from others. How will the utility receive its just compensation (i.e., the not-yet-recovered amount of $60 million) and the associated return? This is the problem of "stranded investment": the book value of obligatory investments rendered potentially unrecoverable by the government's decision to free customers to shop. The concept becomes clear on examination of its components:

1. The "investment" in the phrase "stranded investment" is the utility's original investment in assets; here, $90 million.
2. These assets have a book value and a market value. Book value is that portion of the utility's original investment not yet recovered in rates through depreciation charges—here, $60 million. Market value is the price the assets would fetch in a competitive market: for electric generation, the net present value of the stream of

---

122. U.S. CONST. amend. V.
123. 262 U.S. 276, 290 (1923) (Brandeis, J., concurring). Justice Brandeis's opinion is variously referred to as a concurrence or a dissent. His first and third sentences show that it was both—a concurrence with the outcome and a dissent from the reasoning: "I concur in the judgment of reversal . . . . I differ fundamentally from my brethren concerning the rule to be applied in determining whether a prescribed rate is confiscatory." *Id.* at 289.

earnings the utility would receive from sales of electricity produced by the generation assets. If in our example the asset at issue had a market value of $45 million,
the "stranded investment" would be $15 million ($60 million minus $45 million).

Stranded investment, then, is the excess of book value over market value of these assets.

Caution: This discussion has assumed that the market value will be less than the book
value, leading to "stranded investment." But the opposite is also possible—what some call
"stranded benefits." On the day competition begins, the utility might be sitting on a gold
mine: a well-running, book-depreciated nuclear plant in a capacity-short region with high
market prices. Shareholders would have no constitutional concern about "just compensation." There would be, however, a statutory question: Who, as between shareholders and
customers, should receive the excess of market value over book value? We will address this
question in Chapter 4.B.5.e. For purposes of the present discussion, we will assume that
book value exceeds market value, that there is stranded investment, not stranded benefit.

3.C.3.b. Case law

The case law establishes this principle: Within some vaguely defined boundaries, regulators can place on utility investors the risk that competition will leave prudent investment
unrecovered. That was the message of *Charles River Bridge*. But the judicial guidance is
imperfect, leading policy makers to make compromise calls that have survived judicial
challenge. After discussing three oft-cited cases dealing with ratemaking, we will discuss
the policy compromises made in the electricity and gas industries.

1. Market Street Railway Co. v. Railroad Commission of California:[124] Market Street
Railway operated streetcars and buses in and around San Francisco. Faced with competition from municipal transportation companies and other transportation modes, the
company was losing customers and money under its then-current rates. The state commission lowered the rates, finding that a six-cent fare would "sufficiently stimulate traffic
to leave" a 6 percent return on the rate base. The utility challenged the rate reduction as
an unconstitutional taking without just compensation. The Court upheld the commission. In famous language, the Court explained that the Constitution has no sympathy for
a company whose services are no longer needed:

[I]f there were no public regulation at all, this appellant would be a particularly ailing
unit of a generally sick industry. The problem of reconciling the patrons' needs and
the investors' rights in an enterprise that has passed its zenith of opportunity and usefulness, whose investment already is impaired by economic forces, and whose earning

---

124.   324 U.S. 548 (1945).

possibilities are already invaded by competition from other forms of transportation, is quite a different problem. . . .

The due process clause has been applied to prevent governmental destruction of existing economic values. It has not and cannot be applied to insure values or to restore values that have been lost by the operation of economic forces.[125]

Normally, a utility would be entitled to rates "sufficient to assure confidence in the financial integrity of the enterprise, so as to maintain its credit and to attract capital" and to "enable the company to operate successfully, to maintain its financial integrity, to attract capital, and to compensate its investors for the risks assumed." But these assurances "obviously are inapplicable to a company whose financial integrity already is hopelessly undermined, which could not attract capital on any possible rate, and where investors recognize as lost a part of what they have put in."[126]

2. *Jersey Central Power & Light v. FERC:*[127] After prudently spending $397 million on a nuclear plant, Jersey Central prudently abandoned the project. The utility then asked FERC to approve higher wholesale rates to recover its costs. FERC's then-existing policy on prudent abandoned plant was to allow recovery of, but not return on, the investment. This approach split the pain roughly 50/50 between shareholders and ratepayers.[128] The "no return" meant not only no return on equity, but also no recovery of the carrying charges on the debt incurred to construct the plant. (Jersey Central had voluntarily forgone the return on equity.) FERC applied its policy to Jersey Central summarily, without a hearing into how it would affect the utility financially. The utility went to court.

The D.C. Circuit voted 5–4 to return the case to FERC for a hearing on financial effects. The majority opinion had two key holdings. First, FERC's policy of requiring utilities to absorb costs associated with prudent-but-unuseful investment did not inherently violate the Takings Clause. That finding is consistent with *Market Street Railway* and *Charles River Bridge*. Second, before applying the policy in a specific case, the regulator must inquire into whether the policy would prevent the utility from maintaining its "financial integrity," a test required by *Hope Natural Gas v. Federal Power Commission*.[129]

---

125.   *Id.* at 548, 554, 557, 567. By the "Due Process Clause," the Court means the Fourteenth Amendment, which provides in relevant part: "Nor shall any State deprive any person of life, liberty, or property, without due process of law . . . ." This clause applies the Fifth Amendment's Takings Clause to the states. *See, e.g.,* Chicago, B. & Q.R. Co. v. Chicago, 166 U.S. 226 (1897); Fideicomiso de la Tierra del Cano Martin Pena v. Fortuno, 604 F.3d 7, 12 (1st Cir. 2010) (applying the Takings Clause of the Fifth Amendment to the states and to Puerto Rico through the Fourteenth Amendment).

126.   *Market Street Railway*, 324 U.S. at 566 (quoting Hope Natural Gas v. Fed. Power Comm'n, 320 U.S. 591, 603 (1944)).

127.   810 F.2d 1168 (D.C. Cir. 1987).

128.   FERC stated this sharing policy in New England Power Co., 8 FERC ¶ 61,054 (1979), *aff'd sub nom.* NEPCO Mun. Rate Comm'n v. FERC, 668 F.2d 1327 (D.C. Cir. 1981), *cert. denied sub nom.* New England Power Co. v. FERC, 457 U.S. 1117 (1982).

129.   320 U.S. 591 (1944). *Hope Natural Gas* is discussed in detail at Chapter 6.B.2.a.

Elaborating the first point was Judge Starr's concurrence. He rejected the utility's argument for a "prudent investment rule," that is, a requirement that all prudent investment receive recovery, regardless of the investment's usefulness. While a utility's obligation to serve makes *some type* of investment mandatory, the utility's *specific* investment decisions are voluntary. These voluntary actions, Judge Starr explained, involve ordinary business risk undeserving of government protection, at least in the case of an abandoned plant:

> What is fundamental [in determining whether to authorize full cost recovery] is that the government did not force upon the utility a specified course of action . . . .
>
> Indeed, it would be curious if the Constitution protected utility investors entirely from business dangers experienced daily in the free market, the danger that managers will prove to have been overly sanguine about business prospects or the danger that a particular capital investment will not prove successful . . . . [T]he Fifth Amendment does not provide utility investors with a haven from the operation of market forces . . . . Yet the prudent investment rule, in full vigor, would accomplish virtually that state of insulation, all in the guise of preventing government from effecting a taking without just compensation.[130]

3. *Duquesne Light Co. v. Barasch:*[131] Anticipating demand growth, Duquesne began constructing a nuclear plant. When demand growth slowed, the utility changed its plan and stopped construction. The Pennsylvania Commission found all the utility's actions to be prudent: the decision to build, the decision to choose nuclear, the decision to stop and all costs incurred in between. But a state statute required the plant costs to be absorbed by shareholders (i.e., neither placed in rate base to earn a return, nor amortized as depreciation expense), because they were not "used and useful" to customers.[132] Duquesne challenged the statute under the Fifth Amendment's Takings Clause.

The U.S. Supreme Court upheld the statute, reasoning that the Fifth Amendment does not guarantee recovery of prudent costs. Pennsylvania was free to enact laws that put the risk of prudent-but-unlucky costs on shareholders. Further, the small size of the disallowance (a 0.4 percent reduction in its annual revenue requirement) meant that the disallowance did not violate the "financial integrity" test of *Hope Natural Gas*.[133] We will return to this case when discussing ratemaking in Chapter 6. For purposes of our current

---

130. *Jersey Central*, 810 F. 2d at 1181, 1191 (Starr, J., concurring) (citations omitted).
131. 488 U.S. 299 (1989).
132. The statute stated that "the cost of construction or expansion of a facility undertaken by a public utility producing . . . electricity shall not be made a part of the rate base nor otherwise included in the rates charged by the electric utility until such time as the facility is used and useful in service to the public." *Id.* at 303–04 (quoting 66 PA. CONS. STAT. § 1315).
133. The 8–1 vote in *Barasch* (the dissent was on a procedural point) signals the clarity and certainty of this principle. No subsequent decision has blurred the picture.

topic—the transition to competition—*Duquesne*'s relevance is the same as *Market Street Railway*'s and *Jersey Central*'s: The Constitution does not promise recovery of costs, even prudent costs, incurred to carry out an obligation to serve.

Back to stranded costs: Based on these precedents, some have argued that the Constitution does not require stranded cost recovery in the context of transitions to competition. They assert that by accepting the obligation to serve, the utility necessarily accepts the risk that the government someday will introduce competition. That was the view of a New York State trial judge. The New York Public Service Commission promulgated a rule authorizing retail competition, without promising recovery of stranded costs. Utilities challenged the rule. The Judge upheld it, making three main findings:

1. He rejected the utilities' argument that they had "contracted with New York State to provide safe and reliable service in return for prudent cost recovery; that this constituted a 'regulatory compact'; and that failure to guarantee full recovery of stranded costs constitutes a breach of contract." He concluded that past commission decisions disallowing prudent costs eliminated any notion of a "compact" guaranteeing prudent cost recovery.

2. He found that "[s]ince the turn of the century, electric utilities have been on notice that they are required to serve the public need for electricity, not in return for a particular ratemaking method, but in return for a variety of powers traditionally reserved to the sovereign."

3. He reasoned that (a) "'[j]ust and reasonable' rates do not necessarily guarantee utilities net revenues nor do they immunize utilities from the effects of competition" (citing *Market Street Railway*); (b) "[t]he public have not underwritten the investment"; and (c) "[t]he loss of, or the failure to obtain, patronage, due to competition, does not justify the imposition of charges that are exorbitant and unjust to the public. The . . . Constitution . . . does not protect public utilities against such business hazards."[134]

Some have argued that *Market Street Railway* and *Barasch* should not apply to monopoly-to-competition transitions. When regulators introduce competition into formerly monopoly markets, they assert, the "destruction" of "economic values" arises not from "market forces" but from a change in government policy (these phrases come from *Market Street Railway*). Having induced the utility to make investments when compensation was assured (because customers were dependent), the government then removed that assurance by giving customers options. This change in investment status, from obligatory to

---

134. Energy Ass'n of N.Y. v. Pub. Serv. Comm'n of N.Y., 653 N.Y.S.2d 502, 513–14 (N.Y. Sup. Ct. 1996) (quoting Pub. Serv. Comm'n v. Utils. Co., 289 U.S. 130, 135 (1933); Los Angeles Gas Corp. v. R.R. Comm'n, 289 U.S. 287, 306 (1933)).

unnecessary, was a government action that destroyed "economic values," justifying compensation. *Barasch* anticipated this very concern, giving it a constitutional dimension:

> The risks a utility faces are in large part defined by the rate methodology because utilities are virtually always public monopolies dealing in an essential service, and so relatively immune to the usual market risks. Consequently, a State's decision to arbitrarily switch back and forth between methodologies in a way which required investors to bear the risk of bad investments at some times while denying them the benefit of good investments at others would raise serious constitutional questions.[135]

3.C.3.c. Policy outcomes

In electricity and gas, legal uncertainty and dollar magnitude combined to produce a common solution: allowing stranded-cost recovery, or at least the opportunity to argue for it. Telecommunications did not face the same situation.

3.C.3.c.i. Electricity sales at wholesale

Recall that FERC Order No. 888 required transmission-owning, investor-owned public utilities to provide transmission service to eligible customers.[136] Eligible customers included the transmission owners' so-called "transmission-dependent utilities" (TDUs)—usually non-vertically integrated municipal or cooperative systems that depended on the investor-owned utility for generation supply. Order No. 888 freed them to shop for generation from alternative suppliers. Their shopping decisions, FERC found, could leave their legacy utility supplier with unrecovered generation costs, incurred prior to Order No. 888 on the assumption that the customers would remain dependent.

FERC therefore invited the utilities to apply for "extra-contractual" recovery of stranded costs associated with certain pre-existing wholesale contracts, if the costs were "legitimate, prudent and verifiable." (Why were they "extra-contractual"? A dependent customer's contract obligation might require purchases for only, say, eleven years. But the utility might have incurred costs requiring recovery over thirty years, based on its "reasonable expectation" that its customers would renew their contracts and would pay their share of long-term investments and other incurred costs.) FERC justified this "extra-contractual" recovery because utilities that incurred costs to serve dependent wholesale customers should not now "be held responsible for failing to foresee the actions this Commission would take to alter the use of their transmission systems in response to the fundamental changes that are taking place in the industry." FERC did caution that its offer of "extra-contractual" recovery "will not insulate a utility from the normal risks of competition,

---

135. *Barasch*, 488 U.S. at 315.
136. *See supra* Chapter 3.A.1.

such as self-generation, cogeneration, or industrial plant closure, that do not arise from the new availability of non-discriminatory open access transmission."[137]

3.C.3.c.ii. Electric sales at retail

State retail electricity competition statutes typically offered utilities a chance to recover stranded costs.[138] Electricity stranded costs fell into the following major categories:

1. Generation-related assets;
2. Long-term purchase contracts for power or fuel;
3. "Regulatory assets" like deferred income tax liabilities;
4. "Capitalized investments in some social programs that were made at the direction of a" commission;[139]
5. "the unfunded portion of the utility's projected nuclear generating plant decommissioning costs";[140] and
6. "costs of employee severance, retraining, early retirement, outplacement and related expenses, at reasonable levels, for employees who are affected by changes that occur as a result of the restructuring of the electric industry."[141]

The recovery mechanism was usually a "nonbypassable" charge attached to the still-monopoly distribution service. By requiring all customers—shoppers and non-shoppers—to pay their pro rata share of legacy costs, this device ensured that their decisions whether to shop or stay with the incumbent would focus on prospective facts rather than past costs.[142]

3.C.3.c.iii. Natural gas pipelines

Recall that FERC ordered gas pipelines to "unbundle" gas transportation service from gas sales service.[143] This action enabled pipeline customers to shop elsewhere for gas, but it left pipelines with two types of costs: stranded assets and "take-or-pay" liabilities.

Stranded assets: As defined by FERC, these included "upstream pipeline capacity for which a downstream pipeline cannot find a buyer, and storage capacity that a pipeline

---

137. Order No. 888, 75 FERC ¶ 61,080 at text accompanying nn.581–88.
138. *See, e.g.*, 66 Pa. Cons. Stat. § 2804(13) ("[T]he commission has the power and duty to approve a competitive transition charge [for the recovery of transition] or stranded costs it determines to be just and reasonable to recover from ratepayers.").
139. Congressional Budget Office, Electric Utilities: Deregulation and Stranded Costs (1998), *available at* https://www.cbo.gov/sites/default/files/cbofiles/ftpdocs/9xx/doc976/stranded.pdf.
140. 66 Pa. Con. Stat. § 2808(c)(1).
141. *Id.* § 2803.
142. *See, e.g.*, Del. Code tit. 26, § 1010 (authorizing commission to impose a nonbypassable charge, so as to protect standard-offer customers "from substantial migration away from standard offer service, whereupon they may be forced to share too great a share of the cost of the fixed assets that are necessary to serve them.").
143. *See* Chapters 3.A.2 and 4.B.3.a.

no longer needs when the volume of its sales service shrinks."[144] FERC allowed pipelines to recover the costs of these stranded assets, if the costs were prudently incurred but no longer "used and useful."[145] Costs are "stranded" only if book value exceeds market value. The pipelines therefore had to net positive values against negative values:

> [T]o the extent that [a pipeline] recognizes gains on sales of stranded facilities and later has losses on sales of facilities that it seeks to recover as stranded costs, [the pipeline must, if it files for recovery of stranded costs,] detail the prior gains and reduce the proposed stranded-cost recovery amount by the amount of those gains.[146]

FERC then gave the pipelines two paths to compensation: spin-off or write-down. If the pipeline spun off its asset (i.e., transferred it to its shareholders), it could "apply for stranded cost treatment for any amounts below the book value of the facilities it received. These amounts would, of course, be offset by any amounts received in excess of book value."[147] If the pipeline retained ownership, it could write down the asset's value to an "economically viable level" (meaning a level reflecting market value) and then "propose [for recovery from customers] the difference between the net depreciated original cost of the plant and the lower market value, as a stranded cost." The pipeline could recover "this written down amount over a reasonable period of time, such as five years." Finally, consistent with its policy on abandoned plants (*see* the discussion of *Jersey Central* in Chapter 3.C.3.b), FERC would allow recovery of, but not a return on, the stranded cost: "A rate of return on the amount of written down facilities would be inappropriate since this allows a return on facilities that are not economically viable, and may also result in a competitive advantage for the pipeline."[148]

Take-or-pay costs: The gas transition involved billions in "take-or-pay" costs—pipelines' pre-unbundling obligations to pay producers for gas the pipelines needed to serve their dependent LDC customers:

> Take-or-pay costs are incurred when a pipeline, in order to maintain inventories for its sales customers, enters into a contract with the producer in which it promises either to take or to pay for the gas it has contracted to buy. Pipelines that have built up such

---

144. *See* United Distribution Cos. v. FERC, 88 F.3d 1105, 1178 (D.C. Cir. 1996); *see also* Order No. 636, 59 FERC ¶ 61,030 at text accompanying n.281 (describing stranded assets as "[c]osts of a pipeline's assets [historically] used to provide bundled sales service, such as gas in storage, and capacity on upstream pipelines, that cannot be directly assigned to customers of the unbundled services").
145. *United Distribution Cos.*, 88 F.3d at 1178; *see also* Order No. 636-B, 61 FERC ¶ 62,272, at p. 62,041.
146. Trunkline Gas Co., 95 FERC ¶ 61,337, at p. 62,241 (2001).
147. National Fuel Gas Supply Corp., 71 FERC ¶ 61,031, at p. 61,138 (1995).
148. *Id.* Recall that in *Jersey Central*, FERC had denied recovery of the return on debt. Here, in contrast, "[t]he pipeline would . . . be allowed to recover interest on the unamortized portion of its written-down plant[,] . . . as this will keep the pipeline whole for the direct cost of its investment in the facilities . . . ." *Id.*

inventories find them hard to sell once they have granted access to the pipeline to carry the gas of their competitors; as a result, they are hit with billions of dollars of costs . . . .[149]

FERC required the LDCs to bear part of these costs, a decision the Court of Appeals for the D.C. Circuit upheld as "an acceptable cost-spreading decision requiring those who benefit from the transition to a competitive natural gas market to absorb some of the costs."[150]

3.C.3.c.iv. Telecommunications

The telecommunications transition did not involve stranded cost concerns of the same magnitude as electricity or gas. The issue arose indirectly, as a result of the monopoly-era relationship between long-distance and local phone rates and between local residential and business service rates. Prior to its 1984 divestiture, AT&T's long-distance service rates were set above fully allocated cost,[151] by the FCC for interstate long distance and by state commissions for intrastate long distance. The extra revenues allowed AT&T to lower the rates for its local phone service. When the FCC allowed entrants into the long-distance market, AT&T argued that the resulting price competition would reduce the revenues it formerly used to lower the rates for local service. The Regional Bell Operating Companies made a similar argument at the state level, where they historically had kept rates for both intrastate long-distance and local business phone service above cost, so as to lower local residential rates. After divestiture, the RBOCs expressed concern that competition from CLECs for business customers would lower business rates, reducing revenues and placing upward pressure on local residential rates.

These inter-class concerns aside, stranded investment was not a major issue in telecommunications for several reasons. First, the telecommunications industry is almost exclusively a distribution business; there is no equivalent of generation capacity to be stranded. Second, competitive entry did not produce redundant capacity that would render the incumbents' capacity unused, because the new competitors and their customers still needed to use (and pay for) the incumbents' capacity. (Recall from Chapter 3.A.3 that the 1996 Act allowed CLECs to use the incumbents' capacity, via purchase-for-resale of the incumbent's full bundle, or purchase of "unbundled network elements." In-building wiring was a possible exception to the absence of stranded assets.) Third, the incumbents' networks usually had a market value exceeding their depreciated book value. Fourth, the

---

149.   Pub. Util. Comm'n of Cal. v. FERC, 988 F.2d 154, 157, 166 (D.C. Cir. 1993).
150.   *Id.* at 169; *see also* Associated Gas Distribs. v. FERC, 824 F.2d 981, 1027 (D.C. Cir. 1987) (upholding stranded cost recovery because pipelines were "caught in an unusual transition" due to regulatory changes beyond their control, having "entered into the now uneconomic contracts in an era when government officials berated pipeline management for failures of supply and constantly predicted continuing energy price escalations.").
151.   Fully allocated cost, sometimes called "fully distributed cost," refers to rates designed to recover all costs of production, both variable and fixed.

FCC for interstate services, and the state commissions for intrastate services, established "access charges" (such as the "subscriber line charge" or SLC) to compensate ILECs for originating and terminating traffic on their local networks for the CLECs and for long-distance companies.

For these reasons, stranded costs have not been a major concern in telecommunications.[152] The issues were about how to allocate ILECs' cost recovery between and among residential customers, business customers, and interconnecting competitive local and LD providers. The political goal, at the state and local level, was to keep residential local service rates as low as possible (meaning higher access and interconnection charges for other carriers), while the goal at the national (FCC) level was to promote more competition by shifting the largely fixed costs of access to ILECs' networks to subscribers though the SLC.[153]

3.C.3.d. Contract Clause

The preceding discussion has framed the stranded cost discussion as a question of "just compensation" under the Fifth Amendment's Takings Clause (applied to the states through the Fourteenth Amendment). Some advocates for stranded cost recovery argued that the utility-government relationship was a contract, making stranded cost recovery a government obligation under the Constitution's Contract Clause, which states: "No State shall . . . pass any Law impairing the Obligation of Contracts."[154] A series of writings and counter-writings pursued the point.[155]

The two analyses—Takings Clause and Contract Clause—have some common features. Contract analysis looks to parties' expectations based on their mutual understandings; Takings Clause analysis looks to expectations created by government and relied on by investors. But in the context of public utilities, modern courts concerned with compensation

---

152. More recently, the growth of wireless service and, to a lesser extent, the provision of voice services by cable operators, have reduced the number of ILEC residential phone subscribers, leading to the possibility of stranded investment. But this trend has been offset in part by the ILECs' gain in revenue from unregulated broadband (such as digital subscriber line, or DSL) services offered over the same facilities, especially for larger ILECs like the RBOCs. In addition, local phone service rates for large ILECs are increasingly subject only to non-cost-based price cap regulation, or no price regulation, making the stranded cost comparison between embedded cost and market value irrelevant. The subscriber line loss problem is greater for small rural LECs (RLECs). In that latter context, the forum for resolving this concern has been debates over intercarrier compensation rates, universal service fund and SLC fees rather than retail rate regulation. *See* BROTMAN, *supra* note 35, §§ 5.01[4]-[5]; Connect America Fund, Report and Order and Further Notice of Proposed Rulemaking, 26 FCC Rcd. 17,663 (2011) ("*CAF Order*") (petitions for reconsideration pending).
153. *See generally* BROTMAN, *supra* note 35, § 4.06[2].
154. U.S. CONST. art. 1, § 10, cl. 1.
155. *See, e.g.*, J. GREGORY SIDAK & DANIEL F. SPULBER, DEREGULATORY TAKINGS AND THE REGULATORY CONTRACT: THE COMPETITIVE TRANSFORMATION OF NETWORK INDUSTRIES IN THE UNITED STATES (1997); Timothy J. Brennan & James Boyd, *Stranded Costs, Takings, and the Law and Economics of Implicit Contracts*, 11 J. REG. ECON 41 (1997).

have always applied the Takings Clause, for the simple reason that there is no contract between the utility and the government. As a leading treatise states:

> [C]ourts should not rule that the government has entered into a contract . . . unless it is clear that a governmental entity with authority to do so has contracted with the private party in a way that restricts the power of the government to act in the future. Governmental actions relating to the use of property or business activity normally will be regulatory and not contractual in nature.[156]

The utility-government relationship lacks any evidence of the trio of features producing a contract: offer, acceptance and consideration. In the public utility context, the government-as-regulator promulgates statutes, rules and orders; it does not sign contracts to buy services. There may be contracts granting the franchise to serve; but the financial relationship, other than perhaps addressing franchise fees, is regulatory rather than contractual. No court has applied the Contract Clause of the U.S. Constitution to grant stranded cost recovery.[157]

3.C.4. Concluding constitutional thoughts

We began this Chapter 3.C by distinguishing two possible types of compensation for an incumbent whose exclusive franchise is breached: (1) compensation for the unrecovered sunk costs incurred historically to meet an obligation to serve, and (2) compensation for the future stream of profit associated with the formerly-dependent-now-shopping customers. The solutions reached in electricity and gas all address the former but not the latter.

A closer look at the economics shows why. When the utility receives its unrecovered sunk costs, it can invest those dollars in any enterprise, earning there the profit that it no longer earns from its formerly dependent customers. (That profit is the same "comparable" return that the Fifth Amendment grants the utility a reasonable opportunity to earn—as we will learn from *Bluefield* and *Hope* in Chapter 6.B.2.a.) Were the government to award the unrecovered cost dollars *plus* lost profit dollars, the utility would receive

---

156. Ronald D. Rotunda, et al., Treatise on Constitutional Law: Substance and Procedure § 15.8, at 103 n.74 (2d ed. 1989); *see also* Parker v. Wakelin, 937 F. Supp. 46, 52 (D. Me. 1996) (quoting Nat'l R.R. Passenger Corp. v. Atchison, Topeka & Santa Fe Ry. Co., 470 U.S. 451, 465–66 (1985) ("Analysis of this question must begin with the well-established proposition that absent some clear indication that the legislature intends to bind itself contractually, the presumption is that a law is not intended to create private contractual or vested rights but merely declares a policy to be pursued until the legislature shall ordain otherwise.") (internal quotations omitted).

157. *But see supra* Chapter 3.C.2.a (discussing New Orleans Waterworks Co. v. Rivers, 115 U.S. 674 (1885)); *cf.* Phelps Dodge Corp. v. Ariz. Elec. Power Coop., 207 Ariz. 95, 129 (Ariz. Ct. App. 2004) (finding state constitutional provision that granted "public service corporations" selling electricity the "right to construct and operate [specified] lines" also conferred "property rights . . . protected by the contract clause of the Arizona Constitution"); *id.* at 129 (finding that because this protection applied only to transmission and distribution, not generation, the introduction of competition in generation impaired no rights).

the "foregone" profit twice: once through the government award and again through its investment of the compensation received.

*   *   *

When introducing competition into historically monopolistic markets, policymakers begin by authorizing competition. They do so by changing the laws and regulations that made the prior providers monopolies. Each of the traditional features—exclusivity, consent to regulation, obligation to serve, quality of service, eminent domain and limited liability for negligence—requires attention. Policymakers also must consider the Constitution, which protects private property from a governmental "taking" without "just compensation." When their company is knocked off its historical pedestal, utility shareholders suffer two potential disappointments: non-recovery of sunk costs, and loss of future profits. While not crystal clear, the constitutional case law is sensitive to the former concern, less so to the latter. Compromises reached by policymakers with the parties have kept this "stranded cost" question away from the U.S. Supreme Court; while lower courts, when asked, ultimately upheld the solutions.

CHAPTER FOUR
Making Competition Effective

[P]ipelines continue to possess substantial market power; . . . they have exercised that power to deny their own sales customers, and others without fuel-switching capability, access to competitively priced gas; and . . . this practice has denied consumers access to gas at the lowest reasonable rates. . . . [D]iscrimination in transportation has denied gas users, and the economy generally, the benefits of a competitive wellhead market.[1]

[Transmission owners have engaged in] refusals to wheel, dilatory tactics that so protracted negotiations as to effectively deny wheeling, refusals to provide service priority equal to native load, or refusals to provide service flexibility equivalent to the utility's own use.[2]

It is easy to see why a company that owns a local exchange . . . would have an almost insurmountable competitive advantage not only in routing calls within the exchange, but, through its control of this local market, in the markets for terminal equipment and long-distance calling as well.[3]

Chapter 3 addressed the legal steps necessary to authorize competition. It is necessary to remove statutory exclusivity, grant entry rights to new competitors and address incumbents' sunk costs. But authorizing competition does not promise effective competition—a market structure which rewards merits, not market power. After defining "effective competition," this Chapter 4 describes the three steps necessary to create it. Regulators must "unbundle" the incumbent's competitive services from its monopoly services, grant all entrants access to the monopoly facilities on non-discriminatory terms and reduce non-facility barriers to entry.

Once a market is made potentially competitive, there still is the risk that sellers will behave anti-competitively, weakening the competitive forces that policymakers have authorized. We turn to anti-competitive behavior and its prevention in Chapter 5.

4.A. Effective competition: Definitions, goals and metrics
4.A.1. Definitions of competition

"Competition" has two dimensions: seller behavior and market structure. Businesses vying for customers tend to focus on behavior. They define competition as rivalry, as having

---

1. Associated Gas Distribs. v. FERC, 824 F.2d 981, 1010 (D.C. Cir. 1987).
2. Promoting Wholesale Competition Through Open Access Non-Discriminatory Transmission Services by Public Utilities, Recovery of Stranded Costs by Public Utilities and Transmitting Utilities, Order No. 888, 75 FERC ¶ 61,080, App. C (1996) (citing intervenors' allegations).
3. Verizon Commc'ns v. FCC, 535 U.S. 467, 490–91 (2002).

competitors. For them, competition is "a conscious striving against other business firms for patronage perhaps on a price basis but possibly also (or alternatively) on non-price grounds."[4]

Economists, removed from competition's daily pressures, focus more on market structure. They define pure competition as a market in which "the number of firms selling a homogeneous commodity is so large, and each individual firm's share of the market is so small, that no individual firm itself is able to influence appreciably the commodity's price by varying the quantity of output it sells."[5] Some economists describe market structure by focusing not on the number of players, their sizes and market shares, but on presence or absence of entry barriers. In this view of structure, even a monopolist can perform like a competitor if competition is a threat; that is, if potential competitors can enter easily.[6]

4.A.2. Goals of competition

Whether competition in a particular market is effective depends on one's goals. Defining those goals is difficult:

> [T]he most severe stumbling block in evaluating industrial performance is likely to be securing agreement on what is considered good or bad attributes of performance. Conflicting value judgments concerning performance attributes and their weights undoubtedly underlie many disputes as to the proper public policy toward monopolistic business enterprises.[7]

Some view competition's purpose as "lower prices"; they judge its success on that dimension alone. Doing so misses much richer purposes. Scherer and Ross would ask: Does the market display "greater responsiveness to consumer demands and generate more potent incentives for the frugal use of resources," compared to the predecessor monopoly market?[8] Alfred Kahn argues that competition aims to produce performance that is "*positively good*—efficient, progressive, risk-taking, innovative."[9] Consistent with Kahn, one can view competition as a progression of breakthroughs:

---

4. FREDERIC M. SCHERER & DAVID ROSS, INDUSTRIAL MARKET STRUCTURE AND ECONOMIC PERFORMANCE 16 (1990).
5. *Id.*
6. *See* WILLIAM J. BAUMOL, JOHN C. PANZAR & ROBERT D. WILLIG, CONTESTABLE MARKETS AND THE THEORY OF INDUSTRY STRUCTURE (1982). The authors provide a "formal analytic structure" to support the insight that "potential competition, that is, the *mere threat* of entry, can . . . affect the behavior of firms significantly and beneficially" (emphasis in original). *See also* Ala. Power Co., 13 NRC 1027, 1061 (1981) (reasoning that "the existence of a potential [wholesale] competitor may have an effect on the actions of another distributor"), *aff'd*, Ala. Power Co. v. NRC, 692 F.2d 1362 (11th Cir. 1982).
7. SCHERER & ROSS, *supra* note 4, at 55 (crediting Adam Smith).
8. *Id.* at 54.
9. 2 ALFRED KAHN, THE ECONOMICS OF REGULATION: PRINCIPLES AND INSTITUTIONS 18 (1970, 1988) (emphasis in original).

Competition is, to an important extent, a mechanism by which new ideas emerge and the best ones survive, only to be superseded by other still better ones. . . . When the Berlin Wall came down, West Germans were not amazed at how high prices were in the East; they were amazed at the extraordinary lack of choice and poor quality of the products that were available, suggesting that this had been the real, enduring benefit of a competitive market economy.[10]

Lower prices, innovations and breakthroughs, product quality and diversity, different allocations of risk and reward: these are some of the goals of competition.

4.A.3. Effective competition: Meanings and measurements

To achieve the desired policy goals, competition must be effective. Effective competition describes a market structure where the sellers and buyers lack "market power." Market power is the "power to control prices or exclude competition."[11] Market power can be exercised by a seller or a buyer. For a seller, market power is "the ability profitably to maintain prices above competitive levels for a significant period of time," along with the ability to "lessen competition on dimensions other than price, such as product quality, service, or innovation."[12] A seller also exercises market power when it "hold[s] a price constant and offer[s] an inferior service while excluding competitors."[13] For a buyer, market power is the ability "to depress the price paid for a product to a level that is below the competitive price and thereby depress output."[14] Finally, market power can be exercised by a single firm unilaterally, or by a group of firms coordinating, implicitly or explicitly.[15]

If effective competition requires the absence of market power, by what criteria do we measure our progress toward that result? Kahn tells us that "[t]he effectiveness of competition cannot be simply measured on a single linear scale running from pure monopoly at one end to pure sellers, complete independence of action, perfect standardization of products, zero governmental intervention and zero monopoly power."[16] Scherer and Ross recommend organizing criteria into three categories: structure, conduct, and performance. It is worth the effort to absorb their detail:

---

10.   Stephen C. Littlechild, *The Nature of Competition and the Regulatory Process, in* "Effective Competition" in Telecommunications, Rail and Energy Markets 13 (2011), *available at* http://www.ceps.eu/system/files/article/2011/01/Forum.pdf (quoting Derek Morris, Dominant Firm Behaviour under UK Competition Law 23 (2003) (paper presented to Fordham Corporate Law Institute, Thirtieth Annual Conference on International Antitrust Law and Policy, New York City, October 23–24, 2003)).

11.   United States v. E.I. Du Pont de Nemours & Co., 351 U.S. 377, 391 (1956).

12.   U.S. Dep't of Justice & Fed. Trade Comm'n, Horizontal Merger Guidelines § 0.1 (1992, rev. 1997), *available at* http://www.justice.gov/atr/public/guidelines/horiz_book/01.html.

13.   Portland General Exchange, Inc., 51 FERC ¶ 61,108, at p. 61,244 n.47 (1990).

14.   Horizontal Merger Guidelines, *supra* note 12, § 0.1.

15.   *Id.*

16.   2 Kahn, *supra* note 9, at 114.

Structural criteria

1. "The number of traders should be at least as large as scale economies permit."
2. "There should be no artificial inhibitions on mobility and entry."
3. "There should be moderate and price-sensitive quality differentials in the products offered."

Conduct criteria

1. "Some uncertainty should exist in the minds of rivals as to whether one rival's price moves will be followed by the others."
2. "Firms should strive to attain their goals independently, without collusion."
3. "There should be no unfair, exclusionary, predatory, or coercive tactics."
4. "Inefficient suppliers and customers should not be shielded from competition."
5. "Sales promotion should be informative, or at least not be misleading."
6. "There should be no persistent, harmful price discrimination."

Performance criteria

1. "Firms' production and distribution operations should be efficient and not wasteful of resources."
2. "Output levels and product quality (*i.e.*, variety, durability, safety, reliability, and so forth) should be responsive to consumer demands."
3. "Profits should be at levels just sufficient to reward investment, efficiency, and innovation."
4. "Prices should encourage rational choice, guide markets toward equilibrium, and not intensify cyclical instability."
5. "Opportunities for introducing technically superior new products and processes should be exploited."
6. "Success should accrue to sellers who best serve consumer wants."[17]

The authors acknowledge that their multi-criteria approach, objective on the surface, is susceptible to subjectivity:

How price sensitive must quality differentials be? When are promotional expenses excessive, and when are they not? How long must price discrimination persist before it is persistent? And so on. . . . [H]ow should the workability of competition be evaluated when some, but not all, of the criteria are satisfied? If, for example, performance but not structure conforms to the norms, should we conclude that competition is workable, since

---

17. SCHERER & ROSS, *supra* note 4, at 53–54.

it is performance that really counts in the end? Perhaps not, because with an unworkable structure there is always a risk that future performance will deteriorate. . . ."[18]

* * *

From this opening discussion of definitions, goals and measurements, it should be clear that "competition" is not the same as "effective competition." "Competition," in its loosest layperson sense, is merely two or more suppliers vying for a customer. "Effective competition" is, in contrast, some combination of market structure, seller and buyer conduct, and performance outcomes that achieves the goals sought by the policymaker. The point here is not to recommend any particular combination of definitions, goals and measurements, but to stress that only by specifying that combination can the policymaker know if her competition experiment is succeeding.

We now turn to the steps competition policymakers take to achieve that success. In combination, these materials help the policymaker to answer the questions "Why are we doing this?" and "Is it working?"

---

18. *Id.* A statutory attempt at defining "effective competition" with objective criteria appears in the cable rate regulation section of the Communications Act of 1934. There are four options, three of which are structural and quantitative, the fourth more behavioral and subjective:

> (A) fewer than 30 percent of the households in the franchise area subscribe to the cable service of a cable system;
> (B) the franchise area is—
>> (i) served by at least two unaffiliated multichannel video programming distributors each of which offers comparable video programming to at least 50 percent of the households in the franchise area; and
>> (ii) the number of households subscribing to programming services offered by multichannel video programming distributors other than the largest multichannel video programming distributor exceeds 15 percent of the households in the franchise area;
> (C) a multichannel video programming distributor operated by the franchising authority for that franchise area offers video programming to at least 50 percent of the households in that franchise area; or
> (D) a local exchange carrier or its affiliate (or any multichannel video programming distributor using the facilities of such carrier or its affiliate) offers video programming services directly to subscribers by any means (other than direct-to-home satellite services) in the franchise area of an unaffiliated cable operator which is providing cable service in that franchise area, but only if the video programming services so offered in that area are comparable to the video programming services provided by the unaffiliated cable operator in that area.

Federal Communications Act of 1934, ch. 652, § 623(l)(1), 48 Stat. 1064 (1934) (codified as amended by the Telecommunications Act of 1996 at 47 U.S.C. § 543(l)(1)).

4.B. Unbundling: Reducing the incumbent's control of "essential facilities"
4.B.1. Unbundling defined

Vertically integrated monopolies perform a series of services that they offer to the consumer as a single "bundled" product. Just as Starbucks bundles the barista, beans, grinder, worker and paper cup into a single cup of coffee for sale, a vertically integrated electric utility bundles the generation, transmission, distribution and aggregation into electric power for sale.[19] Over the decades, policymakers have identified some components of these bundled services as appropriate for competition. Examples are wholesale and retail electricity, wholesale and retail natural gas, long-distance and local phone calling, telephone equipment (called "customer premises equipment" or CPE), and information services. But specifying services as appropriate for competition only begins the process of introducing competition. The next step is "unbundling" the monopoly business from the potentially competitive businesses.

"Bundled" means "sold as a package, inseparably." In the pre-competitive era, a customer could not buy the potentially competitive product (e.g., wholesale electricity, natural gas or telephone equipment) without also buying the monopoly product (e.g., electric transmission service, gas transportation service, or local phone service). Conversely: If the customer wanted to buy the incumbent's electric transmission, pipeline or local phone service, she would have to buy the incumbent's electricity, gas, or CPE. The monopoly asset acted as a strategic asset: a physical facility controlled by the incumbent, not economically duplicable by a competitor, the access to which is essential to shop for or market a competitive product. By bundling, the incumbent could exclude from the market, or discriminate against, competing sellers of the potentially competitive product.[20]

If "bundling" is the incumbent's action—combining the monopoly and competitive services into an inseparable package—"unbundling" is the regulator's action, ordering the incumbent to make the monopoly product available for sale separately. Then customers can buy the monopoly service from the incumbent, while buying the competitive service from others. This regulatory action needs a statutory basis: the prohibition against "undue preference or advantage."[21] The risk of "undue preference or advantage" exists because

---

19.   Starbucks does offer some unbundled products. It sells beans and grinders so customers can make coffee at home. You can even bring your own cup to the counter, although doing so gets no discount off the coffee price.

20.   *See* Nat'l Fuel Gas Supply Corp. v. FERC, 468 F.3d 831, 834 (D.C. Cir. 2006) (citations omitted):

>   Like railroads, water pipelines, cable television lines, and telephone lines, natural gas pipelines traditionally have been considered natural monopolies. In other words, the costs of entering the market are so high (because of the large fixed cost of building a pipeline) that it is most efficient for only one firm to serve a given geographical region. . . . As natural monopolies, pipelines if unregulated would possess the ability to engage in monopolistic pricing for transportation services and discriminate against unaffiliated entities that seek to transport gas.

21.   *See, e.g.*, Natural Gas Act, ch. 556, § 4(b)(1), 52 Stat. 822 (1938) (codified at 15 U.S.C. § 717c (b)(1)) ("[n]o natural-gas company shall, with respect to any transportation or sale of natural gas . . . make

in each monopoly-to-competition transition, policymakers have allowed the incumbent to continue owning the monopoly asset, while also competing (directly or through an affiliate) to provide the potentially competitive services. Because a company in this position has the incentive and ability to discriminate against competing providers, regulators need rules to prevent discrimination. With some variations and exceptions, this situation exists in each of the major utility industries.[22] Specifically:

Wholesale gas: By controlling monopoly pipelines, incumbents could bundle transportation with wholesale sales service, making the local distribution companies dependent on the pipeline for both products. FERC's Order No. 636 required incumbent pipelines to provide monopoly transportation service, while allowing them to sell wholesale gas and storage service through marketing affiliates. Order No. 636 therefore required the pipeline owners to provide the transportation service on a non-discriminatory basis.[23]

Wholesale electricity: Incumbent utilities controlled monopoly transmission systems. Because these entities bundled transmission service with wholesale electricity, transmission-dependent wholesale customers had no choice but to buy their power from the transmission owner. In the wholesale competitive electric markets envisioned by FERC's Order No. 888 (discussed in Chapters 3.A.1 above and 4.B.3.a below), incumbent utilities would continue to provide monopoly transmission service, while also owning (directly or through an affiliate) generation and competing in wholesale power markets. Order No. 888 therefore required the transmission owner to provide the transmission service on a non-discriminatory basis.

Retail electricity and gas: In most states that authorized competition in retail electricity and gas, incumbent utilities continued to own and provide monopoly distribution service,

---

or grant any undue preference or advantage to any person or subject any person to any undue prejudice or disadvantage"); Federal Power Act, ch. 285, § 205(b), 49 Stat. 851 (1920) (codified at 16 U.S.C. § 824d(b) ("No public utility shall, with respect to any transmission or sale subject to the jurisdiction of the Commission, (1) make or grant any undue preference or advantage to any person or subject any person to any undue prejudice or disadvantage, or (2) maintain any unreasonable difference in rates, charges, service, facilities, or in any other respect, either as between localities or as between classes of service."); Communications Act, ch. 652, § 202(a), 48 Stat. 1070 (1934) (codified at 47 U.S.C. § 202(a)) ("It shall be unlawful for any common carrier to make any unjust or unreasonable discrimination in charges, practices, classifications, regulations, facilities, or services for or in connection with like communications service . . . , or to make or give any undue or unreasonable preference or advantage to any particular person, class of persons, or locality, or to subject any particular person, class of persons, or locality to any undue or unreasonable prejudice or disadvantage."). Most state statutes have similar prohibitions. *See, e.g.,* D.C. CODE § 34-1101 ("The charge made by any public utility for a facility or service furnished, rendered, or to be furnished or rendered, shall be reasonable, just, and non-discriminatory."); KAN. STAT. ANN. § 66-101b ("Every unjust or unreasonably discriminatory or unduly preferential rule, regulation, classification, rate, charge or exaction is prohibited and is unlawful and void.").

22.   As noted in Chapter 3.A.3, in the telecommunications arena the Modification of Final Judgment departed from this premise by prohibiting the Regional Bell Operating Companies (RBOCs) from providing long-distance service and information services, and from manufacturing CPE. The 1996 Act then permitted the RBOCs to enter these competitive markets subject to conditions.

23.   For details, see Chapter 3.A.2 and sources cited there.

while also providing retail sales service as "default" providers.[24] Some states also allowed the incumbents to be competitive providers (albeit through affiliates). These states required the local utilities to provide the distribution service on a non-discriminatory basis.

Telephone service: As explained in Chapter 3.A.3, the Telecommunications Act of 1996 authorized competitive entry into retail and wholesale telephone service markets. The incumbent local exchange carriers (ILECs) continued to own the "last mile" of telephone wires, providing the monopoly services necessary for switching calls. The Act also allowed ILECs to continue selling local telephone service in competition with the new entrants. (ILECs also were allowed to provide long-distance and information services, subject to conditions.) To prevent the ILECs from using their control over the last mile to block their competitors, Congress required them to grant non-discriminatory access to the noncompetitive services.[25] As the Supreme Court explained:

> Until the 1990s, local phone service was thought to be a natural monopoly. States typically granted an exclusive franchise in each local service area to a local exchange carrier (LEC), which owned, among other things, the local loops (wires connecting telephones to switches), the switches (equipment directing calls to their destinations), and the transport trunks (wires carrying calls between switches) that constitute a local exchange network. Technological advances, however, have made competition among multiple providers of local service seem possible, and Congress recently ended the longstanding regime of state-sanctioned monopolies.
>
> The Telecommunications Act of 1996 . . . fundamentally restructures local telephone markets. States may no longer enforce laws that impede competition, and incumbent LECs are subject to a host of duties intended to facilitate market entry. Foremost among these duties is the LEC's obligation under 47 U. S. C. § 251(c) . . . to share its network with competitors.[26]

* * *

These examples show that in markets historically dominated by vertically integrated monopolies, unbundling is a prerequisite for effective competition. The process of unbundling has three main steps: (1) granting non-discriminatory access to the monopoly service; (2) establishing appropriate rates for the monopoly service; and (3) reorganizing the

---

24. Default service is discussed in Chapter 3.B.2.
25. *See* 47 U.S.C. § 251(c)(3) (requiring the "incumbent local exchange carriers" to unbundle, and offer to competitors at wholesale prices, "network elements" including loops, switches, operational support systems and databases).
26. AT&T v. Iowa Utils. Bd., 525 U.S. 366, 371 (1999).

incumbent's corporate structure, to reduce the opportunities for favoritism. Before addressing these three steps, we describe backbone principles gained from antitrust law: the concepts of "monopolization" and "essential facilities," and their application to utilities through regulatory statutes. Then, after the discussion of access, rates and corporate separation, we address a nagging question: Does unbundling conflict with efficiency, by reducing the benefits from vertical integration? This subchapter closes by applying the principles of unbundling in this era of technological change, focusing on broadband and "smart grid."

Terminology note: The term "non-discriminatory" is regulatory shorthand, but legally inaccurate. In both antitrust law and statutory law, the prohibition is not against all discrimination, but against discrimination that is "undue" or "unjust or unreasonable." "Due" or "reasonable" discrimination is lawful. As we will see, much ink has been spilled over the difference.

4.B.2. The antitrust foundation

Mere unbundling—making the monopoly product for sale separately from the competitive product—does not make a market effectively competitive. Without regulatory conditions, the incumbent still can discriminate against its competitors. Discrimination can take at least four forms: limiting competitors' access to the monopoly facility; providing lower quality, less predictable service; charging rates exceeding own reasonable costs; and declining to expand the facility for its competitors' needs while doing so for its own customers. Regulators counteract these anti-competitive actions with conditions. These regulatory efforts have two legal bases. Antitrust law prohibits "monopolizing," while substantive regulatory law prohibits "undue preferences."

Although legal responsibility for enforcing antitrust law lies with the U.S. Department of Justice and the Federal Trade Commission, antitrust law's principles pervade utility regulation, in three ways. First, a state law protecting a utility from competition does not insulate it from antitrust liability: monopolists may not monopolize. Second, utilities must share their "essential facilities" with their competitors—although only up to a point. Third, the provisions in regulatory statutes referencing the "public interest" and prohibiting undue discrimination require regulators to pursue antitrust's purposes. We discuss each of these concepts now.

4.B.2.a. Monopolists may not monopolize

Section 2 of the Sherman Antitrust Act provides:

> Every person who shall monopolize, or attempt to monopolize, or combine or conspire
> with any other person or persons, to monopolize any part of the trade or commerce
> among the several States, or with foreign nations, shall be deemed guilty of a felony . . . .[27]

This proscription against monopolizing is central to our economy:

> Antitrust laws in general, and the Sherman Act in particular, are the Magna Carta of
> free enterprise. They are as important to the preservation of economic freedom and our
> free-enterprise system as the Bill of Rights is to the protection of our fundamental per-
> sonal freedoms.[28]

A monopoly can be lawful, but monopolizing is not. Consequently, a utility cannot claim
immunity from antitrust law just because the government regulates it as a monopoly. Two
landmark court decisions illustrate this principle: *Otter Tail Power Co. v. United States*
applied the principle to federal regulation, while *Cantor v. Detroit Edison Co.* applied it
to state regulation.[29] These two cases also illustrate two distinct types of monopolizing.
As discussed next, Otter Tail sought to *maintain* its lawful monopoly over municipalities'
attempts to replace it. Detroit Edison sought to *extend* its lawful monopoly over retail
electric sales into an unlawful monopoly over light bulb sales.

   Otter Tail: Otter Tail was a vertically integrated electric utility. It had exclusive franchises to serve retail consumers in 465 towns in Minnesota, North Dakota and South
Dakota. When the franchise expiration dates neared, some towns considered "munici-
palizing": replacing Otter Tail with municipally-owned power systems that would serve
residents directly. To achieve their goal, the municipalities would have to (a) buy out Otter
Tail's physical distribution system within their borders, (b) shop for wholesale power, and
(c) persuade Otter Tail to provide transmission service to carry that wholesale power to
the towns. (Even after the buyout, Otter Tail would own the transmission system essential for imports.) Otter Tail would be a possible wholesale power supplier but would no
longer be the exclusive retail provider. In short, Otter Tail would lose its power supply
monopoly over these towns and their residents.

   Otter Tail declined to cooperate in its competitive demise. After four towns voted to
municipalize, the utility used its "strategic dominance in the transmission of power . . . to

---

27.   Sherman Antitrust Act, ch. 647, § 2, 26 Stat. 209 (1890) (codified at 15 U.S.C. § 2).
28.   United States v. Topco Assocs., Inc., 405 U.S. 596, 610 (1972).
29.   Otter Tail Power Co. v. United States, 410 U.S. 366 (1973); Cantor v. Detroit Edison Co., 428 U.S. 579
      (1976).

foreclose potential entrants into the retail area from obtaining electric power from outside sources of supply."[30] The utility's anti-competitive actions consisted of

> (1) refusals to sell power at wholesale to proposed municipal systems in the communities where it had been retailing power; (2) refusals to "wheel" power to such systems, that is to say, to transfer by direct transmission or displacement electric power from one utility to another over the facilities of an intermediate utility; (3) the institution and support of litigation designed to prevent or delay establishment of those systems; and (4) the invocation of provisions in its transmission contracts with several other power suppliers for the purpose of denying the municipal systems access to other suppliers by means of Otter Tail's transmission systems.[31]

The United States sued Otter Tail under the Sherman Act. The federal trial court found that the utility had attempted to monopolize, and had monopolized, the retail distribution of electric power in its service area. The U.S. Supreme Court affirmed. Although retail electricity supply was a natural monopoly service, competition was still possible: "Otter Tail competes for the right . . . to serve the entire retail market within the composite limits of a town, and that competition is generally between Otter Tail and a prospective or existing municipal system." (Recall the discussion of "franchise competition" in Chapter 2.A.2.f.) Otter Tail had sought to maintain its monopoly by preventing that competition: "The record makes abundantly clear that Otter Tail used its monopoly power in the towns in its service area to foreclose competition or gain a competitive advantage, or to destroy a competitor, all in violation of the antitrust laws."[32]

Otter Tail argued immunity from antitrust liability, because it was regulated as a "public utility" under the Federal Power Act. The Court disagreed: "Repeals of the antitrust laws by implication from a regulatory statute are strongly disfavored, and have only been found in cases of plain repugnancy between the antitrust and regulatory provisions."[33] The Federal Power Act offered no exception from this principle:

> To the contrary, the history of Part II of the Federal Power Act indicates an overriding policy of maintaining competition to the maximum extent possible consistent with the public interest. . . .
>
> Congress rejected a pervasive regulatory scheme for controlling the interstate distribution of power in favor of voluntary commercial relationships. When these relationships

---

30. Otter Tail Power Co. v. United States, 410 U.S. 366, 377 (1973) (quoting United States v. Otter Tail Power Co., 331 F. Supp. 54, 60 (D. Minn. 1971)).
31. *Id.* at 368.
32. *Id.* at 369–70, 377.
33. *Id.* at 372 (quoting United States v. Phila. Nat'l Bank, 374 U.S. 321, 350–51 (1963)).

are governed in the first instance by business judgment and not regulatory coercion, courts must be hesitant to conclude that Congress intended to override the fundamental national policies embodied in the antitrust laws.

The Court supplied additional examples where statutes offered did not insulate utilities from antitrust law:

> In *California v. Fed. Power Comm'n,* 369 U.S. 482, 489 (1962), . . . the Court held that approval of an acquisition of the assets of a natural gas company by the Federal Power Commission pursuant to Sec. 7 of the Natural Gas Act "would be no bar to [an] antitrust suit." Under Sec. 7, the standard for approving such acquisitions is "public convenience and necessity." Although the impact on competition is relevant to the Commission's determination, the Court noted that there was "no 'pervasive regulatory scheme' including the antitrust laws that ha[d] been entrusted to the Commission." . . . Similarly, in *United States v. Radio Corp. of America,* . . . the Court held that an exchange of radio stations that had been approved by the Federal Communications Commission as in the "public interest" was subject to attack in an antitrust proceeding.

Also failing was Otter Tail's self-interest plea, that "without the weapons which it used, more and more municipalities will turn to public power and Otter Tail will go downhill." The Court's response was blunt:

> [The Sherman Act] assumes that an enterprise will protect itself against loss by operating with superior service, lower costs, and improved efficiency. Otter Tail's theory collided with the Sherman Act as it sought to substitute for competition anti-competitive uses of its dominant economic power. . . . "[T]he public interest is far broader than the economic interest of a particular power supplier."[34]

Otter Tail had a counterpart in telecommunications: MCI's antitrust suit against AT&T. MCI competed with AT&T to provide long-distance telecommunications services. To attract and retain customers, MCI needed to interconnect with AT&T's monopoly telephone networks. MCI complained that AT&T was monopolizing—seeking to maintain its monopoly over long-distance service—by creating obstacles to interconnection and by lowering its own long-distance rates to predatory levels.[35] When MCI sued under the federal antitrust laws, AT&T asserted immunity on the grounds that it was regulated by the FCC.

---

34. *Id.* at 373–74, 380, 380 n.10 (quoting Vill. of Elbow Lake v. Otter Tail Power Co., 46 FPC 675, 678 (1971)).
35. Predatory pricing is discussed in Chapter 5.A.2.

The Seventh Circuit disagreed. Both of AT&T's actions (its interconnection obstacles and its rate reductions) were acts of discretion: "[T]he Act gives the carrier sole responsibility for filing a tariff." The FCC merely allowed AT&T's voluntary tariff to go into effect, taking no affirmative action: "By permitting the tariff to go into effect, the FCC does not assert that it has examined the content of the tariff and found it necessary or appropriate to effectuate the regulatory program, nor does it have an obligation under the Act to make such a finding." Moreover, the FCC's policies during the relevant time period "appear designed to promote rather than inhibit competition in the specialized telecommunications field. Thus, the allowance of antitrust liability is likely to complement rather than undermine the applicable statutory scheme." Under these circumstances, the FCC's regulation did not protect AT&T from antitrust liability: "[W]here, as here, the pricing decisions complained of are more the result of business judgment than regulatory coercion, and the FCC has neither dictated nor approved of those decisions, the challenged rate filings are not immune from antitrust scrutiny."[36]

Cantor: The preceding discussion offered *Otter Tail* to demonstrate the proposition that regulated utility status does not insulate a utility from antitrust liability. In *Otter Tail*, the regulatory context was a federal statute. In *Cantor*, the context was state law. Detroit Edison had a state-granted exclusive franchise to provide retail electric service. The utility also gave its customers free lightbulbs—18 million in 1972. The Michigan Public Service Commission had approved the giveaway program. That approval included allowing the utility to recover the lightbulb costs through retail rates and prohibiting any program change without its permission. Cantor owned a local drug store that sold light bulbs. Unable to compete against the giveaways, he sued, claiming that Detroit Edison was monopolizing retail light bulb sales in violation of the Sherman and Clayton Acts. The utility argued it was immune because the state commission had approved the program. The utility relied on the "state action" doctrine of *Parker v. Brown*.[37]

---

36. MCI Commc'ns v. AT&T, 708 F.2d 1081, 1104 (7th Cir. 1983) (quoting Phonetele, Inc. v. AT&T, 664 F.2d 716, 733 (9th Cir. 1981)). Cases with similar holdings, cited by the *MCI* court are *City of Kirkwood v. Union Elec. Co.*, 671 F.2d 1173, 1176–79 (8th Cir. 1982) (holding that the Federal Power Act does not grant immunity from antitrust liability for utility rate filings that have anti-competitive effect), *cert. denied*, 459 U.S. 1170 (1983); and *City of Mishawaka v. Ind. & Mich. Elec. Co.*, 560 F.2d 1314, 1318–21 (7th Cir. 1977) (similar holding applicable to "price squeezing"—an anti-competitive relationship between wholesale and retail rates discussed in Chapter 5.A.1).
      The Seventh Circuit in *MCI* did uphold the trial court's decision (a) "allow[ing] AT&T to assert a defense based on good faith adherence to its regulatory obligations," and (b) instructing the jury that if AT&T "refused the interconnections because [it believed] in good faith" that the interconnections "would have violated established regulatory policies[,] . . . then the refusal to provide the interconnections was not anti-competitive conduct and cannot be considered conduct engaged in for the purpose of maintaining a monopoly." MCI v. AT&T, 708 F.2d at 1109; *see also* United States v. Marine Bancorp., 418 U.S. 602, 627 (1974) (holding that an antitrust court's review of bank merger "must take into account the unique federal and state restraints on entry into" commercial banking).
37. 317 U.S. 341 (1943). The state action doctrine exempts qualifying state and local government regulation from federal antitrust law even in instances where the regulation at issue compels an otherwise clear violation of federal antitrust laws. Underlying the doctrine is a judicial view that federal antitrust

The Court disagreed. The utility's decision to give away light bulbs was voluntary. Although the utility's retail electric service was "pervasively regulated," its sale of light bulbs was not. There was no "statewide policy relating to light bulbs." No Commission order required the program, and nothing prevented the utility from obtaining Commission permission to end it. Nor did the Commission's approval protect the utility. No state may authorize a private party to "restrain interstate or international commerce against

laws should not intrude too deeply into state regulatory process. *See* HERBERT HOVENCAMP, FEDERAL ANTITRUST POLICY: THE LAW OF COMPETITION AND ITS PRACTICE 739–40 (3d ed. 2005). The doctrine was first recognized in *Parker v. Brown*, where the U.S. Supreme Court upheld a California statutory program to allocate production among raisin growers. The Court there noted that nothing in the language or history of the Sherman Antitrust Act revealed an intent to preempt official state action.

The boundaries of state action immunity have been debated for decades. *See, e.g.*, FTC v. Ticor Title Ins. Co., 504 U.S. 621 (1992) (holding that where prices or rates are initially set by private parties, subject to veto only if the state chooses, the party claiming the immunity must show that state officials have undertaken the necessary steps to determine the specifics of the price-fixing or rate setting scheme); Cal. Retail Liquor Dealers Ass'n. v. Midcal Aluminum, Inc., 445 U.S. 97, 105 (1980) (holding that state compulsion is not a prerequisite to exemption, and establishing a two-part test for applying the immunity: the anti-competitive activity must be "clearly articulated" by state regulatory policy, and the private activity involved must be "actively supervised" by the state); Goldfarb v. Va. State Bar, 421 U.S. 773 (1975) (holding that the threshold inquiry in determining whether an activity is state action is whether the activity is compelled by the state acting as sovereign).

The immunity does not automatically apply to state agencies or subdivisions of a state. *See* City of Columbia v. Omni Outdoor Adver., 499 U.S. 365 (1991) (reaffirming the foreseeability test and holding that there is no conspiracy exception to state action immunity; and upholding a city zoning ordinance that was allegedly designed to benefit a billboard company); Town of Hallie v. City of Eau Claire, 471 U.S. 34 (1985) (holding that *Midcal*'s clearly articulated standard as applied to municipalities requires only that the anti-competitive conduct be a foreseeable result of the state statute under which the municipality is acting, and that active state supervision of anti-competitive conduct is not a prerequisite to exemption from the antitrust laws where the actor is a municipality, rather than a private party); Lafayette v. La. Power & Light Co., 435 U.S. 389 (1978) (holding that the doctrine applies only to anti-competitive conduct engaged in by sub-divisions of a state pursuant to a state policy to displace competition with regulation or monopoly service).

Some commentators have asserted that lower courts have applied these tests (especially *Midcal*'s clear articulation standard and the foreseeability test) overbroadly. An example is *FTC v. Phoebe Putney Health System, Inc.*, 663 F.3d 1369 (11th Cir. 2011), where the court held that a hospital acquisition that substantially lessened competition was protected by state action immunity. The court reasoned that the transaction met the clear articulation standard because it was a foreseeable anti-competitive effect of the defendant hospital authority's statutory power to acquire assets. *See* Angela Dively, *Clarifying State Action Immunity under Antitrust Laws: FTC v. Phoebe Putney*, 25 ST. THOMAS L. REV. 73 (2013) (citing FEDERAL TRADE COMM'N OFFICE OF POLICY PLANNING, REPORT OF THE STATE ACTION TASK FORCE 26 (2003), http://www.ftc.gov/os/2003/09/stateactionreport.pdf)); *see also* Herbert Hovenkamp, *Antitrust State Action Doctrine and the Ordinary Powers of Corporations* (University of Iowa Legal Studies Research, Working Paper No. 12-30, 2012), *available at* http://ssrn.com/abstract=2012717. The Supreme Court has upheld the Eleventh Circuit. FTC v. Phoebe Putney Health System, Inc., 133 S. Ct. 1003 (2012).

For in-depth discussions on state action immunity, see 1A PHILLIP E. AREEDA & HERBERT HOVEN-KAMP, ANTITRUST LAW: AN ANALYSIS OF ANTITRUST PRINCIPLES AND THEIR APPLICATION ¶¶ 221–29 (3d ed. 2006 & Supp. 2012); 2 ABA SECTION OF ANTITRUST LAW, ANTITRUST AND DEVELOPMENTS 1271–1303 (7th ed. 2012); Eric L. Richards, *Exploring the Far Reaches of the State Action Exemption: Implications for Federalism*, 57 ST. JOHN'S L. REV. 274 (1983); Barry J. Kessler, *State Action Antitrust Exemption as Applied to Public Utility Regulation: Borough of Ellwood City v. Pennsylvania Power Co.*, 20 URB. L. ANN. 289 (1980); Elizabeth Trujillo, *State Action Antitrust Exemption Collides with Deregulation: Rehabilitating the Foreseeability Doctrine*, 11 FORDHAM J. CORP. & FIN. L. 349 (2006); Aaron C. Stine & Eric D. Gorman, *Putting a Lid on State-Sanctioned Cartels: Why the State Action Doctrine in its Current Form Should Become a Remnant of the Past*, 66 U. MIAMI L. REV. 123 (2011).

the will of the nation as lawfully expressed by Congress." Put another way, a State cannot immunize Sherman Act violators simply "by declaring that their action is lawful." The question, where there is a "mixture of private and public decisionmaking" (i.e., where there is "state participation in the decision") is whether "the private party exercised sufficient freedom of choice to enable the Court to conclude that he should be held responsible for the consequences of his decision." In Detroit Edison's case, "there can be no doubt that the option to have, or not to have, such a program is primarily respondent's, not the Commission's." Indeed, the utility had begun the program years before the Commission even existed. The commission's subsequent approval did not make the program "state action."[38]

Detroit Edison also argued that federal antitrust law should give way to state utility law. The Court disagreed, for three reasons. First, there was no necessary inconsistency between (a) the Sherman Act's ban on monopolizing and (b) state utility law's "public interest standard." Second, "even assuming inconsistency, we could not accept the view that the federal interest must inevitably be subordinated to the State's." Third, "even if we were to assume that Congress did not intend the antitrust laws to apply to areas of the economy primarily regulated by a State, that assumption would not foreclose the enforcement of the antitrust laws in an essentially unregulated area such as the market for electric light bulbs." Outlawing the anti-competitive giveaway would leave the state's legitimate interest in utility regulation "almost entirely unimpaired."[39]

Some regulatory statutes do preclude antitrust law: The afore-discussed cases—*Otter Tail, MCI* and *Cantor*—all held that a company is not relieved of antitrust liability just because it is subject to a regulatory statute. But courts have interpreted some regulatory statutes to have that very effect. In *Verizon Communications Inc. v. Law Offices of Curtis Trinko*,[40] the Supreme Court held that the wholesale service requirements imposed on ILECs by the 1996 Act rendered antitrust law unavailable as an alternative or additional remedy. Trinko, a customer of AT&T (who was, at the time, merely a CLEC) argued that Verizon, an ILEC, violated the Sherman Act by failing to provide AT&T non-discriminatory access to Verizon's operations support systems (OSS) and local loop, as required by the 1996 Act.[41] The FCC and the New York Public Service Commission had already penalized Verizon for its misbehavior. The Supreme Court dismissed Trinko's antitrust claim. In determining whether anti-competitive actions trigger antitrust liability, the Court explained,

> [o]ne factor of particular importance is the existence of a regulatory structure designed
> to deter and remedy anti-competitive harm. Where such a structure exists, the additional

---

38. *Cantor*, 428 U.S at 585, 591–92 n.26 (quoting N. Sec. Co. v. United States, 193 U.S. 197, 346 (1904));
     id. at 591 n.27 (quoting Parker v. Brown, 317 U.S. at 351); *id.* at 593–94.
39. *Id.* at 595–98.
40. 540 U.S. 398 (2004).
41. *See supra* Chapter 3.A.3.

benefit to competition provided by antitrust enforcement will tend to be small, and it will be less plausible that the antitrust laws contemplate such additional scrutiny.

The Court described (a) the ILECs' obligation to provide wholesale services, and (b) the 14-point "competitive checklist" ILECs had to satisfy before receiving permission to provide long-distance service (see Chapter 3.A.3). This regulatory regime "significantly diminishes the likelihood of major antitrust harm" and was "an effective steward of the antitrust function." Against antitrust's "slight benefits" in this context, "we must weigh a realistic assessment of its costs." Those costs include (1) the risk of "false positives" (i.e., penalizing aggressive competitive behavior that enhances rather than weakens competition); (2) "a new layer of interminable litigation, atop the variety of litigation routes already available to and actively pursued by competitive LECs"; and (3) involvement of courts in technical matters beyond their abilities. "The problem should be deemed irremedia[ble] by antitrust law when compulsory access requires the court to assume the day-to-day controls characteristic of a regulatory agency."[42] Those factors counseled against subjecting Verizon's behavior to antitrust law. (*Trinko* also established limits on the antitrust law obligation to share one's facilities with competitors, a subject discussed at Chapter 4.B.2.d.)

The relationship between regulatory statute and antitrust law returned to the Supreme Court in *Credit Suisse Sec. (USA) L.L.C. v. Billing*.[43] Underwriters of an initial public offering allegedly extracted from buyers of the stock a commitment "(1) to buy additional shares of that security later at escalating prices, . . . (2) to pay unusually high commissions on subsequent security purchases from the underwriters, or (3) to purchase from the underwriters other less desirable securities." The Court held that the buyers' antitrust suit was precluded by federal securities law.

Applying four traditional factors, the Court concluded that (1) the defendants' alleged activities constituted "conduct squarely within the heartland of securities regulations;" (2) there existed "clear and adequate SEC authority to regulate" the conduct; (3) there was "active and ongoing agency regulation;" and (4) the facts presented "a serious conflict between the antitrust and regulatory regimes."[44] These factors led the Court to several conclusions. First, "only a fine, complex, detailed line separates activity that the SEC permits or encourages (for which [plaintiff buyers] must concede antitrust immunity) from activity that the SEC must (and inevitably will) forbid (and which, on [plaintiff buyers'] theory, should be open to antitrust attack)." Given this complexity, only the SEC can draw the line "with confidence." If antitrust law were available to plaintiffs, "different

---

42. *Trinko*, 540 U.S. at 413–15 (quoting Phillip Areeda, *Essential Facilities: An Epithet in Need of Limiting Principles*, 58 ANTITRUST L.J. 841, 853 (1989)).
43. 551 U.S. 264 (2007).
44. *Id.* at 285 (citing Gordon v. N.Y. Exch., Inc., 422 U.S. 659 (1975)).

nonexpert judges" and "different nonexpert juries" in "dozens of different courts" could reach different conclusions. There then would be

> no practical way to confine antitrust suits so that they challenge only activity of the kind the investors seek to target, activity that is presently unlawful and will likely remain unlawful under the securities law. Rather, these factors suggest that antitrust courts are likely to make unusually serious mistakes in this respect. And the threat of antitrust mistakes, i.e., results that stray outside the narrow bounds that plaintiffs seek to set, means that underwriters must act in ways that will avoid not simply conduct that the securities law forbids (and will likely continue to forbid), but also a wide range of joint conduct that the securities law permits or encourages (but which they fear could lead to an antitrust lawsuit and the risk of treble damages). . . . By seriously alter[ing] underwriter conduct in undesirable ways, to allow an antitrust lawsuit would threaten serious harm to the efficient functioning of the securities markets.

Second, the Court concluded that "any enforcement-related need for an antitrust lawsuit is unusually small," because the SEC "actively enforces" rules that ban the alleged conduct and because its statute requires it to "take account of competitive considerations," making reliance on antitrust actions "somewhat less necessary."[45]

* * *

Some statutes preserve antitrust's application explicitly, but even these "saving clauses" are themselves subject to limitation.[46] Even if the statute is not explicit, the courts caution against inferring immunity lightly: "Implied antitrust immunity is not favored, and can be justified only by a convincing showing of clear repugnancy between the antitrust laws

---

45. *Credit Suisse*, 551 U.S. at 281–83.
46. *See, e.g.*, Telecommunications Act of 1996 § 601(b)(1) ("[N]othing in this Act or the amendments made by this Act shall be construed to modify, impair, or supersede the applicability of any of the antitrust laws."). Note the term "modify." The *Trinko* Court held that this clause not only *preserves* the application of antitrust law; it declines to *extend* antitrust law. 540 U.S. at 406–07 (holding that "just as the 1996 Act preserves claims that satisfy existing antitrust standards, it does not create new claims that go beyond existing antitrust standards"). The *Trinko* Court found that "Verizon's alleged insufficient assistance in the provision of service to rivals is not a recognized antitrust claim under this Court's existing refusal-to-deal precedents." 540 U.S. at 410 (explaining that (a) Verizon's "prior conduct sheds no light upon the motivation of its refusal to deal—upon whether its regulatory lapses were prompted not by competitive zeal but by anticompetitive malice;" and (b) the services AT&T sought were not ones Verizon already provided to others but was refusing to provide to AT&T, but rather were services requiring unbundled elements that "exist only deep within the bowels of Verizon," involving "new systems" to be designed and implemented. Existing antitrust law, the Court found, did not impose such an obligation, as explained further in Chapter 4.B.2.d.

and the regulatory system."[47] *Trinko* and *Credit Suisse* are examples of how the Supreme Court applies this standard.[48]

The bottom line is that legal monopolies may not monopolize: "[P]ower gained through some natural or legal advantage such as a patent, copyright or business acumen can give rise to [antitrust] liability if 'a seller exploits his dominant position in one market to expand his empire into the next.'"[49] But whether they monopolize, in terms of antitrust law, depends on whether antitrust law applies.

4.b.2.b. Essential facilities doctrine: Origins
In capitalism, a firm is normally free to deal, or refuse to deal, with whomever it wants. Antitrust law inserts an exception. If the firm controls a facility essential for competition (known as an "essential" or "bottleneck" facility), but "denies a second firm reasonable access to a product or service that the second firm must obtain in order to compete with the first," the first firm can be guilty of monopolizing, in violation of the Sherman Act.[50] To prove a violation and compel access, the competitor (or the Department of Justice, if the suit is brought by the government) must show four facts:

> (1) control of the essential facility by a monopolist; (2) a competitor's inability practically or reasonably to duplicate the essential facility; (3) the denial of the use of the facility to a competitor; and (4) the feasibility of providing the facility to competitors.[51]

This subchapter discusses the doctrine's origins, its diverse applications and its limits.

The seminal "essential facility" case, *United States v. Terminal Railroad Association of St. Louis*,[52] echoes the four above-listed factors. Terminal Railroad controlled the only

47. United States v. Nat'l Ass'n of Sec. Dealers, Inc., 422 U.S. 694, 719–20 (1975) (interpreting federal statute to find some mutual fund actions sheltered from the antitrust law, and other actions not sheltered); *see also* Gordon v. N.Y. Stock Exch., Inc., 422 U.S. 659 (1975) (finding that stock exchanges' system of fixed rates for commissions on certain stock transactions was insulated from antitrust liability because the Securities Exchange Act of 1934 granted the SEC authority to oversee these rates); Silver v. N.Y. Stock Exch., 373 U.S. 341, 357 (1963) (interpreting the Securities Exchange Act as not exempting from antitrust law an NYSE rule prohibiting members from having private telephone connections with non-members; repeal "is to be regarded as implied only if necessary to make the Securities Exchange Act work, and even then only to the minimum extent necessary").
48. For a detailed argument that *Trinko* and *Credit Suisse* unnecessarily and excessively limited antitrust action in regulated industries, especially actions by public agencies (like the Federal Trade Commission) whose expertise in case selection limits the risk of unnecessary enforcement, see Howard Shelanski, *The Case for Rebalancing Antitrust and Regulation*, 109 Mich. L. Rev. 683 (2011) (arguing that had *Trinko* and *Credit Suisse* been the law in 1984, it "would likely have blocked the suit by the U.S. Department of Justice ("DOJ") that in 1984 broke up AT&T's monopoly over telephone service, considered among the most important antitrust enforcement actions in history").
49. Eastman Kodak Co. v. Image Technical Servs., Inc., 504 U.S. 451, 479 n.29 (1992) (quoting Times-Picayune Publ'g Co. v. United States, 345 U.S. 594, 611 (1953)).
50. Alaska Airlines, Inc. v. United Airlines, Inc., 948 F.2d 536, 542 (9th Cir. 1991).
51. *MCI Commc'ns*, 708 F.2d at 1132–33.
52. 224 U.S. 383 (1912).

rail access to St. Louis. It used its control to maintain its monopoly. A skeletal summary of the facts illustrates each element of modern essential facility analysis.

Non-duplicability: An essential facility is "essential" because competitors cannot duplicate it economically. The Court's detail set the standard for future assessments of duplicability:

> Though twenty-four lines of railway converge at St. Louis, not one of them passes through. About one-half of these lines have their termini on the Illinois side of the river. The others, coming from the west and north, have their termini either in the city or on its northern edge. To the river the city owes its origin, and for a century and more its river commerce was predominant. It is now the great obstacle to connection between the termini of lines on opposite sides of the river and any entry into the city by eastern lines. The cost of construction and maintenance of railroad bridges over so great a river makes it impracticable for every road desiring to enter or pass through the city to have its own bridge. . . .
>
> The result of the geographical and topographical situation is that it is, as a practical matter, impossible for any railroad company to pass through, or even enter St. Louis, so as to be within reach of its industries or commerce, without using the facilities entirely controlled by the Terminal Company.

Control with intent to monopolize: Terminal Railroad attained and maintained its monopoly by purchasing competing lines. There had been three competing ways to connect railroads terminating on either side of the Missouri River at St. Louis: Terminal's property, a competing ferry company, and an alternative bridge that connected to railroads not owned by Terminal. "The independent existence of these three terminal systems was, therefore, a menace to complete domination as keeping open the way for greater competition. . . . To close the door to competition large sums were expended [by Terminal] to acquire stock control." So Terminal bought the shares of all three and combined them into a single system. With this action, Terminal controlled not only terminals, but also transportation links between railroads on either side of the river. Contracts among the members of the Terminal-controlled combination precluded non-members from using the combined facilities absent unanimous consent among the members. Terminal then had the

> power . . . to exclude independent entrance to the city by any outside company. . . . This control and possession constitutes such a grip upon the commerce of St. Louis and commerce which must cross the river there, whether coming from the east or west as to be both an illegal restraint and an attempt to monopolize.

Remedy: The physical situation—specifically, the non-duplicability of the assets controlled by Terminal—made the unified, exclusive system "an obstacle, a hindrance and a restriction upon interstate commerce, unless it is the impartial agent of all who, owing to conditions, are under such compulsion, as here exists, to use its facilities." That impartiality would not exist "unless the prohibition against the admission of other companies to such control is stricken out and provision made for the admission of any company to an equal control and management upon an equal basis with the present proprietary companies." The Court's solution was to make Terminal Company "the bona fide agent and servant of every railroad line which shall use its facilities." This outcome would require contract revisions, including

> providing for the admission of any existing or future railroad to joint ownership and control of the combined terminal properties, upon such just and reasonable terms as shall place such applying company upon a plane of equality in respect of benefits and burdens with the present proprietary companies[; and]
>
> . . . provid[ing] definitely for the use of the terminal facilities by any other railroad not electing to become a joint owner, upon such just and reasonable terms and regulations as will, in respect of use, character and cost of service, place every such company upon as nearly an equal plane as may be with respect to expenses and charges as that occupied by the proprietary companies.

The Court also issued an ultimatum: If the parties fail to amend the agreements, the court would order the Terminal combination dissolved.[53]

4.B.2.c. Essential facility examples

Essential facilities need not be physical. They can be information sources, cooperative marketing arrangements, selling time, and special services. This diversity is evident in the seven cases discussed next. In each, a federal court either found that an essential facility existed, or granted the plaintiff a chance to prove that one existed. In these cases, the common feature is their focus on facts. These examples will help practitioners assess whether a particular facility is indispensable to competition, warranting judicial or regulatory action to compel non-discriminatory access.

a. Newspaper publishing association: The Associated Press (AP) was a nonprofit cooperative association with 1200 member companies. It engaged in the "collection, assembly and distribution of news." The news was collected by reporter-employees of the members, assembled by the AP and distributed back to the paid-in members. The By-Laws prohibited each member from selling news to non-members. They also gave each member a

---

53. *Id.* at 395–412.

near-veto over membership requests from non-members who competed with that member. (If a member protested a non-member competitor's application, the applicant faced onerous conditions, including a payment equal to 10 percent of the entire dues paid by all members since 1900. In contrast, applicants who were not competitors of members gained membership by simple majority vote of AP's Board, and paid no entry fee.)

The Court found that AP was an essential facility. A non-member's inability to buy news from it or any member "can have the most serious effects." Collecting this news is "practically impossible for any one newspaper alone." While there were other news services, AP was the largest, "universally agreed to be of great consequence." Non-membership was a competitive disadvantage. For the members, competitive success occurred not through individual "enterprise and sagacity" but from "the collective power of an unlawful combination." That the product was not a physical facility but "the creation or product of a man's ingenuity" was irrelevant, because the right to sell or not sell one's output does not include the right to "unduly hinder or obstruct the free and natural flow of commerce. . . ."

Because the By-Laws were an unlawful restraint of trade "on their face," there was no need to show anti-competitive effect; an agreement to restrain trade was unlawful "whether it be 'wholly nascent or abortive on the one hand, or successful on the other.'" That AP had not achieved a "complete monopoly" was "wholly irrelevant." By tying its members' hands, by preventing the sale of news to non-member competitors and by denying access to competing non-members, the AP restrained trade.

The Court fitted the remedy to the violation. Since the violation was agreeing to bar competing non-members, the remedy was to revise the application process to make an applicant's competitive status irrelevant.[54]

b. Newspaper advertising space: The sole daily newspaper in Lorain, Ohio reached 99 percent of the city's families. It enjoyed a "substantial monopoly" over the mass dissemination of news and advertising, both local and national. Its position was a "commanding and an overpowering one." Advertising with the newspaper was essential for local businesses, as there was no other feasible way to reach the city's families.

Then a new radio station arrived. The station's income depended on advertising. The newspaper, to maintain its monopoly over advertising, refused to accept advertising from businesses that advertised with the station. The essential facility was the newspaper. Its owner used its position to monopolize the market for advertising. Forcing local businesses to boycott the radio station was "bold, relentless, and predatory commercial behavior" that violated the Sherman Act. The newspaper claimed a right to select its customers, but that right is not unconditional:

---

54.   Associated Press v. United States, 326 U.S. 1, 12 (1945) (quoting United States v. Socony-Vacuum Oil Co., 310 U.S. 150, 225 (1940)).

[T]he word "right" is one of the most deceptive of pitfalls; it is so easy to slip from a qualified meaning in the premise to an unqualified one in the conclusion. Most rights are qualified. . . . The right claimed by the publisher is neither absolute nor exempt from regulation. Its exercise as a purposeful means of monopolizing interstate commerce is prohibited by the Sherman Act.

For a remedy, the court (a) enjoined the newspaper from refusing to accept advertisements on the grounds that the business also advertised elsewhere; and (b) required the newspaper to publish a notice weekly, for twenty weeks, that described the remedy.[55]

c. Fruit and vegetable warehouse: In Providence, Rhode Island, the most attractive site for wholesaling fruits and vegetables was a warehouse located next to the rail line. The warehouse was owned by a corporation whose shareholders were the building's tenants—produce wholesalers. One tenant, Gamco, pledged its stock as collateral to its lender, a Boston wholesaler. Gamco's financial difficulties led to the forced transfer of its stock to the lender. But Gamco's lease prohibited stock transfer without permission from the warehouse board. The warehouse persuaded the state courts to eject Gamco for violating the lease. Gamco then sued under the Sherman Act, claiming the warehouse was an essential facility whose owners used it to monopolize wholesale produce sales.

The warehouse responded that it was not an essential facility because there were adequate alternative sites. The Court disagreed. Other sites near the railroad were less desirable, because

> it is only at the Building itself that the purchasers to whom a competing wholesaler must sell and the rail facilities which constitute the most economical method of bulk transport are brought together. To impose upon plaintiff the additional expenses of developing another site, attracting buyers, and transhipping his fruit and produce by truck is clearly to extract a monopolist's advantage. . . . The [Sherman] Act does not merely guarantee the right to create markets; it also insures the right of entry to old ones.

The Court acknowledged that an owner's obligation to share access to an essential facility is not unlimited. "Reasonable criteria of selection [of users] . . . such as lack of available space, financial unsoundness, or possibly low business or ethical standards" are permissible. But the burden of justifying exclusion is on the "latent monopolist":

> Where, as here, a business group understandably susceptible to the temptations of exploiting its natural advantage against competitors prohibits one previously acceptable from hawking his wares beside them any longer at the very moment of his affiliation with a

---

55.   Lorain Journal Co. v. United States, 342 U.S. 143, 155 (1951).

potentially lower priced outsider, they may be called upon for a necessary explanation. The conjunction of power and motive to exclude with an exclusion not immediately and patently justified by reasonable business requirements establishes a prima facie case of the purpose to monopolize."

The remedy (in addition to damages and attorneys' fees) was comparable access: "[T]he plaintiff should be accorded space in the building as a tenant on terms similar to those accorded others, at once if available without dispossessing such innocent parties, otherwise as soon as available."[56]

d. Football stadium: The City of Washington, D.C. leased its stadium to the Redskins, a National Football League team. The lease agreement prohibited the City from renting the stadium to any other professional football team. Promoters of a possible American Football League franchise sought access, arguing that the facility was "the only stadium in the D.C. metropolitan area that is suitable for the exhibition of professional football games," and that by refusing to lease, the City was monopolizing. The promoters also presented evidence that "proper agreements regarding locker facilities, practice sessions, choice of playing dates, and so forth would have made sharing of the stadium practical and convenient." The court found that "[t]o be 'essential' a facility need not be indispensable; it is sufficient if duplication of the facility would be economically infeasible and if denial of its use inflicts a severe handicap on potential market entrants." The appellate court ordered the trial court to instruct the jury on the essential facilities doctrine so that they could consider the plaintiff's evidence.[57]

e. Telephone subscriber list: Southwestern Bell (SWB) provided local telephone service. It also published a "white pages" for its telephone customers. To publish the white pages, SWB had to create, and keep current, a database containing names, addresses and telephone numbers of all its customers. SWB licensed this database to its subsidiary Southwestern Bell Yellow Pages and to independent publishers like Great Western, who published a competing yellow pages. The database was important to any yellow page publisher's competitive survival. Said a former Yellow Pages President: "[W]ithout sharing this updated information with competing directory publishers, telephone companies are able to leverage their monopoly position in the telephone service area into the competitive directory market." And a later president asked why the company couldn't raise the price higher, so that "we might [be able] to . . . get rid of some [competing] publishers." Moreover, the database version was always up to date by necessity, because it was based

56. Gamco, Inc. v. Providence Fruit & Produce Building, Inc., 194 F.2d 484, 487–89 (1st Cir. 1952) (citations omitted); *see also* Am. Fed. of Tobacco Growers v. Neal, 183 F.2d 869, 872 (4th Cir. 1950) (requiring access to tobacco warehouse and auction time; "having set up the market in this way, defendants may not be heard to say that they have not established a monopoly merely because they do not interfere with an outside warehouse if it can shift for itself").
57. Hecht v. Pro-Football, Inc., 570 F.2d 982, 985, 992–93 (D.C. Cir. 1977).

on telephone numbers. Plaintiff's only alternative, picking a paper directory up "off the street" and copying it, would yield outdated numbers, disadvantaging it competitively.

When Southwestern Bell raised the price of the data version and imposed restrictions on its use, Great Western sued. The jury found that Southwestern Bell's actions violated the antitrust laws and awarded damages and attorneys' fees, and the court of appeals upheld.[58]

f. Telephone central office services: AT&T's ILEC subsidiaries had a state-granted, lawful monopoly over dial tones and interconnection services. AT&T also owned pay phones. The plaintiff North American Industries (NAI) was an independent provider, and direct competitor of AT&T, in the pay phone service market. AT&T had a special central office service that prevented people from making long-distance calls from pay phones without paying for them. AT&T provided these services to its own pay phones but not to the plaintiff's. The court found that in the pay phone market, AT&T's central office service was an essential facility because the alternative (what then was called "smart phones") were too expensive or unworkable.[59]

g. Downhill ski services: Defendant (Ski Co.) and plaintiff (Highlands) owned ski resorts in the Aspen area. Defendant owned three, plaintiff owned one. They had a joint marketing arrangement that allowed skiers to buy six-day tickets usable on a given day at any of the four resorts. The companies allocated the revenues between them based on skiers' actual usage of the sites. Defendant Ski Co. pulled out of the arrangement, continuing to sell six-day, multi-area tickets for its own three mountains only. If Plaintiff Highlands' customers wanted to ski on Ski Co. slopes, they would have to buy two tickets rather than one. Instead, they stopped buying Highlands tickets. Plaintiff Highlands lost revenue and market share: "Without a convenient all-Aspen ticket, Highlands basically 'becomes a day ski area in a destination resort.'"

The U.S. Supreme Court found that the multi-day, multi-area ticket was an essential facility. The ticket allowed week-long visitors flexibility in skiing options. (Aspen itself stood out unique among ski resorts, said the trial transcript, because of its "reputation for 'super powder,' 'a wide range of runs,' and an 'active night life,' including 'some of the best restaurants in North America.'") Further, opening other ski locations nearby is difficult due to topographical obstacles and environmental and zoning regulation. By eliminating the joint ticket, the defendant was "monopolizing" the market for downhill ski services in Aspen. While "a firm possessing monopoly power has no duty to cooperate with its business rivals," its refusal to cooperate cannot have a "purpose to create or maintain a monopoly." Here, the refusal to cooperate left the defendant as "the only business in Aspen that could offer a multi-day multi-mountain skiing experience." The decision to exclude its three mountains was "a decision by a monopolist to make an important change

---

58. Great W. Directories v. Sw. Bell Tel. Co., 63 F.3d 1378 (5th Cir. 1995).
59. Am. Tel. & Tel. Co. v. N. Am. Indus. of N.Y., 772 F. Supp. 777 (S.D.N.Y. 1991).

in the character of the market." There was no evidence of an efficiency justification or other legitimate business reasons for defendant's decision; the evidence rather showed an intent to reduce competition by damaging a competitor. The action was unlawful under the antitrust laws.[60]

*   *   *

These diverse examples display the essential facility doctrine's flexibility, in two respects. First, the competitor need not go out of business to make its point. In *Aspen Skiing*, the plaintiff's revenues and market share declined but the business didn't fail. In *Associated Press*, the trial court found it "would be possible . . . to conduct some kind of a newspaper without any news service whatever."[61] Second, the essential facility need not be indispensable: "It is sufficient if duplication of the facility would be economically infeasible and if denial of its use inflicts a severe handicap on potential market entrants."[62]

At the same time, the doctrine's applicability to regulated industries is unclear after *Trinko*. In that case (recall from Chapter 4.B.2.a), Verizon had failed to provide its CLEC competitors with non-discriminatory access to wholesale services. That failure triggered regulatory penalties from the FCC and the New York Commission, but the Supreme Court dismissed Trinko's antitrust claim. Describing *Aspen Skiing* as "at or near the outer boundary of [Sherman] § 2 liability," the court gave three reasons for being "very cautious" about forcing firms to share their infrastructure. First, the "opportunity to charge monopoly prices—at least for a short period . . . induces risk taking that produces innovation and economic growth." Forcing sharing reduces incentives to invest. Second, forced sharing requires courts "to act as central planners, identifying the proper price, quantity, and other terms of dealing—a role for which they are ill-suited." Third, "compelling negotiation between competitors may facilitate the supreme evil of antitrust: collusion."

The *Trinko* Court then distinguished Verizon's behavior from Aspen Skiing's. Aspen Skiing withdrew from a presumably profitable arrangement, "suggest[ing] a willingness to forsake short-term profits to achieve an anti-competitive end." Verizon, in contrast, was not sacrificing an existing voluntary business relationship for anti-competitive purposes. Further, the product Aspen refused to provide its rival was one it was already selling—ski lift tickets. For Verizon, the withheld wholesale services were "something brand new," services "not otherwise marketed or available to the public," services which "exist[ed]

60.   Aspen Skiing Co. v. Aspen Highlands Skiing Corp., 472 U.S. 585, 594, 599–611 (1985) (quoting trial transcript).
61.   United States v. Associated Press, 52 F. Supp. 362, 371 (S.D.N.Y. 1943), *aff'd*, 326 U.S. 1 (1945).
62.   Hecht v. Pro-Football, 570 F.2d at 992.

only deep within the bowels of Verizon." Under these circumstances, the refusal to share was not an action barred by antitrust law.[63]

Trinko has led to questions about how to apply the essential facilities doctrine in the regulated industry context. According to two commentators, the opinion

> contains tantalizing hints suggesting how the nature of the party seeking access, the number of network elements to which access is sought, the technological complexity of the interface, and whether the access sought is already being provided to other customers can each affect the analysis. Unfortunately, the opinion merely offered these observations in passing without developing them in a systematic way.[64]

4.B.2.d. Incumbent's refusal to share: Business justifications

An essential facility's owner may decline to share for legitimate business reasons, even if the refusal harms competition. Legitimate business reasons will exist if (a) there is a "lack of available space, financial unsoundness, or possibly [the requestor's] low business or ethical standards";[65] (b) sharing "would be impractical or would inhibit the defendant's ability to serve its customers adequately";[66] or (c) sharing would "erode [the owner's] integrated system and threaten its capacity to serve adequately the public."[67] Here are four examples of antitrust lawsuits that failed because the essential facility's owner had a legitimate business reason for declining to share.

Electricity transmission: Southern California Edison had contractual rights to use part of the Pacific Intertie, enabling SCE to import low-cost hydroelectric power from the Pacific Northwest for its retail customers. Municipally-owned power systems located in SCE's service area depended on the utility's transmission system to import power for their own customer-residents. The municipals asked SCE to sell them firm (i.e., uninterrupted) access to the Intertie's capacity. The utility refused; it "could not transmit all of the power it wanted [for its retail customers] if a portion of its capacity rights were being used by the Cities at the same time." The court of appeals agreed with SCE: "This is not a situation where the capacity is not being used (*MCI*) or the sole reason for the denial of access is to maintain a monopoly (*Otter Tail*). . . . The Cities seem to contend that Edison has to disable itself so that they can get cheap power. The law requires no such thing." Further,

---

63. *Trinko*, 540 U.S. at 409–11.
64. Daniel F. Spulber & Christopher S. Yoo, *Mandating Access to Telecom and the Internet: The Hidden Side of* Trinko, 107 COLUM. L. REV. 1822, 1825–26 (2007) (recommending a "classification system that . . . offers a basis for differentiating among different types of access based on the nature of the party seeking access, the portion of the network to which access is sought, and the nature of the services that the party seeking access intends to provide").
65. Gamco v. Providence Fruit, 194 F.2d at 487.
66. Hecht v. Pro-Football, 570 F.2d at 992–93.
67. Otter Tail v. United States, 410 U.S. at 381.

the court found, "SCE was willing to use other transmission capacity to bring power to the Cities from other locations."[68]

Football franchise locations: The National Football League (NFL) was organized in 1920; the American Football League (AFL) in 1959. In a Sherman Act lawsuit, the AFL argued that the NFL had teams in the most desirable cities and was using that advantage anti-competitively. The AFL wanted the NFL to surrender some of its sites to the AFL. Distinguishing monopoly from monopolizing, the court found no antitrust violation:

> [E]njoy[ing] a natural monopoly does not occasion a violation of the antitrust laws unless the natural monopoly power of those teams was misused to gain a competitive advantage for teams located in other cities, or for the league as a whole. It frequently happens that a first competitor in the field will acquire sites which a latecomer may think more desirable than the remaining available sites, but the firstcomer is not required to surrender any, or all, of its desirable sites to the latecomer simply to enable the latecomer to compete more effectively with it. . . . When one has acquired a natural monopoly by means which are neither exclusionary, unfair, nor predatory, he is not disempowered to defend his position fairly.[69]

Gas pipeline: In the early 1980s (before the "unbundling" era initiated by FERC Order Nos. 436 and 636), Panhandle had entered long-term contracts to buy gas for its customers. When market prices dropped, customers sought to buy gas from lower-cost sources. Panhandle declined to transport the lower-cost gas. The Illinois Attorney General sued, asserting that the pipeline was using its control of the facility to monopolize the market for gas sales. The pipeline prevailed. Panhandle had good business reason for its refusal: allowing its customers access would leave it with large "take-or-pay" liabilities to producers.[70] Further, Panhandle's pipeline was not an essential facility, because "it would have been economically feasible for competitors to duplicate much of Panhandle's system within central Illinois by means of interconnections between competing pipelines and the construction of new pipelines."

No competition, no duty: There is no duty to share if the facility owner does not compete with the requestor. Control for anti-competitive purpose, not mere control, is what triggers the antitrust obligation. Thus, America Online's then-monopoly over electronic

68. City of Anaheim v. S. Cal. Edison Co., 955 F.2d 1373, 1381 (9th Cir. 1992). As discussed in Chapter 4.B.3.a below, this antitrust law basis for rejecting the municipals' requests is less relevant today. FERC's Order No. 888 requires transmission owners to grant access on a non-discriminatory basis, except for a limited, interim priority for "native load."
69. Am. Football League v. Nat'l Football League, 323 F.2d 124, 131 (4th Cir. 1963).
70. Ill. *ex rel.* Burris v. Panhandle E. Pipe Line Co., 935 F.2d 1469, 1482–83 (7th Cir. 1991). For a discussion of take-or-pay liabilities, see Chapter 3.C.3.c.iii.

access to its subscribers did not obligate it to carry email traffic for an advertiser, because AOL did not compete with the advertiser.[71]

* * *

These four illustrations demonstrate a key difference between antitrust law and regulatory law. Antitrust law tolerates an incumbent's refusal to share its essential facility, even where the refusal disadvantages market entrants, if the refusal does not stem from anticompetitive purposes. The purpose of the essential facilities doctrine, and antitrust law generally, is to prevent unfair competition, not to ensure effective competition. Regulatory law is fundamentally different. Regulation can be proactive, creating a competitive structure that precludes market power, whereas antitrust law is reactive, being triggered only after the exercise of market power. As Chapter 4.B.3 will explain, regulators have used their statutes' prohibition against "undue preference" not merely to prevent anticompetitive behavior but to convert monopoly markets to competitive markets—to order remedies not available under antitrust law.

4.B.2.e. Antitrust's role in utility regulation

Enforcement of federal antitrust law is the responsibility of the U.S. Department of Justice and the Federal Trade Commission. But its principles apply to federal utility regulators too. That is the message of the landmark decision in *Gulf States Utilities Co. v. Federal Power Commission.*[72]

Gulf States sought the FPC's approval to issue $30 million in first mortgage, thirty-year bonds to refinance short-term debt. Section 204 of the Federal Power Act authorized the FPC to approve utility financing "only if it finds that such issue . . . is for some lawful object, within the corporate purposes of the applicant and compatible with the public interest, which is necessary or appropriate for or consistent with the proper performance by the applicant of service as a public utility."[73] Municipal wholesale customers of Gulf States argued that the utility, along with other nearby investor-owned utilities, "had engaged in activities 'apparently violative of the anti-trust laws,'" among other statutes. The activities included denying the municipals and other small entities the transmission service they needed to "pool" their generation resources, so as to reduce their dependence on the investor-owned utilities. These anti-competitive activities "would be 'financed or refinanced by the bonds here proposed,'" and were "incompatible with the public interest," in violation of Section 204. The municipals asked the Commission for a hearing, to determine whether the FPC should condition the financing to end the anti-competitive behavior.

71. Am. Online, Inc. v. GreatDeals.net, 49 F. Supp. 2d 851, 862 (E.D. Va. 1999).
72. 411 U.S. 747 (1973).
73. 16 U.S.C. § 824c(a).

The FPC denied the hearing and approved the financing. The alleged violations, said the FPC, "are irrelevant to a requested authorization of securities. There is no relief that the Commission can order in authorizing the issuance of the Bonds for refinancing purposes that would have any effect on the interest of the Petitioners, or solve any of the problems outlined by them."

The Supreme Court reversed. The Commission must "inquire into and []be satisfied with the purposes of the [bond] issue and its lawfulness." In oft-quoted language, the Court explained:

> Under the express language of § 204 the public interest is stressed as a governing factor. There is nothing that indicates that the meaning of that term is to be restricted to financial considerations, with every other aspect of the public interest ignored. Further, there is the section's requirement that the object of the issue be lawful. The Commission is directed to inquire into and to evaluate the purpose of the issue and the use to which its proceeds will be put. Without a more definite indication of contrary legislative purpose, we shall not read out of § 204 the requirement that the Commission consider matters relating to both the broad purposes of the Act and the fundamental national economic policy expressed in the antitrust laws. . . .
>
> [T]he Commission's broad authority to consider anti-competitive and other conduct touching the "public interest" under the other sections of the Act emphasizes the breadth of its authority under the public interest standard generally and as embodied in § 204.[74]

Gulf States thus established that a regulator's "public interest" duties include applying the principles and furthering the policies of other statutes; here, the antitrust laws. But there is a limit to a regulator's "public interest" duties. Absent statutory authorization, the mere presence of the phrase "public interest" does not authorize an economic regulator to enter areas unrelated to economic regulation, such as prohibiting racial discrimination.[75]

4.B.3. Statutory foundation: The prohibition against "undue preference"

Antitrust law prevents anti-competitive behavior, but it does not ensure competition. It is "not designed to replicate the results of competition or to correct inherent structural defects such as natural monopoly."[76] The market in which the NFL and AFL competed

---

74. Gulf States Utilities Co. v. FPC, 411 U.S. 747, 751, 753, 756–59 (1973) (quoting municipalities' pleadings to the FPC).
75. National Association for the Advancement of Colored People v. FPC, 425 U.S. 662 (1976) ("public interest" phrase in the Federal Power Act does not authorize FPC to remedy racial discrimination by regulatees).
76. RICHARD J. PIERCE, JR. & ERNEST GELLHORN, REGULATED INDUSTRIES IN A NUTSHELL 21 (4th ed. 1999). As the Supreme Court explained in *Trinko*, 540 U.S. at 415–16 (emphasis in original, citations omitted):

for franchise locations was not an effectively competitive market, not because the NFL competed unfairly but because the NFL arrived first.[77] Anaheim and other municipal power systems were competitively disadvantaged, not (according to the court) because Southern California Edison acted anti-competitively but because the utility lawfully used its transmission rights for its own customers rather than its competitors.[78]

To convert a market structure from monopolistic to competitive, therefore, policymakers could not depend on antitrust law; they turned to their substantive statutes. Their solutions have taken several forms. For competition in wholesale gas and wholesale electricity, FERC relied on its longstanding authority, under the Natural Gas Act of 1938 and the Federal Power Act of 1935, to eliminate "undue preference and advantage" in access to pipeline and transmission systems, respectively. For competition in retail electricity and gas service, state legislatures amended early 20th-century statutes to require incumbents to share distribution facilities. For telecommunications, the bottlenecks were opened through a combination of antitrust litigation, the federal Telecommunications Act of 1996, state legislation, and regulatory actions by the FCC and state commissions under their respective statutes.

These actions all aimed to solve the same problem: the incumbent monopolist's incentive and opportunity to use its bottleneck facilities to protect its monopoly, to extend that monopoly into new markets, or both. Each regulatory solution incorporated some version of the essential facilities doctrine's two-part solution: (1) requiring the monopolist to provide non-discriminatory access to the bottleneck facility at reasonable rates, and (2) limiting that obligation to avoid interfering with the monopolist's legitimate, preexisting businesses. This subsection discusses these legislative and regulatory steps in the electric, gas and telecommunications industries.[79]

The 1996 Act is in an important respect much more ambitious than the antitrust laws. It attempts "to *eliminate the monopolies* enjoyed by the inheritors of AT&T's local franchises." Section 2 of the Sherman Act, by contrast, seeks merely to prevent *unlawful monopolization*. It would be a serious mistake to conflate the two goals. The Sherman Act is indeed the "Magna Carta of free enterprise," . . . but it does not give judges *carte blanche* to insist that a monopolist alter its way of doing business whenever some other approach might yield greater competition. We conclude that respondent's complaint fails to state a claim under the Sherman Act.

77. Am. Football League v. Nat'l Football League, 323 F.2d 124 at 131.
78. *See* discussion of City of Anaheim v. Southern California Edison Co., *supra* Chapter 4.B.2.d.
79. The intent here is to illustrate the common principles, not to substitute for the many writings that detail the specifics of particular industries. *See, e.g.,* STUART M. BENJAMIN ET AL., TELECOMMUNICATIONS LAW AND POLICY chs. 8–12 (3d ed. 2012); PETER BLUHM, NATIONAL REGULATORY RESEARCH INSTITUTE, FUNDAMENTALS OF TELECOMMUNICATIONS REGULATION: MARKETS, JURISDICTION, AND CHALLENGES (2011); JOSEPH P. TOMAIN & RICHARD D. CUDAHY, ENERGY LAW IN A NUTSHELL (2d ed. 2011); Harvey Reiter, *The Contrasting Policies of the FCC and FERC Regarding the Importance of Open Transmission Networks in Downstream Competitive Markets,* 57 FED. COMM. L.J. 243 (2005); Richard J. Pierce, Jr., *Reconstituting the Natural Gas Industry from Wellhead to Burnertip,* 25 ENERGY L.J. 57 (2004); Richard J. Pierce, Jr., *The State of the Transition to Competitive Markets in Natural Gas and Electricity,* 15 ENERGY L.J. 323 (1994); Harvey Reiter, *Competition and Access to the Bottleneck: The Scope of Contract Carrier Regulation Under the Federal Power and Natural Gas Acts,* 18 LAND & WATER L. REV. 1 (1983).

4.B.3.a. Gas and electricity at wholesale

Prior to the 1980s, owners of natural gas pipelines and electric transmission lines used their legitimate monopolies over transportation to diminish competition in energy sales.[80] To end this practice, FERC used a four-part approach: findings of undue discrimination, reliance on its statutory authority to act, references to antitrust law, and generic rules rather than case-by-case findings. We address FERC electricity and gas efforts together because they flow from similar statutory language.[81]

Findings of discrimination: FERC's findings on pipeline discrimination were blunt. As the court of appeals summarized:

> Pipelines were using their market power in the transportation market to discriminate (indirectly) in the sale of gas, a commodity that Congress had concluded was produced under roughly competitive conditions. In the sale of such a commodity there is no economic justification for charging different prices based on the purchasers' differing access to substitutes (*i.e.*, their price elasticity of demand). Indeed, if a product is produced under competitive conditions, such price discrimination cannot occur unless a bottleneck with market power stands between it and the customers.

These conditions led the Commission to conclude—

> (a) that pipelines continue to possess substantial market power; (b) that they have exercised that power to deny their own sales customers, and others without fuel-switching capability, access to competitively priced gas; and (c) that this practice has denied consumers access to gas at the lowest reasonable rates. Thus, despite the removal of regulation over the price and non-price aspects of wellhead transactions [as a result of the Natural Gas Policy Act of 1978], and the evolution of an interconnected nationwide pipeline grid, discrimination in transportation has denied gas users, and the economy generally, the benefits of a competitive wellhead market.[82]

Similarly, in electricity FERC described how transmission owners discriminated against their customers. The alleged actions included:

1.   refusing to offer firm transmission service;
2.   using the generation dispatching process to make transmission unavailable;

---

80.   *See supra* Chapters 3.A.1 and 3.A.2.
81.   Because the Natural Gas Act of 1938 was based on the Federal Power Act of 1935, their common provisions are interpreted consistently. FPC v. Sierra Pac. Power Co., 350 U.S. 348, 353 (1956); Ark. La. Gas Co. v. Hall, 453 U.S. 571, 577 n.7 (1981); Ky. Utils. Co. v. FERC, 760 F.2d 1321, 1325 n.6 (D.C. Cir. 1985).
82.   Associated Gas Distribs. v. FERC, 824 F.2d at 1010 (citations omitted).

3. refusing to transmit power from the transmission owners' own generators to customers with emergencies, even when the capacity was available, instead buying the power elsewhere and reselling it to the customer at a high rate;

4. retaliating against customers who complained about discrimination;

5. requiring customers to schedule transmission service by noon of the preceding day, while imposing no such deadline when the utility served its own customers;

6. buying up transmission capacity that a captive customer had sought to buy; and

7. overstating the cost of transmission improvements necessary to accommodate service requests.[83]

Statutory authority to act: The Natural Gas Act "has the fundamental purpose of protecting interstate gas consumers from pipelines' monopoly power."[84] Section 4(b) prohibits any "undue preference" and any "unreasonable difference in rates, charges, service, facilities, or in any other respect;" authorizes the Commission to disapprove pipeline tariffs that fail these tests; and requires the Commission to correct any "rate, charge or classification," or any "rule, regulation, practice, or contract" affecting the same, that is "unjust, unreasonable, unduly discriminatory, or preferential."[85] Similarly, Sections 205 and 206 of the Federal Power Act grant FERC "a mandate . . . to ensure that . . . no person is subject to any undue prejudice or disadvantage" with respect to its two jurisdictional services: transmission and wholesale power sales. This mandate translates into a duty to "determine whether any rule, regulation, practice or contract affecting rates for such transmission or sale for resale is unduly discriminatory or preferential, and [then to] . . . prevent those contracts and practices that do not meet this standard."[86] Based on these statutory provisions, FERC imposed obligations to provide transportation service non-discriminatorily.[87]

Opponents objected that Congress had neither mandated "common carriage" nor explicitly granted FERC power to order access.[88] The Court was unimpressed: "The [Natural

---

83. *See* Order No. 888, 75 FERC ¶ 61,080, App. C (section entitled "Allegations of Public Utilities Exercising Transmission Dominance). Appendix C contains several dozen examples of "refusals to wheel, dilatory tactics that so protracted negotiations as to effectively deny wheeling, refusals to provide service priority equal to native load, or refusals to provide service flexibility equivalent to the utility's own use." *Id.*

84. Associated Gas Distribs. v. FERC, 824 F.2d at 995.

85. 15 U.S.C. §§ 717c(b), 717d(a).

86. Order No. 888, 75 FERC ¶ 61,080 at text accompanying n.195.

87. The Order No. 436 obligation attached to any pipeline that (1) has a "blanket certificate" to provide gas transportation under section 7 of the NGA, or (2) provides transportation under section 311 of the Natural Gas Policy Act. The court of appeals described "blanket certification" as "a certificate authorizing transportation services generically and thus obviating the need for unwieldy individual certification." Associated Gas Distribs. v. FERC, 824 F.2d at 996. The Order No. 888 obligation applied to investor-owned utilities, as well as to non-investor-owned utilities that chose to take Order No. 888 service from investor-owned utilities. The D.C. Circuit thus described Order No. 888 as "seek[ing] to break a utility's monopoly over the transmission of electric power by requiring that the utility permit wholesale sellers to transmit power over its facilities under the same terms and conditions as the utility itself transmits power." Louisiana Energy & Power Authority v. FERC, 141 F.3d 364, 370 (D.C. Cir. 1998).

88. Often cited for this proposition was Richmond Power & Light Co. v. FERC, 574 F.2d 610 (D.C. Cir. 1978).

Gas] Act fairly bristles with concern for undue discrimination," and therefore gives the Commission "power to stamp out" such behavior. To argue that the absence of an explicit mandate disables FERC from remedying undue discrimination "turns statutory construction upside down, letting the failure to grant a general power prevail over the affirmative grant of a specific one."[89] The Commission distinguished the prior cases:

> In the FPA, while Congress elected not to impose common carrier status on the electric power industry, it tempered that determination by explicitly providing the Commission with the authority to eradicate undue discrimination—one of the goals of common carriage regulation. By providing this broad authority to the Commission, it assured itself that in preserving "the voluntary action of the utilities" it was not allowing this voluntary action to be unfettered.[90]

The role of antitrust law: While the statutory ban on undue preference was FERC's main statutory basis, there was also its duty to consider antitrust principles. FERC recognized that under *Gulf States Utilities Co.*, the Federal Power Act's "public interest" language "clearly carries with it the responsibility to consider, in appropriate circumstances, the anti-competitive effects of regulated aspects of interstate utility operations." FERC then described the relationship between undue discrimination and anti-competitive effects:

> In most situations, discrimination that precludes transmission access or gives inferior access will have at least potential anti-competitive effects because it limits access to generation markets and thereby limits competition in generation. Similarly, it is probable that any transmission provision that has anti-competitive effects would also be found to be unduly discriminatory or preferential because the anti-competitive provision would most likely favor the transmission owner vis-à-vis others.[91]

When Order No. 888 was issued in 1996, most transmission owners were also generation owners. Companies in this position had incentive and opportunity to discriminate in transmission service to gain advantage in generation markets. Today, some transmission facilities are owned by transmission-only companies. They too must comply with Order

---

89. Associated Gas Distribs. v. FERC, 824 F.2d at 998.
90. Order No. 888, 75 FERC ¶ 61,080 at text accompanying n.203 (footnote omitted). FERC distinguished *Richmond* as a situation in which the transmission owner had already volunteered to provide access for some purposes, but not for Richmond's purposes. As the *Richmond* court said, "[i]f Congress had intended that utilities could inadvertently bootstrap themselves into common-carrier status by filing rates for voluntary service, it would not have bothered to reject mandatory wheeling." 574 F.2d at 620. Nowhere did the *Richmond* court foreclose FERC from ordering transmission service as a remedy for undue discrimination.
91. Order No. 888, 75 FERC ¶ 61,080 at text accompanying nn.195–96 (quoting Gulf States v. FPC, 411 U.S. at 758–59).

No. 888, because a transmission-only company can distort generation competition by favoring some generators over others.

Generic rule rather than case-by-case findings: In both the gas and electricity efforts, opponents attacked FERC for issuing industry-wide orders based on unproven anecdotes,[92] instead of evaluating each utility's practices case-by-case. The court dismissed these concerns: "Courts reviewing an agency's selection of means are not entitled to insist on empirical data for every proposition on which the selection depends."[93] And in Order No. 888 FERC responded as follows:

> The inherent characteristics of monopolists make it inevitable that they will act in their own self-interest to the detriment of others by refusing transmission and/or providing inferior transmission to competitors in the bulk power markets to favor their own generation, and it is our duty to eradicate unduly discriminatory practices. As the *Associated Gas Distributors* court stated: "Agencies do not need to conduct experiments in order to rely on the prediction that an unsupported stone will fall."[94]

4.B.3.b. Gas and electricity at retail

In retail energy services, the bottleneck is the physical distribution system: the pipes and wires that carry gas and electricity directly to consumers. For the dozen or so states that enacted retail competition statutes, the solution was statutory. This Pennsylvania provision is typical:

> [T]he commission shall require that a public utility that owns or operates jurisdictional transmission and distribution facilities shall provide transmission and distribution service to all retail electric customers in their service territory and to electric cooperative corporations and electric generation suppliers, affiliated or nonaffiliated, on rates, terms of access and conditions that are comparable to the utility's own use of its system.[95]

4.B.3.c. Telecommunications

As Chapter 3.A.3 explained, the Modification of Final Judgment required AT&T to divest its local exchange carrier subsidiaries from its long-distance service subsidiary.

---

92. Order No. 888's "Appendix C" listed allegations that were not proven at hearings.
93. Associated Gas Distribs. v. FERC, 824 F.2d at 1008.
94. Order No. 888, 75 FERC ¶ 61,080 at text accompanying n.258 (quoting Associated Gas Distribs. v. FERC, 824 F.2d at 1008); *see also* New York v. FERC, 535 U.S. 1, 14 (2002) (upholding Order No. 888 and noting that the court of appeals below had found that FERC's ordering of non-discriminatory access was "premised not on individualized findings of discrimination by specific transmission providers, but on FERC's identification of a fundamental systemic problem in the industry").
95. Pa. Cons. Stat. tit. 66, § 2804(6).

The divestiture would make AT&T solely a long-distance and equipment company. The divested local exchange carriers would be limited to providing local telephone service.[96] Consistent with the distinction drawn above between antitrust law and regulatory law,[97] the MFJ "did nothing . . . to increase competition in the persistently monopolistic local markets, which were thought to be the root of natural monopoly in the telecommunications industry."[98]

Twelve years after divestiture, Congress ordered bottleneck access statutorily. The Telecommunications Act of 1996 subjected incumbents to "a host of duties intended to facilitate market entry," including sharing their "networks" with competitors.[99] That sharing consisted of offering competing carriers three options: (1) purchase local telephone services from the incumbent, at wholesale rates, for resale to end users; (2) lease individual "elements" of the incumbent's network on an unbundled basis; or (3) interconnect their own facilities with the incumbent's network.[100] As with FERC Order Nos. 436, 636 and 888, the mandate's purpose was to stimulate competition by preventing discrimination:

> It is easy to see why a company that owns a local exchange . . . would have an almost insurmountable competitive advantage not only in routing calls within the exchange, but, through its control of this local market, in the markets for terminal equipment and long-distance calling as well. A newcomer could not compete with the incumbent carrier to provide local service without coming close to replicating the incumbent's entire existing network, the most costly and difficult part of which would be laying down the last mile of feeder wire, the local loop, to the thousands (or millions) of terminal points in individual houses and businesses. The incumbent company could also control its local-loop plant so as to connect only with terminals it manufactured or selected, and could place conditions or fees (called access charges) on long-distance carriers seeking to connect with its network. In an unregulated world, another telecommunications carrier would be forced to comply with these conditions, or it could never reach the customers of a local exchange.[101]

---

96. United States v. AT&T, 552 F. Supp. 131 (D.D.C. 1982), *aff'd sub nom.* Maryland v. United States, 460 U.S. 1001 (1983).
97. *See* PIERCE & GELLHORN, *supra* note 76, at 21 (antitrust law is "not designed to replicate the results of competition or to correct inherent structural defects such as natural monopoly").
98. Verizon Commc'ns v. FCC, 535 U.S. 467, 475–76 (2002).
99. AT&T v. Iowa Utils. Bd., 525 U.S. at 371.
100. 47 U.S.C. § 251(c).
101. Verizon Commc'ns v. FCC, 535 U.S. at 490–91 (footnotes omitted). See also the remarks of Senator Breaux on the Senate Floor, quoted in *Verizon v. FCC*, 535 U.S. at 488 (quoting 141 CONG. REC. 15,572 (1995)):

> This is extraordinary in the sense of telling private industry that this is what they have to do in order to let the competitors come in and try to beat your economic brains out. . . .
> It is kind of almost a jump-start. . . . I will do everything I have to let you into my business, because we used to be a bottleneck; we used to be a monopoly; we used to control everything.
> Now, this legislation says you [i.e., the ILECs] will not control much of anything. You will have to allow for non-discriminatory access on an unbundled basis to the network functions and

* * *

Figure 4 is a simple display of bottleneck facilities, and the regulatory actions to open them up to competitors, in electricity, gas and telecommunications.

4.B.3.d. Limits on incumbent's obligation to share facilities

As explained in Chapter 4.B.2.d, antitrust law relieves a monopolist of the duty to share (a) if there is "lack of available space";[102] (b) if the sharing "would be impractical or would inhibit the defendant's ability to serve its customers adequately";[103] or (c) if sharing would "erode its integrated system and threaten its capacity to serve adequately the public."[104] Regulatory actions replicated those limits.

Under Order No. 888, the incumbent transmission owner need not provide non-discriminatory access to competitors if doing so impairs its ability to serve its "native load." (The phrase "native load" refers to customers for whom the utility historically built capacity to fulfill its obligation to serve—and whose customers paid for that capacity.) "[Transmission-owning] utilities may reserve existing transmission capacity needed for native load growth and network transmission customer load growth reasonably forecasted within the utility's current planning horizon." For future capacity, however, the utility must give all customers, native and competitive, the opportunity to reserve and pay. Over time, then, the treatment differential would disappear.[105]

In telecommunications, limits on the incumbent's duty to share appear in the area of "collocation." The 1996 Telecommunications Act imposed on incumbent local exchange carriers

[t]he duty to provide, on rates, terms, and conditions that are just, reasonable, and non-discriminatory, for physical collocation of [CLEC] equipment necessary for interconnection or access to unbundled network elements at the premises of the local exchange carrier, except that the carrier may provide for virtual collocation if the local exchange carrier demonstrates to the State commission that physical collocation is not practical for technical reasons or because of space limitations.[106]

---

services of the Bell operating companies network that is at least equal in type, quality, and price to the access [a] Bell operating company affords to itself.
102. Gamco v. Providence Fruit, 194 F.2d at 487.
103. Hecht v. Pro-Football, 570 F.2d at 992–93.
104. Otter Tail v. United States, 410 U.S. at 381.
105. Order No. 888, 75 FERC ¶ 61,080 at text accompanying n.309.
106. 47 U.S.C. § 251(c)(6). "Network element" is defined as "a facility or equipment used in the provision of a telecommunications service. Such term also includes features, functions, and capabilities that are provided by means of such facility or equipment, including subscriber numbers, databases, signaling systems, and information sufficient for billing and collection or used in the transmission, routing, or other provision of a telecommunications service." 47 U.S.C. § 153(29).

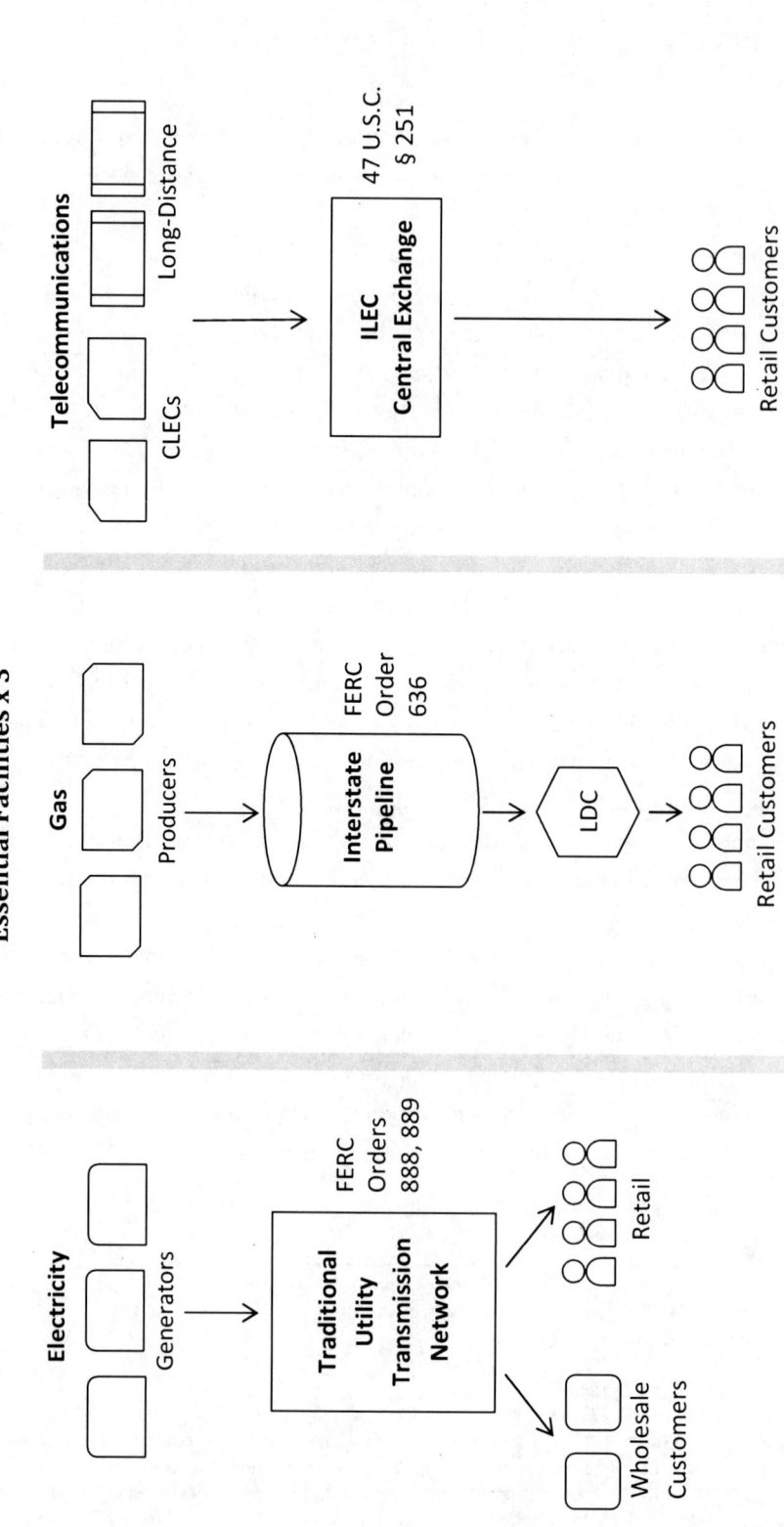

Figure 4
Essential Facilities x 3

Access to incumbent's central exchange was necessary for competition, but when "physical" collocation is not "practical," "virtual" collocation will have to suffice. ("Virtual collocation" means having the CLEC rely on the incumbent's existing equipment rather than placing the CLEC's equipment on the incumbent's premises.)

4.B.4. Unbundled rates for competitive neutrality

As just discussed, the incumbent's obligation to grant non-discriminatory access can stem from two legal sources: (a) antitrust law's prohibition against monopolization, and (b) an industry-specific regulatory statute. Regardless of the legal source, regulators cannot simply commandeer the incumbent's assets; an access directive must satisfy the Constitution's requirement of "just compensation."[107] Regulators provide that compensation by setting rates for the unbundled, non-competitive service. Thus FERC's orders on gas and electric unbundling, state statutes and orders on retail electric and gas unbundling, and the 1996 Telecommunications Act all established ratemaking procedures and methods. Even when the access order comes from an antitrust court, the job of rate-setting lies with the regulatory agency.[108]

The special challenge in setting rates for the newly unbundled, non-competitive services is to achieve competitive neutrality. If a statute or order allows incumbents to provide both monopoly and competitive services, their incentive is to recover competitive costs from the monopoly customers, so they can offer artificially low prices in the competitive markets. Regulators have addressed this concern in different ways. Discussed next is "cost unbundling," used mostly in electricity and gas, followed by the unique contribution from telecommunications—unbundling based on "total element long-run incremental cost."

4.B.4.a. Cost unbundling

"Cost unbundling" removes non-monopoly costs from the monopoly service rate. This technique protects customers of the monopoly service from excess charges and new competitors from unfair competition. Two statutory examples appear in the margin.[109]

---

107. See Chapter 6.B.2 for a discussion of the Fifth Amendment's Takings Clause.
108. In *Terminal Railroad*, the Supreme Court upheld the trial court's order that Terminal grant access to its rails, but made clear that the Interstate Commerce Commission would set the rates. "[N]othing therein shall be taken to affect in any wise or at any time the power of the Interstate Commerce Commission over the rates to be charged by the Terminal Company, or the mode of billing traffic passing over its lines, or the establishing of joint through rates or routes over its lines." United States v. Terminal R.R. Ass'n of St. Louis, 224 U.S. 383, 412 (1912). As we will learn in Chapter 9, concerning the filed rate doctrine, the exclusive authority for rate-setting lies with regulatory agencies.
109. PA. CON. STAT. tit. 66, § 2804(3) provides:

   The commission shall require the unbundling of electric utility services, tariffs and customer bills to separate the charges for generation, transmission and distribution. The commission may require the unbundling of other services.

   N.J. STAT. § 48:3-52(a) provides:

These unbundled costs fall into two categories. Sunk costs are already stated on a utility's books of account; they represent the original costs of existing assets less accumulated depreciation. Operating costs are the predicted costs of operating those assets. In each category, the regulator must separate the competitive from the non-competitive costs. There are two steps. The first step is "direct assignment," to the monopoly service, of costs uniquely associated with the monopoly service. These costs would include the transmission and distribution system, and its operators and maintenance personnel. The second step is "allocation" of "common costs"—costs that are necessary to the entire utility business, including both the monopoly and non-monopoly services. Examples are the utility's headquarters building and its CEO's salary. Accountants allocate these costs using special ratios.[110]

4.B.4.b. Total element long-run incremental cost

While electric and gas regulators set rates for monopoly services using sunk or predicted costs, telecommunications regulators implementing the unbundling provisions of the 1996 Act used future-oriented costs. As explained in Chapter 3.A.3, the Telecommunications Act of 1996 required each ILEC to offer local phone service competitors non-discriminatory access to its "local loop" or "last mile." That offer had to include three options: (1) purchase local telephone services at wholesale rates for resale to end users; (2) lease elements of the incumbent's network "on an unbundled basis"; or (3) interconnect the CLEC's own facilities with the incumbent's network.[111] Options (2) and (3), "leasing" unbundled elements and interconnection, provide the context for price-setting based on future-oriented costs. (When a CLEC makes a wholesale purchase of network elements, Section 252(d)(3) of the Act bases the purchase price on the incumbent's retail rates.)

If the ILEC and CLEC cannot reach agreement on a rate, the 1996 Act requires the state commission to set it, using an FCC-mandated method called "total element long-run incremental cost" (TELRIC).[112] TELRIC departed from actual cost, that is, the historical

---

[E]ach electric public utility shall unbundle its rate schedules such that discrete services and charges provided, which were previously included in the bundled utility rate, are separately identified and charged in its tariffs. Such discrete services and charges shall include, at a minimum, customer account services and charges, distribution and transmission services and charges and generation services and charges, and the board may require that additional services and charges be unbundled and separately billed. . . . All competitive services offered by an electric public utility shall be charged separately from non-competitive services.

110.   Readers seeking technical detail should consult texts on accounting and economics. Legal issues have arisen, however, over methods of cost accounting. We will visit these issues in Chapter 8, concerning discrimination in ratemaking.

111.   *See* 47 U.S.C. § 251(c).

112.   The Act defines "network element" as "a facility or equipment used in the provision of a telecommunications service. Such term also includes features, functions, and capabilities that are provided by means of such facility or equipment, including subscriber numbers, databases, signaling systems, and information sufficient for billing and collection or used in the transmission, routing, or other provision of a

cost of the ILEC's equipment and plant, plus the ILEC's predicted costs of operating those assets. TELRIC is based instead "on the use of the most efficient telecommunications technology currently available and the lowest cost network configuration, given the existing location of the incumbent LEC's wire centers."[113] The FCC chose TELRIC based on its interpretation of the statute, which requires that the rate be based on "the cost . . . of providing the . . . network element," which "may include a reasonable profit," but which must be "determined without reference to a rate-of-return or other rate-based proceeding."[114]

Determining a rate "without reference to a rate-of-return or other rate-based proceeding" was, according to the Supreme Court, an "important limitation previously unknown to utility regulation." Why did the 1996 Act take this unconventional approach? Congress felt that "the traditional rate-based methodologies gave monopolies too great an advantage," because they controlled information about their costs. The solution to this control was to "mov[e] away from the assumption common to all the rate-based methods, that the monopolistic structure within the discrete markets would endure." Using a form of "rate making different from any historical practice [would] achieve the entirely new objective of uprooting the monopolies that traditional rate-based methods had perpetuated." Congress wanted "not just to balance interests between sellers and buyers, but to reorganize markets by rendering regulated utilities' monopolies vulnerable to interlopers, even if that meant swallowing the traditional federal reluctance to intrude into local telephone markets."[115]

4.B.5. Separation to reduce temptation

Unbundling makes competition possible, but it does not make competition effective. If the incumbent enters the newly competitive markets while still controlling the bottleneck, it has the incentive and opportunity to run its bottleneck business in a way that favors its competitive business. The common response, as detailed in Chapters 4.B.3 and 4.B.4, is to require non-discriminatory access to the bottleneck at competitively neutral prices, with those prices determined through cost unbundling. But the incumbent still can use its other resources—employees, equipment, historic customer data, business relationships, and reputation—to gain and maintain an advantage over newcomers. To the extent that advantage is unearned—because it arises not from merits but from a history of government protection from competition—competition is distorted.

To address this concern, regulators have chosen among four forms of separation. The first two, "functional unbundling" and "corporate unbundling," are typically supplemented

---

telecommunications service." 47 U.S.C. § 153(35).
113. *See* Forward-looking economic cost, 47 C.F.R. § 51.505(b)(1).
114. 47 U.S.C. § 252(d)(1). The Supreme Court previously had upheld the FCC's jurisdiction to determine the methodology states would use. AT&T v. Iowa Utils. Bd., 525 U.S. at 384–85.
115. Verizon v. FCC, 535 U.S. at 488–89, 493. We will discuss rate of return regulation in detail in Chapter 6.

by a "code of conduct" that regulates relationships between the incumbent's competitive and non-competitive businesses. A third approach allows the utility to continue owning both types of business, but transfers "functional control" of the monopoly business to an independent entity. The fourth option, divestiture, eliminates all risk of favoritism by requiring or encouraging the incumbent to sell off either the competitive or the non-competitive business to an unaffiliated entity. This subchapter describes the four options, then closes with a concern. Separation can have a cost: the loss of economies associated with jointly owning vertically related businesses, even if one is monopolistic and one is competitive.

4.B.5.a. Functional unbundling

Sometimes referred to as "divisional unbundling," the competitive and non-competitive services are provided by the same corporation, but by separate employees. FERC's Order Nos. 888 and 889 require functional unbundling. A vertically integrated utility can provide both competitive wholesale generation and non-competitive transmission service from a single corporation. Preventing favoritism depends on compliance with a code of conduct, discussed in Chapter 4.B.5.c. below. In telecommunications, the analogy to functional unbundling is the "non-structural safeguards" adopted by the FCC in *Computer III*.[116] These safeguards prescribe company behavior rather than build structural walls.[117]

4.B.5.b. Corporate unbundling

Sometimes referred to as "affiliate unbundling," "structural separation" or "structural safeguards," the competitive and non-competitive services are provided by separate corporate affiliates within the same corporate family. When FERC required gas pipelines to unbundle transportation service from gas supply sales, pipelines wishing to conduct both activities formed separate "marketing affiliates" to carry out the sales activities. These affiliates purchased gas from producers (including affiliated producers), purchased transportation from pipelines, then sold the gas to local distribution companies and other customers. Similarly, in states that have authorized retail gas competition, local gas distribution companies have formed retail marketing affiliates to sell gas directly to consumers. And in telecommunications, the FCC's *Computer II* rules required structural separation.[118]

---

116. *See* discussion Chapter 3.A.3; Amendment of Section 64.702 of the Commission's Rules and Regulations (*Computer III*), Report & Order, 104 F.C.C.2d 958 (1986); *on recon.*, Phase I Reconsideration Order, 2 FCC Rcd. 3035 (1987), *on further recon.*, Order on Further Reconsideration, 3 FCC Rcd. 1135 (1988), *on second further recon.*, Order on Second Further Reconsideration, 4 FCC Rcd. 5927 (1989), *vacated in part sub nom.* California v. FCC, 905 F.2d 1217 (9th Cir. 1990), *cert. denied*, 514 U.S. 1050 (1995) (vacating Report & Order and Phase I Reconsideration Order).

117. The primary *Computer III* non-structural safeguards were comparably efficient interconnection ("CEI") and open network architecture ("ONA") requirements. *See* PETER W. HUBER, MICHAEL K. KELLOGG & JOHN THORNE, FEDERAL TELECOMMUNICATIONS LAW § 12.5.2 (2d ed. 1999).

118. Amendment of Section 64.702 of the Commission's Rules and Regulations (*Computer II*), Final Decision, 77 F.C.C.2d 384 (1980), *on recon.*, Memorandum Opinion and Order, 84 F.C.C.2d 50 (1981), *on further recon.*, Order on Further Reconsideration, 88 F.C.C.2d 512 (1981), *aff'd sub nom.* Computer &

These first two structural options, functional unbundling and corporate unbundling, appear in state statutes and rules as well. For example:

Maine requires utilities to place competitive electric supply activities in an affiliate separate from the incumbent electric distribution company. That competitive affiliate can market without limit, outside the utility's monopoly service territory. Within the utility's monopoly service territory, the affiliate's sales may not exceed 33 percent of the total kilowatt-hours sold within the service territory, and its share of "standard-offer service" load within the monopoly affiliate's service territory cannot exceed 20 percent.[119]

New Jersey requires Board approval for any mixing of competitive and non-competitive services within the same corporate family, with or without separate affiliates. The Board must ensure that (a) tariffs for the competitive services do not "adversely impact the ability of the electric public utility to offer its non-competitive services to customers in a safe, adequate and proper manner"; and (b) those tariff prices are not lower than the fully allocated cost of the competitive service.[120]

Rhode Island requires separate affiliates for the competitive and non-competitive functions, unless the commission has granted a "public interest" exception.[121]

A variation on corporate unbundling is to place the bottleneck asset in a separate corporation, owned jointly by the utilities that need the asset. Vermont uses this approach for its transmission system, which is owned by the Vermont Electric Company (VELCO). The Vermont utilities created VELCO in the 1950s to ensure that the low-cost power generated by the St. Lawrence River Project would be available to all the state's utilities. When the two largest VELCO shareholders, Central Vermont Public Service and Green Mountain Power, proposed to merge in 2012, they would own 78 percent of VELCO, posing a market power problem. To solve it, the Vermont Public Service Board required (a) a transfer of nearly half the companies' shares to an independent, public purpose entity; (b) a reduction in their VELCO Board seats; and (c) the appointment of three independent members to the VELCO Board.[122]

Commc'ns Indus. Ass'n v. FCC, 693 F.2d 198 (D.C. Cir. 1982), *cert. denied*, 461 U.S. 938 (1983), *aff'd on second further recon.*, 56 Rad. Reg. 2d (P&F) 301 (1984).

119. ME. REV. STAT. tit. 35-A, § 3205(2)(B). Standard service is the service for customers who do not shop with a non-incumbent. See *supra* Chapter 3.B.1.

120. N.J. STAT. § 48:3-55(a). Fully allocated cost, sometimes called "fully distributed cost," refers to rates designed to recover all costs of production, both variable and fixed. *See* Associated Gas Distribs. v. FERC, 824 F.2d at 1007 (D.C. Cir. 1987) (citing 18 C.F.R. § 284.7(c)(3)) (defining fully allocated cost as a rate such that, "if the pipeline carries projected volume at the specified unit price, it should exactly recover all costs allocable to the relevant service for the period").

121. R.I. GEN. LAWS § 39-1-27(a).

122. *See* Cent. Vt. Pub. Serv. Corp., Gaz Metro & Green Mountain Power Corp., Docket No. 7770, 2012 Vt. PUC LEXIS 279, at *272, *276–80, 299 P.U.R.4th 204 (Vt. Pub. Serv. Bd. June 15, 2012).

4.B.5.c. Codes of conduct

Even after granting regulated access to its bottleneck facility, and even with functional or corporate separation, the incumbent can still find ways to favor its own competitive activities over its competitors'. To reduce the risk of favoritism further, regulators have issued "codes of conduct." The aim is to create an "arm's-length relationship" between the incumbent's monopoly and competitive activities. FERC's Order No. 888, for example, required transmission-providing utilities to adopt three structural measures:

1. "a public utility must take transmission services (including ancillary services) for all of its new wholesale sales and purchases of energy under the same tariff of general applicability as do others;"
2. "a public utility must state separate rates for wholesale generation, transmission, and ancillary services;" and
3. "a public utility must rely on the same electronic information network that its transmission customers rely on to obtain information about its transmission system when buying or selling power."[123]

FERC accompanied Order No. 888, whose focus was the transmission tariff, with Order No. 889, whose focus was structural separation.[124] Order 889 has three major components:

1. standards to ensure that transmission employees "function independently" of purchase and sale employees;
2. an "open access same time information system," which is a web-based information source providing "transmission customers with information, . . . by electronic means, about available transmission capacity, prices, and other information" at the same time that information became available to the transmission owner's own marketing employees; and
3. communications standards and protocols necessary to ensure that this information becomes accessible to all customers simultaneously.

As for gas, FERC issued Order No. 497, prohibiting pipelines from giving their marketing affiliates or wholesale merchant functions undue preferences over non-affiliated customers.[125]

---

123. Order No. 888, 75 FERC ¶ 61,080 at text accompanying n.117.
124. Open Access Same-Time Information System (formerly Real-Time Information Networks) and Standards of Conduct, Order No. 889, 75 FERC ¶ 61,078 (1996), *order on reh'g*, Order No. 889-A, 78 FERC ¶ 61,221 (1997), *order on reh'g*, Order No. 889-B, 81 FERC ¶ 61,253 (1997).
125. Inquiry Into Alleged Anti-competitive Practices Related to Marketing Affiliates of Interstate Pipelines, Order No. 497, 43 FERC ¶ 61,420 (1988), *order on reh'g*, Order No. 497-A, 49 FERC ¶ 61,334 (1989). In its Order No. 2004, FERC sought to extend its gas code of conduct of Order No. 497 to

FERC later combined its separation principles for gas and electricity into a single code of conduct. These principles apply to providers of pipeline transportation service and providers of electricity transmission (both called "transmission providers"), if they conduct "transmission transactions with an affiliate that engages in marketing functions." Order No. 717 established three main requirements:

1. The "transmission function employees must function independently from its marketing function employees, except as permitted in this part or otherwise permitted by Commission order."

2. A "transmission provider and its employees, contractors, consultants and agents are prohibited from disclosing, or using a conduit to disclose, non-public transmission function information to the transmission provider's marketing function employees."

3. The transmission provider must "provide equal access to non-public transmission function information disclosed to marketing function employees to all its transmission customers, affiliated and non-affiliated, except as permitted in this part or otherwise permitted by Commission order."[126]

States implementing retail gas or electric competition also adopted codes of conduct. Ohio's retail electric competition statute, for example, prohibits an electric utility from engaging in both competitive and noncompetitive services, directly or through an affiliate, without a Commission-approved "corporate separation plan." The plan must include full

---

non-marketing affiliates, labeled "energy affiliates." Standards of Conduct for Transmission Providers, Order No. 2004, 105 FERC ¶ 61,248 (2003), *order on reh'g*, Order No. 2004-A, 107 FERC ¶ 61,032 (2004), *order on reh'g*, Order No. 2004-B, 108 FERC ¶ 61,118 (2004), *order on reh'g*, Order No. 2004-C, 109 FERC ¶ 61,325 (2004), *order on reh'g*, Order No. 2004-D, 110 FERC ¶ 61,320 (2005), *vacated and remanded as it applies to natural gas pipelines sub nom.* National Fuel Gas Supply Corp. v. FERC, 468 F.3d 831 (D.C. Cir. 2006). This was a broad category that included any affiliate of a gas pipeline or electric transmission company, which affiliate (1) engages in or is involved in transmission transactions in U.S. energy or transmission markets; (2) manages or controls transmission capacity of a transmission provider in U.S. energy or transmission markets; (3) buys, sells, trades or administers natural gas or electric energy in U.S. energy or transmission markets; or (4) engages in financial transactions relating to the sale or transmission of natural gas or electric energy in U.S. energy or transmission markets. 18 C.F.R. § 358.3(d), *revised by* Standards of Conduct for Transmission Providers, Order No. 717, 125 FERC ¶ 61,604, at P 12 (2008), *order on reh'g*, Order No. 717-A, 129 FERC ¶ 61,043 (2009), *order on reh'g*, Order No. 717-B, 129 FERC ¶ 61,123 (2009), *order on reh'g*, Order No. 717-C, 131 FERC ¶ 61,045 (2010), *order on reh'g*, Order No. 717-D, 135 FERC ¶ 61,017 (2011).

In ordering this extension of its gas code of conduct, FERC had relied on "both an asserted theoretical threat of undue preferences and a claimed record of abuse." Nat'l Fuel Gas Supply Corp. v. FERC, 468 F.3d 831, 839 (D.C. Cir. 2006). Because a theoretical threat alone is not a sufficient basis for an order, and because the record did not have the evidence of abuse that FERC claimed, the court of appeals invalidated Order 2004 as "arbitrary and capricious." In response, FERC promulgated Order No. 717, discussed in the text next.

126. 18 C.F.R. § 358.2(b)–(d); Standards of Conduct for Transmission Providers, Order No. 717, 125 FERC ¶ 61,604 (2008). Note that FERC defined "affiliate" to "include[] a division of the specified entity that operates as a functional unit." 18 C.F.R. § 358.3(a)(1).

corporate separation, including separate accounting requirements, sufficient to prevent "unfair competitive advantage" and "the abuse of market power." There can be no "undue preference or advantage to any affiliate, division, or part of its own business" in the provision of "utility resources," including but not limited to "trucks, tools, office equipment, office space, supplies, customer and marketing information, advertising, billing and mailing systems, personnel, and training."[127]

4.B.5.d. Transfer of control to independent entity

Even with functional separation, corporate separation and codes of conduct, control over monopoly assets remains with an incumbent motivated to favor its family's competitive businesses. These regulatory devices work only to the extent they eliminate opportunities to discriminate. And they don't always work. Three years after Order Nos. 888 and 889, FERC admitted that functional separation and codes of conduct are "not the best way to correct vertical integration problems":

> [W]e acknowledge that many utilities are making good-faith efforts to properly implement standards of conduct. However, we also believe that there is great potential for standards of conduct violations that will never even be reported or detected. . . . The fact remains that claims of undue discrimination have not diminished [since issuance of Order Nos. 888 and 889], and there is no evidence that discrimination is becoming a non-issue.

Meanwhile, regulatory attention was proving burdensome, impractical and insufficient:

> [W]e are increasingly concerned about the extensive regulatory oversight and administrative burdens that have resulted from policing compliance with standards of conduct. . . .
>
> [T]he cost and time [to complainants] required to pursue legal channels to prove discrimination will often provide an inadequate remedy because, among other things, the competition may have already been lost.[128]

---

127. OHIO REV. CODE § 4928.17.
128. Regional Transmission Organizations, Order No. 2000, 89 FERC ¶ 61,285 at text accompanying n.93 (1999), *order on reh'g*, Order No. 2000-A, 90 FERC ¶ 61,201 (2000). Footnotes 91 and 92 in Order No. 2000 give details:

>   n.91 *See* Wisconsin Public Power Inc. SYSTEM v. Wisconsin Public Service Corporation, 83 FERC ¶ 61,198 at p. 61,855, 61,860 (1998), *order on reh'g*, 84 FERC ¶ 61,120 (1998) (WPSC's actions raised "serious concerns" as to functional separation; WP&L's actions demonstrated that it provided unduly preferential treatment to its merchant function); Washington Water Power Co., 83 FERC ¶ 61,097 at p. 61,463, *further order*, 83 FERC ¶ 61,282 (1998) (utility found to have violated standards in connection with its marketing affiliate); Utah Associated Municipal Power Systems v. PacifiCorp, 87 FERC ¶ 61,044 (1999) (finding that PacifiCorp had failed to maintain functional separation between merchant and transmission functions).

>   n.92 *See, e.g.*, Communications of Market Information Between Affiliates, 87 FERC ¶ 61,012

The surest way to eliminate discrimination is to divest the monopoly or the competitive business, because then the owner of the monopoly asset no longer has a competitive business to favor. We will discuss divestiture in Chapter 4.B.5.e. But first, there is a step short of divestiture: Transfer control of the monopoly assets to an independent entity.

The prominent example of this is FERC's Order No. 2000, which encourages transmission owners to create or join "regional transmission organizations." In these arrangements, the utility retains passive ownership of its transmission assets (including the right to profits associated with sales of transmission service over those assets), but transfers "functional control" of the assets to a corporately independent RTO. On receiving this control, the RTO becomes the exclusive transmission service provider for customers seeking service over the transferred facilities: a "public utility" whose prices, terms, conditions and performance would be regulated by FERC under the Federal Power Act. It would be independent from all market participants, with exclusive authority to (a) receive, evaluate, and approve or deny all requests for transmission service and interconnection; and (b) file tariffs with FERC to set the rates, terms and conditions of service provided over the facilities it controlled. So fashioned, the RTO would not only prevent transmission owners from favoring their own products and customers, it would encourage power supply trading over larger territories, thereby increasing competition. The sum of individual utility transfers in a region will create, FERC said, "independent regionally operated transmissions grids [that] will enhance the benefits of competitive electricity markets."[129]

4.B.5.e. Divestiture

Divestiture is the ultimate separation. The utility sells off either its monopoly or its competitive business to an unaffiliated corporation. Doing so eliminates both the incentive and

---

(1999) (FERC issued declaratory order based on hot-line complaint, clarifying that it is an undue preference in violation of section 205 of the FPA for a public utility to tell an affiliate to look for a marketing offer prior to posting the offer publicly).

See also Order No. 2000, 89 FERC ¶ 61,285 at nn.95, 96 (citing a commenter's statement that "[f]unctional unbundling and enforcement of [standard of] conduct standards require herculean policing efforts, and they are not practical").

129. Order No. 2000, 89 FERC ¶ 61,285 at text accompanying n.2. States, as well as FERC, had recognized the problem of continued incumbent bias, and the benefit of transferring control to an independent entity. As Order No. 2000 noted, Illinois, Wisconsin, Virginia, Arkansas and Ohio all had passed statutes requiring their transmission-owning utilities to join an independent system operator or take other measures to ensure transmission independence. *Id.* at text accompanying n.42.

As of this writing, there are seven RTOs or ISOs in the United States, covering all regions except the Northwest, Southwest and Southeast: ISO New England, New York ISO, PJM Interconnection, Electric Reliability Council of Texas, Southwest Power Pool, Midwest ISO and California ISO. Canada has three: New Brunswick System Operator, Ontario Independent Electric System Operator, and Alberta Electric System Operator. *See Regional Transmission Organizations (RTO)/Independent System Operators (ISO)*, FERC, http://www.ferc.gov/industries/electric/indus-act/rto.asp (last visited Jan. 25, 2013).

opportunity to use its bottleneck to favor its competitive business.[130] Regulatory decisions on divestiture involve at least six variables, represented by the questions that follow.[131]

Should the divestiture be mandatory or discretionary? In state and federal proceedings, there have been examples of both:

1.   The Public Utility Holding Company Act of 1935 (PUHCA) required each public utility holding company to divest assets and businesses that were not part of a holding company's single "integrated public-utility system."[132]

2.   The FERC-instituted transitions to competition in electricity and gas, begun in the 1980s, did not mandate divestiture. Some companies have responded to these transitions by divesting voluntarily.

3.   The AT&T restructuring required by the 1984 MFJ (discussed in Chapter 3.A.3) involved divestiture under a court-approved settlement of an antitrust lawsuit, rather than a statutory or regulatory requirement.

4.   States that introduced competition in electricity and gas varied, not only in whether divestiture was mandatory or voluntary, but also whether the mandate came from the statute or the commission. Maine's statute ordered divestiture;[133] New Jersey's statute authorized commission-ordered divestiture.[134] Connecticut's and Massachusetts' statutes conditioned the utility's stranded cost recovery on voluntary divestiture.[135] Pennsylvania's and Virginia's statutes prohibited the state commissions from ordering divestiture.[136]

---

130.   Some conversationalists include in "divestiture" the utility's transfer of assets to an affiliate. Transferring to an affiliate does not eliminate the possibility of favoritism. It therefore is clearer to label this latter action "affiliate separation," reserving "divestiture" for the disposition of assets to an unaffiliated entity.

131.   *Context note*: This discussion focuses on divestitures associated with the government-induced conversion of monopoly markets to competitive markets. A separate set of divestiture questions arises in the area of mergers and acquisitions, to be discussed in the companion volume.

132.   Public Utility Holding Company Act of 1935 (codified at 15 U.S.C. §§ 79 *et seq.*) (repealed 2005). We will discuss PUHCA, and its exceptions and exemptions, in the companion volume on corporate structure, mergers and acquisitions.

133.   *See* ME. REV. STAT. tit. 35-A, § 3204(1), (5), (6) (requiring generation divestiture, subject to limited exceptions for nuclear plants, facilities necessary to carry out transmission and distribution obligations, and "qualifying facilities" subject to the Public Utility Regulatory Policies Act of 1978).

134.   New Jersey's Electric Discount and Energy Competition Act (1999) (codified at N.J. STAT. § 48:3-59(a)(2)), authorized the Board to require divestiture if:

> necessary because the concentration or location of electric generation facilities under the electric public utility's ownership or control enable it to exercise market control that adversely affects the formation of a competitive electricity generation market and adversely affects retail electric supply customers by enabling the electric public utility or its related competitive business segment to gain an unfair competitive advantage or otherwise charge non-competitive prices.

135.   *See* CONN. GEN. STAT. § 16-244f(b)(1), (5) (conditioning stranded cost recovery on commission approval of divestiture plan and submittal of all non-nuclear generation to a public auction, in which affiliates may bid); MASS. GEN. LAWS ch. 164, § 1G(d)(1) (similar, and requiring that sales proceeds "be dedicated to reducing such company's total transition cost").

136.   *See* PA. CON. STAT. tit. 66, § 2804(5) ("The commission may permit, but shall not require, an electric

Which should be divested: The monopoly or the competitive business? In retail competition states, policymakers seeking divestiture emphasized competitive assets; namely, generation. The utility retained the distribution and transmission assets, as well as its state law obligation to serve non-shopping customers. No state required the utility to divest its retail sales and customer service activities, although some states did require some form of functional or corporate separation between the retail sales activity and the monopoly distribution service.

In contrast, FERC has encouraged divestiture of the monopoly asset, electricity transmission, by offering financial "incentives" to transmission-only companies, called "Transcos":

> By eliminating competition for capital between generation and transmission functions and thereby maintaining a singular focus on transmission investment, the Transco model responds more rapidly and precisely to market signals indicating when and where transmission investment is needed. We agree that Transcos have no incentive to maintain congestion in order to protect their owned generation. Moreover, Transcos' for-profit nature, combined with a transmission-only business model, enhances asset management and access to capital markets and provides greater incentives to develop innovative services. By virtue of their stand-alone nature, Transcos also provide non-discriminatory access to all grid users.[137]

Who should be allowed to buy the assets? There are four major possibilities: (a) an existing company in the region seeking to expand its market share; (b) an existing company from some other region, seeking to expand into a new territory; (c) a new company, seeking first-time market entry; and (d) a new corporation owned by the incumbent's existing shareholders, who receive shares in a "spin-off" and then are free to sell their shares in the new company to others.

Should the divestiture process be a public auction or a private deal? In both mandatory and voluntary divestitures, the regulator expects the divesting utility to use the sales procedure likely to produce the highest price. Doing so produces the largest possible reduction in the utility's rates to its monopoly service customers. (Chapter 6.C.3 will detail this relationship between sales proceeds and rates.) Some state commissions have run auctions, using consultants to design the bidding process and then ordering the utility to accept the

---

utility to divest itself of facilities or to reorganize its corporate structure."); Va. Code § 56-590(A) ("The Commission shall not require any incumbent electric utility to divest itself of any generation, transmission or distribution assets pursuant to any provision of this chapter.").

137. Promoting Transmission Investment through Pricing Reform, Order No. 679, 116 FERC ¶ 61,057, at PP 221, 224 (2006). FERC has issued a Notice of Inquiry to revisit various aspects of this 2006 rule. *See* Promoting Transmission Investment Through Pricing Reform, Notice of Inquiry, 135 FERC ¶ 61,146 (2011). The context here is FERC's efforts to bring competition to wholesale electricity markets. In the context of mergers, FERC has focused its divestiture attention on generation.

bid results. Other state commissions have defined general parameters for the sales process, but left the utility free to choose the method.

Who gets the gain or bears the loss—customers or shareholders? Divestiture produces proceeds. Those proceeds will be either above or below the divested asset's book cost. Who gets the gain or bears the loss? Chapter 3.C.1 explained that most statutes and commission decisions on retail competition make customers responsible for "stranded investment"— the excess of book cost over market value. What if the opposite occurs—sales proceeds exceed book value? A symmetrical policy would require that those who bear the loss also get the gain. This subject returns in Chapter 6.C.3, which addresses the utility's obligation under "just and reasonable" ratemaking to minimize its costs by maximizing its revenues.

How do the utility and its regulator handle the utility's post-divestiture dependence on others? A retail electric utility that divests its generation now must shop for its power in wholesale markets. When an LDC's pipeline unbundles transportation from sales, the LDC must shop for wholesale gas. In each situation, the retail utility must become proficient at procurement. It must choose the right mix of short-, medium- and long-term products, design requests for proposals, compare offers and negotiate purchase terms. Its skill and prudence become new subjects for regulatory attention. (We will discuss prudence, and its effects on rates, in Chapter 6.B and C.)

4.B.6. Unbundling's effects on vertical economies

Unbundling has a potential downside: Separating services formerly provided together could create problems of physical feasibility or increase total cost. Put another way: Does vertical integration create efficiencies that are lost through unbundling? Restructuring efforts in electricity, gas and telecommunications all addressed this question.

4.B.6.a. Electricity's ancillary services and efficiency losses

Recall that FERC's Order No. 888 requires "functional unbundling" of generation from transmission: The same utility corporation may provide both monopoly transmission service and competitive generation service, subject to a code of conduct.[138] FERC also required transmission service providers to establish separate prices for each of six "ancillary services."[139] In this context, FERC fine-tuned its unbundling requirement. For four

---

138. *See supra* Chapter 4.B.5.c.
139. Ancillary services are generation services necessary to maintain the stability of the transmission system. The FERC-ordered tariff accompanying Order No. 888 defines and describes them as follows:
    1. Scheduling, System Control and Dispatch Service ("This service is required to schedule the movement of power through, out of, within, or into a Control Area.")
    2. Reactive Supply and Voltage Control from Generation Sources Service ("In order to maintain transmission voltages on the Transmission Provider's transmission facilities within acceptable limits, generation facilities (in the Control Area where the Transmission Provider's transmission facilities are located) are operated to produce (or absorb) reactive power.")
    3. Regulation and Frequency Response Service ("Regulation and Frequency Response Service is necessary

of these services, the customers could buy them from the utility or from third parties, or self-supply them. For the other two, the customer had to buy them from the utility. For these latter two services (Scheduling, System Control and Dispatch Service; and Reactive Supply and Voltage Control Service from Generation Sources), FERC found it is (a) physically impossible for a customer to take any transmission service without also taking these two services; and (b) physically infeasible for anyone but the transmission provider to provide them. (The transmission provider, however, can procure these services competitively from third parties.) Unbundling had to give way to physical reality.

Turning from physical issues to economics: John Kwoka of Northeastern University has used econometrics to study whether mandatory generation divestiture has affected efficiencies in electric distribution. Examining 73 utilities in the period 1994–2003, he and his co-authors found that "the major divestitures that were required by state regulators had large adverse effects on efficiency, whereas utilities that divested at their own initiative had at worst neutral efficiency outcomes. These results raise serious questions about one of the centerpieces of electricity restructuring," that is, mandatory divestiture. The specific "adverse effects" were "declines in . . . operating efficiency, measured both by operating costs and also by total costs including capital expenditures."[140] (To be clear, this study focused on generation divestiture's effect on distribution system efficiency, not on generation efficiency. It is possible, of course, for one of these effects to be positive, the other negative, and for one effect to outweigh the other.)

---

to provide for the continuous balancing of resources (generation and interchange) with load and for maintaining scheduled Interconnection frequency at sixty cycles per second (60 Hz). Regulation and Frequency Response Service is accomplished by committing on-line generation whose output is raised or lowered (predominantly through the use of automatic generating control equipment) as necessary to follow the moment-by-moment changes in load.")

4. Energy Imbalance Service ("Energy Imbalance Service is provided when a difference occurs between the scheduled and the actual delivery of energy to a load located within a Control Area over a single hour.")

5. Operating Reserve—Spinning Reserve Service ("Spinning Reserve Service is needed to serve load immediately in the event of a system contingency. Spinning Reserve Service may be provided by generating units that are on-line and loaded at less than maximum output.")

6. Operating Reserve—Supplemental Reserve Service. ("Supplemental Reserve Service is needed to serve load in the event of a system contingency; however, it is not available immediately to serve load but rather within a short period of time. Supplemental Reserve Service may be provided by generating units that are on-line but unloaded, by quick-start generation or by interruptible load.")

Order No. 888, 75 FERC ¶ 61,080 at app. D, § 3.

140. John Kwoka, Michael Pollitt & Sanem Sergici, *Divestiture Policy and Operating Efficiency in U.S. Electric Power Distribution*, 38 J. REG. ECON. 86, 106 (2010). This 2010 study confirmed, with updated data, the conclusions in his earlier study. *See* John Kwoka, *Vertical Economies in Electric Power: Evidence on Integration and Its Alternatives*, 20 INT'L J. INDUSTRIAL ORG. 653 (2002).

4.B.6.b. Gas marketing data

Recall that FERC's Order No. 497 issued a rule prohibiting a natural gas pipeline from favoring its marketing affiliate over non-affiliated marketers.[141] Pipelines must share "transportation information" (i.e., data on available pipeline capacity) with affiliates and non-affiliates contemporaneously. The D.C. Circuit upheld this requirement. There was both (1) a "theoretical danger that pipelines will favor their marketing affiliates in providing information, and that the result would be anti-competitive," and (2) "evidence that the discriminatory and anti-competitive distribution of information is not just a theoretical danger, but a real one."[142] But the court rejected a different component of the rule, one requiring "contemporaneous sharing" of "gas sales and gas marketing information." In adopting that component, FERC had given short shrift to the incumbent's legitimate use of vertical economies. As the court explained:

> We suspect that the difficulties we have identified [with the requirement of contemporaneous disclosure of gas sales and gas marketing information] may have their source in a basic misconception held by FERC. The Commission appears to believe that any advantage a pipeline gives its marketing affiliate is improper. . . . But advantages a pipeline gives its affiliate are improper only to the extent that they flow from the pipeline's anti-competitive market power. Otherwise vertical integration produces permissible efficiencies that cannot by themselves be considered uses of monopoly power. . . . As it stands, therefore, [the requirement to share sales and marketing information] may well reflect a remedy improperly disproportionate to the identified ailment, pipeline's market power over transportation.

The court emphasized that "the sharing of information between pipelines and their marketing affiliates has efficiency benefits," and that "any separation reduces those benefits to some extent." Unless FERC could connect that sharing to pipeline market power, the ban on sharing "would undermine the efficiencies of pipeline-affiliate integration without promising any compensating benefits." FERC had conceded that pipelines did not have market power over sales or marketing, and that some marketing and sales information comes not from their market power over transportation, but rather from "ongoing customer calls and reviews of filings with state and federal regulator[y] agencies, trade publications, and market reports."[143]

---

141.   *See supra* Chapter 4.B.5.c (discussing Codes of Conduct).
142.   Tenneco Gas Co. v. FERC, 969 F.2d 1187, 1197 (D.C. Cir. 1992).
143.   *Id.* at 1197, 1199–1201, 1205 (citations omitted).

4.B.6.c. Telecommunications: From alien attachments to broadband

In the telecommunications arena, arguments about vertical integration's benefits span a century, with claims ranging from valid to illusory to laughable. The story begins with "alien attachments." It continues today with debates about integrating "information services" into the telecommunications network.

Alien attachments: For decades, Bell Telephone used the "vertical economies" argument to keep equipment competitors away from its customers. The FCC's evolving reactions, only partly digested here, are worth the reader's patience.

The original Bell System included, all in one corporate family, local exchange companies (LECs), a long-distance company and an equipment manufacturing company.[144] Bell owned all the equipment—wires (both external and internal to the customer's premises), switches, central offices, and customer premises equipment (CPE). A telephone customer bought service, and only service. Beginning in 1899, Bell enforced its vertical control through tariff provisions, approved by regulators, forbidding its customers from connecting "foreign attachments" (also known as "alien attachments"). Alien attachments were defined as CPE made by anyone other than Bell. Bell defended its tariffs with the argument that alien attachments would degrade the system. The tariffs' "practical effect was to eliminate all competitive suppliers of CPE."[145] With this vertical integration argument, and the FCC's approval, Bell extended its monopoly into the home.

Not without opposition. Between 1947 and 1976 the FCC addressed Bell's vertical integration claims in a series of challenges, acceptances and judicial reversals, not all of them consistent. In 1947, the FCC rejected all Bell tariffs that barred recording devices connected to interstate calls, finding that these devices did not cause "any perceptible effect on the functioning of the telephone apparatus or the quality of the telephone service."[146] But in 1954, the Commission allowed Bell to ban, for interstate calls, a "telephone answering device" called "Telemagnet."[147] (At the same time that Bell was barring these devices,

---

144.   See *supra* Chapter 3.A.3.
145.   HUBER, KELLOGG & THORNE, *supra* note 117, at 663–70. Here was a typical tariff provision, used in Bell's interstate and intrastate tariffs:

> Equipment, apparatus and lines furnished by the Telephone Company shall be carefully used and no equipment, apparatus or lines not furnished by the Telephone Company shall be attached to, or used in connection therewith, unless specifically authorized in this tariff. When equipment, apparatus or lines furnished by the customer or subscriber are used in connection with equipment, apparatus or lines furnished by the Telephone Company, the equipment, apparatus and lines furnished by the customer or subscriber must be connected solely with the Telephone Company's system. Any equipment furnished by the Telephone Company shall remain the property of the Telephone Company and upon termination of service for any cause whatsoever be returned to it, in good condition, reasonable wear and tear thereof excepted.

Jordaphone Corp. v. AT&T, 18 F.C.C. 644, ¶ 9 (1954).
146.   In the Matter of Use of Recording Devices in Connection with Telephone Services, 11 F.C.C. 1033, 1036 (1947).
147.   Jordaphone v. AT&T, 18 F.C.C. 644, ¶ 36. Jordaphone's complaint was supported by other answering

Bell was offering its own answering machine on a test basis.) Telemagnet's answering machine differed from previously approved recording devices, the FCC said, because it "opens and closes the telephone circuit," and "after opening the telephone circuit, [it] may fail to close it or may keep the circuit open after the calling party hangs up, creating a 'receiver-off-the-hook' condition, which, if it lasts for a given length of time, will cause interference with the normal operation of the telephone circuit." The Commission upheld Bell's tariff ban of the device, as applied to interstate and foreign calls, not because of the off-the-hook effect but because there was not a "public need and demand . . . [for the device] in connection with interstate and foreign telephone service." The predominant use of answering devices, the FCC said, would be for intrastate toll calls and local exchange service. The Commission then found Bell's ban "unjust and unreasonable" as applied to intrastate or exchange service, because when used for that purpose it would cause no "substantial harm" to interstate or foreign service.[148]

Then there was Hush-a-Phone, "a cup-like device . . . which snaps on to a telephone instrument and makes for privacy of conversation, office quiet and a quiet telephone circuit." Bell's tariff prohibited the device. The Commission upheld the tariff, not because the device impaired the network, but because the listener "hears a lower and somewhat distorted sound." (Court's paraphrasing of the FCC's order.) The court of appeals reversed. Trying not to smile, the court said the caller would achieve the same voice distortion "by cupping his hand between the transmitter and his mouth and speaking in a low voice into this makeshift muffler," a bodily act over which neither Bell nor the FCC had control. "To say that a telephone subscriber may produce the result in question by cupping his hand and speaking into it, but may not do so by using a device which leaves his hand free to write or do whatever else he wishes, is neither just nor reasonable." The court's principle: Bell's tariffs could not lawfully interfere with the "subscriber's right reasonably to use his telephone in ways which are privately beneficial without being publicly detrimental."[149]

Bell's anti-competitive acts thus attracted judicial attention well before the 1984 Bell breakup. In *Hush-a-Phone*, the FCC had acknowledged the device's key benefit—it "makes for a quiet line"—but upheld Bell's ban because customers could purchase quieting devices from Bell. The court didn't bite:

---

machine makers, including "The Electronic Secretary," "Telemaster" and a Liechtensteinian company that made "Notaphone."

148. *Id.* The FCC tested the devices with five callers, noting that "[o]ne of the women selected had a 'soft' voice, believed to be typical of some women's voices." *Id.* ¶ 67. The Wisconsin Commission, regulating intrastate service, had suspended the tariff prohibition so as to allow use of the Electronic Secretary. As a result, the P.A. Stark Piano Company advertised that anyone calling any time, day or night, "will hear a famous pianist demonstrate the tone quality of the new spinet piano." And in Milwaukee people with dirty clothes could call the local laundry during the night, leave a message, and have their clothes picked up the next morning. *See* Jordaphone v. AT&T, 18 F.C.C. 644, ¶¶ 26–27.

149. Hush-a-Phone Corp. v. FCC, 238 F.2d 266, 267–69 (D.C. Cir. 1956).

The mere fact that the [Bell] telephone companies can provide a rival device would seem to be a poor reason for disregarding Hush-A-Phone's value in assuring a quiet line. . . . A system whereby [Bell] may market equipment until such time as the Commission orders a halt, while [rival] petitioners may not market competitive equipment until the Commission gives them an authorization, seems inherently unfair. The unfairness is enhanced from time to time when the Commission's adjudicatory process bogs down.[150]

The next chapter in this CPE version of the vertical benefits debate was *Carterfone*. Bell had barred customers' use of a device that allows communication between a mobile radio system and the telephone network. The FCC removed the ban, finding that Bell's "tariff is unreasonable in that it prohibits the use of interconnecting devices which do not adversely affect the telephone system, . . . there being no material distinction between a foreign attachment such as the Hush-A-Phone [which the court of appeals had required the FCC to allow] and an interconnection device such as the Carterfone." The tariff prohibition was also unduly discriminatory because Bell allowed customers to use Bell-made devices that performed the same function. Further, the tariff was overbroad because "it prohibits the use of harmless as well as harmful devices." The Commission then went beyond Carterfone's proposal. Referring to Bell's foreign attachments tariff as a whole, the Commission threw this thunderbolt:

> The present unlawfulness of the tariff also permeates its past. It has been unreasonable and unreasonably discriminatory since its inception, for the reasons given above. . . .
>
> In view of the unlawfulness of the tariff there would be no point in merely declaring it invalid as applied to the Carterfone and permitting it to continue in operation as to other interconnection devices. This would also put a clearly improper burden upon the manufacturers and users of other devices. The appropriate remedy is to strike the tariff and permit the carriers, if they so desire, to propose new tariff provisions in accordance with this opinion.[151]

This was a high-watermark in efforts to subject Bell to CPE competition, but it soon receded. Bell promulgated new tariffs that

> permitted customers to connect to the telephone network, but only through interconnecting devices called protective connecting arrangements (PCAs) [sold only by Bell]. Further, any network control signaling devices—devices, like the ordinary dial telephone, that actually put electronic signals onto the phone network—still had to be furnished,

---

150.   *Id.* at 269 n.9.

151.   Carter Elecs. Corp. v. AT&T, 13 F.C.C.2d 420, 423–25 (1968) ("*Carterphone*").

installed, and maintained by Bell. The Commission turned aside the immediate challenges to these tariffs. *Carterfone*, the Commission reasoned, permitted interconnections with—but not substitutions or replacements for—the system, expansively defined. This substantially eviscerated *Carterfone.*[152]

Attempting again to clear the air, the FCC in 1976 created a program of "technical registrations" for CPE, replacing Bell's tariff-based CPE restrictions. As a result, "CPE suppliers had a choice: they could purchase a 'protective connecting arrangement' (PCA) interface from Bell, or they could register their CPE with the Commission and show that the equipment would not harm the telephone network. Bell's stranglehold on the CPE market was thereby broken."[153]

The "stranglehold" may have been "broken," but opportunity for anti-competitive influence remained. In 1974, the U.S. Department of Justice's antitrust lawsuit alleged that Bell was still using its vertical control, especially its ownership of local exchange facilities, to monopolize the CPE, long-distance and computer markets. The suit was finally resolved by the 1984 Modification of Final Judgment. The MFJ left Bell with its long-distance and equipment businesses but divested its local exchange monopolies to the Regional Bell Operating Companies. It also prohibited the post-divestiture RBOCs from (1) making or marketing CPE, (2) providing interexchange services, (3) providing directory advertising, (4) providing information service, and (5) providing "any other product or service that is not a 'natural monopoly service actually regulated by tariff.'"[154]

From alien attachments to broadband: The question that permeates the "alien attachments" story—Are there vertical economies, and if so how do we preserve them?—is central to today's debates over telecommunications competition. Recall that in *Computer III*,[155] the FCC replaced *Computer II*'s structural safeguards (applicable to ILECs' provision of enhanced services) with non-structural measures. The chief reason was vertical economies: The transformation of telephone switches into computers made it possible to integrate basic service and enhanced service more economically than before. Structural separation, the FCC found, inhibited ILECs from doing so; so it substituted behavioral rules for structural restrictions.[156]

The modern version of this question is the effort to integrate basic services and enhanced services into broadband "information services." In electricity, a comparable technology-driven example is the so-called "smart grid." Both subjects are addressed next.

---

152.   Huber, Kellogg & Thorne, *supra* note 117, at 663–70.
153.   Benjamin et al., *supra* note 79, at 346.
154.   United States v. AT&T, 552 F. Supp. 131, 143 (D.D.C. 1982), *aff'd sub nom.* Maryland v. United States, 460 U.S. 1001 (1983), described in Chapter 3.A.3.
155.   *See supra* Chapter 3.A.3.
156.   *Computer III*, 104 F.C.C.2d at 985–86, 1004, 1008–09; *see also* Huber, Kellogg & Thorne, *supra* note 117, § 12.7.7.

4.B.7. New bottlenecks and new tensions

Our unbundling discussion so far has emphasized the traditional physical bottlenecks—pipelines, transmission, distribution systems, central exchanges and the "local loop." As technology creates new service and product markets, analysts are identifying new forms of bottleneck monopolies.

4.B.7.a. Broadband

In the 1980s and for most of the 1990s, telecommunications services were more important than information services. The latter category included dial-up e-mail and voice messaging, activities incidental to telecommunications. This picture has changed. Broadband is supplanting traditional telecommunications voice and data services as the primary means by which individuals, businesses and governments communicate electronically. Dial-up providers have been replaced by facilities-based entities—cable operators, ILECs, and wireless carriers—who combine Internet access with local broadband transport as an integrated service.[157]

These developments bring us back to this Chapter's main question: How do regulators make competition effective in markets where the major incumbent providers are positioned to gain and exercise market power? While local broadband service is unlikely to be the exclusive monopoly that local telephone service was, many geographic areas have only a few facilities-based providers. Economies of scale and density associated with distribution wirelines limit the number of cable operators and landline broadband providers, while radiofrequency licensing restrictions limit the number of wireless providers. When a market has few providers and high entry barriers, market power is a risk.

The regulatory solution is a work in progress. The FCC (in its *Computer Inquiries*) and Congress (in the 1996 Act) distinguished "telecommunications service" (pure information transport) from "information service" (electronic transport integrated with information storage, content manipulation or content generation). "Telecommunications services" are subject to Title II common-carrier regulation (and state commission regulation for intrastate telecommunications services), while "information services" are subject only to the FCC's Title I "ancillary" jurisdiction. Applying that jurisdiction, the FCC has determined that information services are "inherently interstate," and thus by statute preemptively immune, for the most part, from state commission regulation.[158]

Beginning in 2002, the FCC classified broadband services as an "information service,"[159] meaning it was not subject to Title II common carrier-type regulation. In 2010 the FCC

---

157. *See* TILLMAN L. LAY, TAKING ANOTHER LOOK AT FEDERAL/STATE JURISDICTIONAL RELATIONSHIPS IN THE NEW BROADBAND WORLD 5–7 (National Regulatory Research Institute 2011).

158. *See* LAY, *supra* note 157, at 1, 6–7; Lee Selwyn & Helen Golding, *Revisiting the Regulatory Status of Broadband Internet Access: A Policy Framework for Net Neutrality and an Open Competitive Internet,* 63 FED. COM. L.J. 91, 94–95, 95 n.8 (2010) ("*Broadband Internet Access*").

159. The FCC first classified cable operator-provided broadband as an information service. Internet Order

had considered reclassifying broadband transmission as a "telecommunications service."[160] Instead, its 2010 Open Internet Order used common-carrier-like, "light touch" regulation based on its Title I ancillary jurisdiction.[161]

The future of broadband regulation therefore remains unclear. If the court of appeals holds that the Open Internet Order is outside the FCC's jurisdiction, there could be amendments to the Communications Act to grant that jurisdiction. Or the FCC could try to reclassify the transmission component of broadband as a "telecommunications service" subject to regulation, likely prompting more court challenges. Or there could be neither congressional nor FCC action, leaving broadband service outside FCC jurisdiction. If, on the other hand, the FCC's Open Internet Order is upheld, much work will remain to shape the FCC regulation—leading possibly to separate court challenges or legislative override.

4.B.7.b. Smart grid

Another area where technology and incumbency combine to raise market power issues is the so-called "smart grid." The German scholars Johann Kranz and Arnold Picot see the smart grid as

> a communications layer's virtual overlay on the existing power grid. This overlay allows all actors and components within the electricity value chain to exchange information, thereby facilitating supply and demand's coordination. This overlay closes the communication gap between consumers' premises and the rest of the network, but requires the deployment of an [advanced metering] infrastructure.[162]

Cable Modem Declaratory Ruling, 17 FCC Rcd. 4798 (2002), *aff'd in part, rev'd in part sub nom.* Brand X Internet Servs. v. FCC, 345 F.3d 1120 (9th Cir. 2003), *rev'd sub nom.* Nat'l Cable & Telecomms. Ass'n v. Brand X Internet Serv., 545 U.S. 967 (2005). It then reclassified landline telephone company-provided broadband from a telecommunications service to an information service, *Appropriate Framework for Broadband Access to the Internet over Wireline Facilities,* Report and Order, 20 FCC Rcd. 14853 (2005), and thereafter did likewise with respect to wireless broadband service, *Appropriate Regulatory Treatment for Broadband Access to the Internet Over Wireless Networks,* Declaratory Ruling, 22 FCC Rcd. 5901 (2007).

160. *See* Framework for Broadband Internet Services, Notice of Inquiry, 25 FCC Rcd. 7866 (2010).
161. Preserving the Open Internet Broadband Industry Practices, Report and Order, 25 FCC Rcd. 17905 (2010) ("Open Internet Order"), *pet. for review pending sub nom.* Verizon v. FCC, No. 11-1355 (D.C. Cir.). *See also* Lay, *supra* note 157, at 5–7.
162. Johann J. Kranz & Arnold Picot, National Regulatory Research Institute, Toward an End-to-End Smart Grid: Overcoming Bottlenecks to Facilitate Competition and Innovation in Smart Grids 1 (2011), *available at* http://www.nrri.org/pubs/telecommunications/NRRI_End_to_End_Smart_Grid_june11-12.pdf. For additional definitions of "smart grid" *see* U.S. Dep't of Energy, The Smart Grid: An Introduction (2008), *available at* http://www.oe.energy.gov/SmartGridIntroduction.htm; and Me. Rev. Stat. tit. 35-A, § 3143(1)(A) ("'Smart grid' means the integration of information and communications innovations and infrastructure with the electric system to enhance the efficiency, reliability and functioning of the system through smart grid functions.").

In the developing markets for smart grid services, the authors identify three bottlenecks critical to new entrants: the last mile, meter data, and interoperability. Their description of these bottlenecks, and their regulatory recommendations, illustrate the type of analysis required to nurture competition in these new markets. A summary follows.

Last mile: The "last mile" of infrastructure, and the associated data, are essential for competition but not economically duplicable by competitors:

> End-to-end communication requires initially developing the missing communications link between consumers' premises and the rest of the energy network (the last mile) by deploying an Advanced Metering Infrastructure (AMI), along with smart meters. . . . The last mile infrastructure cannot be substituted or replicated within a reasonable time and cost frame. Moreover, together with the meter data, the infrastructure provides an essential input allowing efficient downstream markets, *i.e.* complementary services, products, and applications, to emerge.

Their recommended solution is non-discriminatory access:

> Regulatory intervention, in the form of open (or mandated) access, is needed to secure transparent and non-discriminatory third party access to a smart grid's last mile infrastructure. . . . If the entry does work out, the transitory entry assistance can be gradually withdrawn to increase the entrants' economic and strategic incentives to invest in their own infrastructure.[163]

Meter data: Non-duplicable bottlenecks can consist not only of tangible assets like poles and wires, but also "intangible" assets like—

> intellectual property rights, such as proprietary standards, protocols, or interfaces. . . . The data retrieved from smart meters can also be regarded as essential inputs for authorized actors. The data aids them in improving grid management and monitoring, streamlining business processes, and enabling innovative energy efficiency measures and value-added services.

These conditions allow incumbent utilities to—

> deter entry by raising rivals' costs through practices such as exclusive dealing, refusals to deal, tying, or defining of proprietary protocols and standards to artificially increase rivals' transactions and consumers' switching costs. . . . They could also define incompatible

---

163.   Kranz & Picot, *supra* note 162, at ii, 23.

data formats or interfaces for each distribution area, or they could intentionally delay data access and provision.

Their recommended solution is data access:

> [T]o enable an efficient applications market in a future smart grid requires that all authorized parties are guaranteed equal access to an (online) data platform to recall data in (1) as close to real time as possible, (2) a standardized and machine-readable format, and (3) the same granularity in which it is collected. . . .
>
>   Furthermore, consumers should have access to this data and determine the respective parties' data access rights if the information needs go beyond essential data for billing, or essential technical information.

Another structural solution is to place data access questions within the control of an independent platform or party:

> Several regulatory agencies have recommended establishing an independent data platform accessible to third parties, or have already established such a platform. Others have suggested that the function of data collection, management, and access should be completely decoupled by establishing an independent and neutral data service provider . . . . Moreover, an independent single platform provider may be able to provide the data more cost-effectively, due to economies of scale. This provider can also perform tasks such as meter registration and consumer switching.[164]

An example of an independent data platform is where the customer and her appliances communicate directly with third parties through the Internet. The utility's meter is no longer a bottleneck, and the utility's control of customer information is no longer exclusive.

Interoperability: New entrants need to connect to and communicate with the distribution system's components:

> Data's seamless exchange requires open and nonproprietary standards and communication protocols that allow each component and actor within the smart grid to communicate end-to-end. . . . [P]rotocols and standards can resemble essential inputs. . . . Open systems benefit modular innovation, the number of potential market entrants, and market

---

164.   Kranz & Picot, *supra* note 162, at 13, 17, 21 (citing European Regulators' Group for Electricity and Gas (ERGEG), Smart Metering with a Focus on Electricity Regulation (2007), *available at* http:// http://www.e-control.at/portal/page/portal/medienbibliothek/strom/dokumente/pdfs/E07-RMF-04-03_SmartMetering_2007-10-31_0_0.pdf).

dynamics. . . . [Incumbent utilities] may use protocols and standards as strategic weapons to build closed systems in which they safeguard interface information.[165]

Another regulatory solution is to appoint an independent entity to control bottleneck functions associated with smart grid services. Recall the regional transmission organization concept, created by FERC as a means of separating transmission control from ownership.[166] An analogous concept is a "smart grid coordinator." A new Maine statute defines this phrase to mean an "entity, authorized by the commission in accordance with [ME. REV. STAT. tit. 35-A, § 3143(5)], that manages access to smart grid functions and associated infrastructure, technology and applications within the service territory of a transmission and distribution utility." Under this statute, the Maine Public Utilities Commission is investigating "whether it is in the public interest of the State to have one or more smart grid coordinators." If the Commission makes that finding and appoints a coordinator, the entity "may operate as a transmission and distribution utility, under a commission-approved contract with a transmission and distribution utility or in some other manner approved by the commission."[167]

4.C. Reducing non-facility entry barriers

Authorizing competition (Chapter 3), and granting access to incumbent essential facilities (Chapter 4.B), make competition possible. But competition will be certain only if there is entry, by competitors who are viable, capable, confident and well-resourced—companies willing to risk capital and enter. Markets long served by a dominant firm tend to have non-physical features that deter entry. Economists call these features entry barriers: "any market condition that makes entry more costly or time-consuming and thus reduces the effectiveness of potential competition as a constraint on the pricing behavior of the dominant firm."[168] This subchapter defines the concept and provides illustrations, along with regulatory solutions.

---

165. KRANZ & PICOT, *supra* note 162, at 22 (citing Andrea Renda, *Catch Me If You Can! The Microsoft Saga and the Sorrows of Old Antitrust*, 1 ERASMUS L. AND ECON. REV. 1 (2004); Andrea Renda, *Competition-Regulation Interface in Telecommunications: What's Left of the Essential Facility Doctrine*, 34 TELECOMM. POLICY 23 (2010)).
166. See *supra* Chapters 2.F.5, 3.A.1 and 4.B.5.d.
167. ME. REV. STAT. tit. 35-A, § 3143(1)(B), (5). Investigation into Need for Smart Grid Coordinator and Smart Grid Coordinator Standards, Dkt. No. 2010-267 (Me. Pub. Utils. Comm'n). The Maine Commission has suspended the investigation, pending the outcome of a related pilot program being conducted in a different proceeding, Central Maine Power Request for Approval of Non-Transmission Alternative (NTA) Pilot Projects for the Mid-Coast and Portland Areas, Dkt. No. 2011-138 (Me. Pub. Utils. Comm'n) (opened April 11, 2011).
168. S. Pac. Commc'ns Co. v. AT&T, 740 F.2d 980, 1001 (D.C. Cir. 1984).

4.C.1. Entry barriers defined

"There is perhaps no subject that has created more controversy among industrial organization economists than that of barriers to entry."[169] The controversies involve both definitions
and measurement. As for definitions, consider these different notions:

- the extent to which, in the long run, established firms can elevate their selling prices
  above minimal average costs of production and distribution . . . without inducing
  potential entrants to enter the industry. (Joe Bain)
- a cost of producing (at some or every rate of output) which must be borne by firms
  which seek to enter an industry but is not borne by firms already in the industry.
  (George Stigler)
- socially undesirable limitations to entry of resources which are due to protection
  of resource owners already in the market. (Carl von Weizsacker)[170]

As for measurement, the economists Scherer and Ross have described two main approaches:

> One entails a more or less careful study of an industry's technology, raw material avail-
> ability, spatial configuration, consumer buying practices, and legal environment followed
> by subjective judgments as to whether entry barriers are, say, very high, substantial, or
> moderate to low.
>
> The other approach seeks objectively measurable indices consonant with the theory of
> entry deterrence. For example, scale economies limit the number of firms that can oper-
> ate in an industry at minimum average cost. The Bain-Sylos-Modigliani theory suggests
> that prices can be held persistently above costs by a greater margin, the larger a mini-
> mum efficient scale firm is relative to the size of the market, the steeper the cost curves
> are at less than minimum efficient scale, and the less elastic demand is.[171]

An entry barrier is not inherently undesirable. Policymakers sometimes build them to benefit the public. Professional licensing creates a barrier between incumbents and newcomers,
because the newcomer has to spend money and years studying law, medicine or religion
to become a certified lawyer, doctor or preacher. The barrier benefits society because it
distinguishes the trained from the untrained. The patent system bars imitators for seventeen years or more, on the premise that the brass ring of a product monopoly will inspire
the inventor (and her investors) to risk the money and time necessary for breakthroughs.
And any vigorous competitor aspires to build her own entry barrier, lawfully: longstanding,

---

169.   W. Kip Viscusi, Joseph E. Harrington & John M. Vernon, Economics of Regulation and Anti-
       trust 159 (4th ed. 2005).
170.   *Id.*
171.   Scherer & Ross, *supra* note 4, at 424.

outstanding performance builds customer loyalty, discouraging competitors unwilling to spend comparable effort. Entry barriers are not inherently anti-competitive; the prospect of erecting them is what attracts competitors to begin with.[172]

What about entry barriers that exist because of a utility's century-long status as the government-sanctioned incumbent? To convert regulated monopoly markets into competitive markets, regulators must identify those barriers and find ways to reduce them. In this effort, three examples from non-utility industries are worth considering.

4.C.2. Product promotion advantages

Procter & Gamble was a large, diversified manufacturer of household products. The firm was a "dominant factor" in soaps, detergents and cleaners. Its large advertising budget brought it large media discounts. P&G acquired the assets of Clorox, the leading maker of household liquid bleach with 48.8 percent of the national market. This "product extension merger," said the Federal Trade Commission, violated Section 7 of the Clayton Act because it substantially lessened competition in the national market for household liquid bleach.[173] The Supreme Court upheld the Commission. Among the reasons was that Procter's access to advertising discounts, unavailable to its competitor, was a barrier to entry:

> Since all liquid bleach is chemically identical, advertising and sales promotion are vital. . . . The major competitive weapon in the successful marketing of bleach is advertising. . . . Procter would be able to use its volume discounts to advantage in advertising Clorox. Thus, a new entrant would be much more reluctant to face the giant Procter than it would have been to face the smaller Clorox.[174]

---

172. *See Trinko*, 540 U.S. at 407 ("The opportunity to charge monopoly prices—at least for a short period—is what attracts 'business acumen' in the first place; it induces risk taking that produces innovation and economic growth.").

173. Section 7 of the Clayton Act provides:

> No corporation engaged in commerce shall acquire, directly or indirectly, the whole or any part of the stock or other share capital and no corporation subject to the jurisdiction of the Federal Trade Commission shall acquire the whole or any part of the assets of another corporation engaged also in commerce, where in any line of commerce in any section of the country, the effect of such acquisition may be substantially to lessen competition, or to tend to create a monopoly.

Clayton Act, ch. 323, § 7, 38 Stat. 730 (1914) (codified as amended at 15 U.S.C. § 18).

174. FTC v. Procter & Gamble Co., 386 U.S. 568, 572, 579 (1967); *see also* Gen. Foods Corp. v. FTC, 386 F.2d 936, 945 (3d Cir. 1967) (upholding FTC finding that General Foods' "mixed conglomerate merger" with S.O.S. would substantially lessen competition in the household steel wool submarket, in part because General Foods' television discounts—due to "pooled purchases" from its various divisions—would allow the merged company to "advertise and promote S.O.S. less expensively than the pre-merger S.O.S."); S. Pac. v. AT&T, 740 F.2d at 1002 (incumbent's extensive image advertising expenditures constituted a barrier to entry).

A related entry barrier is the cost of "corrective advertising." If the incumbent misleads the public about its new competitor, the new entrant must incur costs to correct the misimpressions.[175]

4.C.3. Entrenched customer preferences

In the AT&T divestiture lawsuit, Judge Greene found that AT&T's monopoly position was protected not only by its control of the bottleneck, but also by "entrenched customer preferences."[176] Courts have observed similar entry barriers in diverse cases. To promote its discount perfumes to distributors, the R.G. Smith Company claimed it had

> duplicat[ed] 100% perfect the exact scent of the world's finest and most expensive perfumes and colognes at prices that will zoom sales to volumes you have never before experienced! . . . We dare you to try to detect any difference between Chanel #5 ($25.00) and Ta'Ron's 2nd Chance ($7.00).

Chanel sued, arguing that R.G. Smith's ads violated Chanel's trademark. Chanel lost. Its effort to protect its trademark actually impaired competition:

> The object of much modern advertising is "to impregnate the atmosphere of the market with the drawing power of a congenial symbol[,]" . . . rather than to communicate information as to quality or price. The primary value of the modern trademark lies in the "conditioned reflex developed in the buyer by imaginative or often purely monotonous selling of the mark itself." . . . To the extent that advertising of this type succeeds, it is suggested, the trademark is endowed with sales appeal independent of the quality or price of the product to which it is attached; economically irrational elements are introduced into consumer choices; and the trademark owner is insulated from the normal pressures of price and quality competition. In consequence the competitive system fails to perform its function of allocating available resources efficiently.[177]

By associating itself with Chanel's good name, therefore, R.G. Smith broke down a barrier, channeling customers' awe of Chanel toward a cheaper but olfactorily equivalent product.[178]

---

175. *See* Davis v. S. Bell Tel. & Tel. Co., 1994 U.S. Dist. LEXIS 13,257, at *6–7 (S.D. Fla. 1994) (finding an entry barrier where a new competitor had to spend advertising money to correct the incumbent's "misleading marketing").
176. United States v. AT&T, 524 F. Supp. 1336, 1348 (D.D.C. 1981).
177. R.G. Smith v. Chanel, 402 F.2d 562, 566–67 (9th Cir. 1968) (quoting R.G. Smith's ads) (citations omitted).
178. *See also* S. Pac. v. AT&T, 740 F.2d at 1002 (describing competitors' "need to overcome brand preference established by the defendant's having been first in the market or having made extensive 'image' advertising expenditures").

Customer entrenchment can arise not only from advertising but from long-term working relationships. "Attracting customers and dealers and building customer and dealer loyalty require of any new entrant into a given market more time and capital than is necessary in markets where customer and dealer ties are less significant."[179]

4.C.4. Long-term contracts

By ensuring stable revenue, long-term contracts can attract investment. This feature makes them pro-competitive. They can be anti-competitive, though: When the incumbent ties up favored customers, the new entrants have less fruit to pick. During the natural gas transition, local distribution companies explained that the pipelines' long-term contracts "lock[ed] in customers and serve[d] as a barrier to entry into the pipeline market by potential competitors. Rival pipelines will not build extensions to their system if the market for additional capacity has been foreclosed by long-term contracts with the existing pipeline."[180]

4.C.5. Entry barriers in regulated utility markets

The foregoing examples of entry barriers—product promotion advantages, entrenched customer preferences, name recognition and long-term contracts—have counterparts in utility regulators' efforts to introduce competition into monopoly markets. In the midst of its conversion efforts, the California Commission made this observation:

> By the very nature of SoCal's monopoly position in the energy and energy services market, its access to comprehensive customers records, its access to an established billing system and its "name brand" recognition, it may be that SoCal enjoys significant market power with respect to any new product or service in the energy field.[181]

---

179. Pargas, Inc. v. Empire Gas Corp., 423 F. Supp. 199, 215 (D. Md. 1976) (describing evidence, in proposed acquisition, of "barriers to successful entry into LP-gas distribution, . . . [where] long-standing customer and dealer ties with established competitors provide advantages for existing firms").

180. United Distribution Co. v. FERC, 88 F.3d 1105, 1140 (D.C. Cir. 1996). Other examples of entry barriers arising from long-term contracts include stadium concessions and waste management arrangements. *See* Twin City Sportservice, Inc. v. Charles O. Finley & Co., 676 F.2d 1291, 1301 (9th Cir. 1982) (1982) (quoting district court finding that stadium owner's insistence on long-term franchise contracts with its concessionaires represent "classic examples of artificially created barriers to effective entry into and competition within the [concession franchise] market"); *see also* Tri-State Rubbish v. Waste Mgmt., 998 F.2d 1073, 1081 (1st Cir. 1993) (noting that in the waste business, "the efficiencies of collecting from a number of closely located customer sites could make new entry difficult, especially if the community were small and many customers were tied to an existing dominant hauler by long-term contracts").

181. Order Instituting Rulemaking to Establish Standards of Conduct Governing Relationships Between Energy Utilities and Their Affiliates, 183 P.U.R.4th 503, 1997 Cal. PUC LEXIS 1139, at *79 (Cal. Pub. Util. Comm'n Dec. 16, 1997) ("*California Standards*") (quoting Southern California Gas Company Performance-based Ratemaking Decision, D. 97-07-054, slip op. at 63 (Cal. July 16, 1997)).

Among the many battlegrounds where solutions emerged are four discussed here: customers' ability to change suppliers, the monthly billing relationship, incumbent's control of customer information, and use of the incumbent's name.

4.C.5.a. Changing suppliers

For competition to thrive, customers must find supplier-switching convenient and low-cost. Regulatory solutions have included:

1.   requiring LECs to provide number portability (the ability to keep one's phone number when switching phone companies) and dialing parity (no requirement to dial multiple extra numbers when using non-incumbent providers).[182]

2.   requiring ILECs to give competitive local exchange carriers access to "office support systems" that process customer orders at a speed and effectiveness comparable to that provided by the incumbent to its own customers; and[183]

3.   creating customer education programs to compensate for customers' lack of shopping experience.[184]

4.C.5.b. Monthly billing

The monthly billing task can be both an entry barrier and a competitive opportunity.[185] Some new electricity sellers will excel in procuring electricity resources and gathering customers, but lack an infrastructure to invoice customers and collect payments. Or, their small size may preclude them from realizing economies of scale in the billing function.[186] One barrier-reducing solution is to require the incumbent utility to provide consolidated billing services, that is, to include the competitive provider's invoice for electric service in the utility's monthly bill for distribution service. Other sellers, in contrast, may want to differentiate themselves through their bills.[187] Some states have allowed both options:

---

182.   *See* 47 U.S.C. §§ 251(b)(2)–(3).

183.   *See* AT&T v. FCC, 220 F.3d 607, 613 (D.C. Cir. 2000) (listing cases where FCC rejected ILEC applications to provide long-distance service, on the grounds that ILEC had failed to provide non-discriminatory access to operations support systems).

184.   *See* Regina R. Johnson & Bruce W. Radford, *Rating the Consumer Education Campaigns*, 138 PUB. UTIL. FORTNIGHTLY 38, 40 (2000). I am grateful to Nalani Still, a student in my 2011 public utility law class at Georgetown University Law Center, for identifying this and other sources.

185.   I am grateful to Matthew Bisanz, a student in my 2011 public utility law class at Georgetown University Law Center, for allowing my use in this paragraph of ideas and research from his semester paper.

186.   *See* Central Hudson Gas & Electric Corp., No. 05-M-0332 (N.Y. Pub. Serv. Comm'n June 1, 2005) (indicating competitive providers' preference for consolidated billing and collection to more quickly implement enhanced competition).

187.   *See* Metering, Billing and Other Customer Services, No. 00-054-U (Ark. Pub. Serv. Comm'n May 17, 2000) (recognizing that competitive billing may increase competition in the retail services market), *available at* http://www.apscservices.info/pdf/00/00-054-u_31_1.pdf; P. Grey, *Retailers Should Own The Bill*, 3 POWER & GAS 22–23 (2003) (discussing the competitive advantage of impressing the consumer through the billing process).

requiring the incumbent to prepare the bills at a new entrant's request, while also allowing new entrants to send their own bills.[188]

Separate from the goal of reducing the billing barrier is preventing the incumbent from raising the barrier. An incumbent utility might use its own billing systems, created for its monopoly business, to assist its competitive business. Kansas City Power & Light marketed to its customers a competitive heating, ventilation and air conditioning program, called "Worry Free Service." Customers could pay for the service on their regular electric bill. The problem was that non-utility providers of such services could not offer the same convenience.[189] The California Commission prohibited a similar practice, unless the utility made the option available to its competitors.[190]

4.C.5.c. Knowledge of the customer base

A market entrant needs market information. The incumbent utility has decades of data about customer locations, consumption patterns and payment histories. In a competitive context, this information allows the utility to target its marketing: "[A]ccess to usage data is a critical component of an effective competitive retail market."[191] Next are three examples of utilities using knowledge gained from their legacy monopoly status to advance their competitive objectives.

Energy services: In 1995, Virginia Power formed an energy services division, Evantage, to "prepare for unbundling of services." The company "aim[ed] to get out early, establish a reputation and a long list of clients before, as is expected, numerous competitors organize their own deregulated energy services." The company formed a national alliance with Westinghouse to provide electrical systems services in the unregulated retail market: "maintenance and supply services, information systems, on-site generation plants, lighting replacements and energy efficiency products and services including planning, design and installation." The company also contracted with 150 Shop 'n' Save stores to "share energy efficiency savings resulting from installing lighting and [heating, ventilation and air conditioning] systems."[192]

Heating, ventilation and air conditioning: When Delmarva Power and Light merged with Atlantic Energy in 1996, the resulting "Connectiv Company" became a major presence in

---

188. *See* VIRGINIA STATE CORP. COMM'N, REPORT TO THE GENERAL ASSEMBLY: COMPETITION FOR ELECTRIC METERING, MILLING, AND OTHER SERVICES 5 (1999), *available at* http://www.scc.virginia.gov/comm/reports/mandb1.pdf.

189. *KCP&L Pushes its Worry Free HVAC Service into Houston, Dallas Markets*, ENERGY SERVS. & TELECOM REP., May 27, 1997.

190. *California Standards*, 1997 Cal. PUC LEXIS 1139 at *94–95 ("[U]tility affiliates may have access to the billing envelopes [of the incumbent utility] if other competitors are offered the same access on the same terms and conditions.").

191. In the Matter of Competitive Opportunities Regarding Electric Service, 181 P.U.R.4th 324, 1997 N.Y. PUC LEXIS 450 (N.Y. Pub. Util. Comm'n Aug. 1, 1997) ("New York Competitive Opportunities Order").

192. *Utilities Prepare Competition Strategies to Expand Deregulated Market Share*, THE ENERGY REPORT, Aug. 25, 1997.

the Mid-Atlantic heating, ventilation and air condition market by going on an "acquisition spree." Its general manager stated: "Customers recognize the [utility's] brand. . . . With all of those mergers, we were able to drive total operating costs down. That gave us a lot of synergies. It also gave us a bigger customer base to which we could market our products and a bigger media presence. We can now advertise in the Philadelphia market and reach a million of our customers instead of a couple hundred thousand."[193]

Home security: Kansas City Power & Light created a marketing partnership with Westar, a Western Resources subsidiary providing security services. According to KCP&L's vice-president for marketing: "We have good feedback from our [utility] customers that security services is something we can bring to them. They do see KCPL bringing enhanced value, and that is where our Promise [i.e., the home alarm service] adds significant value to what is already an excellent product. We very much have interest in marketing it in this region. The question is: How far does the equity in our brand reach?"[194]

In each of these examples, the utility's market entry was eased by its customer data. Because of the utility's franchised status, the data was acquired from customers involuntarily, and the gathering cost was charged to customers through their rates. To acquire comparable information, new competitors would have to incur major costs—and somehow persuade customers to volunteer their information. Recognizing this entry barrier, the New York Commission directed utilities to make 24 months of usage and load profile data available to competitors, with the customers' consent, at no charge.[195] Similarly, the California Commission ordered the utilities to create a database, consisting of zip codes, rate categories, monthly usage, meter reading dates and billing cycles (without customer names), for use by competitors. There also was an "opt-in" database with confidential information about customer usage, to be released to a competitor except only at a customer's request.[196]

4.C.5.d. Incumbent's name

For a utility with a positive reputation, its name has economic value. Customers associate it with a century of solid service. Adding value is the utility's regulated status, which customers can associate with government endorsement. A utility can leverage this value by creating competitive affiliates having the same name. The name then creates an entry barrier, because newcomers would have to serve for a similar century, or spend many dollars for advertising, in hopes of attaining similar recognition and status.

193.   *Id.*
194.   *Kansas City P&L, Westar Security Ink Marketing Deal For Own, Other Customers,* ENERGY SERVS. & TELECOM REP., July 3, 1997.
195.   *New York Competitive Opportunities Order,* 1997 N.Y. PUC LEXIS 450.
196.   Order Instituting Rulemaking on the Commission's Proposed Policies Governing Restructuring California's Electric Services Industry and Reforming Regulation, Decision No. 97-10-031, 1997 Cal. PUC LEXIS 960 (Cal. Pub. Util. Comm'n Oct. 9, 1997).

Compared to the problems of supplier-switching, monthly billing and customer information, the incumbent's name has proved a harder nut to crack. Prohibiting the affiliate from using the corporate name raises questions under the U.S. Constitution's First Amendment.[197] When a conservation-minded New York Public Service Commission blocked utilities from advertising to promote electricity consumption, the Supreme Court struck the prohibition. The Court outlined a four-part test:

> For commercial speech to come within [the First Amendment's protection], it at least must concern lawful activity and not be misleading. Next, we ask whether the asserted governmental interest is substantial. If both inquiries yield positive answers, we must determine whether the regulation directly advances the governmental interest asserted, and whether it is not more extensive than is necessary to serve that interest.[198]

The Court then applied the four criteria. First, the Commission did not claim that the utility's promotion of its services was misleading or related to unlawful activities. Second, the commission's interests in energy conservation and fair and efficient rates were substantial governmental interests. Third, while the restriction did directly advance the government's interest in energy conservation, the relationship between the ban and rates was too tenuous and speculative. Fourth, the restriction was more extensive than necessary to further the asserted state interest:

> [T]he energy conservation rationale, as important as it is, cannot justify suppressing information about electric devices or services that would cause no net increase in total energy use. In addition, no showing has been made that a more limited restriction on the content of promotional advertising would not serve adequately the State's interests.[199]

While courts routinely organize their analyses of restrictions on commercial speech around the *Central Hudson* test, they have applied the factors differently. The result is an "absence of clearly defined rules for applying each test" and "considerable room for interpretation at almost every state of the analysis process, making predictable outcomes difficult to achieve."[200]

The California Commission recognized the competitive advantage to a utility's affiliate of using the utility's name. To avoid First Amendment problems, the Commission focused on the risks of deception, confusion and unfair competition, arriving at this requirement:

---

197. The First Amendment provides in part: "Congress shall make no law . . . abridging the freedom of speech."
198. Cent. Hudson Gas and Elec. Corp. v. Pub. Serv. Comm'n of N.Y. 447 U.S. 557, 566 (1980).
199. *Id.* at 566–70.
200. 6 James B. Astrachan, et al., The Law of Advertising § 6.01 (2012).

[A] utility shall not trade upon, promote, or advertise its affiliate's affiliation with the utility, nor allow the utility name or logo to be used by the affiliate or in any material circulated by the affiliate, unless it discloses in plain legible or audible language, on the first page or at the first point where the utility name or logo appears that:

- "the affiliate 'is not the same company as [*i.e.*, PG&E, Edison, the Gas Company, etc.] the utility'";
- "the affiliate is not regulated by the California Public Utilities Commission"; and
- "you do not have to buy [the affiliate's] products to continue to receive quality regulated services from the utility."

The application of the name/logo disclaimer is limited to the use of the name or logo in California.[201]

Similar concerns arose around joint marketing by the utility and a competitive affiliate. According to the California Commission:

Joint marketing by a utility and affiliate creates opportunities for cross-subsidization, and also has the strong potential to mislead the consumer, for example, by implying that taking affiliate services is somehow related to the provision of the monopoly utility service. Joint marketing opportunities, especially when coupled with the joint use of a name and logo, will promote customer confusion by allowing affiliates to capitalize on the public perception that their products are closely associated with the regulated utility's.

The Commission therefore adopted this rule:

A utility shall not participate in joint advertising or joint marketing with its affiliates. This prohibition means that utilities may not engage in activities which include, but are not limited to the following:

a.   A utility shall not participate with its affiliates in joint sales calls, through joint call centers or otherwise, or joint proposals (including responses to requests for proposals (RFPs)) to existing or potential customers. At a customer's unsolicited request, a utility may participate, on a non-discriminatory basis, in non-sales meetings with its affiliates or any other market participant to discuss technical or operational subjects regarding the utility's provision of transportation service to the customer;

---

201.   *California Standards*, 1997 Cal. PUC LEXIS 1139 at *84.

b.   Except as otherwise provided for by these Rules, a utility shall not participate in any joint activity with its affiliates. The term "joint activities" includes, but is not limited to, advertising, sales, marketing, communications and correspondence with any existing or potential customer;

c.   A utility shall not participate with its affiliates in trade shows, conferences, or other information or marketing events held in California.[202]

* * *

Authorizing competition does not produce effective competition—not when the incumbent has held a monopoly for a century. The regulatory work begins with defining the goals. Is the purpose of competition lower rates, more innovation, diversity of offerings, improved quality, or all of the above? With goals made clear, policymakers can measure whether competition is working. The next step is unbundling: requiring the incumbent to offer the monopoly and non-monopoly products for sale separately. This step involves (a) establishing non-discriminatory terms and conditions for the monopoly product, and (b) determining how to separate the incumbent's monopoly and competitive activities so as to remove any unearned advantage in the newly competitive markets.

In these efforts, regulatory actions are informed by antitrust principles. Antitrust law itself may be available as a distinct tool, but it has limits. Its purpose is to prevent anti-competitive behavior, not to make markets competitive. Further, antitrust courts do not force incumbents to share their assets when doing so undermines the owner's legitimate business activities. Moreover, while a utility's regulated status does not necessarily insulate utilities from antitrust liability, recent case law has limited antitrust's applicability to regulated industries. Regulators also remain aware that while unbundling lowers entry barriers, it can lead to cost increases and inconveniences if vertical economies are lost.

Even after granting competitors' access to the incumbent's bottleneck facilities, there can be non-physical entry barriers, arising from product promotion advantages, entrenched customer preferences and the incumbent's long-term contracts and its access to customer data. Commissions have developed solutions to some of these barriers, but others, like the incumbent's name recognition, cannot be removed due to First Amendment protection.

These legal and factual questions, over what constitutes effective competition and how to nurture and protect it, are as old as the Supreme Court's 1912 decision in *Terminal Railroad*, and as new as the current debates over the appropriate market structures for broadband and smart grid.

---

202.   *Id.* at *205–06.

CHAPTER FIVE

Monitoring Competition for Anti-competitive Behaviors

[C]ompetition in the unregulated enhanced services market does nothing to decrease the [Bell Operating Companies'] monopoly power in the basic services market . . . . If anything, increased competition in the enhanced services market simply increases the BOCs' incentive to shift costs so they can engage in predatory price-cutting as a means of maintaining or increasing their share of the market for enhanced services.[1]

To convert an historically monopoly market into a competitive market, the first step is to authorize competition, by removing legal barriers to entry. The second step is to make competition effective, by "unbundling" competitive services from noncompetitive services and reducing entry barriers. We addressed those steps in Chapters 3 and 4, respectively. A third step remains: monitoring the new competition.

Monitoring is necessary because market imperfections are inevitable, and because imperfections invite misbehavior. To be perfectly competitive, a market must meet four conditions: standardized products, many sellers and buyers, perfect knowledge by all participants, and no entry barriers.[2] Utility industries undergoing conversion from monopoly to competitive market structures will not meet all these conditions. Consider:

- *Standardized products*: In their physical form, electrons, gas molecules and bits are uniform across sellers, but electricity and gas *services* are not. There are short-term and long-term arrangements, deliveries at different voltages and pressures, varying rate structures and payment plans, and sources with different environmental attributes. Telecommunications services are even more differentiated, with a mind-numbing variety of options for prices, contract term length and customer service quality.

- *Many buyers and sellers*: This factor varies by geographic and product market. In energy, it can vary by time of season and even time of day: On hot August afternoons only a few sellers may have reserve capacity available.

- *Perfect information*: The time necessary to master information about sources, pricing, seller viability and contract terms exceeds what the typical retail customer is

---

1. California v. FCC, 905 F.2d 1217, 1234 (9th Cir. 1990).
2. 2 Alfred Kahn, The Economics of Regulation 114 (1970; 1988); *see also* Darren Bush & Carrie Mayne, *In (Reluctant) Defense of Enron: Why Bad Regulation Is to Blame for California's Power Woes (or Why Antitrust Law Fails to Protect Against Market Power When the Market Rules Encourage Its Use)*, 83 Or. L. Rev. 207, 233–34 (2007) (listing four factors for perfect competition: "(1) [T]he product sold must be uniform across all sellers, or, in other words, consumers are not compelled to choose one producer's output over the other based on product differentiation; (2) there must be many buyers and sellers, such that no one seller's or buyer's actions alone will change the prevailing market price; (3) all agents participating in the market must have perfect information; and (4) no barriers of entry may exist for sellers considering entering the market.") (citations omitted).

willing to invest. Even sophisticated wholesale customers, like municipal electric power systems and local gas distribution companies, often have less information about wholesale markets than the generating companies, pipelines and producers that sell in those markets.

- *No entry barriers*: As illustrated in Chapter 4.C, utility industries have non-physical entry barriers typical of retail markets with a longstanding, dominant player: incumbent branding, advertising costs, customer inertia and long-term contracts.

These imperfections breed misbehavior, such as pricing anti-competitively, tying competitive services to monopoly services, and manipulating market outcomes. (A distinct category of behaviors in developing markets—mergers, acquisitions and other corporate reorganizations—will be discussed in the companion volume.) This Chapter describes these behaviors and the actions regulators take to detect and deter them—if they have the statutory authority.[3] Monitoring also can lead to rethinking, about whether and how to separate the monopolist from its competitive business activities. Examples of such rethinking—and revising policies on separation—close this chapter.

---

3. See, for example, the statutes in New Jersey and Connecticut, which make market monitoring mandatory:

> The board shall monitor the retail supply market in this State, and shall consider information available from the PJM Interconnection . . . with respect to the conduct of electric power suppliers. The board shall monitor proposed acquisitions of electric generating facilities by electric power suppliers as it deems necessary, in order to ascertain whether an electric power supplier has or is proposed to have control over electric generating facilities of sufficient number or strategic location to charge noncompetitive prices to retail customers in this State. The board shall have the authority to deny, suspend or revoke an electric power supplier's license, after hearing, if it determines that an electric power supplier has or may acquire such control, or if the electric power supplier's violations of the rules, regulations or procedures of the PJM Interconnection . . . may adversely affect the reliability of service to retail customers in this State or may result in retail customers being charged noncompetitive prices.

New Jersey Electric Discount and Energy Competition Act, § 29(f), 1999 N.J. Laws 23 (1999) (codified at N.J. Rev. Stat. § 48:3-78).

> Upon complaint or upon its own motion, for cause shown, the department shall conduct an investigation of any possible anti-competitive or discriminatory conduct affecting the retail sale of electricity or any unfair or deceptive trade practices. Such investigations may include, but are not limited to, the effect of mergers, consolidations, acquisition and disposition of assets or securities of electric suppliers, as defined in section 16-1 of the general statutes, as amended by section 1 of this act, or transmission congestion on the proper functioning of a fully competitive market.

Substitute House Bill No. 5005 § 20 (b)(1), 1998 Ct. P.A. 28 (1998) (codified at Conn. Gen. Stat. § 16-245u(b)(1).

5.A. Anti-competitive pricing
5.A.1. Price squeeze

"Price squeeze" is an anti-competitive pricing action by a wholesale seller. It occurs under a unique set of market conditions: The wholesale seller is also a retail seller, competing with its wholesale customer for consumers; and the wholesale customer depends on the wholesale seller for supply. Under these conditions, the wholesale seller has the incentive and opportunity to charge its dependent wholesale customer a discriminatory price designed to damage the wholesale customer's ability to compete at retail.

To digest this mouthful, consider a hypothetical. A distribution-only municipal power system is adjacent to a vertically integrated investor-owned utility (IOU), where the IOU is the municipal's only generation source. These adjacent entities compete for retail customers, in at least three ways: franchise competition (where the investor-owned utility seeks to replace the municipal system as the franchised seller to the municipality's residents); fringe area competition (where state law allows customers near the service territory boundary to choose between adjacent suppliers); and industrial location competition (where the two entities compete to attract industries seeking to locate or expand in the area).[4]

Now consider the IOU's pricing strategy:

1. Assume the retail rate charged by both the municipal system and the investor-owned utility is 7 cents/kWh.

2. Assume (simplistically) that of the municipal system's 7 cent retail price, 1 cent is attributable to the municipal's distribution costs, and 2 cents are attributable to its transmission cost. The remaining 4 cents are attributable to the purchase of power from the IOU.

3. The IOU's strategy is simple: Raise the wholesale price of power to the municipal to a point where the municipal's retail price becomes unattractive relative to the IOU's retail price. Specifically: Raise the wholesale sale price from 4 cents to 5 cents, forcing the municipal to raise its retail price from 7 cents to 8 cents.

4. The municipal's retail price will now be a full 1 cent higher than the investor-owned utility's retail price. Competitively disadvantaged, it is at risk of (a) having its citizens vote to invite the investor-owned utility to replace the municipal as the franchised supplier, and (b) losing industrial customers to fringe area competition or locational competition.

---

4. These types of competition are discussed in Chapter 2.A.2. *See also* Conway Corp. v. Fed. Power Comm'n, 510 F.2d 1264, 1268 (D.C. Cir. 1975) (wholesale competitors "seek to maintain customer satisfaction with the quality and price of their service in order to attract new industries and to retain existing customers"), *aff'd*, 426 U.S. 271 (1976).

Figure 5
Price Squeeze Strategy

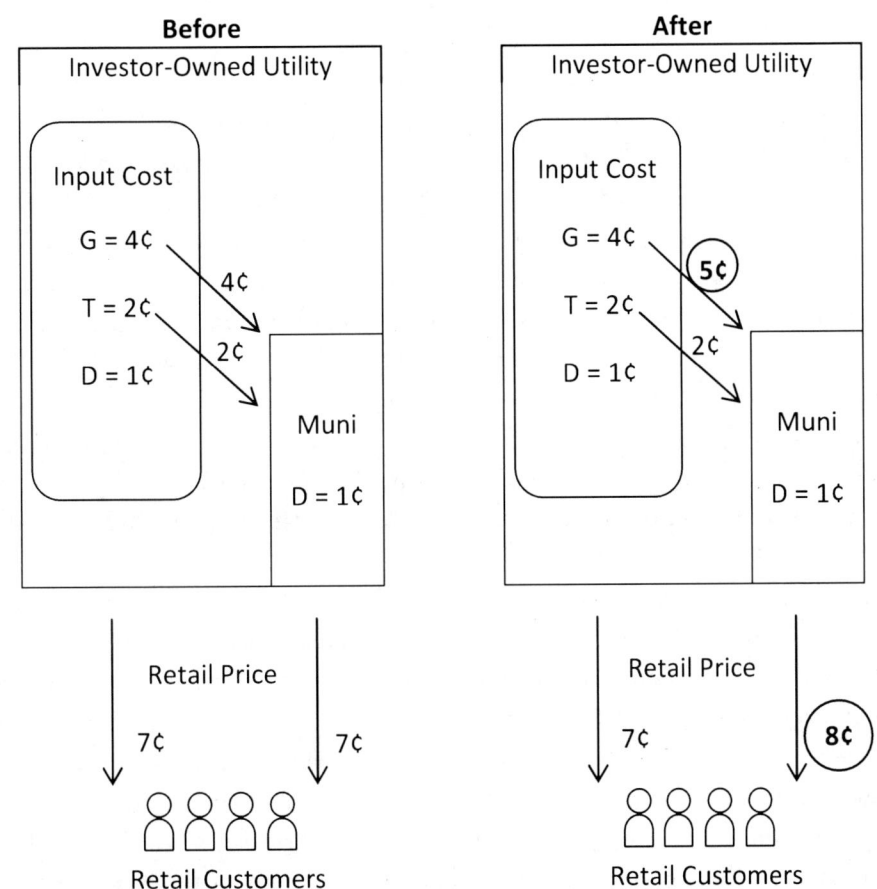

This relationship among vertically integrated utility, distribution-only municipal system, wholesale price and retail price is displayed in Figure 5.

Price squeeze can be intentional or inadvertent (such as when the wholesale seller's retail regulator has set the retail price low). Either way, the squeeze distorts competition in the retail market:

Because of such price discrimination, it becomes difficult for the wholesale customer to pay the wholesale rate and resell the power at rates competitive with its supplier's retail rates. Price discrimination becomes price squeeze when the disparity between wholesale and retail rates causes an anti-competitive effect, *i.e.*, the wholesale customer loses or is likely to lose retail load, thereby squeezing the wholesale customer out of the retail market. Price squeeze may be caused by intentional actions of a wholesale supplier (predatory price squeeze) or by differences between the ratemaking policies and procedures of this Commission and state commissions (regulatory price squeeze).[5]

Whether intentional or inadvertent, a regulator—FERC at least—is obliged by statute to respond. That was the Supreme Court's message in the landmark case of *Federal Power Commission v. Conway Corp.*[6] Gulf States sold retail electricity to its service territory customers, and wholesale electricity to nearby city-owned power systems. The cities and the utility were in competition for industrial retail customers. Gulf States asked the Federal Power Commission for permission to raise its wholesale rate to the city systems. The cities protested, arguing that the new wholesale price, when compared to Gulf States' retail price, would leave them unable to compete. Gulf States' pricing was "an attempt to squeeze [the wholesale Customers] or some of them out of competition and to make them more susceptible to the persistent attempts of [Gulf States] to take over the public[ly] owned systems in the State." Under the Federal Power Act, the Federal Power Commission had to determine whether Gulf States' proposed wholesale rate was "just and reasonable." The cities insisted that the FPC consider the wholesale price's anti-competitive effect, and lower that wholesale rate to reduce that effect. The FPC declined, saying it lacked jurisdiction to consider the wholesale price's anti-competitive effect because the relief—adjusting the wholesale rate based on its relationship to the retail rate—was outside the Commission's wholesale-only jurisdiction.

The Supreme Court saw it differently: The Commission had the jurisdiction and the duty to consider whether the rates it authorized at wholesale had an anti-competitive effect at retail; and if so, to correct the problem. Section 205 of the Federal Power Act prohibits any "unreasonable difference in rates" or service "with respect to any . . . sale subject to the jurisdiction of the Commission." Referring to this provision, the Supreme Court declared:

[A] jurisdictional [i.e., wholesale] sale is necessarily implicated in any charge that the difference between wholesale and retail rates is unreasonable or anti-competitive. If the undue preference or discrimination is in any way traceable to the level of the jurisdictional rate, it is plain enough that the section would to that extent apply; and to that extent

---

5. Southern California Edison Co., 40 FERC ¶ 61,371, at p. 62,151 (1987), *reh'g granted in part*, 50 FERC ¶ 61,275 (1990); *see also* Cities of Anaheim v. FERC, 941 F.2d 1234, 1237 (D.C. Cir. 1991) (describing price squeeze as "an unjustified disparity between a public utility's wholesale and retail electric power rates ('price discrimination') that harms the ability of wholesale customers to compete with the utility in the retail market").
6. 426 U.S. 271 (1976).

the Commission would have power to effect a remedy under sec. 206 by an appropriate order directed to the jurisdictional rate.

Because Gulf States and its city wholesale customers were competing for retail customers, Gulf States' retail rates "are part of the factual context in which the proposed wholesale rate will function." The Commission was obligated to consider that context. The FPC had reasoned that once it set the wholesale rate properly, the blame for any discriminatory or anti-competitive effect was solely with the retail rate, which is outside the Commission's wholesale jurisdiction. The Court again disagreed:

> This argument assumes . . . that ratemaking is an exact science and that there is only one level at which a wholesale rate can be said to be just and reasonable and that any attempt to remedy a discrimination by lowering the jurisdictional rate would always result in an unjustly low rate that would fail to recover fully allocated wholesale costs. . . . [T]here is no single cost-recovering rate, but a zone of reasonableness. . . .

The Court then quoted the Commission's own words from a prior case:

> It occurs to us that one rate in its relation to another rate may be discriminatory, although each rate per se, if considered independently, might fall within the zone of reasonableness. There is considerable latitude within the zone of reasonableness insofar as the level of a particular rate is concerned. The relationship of rates within such a zone, however, may result in an undue advantage in favor of one rate and be discriminatory insofar as another rate is concerned. When such a situation exists, the discrimination found to exist must be removed.[7]

Although regulatory agencies must consider the effects of price squeeze, the practice does not necessarily violate antitrust law. That was the Supreme Court's conclusion in *Pacific*

---

7. *Id.* at 274–78 (quoting Otter Tail Power Co., 2 F.P.C. 134, 149 (1940). Several circuit courts have also recognized that federal–state differences in ratemaking offer dominant sellers opportunities to manipulate prices. *See, e.g.,* City of Anaheim v. S. Cal. Edison Co., 955 F.2d 1373, 1377 (9th Cir. 1992) (describing various courts' hesitance to apply price squeeze theory in regulated settings, but acknowledging that "because the regulatory systems do not work in perfect harmony, it is possible for a utility to manipulate its filings and requests in a manner that causes an, at least temporary, squeeze which might be just as effective as one perpetrated by an unregulated actor"); Cities of Bethany v. FERC, 727 F.2d 1131, 1141 (D.C. Cir. 1984) ("When a utility competes with a wholesale customer in a retail market, FERC presumes anti-competitive effects from a rate disparity that burdens the customer-competitor."); Cities of Mishawaka v. American Electric Power Co., 616 F.2d 976, 983–84 (7th Cir. 1980) (finding that because "wholesale rates under federal control go into effect automatically without agency approval, but the state retail rates must await state approval," this "dual system also offers an obvious, ready made illegal opportunity with a legitimate gloss").

Bell Telephone Co. v. Linkline Communications.[8] Linkline was an independent seller of digital subscriber line (DSL) service. (DSL is a method for connecting to the Internet at high speeds over telephone lines.) Linkline and other independent Internet service providers (ISPs) accused Pacific Bell of practicing price squeeze in the DSL market. Here were the facts:

1.   AT&T (through Pacific Bell) owned the telephone lines necessary to provide DSL service.
2.   Pacific Bell also sold DSL service at retail, in competition with ISPs.
3.   Pacific Bell also sold DSL service at wholesale to ISPs. It had a regulatory obligation (accepted as a condition of an FCC merger approval) to offer this wholesale DSL service at a price no greater than Pacific Bell's retail price.
4.   Pacific Bell raised its wholesale DSL price while cutting its retail DSL price.
5.   The ISPs sued under the Sherman Antitrust Act, alleging price squeeze.

The courts rejected the ISPs' claim. AT&T had no *antitrust law* obligation to provide the wholesale DSL service in the first place; their obligation arose from the FCC condition only. And, "if a firm has no antitrust duty to deal with its competitors at wholesale, it certainly has no duty to deal under terms and conditions that the rivals find commercially advantageous." The Court also did not want to be dragged into rate proceedings. Noting that "[t]he most commonly articulated standard for price squeezes is that the defendant must leave its rivals a 'fair' or 'adequate' margin between the wholesale price and the retail price[,]"[9] it quoted Justice (then Judge) Breyer's summary of the difficulties:

[H]ow is a judge or jury to determine a "fair price?" Is it the price charged by other suppliers of the primary product? None exist. Is it the price that competition 'would have set' were the primary level not monopolized? How can the court determine this price without examining costs and demands, indeed without acting like a rate-setting regulatory agency, the rate-setting proceedings of which often last for several years? Further, how is the court to decide the proper size of the price 'gap?' Must it be large enough for all independent competing firms to make a 'living profit,' no matter how inefficient they may be? . . . And how should the court respond when costs or demands change over time, as they inevitably will?[10]

---

8.   555 U.S. 438 (2009).
9.   *Id.* at 440, 448 and n.2 (citing Verizon Commc'ns, Inc. v. Law Offices of Curtis V. Trinko, LLP, 540 U.S. 398, 410 (2004) (discussed in Chapter 4.B.2.a above)). The *Pacific Bell* Court also found that "the market for high-speed Internet service is now quite competitive; DSL providers face stiff competition from cable companies and wireless and satellite providers."
10.   *Id.* at 454 (quoting Concord v. Boston Edison Co., 915 F.2d 17, 25 (1st Cir. 1990)); *see also Concord,*

* * *

In our context of converting a monopoly market to a competitive market, price squeeze problems can arise where the incumbent monopoly controls a wholesale resource essential to its retail competitor. The incumbent will have incentive and opportunity to price its monopoly inputs to damage its competitors. This action might not violate antitrust laws (*Pacific Bell v. Linkline*), but it can undermine the regulator's competitive efforts. Alertness to the problem, and statutory authority to fix it (as the *Conway* Court read into the Federal Power Act), are necessary.

5.A.2. Predatory pricing

Predatory pricing is "pricing below an appropriate measure of cost for the purpose of eliminating competitors in the short run and reducing competition in the long run."[11] To violate antitrust law, predatory pricing must meet two conditions:

1. The prices are "below an appropriate measure of its rival's costs." The "appropriate measure" is much debated. As long as the price exceeds seller's cost ("appropriate[ly] measure[d]"), there is no valid antitrust claim merely because the challenged price is below general market levels or below the costs of the firm's competitors. In those situations, the price's competitor-defeating effect "either reflects the lower cost structure of the alleged predator, and so represents competition on the merits, or is beyond the practical ability of a judicial tribunal to control without courting intolerable risks of chilling legitimate price cutting." The Court warned:

> Even in an oligopolistic market, when a firm drops its prices to a competitive level to demonstrate to a maverick the unprofitability of straying from the group, it would be illogical to condemn the price cut: The antitrust laws then would be an obstacle to the chain of events most conducive to a breakdown of oligopoly pricing and the onset of competition. Even if the ultimate effect of the cut is to induce or reestablish supracompetitive pricing, discouraging a price cut and forcing firms to maintain supracompetitive prices, thus depriving consumers of the benefits of lower prices in the interim, does not constitute sound antitrust policy.[12]

---

915 F.2d at 25 ("[A]ntitrust courts normally avoid direct price administration, relying on rules and remedies . . . that are easier to administer.")).

11.   Cargill, Inc. v. Monfort of Colo., Inc., 479 U.S. 104, 117–18 n.12 (1986); *see also* Brooke Grp. v. Brown & Williamson Tobacco, 509 U.S. 209, 222 (1993) (predatory pricing occurs when "[a] business rival has priced its products in an unfair manner with an object to eliminate or retard competition and thereby gain and exercise control over prices in the relevant market").

12.   *Brooke Group*, 509 U.S. at 222–24 and n.1 (citing numerous cases creating a conflict among lower courts over the appropriate measure of costs). *Id.* at 223–24 (citing other sources).

2. *"[T]he competitor had a reasonable prospect, or, . . . a dangerous probability, of recouping its investment in below-cost prices."* The Court distinguished consumer-harmful predation from consumer-helpful price-cutting: "Recoupment is the ultimate object of an unlawful predatory pricing scheme; it is the means by which a predator profits from predation. Without it, predatory pricing produces lower aggregate prices in the market, and consumer welfare is enhanced."[13] But proving the likelihood of recoupment is no simple matter. The plaintiff first needs to show that, "given the aggregate losses caused by the below-cost pricing, the intended target would likely succumb," thus enabling the predator, potentially, to raise its prices to recover its prior loss. The target's departure, however, would not by itself enable recoupment: New competitors might enter, or other competitors might remain, the latter having survived the predator's price cutting by becoming more efficient. If so, the original price cut would have benefited consumers and the predator's strategy would have failed, making it non-predatory. A plaintiff therefore needs also to show that the predation

> would cause a rise in prices above a competitive level that would be sufficient to compensate for the amounts expended on the predation, including the time value of the money invested in it. As we have observed on a prior occasion, "in order to recoup their losses, [predators] must obtain enough market power to set higher than competitive prices, and then must sustain those prices long enough to earn in excess profits what they earlier gave up in below-cost prices."[14]

In short, courts are tough on predation plaintiffs. The judicial standards "are not artificial obstacles to recovery; rather, they are essential components of real market injury. . . . It would be ironic indeed if the standards for predatory pricing liability were so low that antitrust suits themselves became a tool for keeping prices high."[15]

But the limits on antitrust do not confine regulation. Antitrust law aims at anti-competitive behavior in markets as they exist; it does not purport to convert historically monopoly markets into competitive markets. In contrast, regulatory law, particularly its prohibition against "undue preference," authorizes regulators to take actions to inject competition.[16] When applying substantive regulatory law, courts and commissions have more flexibility to act against predatory pricing, so as to protect and nurture competition in transitional markets.

---

13. *Id.* at 224.
14. *Brooke Group*, 509 U.S. at 225–27 (quoting Matsushita Elec. Indus. Co. v. Zenith Radio Corp., 475 U.S. 574, 590–91 (1986)).
15. *Id.*
16. See Chapter 4.B.3 for more explanation of, and references on, this point.

Telecommunications presents an example. In its *First Computer Inquiry (Computer I)*,[17] the FCC required all telephone carriers with revenues exceeding $1 million to use "corporate separation" to separate their "basic" from "enhanced" services.[18] In its *Second Computer Inquiry (Computer II)*,[19] the FCC maintained structural separation, but restricted it to members of the Bell System. In its *Third Computer Inquiry (Computer III)*,[20] the FCC eliminated the structural separation requirement entirely, in favor of (a) cost accounting regulations, requiring the companies to separate competitive from noncompetitive costs on their books; and (b) behavioral requirements, primarily requirements for open network architecture (ONA) and comparably efficient interconnection (CEI).[21]

Challengers to *Computer III* argued that without structural, that is, corporate, separation, the RBOCs could engage in predatory pricing—using their monopoly profits from "basic services" to subsidize predatory prices for enhanced services.[22] The Commission rejected this concern, stating that the market for enhanced services was "extremely competitive." The Court of Appeals found the FCC's response illogical:

> The Commission does not explain how the fact that the enhanced services market is "extremely competitive" reduces the BOCs' [Bell Operating Companies'] ability to cross-subsidize their unregulated enhanced services businesses by misallocating costs to their regulated activities. The BOCs' ability to shift costs derives from the fact that they are monopoly providers of basic telephone service. Because competition in the unregulated enhanced services market does nothing to decrease the BOCs'

---

17. Regulatory and Policy Problems Presented by the Interdependence of Computer Services and Facilities, Final Decision and Order, 28 F.C.C.2d 267 (Mar. 18, 1971) (*Computer I* Final Decision), *aff'd in part and rev'd in part*, GTE Serv. Corp. v. FCC, 474 F.2d 724 (2d Cir. 1973).

18. See Chapter 4.B.5 for a discussion of forms of separation. The terms "basic" and "enhanced" were, at the time, the telecommunications world's rough synonyms for monopoly regulated services and competitive new services, or POTS and PANS—"plain old telephone service" and "pretty amazing new stuff."

19. Amendment of Section 64.702 of the Commission's Rules and Regulations, 77 F.C.C.2d 384, 420 (1980) (*Computer II* Final Decision), on reconsideration, 84 F.C.C.2d 50 (Apr. 7, 1980) (*Computer II* Reconsidered Decision); 88 F.C.C.2d 512 (Oct. 7, 1981) (*Computer II* Further Reconsidered Decision), *aff'd*, Computer & Commc'ns Indus. Ass'n v. FCC, 693 F.2d 198 (D.C. Cir. 1982), *cert. denied*, 461 U.S. 938 (1983).

20. Amendment of Sections 64.702 of the Commission's Rules and Regulations, 104 F.C.C.2d 958 (May 15, 1986) (Phase I Order), on reconsideration, 2 FCC Rcd. 3,035 (Mar. 26, 1987) (Phase I Reconsideration); 2 FCC Rcd. 3072 (Mar. 26, 1987) (Phase II Order) (in addition to various other orders on reconsideration).

21. Open network architecture required ILECs to unbundle the basic service elements of their local networks. *See* PETER W. HUBER ET AL., FEDERAL TELECOMMUNICATIONS LAW § 12.5.2, nn.133–35 & sources cited therein (2d ed. Supp. 2013). The *Computer III* ONA requirements were eventually codified (in modified form) in Section 251, added by the 1996 Act. Comparably efficient interconnection required ILECs to provide to competing information service providers interconnection to the ILECs' facilities that was technically comparable to that which the ILEC provided to its own information service operation, and at the same rates. *See id.* § 12.5.2, nn.136–38 & sources cited therein.

22. The distinction between corporate separation and accounting separation will be treated in the companion volume, concerning corporate structure.

monopoly power in the basic services market, we fail to see how it can diminish the BOCs' ability to shift costs to their regulated services without detection in ratemaking proceedings. If anything, increased competition in the enhanced services market simply increases the BOCs' incentive to shift costs so they can engage in predatory price-cutting as a means of maintaining or increasing their share of the market for enhanced services.

The Court invalidated the FCC's elimination of structural separation as "arbitrary and capricious."[23]

The point is that regulatory commissions, using their statutory authority to ensure that rates are "just and reasonable" and that utilities do not practice "undue preference," can consider the risk of predatory pricing without meeting the more stringent (and still debated) standards of antitrust law.

5.B. Tying
5.B.1. Definition and examples

Tying occurs when a seller of Product X requires its buyer to buy the seller's Product Y. If the seller has a monopoly over Product X (the tying product), then the buyer has no choice but to buy the seller's Product Y (the tied product). The practice then undermines competition in the tied product market:

> The essential characteristic of an invalid tying arrangement lies in the seller's exploitation of its control over the tying product to force the buyer into the purchase of a tied product that the buyer either did not want at all, or might have preferred to purchase elsewhere on different terms. When such forcing is present, competition on the merits in the market for the tied item is restrained and the Sherman Act is violated.[24]

Tying is a "per se" violation of antitrust law—monopolizing barred by the Sherman Act—if four factors are present: "(1) the tying and tied goods are two separate products; (2) the defendant has market power in the tying product market; (3) the defendant affords consumers no choice but to purchase the tied product from it; and (4) the tying arrangement forecloses a substantial volume of commerce."[25]

Tying is not always anti-competitive. It can be pro-competitive and pro-consumer if grounded in efficiencies.[26] By reducing production and transaction costs, tying induces

---

23. California v. FCC, 905 F.2d 1217, 1234, 1238 (9th Cir. 1990). As noted in Chapter 3.A.3, however, on remand the FCC successfully justified and re-imposed its *Computer III* nonstructural safeguards.
24. Jefferson Parish Hosp. Dist. No. 2 v. Hyde, 466 U.S. 2, 12 (1984).
25. United States v. Microsoft Corp., 253 F.3d 34, 85 (D.C. Cir. 2001).
26. *See* 9 PHILLIP E. AREEDA & HERBERT HOVENKAMP, ANTITRUST LAW ¶ 1703g, at 51–53 (2d ed. 2000).

competitors to bring consumers more convenience at lower prices. As long as neither product is a monopoly product, there is no harm to competition: "[I]f one of a dozen food stores in a community were to refuse to sell flour unless the buyer also took sugar it would hardly tend to restrain competition in sugar if its competitors were ready and able to sell flour by itself."[27]

The key distinction between lawful and unlawful tying is whether "forcing is present." The plaintiff must prove market power in the tying market.[28] In *Jefferson Parish Hospital District No. 2 v. Hyde*,[29] the tying product was a hospital's surgeries, while the tied product was anesthesiology services. The hospital had an exclusive contract with an anesthesiology firm. Any patient having surgery at the hospital had to use an anesthesiologist supplied by the firm. When an unaffiliated anesthesiologist was denied hospital privileges, he challenged the arrangement as illegal tying. The Supreme Court held for the hospital. There was no showing that the hospital had market power in the surgery market sufficient to force patients to use the hospital's anesthesiologist firm; they were free to seek surgeries at other hospitals. (And they did—seventy percent of patients living in the parish went to other hospitals.)[30]

Turning to regulated utilities: discussing "unbundling," Chapter 4.B provided several examples of tying and the regulatory responses. FERC's Order No. 888 "untied" generation from transmission. No longer can a transmission-owning utility force customers needing transmission service (the tying product) to buy the utility's generation service (the tied product). The Telecommunications Act of 1996 sought to untie retail local telephone service from the incumbent's control of the "last mile," by allowing customers to buy local and long-distance services from competitive local exchange companies who purchased access to the last mile. FERC's Order No. 636 untied natural gas sales from pipeline transportation service. States that introduced retail competition in gas and electricity untied energy sales from the incumbent's control of monopoly distribution facilities. Unbundling, then, is the regulatory response to a monopoly utility's ability to tie.[31]

---

27. *Jefferson Parish*, 466 U.S. at 12 (quoting N. Pac. Ry. Co. v. United States, 356 U.S. 1, 7 (1958) (internal quotation marks omitted)).
28. *See* Ill. Tool Works v. Indep. Ink, 547 U.S. 28, 44 (2006) (tying the sale of non-patented ink to a patented ink jet print-head is not necessarily illegal tying because "a patent does not necessarily confer market power").
29. 466 U.S. 2, 12 (1984).
30. *Id.* at 26.
31. Tying was the claim when the U.S. Department of Justice sued the City of Stilwell, Oklahoma. The City was the sole supplier of public water and sewer services to premises in the city area. In 1985 it initiated an all-or-none utility policy, refusing to extend or connect water or sewer lines to premises unless the developer, owner or occupant also agreed to purchase electric service from the City's Utility Department. A consent agreement prohibits Stillwell from tying the utility services to the water and sewer services, or discriminating or retaliating against customers who do not purchase both services. United States v. City of Stilwell, No. CIV 96-196-B (E.D. Okla. Nov. 5,1998), *available at* http://www.justice.gov/atr/cases/stilwe0.htm.

5.B.2. "Technology tying" in utility industries

Technological advances are introducing knotty problems in the tying context. Professors Kranz and Picot, introduced in Chapter 4.B.7, have described new product and service opportunities made possible by "smart grid." But they also emphasized the risk that an incumbent electricity or telecommunications company could use its control of essential facilities to exclude competitors from nascent product markets. These actions can take the form of tying, where the incumbent says—

1.   to retail customers: "If you want electricity delivered over my distribution lines you have to buy my meter";
2.   to meter providers: "If you want me to connect your meter you must let me have exclusive access to your data"; or
3.   to marketers of new products: "If you want access to the customer's data you must let me own your technology."

Similar concerns are presented in the transition to broadband. The provider of broadband transmission can integrate web applications or other services with broadband service, integrating meaning forcing the customer to buy the web applications if they want broadband. Its customers then would be less likely to buy the web applications or services from third parties.[32]

Compounding the risks to competition in developing product markets is the practice of "technology tying": "where a firm designs a product so that it functions only when used with a complementary product."[33] An early example (likely to cause pleasant memories for readers of a certain age) was the Nintendo Entertainment System (NES). The operating system (including hardware) was the tying product and the game software was the tied product. As described in an FTC staff paper:

> When Nintendo introduced the NES to the U.S. in 1986, the system's hardware component included the 10-NES security chip whose only function was to prevent non-Nintendo authorized games from being used with the Nintendo hardware. This security chip was a technological tie that permitted Nintendo to generate additional system revenue through sales of the Nintendo System's software component.[34]

---

32.   Indeed, broadband Internet access provided by facilities-based carriers and cable operators has rendered standalone, non-carrier dial-up ISPs like AOL and CompuServe largely obsolete.
33.   Sarita Frattaroli, Note, *Dodging The Bullet Again: Microsoft III's Reformulation of the Foremost Technological Tying Doctrine*, 90 B.U.L. Rev. 1909, 1916–17 (2010) (citing Daniel E. Gaynor, *Technological Tying* 1 (FTC Bureau of Econ., Working Paper No. 284, 2006), *available at* http://www.ftc.gov/be/work-papers/wp284.pdf.
34.   *Id.*

Then there was Microsoft's Windows operating system (the tying product) and its Internet Explorer (the tied product). Microsoft bundled the two products under a single price; anyone buying the operating system was also buying the browser.[35] Among the issues was whether to apply the "rule of reason" test or the "per se" test.[36] The Supreme Court has warned that "it is only after considerable experience with certain business relationships that courts classify them as per se violations."[37] The court of appeals in *Microsoft* therefore used the rule of reason, reversing the trial court (which had applied the per se rule). The court reasoned that Microsoft's Windows-Internet Explorer tie

> offer[ed] the first up-close look at the technological integration of added functionality into software that serves as a platform for third-party applications. . . . There being no close parallel in prior antitrust cases, simplistic application of per se tying rules carries a serious risk of harm.[38]

One reason for the judicial caution imposed by rule of reason analysis is that technology tying can be pro-competitive. Given "the pervasively innovative character of platform software markets, tying in such markets may produce efficiencies that courts have not previously encountered."[39] As one author has explained:

> Many technology products run on a common platform. The more individuals that buy that particular platform, the more products will be produced and available to the consumer. Technology markets therefore have network effects, where the value of a product to an individual consumer increases with the number of consumers that adopt that same product. The integration of two products may provide other efficiency benefits, such as convenience to the consumer or increased functionality. Given rapid innovation and shifting understanding of consumer preferences in the

---

35. *See* U.S. v. Microsoft Corp., 253 F.3d 34, 84–85 (D.C. Cir. 2001).
36. The "rule of reason" analysis balances pro-competitive benefit against anti-competitive harm; the "per se" rule finds an antitrust violation based on the act alone. *See* Phillip E. Areeda & Herbert Hovenkamp, Antitrust Law ¶¶ 1500–1512 (3d ed. 2006).
37. Broadway Music, Inc. v. CBS, 441 U.S. 1, 9 (1979) (quoting United States v. Topco Assocs., 405 U.S. 596, 607–08 (1972)).
38. *Microsoft Corp.*, 253 F.3d at 84 (quoting earlier cases); *see also id.* at 95 ("[P]laintiffs must show that Microsoft's conduct was, on balance, anti-competitive. Microsoft may of course offer pro-competitive justifications, and it is plaintiffs' burden to show that the anti-competitive effect of the conduct outweighs its benefit."); *id.* at 93 (explaining that "[t]he ubiquity of bundling in competitive platform software markets should give courts reason to pause before condemning such behavior in less competitive markets."). The court of appeals did uphold the trial court's finding that Microsoft had monopoly power in the tying product market (i.e., the operating system), but that finding alone did not make the tying unlawful.
39. *Id.* at 93.

technology industry, technological integration may be particularly likely to foster efficiencies and increase consumer welfare.[40]

In sum: the combination of antitrust tolerance, factual complexity and rapid technological change will require regulatory attention, but not necessarily regulatory intervention.[41]

5.C. Market manipulation

Imperfect markets invite manipulation by sellers who have, or want, market power. Wholesale energy markets offer an illustration. Their imperfections, or potential to acquire imperfections, are not disputed. Consider this list:

1. "[E]nergy is not storable. Thus, market power in electricity has a temporal element not found in many other industries, where inventories may be able to limit the exercise of market power."

2. "[D]emand in electricity markets has been virtually inelastic, at least thus far. Therefore, market power is not limited by consumer reaction, as it typically is in other industries."

3. "[M]arket power can be exercised in numerous ways in electricity markets. For example, market power can be exercised by withholding capacity or by raising the price at which the capacity is offered for sale."

4. "[M]arket power may be enhanced in electricity markets because supply response may be limited. This is especially true during peak hours, when demand is high and all available alternative resources may already be on-line."

5. "[N]ot all generation plants are created equally. Generation plants all have different heat rates and fuel costs, and because of these differences in efficiency levels their marginal costs are different. Withholding of a generation plant, therefore, may increase the price of electricity as the next highest-cost generator is brought on-line to replace it."

6. "[S]ome power plants have 'locational market power' because they are necessary in order to assure system stability. A plant with locational market power may be called upon to run to assure voltage stability or to assure adequate transmission capacity (e.g., because the plant provides counterflow)."[42]

---

40. Frattaroli, *supra* note 33, at 1917.
41. Along with rethinking current statutory authority. In the telecommunications area, guidance may emerge when the courts decide the challenges to the FCC's authority to issue open Internet rules. *See supra* Chapter 4.B.7.a.
42. Bush & Mayne, *supra* note 2, at 256–57 (2007).

Three other common imperfections, some overlapping with the foregoing, are: (a) In particular combinations of season, time of day and location, demand can exceed supply due to transmission or generation shortages; (b) retail utilities are able to recover wholesale price increases from their captive customers, and therefore have weak incentives—absent regulatory pressures—to bargain prices down; and (c) state-set retail prices are usually based on average annual costs, rather than actual hourly costs. (Average costs mask the actual wholesale hourly (variable) costs, causing customers to demand and buy more than they would if they faced an hourly price reflecting hourly cost. Only when they receive their monthly bill do they learn how much their consumption cost them.)

These conditions can lead to a form of market manipulation known as "withholding," both physical and economic. Here is how it works. In an organized wholesale energy market, sellers submit, a day ahead, hourly bids stating the quantity they are willing to sell at the price they require. The wholesale buyers are retail utilities (known as "load-serving entities"); they state, also a day ahead for each hour, the quantities they need to buy to serve their obligatory load. The market administrator runs a computer that selects sellers in merit order (lowest price first), until the quantity selected equals the quantity the buying utilities need. The market price—the price that all sellers receive, regardless of their bid price—is the price bid by the last selected seller, that is, the selected seller with the highest price. In physical withholding, a seller withholds some of his generation capacity from the market. Doing so moves the bid stake up one notch, raising the market clearing price. The withholding seller hopes that this higher price increases the profits earned by his other generation by more than the profits forgone from withholding generation. In economic withholding, the seller bids a price above his marginal cost, risking non-selection[43] but again hoping that the resulting shortage drives up the price received by his non-withheld generation.[44]

---

43.   Economic theory holds that a rational, non-manipulating seller facing competitive pressure will bid a price equal to his marginal cost—the additional cost of producing one more unit. The logic is simple: If he bids a price less than his marginal cost, he loses money on every sale. If he bids a price more than his marginal cost, he risks losing the sale, to a competitor who bids a lower price.

44.   Withholding will be profitable when "the percentage increase in price received by the supplier exceeds the percentage decrease in quantity of units sold by the supplier." New York Independent System Operator, 122 FERC ¶ 61,211, P 20, 2008 FERC LEXIS 483 (citing market monitor's explanation). To block physical and economic withholding, FERC has imposed "must offer" obligations and "offer caps," respectively. *See, e.g., id.* at ¶ 21. For a detailed (and depressing) description of types of market manipulation, see *Final Report on Price Manipulation In Western Markets, Fact-Finding Investigation of Potential Manipulation of Electric and Natural Gas Prices,* Dkt. No. PA02-2-000 (March 2003), *available at* www.ferc.gov/legal/maj-ord-reg/land-docs/PART-I-3-26-03.pdf. While this FERC Staff Report focused on the California market crisis of 2000–2001, it describes types of seller manipulation that are possible in other organized markets. In addition to physical and economic withholding, the Staff Report describes pipeline-generation manipulation, artificial congestion, megawatt laundering (also known as "Ricochet" and "round trip trading"), and churning.

5.D. Rethinking separation

Chapters 3, 4, and 5 have addressed the prerequisites for bringing competition successfully to formerly monopoly markets. Policymakers first must define the rights and responsibilities of the incumbents and their new competitors (Chapter 3), then remove or reduce the incumbents' unearned advantages (Chapter 4). Reducing incumbents' unearned advantages involves both (a) unbundling (non-discriminatory access at non-discriminatory, compensatory rates, and some form of structural separation); and (b) reducing other entry barriers. This Chapter 5 has focused on the need to monitor the new markets, because their inevitable imperfections allow such misbehaviors as anti-competitive pricing, tying and market manipulation.

A key factor making immature markets vulnerable to misbehavior, and justifying continued regulatory involvement, has been the market presence of incumbents—specifically, incumbents that simultaneously provide the new competitive services and the traditional non-competitive services. In the early days of competition, policymakers sought to separate these services, in the three ways discussed in Chapter 4.B.5: divisional separation, corporate separation, and divestiture. Market monitoring has led some policymakers to revise their prior separation decisions, sometimes for different reasons. Some have determined that competition is sufficiently vigorous that allowing the separated functions to reintegrate will increase efficiencies without harming competition. Others have decided that competition is sufficiently uneven that reintegration, and a return to dependence on the local monopoly, is their best protection. These two different reactions are discussed next.

5.D.1. Sufficient competition scenario

A regulator orders separation based on this factual premise: An incumbent selling in both the monopoly and competitive markets will use its monopoly to discriminate against competitors. But facts can change. If access to the bottleneck facility becomes non-discriminatory in fact (and not merely on paper); if the former bottleneck becomes a non-bottleneck because competitors can replicate it economically; if other entry barriers have lowered, allowing competitors to enter and thrive; if there is no evidence of anti-competitive pricing, tying, or market manipulation; if one or more of these factors exists, then the case for separation weakens. This possibility has been recognized in federal statutes addressing telecommunications, electricity, and gas.

Telecommunications: Recall that the Modification of Final Judgment (MFJ) barred the Regional Bell Operating Companies (RBOCs) from entering the newly competitive long-distance markets.[45] With divestiture, the RBOCs no longer could use their lawful

---

45.   As explained in Chapter 3.A.3, the MFJ was a consent decree settling the U.S. Government's antitrust suit against AT&T. It required AT&T to divest its local exchange carrier subsidiaries from the rest of AT&T (including its long-distance service and CPE subsidiaries). The divestiture made AT&T solely

monopolies over the "last mile" to (a) deny independent long-distance companies the interconnection services needed to connect to local telephone customers, or (b) allocate the costs of competitive long-distance service to customers of monopoly local telephone service, gaining an unfair competitive advantage in the long-distance market. But the MFJ recognized that facts could change. It described the probability that

> over time, the Operating Companies will lose the ability to leverage their monopoly power into the competitive markets from which they must now be barred. This change could occur as a result of technological developments which eliminate the Operating Companies' local exchange monopoly or from changes in the structure of the competitive markets. Thus, a restriction [in the MFJ] will be removed upon a showing that there is no substantial possibility that an Operating Company could use its monopoly power to impede competition in the relevant market.[46]

Congress came to the same conclusion. The 1996 Act therefore provided a path for the RBOCs' reentry into competitive long-distance markets. Section 271(b)(2) of the Communications Act of 1934 (as amended by the 1996 Act) allowed the RBOCs to provide long-distance service to customers located outside their regions. Section 271(c)(2)(B) allowed an RBOC to provide long-distance service to customers within their regions, if the FCC found them in compliance with the 14-point "Competition Checklist." The Checklist reflects the market characteristics necessary to prevent the RBOCs from using a dominant position in the local telephone service to gain an unearned

---

a long-distance, CPE and data-processing company. The divested local exchange carriers were limited to providing local telephone service. United States v. AT&T, 552 F. Supp. 131 (D.D.C. 1982), *aff'd sub nom.* Maryland v. United States, 460 U.S. 1001 (1983).

46. United States v. AT&T, 552 F. Supp. at 194–95.

advantage in long-distance markets.[47] All RBOCs have now been authorized to enter the long-distance market.[48]

Electricity and gas: The federal Public Utility Holding Company Act of 1935 (PUHCA) limited each electric and gas holding company to a single "integrated public-utility system."[49] In the 1980s and 1990s, utilities seeking PUHCA's repeal emphasized that (a) the emerging wholesale competition in electric generation would protect against incumbents' monopolistic expansion; and (b) by allowing incumbents to enter new geographic markets, repeal would increase competition.[50] These arguments eventually prevailed, leading to PUHCA's

---

47.   The 14 checklist items in 47 U.S.C. § 271(c)(2)(B) are:

    (i) Interconnection in accordance with the requirements of sections 251(c)(2) and 252(d)(1).
    (ii) Non-discriminatory access to network elements in accordance with the requirements of sections 251(c)(3) and 252(d)(1).
    (iii) Non-discriminatory access to the poles, ducts, conduits, and rights-of-way owned or controlled by the Bell operating company at just and reasonable rates in accordance with the requirements of section 224.
    (iv) Local loop transmission from the central office to the customer's premises, unbundled from local switching or other services.
    (v) Local transport from the trunk side of a wireline local exchange carrier switch unbundled from switching or other services.
    (vi) Local switching unbundled from transport, local loop transmission, or other services.
    (vii) Non-discriminatory access to—
        (I) 911 and E911 services;
        (II) directory assistance services to allow the other carrier's customers to obtain telephone numbers; and
        (III) operator call completion services.
    (viii) White pages directory listings for customers of the other carrier's telephone exchange service.
    (ix) Until the date by which telecommunications numbering administration guidelines, plan, or rules are established, non-discriminatory access to telephone numbers for assignment to the other carrier's telephone exchange service customers. After that date, compliance with such guidelines, plan, or rules.
    (x) Non-discriminatory access to databases and associated signaling necessary for call routing and completion.
    (xi) Until the date by which the Commission issues regulations pursuant to section 251 to require number portability, interim telecommunications number portability through remote call forwarding, direct inward dialing trunks, or other comparable arrangements, with as little impairment of functioning, quality, reliability, and convenience as possible. After that date, full compliance with such regulations.
    (xii) Non-discriminatory access to such services or information as are necessary to allow the requesting carrier to implement local dialing parity in accordance with the requirements of section 251(b)(3).
    (xiii) Reciprocal compensation arrangements in accordance with the requirements of section 252(d)(2).
    (xiv) Telecommunications services are available for resale in accordance with the requirements of sections 251(c)(4) and 252(d)(3).

48.   *See, e.g.,* BellSouth Corp., 13 FCC Rcd. 20,599 (1998).
49.   We introduced PUHCA in Chapter 3.A.1. We will return to that Act in the companion volume on corporate structure, mergers and acquisitions.
50.   The Public Utility Regulatory Policies Act of 1978 exempted "qualifying facilities" from PUHCA. Then the Energy Policy Act of 1992 created a category of "exempt wholesale generators" that also were exempt from PUHCA. The EWGs did not have to meet PURPA's renewable energy or cogeneration requirements; but they did not have the QFs' right to require a host utility to buy their output. *See supra* Chapter 3.A.1.

repeal in 2005. But unlike the 1996 Telecommunications Act, which required an RBOC to prove that it had taken the prescribed steps to open its local telephone service market to competition before it could reenter long-distance markets, PUHCA's repeal allowed utilities to enter all markets without federal review.[51]

The point: In all three of these industries, then, policymakers removed prior bans on simultaneous ownership of monopoly and competitive businesses, on the theory that more competition would result. But as discussed next, some policymakers have moved in the opposite direction, on the grounds that sufficient competition did not result.

5.D.2. Insufficient competition scenario

When a retail electric utility divests its generation, it depends for its power supply on wholesale markets. If those markets are competitive and efficient, customers benefit. But where these markets are non-competitive or inefficient—or perceived as such—states that previously ordered or approved divestiture rethink their decisions. States have responded to these risks in different ways.

In the late 1990s, California's utilities had divested much of their generation. In summer 2000, California residents faced volatile wholesale prices. The Legislature then prohibited any further generation divestiture at least until 2006.[52] Some states have pressed their previously divested utilities to become generation owners again. Other states, such as Ohio, Illinois and the District of Columbia, manage their wholesale market risks directly, by overseeing their utilities' procurement of power at wholesale.[53]

In a variant of state-managed procurement, New Jersey (by statute) and Maryland (by Commission order) have sought to influence the wholesale market price by creating state-guaranteed revenue floors for selected generation bidders. Each state runs a process with these steps:

---

51. There remain some federal reviews for certain mergers and acquisitions under Section 203 of the Federal Power Act. Moreover, the federal repeal does not preclude states from conducting their own reviews. We will discuss these issues in the companion volume on corporate structure, mergers and acquisitions.

52. *See* Cal. Pub. Util. Code § 273 (providing, in part: "Notwithstanding any other provision of law, no facility for the generation of electricity owned by a public utility may be disposed of prior to January 1, 2006. The commission shall ensure that public utility generation assets remain dedicated to service for the benefit of California ratepayers.")

53. *See* Ohio Edison Co., No. 12-1230-EL-SSO, 299 P.U.R.4th 1 (July 18, 2012) (authorizing a process in which the Commission approves the utility's request for proposals, and then a commission-appointed auction manager selects the winner (subject to a Commission veto within 48 hours); Illinois Public Utilities Act, 220 Ill. Comp. Stat. 5/16-111.5 (detailing generation procurement process, including roles for "procurement administrator" and "procurement monitor," the latter retained by the Commission); D.C. Mun. Regs. tit. 15 § 4101 (establishing procedures for utilities' competitive procurement of wholesale power).

(a)   The retail utilities select generation suppliers through an auction.

(b)   Each selected generation owner will receive for its capacity and energy a utility-guaranteed price high enough to attract generation sellers. The utility's payments to the generators are recoverable from its retail customers through rates set by the state commission.

(c)   Each selected generation bidder is required to bid its capacity and energy into the organized PJM wholesale market.[54]

The state-guaranteed revenue stream enables the generators to bid a price lower than normal. A lower-than-normal bid lowers the stack of chosen bidders, so that the last chosen bidder is a seller with a lower price bid than would be the case absent the state-assisted lower-than-normal bid. The result is a lower "market clearing" price.[55]

FERC has expressed concern that these actions might benefit the acting states in the short run but undermine wholesale competition in the long run.[56] To discourage artificial bids, FERC has established a "minimum offer price rule" (MOPR) explaining:

> A capacity market will not be able to produce the needed investment to serve load and reliability if a subset of suppliers is allowed to bid noncompetitively to suppress market clearing prices. . . . The lower prices that would result [if we eliminated the MOPR] would undermine the market's ability to attract needed investment over time. Although capacity prices might be lower in the short run, in the long run, such a strategy will not attract sufficient private investment to maintain reliability. The MOPR does not punish load, but maintains a role for private investment so that investment risk will not be shifted to captive customers over time.[57]

* * *

The regulatory work to make markets work is continuous. Once competition is authorized, once competitive services are unbundled from monopoly services, once entry barriers are reduced, it is necessary to monitor the markets. Immature markets are imperfect markets,

---

54.   In 2010, the New Jersey Legislature enacted S. 2381 (New Jersey Statute), authorizing the establishment of a Long-Term Capacity Agreement Pilot Program (LCAPP). N.J. Stat. § 48:3-98.3. The Maryland Commission issued Order No. 84,815 in its proceeding entitled Whether New Generating Facilities are Needed to Meet Long-Term Demand for Standard Offer Service, Case No. 9214, 297 P.U.R.4th 336 (Md. Pub. Serv. Comm'n Apr. 12, 2012).
55.   As of this writing (spring 2013), both of these state efforts are in federal court, challenged by sellers who object to the price-lowering effects of the state actions. PPL Energy Plus v. Nazarian, No. MJG-12-1286, 2012 U.S. Dist. LEXIS 135756 (D. Md. Aug. 3, 2012); PPL Energy Plus, LLC v. Solomon, No. 11-745, 2012 U.S. Dist. LEXIS 140335 (D.N.J. Sept. 28, 2012). The challenges are based on the Supremacy Clause and Commerce Clause. For a discussion of those two constitutional clauses, see Chapter 12.
56.   PJM Interconnection, LLC, 135 FERC ¶ 61,022, at P 6 (2011).
57.   PJM Interconnection, LLC, 128 FERC ¶ 61,157, at PP 90–91 (2009).

and market imperfections lead to market misbehavior. This chapter has addressed three forms of misbehavior: (a) anti-competitive pricing, specifically price squeeze and predation; (b) product tying, where the seller of the monopoly product forces its customer to buy the seller's competitive product; and (c) market manipulation, in particular the physical and economic withholding that can occur in organized wholesale markets.

Common to these problems is concern over the role of the incumbent—as the owner of monopoly facilities and the potential entrant in competitive markets. In telecommunications, policymakers' confidence in competition, a confidence disputed by some, has led them to authorize companies to reintegrate business activities that the MFJ had separated. In wholesale electricity, some states have moved to reintegrate, for the opposite reason: to reduce their dependence on a wholesale market they deem unpredictable. Common to both reactions is the regulatory role, of testing, monitoring and adjusting.

PART TWO

Pricing
How Much Can Sellers Charge—
and Who Decides?

Setting prices for utility services is time-consuming and contentious. The applicable law boils down to three simple-sounding phrases. The first two appear in nearly every regulatory statute: Rates must be "just and reasonable," and they must not grant any "undue preference or advantage." The third phrase appears in the U.S. Constitution's Fifth Amendment: once a utility has spent money to perform an obligatory public service, it is entitled to "just compensation."

Empowered and constrained by these phrases, and the hundreds of court opinions interpreting them, regulatory rate-setters have used two major approaches:

- *Cost-based rates and their variants*: The regulator sets or caps the price based on some measure of cost. The permissible cost bases range from "embedded cost" of sunk investments to long-run incremental cost of future technologies. Rates in this cost-based category include variants of "performance-based rates" like "price caps" and "alternative forms of regulation"—concepts that use cost as a starting point but give the seller some degree of pricing discretion.
- *Market-based rates*: The regulator authorizes the seller to set its own prices, subject to regulatory oversight. That oversight has two components: an advance finding that the seller has no "market power," and subsequent monitoring to prevent the seller from gaining and exploiting market power.

Cost-based and market-based ratemaking have a common purpose: to induce all sellers to perform cost-effectively. Each method draws from the other. When setting cost-based rates, regulators look to market prices for benchmark comparisons. When monitoring market-based rates, regulators compare them to generic costs to see if sellers are pricing above reasonable costs—evidence of possible market power. And in markets where sellers might gain market power due to shortages or other factors, regulators might allow market prices but cap them at ceilings that bear some relationship to costs.

There is of course a third approach to price-setting—no regulation: Repeal the regulatory role entirely, leaving consumer protection to market forces and antitrust enforcement. All three approaches co-exist, for one or more types of transactions, in each of the electric, gas and telecommunications industries.

Chapters 6 and 7 describe the many legal features of cost-based ratemaking and market-based ratemaking, respectively. We then turn to four subjects that apply, to a lesser or greater degree, to both cost-based ratemaking and market-based ratemaking:

- The *prohibition against undue discrimination* requires that similar customers be treated similarly, but also allows due discrimination—treating dissimilar customers dissimilarly. (Chapter 8)
- Under the *filed rate doctrine*, a utility may charge only the rate officially filed with and accepted by the regulator. Simple in principle, the doctrine's applications are complex. It constrains not only the utility but also federal and state courts, and the rate-setting commission itself. It bars these bodies from approving any form of compensation, whether in the form of contract damages, tort damages, rate refunds or rate surcharges, that varies from the filed rate. (Chapter 9)
- The *prohibition against retroactive ratemaking* prohibits regulators from allowing refunds or surcharges when past rates do not produce their intended results. (Chapter 10)
- The *Mobile-Sierra doctrine*, an interpretation of federal regulatory statutes, limits the regulator's authority to relieve a contracting party of its contract obligations. (Chapter 11)

CHAPTER SIX
"Just and Reasonable" Prices in Non-competitive Markets
Cost-Based Rates Set by the Regulator

The corporation may not be required to use its property for the benefit of the public with-
out receiving just compensation for the services rendered by it. How such compensation
may be ascertained, and what are the necessary elements in such an inquiry, will always
be an embarrassing question.[1]

Without competitors, an unregulated utility could raise prices at will, restrained only by its customers' readiness to reduce consumption. To prevent this abuse, statutes direct regulators to set rates that are "just and reasonable." In this no-competition context, regulators base rates on some measure of "cost." The law places on regulators a dual obligation: to protect the consumer from unreasonable costs, and to provide the utility a reasonable opportunity to earn a fair return. These obligations are the subject of this chapter. They apply to both state and federal regulators—to any commission engaged in cost-based ratemaking.

The phrase "cost-based rates" can confuse newcomers because there are different types of "costs" and different types of "bases." The phrase refers to rates set by the regulator based on some measure of costs. Contrast the phrase "market-based rates" (the subject of Chapter 7), which refers to rates set by the seller and disciplined by competitive forces. More specifically, the phrase "cost-based rates" is usually shorthand for "embedded cost rates": rates based on costs that a specific utility has actually incurred or expects to incur—including both fixed costs (e.g., generators, pipelines, pumps, land, headquarters building and vehicles) and variable costs (e.g., fuel, labor and taxes). But as this chapter will discuss, "embedded cost" is not the only path to "cost-based" rates. We will encounter "area rates," "rate caps," "performance-based rates," and FCC-mandated wholesale rates based on "total element long-run incremental cost" (TELRIC). Each variant has some connection to some type of "cost," and each has satisfied the statutory test of "just and reasonable."[2]

To explain the legal principles and their applications to the "cost-based" variations, this Chapter covers the following topics:

(a)   The rate-setting equations for embedded cost rates

(b)   What does "just and reasonable" mean? Statutory purpose and constitutional limit

(c)   Imprudent actions and inactions: Who bears the costs of inefficiency and waste?

(d)   Prudent actions but uneconomic outcomes: Who bears the costs of bad luck?

---

1.   Smyth v. Ames, 169 U.S. 466, 546 (1898).
2.   For a peerless discussion of ratemaking from an economic perspective, see the first volume of ALFRED KAHN, THE ECONOMICS OF REGULATION: PRINCIPLES AND INSTITUTIONS (1970, 1988). Every page is worth the reader's attention. For this author's eulogy of Alfred Kahn, see http://www.scotthemplinglaw.com/essays/alfred-kahn.

(e)   Variations on costs and their bases

(f)   Departures from cost bases

6.A. The rate-setting equations

The most common method for setting cost-based rates is utility-specific ratemaking, known variously as "rate of return regulation," "rate base regulation," "embedded cost regulation" or "revenue requirement regulation." Using data on the utility's fixed and variable costs (sometimes historic, sometimes predicted, sometimes both), the regulator sets rates calculated to give the utility a reasonable opportunity to recover its prudent costs and earn a "fair" return on capital invested. Those calculations are based on assumptions about the likely number and type of customers and level of sales.

Embedded cost ratemaking uses two simple equations. The first equation describes the "annual revenue requirement": the total dollars the utility must receive during a specified future year (called a "rate year") as reasonable compensation for providing obligatory service. If the utility sells enough service to earn those dollars, it can cover its reasonable expenses (e.g., operating expenses, taxes and depreciation) and the interest on its debt and still have enough left for its shareholders to receive a reasonable return on their investment. Here is the equation:

$$\text{Annual revenue requirement} = \text{expenses} + \text{cost of capital}$$

where—

- expenses include operations and maintenance costs (e.g., labor and fuel), taxes, and depreciation; and

- cost of capital includes (a) interest payments to lenders plus (b) return on shareholder equity (the latter defined as commission-authorized return on equity multiplied by total equity).

Terminology note: The phrase "cost of capital," which refers to the cost of debt plus the return on equity, is sometimes referred to as "rate of return" multiplied by "rate base." In that definition,

- rate of return is the weighted rate of return for debt and equity; and

- rate base is the sum of all capital investment, whether funded by debt or equity, less accumulated depreciation.[3]

---

3.   An excellent explanation of depreciation and its role in the revenue requirement appears in Louisiana Public Service Commission v. FCC, 476 U.S. 355, 364–65 (1986):

The second equation converts the revenue requirement the utility needs to receive into the rates customers must pay. The utility receives its revenue because its customers pay for their service. The second equation therefore converts the annual revenue requirement into a rate per unit consumed:

$$\frac{\text{Annual Revenue Requirement (in \$)}}{\text{Expected sales in units of volume}}$$

where units of volume could be in kWh, gallons, minutes, Mcfs. This fraction produces a $/unit rate, such as $/kWh, $/gallons, $/Mcf.

In real life, the conversion of annual revenue requirement to rates is more complicated, for at least four reasons:

1. Some costs are allocated on a per-customer basis rather than a per-unit-consumed basis. Most customers pay a fixed "customer charge," say $10 a month, even if their usage is zero. This type of charge recovers certain costs (known as "fixed costs") that do not vary with consumption, like the physical connection between a resident and the nearest transformer.

2. For large customers, a portion of the utility's revenue requirement is allocated on a demand basis rather than a usage basis. These customers will pay, in addition to a usage charge, a demand charge. The demand charge reflects each customer's pro rata share of the utility's cost of meeting demand in a peak period. Its supporting logic is that (a) the utility must have sufficient capacity to meet demand at its peak (otherwise lights and ovens would go out, busy signals would dominate, and no water would flow from faucets); and (b) it makes sense, in terms of economic efficiency and fairness, to allocate the cost of that plant in proportion to a customer's contribution to the peak.

Depreciation is defined as the loss in service value of a capital asset over time. In the context of public utility accounting and regulation, it is a process of charging the cost of depreciable property, adjusted for net salvage, to operating expense accounts over the useful life of the asset... [A] regulated carrier is entitled to recover its reasonable expenses and a fair return on its investment through the rates it charges its customers, and . . . depreciation practices contribute importantly to the calculation of both the carrier's investment and its expenses. [citations omitted]

The total amount that a carrier is entitled to charge for services, its "revenue requirement," is the sum of its current operating expenses, including taxes and depreciation expenses, and a return on its investment "rate base." The original cost of a given item of equipment enters the rate base when that item enters service. As it depreciates over time—as a function of wear and tear or technological obsolescence—the rate base is reduced according to a depreciation schedule that is based on an estimate of the item's expected useful life. Each year the amount that is removed from the rate base is included as an operating expense.

We will return to this case in Chapter 12, concerning the relationship between federal and state regulation.

3.   The remaining costs are collected on the basis of actual consumption. Large customers, therefore, usually have a three-part charge: a customer charge (which does not vary with usage), a demand charge (representing their proportionate contribution to peak), and a usage charge (representing the variable cost associated with each unit of consumption).

4.   Regulators usually create different rates for different customer categories, such as commercial, industrial, residential, and streetlighting, with those categories further subdivided into large and small. To develop rates for each class, the regulator takes the annual revenue requirement and allocates it among the classes based on their share of demand in some defined peak period, then sets rates separately for each class.

This cost allocation process has many variations. The legal principle guiding those variations is the statutory prohibition against undue discrimination. We will address discrimination in Chapter 8.

The equations, once read and used a few times, are simple. What is not simple is deciding what number belongs in each slot. The legal principles guiding those decisions fill the remainder of this chapter.

6.B. What does "just and reasonable" mean?
6.B.1. Statutory purpose: Seller and buyer interests
The phrase "just and reasonable" appears in most economic regulatory statutes, both federal and state. Its ancestor is the Interstate Commerce Act of 1887: "[A]ll charges made for any service rendered in the transportation of passengers or property . . . shall be reasonable and just; and every unjust and unreasonable charge for such service is prohibited and declared to be unlawful."[4] To assist in applying these words, legislative history and case law give us three principles:

a. The phrase has no fixed meaning: The "just and reasonable" standard is "not very precise, and does not unduly confine FERC's ratemaking authority. . . . [T]he necessity for an anchor to 'hold the terms "just and reasonable" to some recognizable meaning' is plain, for the words themselves have no intrinsic meaning applicable alike to all situations."[5]

---

4.   Interstate Commerce Act of 1887, ch.104, § 1, 24 Stat. 379 (1887) (current version at 49 U.S.C. § 10701).
5.   Farmers Union Cent. Exch. v. FERC, 734 F.2d 1486, 1501 (D.C. Cir. 1984) (quoting earlier cases). *But see id.* at 1505 (quoting The Economic Regulation of Business and Industry: A Legislative History of U.S. Regulatory Agencies 906 (B. Schwartz ed. 1973) [hereinafter Legislative History] (quoting Senator LaFollette in the 1906 debate over the Hepburn Act's amendment to the Interstate Commerce Act to expand the Commission's authority to include oil pipelines: "The phrase 'just and reasonable' has a clear and well defined meaning in the law. It measures what the public must pay. It measures all that the carrier is entitled to receive.")).

b. It means more than abuse-prevention, it takes into account the interests of both buyers and sellers: The legislative history of the Interstate Commerce Act indicates that the "just and reasonable" phrase "meant more than a ban on prohibitive pricing. . . . [Legislative] [d]iscussions . . . focused not upon prohibitive pricing practices, but instead on setting a fair price that would be neither excessive to the shipper nor threatening to the financial integrity of the carrier." Congress wanted rates "that would permit the carriers to earn a fair return, while protecting the shippers and the public from economic harm."[6] This dual purpose also informs the Natural Gas Act (sections 4(e) and 5(a) of which also require rates to be "just and reasonable"[7]):

> When the inquiry is on whether the rate is reasonable to a producer, the underlying focus of concern is on the question of whether it is *high* enough to both maintain the producer's credit and attract capital. To do this, it must, *inter alia*, yield to equity owners a return "commensurate with returns on investments in other enterprises having corresponding risks," as well as cover the cost of debt and other expenses. . . . As has been indicated, however, the primary purpose of the Natural Gas Act is to protect consumers. Thus when the inquiry is whether a given rate is just and reasonable to the consumer, the underlying concern is whether it is *low* enough so that exploitation by the producer is prevented. Accordingly, the Commission must weigh the sometimes conflicting interests of both producer and consumer before it can say that a particular rate is "just and reasonable" within the meaning of the Natural Gas Act.[8]

c. "Just and reasonable" establishes a "zone" rather than a fixed point: Under the umbrella of "just and reasonable,"

> an agency may issue, and courts are without authority to invalidate, rate orders that fall within a "zone of reasonableness," where rates are neither "less than compensatory"

---

6. Farmers Union Cent. Exch. v. FERC, 734 F.2d at 1504–05 (citing Senator Elkins's statement that the rates should allow "the shipper and producer [to] make a fair profit on their products, the [carrier] a fair return for the service rendered, and the consumer get what he buys at a fair price"). *See also id.* (quoting Legislative History, *supra* note 5, at 854 (remarks of Senator Clay) (Under the "just and reasonable" standard, ICC must determine "whether or not the rate so fixed is confiscatory or not compensatory for the services performed.")); *id.* (quoting Legislative History at 859 (remarks of Senator Clay) ("Can the [ICC's] power be exercised either to oppress the roads or the shippers? Can this power be exercised either to wrong or injure the carrier or the shipper? . . . . Can the Commission fix a rate that would prevent the railroads from making operating expenses and denying to them just compensation for the services performed? I answer, 'No.' . . . The object and purpose of this legislation is to make [carriers] do right and to make shippers do right.")); *id.* (quoting Legislative History at 880 (remarks of Senator Culberson) ("The Supreme Court has held that the words 'just and reasonable' have relation both to the rights of the public and of the companies, and that the rate must be fixed with reference to the rights of each.")).
7. 15 U.S.C. §§ 717c(e), 717d(a).
8. City of Chi. v. FPC, 458 F.2d 731, 750–51 (D.C. Cir. 1971) (emphasis in original).

nor "excessive." . . . The "zone of reasonableness" is delineated by striking a fair balance between the financial interests of the regulated company and "the relevant public interests, both existing and foreseeable."[9]

6.B.2. Constitutional constraint: The Takings Clause

A statute's "just and reasonable" phrase grants regulators discretion, but that discretion is bounded by the Takings Clause of the Fifth Amendment: "[N]or shall private property be taken for public use, without just compensation."[10] This provision binds federal regulators directly; it binds state regulators through the Fourteenth Amendment.[11] Here is how the Takings Clause applies to regulatory price-setting:

1. Shareholder investment in the utility is "private property."
2. When the government imposes on the utility an obligation to invest funds, there is a "taking" of "private property" in the amount of funds invested.
3. The revenue produced by the rates authorized by the regulator is the "compensation."

The Constitution requires this compensation to be "just compensation." To explore the concept, we first describe the relationship between just compensation and shareholders' legitimate expectations. Those expectations have a substantive and a procedural component. We then discuss the limits on those expectations, for not every shareholder disappointment is a constitutional breach. Since 1944, the case law has delivered a consistent message: regulators have flexibility. No single ratemaking method is constitutionally required; what matters is a regulatory decision's "end result," its "total effect."

6.B.2.a. Regulator's duty: Honor shareholders' legitimate expectations

6.B.2.a.i. Substantive expectation: Opportunity to earn fair return
Applying the Takings Clause to public utility ratemaking, the law asks three questions: What is the "property"? How is it "taken"? and What is "just compensation"? Justice Brandeis supplied the answers:

> The thing devoted by the investor to the public use is not specific property, tangible and intangible, but capital embarked in the enterprise. Upon the capital so invested the Federal Constitution guarantees to the utility the opportunity to earn a fair return.[12]

---

9. Farmers Union Cent. Exch. v. FERC, 734 F.2d at 1502 (citing FERC v. Pennzoil Producing Co., 439 U.S. 508, 517 (1979) (quoting Permian Basin Area Rate Cases, 390 U.S. 747, 797 (1968))).
10. U.S. Const. amend. V.
11. Chi., B. & Q.R. Co. v. Chicago, 166 U.S. 226 (1897).
12. Mo. *ex rel.* Sw. Bell Tel. Co. v. Pub. Serv. Comm'n of Mo., 262 U.S. 276, 290 (1923) (Brandeis, J., concurring).

The "property" is the shareholder's investment, the "taking" occurs when the utility invests capital to carry out its public service obligation, and the "just compensation" occurs when the regulator sets rates sufficient to "guarantee[] to the utility the opportunity to earn a fair return."

Historical background: Justice Brandeis's reasoning is applied today routinely. The reasons why are best grasped by reviewing ratemaking's first five difficult decades.[13]

1. *The "fair value" rule of* Smyth v. Ames: In 1898, the Supreme Court announced that regulators must allow a reasonable return on the "fair value" of utility property invested.[14] Described by Justice Souter as a "troublesome mandate" of "mind-numbing complexity," imposed "without irony," *Smyth* required consideration of the

> original cost of construction, the amount expended in permanent improvements, the amount and market value of its bonds and stock, the present as compared with the original cost of construction, the probable earning capacity of the property under particular rates prescribed by statute, and the sum required to meet operating expenses.[15]

"To the bewildered," Justice Souter recounted, "*Smyth* simply threw up its hands, prescribing no one method for limiting use of these numbers but declaring all such facts to be 'relevant.'"[16]

The fair value rule depended on either (a) circular reasoning, or (b) guesses about construction cost, reproduction cost, or replacement cost. As Justice Brandeis explained (with evident frustration because the *Southwestern Bell* majority did not reject *Smyth*):

> The rule of *Smyth v. Ames* sets the laborious and baffling task of finding the present value of the utility. It is impossible to find an exchange value for a utility, since utilities, unlike merchandise or land, are not commonly bought and sold in the market. Nor can the present value of the utility be determined by capitalizing its net earnings, since the earnings are determined, in large measure, by the rate which the company will be permitted to charge; and, thus, the vicious circle would be encountered. So, under the rule of *Smyth v. Ames*, it is usually sought to prove the present value of a utility by ascertaining what it actually cost to construct and install it; or by estimating what it should have cost; or by estimating what it would cost to reproduce, or to replace, it. . . . [The] galactic notion of

---

13. For a fuller history, see Justice Souter's extraordinarily clear discussion in Verizon Commc'ns, Inc. v. FCC, 535 U.S. 467, 481–86 (2002).
14. Smyth v. Ames, 169 U.S. at 546.
15. *Id.* at 547.
16. Verizon Commc'ns v. FCC, 535 U.S. at 481–82 (citing Mo. *ex rel.* Sw. Bell v. Pub. Serv. Comm'n of Mo., 262 U.S. at 294–98, 294 n.6 (Brandeis, J., concurring).

fair value could produce revenues grossly excessive or insufficient when gauged against the costs of capital.[17]

A generation later, Justice Douglas echoed the point, summing up fair value's essential circularity as follows: "The heart of the matter is that rates cannot be made to depend upon 'fair value' when the value of the going enterprise depends on earnings under whatever rates may be anticipated."[18]

2. Brandeis's "prudent investment" rule: Twenty-five years after *Smyth*, Justice Brandeis presented his alternative to fair value's agony. His approach laid the foundation for much of cost-based ratemaking today:

> The adoption of the amount prudently invested as the rate base and the amount of the capital charge as the measure of the rate of return would give definiteness to these two factors involved in rate controversies which are now shifting and treacherous, and which render the proceedings peculiarly burdensome and largely futile. Such measures offer a basis for decision which is certain and stable. The rate base would be ascertained as a fact, not determined as matter of opinion. It would not fluctuate with the market price of labor, or materials, or money. It would not change with hard times or shifting populations. It would not be distorted by the fickle and varying judgments of appraisers, commissions, or courts. It would, when once made in respect to any utility, be fixed, for all time, subject only to increases to represent additions to plant, after allowance for the depreciation included in the annual operating charges. The wild uncertainties of the present method of fixing the rate base under the so-called rule of *Smyth v. Ames* would be avoided; and likewise the fluctuations which introduce into the enterprise unnecessary elements of speculation, create useless expense, and impose upon the public a heavy, unnecessary burden.[19]

3. The "end result" test of Hope: Two more decades passed. As the *Verizon* Court notes, poignantly: "[A]lthough [Justice Brandeis] did not live to enjoy success, his campaign against *Smyth* came to fruition in . . . *Hope Natural Gas Co.*"[20] The Federal Power Commission set Hope's rates using Justice Brandeis's approach: a rate base consisting of historical (original) cost less accumulated depreciation, an authorized return on equity based on market facts, and expenses based on reasonable projections. The utility attacked the Commission's

---

17. Mo. *ex rel.* Sw. Bell v. Pub. Serv. Comm'n of Mo., 262 U.S. at 292–93 (Brandeis, J., concurring).
18. FPC v. Hope Natural Gas Co., 320 U.S. 591, 601 (1944). *See also* Duquesne Light Co. v. Barasch, 488 U.S. 299, 309 (1989) ("According to Brandeis, the *Smyth v. Ames* test usually degenerated to proofs about how much it would cost to reconstruct the asset in question, a hopelessly hypothetical, complex, and inexact process.").
19. Mo. *ex rel.* Sw. Bell v. Pub. Serv. Comm'n of Mo., 262 U.S. at 306–07 (Brandeis, J., concurring).
20. Verizon Commc'ns v. FCC, 535 U.S. at 483.

authorized return, arguing it was unconstitutionally low when calculated under *Smyth*'s "fair value" method. The Court upheld the Commission, rejecting not only *Smyth*'s insistence on fair value, but more broadly, the need for any "single formula or combination of formulae." The constitutional focus must be not on methodology, but on the "end result" and "total effect" of the rate order. Here is the famous language, repeated countless times by courts and commissions:

> [T]he Commission was not bound to the use of any single formula or combination of formulae in determining rates. Its rate-making function, moreover, involves the making of "pragmatic adjustments." . . . And when the Commission's order is challenged in the courts, the question is whether that order "viewed in its entirety" meets the requirements of the Act. . . . Under the statutory standard of "just and reasonable" it is the result reached not the method employed which is controlling. . . . It is not theory but the impact of the rate order which counts. If the total effect of the rate order cannot be said to be unjust and unreasonable, judicial inquiry under the Act is at an end. The fact that the method employed to reach that result may contain infirmities is not then important. . . .
>
> Rates which enable [a] company to operate successfully, to maintain its financial integrity, to attract capital, and to compensate its investors for the risk assumed certainly cannot be condemned as invalid, even though they might produce only a meager return on the so called 'fair value' rate base.[21]

4. *Brandeis to* Bluefield *to* Hope: If Justice Brandeis provided the constitutional blueprint, Bluefield and Hope did the construction. In *Bluefield Water Works & Improvement Co. v. Public Service Commission of West Virginia*,[22] the Commission authorized rates that produced a return on equity of under 6 percent. This was too low to constitute "just compensation," the Court found. The low and irregular income resulting from the rates would reduce the prices of the utility's securities, causing investors to demand higher rates of return. The Court described the utility's entitlement and the regulator's obligation:

> [A] public utility is entitled to such rates as will permit it to earn a return on the value of the property which it employs for the convenience of the public equal to that generally being made at the same time and in the same general part of the country on investments in other business undertakings which are attended by corresponding risks and uncertainties.[23]

---

21. FPC v. Hope Natural Gas, 320 U.S. at 602, 605 (citations omitted). *See also* FPC v. Natural Gas Pipeline Co., 315 U.S. 575, 586 (1942) ("The Constitution does not bind rate-making bodies to the service of any single formula or combination of formulas").
22. 262 U.S. 679 (1923).
23. *Id.* at 692–93.

In *Hope*, the Court emphasized the investor's interest in the utility's "financial integrity." Financial integrity requires "enough revenue not only for operating expenses but also for the capital costs of the business." The capital costs, in turn, "include service on the debt and dividends on the stock." The equity owner's return, further, "should be commensurate with returns on investments in other enterprises having corresponding risks. That return, moreover, should be sufficient to assure confidence in the financial integrity of the enterprise, so as to maintain its credit and to attract capital."[24]

5. *The importance of expectations*: These passages from *Bluefield* and *Hope* create expectations for investors. The regulator's duty is to honor those expectations. Reviewing courts thus consider the "economic impact of the regulation on the claimant and, particularly, the extent to which the regulation has interfered with distinct investment-backed expectations."[25]

A note on "risk": *Bluefield* requires the regulator to authorize a return (profit) commensurate with the utility's risks, taking into account "other business undertakings which are attended by corresponding risks and uncertainties."[26] What are these risks? For any utility investment, there are three main risks: (a) not recovering the entire investment, (b) recovering it later than expected, and (c) earning a return lower than expected. These risks exist because the utility can experience one or more of following possibilities:

1.   Actual sales volume is less than the level assumed by the Commission when setting the revenue requirement (unless the rates are "decoupled").[27] A sales drop can occur for multiple reasons: a slow economy, structural changes in customer consumption due to new energy-efficient building stock and appliances, and unexpected outages.

2.   Actual demand is less than the level assumed (for customers whose bills are based in whole or in part on demand). The potential causes are similar to those for sales volume.

3.   Actual costs are higher than assumed. Possible causes include general inflation greater than predicted, special inflation associated with input costs, labor productivity below assumptions and unanticipated accidents and repairs.

4.   Actual delinquencies are higher than assumed. Possible causes include an unanticipated economic slowdown and the loss of a major employer in the service territory.

5.   The regulator reduces revenues for reasons other than imprudence. As Chapter 6.D will discuss, the Supreme Court in *Duquesne Light Co. v. Barasch*, 488 U.S.

---

24.   FPC v. Hope Natural Gas, 320 U.S. at 603.
25.   Penn Central Transp. Co. v. New York, 438 U.S. 104, 124 (1978).
26.   Bluefield Water Works & Improvement Co. v. Pub. Serv. Comm'n of W. Va., 262 U.S at 692.
27.   A "decoupled" rate structure makes recovery of fixed costs (including profit) independent of sales. *See* REGULATORY ASSISTANCE PROJECT, REVENUE REGULATION AND DECOUPLING: A GUIDE TO THEORY AND APPLICATION (2011).

299 (1989), declared that a statute or commission can constitutionally disallow prudent costs under the "used and useful" and "utility bears the risk" approaches. (A utility also faces the risk of non-recovery due to imprudence or poor performance, but this risk is not compensated for in the authorized return on equity because protection from imprudence disallowance is not within shareholders' "legitimate" expectations.)

6.B.2.a.ii. Procedural expectation: Opportunity for hearing

The regulator owes the utility an opportunity to present facts to support its claim for compensation. That was the court's ruling in *Jersey Central Power & Light Co. v. FERC.*[28] Jersey Central spent $397 million building a nuclear plant, then canceled the project. The utility asked FERC for a rate increase to recover, and receive a return on, the investment. (The rate case occurred at FERC because the plant was owned by a wholesale affiliate; FERC has exclusive jurisdiction over wholesale sales.[29]) FERC had an existing policy on canceled plants: Allow amortization (i.e., gradual recovery) of the investment but disallow a return, because a canceled plant is not "used and useful." Jersey Central argued that FERC should not apply this policy automatically, without holding a hearing to consider the utility's weak financial condition. The utility told FERC it was relying wholly on short-term capital from a revolving credit arrangement that could be canceled at any time, and had been unable to issue dividends for four years. FERC rejected the hearing request, then limited Jersey Central's rate increase by applying its recovery-but-no-return policy.

The court of appeals reversed. Without holding a hearing on the utility's financial condition, FERC could not know whether its policy of "no return" would meet *Hope*'s required "end result": just and reasonable rates as required by statute, and just compensation as required by the Constitution.[30]

The constitutional hearing requirement also appears in *Permian Basin Area Rate Cases.*[31] Recall from Chapter 3.A.2 that under the *Phillips* decision, the Federal Power Commission set natural gas producer rates under the Natural Gas Act.[32] One of the FPC's ratemaking techniques was to set general price ceilings, called "maximum rates," for each of several gas-gathering areas. An area's maximum rate applied to all producers in that area, regardless of an individual producer's costs. Some producers challenged the concept, arguing that if their costs were high relative to these ceilings, the constitutional requirement of "just

---

28.   810 F.2d 1168 (D.C. Cir. 1987).
29.   *See* Federal Power Act § 201(b)(1), 16 U.S.C. § 824(b)(1).
30.   Jersey Cent. Power & Light Co. v. FERC, 810 F.2d 1168, 1177–78 (D.C. Cir. 1987) (finding that the Commission "resists 'end result' examination at the agency level, and is deeply antagonistic to court review of ratemaking under the guidelines laid down by *Hope*").
31.   390 U.S. 747 (1968).
32.   Congress repealed this authority in 1989 with the Natural Gas Wellhead Decontrol Act, amending the NGPA to eliminate all wellhead price controls as of January 1, 1993.

compensation" entitled them either to cease production (regardless of any contractual obligation to produce), or to seek from the FPC "special relief," that is, a producer-specific rate increase. The FPC's policy indeed allowed producers to request special relief hearings. As the Supreme Court explained:

> The Commission acknowledged [these area rates] might in individual cases produce hardship, and declared that it would, in such cases, provide special relief. It emphasized that exceptions to the area rates would not be readily or frequently permitted, but declined to indicate in detail in what circumstances relief would be given.

The Court did not decide whether actually granting special relief would be "in every situation constitutionally imperative, for such arrangements have here been provided by the Commission, and we cannot now hold them inadequate."[33] The Commission's procedure protected its policy against constitutional attack.

The FCC took a similar tack when it allowed incumbent local exchange carriers to argue, on a company-specific basis, that the TELRIC methodology would produce unconstitutionally confiscatory rates.[34] The Supreme Court described the FCC's order as "more hospitable to early taking claims than any court would be under *Duquesne*.... The FCC ... is willing to consider a challenge to TELRIC in advance of a rate order, but any challenger needs to go beyond general criticism of a method's tendency, and to show with 'specific information' that a confiscatory rate is bound to result."[35]

Bottom line: When a utility makes a credible, specific claim that a rate order's "end result" would be to violate its constitutional right—a right to a rate "sufficient to assure confidence in the financial integrity of the enterprise"[36]—the regulator must (a) provide the utility an opportunity to prove the facts at hearing, and then (b) take those facts into account when setting the rate.

6.B.2.b. Limits on shareholders' legitimate expectations

When applying *Hope*'s "end result" test to regulatory decisions, courts will consider "economic impact of the regulation on the claimant and, particularly, the extent to which the regulation has interfered with distinct investment-backed expectations."[37] In the context of cost-based ratemaking, what are a utility's "distinct investment-backed expectations"? And what are the limits on those expectations?

---

33. *Permian Basin Area Rate Cases*, 390 U.S. at 764, 770.
34. TELRIC first appeared in Chapter 4.B.4.b, concerning non-discriminatory rates for access to the "last mile."
35. Verizon Commc'ns v. FCC, 535 U.S. at 528 n.39.
36. *Hope*, 320 U.S. at 603.
37. Penn Cent. Transp. Co. v. New York, 438 U.S. at 124.

The central expectation is that the rates will produce a return on the investment required for utility service that (a) is "equal to that generally being made at the same time and in the same general part of the country on investments in other business undertakings which are attended by corresponding risks and uncertainties";[38] and (b) enables the utility to "operate successfully, to maintain its financial integrity, to attract capital."[39] Judicial applications of this language have produced five overlapping limits.

a. In the constitutional calculation, only prudent costs are counted: Justice Brandeis's alternative to *Smyth*'s "fair value" method was "[t]he adoption of the amount *prudently* invested as the rate base" on which the rate of return is authorized.[40]

b. The Constitution does not protect against economic bad luck: Recall *Market Street Railway*—"The due process clause has been applied to prevent governmental destruction of existing economic values. It has not and cannot be applied to insure values or restore values that have been lost by the operation of economic forces."[41] Fifty years earlier, the Supreme Court sounded the same theme:

> If the establishing of new lines of transportation should cause a diminution in the number of those who need to use a turnpike road, and consequently, a diminution in the tolls collected, that is not, in itself, a sufficient reason why the corporation, operating the road, should be allowed to maintain rates that would be unjust to those who must or do use its property. . . . If a corporation cannot maintain such a highway and earn dividends for stockholders, it is a misfortune for it and them which the Constitution does not require to be remedied by imposing unjust burdens on the public.[42]

c. Financial success, even survival, is not guaranteed: As the Louisiana Supreme Court declared: "The Supreme Court decisions in *Hope* and the subsequent case of *Permian Basin Area Rate Cases* . . . have been construed to mean that there is no requirement that the end result of a rate-making body's adjudication must be the setting of rates at a level that will guarantee the continued financial integrity of the utility."[43]

d. Regulators can change their policies: An historic approach to price regulation need not continue indefinitely. The incumbent phone companies attacked TELRIC[44] for departing from the FCC's past cost recovery methods. The Supreme Court responded:

---

38. Bluefield Water Works & Improvement Co. v. Pub. Serv. Comm'n of W. Va., 262 U.S. at 692–93.
39. FPC v. Hope Natural Gas, 320 U.S. at 605.
40. Mo. *ex rel.* Sw. Bell Tel. Co. v. Pub. Serv. Comm'n of Mo., 262 U.S. at 306–08 (emphasis added).
41. Market St. Ry. Co. v. R.R. Comm'n of Cal., 324 U.S. 548, 567 (1945) (discussed in Chapter 3.C.3.b).
42. Covington & Lexington Tpk. Rd. Co. v. Sandford, 164 U.S. 578, 596–97 (1896).
43. Gulf States Utils. Co. v. La. Pub. Serv. Comm'n, 578 So. 2d 71, 95 (La. 1991). *See also* Kan. Gas & Elec. Co. v. State Corp. Comm'n, 720 P.2d 1063 (Kan. 1986); Pa. Elec. Co. v. Pa. Pub. Util. Comm'n, 502 A.2d 130 (Pa. 1985).
44. Discussed in Chapter 4.B.4.b.

[T]o the extent that the incumbents argue that there was at least an expectation that some historically anchored cost-of-service method would set wholesale lease rates, no such promise was ever made. . . . Any investor paying attention had to realize that he could not rely indefinitely on traditional rate making methods but would simply have to rely on the constitutional bar against confiscatory rates.[45]

The possibility that a regulator can change its methodology flows inevitably from *Hope*'s ruling that methodology is constitutionally irrelevant. The emphasis on "end result" means that "[t]he [judicial] inquiry is essentially . . . ad hoc [and] factual."[46] "Ad hoc" means that mere change cannot be constitutionally suspect.

The Fifth Amendment's flexibility is not unlimited, however. A regulatory "decision to arbitrarily switch back and forth between methodologies in a way which required investors to bear the risk of bad investments at some times while denying them the benefit of good investments at others" would certainly raise constitutional eyebrows.[47] In the TELRIC appeal, this concern did not arise because the petitioners

fail[ed] to present any evidence that the decision to adopt TELRIC was arbitrary, opportunistic, or undertaken with a confiscatory purpose. . . . [T]here was no "switch" of methodologies, since the wholesale market for leasing network elements is something brand new under the 1996 Act. There was no replacement of any predecessor methods, much less an opportunistic switch "back and forth."[48]

e. Compensation claims must be accurate claims: When Verizon attacked TELRIC as insufficiently compensatory, the Supreme Court found the claims "spurious" and "patently misstated."[49]

---

45. Verizon Commc'ns v. FCC, 535 U.S. at 528 (noting prior FCC statement that "regulation does not and should not guarantee full recovery of their embedded costs") (citing *Duquesne Light Co. v. Barasch*, 488 U.S. at 315 (holding that the Constitution does not guarantee recovery of prudent costs)). *See also* L.A. Gas & Elec. Corp. v. R.R. Comm'n of Cal., 289 U.S. 287, 305 (1933) ("Mindful of its distinctive function in the enforcement of constitutional rights, the Court has refused to be bound by any artificial rule or formula which changed conditions might upset").

46. Jersey Cent. Power & Light Co. v. FERC, 810 F.2d at 1192 (Starr, J., concurring) (quoting *Kaiser Aetna v. United States*, 444 U.S. 164, 175 (1979)).

47. Duquesne Light Co. v. Barasch, 488 U.S. at 315.

48. Verizon Commc'ns v. FCC, 535 U.S. at 527–528.

49. Verizon had complained that its balance sheet figure for "total plant" was $342 billion, while its TELRIC compensation would only be $180 billion. The Court blew away both figures. The $342 billion did not reflect depreciation or net current liabilities; adjusting for those factors lowered the number to $166 billion. The $180 billion was based on a "barebones universal-service telephone network" which did not reflect the more advanced elements that incumbents would be leasing under TELRIC. *Id.* at 525–26.

6.B.3. Regulatory discretion under the "just and reasonable" standard

Both the "just and reasonable" standard and *Hope*'s focus on "end result" lead to the same place: regulatory discretion over method selection. This purpose is embodied in *Hope*'s conclusion: "Since there are no constitutional requirements more exacting than the standards of the Act, a rate order which conforms to the latter does not run afoul of the former."[50] The regulatory decisions accommodated by this statutory-constitutional deference occupy many different points on the customer-shareholder spectrum. Five examples follow.

 a. A commission can disallow prudent investments if they are not "used and useful": In *Duquesne Light Co. v. Barasch* (facts detailed in Chapter 3.C.3.b), the utility prudently initiated construction of a nuclear plant, prudently incurred construction costs, then prudently abandoned the project. Duquesne's prudence made no difference, though, because Pennsylvania's statute required the Commission to disallow a return on investment that was not "used and useful" to customers. (An abandoned plant is not used and useful.) The U.S. Supreme Court upheld the statute's constitutionality. The statute was a "hybrid system," a "slightly modified form of the historical cost/prudent investment system."[51] The "modification" was that prudent investment was not eligible for recovery (through amortization as depreciation expense) or to earn a return (by placing it in rate base), if it was not used and useful. Further, the cost disallowance caused but a nick in the company's financials: It reduced annual revenue by only 0.4 percent to 0.5 percent a year, whereas the two utilities were earning 16.14 percent and 15.72 percent on common equity and an 11.64 percent and 12.02 percent overall return on rate base, respectively. Applying *Hope*'s "end result" test, the Court found that the

> overall impact of the rate orders . . . is not constitutionally objectionable. No argument has been made that these slightly reduced rates jeopardize the financial integrity of the companies, either by leaving them insufficient operating capital or by impeding their ability to raise future capital. Nor has it been demonstrated that these rates are inadequate to compensate current equity holders for the risk associated with their investments under a modified prudent investment scheme.[52]

---

50. FPC v. Hope Natural Gas, 320 U.S. at 607.
51. Duquesne Light Co. v. Barasch, 488 U.S. at 310, 316 n.10 (referring to the Brandeis model described in Chapter 3.C.3.a).
52. *Id.* at 312. Was the Supreme Court correct to focus on the small magnitude of Duquesne's loss? Two economists say the Court here made three errors. First, by considering only Duquesne's loss, the Court ignored the "cumulative impact industry-wide," specifically, the opinion's influence on settlements of other nuclear cost cases. Second, by emphasizing that Duquesne's loss was "slight," the Court "did not limit the number of 'slight' losses that could be imposed. Many small losses could add up to a large one in a hurry, especially given the third problem." Third, in relying on 0.4 percent point figure, the Court confused total return with shareholder return. The 0.4 percent figure was associated with the entire rate base. But rate base consists of contributions from bondholders, preferred shareholders and common shareholders. The first two categories "expect to be paid," because their payments are guaranteed by contract. The real loss-bearers are, therefore, the owners of common stock, who contributed only around

This passage leaves open the possibility that a disallowance of prudent-but-not-used-and-useful costs might trigger constitutional alarms if it caused the utility financial distress.

b. A utility's cost-based rates need not reflect its specific costs: After the *Phillips* decision,[53] the Federal Power Commission initially based each gas producer's rates on its specific costs. This involved thousands of cases and years of backlog. The Commission switched to an "area rate" methodology, setting a maximum rate for all gas from a defined area, based on general costs associated with that area's production. Upholding the program, the Supreme Court stated:

> This Court has repeatedly recognized that legislatures and administrative agencies may calculate rates for a regulated class without first evaluating the separate financial position of each member of the class; it has been thought to be sufficient if the agency has before it representative evidence, ample in quantity to measure with appropriate precision the financial and other requirements of the pertinent parties.[54]

c. Cost-based rates can lawfully depart from embedded cost: Recall that the FCC requires states to set rates for unbundled network elements using TELRIC.[55] TELRIC rates are based not on the carrier's actual cost, but on "forward-looking economic cost of an element." That forward-looking economic cost "should be measured based on the use of the most efficient telecommunications technology currently available and the lowest cost network configuration, given the existing location of the incumbent's wire centers."[56] Dissatisfied with the revenue levels yielded by TELRIC, the incumbent local exchange carriers pressed the Supreme Court to interpret the term "cost" in the 1996 Act to mean embedded cost (which produced a higher rate). Doing so, they argued, would avoid a "serious constitutional question" arising from the alleged revenue insufficiency.[57]

The Court saw no serious constitutional question. The petitioners were challenging an entire method; but under *Hope* what mattered was not the method but the "end result."

34–36 percent of the rate base. The effect on common shareholders, they calculate, was not 0.4 percent but 5.3 percent. A. Lawrence Kolbe and William B. Tye, *The* Duquesne *Opinion: How Much "Hope" is There for Investors in Regulated Firms?*, 8 YALE J. ON REG. 113 at text accompanying nn.108–11 (1991).

53. Phillips Petrol. Co. v. Wisconsin, 347 U.S. 672 (1954) (interpreting the Natural Gas Act to require Federal Power Commission to set rates for natural gas producers). *See* Chapter 3.A.2.

54. *Permian Basin Area Rate Cases*, 390 U.S. at 768–70.

55. Readers encountered TELRIC in Chapters 4.B.4.b (non-discriminatory rates for essential facilities) and 6.B.2.a.ii (hearing requirement).

56. 47 C.F.R. § 51.505(b)(1).

57. Under the doctrine of "constitutional avoidance," courts try to interpret statutes to avoid finding them unconstitutional. A famous recent example is Chief Justice Roberts's opinion in *National Federation of Independent Business v. Sebelius*, 132 S. Ct. 2566 (2012), interpreting the health insurance mandate as a "tax" authorized by the Constitution's Taxing and Spending Clause, Article I, Section 8, Clause 1, to avoid striking the provision as unconstitutional under the Commerce Clause.

The carriers had presented no specific end result for a specific company; and the numbers they presented showing industry-wide effects were "spurious" and "misstated."[58]

d. Zone of reasonableness includes fully allocated cost: No single rate commands statutory or constitutional approval; there is instead a "zone of reasonableness" accommodating a range of lawful rates.[59] While the zone has no precise boundaries, we know it includes "fully allocated cost." Cable television systems need to attach their cables to existing poles. Those poles are owned by electric utilities, who charge the cable companies for the attachments. Under the federal Pole Attachments Act, a cable company alleging overcharge by the electric utility can petition the FCC for "just and reasonable" rates, if the state commission is unavailable to set the rate. The Act authorized the FCC to set rates within a range, bounded by (a) the marginal cost of providing the attachment, and (b) the fully allocated cost of constructing and operating each pole hosting an attachment.[60] Concerning the maximum rate, the Supreme Court declared that it could not "seriously be argued, that a rate providing for the recovery of fully allocated cost, including the actual cost of capital, is confiscatory." (The Court did not address whether a compelled rate as low as incremental cost would be constitutional.)[61]

e. "End result" can involve many financial factors: Under *Hope*, commission-set rates must "enable [a] company to operate successfully, to maintain its financial integrity, to attract capital, and to compensate its investors for the risk assumed."[62] Applying this standard, courts and commissions have relied on a host of financial factors. Here are eight questions courts have examined:

1.   Is the revenue surplus sufficient to expand service and maintain working capital?[63]
2.   Is revenue sufficient to ensure that service to customers will not be impaired?[64]
3.   Is cash flow sufficient for operations and debt payment?[65]

---

58.   Verizon Commc'ns v. FCC, 535 U.S. at 525–26. Challenging the method rather than the result was the same error committed in *Barasch* by the Pennsylvania Electric Association, which challenged as facially unconstitutional a state statute that disallowed prudent cost.

59.   We previously encountered "zone of reasonableness" in Chapter 5.A.1, discussing the Supreme Court's decision in *Conway*. There the Federal Power Commission was obligated to set wholesale rates at the low end of the zone to avoid price squeeze caused by the relationship between wholesale and retail rates in the same market; and in Chapter 6.B.1, citing *Farmers Union* and *City of Chicago* to discuss the statutory need to accommodate both seller and buyer interests when establishing rates within the zone.

60.   47 U.S.C. § 224(d)(1). The Act defines "fully allocated cost" as the product of "multiplying the percentage of the total usable space, or the percentage of the total duct or conduit capacity, which is occupied by the pole attachment by the sum of the operating expenses and actual capital costs of the utility attributable to the entire pole, duct, conduit, or right-of-way." *Id.*

61.   FCC v. Fla. Power Corp., 480 U.S. 245, 254 & n.7 (1987).

62.   FPC v. Hope Natural Gas, 320 U.S. at 605.

63.   *See* Ark. Pub. Serv. Comm'n v. Cont'l Tel. Co., 561 S.W.2d 645, 652 (Ark. 1978).

64.   *See* Potomac Elec. Power Co. v. Pub. Serv. Comm'n of the D.C., 457 A.2d 776, 785 (D.C. 1983); Tenn. Cable Television Ass'n. v. Tenn. Pub. Serv. Comm'n, 844 S.W.2d 151, 159–60 (Tenn. Ct. App. 1992).

65.   *See* N.C. Utils. Comm'n v. Thornburg, 342 S.E.2d 28, 34 (N.C. 1986).

4.   Does the debt-equity ratio reflect financial strength?[66]

5.   Are the bond ratings sufficient to maintain financial integrity?[67]

6.   Is the quality of earnings—specifically, construction work in progress (CWIP) and allowance for funds used during construction (AFUDC) as a percentage of net income—sufficient to maintain financial integrity?[68]

7.   How strong is the interest coverage ratio, which measures the net earnings available for interest payments?[69]

8.   Are there other factors affecting company value?[70]

6.B.4. Roles of legislature, commission and court

Ratemaking decisions involve legislatures, regulators and courts. A century of discussion reveals some general principles about who plays what roles.

Legislatures declare the policies. They can define methodologies, or leave that decision to the regulator. The Pennsylvania statute in *Barasch* limited the Commission's discretion by prohibiting recovery of, or return on, the prudent investment in the canceled plant.[71]

---

66.   *See* New England Tel. & Tel. Co. v. State, 97 A.2d 213, 220 (N.H. 1953); Conn. Natural Gas Corp. v. Pub. Utils. Control Auth., 439 A.2d 282, 291 (Conn. 1981).

67.   *See* N.C. Utils. Comm'n v. Thornburg, 342 S.E.2d at 34–36.

68.   *See id.* at 34–35. CWIP and AFUDC are alternative methods for treating the cost of financing the construction of a capital plant. The financing for a capital plant comes from lenders and shareholders. Financing costs are the interest payments to the lenders and the return on equity to the shareholders. The difference between CWIP and AFUDC concerns the point in time at which the utility collects those financing costs through its rates, as well as the calculation of those costs which are collected. Under CWIP, the utility collects the costs during the construction period. Variations on CWIP include recovering only the interest owed on short-term debt incurred to finance the construction, or recovering the utility's then-authorized rate of return, applied to construction costs as incurred. Under AFUDC, the utility collects the financing costs only when the plant begins commercial operation, as follows: During the construction period, the utility accrues the financing costs on its books. When the plant enters commercial operation, the total accrued financing costs enter the utility's rate base. The commission-authorized return on that rate base (which includes not only the accrued financing costs but also the direct construction costs) then enters the revenue requirement that is the basis for rates. Although both CWIP and AFUDC are reflected in the utility's official "earnings," CWIP has a more positive effect on "*quality* of earnings" because it enhances cash flow during the construction period. The difference in the quality of earnings can affect the utility's financial strength.

69.   *See* Potomac Elec. Power Co. v. Pub. Serv. Comm'n of the D.C., 457 A.2d at 788 (ruling that because ratio of earnings to interest and property retirement of 2.86:1 was greater than indenture agreements, financial integrity was not impaired); Walnut Hill Tel. Co. v. Ark. Public Serv. Comm'n, 709 S.W.2d 96, 100 (Ark. Ct. App. 1986) (noting the use of ratio showing how many times interest is covered by earnings).

70.   *See* Potomac Elec. Power Co. v. Pub. Serv. Comm'n of the D.C., 457 A.2d at 788 (noting that earnings exceeding common stock dividend rate indicated non-impairment of financial integrity); New England Tel. & Tel. Co. v. Mass. Dep't of Pub. Utils., 354 N.E.2d 860, 867 (Mass. 1976) (holding that market-to-book ratio of 1.2 to 1 for newly issued stock is the minimum necessary to compensate the Company adequately for selling costs and market pressure).

71.   *See* Duquesne Light Co. v. Barasch, 488 U.S. at 313 (state legislatures can "giv[e] specific instructions to their utility commissions. . . . [They] are competent bodies to set utility rates." (citing Barasch v. Pa. Pub. Util. Comm'n, 532 A.2d 325, 339 (Pa. 1987) ("The Commission is but an instrumentality of the state legislature for the performance of [ratemaking]"))).

Regulators carry out the legislature's policies. A commission "must be free, within the limitations imposed by pertinent constitutional and statutory commands, to devise methods of regulation capable of equitably reconciling diverse and conflicting interests. . . . [T]he breadth and complexity of the Commission's responsibilities demand that it be given every reasonable opportunity to formulate methods of regulation appropriate for the solution of its intensely practical difficulties."[72]

Courts confine regulators to their delegated authority and enforce constitutional limits, but also defer to regulators' judgments. The ultimate enforcers of the statutory "just and reasonable" standard and the constitutional command of "just compensation" are the courts. Where a regulatory decision complies with those constraints, courts must defer to the regulator's policy judgments."[73] The relationship between commission and courts was articulated with clarity in *Permian Basin*:

> [T]he responsibilities of a reviewing court are essentially three. First, it must determine whether the Commission's order, viewed in light of the relevant facts and of the Commission's broad regulatory duties, abused or exceeded its authority. Second, the court must examine the manner in which the Commission has employed the methods of regulation which it has itself selected, and must decide whether each of the order's essential elements is supported by substantial evidence. Third, the court must determine whether the order may reasonably be expected to maintain financial integrity, attract necessary capital, and fairly compensate investors for the risks they have assumed, and yet provide appropriate protection to the relevant public interests, both existing and foreseeable. The court's responsibility is not to supplant the commission's balance of these interests with one more nearly to its liking, but instead to assure itself that the Commission has given reasoned consideration to each of the pertinent factors.[74]

---

72. Permian Basin Area Rate Cases, 390 U.S. at 767, 790. *See also* Farmers Union Cent. Exch. v. FERC, 734 F.2d at 1501 (explaining that a regulator "enjoys substantial discretion in its ratemaking determinations; but, . . . this discretion must be bridled in accordance with the statutory mandate that the resulting rates be "just and reasonable.").

73. Bus. & Prof'l People for the Pub. Interest v. Ill. Commerce Comm'n, 585 N.E.2d 1032, 1039 (Ill. 1991) (citations omitted) (explaining that "setting utility rates is a legislative rather than a judicial function. . . . [T]he Commission and not the court is the fact-finding body. . . . [The Commission's] findings of fact are to be accepted as *prima facie* true and cannot be set aside on appeal unless they are against the manifest weight of the evidence. *See also* Permian Basin Area Rate Cases, 390 U.S. at 767 ("A presumption of validity therefore attaches to each exercise of the Commission's expertise, and those who would overturn the Commission's judgment undertake 'the heavy burden of making a convincing showing that it is invalid because it is unjust and unreasonable in its consequences.'") (quoting *FPC v. Hope Natural Gas*, 320 U.S. at 602)).

74. Permian Basin Area Rate Cases, 390 U.S. at 791–92. *See also* Farmers Union Cent. Exch. v. FERC, 734 F.2d at 1501 n.42 (citing Senator Elkins's statement, during the Hepburn Act debates, that the "just and reasonable" standard is vague, but still it is a standard because "it is a thing judicially ascertainable which the courts have always recognized it was their right and duty to ascertain in proper cases").

6.C. Imprudent actions and inactions: Who bears the costs of inefficiency and waste?

When establishing the annual revenue requirement, commissions exclude imprudent costs. This subchapter defines the prudence standard, providing illustrations of imprudent actions and inactions. It then addresses the question whether prudence review interferes with management's right to run its business. Next, we discuss a procedural question that can affect outcomes: When prudence issues arise, who has the burden of proof and the burden of going forward? The subchapter closes with the "too-big-to-fail" question: If a disallowance of imprudent costs would sink the utility, does the "just and reasonable" standard allow, or compel, the regulator to allow their recovery in rates?

6.C.1. Prudence principles

Prudence review is regulation's substitute for competitive forces. This purpose is echoed in decades of court decisions:

> Managements of unregulated business subject to the free interplay of competitive forces have no alternative to efficiency. If they are to remain competitive, they must constantly be on the lookout for cost economies and cost savings . . . . Public utility management, on the other hand, does not have quite the same incentive.[75]
>
> [Price regulation substitutes for the] pressures of competitive markets, to prevent regulated companies from becoming "high cost-plus compan[ies]" and to secure efficiency in the allocation of resources.[76]
>
> The principle of prudence has developed in part to counterbalance the monopoly power of public utilities. As one Public Service Commission has observed: "If a competitive enterprise tried to impose on its customers costs from imprudent actions, the customers could take their business to a more efficient provider. A utility's ratepayers have no such choice. A utility's motivation to act prudently arises from the prospect that imprudent costs may be disallowed."[77]

---

75. Midwestern Gas Transmission Co. v. E. Tenn. Natural Gas Co., 36 FPC 61, 70 (1966), *aff'd sub nom.* Midwestern Gas Transmission Co. v. FPC, 388 F.2d 444 (7th Cir. 1968). The Commission later rescinded its decision on unrelated grounds. Knoxville Utils. Bd. v. E. Tenn. Natural Gas Co., 40 FPC 172 (1968).

76. Democratic Cent. Comm. of the D.C. v. Wash. Metro. Area Transit Comm'n, 485 F.2d 886, 907 (D.C. Cir. 1973).

77. *Gulf States Utilities Co.*, 578 So. 2d at 85 n.6 (upholding commission finding that "given the information available at the time, prudent managers would not have chosen in 1979 to construct a nuclear power plant") (quoting Long Island Lighting Co., Case No. 27563, 71 P.U.R.4th 262 (N.Y. Pub. Serv. Comm'n Nov. 16, 1985)).

To achieve this competition-emulating purpose, commissions exclude imprudent costs from the utility's revenue requirement. They reject costs that are "unreasonable,"[78] "extravagant" or "wasteful."[79] These disallowances imply that utilities have affirmative obligations: "to operate with all reasonable economies,"[80] to charge prices based on "lowest feasible cost"[81] and to use "all available cost savings opportunities . . . as well as general economies of management."[82] To satisfy these affirmative obligations, a utility seeking cost recovery through rates must show that it "went through a reasonable decision making process to arrive at a course of action and, given the facts as they were or should have been known at the time, responded in a reasonable manner."[83]

The many prudence cases share four features.

a. The prudence standard requires reasonable behavior based on industry norms: Two days after VEPCO started up its new coal-fired generator, the boiler imploded. FERC allowed rate recovery of repair costs. There was "no showing that . . . VEPCO violated some standard of good engineering judgment, some norm of prudent public-utility behavior."[84] In contrast, when a utility acquired pollution control equipment for its coal plant, FERC disallowed the cost because of industry-wide concerns about the equipment's adequacy.[85]

Adhering to industry norms includes taking into account the consequences of error. Baltimore Gas & Electric's nuclear plant (Calvert Cliffs) suffered a two-week outage due to employee error. The utility had to buy expensive replacement power. The Maryland Commission disallowed part of the cost, because the utility

> did not account satisfactorily for such glaring human error . . . of allowing two sizable rags to get into equipment associated with the generator's cooling water system and remain undetected, thus causing the incurrence of clearly foreseeable substantial replacement power costs at a nuclear plant. The worker's or workers' carelessness was so great as to call into question the Company's procedures for instilling appropriate awareness, alertness and diligence among employees.

The Commission "stress[ed] the high standard of care which must be exercised in regard to maintenance practices and procedures at base load generating plants, such as nuclear

---

78. Gen. Tel. Co. of Upstate N.Y., Inc. v. Lundy, 218 N.E.2d 274, 277 (N.Y. 1966).
79. Acker v. United States, 298 U.S. 426, 430–31 (1936) (upholding disallowance of certain costs for marketing agencies in the Chicago stockyards).
80. El Paso Natural Gas Co. v. FPC, 281 F.2d 567, 573 (5th Cir. 1960).
81. Potomac Elec. Power Co. v. Pub. Serv. Comm'n of the D.C., 661 A.2d 131, 137 (D.C. 1995).
82. *Midwestern Gas Transmission Co.,* 36 FPC at 70.
83. Cambridge Elec. Light Co., D.P.U. 87-2A-1, 86 P.U.R.4th 574 (Mass. Dep't of Pub. Utils. Sept. 3, 1987).
84. Virginia Electric Power Co., 11 FERC ¶ 63,028, at p. 65,189 (1980) (initial decision), *aff'd in relevant part,* 15 FERC ¶ 61,052 (1981).
85. Minnesota Power & Light Co., 11 FERC ¶ 61,313, at p. 61,659 (1980).

plants, in recognition of the high cost consequences of outages at such plants," as compared to cycling or peaking units.[86]

The prudence standard, in short, is "akin to the common-law standard for negligence: Did the utility act in a manner consistent with the performance of other similarly-situated contemporary utilities? If it did, its action cannot fairly be deemed the result of imprudent management."[87]

b. The utility is deemed to know only those facts available at the time of its decision: A "reasonable utility" can act only on what it knows or should know. "A decision may be viewed as prudent even though a different course of action would ultimately have been more advantageous to the utility or its ratepayers. In this regard, hindsight is irrelevant to a prudence analysis because the utility must make a determination that addresses its business prospectively."[88] A prudence inquiry's focus, therefore, "is not whether a decision produced a favorable or unfavorable result, but rather, whether the process leading to the decision was a logical one, and whether the utility company reasonably relied on information and planning techniques known or knowable at the time."[89]

c. In assessing prudence, commissions must take into account a utility's unique roles and duties: A utility delivers essential services, usually to customers lacking alternatives. It operates in a context where errors can be costly.[90] The utility's duties, therefore, include "respond[ing] prudently to changing circumstances or new challenges that arise as a project progresses."[91]

d. Prudence analysis is fact-intensive: When the Ohio Commission reduced a natural gas utility's allowance for lost gas, the U.S. Supreme Court reversed: "The waste or

---

86. Balt. Gas & Electric Co., Case No. 8520/8520A, 1989 Md. PSC LEXIS 85, at *6–7, *24 (Md. Pub. Serv. Comm'n June 5, 1989).

87. Arizona Public Service Corp., 21 FERC ¶ 63,007, at p. 65,103 (1982) (initial decision) (rejecting customer's claim that utility was imprudent for investing in a nuclear plant instead of conservation), *aff'd in relevant part*, 23 FERC ¶ 61,419 (1983). *See also* Appeal of Conservation Law Found., Inc. 507 A.2d 652, 673 (N.H. 1986) (describing the prudence standard as "essentially apply[ing] an analogue of the common law negligence standard for determining whether to exclude value from rate base").

88. Nat'l Fuel Gas Distrib. Corp. v. Pub. Serv. Comm'n of N.Y., 947 N.E.2d 115, 120 (N.Y. 2011). *See also* Bos. Edison Co., D.P.U. 906, 46 P.U.R.4th 431 (Mass. Dep't of Pub. Utils. Apr. 30, 1982) (prudence analysis must consider "that the company had to operate at each step of the way prospectively rather than in reliance on hindsight . . . . [and] in light of all conditions and circumstances which were known or which reasonably should have been known at the time the decisions were made"), *aff'd sub nom.* Att'y Gen. v. Mass. Dep't of Pub. Utils., 455 N.E.2d 414 (Mass. 1983).

89. *Gulf States Utils. Co.*, 578 So. 2d at 85 (upholding commission finding that "given the information available at the time, prudent managers would not have chosen in 1979 to construct a nuclear power plant").

90. Consol. Edison Co. of N.Y., Case 27869, 45 P.U.R.4th 325, 332 (N.Y. Pub. Serv. Comm'n Jan. 21, 1982) (in Indian Point nuclear outage case, determining what "reasonable people" would have done "must take into account the risks associated with operation and maintenance of the nuclear plant and the consequences of imprudence or mismanagement relating to that facility").

91. *Gulf States Utilities Co.*, 578 So. 2d at 85 (citing Long Island Lighting Co., Case No. 27563, 71 P.U.R.4th 262 (N.Y. Pub. Serv. Comm'n Nov. 16, 1985); and Central Vermont Public Service Corp., Docket No. 5132, 83 P.U.R.4th 532 (Vt. Pub. Serv. Bd. May 15, 1987)).

negligence . . . must be established by evidence. . . . In all the pages of this record, there is neither a word nor a circumstance to charge the management with fault. There is not even a shadow of a warning to the company that fault was imputed and that it must give evidence of care."[92]

* * *

These four prudence principles—consistency with industry norms, no hindsight, the utility's special role, and factual intensity—all are illustrated in the examples of imprudent action and inaction that follow.

6.C.2. Imprudent actions

Imprudence comes in different forms. Here are five broad categories, with illustrations from state and federal cases.

6.C.2.a. Poor performance relative to objective indices

Performance can sometimes be quantified, such as with costs, outage frequency and duration, busy signals, and response time. In those situations, imprudence can be inferred, tentatively, from industry indices. When airlines were price-regulated, the Civil Aeronautics Board limited each airline's allowable selling expenses based on comparison with other airlines, adjusted for relevant differences.[93] And when rider representatives alleged that their bus company had the highest operating costs among major urban transit operators, a reviewing court declared: "If this is true, it raised obvious questions about efficiency."[94]

Caution: Indices cannot determine prudence definitively if the comparison companies have factual differences. A Pennsylvania utility argued that the per-kilowatt cost of its nuclear plant compared well with other plants in the Northeast. The state commission criticized the comparison as "rather gross. . . . [It] fail[s] to reflect those costs or economies which are unique to each individual construction project. . . . We know of no axiom which states that comparable costs are reasonable by definition." The Commission instead evaluated the utility's specific cost-causing decisions.[95] Nor are objective indices helpful if the imprudence is obvious. Florida Power Corporation knew that its pumps had a history of failure, but failed to order spare parts. Its defense—"national data bank information" showing that other companies maintained incomplete spare parts inventories—did not persuade the court.[96]

---

92. W. Ohio Gas Co. v. Pub. Utils. Comm'n of Ohio, 294 U.S. 63, 68 (1935).
93. Trans World Airlines, Inc. v. Civil Aeronautics Bd., 385 F.2d 648, 657–58 (D.C. Cir. 1967).
94. *Democratic Cent. Comm. of the D.C.*, 485 F.2d at 907.
95. Pa. Pub. Util. Comm'n v. Phila. Elec. Co., Docket No. 438, 31 P.U.R.4th 15, 28 (Pa. Pub. Util. Comm'n May 7, 1989).
96. Fla. Power Corp. v. Cresse, 413 So. 2d 1187, 1189 (Fla. 1982).

6.C.2.b. Failure to use reasonable management practices

Relying on expert testimony from management experts, regulators have made detailed findings about management practices that cause imprudent costs. Examples include the utility—

(a) failing to use a physical model or to review the vendor's pipe fabrication drawings.[97]

(b) failing to exercise care in acquiring generating units.[98]

(c) using unreliable cost estimates, incurring excess expenditures designed to overcome delays, making unnecessary design changes, conducting poor relations with the contractor and maintaining inadequate quality control.[99]

6.C.2.c. Failure to oversee contractors and employees

Every utility selects and supervises contractors and employees. When they err, the utility cannot avoid an imprudence disallowance simply by shifting blame. Some jurisdictions make a difference, however, between contractor error and employee error.

a. Contractor error: When Virginia Power's new oil-fired generator imploded,[100] FERC allowed Virginia Power to recover its repair costs (less insurance proceeds) over five years. But the Commission criticized the utility because it had indemnified the contractor for the latter's imprudence:

> [T]his Commission cannot, consistent with its legal duties, approve passing through to jurisdictional ratepayers higher costs incurred as a result of negligence, mismanagement or inefficiency. It makes no difference whether such increased costs are incurred directly by the company, as a result of the utility's failure to pursue its contractual remedies for negligence by its agent, or through the utility's structuring of a contract which left it without remedies, thus allowing the agent to pass on such costs to its principal (the utility) and thence to the ratepayers. The contract is not in evidence and there was no examination in the hearing of the prudency of VEPCO's having entered into the type of contract that underlies the assignment of costs here. . . . Disallowance of the repair costs would be a compelling conclusion had it been demonstrated that VEPCO executed a contract that left it without remedy for the negligent acts of its contractor and left the ratepayers to pay the bill.[101]

---

97. Pa. Pub. Util. Comm'n v. Phila. Elec. Co., 31 P.U.R.4th 15 (deducting $1.6 million from a utility's rate base for "rework" costs attributable to incorrect construction and unnecessary design changes).

98. Long Island Lighting Co. v. N.Y. Pub. Util. Comm'n, 134 A.D.2d 135 (N.Y. App. Div. 1987) (upholding commission's disallowance of cost recovery for unnecessary repair and replacement of generators).

99. Consumers Power Co., Case No. U-4717, 14 P.U.R.4th 1, 18–19 (Mich. Pub. Serv. Comm'n Mar. 8, 1976), *remanded on other grounds*, 261 N.W.2d 10 (Mich. Ct. App. 1977) (disallowing construction costs for a gas distribution plant).

100. *See supra* Chapter 6.C.1.

101. Virginia Electric Power Co., 15 FERC ¶ 61,052 at p. 61,112.

Minnesota Power & Light hired a contractor to design and procure scrubbers for the utility's coal-fired plants. There was industry-wide concern about the reliability of the contractor's chosen scrubbers. The contractor had had experience only with mining companies, not utilities. Its principal shareholder sat on the utility's Board. The scrubbers didn't work. The utility had failed to obtain a performance guarantee from the contractor and never sued the contractor for damages. FERC found imprudence.[102]

Philadelphia Electric Company was a minority owner in a nuclear plant built by Public Service Electric & Gas (a New Jersey utility). PECO had 4000 workers at the construction site and its annual cost share was $46 million. But it had no permanent on-site representatives. From 1970 through 1977, PECO averaged only three site visits per year. Cost overruns at the plant led to findings of PSEG imprudence. The Pennsylvania Commission imputed PSEG's imprudence to PECO, due to PECO's "total abdication of responsibility for the management of the construction of . . . the project."[103]

A turbine failure in Carolina Power & Light's nuclear generating unit doubled the length of an outage during a period of peak demand. The North Carolina Commission found imprudence due to the Company's inadequate staffing and supervision. The utility had failed to (a) respond to an "increasing backlog of plant equipment, construction, and regulatory problems in a timely manner"; (b) supervise and plan outages to ensure the most expeditious use of "down" time; and (c) supervise the turbine repairs. The Commission quoted from the log of a floor supervisor detailing the construction errors made by an untrained workforce:

> I wish Santa Claus would come early and bring me ten good turbine mechanics and at least one rigger who knows how to rig. These High Valley men are not turbine men nor can they rig. Help.[104]

b. Employee error: Whereas commissions normally impute contractor errors to the utility, their treatment of employee errors varies between penalizing and not penalizing the utility. Here are three examples.

Commonwealth Edison's nuclear plants suffered four unplanned shutdowns, all due to employee errors. As summarized by the reviewing court: "(1) [A] technician deenergized the wrong circuit breaker, causing a two-day outage; (2) an employee or contractor improperly installed a screw, causing a leak that resulted in a 19-day shutdown; (3) an

---

102. Minnesota Power & Light Co., 11 FERC ¶ 61,313 at p. 61,659 ("The combination of self-dealing, the selection of a questionable pollution control process, and the failure either (or both) to secure a performance guarantee and to seek damages constitutes overwhelming evidence of imprudence by MP&L and its Board of Directors.").
103. Pa. Pub. Util. Comm'n v. Phila. Elec. Co., 31 P.U.R.4th at 29.
104. Carolina Power & Light Co., Docket No. E-2, Sub 444, 49 P.U.R.4th 188, 199–203 (N.C. Utils. Comm'n Sept. 24, 1982).

employee or contractor installed a defective turbine test switch that caused a two-day outage; and (4) an admitted 'management deficiency' when a reactor was not pressurized correctly caused a two-day extension of a planned five-day maintenance period." These outages forced the utility to buy costly fuel to run substitute plants. Consumer representatives sought disallowance of the fuel cost, arguing that employee errors necessarily mean utility imprudence. The court disagreed: "Edison cannot be faulted for the human error of its employees unless the evidence shows that Edison failed to adequately hire and train the proper employees." To equate all employee error with management imprudence, the court reasoned, is to defy cost-effectiveness:

> Two of the dictionary definitions of "prudence" are "sagacity or shrewdness in management of affairs" and "skill or good judgment in the use of resources." . . . When determining employee management practices, the most efficient management of resources will minimize the sum of (1) the costs of human error, and (2) the costs of preventing human error. The latter includes extra salary to hire more qualified employees, increased training for employees, and additional management personnel for greater oversight. When the sum of costs in (1) and (2) is minimized, the utility will be able to provide its service for the least possible cost to consumers. Thus, a utility at maximum efficiency will still encounter costs from human error.[105]

In other words, perfect is not worth paying for.

Employee error does become utility imprudence if the utility failed to prepare and oversee its workers. A Consolidated Edison employee miswired a reactor cavity pump, blowing a fuse and causing an extended plant outage requiring expensive replacement power. The New York Commission found that management's written instructions were insufficient. Care in wire installation was especially important in a system providing a critical defense against flooding, said the Commission; the utility should have had the job performed by qualified electricians and checked it upon completion.[106] Similarly, a utility employee responsible for interpreting data failed to spot dented steam generator tubes, resulting in an outage and expensive replacement fuel. The Virginia Commission found the utility imprudent. Because the employee worked long hours and his work was "critical to the avoidance of costly shutdowns," the utility should have safeguarded against inevitable errors.[107]

Recall Baltimore Gas & Electric's nuclear outage at Calvert Cliffs. Mechanics had left two rags in the pipes, leading to an outage. The Commission stated: "[T]he egregious inattention that their misplacement demonstrates leads us to draw the inference that management's procedures and supervision do not conform to the strict standards which we

---

105. Bus. & Prof'l People for the Pub. Interest v. Commerce Comm'n, 665 N.E.2d at 556, 558.
106. *Consol. Edison Co. N.Y.*, 45 P.U.R.4th at 344–45.
107. Va. Elec. & Power Co. v. Div. of Consumer Counsel, 265 S.E.2d 697, 700 (Va. 1980).

previously described as being necessary for work on nuclear generating plants." Objecting
to this inference, the utility said it had trained employees to avoid putting things in pipes,
that people make mistakes, and that to impute all such mistakes to managerial imprudence
is to expect perfection. The Commission responded tartly:

> BG&E's defense, in essence, boils down to: We told our employees not to leave foreign
> objects in generators, but they did it anyway. Management cannot be held responsible
> unless the Commission can cite with unerring particularity the precise action management
> should have taken or inappropriately took, and that management's action or failure to
> act caused the outage. Inasmuch as the Commission has failed in that respect, manage-
> ment cannot be held responsible and the ratepayers must pay the millions of dollars in
> replacement power costs that resulted from the outage.

The Commission disagreed, found imprudence, and disallowed costs.[108]

6.C.2.d. Failure to secure remedies against erring supplier

Public Service of New Hampshire's coal supplier insisted that its contract limited the quantity the utility could buy. To fill its needs, the utility had to buy spot market coal at high
prices. Instead of suing the coal supplier for contract breach, the utility hired the supplier
to make the spot purchases. FERC found the failure to sue imprudent and disallowed
recovery of the spot costs.[109]

6.C.2.e. Failure to heed official criticisms

In the Santa Claus case,[110] involving nuclear plant outages, the North Carolina Commission
cited a "persistent pattern of the company's inability to recognize and cure its problems."
The Commission cited five years of regulatory concern, memorialized in a Commission-
ordered management audit, Nuclear Regulatory Commission appraisals, and assessments
by the Institute of Nuclear Power Operations. Penalizing the utility by lowering its authorized return on equity, the Commission concluded that "the sooner company management
faces up to inefficiencies and problems in its own nuclear program, the sooner nuclear
production will improve."[111]

---

108.   Balt. Gas & Electric Co., 1989 Md. PSC LEXIS 85 at *21–22.
109.   Public Service Co. of New Hampshire, 6 FERC ¶ 61,299, at pp. 61,714–15 (1979). *See also* Minnesota
       Power & Light Co., 11 FERC ¶ 61,313 (finding utility imprudent for, among other things, failing to sue
       its affiliated contractor when the pollution control equipment proved defective).
110.   *See supra* Chapter 6.C.2.c.
111.   *Carolina Power & Light Co.*, 49 P.U.R.4th at 207.

6.C.3. Imprudent inaction

Regulators penalize not only imprudent action, but also imprudent inaction. Consider the problem of surplus capacity. Public utilities are capital intensive. Like families buying houses to grow into, utilities bring on new capacity in "lumps." The economic size of a new plant typically exceeds the immediate need for its entire capacity. The resulting capacity surplus can last for years, until load grows to use all the new capacity. Then it is time to bring on new capacity. So surplus is common. Who pays for it?

If the temporary surplus was unavoidable and its cost prudent, the cost responsibility is usually the customers'.[112] The regulator therefore places the full plant cost into rate base (where it adds to the revenue requirement by earning a return and generating depreciation expense).[113] But the utility is obligated to minimize its customers' costs.[114] Given this obligation, the prudent utility will seek temporary buyers for the output made possible by the surplus, then use the resulting revenue to defray its customers' cost. Failure to do so risks regulatory penalty in one of two forms. One form is easy to understand: remove the marketable surplus from rate base (thereby shifting its cost to the shareholders). The second form, "imputing unearned revenues" (sometimes called "crediting revenues to customers") takes a bit more explanation.

6.C.3.a. The imputation solution

Imputing unearned revenues means reducing the utility's revenue requirement by the revenues a prudent utility would have earned through prudent efforts to sell the surplus temporarily. To understand revenue imputation, we need to amend the revenue requirement equation. The original equation, explained in Chapter 6.A, was:

$$\text{Annual revenue requirement} = \text{expenses} + \text{cost of capital}$$

The amended revenue requirement subtracts the imputed revenues, as follows:

$$\text{Annual revenue requirement} = \text{expenses} + \text{cost of capital, } \textit{less revenue that the utility earned (or that a prudent utility should have earned) from selling its surplus temporarily}$$

---

112. *See supra* Chapters 3.C.3.b, 6.B.3 and *infra* 6.D.1 for discussions of the "used and useful" exception to this statement.
113. As explained in Chapter 6.A.
114. Utilities must "operate with all reasonable economies," El Paso Natural Gas Co. v. FPC, 281 F.2d at 573; charge prices based on "lowest feasible cost," Potomac Electric Power Co. v. Public Service Commission of the District of Columbia, 661 A.2d at 137; and use "all available cost savings opportunities . . . as well as general economies of management," *Midwestern Gas Transmission Co.*, 36 FPC at 70.

Illustrating imputation is a New York Commission decision involving Rochester Gas and Electric. The Commission forecasted that during the rate year, RGE would be able to make $36 million from wholesale sales of electricity, using surplus capacity that was in retail rate base. The Commission subtracted the $36 million from the utility's revenue requirement. The utility contested the Commission's action on two constitutional grounds. First, the order compelled it ("economic coercion" was the utility's phrase) to make wholesale sales. Such coercion was preempted by the Federal Power Act, said the utility, because the regulation of wholesale sales is exclusively FERC's domain. The court disagreed: The state commission could "take into account activities it cannot regulate [i.e., wholesale sales] in setting rates for activities that it may regulate [i.e., retail sales]." Second, the utility argued that the Commission's order violated the Commerce Clause because it "burdened interstate commerce." Again the court disagreed: "[B]ecause [the Commission's imputation] policy fosters a clearly legitimate local interest, does not implicate core Commerce Clause concerns and, if anything, indirectly encourages interstate commerce, we cannot say that it violates the Commerce Clause."[115]

6.C.3.b. Imputation analogy: Who gets the gain on sold-off capacity?
Imputation makes the utility responsible for revenues it should have earned from surplus that sits in rate base. This principle applies not only to sales of output from surplus capacity, but also to sales of the assets themselves.[116] Consider this hypothetical:

1. In 2003, the utility constructed a headquarters building for $90 million. All costs were prudent.
2. The building entered rate base that year with a 30-year straight line depreciation rate. Each year, therefore, the utility's rates recover $3 million (1/30 of the original cost) as depreciation expense, plus a return on the undepreciated amount.
3. In 2013, ten years and $30 million in depreciation expenses later, the asset's book value (original cost less accumulated depreciation) will have declined to $60 million.
4. In 2013, the utility sells the building for $100 million: a $40 million gain over book value at that time.

---

115. Rochester Gas & Elec. Corp. v. Pub. Serv. Comm'n of N.Y., 754 F.2d 99, 101–06 (2d Cir. 1985). *See also* Gulf Power Co. v. Fla. Pub. Serv. Comm'n, 453 So. 2d 799, 802, 804 (Fla. 1984) (upholding commission decision to remove portion of new plant from rate base because, although the capacity "will benefit rate payers [sic] in the long run," the utility "failed to prove that, if it had made a timely effort to sell an additional 186 MW off-system at marginal cost, it would have been unable to do so"). For more discussion of the Commerce Clause as it restricts state regulation, see Chapter 12.B.1.
116. We encountered asset sales in Chapters 3.C.1 and 3.C.3.a, concerning monopoly-to-competition transition. There, the proceeds from the asset sales were subtracted from retail customers' stranded cost obligation.

How do we handle the proceeds? The first $60 million indisputably goes to the utility, to recover the $60 million in still-unrecovered book value. But who gets the $40 million gain—shareholders or customers? Opinions differ. Utilities sometimes argue that gain goes with ownership: Since they own the asset, they keep the gain. Some commissions and courts, in contrast, look past the legal labels. They require that "benefit follow burden." Since the ratepayers bore the burden (paying for ten years' depreciation and return regardless of the building's value to them), they now should get the benefits. Conversely, the utility bore no risk (the plant was in rate base earning a normal profit), so it deserves no gain; a gain now would be windfall because the utility already received "just compensation" for its investment (the ten years of rate-based profit plus depreciation expense, plus the $60 million to retire the remaining book value).

Exemplifying this latter view is an oft-cited opinion of the U.S. Court of Appeals for the District of Columbia Circuit. Overturning a commission decision awarding gain to shareholders, the court stated:

> Ratepayers bear the expense of depreciation, including obsolescence and depletion, on operating utility assets through expense allowances to the utilities they patronize. It is well settled that utility investors are entitled to recoup from consumers the full amount of their investment in depreciable assets devoted to public service. This entitlement extends, not only to reductions in investment attributable to physical wear and tear (ordinary depreciation) but also to those occasioned by functional deterioration (obsolescence) and by exhaustion (depletion). . . .
>
> [Since customers] have shouldered these burdens, . . . it is eminently just that consumers, whose payments for service reimburse investors for the ravages of wear and waste occurring in service, should benefit in instances where gain eventuates—to the full extent of the gain.[117]

---

117. *Democratic Cent. Comm. of the D.C.*, 485 F.2d at 808–09, 810–11, 822 (footnotes omitted); *id.* at 808 ("[I]f the land no longer useful in utility operations is sold at a profit, those who shouldered the risk of loss are entitled to benefit from the gain."). *See also* Separation of Costs of Regulated Telephone Service from Costs of Nonregulated Activities, 2 FCC Rcd. 6283, 6295 ¶¶ 113–14 (Sept. 17, 1987) (order on reconsideration) (observing that "[t]he equitable principles identified in [Democratic Central Committee] have direct application to a transfer of assets out of regulation that produces gains to be distributed," and requiring "that ratepayers receive the gains on assets when the market value of the assets exceeds net book cost."); N.Y. Water Serv. Corp. v. Pub. Serv. Comm'n of N.Y., 12 A.D.2d 122, 129 (N.Y. App. Div. 1960) (allocating gain on sale to ratepayers when ratepayers bore the risk of a loss in value of the assets); N.Y. State Elec. & Gas, Case No. 96-M-0375, 1996 N.Y. PUC LEXIS 671, at *8 (N.Y. Pub. Serv. Comm'n Nov. 19, 1996) (memorandum opinion) (reserving the net gains on the sale of land for ratepayers is "equitable and reasonable"); N.Y. Tel. Co. v. N.Y. Pub. Serv. Comm'n, 530 N.E.2d 843 (N.Y. 1988) (ratepayers entitled to benefits on sale of yellow pages advertisements).
    But see Bd. of Pub. Util. Comm'rs v. N.Y. Tel. Co., 271 U.S. 23 (1926) ("Customers pay for service, not for the property used to render it. Their payments are not contributions to depreciation or other operating expenses or to capital of the company. By paying bills for service they do not acquire any interest, legal or equitable, in the property used for the convenience or in the funds of the company.").

When the utility bears the risk of loss, the situation reverses. If a commission removes an asset from rate base (due to imprudence or non-usefulness), the utility's shareholders thenceforth bear the economic burdens. If they then sell the asset for a gain, they keep the benefit (at least that portion of the benefit allocable to the period of time when the asset was out of rate base).

6.C.4. Defense against disallowance: The "management prerogative"

Recall that commissions that penalize utilities on quality of service grounds risk court reversal based on "management prerogative": the notion that regulators set standards, but management runs the business.[118] The same tension arises in the area of prudence disallowances.

Concerned about imminent natural gas shortages, Consumers Power hired contractors to build a synthetic natural gas plant that would convert liquid hydrocarbons into natural gas. Large cost overruns prompted the Michigan Commission to find and disallow imprudent costs. Did the disallowances violate the utility's management prerogative? The reviewing court said no:

> It remains clear based upon the commission's statutory authority that decisions regarding the planning and construction of utility plant lie within the prerogative of management. It is equally clear, however, that the exercise of management prerogative does not relieve a regulated entity from justifying those decisions in terms of ultimate cost of ratepaying customers. Extensive authority . . . establishes that . . . this commission has an obligation to scrutinize the [Company's] expenditures. . . . Arguments which on the one hand caution against interference with management prerogatives while at the same time fail to demonstrate sufficiently the prudent exercise of those prerogatives do not provide a sufficient foundation for the inclusion of plant in rate base for the purpose of establishing just and reasonable rates.[119]

6.C.5. Burdens of proof on prudence and imprudence
6.C.5.a. General rule: Rebuttable presumption of prudence

When a utility seeks a rate increase it bears the burden of proof. The burden can be explicit, as in the Federal Power Act ("the burden of proof to show that the increased rate or charge

---

118. *See supra* Chapter 2.D.3.d.
119. *Consumers Power Co.*, 14 P.U.R.4th at 20. *See also* City of Detroit v. Mich. Pub. Serv. Comm'n, 14 N.W.2d 784 (Mich. 1944) ("It could not have been the intent of the legislature that the Commission should lack any necessary power to fix reasonable rates, and the Commission should not be permitted to declare itself impotent. It clearly possesses such discretionary power, and that power should be exercised.").

is just and reasonable shall be upon the public utility");[120] or implicit, as in the Interstate Commerce Act ("[A]ll charges made for any service rendered . . . in the transportation of passengers or property. . . *shall be* just and reasonable.").[121] Also known as the "risk of non-persuasion,"[122] the utility's burden of proof is usually lightened by a rebuttable presumption of prudence.[123] This presumption puts a burden on the intervenor, or the regulator, to produce enough evidence of imprudence to create "serious doubt" about the utility's prudence. Creating that "serious doubt" rebuts the prudence presumption, forcing the utility then to produce evidence of its prudence or suffer the "risk of non-persuasion."[124] On the other hand, if the intervenor produces no evidence of imprudence, thus creating no "serious doubt," then the presumption of prudence remains unrebutted, allowing the utility to meet its burden of proof.[125]

This approach to burdens is followed by both state and federal agencies. As the New York Court of Appeals explained:

> A utility company seeking a rate change has the burden of proving that the requested regulatory action is "just and reasonable." . . . However, a utility's decision to expend monetary resources is presumed to have been made in the exercise of reasonable managerial judgment. [The Department of Public Service, an intervenor] carries the initial burden of providing a rational basis to infer that the utility may have acted imprudently before the burden shifts to the utility to demonstrate that its decision was prudent when made.[126]

---

120. Federal Power Act § 205(e), 16 U.S.C. § 824d(e).
121. Interstate Commerce Act § 1 (emphasis added).
122. *See* James Fleming, Jr., *Burdens of Proof*, 47 Va. L. Rev. 51 (1961).
123. *Mo. ex rel.* Sw. Bell Tel. Co. v. Pub. Serv. Comm'n of Mo., 262 U.S. at 290 n.1 ("The term 'prudent investment' is not used in a critical sense. There should not be excluded, from the finding of the base, investments which, under ordinary circumstances, would be deemed reasonable. The term is applied for the purpose of excluding what might be found to be dishonest or obviously wasteful or imprudent expenditures. Every investment may be assumed to have been made in the exercise of reasonable judgment, unless the contrary is shown.") (Brandeis, J., concurring). Justice Brandeis gave no rationale for the presumption. Possible rationales are discussed at Chapter 6.C.5.b below.
124. *Mo. ex rel.* GS Techs. Operating Co. v. Pub. Serv. Comm'n of Mo., 116 S.W.3d 680, 694 (Mo. Ct. App. 2003) (explaining that if the intervenor creates "serious doubt," the utility has "the burden of dispelling these doubts and proving the questioned expenditure to have been prudent").
125. Some describe the intervenor's burden as a "burden of proof," but that is technically inaccurate. The utility always has the burden of proof—to show that its proposed rate is just and reasonable. The intervenor's burden is more accurately labeled the "burden of going forward," the "burden of producing evidence" or the "production burden." Fleming, *supra* note 122, at 55.
126. Nat'l Fuel Gas Distrib. Corp. v. Pub. Serv. Comm'n of N.Y., 947 N.E.2d at 120. *See also* State *ex rel.* Pub. Counsel v. Pub. Serv. Comm'n of Mo., 274 S.W.3d 569, 577–78 (Mo. Ct. App. 2009) (quoting Commission's reasoning that while the utility has "the overall burden of prov[ing] that the rates it is proposing are just and reasonable, . . . [the] commission properly presumed that UE was prudent in its purchase of the [combustion turbine generators], until the State or Public Counsel presented evidence that raised a 'serious doubt' concerning the prudence of its expenditure").

For FERC's similar take, we return to Virginia Power's imploded gas plant. FERC rejected its staff's request for disallowance:

> VEPCO has carried its initial burden to support the repair costs. The burden of going forward to show that the incurrence of the repair costs was occasioned by imprudence or negligence properly attributable to VEPCO, or that VEPCO was remiss in not recovering damages from Brown and Root, or in so structuring a contract that damages could not be recovered, thereupon shifted to those opposed to the allowance, in this case staff. . . . [S]taff simply did not carry its burden in this instance.[127]

FERC will treat the prudence presumption as rebutted if, among other reasons, a state commission has found imprudence. With its presumption rebutted, the utility must offer evidence of its prudence, or it loses. When Southern California Edison abandoned its partly-constructed nuclear plant, the California Commission found the utility imprudent for retail rate purposes. In the companion wholesale rate case at FERC,[128] the Administrative Law Judge warned the utility that given the state commission decision, the utility needed to produce evidence of its prudence. But the utility offered only "vague generalizations about the problems inherent in all building projects. No specific evidence regarding the . . . project was ever introduced." FERC disallowed the costs from the utility's wholesale rates.[129]

This obligation to present facts, not "vague generalizations," applies to the commission as well as to the utility. When the Ohio Commission reduced a natural gas utility's allowance for lost gas, the U.S. Supreme Court reversed: "The waste or negligence . . . must be established by evidence. . . . In all the pages of this record, there is neither a word nor a circumstance to charge the management with fault. There is not even a shadow of a warning to the company that fault was imputed and that it must give evidence of care."[130]

6.C.5.b. Deference to utility expertise

The presumption of prudence reflects deference to utility expertise: "Good faith is to be presumed on the part of the managers of a business. In the absence of a showing of inefficiency or improvidence, a court will not substitute its judgment for theirs as to the measure of a prudent outlay."[131] Deference has its limits, however. A Florida utility sought rate base

---

127.   Virginia Electric Power Co., 15 FERC ¶ 61,052, at p. 61,112.
128.   Most electric utilities have both retail and wholesale customers. The retail rates are set by the state commission under state law; the wholesale rates by FERC under the Federal Power Act.
129.   Southern California Edison Co., 8 FERC ¶ 61,198, at p. 61,680 (1979). FERC was upheld by the court of appeals. City of Anaheim v. FERC, 669 F.2d 799 (D.C. Cir. 1981).
130.   W. Ohio Gas Co. v. Pub. Utils. Comm'n of Ohio, 294 U.S. at 68.
131.   *Id.* at 72 (internal citations omitted) (reversing commission disallowance of a $7,000 expense incurred to attract new business).

recovery of its coal inventory, citing "the collective wisdom of the company's management." The Commission, unimpressed, insisted on evidence, not wisdom:

> With all deference to Gulf's management, a policy followed by management that has such a tremendous financial impact on ratepayers must be substantiated with more than an assertion that it is the result of collective management wisdom. We do not wish to substitute our judgment for that of management. However, we insist that management's judgment be substantiated in a way that permits intelligent review of it. In this context, this can best be accomplished by performance of an analysis or study that identifies all of the major factors that influence development of a coal inventory policy, indicates the relative weight that should be attached to each factor, and evaluates the benefits and costs, in light of these factors, associated with a range of alternate coal inventory levels. . . . In the absence of that kind of empirical support for its position, we find that the Company failed to carry its burden of proof.[132]

The affiliate exception: In a transaction between the utility and its affiliate, the risk of abuse makes deference inappropriate. Then, the burden on proving reasonableness is on the utility.[133]

Is there a legal difference between (a) failing to prove prudence and (b) being found imprudent? Not according to the Texas Supreme Court. Gulf States Utilities built the River Bend nuclear power plant for $4.5 billion. The Texas Commission found that the utility had proved prudence for $2.273 billion of the total, but disallowed another $1.454 billion because of a "lack of sufficient evidence" supporting its prudence. Two of the three Commissioners then voted to allow the utility an opportunity to prove the prudence of that amount. On review, the court held that the utility had no right to present a new case: "By stating that GSU failed to meet its burden of proof on the prudence of the $1.454 billion, the PUC effectively disallowed that amount from the rate base." As a legal matter, the case was over.[134]

---

132. Gulf Power Co. v. Fla. Pub. Serv. Comm'n, 453 So. 2d 799, 802, 804 (Fla. 1984).
133. *See* Boise Water Corp. v. Idaho Pub. Utils. Comm'n, 578 P.2d 1089, 1091 (Idaho 1978) (holding that once the utility has proven that claimed expenses were actually incurred, the burden of proving unreasonableness is with the Commission or intervenor if the expense stems from transactions with non-affiliates; but if the expense was a payment to an affiliate, the burden of showing reasonableness is with the utility); New England Tel. & Tel. Co. v Mass. Dep't of Pub. Utils., 354 N.E.2d at 868 (holding that the utility had the statutory burden of proof as to the reasonableness of any expenses incurred in transactions with affiliates); Application of Peoples Natural Gas Co., 413 N.W.2d 607, 617 (Minn. Ct. App. 1987) (upholding Minnesota Commission's exclusion of utility costs incurred under an affiliated administrative services agreement). The companion book on corporate structure, mergers and acquisitions will address affiliate relations in detail.
134. Coal. of Cities for Affordable Util. Rates v. Pub. Util. Comm'n of Texas, 798 S.W.2d 560, 562–64 (Tex. 1990). These numbers are those used by the court, but they do not add up. The court's opinion does not explain why. The reason is likely the difference between the plant's total cost and what the court describes as Gulf State's 70 percent share of those costs. (Other utilities were co-owners.) The discrepancy in the numbers does not affect the court's reasoning.

6.C.6. Financial consequences of cost disallowance

The same River Bend nuclear plant, and the same utility (Gulf States) reappear in a Louisiana Commission case, because the utility sold retail electricity in both Texas and Louisiana. The Louisiana Commission quantified Gulf States' imprudence at $2 billion. But it disallowed only $1.4 billion, to "allow the company to remain financially viable." The Louisiana Attorney General appealed, arguing that the statutory standard of "just and reasonable rates" required the Commission to disallow the full imprudent amount.

The Louisiana Supreme Court upheld the Commission. The purpose of the "just and reasonable" standard is to protect consumers. Here, the consumer interest could favor a viable utility over a full imprudence disallowance:

> [T]here is no requirement that the end result of a rate-making body's adjudication must be the setting of rates at a level that will guarantee the continued financial integrity of the utility. . . . However, it is also true that it is the Public Service Commission which is constitutionally accorded the authority to decide how the interests of ratepayers and the utility should be balanced in any given rate case. In the exercise of that authority, the Commission may, within its discretion, make a policy determination concerning whether the interests of the ratepayers are better served by disallowing the full damages flowing from a utility's imprudence, or by tempering the disallowance in order to maintain the utility's solvency. . . . [T]he Commission could reasonably have concluded that consumer interests were better served by maintaining Gulf States in a position to provide a reliable supply of electric service than by resorting to the uncertainties of the bankruptcy court.[135]

While recovery of imprudent costs could be consistent with the "just and reasonable" standard (at least in the view of the Louisiana Supreme Court—and then only if the basis is consumer benefit), the courts have established no statutory or constitutional *right* to that recovery, even if that recovery is necessary to maintain its financial integrity. Consumers Power asserted such a right—a constitutional right to the recovery of imprudent costs—when seeking to recover the costs of its canceled Midland nuclear plant. Citing *Duquesne Light Co. v. Barasch*,[136] the utility argued that

> the end result of any rate order must be considered in determining whether a constitutional deprivation exists. . . . [T]o fulfill its constitutional obligations, the Commission must assess the consequences of any disallowance in terms of its effects on the company's

---

135. Gulf States Utils. Co. v. La. Pub. Serv. Comm'n, 578 So. 2d. at 89, 95–96 (citations omitted). Note the reference to the Commission's authority being "constitutionally accorded." Louisiana is one of a minority of states whose utility commission is created by the state Constitution. In most states, the commission is created by statute.

136. *Barasch* is discussed in Chapters 3.C.3.b and 6.B.3.

debt and equity ratios, earnings on common equity, bond ratings, and ability to compete in the financial markets.[137]

The Michigan Commission disagreed, emphatically:

> The [federal and state] constitutions do not guarantee that Consumers will earn, or have the opportunity to earn, its authorized rate of return if it engages in unreasonable or imprudent activities. Likewise, the constitutions do not require the Commission to establish Consumers' rates based on whether those will permit it to achieve a particular coverage ratio or common equity ratio. Rather, the constitutions permit the Commission to use the ratemaking methodology of its choice as long as it abides by Michigan rate-setting statutes, refrains from arbitrarily switching back and forth between methodologies, and allows Consumers an opportunity to earn a reasonable rate of return on its prudent investments in light of the risks inherent in the methodology used.[138]

6.D. Prudent actions but uneconomic outcomes: Who bears the cost of bad luck?

Prudent actions can produce uneconomic outcomes. A new pipeline overruns its budget, due to unpredicted and unavoidable siting disputes. A new power plant ends up with excess capacity, because customer demand falls below reasonable forecasts. A trusted fuel supplier goes bankrupt, forcing the utility to buy high-cost substitutes on the spot market. A gas company's financial hedges become unnecessary (expensively so), because fuel prices drop. An experimental power plant technology fails, forcing the utility to abandon construction. When prudence combines with disappointment, who bears the extra cost—shareholders or customers?

Recall that when regulators assess a decision's prudence, they look only at the facts known or knowable when the decision was made. (See Chapter 6.C.1.) This "no-hindsight" rule means that facts arising after the utility's decision cannot support a prudence disallowance. But post-decision facts can support a different type of disallowance: one based not on imprudence, but on making the utility the risk-bearer of uneconomic outcomes.

The courts have preserved this option, repeatedly. Readers hoping for clear "dos" and "don'ts" will be disappointed; those hoping for broad regulatory discretion will be pleased. After summarizing the judicial precedent, we discuss the regulatory options, followed by the legal limits on those options. The consistent principle across the cases is this: With respect to prudent actions with uneconomic outcomes, commissions have a range of options, from full

---

137. Consumers Power Co., Case No. U-7830 Step 3B, 1991 Mich. PSC LEXIS 119, at *133–34 (Mich. Pub. Serv. Comm'n May 7, 1991) (Commission paraphrasing of utility's argument).
138. *Id.* at *135–36.

recovery plus profit, to no recovery and no profit, and all points in between. What matters, constitutionally, is honoring shareholders' legitimate expectations—as those expectations are influenced by regulatory actions.

6.D.1. Prudence does not guarantee cost recovery

The leading case is *Duquesne Light Co. v. Barasch*.[139] Chapter 3.C.3.b discussed the facts. To recap: A Pennsylvania statute prohibited return on, and recovery of, investment in assets not "used and useful" to customers. An abandoned or canceled plant is not used and useful, so the Commission disallowed the utility's cost, while acknowledging its prudence. The Supreme Court upheld the statute: "[A] state scheme of utility regulation does not 'take' property simply because it disallows recovery of capital investments that are not 'used and useful in service to the public.'"[140] Focusing on the "end result" as required by *Hope*, the Court found the economic effect of disallowance non-confiscatory because it was so small.

The intervenor, Pennsylvania Electric Association, separately sought a ruling that the Constitution necessarily requires recovery of prudent costs, regardless of their usefulness and regardless of the economic effect of a disallowance. That argument, if accepted by the Court, would have prohibited regulators from allocating to shareholders the risk of prudent but uneconomic outcomes. The Court rejected the argument as inconsistent with *Hope*:

> We think that the adoption of any such rule would signal a retreat from 45 years of decisional law in this area which would be as unwarranted as it would be unsettling. *Hope* clearly held that "the Commission was not bound to the use of any single formula or combination of formulae in determining rates . . . ."[141]

The Court thus reaffirmed a line of cases holding that that the Constitution does not insulate a utility from uneconomic outcomes, whether in the form of market forces, obsolescence or bad luck, even when the utility has acted prudently. If an asset is not "used and useful," the Constitution does not make customers pay.[142]

6.D.2. Three points on the risk-assignment spectrum

Barasch and its ancestors tell us that, faced with a non-used and useful asset, the regulator can choose among three results (and points in between, all dependent on the facts): (1) full

---

139.   488 U.S. 299 (1989).
140.   *Id.* at 301–02.
141.   *Id.* at 315 (citing FPC v. Hope Natural Gas, 320 U.S. at 602).
142.   *See* Denver Union Stock Yard Co. v. United States, 304 U.S. 470, 475 (1938) (upholding Agriculture Secretary's exclusion from rate base of "land and improvements used for a stock show and for trackage and facilities for unloading and loading livestock" because they were not "used and useful" for the regulated service); Mkt. St. Ry. Co. v. R.R. Comm'n of Cal., 324 U.S. at 567 ("The due process clause has been applied to prevent governmental destruction of existing economic values. It has not and cannot be applied to insure values that have been lost by the operation of economic forces.").

amortization plus return on the unamortized amount, (2) amortization only, and (3) no amortization and no return. Each of these options (and hybrids of them) can satisfy both the statutory command of "just and reasonable" rates and the constitutional command of "just compensation." A variety of appellate court decisions illustrate this flexibility.

a. Amortization but no return: FERC's decisions to unbundle pipeline transportation service from pipeline gas sales left the pipelines with "sunk" (or "stranded") costs.[143] State commissions argued that because the costs were not "used and useful," the Natural Gas Act bars their recovery from customers. The court of appeals disagreed. It described a middle ground: The Act allowed FERC to remove non-used-and-useful assets from rate base (where they would have earned a profit) but allow recovery of the cost through amortization expense. Granting a profit on non-used-and-useful facilities "would be inappropriate since this allows a return on facilities that are not economically viable, and may also result in a competitive advantage for the pipeline." But allowing cost amortization "will keep the pipeline whole for the direct cost of its investment in the facilities. . . . Investor interests have not, therefore, been entirely ignored."[144]

b. No recovery, no return: A pipeline spent $13 million on unsuccessful synthetic gas supply projects. FERC disallowed both amortization and return. Upholding the Commission, the court of appeals distinguished between imprudence and bad luck: "[T]he problem of risk allocation in this case is not a problem of fault. . . . The Natural Gas Act simply does not guarantee the shareholders of even a prudently managed utility that ratepayers can always be stuck with the bill for supply projects that turn out to be total failures, however praiseworthy the utility's motives for undertaking those projects may have been." The court cited a prior FERC decision holding that to be included in rate base (and thus to earn a return), "expenditures must satisfy not only the necessary condition of prudent investment but must also be 'used and useful' in providing service."[145]

c. Full recovery and return: The court of appeals also has said that the Commission "might also allow the pipeline to recover not only the amortization, but also interest, i.e., the 'cost' of the unamortized portion of the investment. The Commission could further decide to include stranded investments in the utility's rate base and thereby generate a profit for investors."[146]

---

143. *See supra* Chapter 3.C.1.
144. United Distrib. Cos. v. FERC, 88 F.3d 1105, 1179–80 (D.C. Cir. 1996) (quoting Equitrans, Inc., 64 FERC ¶ 61,374, at p. 63,601 (1993), National Fuel Gas Supply Corp., 71 FERC ¶ 61,031, at p. 61,138 (1995), and Jersey Cent. Power & Light Co. v. FERC, 810 F.2d at 1192 (Starr, J., concurring)). *See also* NEPCO Mun. Rate Comm. v. FERC, 668 F.2d 1327, 1333 (D.C. Cir. 1981) ("FERC's refusal to include project expenditures in the rate base, while allowing their recovery as costs over time, is a valid approach to allocating the risks of project cancellation.").
145. Natural Gas Pipeline of Am. v. FERC, 765 F.2d 1155, 1163–64 (D.C. Cir. 1985) (citing Transcontinental Gas Pipe Line Corp., 58 F.P.C. 2038 (1977), *aff'd in relevant part and remanded on other grounds sub nom.* Tenn. Gas Pipeline Co. v. FERC, 606 F.2d 1094 (D.C. Cir. 1979)).
146. United Distrib. Cos. v. FERC, 88 F.3d at 1179.

To summarize: Like the Supreme Court's opinions in *Hope* and *Barasch*, subsequent court of appeals decisions have declined to reject or anoint any specific rule. The courts will review the regulator's inclusion or exclusion of costs based on the facts, subject to the requirement that the regulator's decision be "based on substantial evidence and . . . adequately balance[] the interests of investors and ratepayers."[147]

6.D.3. Four limits on regulatory actions

The regulator's discretion to assign the risk of bad luck is not unbounded. Here are four limiting principles.

a. Honor legitimate shareholder expectations: When commissions allocate the risk of prudent but uneconomic outcomes, they must do so clearly and consistently over the life of an investment. If the commission commits, pre-investment, to full recovery of prudent costs regardless of the outcome, it must honor that commitment when setting rates. Failure to do so risks reversal under state law ("arbitrary and capricious" decisionmaking) or the Constitution (undermining "distinct, investment-backed expectations" created by the prior regulatory commitment).[148] As *Barasch* warned:

> The risks a utility faces are in large part defined by the rate methodology because utilities
> are virtually always public monopolies dealing in an essential service, and so relatively
> immune to the usual market risks. Consequently, a State's decision to arbitrarily switch
> back and forth between methodologies in a way which required investors to bear the risk
> of bad investments at some times while denying them the benefit of good investments at
> others would raise serious constitutional questions.[149]

b. Reflect shareholder risks in the authorized return on equity: Investors legitimately expect higher returns for higher risks. A commission that assigns to shareholders the risk of prudent but uneconomic outcomes must compensate for that risk when it determines the authorized return on equity.[150]

---

147.   *Id.* at 1180. *See also Permian Basin Area Rate Cases*, 390 U.S. at 792 ("Judicial review of the Commission's orders will therefore function accurately and efficaciously only if the Commission indicates fully and carefully the methods by which, and the purposes for which, it has chosen to act, as well as its assessment of the consequences of its order for the character and future development of the industry.").

148.   *See* Penn. Cent. Transp. Co. v. New York, 438 U.S. at 124 (Takings Clause analysis must consider the "economic impact of the regulation on the claimant and, particularly, the extent to which the regulation has interfered with distinct investment-backed expectations").

149.   Duquesne Light Co. v. Barasch, 488 U.S. at 315. *See also Verizon Commc'ns, Inc. v. FCC*, 535 U.S. at 527 ("[T]here may be a taking challenge distinct from a plain-vanilla objection to arbitrary or capricious agency action if a rate making body were to make opportunistic changes in rate setting methodologies just to minimize return on capital investment in a utility enterprise.").

150.   *See, e.g.*, Duquesne Light Co. v. Barasch, 488 U.S. at 312 (Pennsylvania's statute "slightly increases the overall risk of investments in utilities over the pure prudent investment rule. Presumably the PUC adjusts the risk premium element of the rate of return on equity accordingly."). *See also* SCOTT HEMPLING, RIDERS, TRACKERS, SURCHARGES, PRE-APPROVALS AND DECOUPLING: HOW DO THEY AFFECT THE

c. Allow for "lumpiness": A new investment will rarely match existing demand perfectly. Major capacity additions come on line in lumps that create surplus. To treat this surplus automatically as not used and useful, and deny recovery and return, ignores physical reality. As the Wisconsin Supreme Court declared:

> [A] public utility, being required to provide service when and as demanded by the public, must have some latitude with respect to plant management; . . . in determining the rate base, property should not be excluded merely because at the moment it is not in actual service. We held that the commission could not construct a hypothetical plant which would theoretically render equivalent service and on that basis hold that any portion of the existing property was excess."[151]

d. Regulatory flexibility can create regulatory uncertainty, which also raises the cost of capital. This uncertainty has led some state legislatures to authorize, or direct, their commissions to declare up front, prior to major capital investments, what type risk allocation will apply. Here are four examples:

1. Indiana's Environmental Compliance Plan Pre-Approval Act authorizes the Commission to approve a utility's costs in advance, if they form part of an Environmental Compliance Plan that will "constitute[] a reasonable and least cost strategy over the life of the investment consistent with providing reliable, efficient and economical electric service." The Commission can also limit rate challenges to utility-incurred costs to issues of fraud, concealment or gross mismanagement.[152]

2. A Florida statute authorizes cost recovery, prior to a plant's commercial operation, for the siting, design, licensing and construction of electric generating plants based on either nuclear or integrated gasification combined cycle power technologies.[153]

3. A North Carolina statute authorizes recovery, before a plant's commercial operation, of "project development" costs for nuclear plants, subject to certain conditions on types and timing of activities. Eligible activities include (but are not limited to) "evaluation, design, engineering, environmental analysis and permitting, early site permitting, combined operating license permitting, and initial site preparation costs."[154]

COST OF EQUITY? (ElectricityPolicy.com Jan. 2012), *available at* http://www.scotthemplinglaw.com/files/pdf/ppr_riders_oge_hempling112711.pdf.

151. Milwaukee & Suburban Transp. Corp. v. Pub. Serv. Comm'n of Wisconsin, 108 N.W.2d 729, 733–34 (Wis. 1961) (reversing commission disallowance of costs of "shops and yards" rendered unused due to conversion of transportation system from streetcars to trackless trolleys and buses) (citing Wisconsin Telephone Co. v. Public Service Comm'n of Wis., 287 N.W. 122, 158 (Wis. 1939)).

152. IND. CODE § 8-1-27-8(1)(B).

153. FLA. STAT. § 366.93.

154. N.C. GEN. STAT. § 62-110.7.

4.   Mississippi's Baseload Act authorizes the Commission to allow recovery, prior to a plant's commercial operation, of all or some of prudent costs (both pre-construction and construction) associated with a baseload electricity plant—as distinct from the traditional approach, which is to defer decisions about recovery, and actual recovery, until the plant is operating for the customers. The statute also authorizes periodic Commission reviews and approvals of construction prudence, to reduce the uncertainty associated with future cost recovery.[155]

* * *

Chapters 6.C and 6.D. have described regulators' options for disallowing costs under the "just and reasonable" standard, along with the constitutional constraints on disallowance. Figure 6 displays these options as a decision tree. Once the utility requests cost recovery through rates, the commission decides whether the cost is prudent, and whether the associated asset is used and useful. Those factual determinations generate a series of possible outcomes that vary with statutory constraints and commission discretion, all bounded by the Constitution's requirement that state and commission honor investors' legitimate expectations.

6.E. Variations on cost bases

This chapter has focused on traditional cost-based ratemaking (sometimes called "rate of return" or "rate base" or "embedded cost" ratemaking), where the commission bases a utility's revenue requirement on that utility's specific costs, both past or predicted. In several contexts, dissatisfaction with this method has spawned alternatives. Three examples are area rates, price caps, and "alternative forms of regulation." Each varies from, but retains some connection to, some measure of "cost."

6.E.1. Area rates

After the Supreme Court's *Phillips* decision,[156] the Federal Power Commission began to set each gas producer's rates based on its specific costs. Processing individual rate cases for numerous producers caused complexity, workload and backlog. The Commission therefore turned to "area rates." An area rate was based on the average production costs for a specified production region. The rate was applicable to all producers in that region, regardless of

---

155.   Miss. Code Ann. § 77-3-105. For additional discussion of regulatory issues associated with "pre-approval," see Scott Hempling & Scott Strauss, Pre-Approval Commitments: When And Under What Conditions Should Regulators Commit Ratepayer Dollars to Utility-Proposed Capital Projects? (National Regulatory Research Institute, 2008), *available at* http://nrri.org/pubs/electricity/nrri_preapproval_commitments_08-12.pdf.

156.   *See supra* Chapter 3.A.2.

Figure 6
Paths to Cost Recovery

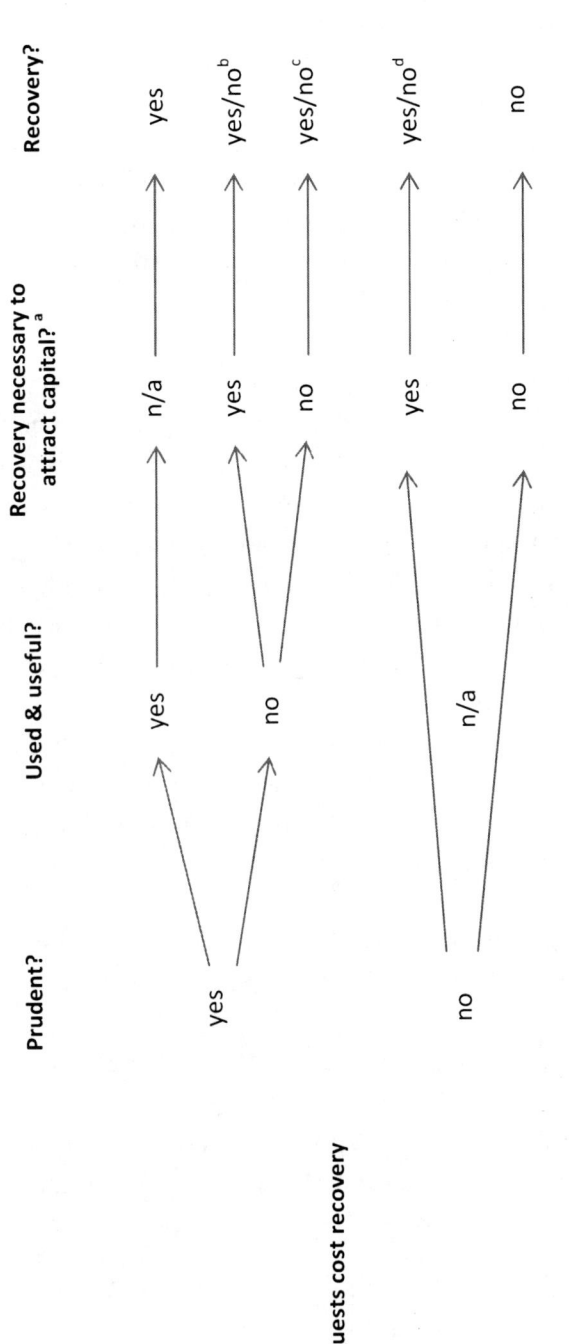

a. *Jersey Central*: Hearing is necessary if utility offers evidence that recovery is necessary for financial integrity; i.e., absent recovery, it cannot attract capital or maintain credit.

b. *Market St. Railway*: Constitution does not "insure values that have been lost by the operation of economic forces." But statutes might permit recovery.

c. *Barasch*: Constitution does not guarantee recovery of prudent costs. A statute therefore can allow or disallow recovery of costs that are prudent but not used and useful.

d. Normally, commissions disallow imprudent costs regardless of effect on utility's finances. But some commissions have allowed recovery where disallowance would leave the company unable to serve adequately. *See, e.g.*, Gulf States Utilities Co. v. Louisiana Pub. Serv. Comm'n, 578 So. 2d 71 (La. 1991).

any specific producer's actual costs. If a producer faced financial difficulty because its costs exceeded the area rate, it could apply for "special relief." The Supreme Court has upheld these area rates as consistent with the Natural Gas Act's "just and reasonable" standard.[157]

6.E.2. Price caps

Price caps give the seller discretion to set its own rates, subject to a commission-set ceiling, for one or more commission-specified services. In the early 1990s, the FCC established price caps for service provided by local exchange carriers to long-distance companies.[158] The FCC's action was prompted by perceived problems with traditional cost-based regulation. As the court of appeals explained:

1. Regulatory efforts to apply the prudent investment rule (where the commission granted recovery of all prudent costs) were "in practice often . . . no match for the capacity of utilities having all the relevant information to manipulate the rate base and renegotiate the rate of return every time a rate was set."

2. "Because a firm can pass any cost along to ratepayers (unless it is identified as imprudent), its incentive to innovate is less sharp than if it were unregulated."

3. "There is even a temptation toward 'gold-plating'—using equipment or services that are not justifiable in purely economic terms, especially when their use improves the lot of management (elegant offices, company jets, etc.)."

4. "Firms can gain by shifting costs away from unregulated activities (where consumers would react to higher prices by reducing their purchases) into the regulated ones (where the price increase will cause little or no drop in sales because under regulation the prices are in a range where demand is relatively unresponsive to price changes)."

5. "Rate-of-return regulation is costly to administer, as it requires the agency endlessly to calculate and allocate the firm's costs."[159]

The FCC's price cap regime worked like this:

1. The FCC grouped the local exchange carriers' services into four major baskets: (1) common line services, (2) traffic sensitive services, (3) special access services, and (4) interexchange services.[160]

---

157. *Permian Basin Area Rate Cases*, 390 U.S. at 813–22.
158. *See* Policy & Rules Concerning Rates for Dominant Carriers, 5 FCC Rcd. 6786 (1990) (Second Report & Order), *order on recon.*, 6 FCC Rcd. 2637 (1991).
159. Nat'l Rural Telecom Ass'n v. FCC, 988 F.2d 174, 178 (D.C. Cir. 1993). *See also* Verizon Commc'ns v. FCC, 535 U.S. at 486.
160. Policy & Rules Concerning Rates for Dominant Carriers, 5 FCC Rcd. at 6811.

2. Each basket had an FCC-set price cap, based in part on the carrier's costs. For any service within the basket, the carrier could charge any price below that basket's cap, keeping whatever profits resulted if it incurred costs lower than the price (and absorbing any losses if things went the other way). That profit retention was subject to the "sharing" and "low end" adjustments noted below. The separate basket caps reduced a company's ability to discriminate by recovering more of its costs from services whose customers had fewer alternatives.[161]

3. Each basket cap was adjusted annually: upward for inflation and for factors outside the seller's control ("exogenous" factors), and downward for anticipated productivity gains ("X factor").

4. A "sharing" mechanism required the carrier to rebate a portion of its profits if its overall rate of return in the previous year exceeded specified levels. This sharing protected against setting the productivity factor too low.[162] Mirroring the sharing adjustment was a "low-end" adjustment, which raised the price cap if the prior year's earnings were much lower than expected.[163]

5. A local exchange carrier could still seek rates exceeding the cap, but the approval process was more intensive and cumbersome.

While the price cap initiatives reflected dissatisfaction with embedded cost regulation, both price cap and embedded cost regulation have two important features in common: (1) The authorized rate uses the seller's specific costs as a starting point; and (2) if the seller's actual cost deviates from the authorized rate, the utility retains profits or absorbs losses, for some period of time. In traditional embedded cost ratemaking, that time period lasts until the commission sets new rates; in price cap regulation the time period lasts until the commission sets a new cap. The time period may or may not be specified at the time the rate or cap is set. These commonalities create some overlap between the two methods. As one text describes:

> How different are price caps from rate of return regulation in practice? After all, . . . rate of return regulation begins to resemble price cap in instances where the relevant regulators

---

161. Nat'l Rural Telecom Ass'n v. FCC, 988 F.2d at 182.

162. *See* Bell Atl. Tel. Cos. v. FCC, 79 F.3d 1195, 1202 (D.C. Cir. 1996) ("By 1993, all seven Bell Operating Companies were in the sharing zone, leading the Commission to believe that the original X-factor had been too low.").

163. *See also id.* at 1198–99 (upholding Commission's adjustments to the productivity factor); U.S. Tel. Ass'n v. FCC, 188 F.3d 521, 524 (D.C. Cir. 1999) (remanding for further explanation of productivity adjustment). The FCC later eliminated the sharing mechanism for carriers choosing specified productivity factors. Price Cap Performance Review for Local Exchange Carriers, 10 FCC Rcd. 8961, 9058, ¶ 222 (1995). The D.C. Circuit upheld this action as consistent with "just and reasonable" ratemaking. *See* U.S. Tel. Ass'n v. FCC, 188 F.3d at 527.

are slow to adjust prices in response to changes in costs. Similarly, price cap regulation begins to resemble rate of return in instances where regulators respond to changes in cost.[164]

6.E.3. Alternative form of regulation

For local telephone and intrastate interexchange service, a cousin to price cap regulation was "alternative form of regulation" (AFOR). The states that chose AFOR had multiple objectives, including "provid[ing] . . . customers with service of a quality consistent with commission rules at affordable rates, . . . facilitat[ing] the development of telecommunication alternatives for customers, and . . . provid[ing], where appropriate, a regulatory environment with greater flexibility than is available under traditional rate-of-return regulation."[165] Because AFOR plans envisioned rates untied from a utility's actual costs, statutory authorization was usually necessary.

A company's AFOR typically included features similar to those in rate caps, including (a) a methodology for calculating rate levels (usually a base rate with period adjustments— upward for inflation and downward for productivity); (b) sharing of profits or losses relative to a specified return on equity; (c) a specified term of years; and (d) measures of service quality (including penalties for shortfalls). The need for a service quality component was explained by the Maryland Commission:

> [T]he present AFOR fails to condition rate increases on any level of service quality, instead permitting Verizon to increase rates according to the passage of time and the application of certain indexing formulas. This disengagement of service quality from rate increases caused, and causes, us to question whether the present AFOR "ensur[es] the quality, availability, and reliability of telecommunications services throughout the state," as the governing statute requires.[166]

6.F. Departures from cost bases

For decades, regulated rates (i.e., rates subject to a statutory "just and reasonable" standard) have departed from cost with judicial approval. The courts' tolerance has rested on two legal bases previously discussed. Lawfulness depends on "the result reached not the

---

164. STUART BENJAMIN, HOWARD SHELANSKI, JAMES SPETA & PHILIP WEISER, TELECOMMUNICATIONS LAW AND POLICY 368 (3d ed. 2012).

165. MINN. STAT. § 237.76. *See also* REV. CODE WASH. § 80.36.135(1)(a) (finding that "[c]hanges in technology and the structure of the telecommunications industry may produce conditions under which traditional rate of return, rate base regulation of telecommunications companies may not in all cases provide the most efficient and effective means of achieving the public policy goals of this state").

166. Appropriate Forms of Regulating Telephone Cos., Order No. 81776, Case No. 9133, 2008 Md. PSC LEXIS 2 (Md. Pub. Serv. Comm'n Jan. 3, 2008) (finding that "the current AFOR no longer serves the public interest").

method employed";[167] and the just and reasonable rates occupy a "zone" rather than a fixed point.[168]

But departing from cost cannot occur casually. Because the regulator's "primary aim" is "to guard the consumer against excessive rates,"[169] courts evaluate rates that depart from cost by asking two questions: (1) Is the departure necessary, and no more than necessary, to carry out a statutory purpose? and (2) How does the rate compare to cost? After discussing these two questions, we describe how recent court decisions have loosened the required connection between rates and costs, and rates and results.

6.F.1. Is the departure necessary to carry out a statutory purpose?

Protecting consumers does not necessarily mean minimizing prices. It can mean raising prices to spur exploration and production.[170] When the FPC began regulating gas producer prices after *Phillips*,[171] consumers challenged these exploration inducements. An early D.C. Circuit opinion urged caution: "If the Commission contemplates increasing rates for the purpose of encouraging exploration and development . . . it must see to it that the increase is in fact needed, and is no more than is needed, for the purpose." The court remanded the case because the FPC, in basing rates on market prices that exceeded cost-based compensation, failed to determine "whether a lesser amount [of price increase] would suffice."[172]

Later cases loosened this requirement. In *Mobil Oil Corp. v. Federal Power Commission*,[173] the Supreme Court upheld certain production "incentives," including price escalators. It found that the Commission could "employ price functionally in order to achieve relevant regulatory purposes." Prices just high enough to satisfy the *Hope-Bluefield* standards (i.e., "sufficient to assure confidence in the financial integrity of the enterprise, so as to maintain its credit and to attract capital") "may not be sufficient also to encourage an increase in production." The statute allowed higher prices, if the Commission could "assur[e] that such increases would not be levied upon consumers unless accompanied by increased supplies of gas." And the calibration of price increase to supply induced need not be precise; it

---

167. FPC v. Hope Natural Gas, 320 U.S. at 602.
168. FPC v. Natural Gas Pipeline, 315 U.S. 575 (1942). *See also* Blumenthal v. FERC, 552 F.3d 875, 883 (D.C. Cir. 2009) ("[T]he Supreme Court has repeatedly rejected the argument 'that there is only one just and reasonable rate possible . . . and that this rate must be based entirely on some concept of cost plus a reasonable rate of return.'") (quoting Mobil Oil Corp. v. FPC, 417 U.S. 283, 316 (1974)).
169. City of Detroit v. FPC, 230 F.2d 810, 817 (D.C. Cir. 1955) (referring to the "just and reasonable" standard of the Natural Gas Act).
170. *See, e.g., Permian Basin Area Rate Cases*, 390 U.S. at 798 (noting that "the Commission's responsibilities include the protection of future, as well as present, consumer interests," the Court upheld a Commission rate structure that "will both provide a useful incentive to exploration and prevent excessive producer profits").
171. In Phillips Petrol. Co. v. Wis., 347 U.S. 672 (1954), discussed in Chapter 3.A.2, the Supreme Court interpreted the Natural Gas Act to require the FPA to regulate gas producer prices. Prior to *Phillips*, the Commission had regulated the prices of pipeline transportation and pipeline sales only.
172. City of Detroit v. FPC, 230 F.2d at 817.
173. 417 U.S. 283 (1974).

was enough to find "a positive relationship between gas contract price levels and exploratory effort."[174]

The D.C. Circuit responded to *Mobil* with gritted teeth:

> Under the shadow of the nationwide shortage of natural gas, the incentive device has
> been seized upon increasingly by the FPC and paraded before the courts in a number of
> guises, perhaps on the assumption that the courts would not be inclined to reject them
> all. . . . Although we continue to view this spectacle with some skepticism, we are inclined
> to test these incentive schemes somewhat less rigorously after the *Mobil Oil* decision. . . . If
> the bars are not down after *Mobil*, the spaces between them are perceptibly wider.[175]

The D.C. Circuit's solution was a "necessity" test: The Commission must "protect consumers from paying substantially more than necessary to bring forth the needed supplies."
Further, the Commission's price increases must be supported with substantial evidence, to
"prevent[] us from 'acquiescing in a charade or a rubber stamping of non-regulation in
agency trappings.'"[176]

This connection between price increase and new supplies was tested by Panhandle's
transfer-and-buyback scheme. This multistate pipeline company also owned gas-producing
properties. Historically, the FPC had required that pipeline-produced gas be priced on a
traditional cost-of-service basis. Panhandle proposed to transfer its gas-producing properties to Pan Eastern, a production-only affiliate. Pan Eastern would produce the gas and
sell it back to the pipeline at the "area rate" price, which exceeded the cost-based price.
The "proposal was viewed from the outset as nothing more than a device for revising the
applicable rates." The court largely approved the scheme because, among other reasons,
there would be "symmetry" between customer burden and benefit: the customers would
receive the "plowback" of all the new production resulting from their higher payment.[177]

The D.C. Circuit's tolerance for pricing "incentives" had limits, however. In computing pipeline revenue requirements, FERC assigned consolidated tax return savings to a
pipeline's shareholders. Giving the money to customers, said FERC, would act as "a dis-
incentive to continued gas supply development activities by pipelines and other regulated
utilities." Reminding readers that "[t]his Court has never allowed rhetoric as a substitute
for a record," the court sent the case back:

---

174. *Id.* at 305–06, 316–19.
175. City of Fulton v. FPC, 512 F.2d 947, 950–51 (D.C. Cir. 1975) (footnotes omitted).
176. *Id.* (citations omitted). See *also* MacDonald v. FPC, 505 F.2d 355, 364 (D.C. Cir. 1974) (where the Com-
      mission allows a producer to depart from normal ratemaking, "its regulatory trust requires it to give
      complete consideration to that producer's individual costs in order to ensure that the producer's profit
      margin is not thereby raised to an unreasonable level").
177. City of Fulton v. FPC, 512 F.2d. at 950, 952 (distinguishing *MacDonald v. FPC*, 505 F.2d at 365, where
      the Commission had made no attempt "to ensure that all the proceeds would be sunk into exploration
      and development").

There is no indication that [the pipeline's exploration and development] investments were any greater after FERC's change in tax cost policy than before the supposed incentive was created. And . . . [t]he FERC ALJ found that only a portion of the tax savings were routed to [exploration and development] companies, with the remainder being used for general corporate purposes. . . .

The Commission urged in its brief that tax savings not directly reinvested eventually find their way to the [exploration and development] companies since the parent company finances exploration and development. The Commission cites no evidence that tax savings "trickle down" from the parent e & d affiliates. FERC asks this Court to take it on faith that such funneling of tax savings does occur.[178]

One more example, perhaps defining the outer edge of commission carelessness: seeking to boost oil pipeline construction, FERC set ceiling prices for oil transportation at levels intended to prevent, in FERC's words, "egregious exploitation and gross abuse" and "gross overreaching and unconscionable gouging." In other words, "exploitation," "abuse" and "gouging" were acceptable unless "egregious," "gross" or "unconscionable." FERC intended its rates to produce "handsome rate base writeups" and "creamy returns on book equity."[179] FERC's standing with the court could not have been helped by its own befuddlement over its role, as the court explained:

On the one hand, FERC declared that "oil pipeline rate regulation is not a consumer-protection measure. It probably was never intended to be. It is and was a producer-protection measure." On the other hand, when FERC began its examination of the unimportance to the public of the cost of oil pipeline transportation, FERC stated, "we look at it through the consumer's glasses. We do so because we are ourselves consumers and because they are the people we are here to protect."

The court of appeals could not square FERC's odd nouns, adjectives and reasoning with the statute's "just and reasonable" test. Pipeline construction was a valid goal, but "in this case FERC failed to forecast or otherwise estimate the dimensions of the need for additional capacity, and did not even attempt to calibrate the relationship between increased rates and the attraction of new capital."[180]

6.F.2. How does the rate compare to cost?

If "just and reasonable" does not mandate a cost basis, can cost be ignored? Early on, the court of appeals said no: "Unless [cost] is continued to be used at least as a point of

---

178.   City of Charlottesville v. FERC, 661 F.2d 945, 953–54 & n.47 (D.C. Cir. 1981).
179.   Williams Pipe Line Co., 21 FERC ¶ 61,260, at pp. 61,649–50 (1982).
180.   Farmers Union Cent. Exch. v. FERC, 734 F.2d at 1503, 1507 n.48 (citations to FERC's opinion omitted).

departure, the whole experience under the [Natural Gas] Act is discarded and no anchor, as it were, is available by which to hold the terms 'just and reasonable' to some recogniz-able meaning."[181] With this "anchor" of objective costs, the regulator can treat sellers and buyers evenhandedly:

> While rather concrete factors such as the ability to maintain and attract capital are avail-able to gauge whether a rate is just and reasonable to a producer, no factors apart from producer costs are available to guide efforts to make that determination from the stand-point of the consumer. Thus the [D.C. Circuit in *City of Detroit*] feared that, if a rate based on market prices were not compared to one based on producer costs, the entire framework for evaluation of the reasonableness of the rate from the standpoint of the consumer would be lost, leaving without protection the segment of society which was supposedly the prime beneficiary of the Natural Gas Act's system of regulation.[182]

The Commission had substituted area rates for seller-specific cost-of-service rates. The change was lawful, because "area rates are essentially rates based on composite cost of service for all producers in a given geographic area. Producer costs thus remain at the heart of the regulatory system."[183] The court again emphasized cost in rejecting FERC's "quite novel principle that oil pipeline ratemaking should protect against only 'egregious exploitation and gross abuse . . . [and] gross overreaching and unconscionable gouging.'" Seller's costs "often offer the principal points of reference for whether the resulting rate is 'less than compensatory' or 'excessive,' the most useful and reliable starting point for rate regulation is an inquiry into costs."[184]

Even in "market pricing," where sellers can charge what they want, FERC monitors prices for lawfulness by comparing them to likely cost. We will discuss this concept in Chapter 7.B and C.

6.F.3. Loosening the connection between rate and result

These cost departure cases have a consistent theme: The regulator must calibrate price "incentive" to customer benefit. But the alert reader will have noticed that these cases average about 40 years in age. More recent appellate decisions give the regulator more running room.

Consider FERC's order granting New England transmission owners a "bonus" of one percentage point in the authorized equity return, for investments made to carry out the

---

181. City of Detroit v. FPC, 230 F.2d at 818–19.
182. City of Chicago v. FPC, 458 F.2d at 751.
183. *Id.*
184. Farmers Union Cent. Exch. v. FERC, 734 F.2d at 1502 (citing *Mobil Oil Corp. v. FPC*, 417 U.S. at 605–06, and FPC v. Hope Natural Gas, 320 U.S. at 591, 602–03).

region's transmission expansion plan.[185] A FERC administrative law judge had rejected the incentive because the utility failed to show that "but for" the extra money, the project would not go forward. The Commission reversed. The applicable test was not "but for," but whether, in the Commission's words, "(i) the proposed incentive falls within the zone of reasonable returns; and (ii) there is some link or nexus between the incentives being requested and the investment being made, i.e., to demonstrate that the incentives are rationally related to the investments being proposed." FERC found that "the proposed incentive will give project owners a significant impetus to push hard for their projects at all phases of the approval process."[186] The D.C. Circuit upheld the Commission:

> We are sympathetic to petitioners' concern about the "rationally related" formulation's facial vagueness. But the Commission's application of the standard in this case belies the notion that it employed the phrase as a fig leaf for accepting any link, however nominal or trivial. Rather, FERC made findings—uncontested by petitioners—of the proposed projects' exceptional value under circumstances of congestion and unreliability. . . . The experts' calculation of dramatic savings from a mere two-year acceleration of the facilities' availability seems to confirm this sense of urgency. . . . [T]he Commission linked the urgency of bringing the projects on line to the incentive's likely tendency to speed up that event.

The court declined to require either a "but for" test or a quantitative benefit-cost fit: "Certainly the Commission's failure to pinpoint specific actions that utilities would take only because of the incentive is of no moment." (Here the court relied—to the likely chagrin of its *Fulton* predecessors—on the Supreme Court's *Mobil Oil* opinion for a "less demanding view of conventional ratemaking.") The Applicants' witness could not connect the rider to any action he would take ("I can't sit here and give you a shopping list now, looking forward, to exactly what we are going to do, specifically in response to this incentive."), but FERC still expected the incentive to accelerate the project. That was enough for the court, which quoted the Commission's statement that "utilities can be expected to respond to financial motivations and, in so doing, to expend the time and effort necessary to sell the importance of their projects at the local level."

Still, the court left an opening: "We note that petitioners' "causal link" argument might be thought to suggest that the Commission should have applied a de facto cost-benefit analysis to the adder and demanded proof that the incremental cost of the adder would be

---

185. FERC authorizes transmission incentives on a case-by-case basis, based on the criteria in Order No. 679-A, which implemented section 219 of the Federal Power Act, added in 2005. Section 219 required the Commission to issue a rule on incentives for transmission projects that increased reliability or reduced congestion. *See* Promoting Transmission Investment Through Pricing Reform, Order No. 679, 116 FERC ¶ 61,057 (2006), *order on reh'g*, Order 679-A, 117 FERC ¶ 61,345 (2006).

186. Bangor Hydro-Electric Co., 117 FERC ¶ 61,129, at P 109 (2006), *order on reh'g*, 122 FERC ¶ 61,265 (2008).

matched by at least equivalent incremental benefits for the customers (see, e.g., the apparent demand for 'symmetry' between the incentive payment and the resulting benefits . . . .)."[187] The court did not address this argument because the petitioners did not raise it before the Commission on rehearing, as required by statute.

* * *

When engaged in cost-based ratemaking, regulators must satisfy two bodies of law. Statutes say that rates must be "just and reasonable," while the Constitution commands that a regulatory "taking" of private property be accompanied by "just compensation." The "just and reasonable" standard protects consumers from exploitation and waste; it protects shareholders from decisions that are arbitrary, inconsistent, and lacking in factual support. The Constitution protects shareholders from confiscation. Within these constraints, regulators have discretion over methodologies.

That discretion has produced rates based on embedded, utility-specific cost; performance-based (but still cost-linked) methods like rate caps and "alternative forms of regulation;" area rates based on average costs; rates based on the long-run costs of developing technologies; incentives for production and construction; and other methods. While it is common for regulators to disallow imprudent costs, views vary on what "prudence" means and who has to prove it. The courts have repeatedly upheld disallowance of prudent costs as permissible both statutorily and constitutionally; in these instances, commissions assign the risk of bad-luck business decisions to the entities making those decisions.

---

187.   Conn. Dep't of Pub. Util. Control v. FERC, 593 F.3d 30, 33–34, 37 (D.C. Cir. 2010).

CHAPTER SEVEN
"Just and Reasonable" Prices in "Competitive" Markets
Market-Based Rates Set by the Seller

Without empirical proof that . . . existing competition would ensure that the actual price is just and reasonable, [the Commission's approach] retains the false illusion that a government agency is keeping watch over rates, . . . when it is in fact doing no such thing.[1]

7.A. Seller-set prices can be "just and reasonable"— if seller lacks market power

7.A.1. Paths to regulatory withdrawal

When policymakers convert monopoly markets to competitive markets, they begin with market structure. They (1) authorize entry by new competitors; (2) make competition effective by unbundling the competitive from noncompetitive services and reducing entry barriers; and (3) monitor the results to prevent anti-competitive action like price squeeze, predatory pricing and tying. Those were the subjects of Chapters 3, 4 and 5. We now turn from structure to pricing. Chapter 6 explained how, in regulated monopoly markets, the regulator sets the prices. When we authorize competition in previously monopolistic markets, should we let sellers set the prices?

The answer has been yes, with two distinct approaches to the regulator's role: statutory repeal and administrative withdrawal. *Statutory repeal* is straightforward: A legislative body repeals price regulation. Doing so removes the regulator's rate authority entirely, leaving entrants to price at will. Examples are state statutes authorizing retail competition in gas and electricity. In those markets, the new competitors set their prices without regulatory review. There is no "just and reasonable" limit and no regulatory role.[2] *Administrative withdrawal* is less straightforward. The statutory "just and reasonable" standard remains on the books; but the regulator, using implicit or explicit authority and subject to varying procedures, withdraws from price-setting. The assumption is that competitive market forces will keep prices just and reasonable. Under this administrative withdrawal umbrella, there are four main variations.[3]

---

1. Farmers Union Cent. Exch., Inc. v. FERC, 734 F.2d 1486, 1510 (D.C. Cir. 1984).
2. Caution: While the competitive retail sellers in these states can price at will, the provider of "default" service (also known as "standard offer" service or "last resort" service) is usually subject to some state commission price regulation. *See supra* Chapter 3.B.2.
3. In each of these variations, the regulator puts no boundaries on the prices. Recall from Chapter 6.E that regulators can also grant sellers pricing discretion within regulator-set boundaries. These price caps and their cousin "alternative form of regulation" (AFOR) are actually a variation on cost-based rates, because they have a foundation in some measure of cost, such as the carrier's last cost-justified rate. Price caps and their relatives have at least three common features: (1) The statutory just and reasonable standard remains in place, (2) the regulator assumes that competitive forces will keep prices just and reasonable, and (3) the formulas and quantities used to set the caps are periodically reviewed to see if they are producing excess or insufficient profit because of the relationship of price to cost.

Variation #1: Regulator removes price regulation for some but not all sellers. In the 1980s and early 1990s, the FCC allowed "non-dominant" (mostly long-distance) carriers to set their prices, but continued to subject the "dominant" carriers (such as the RBOCs and other ILECs) to price regulation (the form of which changed over time).[4] The non-dominant carriers' pricing freedom was not unlimited. They remained subject to (a) Title II's requirements relating to "common carrier" status, including the requirements that rates be just and reasonable and non-discriminatory; and (b) enforcement of those requirements through Title II's complaint procedures.[5]

Variation #2: Regulator removes price regulation for an entire category of services. Two examples are wireless and long distance. Commercial mobile radio service (CMRS) is wireless common carrier telephone service available to the public (as opposed to "private" wireless used to dispatch emergency vehicles and taxis). In 1982, Congress authorized the FCC to exempt CMRS from the Act's tariff-filing requirement, but not from the Act's common carrier obligation or its requirement that rates be just, reasonable and non-discriminatory. Congress also retained customers' ability to enforce those requirements by complaint.[6] Before allowing the exemption, the FCC had to find that (a) the tariff-filing requirement was not necessary (i) to ensure just and reasonable and non-discriminatory charges and practices or (ii) for the protection of consumers; and that (b) its removal was consistent with the public interest.[7] The FCC granted the exemption to wireless in 1994, finding that "market forces are generally sufficient to ensure the lawfulness of rate levels, rate structures, and terms and conditions of service set by carriers who lack market power."[8] Thus exempted from the tariff filing requirement, wireless providers could offer

---

4. In allowing the non-dominant carriers to set their own prices, the FCC relied on its general authority under the Communications Act to construe, administer and adopt rules. 47 U.S.C. §§ 151, 154(i), 201(b). The terms "dominant" and "non-dominant" distinguished between carriers with and without market power. *See* Policy & Rules Concerning Rates for Competitive Common Carrier Services & Facilities Authorizations Therefor (*"Competitive Carriers"*), First Report and Order, 85 F.C.C.2d 1 (1980); Second Report and Order, 91 F.C.C.2d 59 (1982); Policy Statement and Third Report and Order, 48 Fed. Reg. 46,791 (1983); Fourth Report and Order, 95 F.C.C.2d 554 (1983), *vacated*, AT&T v. FCC, 978 F.2d 727 (D.C. Cir. 1992); *Competitive Carriers*, Fifth Report and Order, 98 F.C.C.2d 1191 (1984); Sixth Report and Order, 99 F.C.C.2d 1020 (1985), *rev'd*, MCI Telecomms. Corp. v. FCC, 765 F.2d 1186 (D.C. Cir. 1985). *See also* Policy & Rules Concerning Rates for Dominant Carriers, 5 FCC Rcd. 6786, 6787, P 1 (1990); U.S. Tel. Ass'n v. FCC, 188 F.3d 521, 524 (D.C. Cir. 1999).
5. The FCC attempted to prohibit tariff filings by non-dominant carriers, and later, to make their tariff filings optional. The courts rejected the FCC both times, because 47 U.S.C. § 203(a) required that carriers "shall" file tariffs. MCI Telecomms. Corp. v. FCC, 765 F.2d 1186; MCI Telecomms. Corp. v. AT&T Co., 512 U.S. 218 (1994). This problem was resolved by Section 10 of the Communications Act, 47 U.S.C. §160, added by the Telecommunications Act of 1996. It gave the FCC authority to forbear from applying the requirements of Title II of the Act, including the tariff-filing requirement.
6. Section 203(a) of the Communications Act has the tariff-filing requirement; Section 201 the common carrier obligation; Section 202 the just, reasonable and non-discriminatory rate obligation; and Section 208 the enforcement of these obligations by complaint.
7. 47 U.S.C. § 332(c)(1)(A).
8. Implementation of Sections 3(n) & 332 of the Communications Act, Regulatory Treatment of Mobile Services, 9 FCC Rcd. 1411 (1994) (Second Report and Order).

different terms to different customers, without necessarily violating the statutory prohibition (which still applied) against undue preference. A wireless's provider could still violate the prohibition if, for example, it "'unreasonably discriminated against rural customers, who lacked adequate choice of providers, in favor of urban customers,' or if 'a CMRS market were inadequately competitive' or if there were other market failures limiting 'consumers' abilities to protect themselves.'"[9]

While the FCC has exempted CMRS providers from the tariff-filing requirement, it has not exercised its forbearance authority, added in 1996,[10] to exempt them from Sections 201 and 202 (common carrier status and the standards of justness and reasonableness and non-discrimination.) In theory the FCC could re-impose price regulation on wireless sellers, generically or in response to case-by-case complaints.[11]

Turning to non-dominant long-distance providers, the FCC has used its forbearance authority to eliminate their tariff-filing obligation.[12] As with wireless, the FCC found that competition provides sufficient discipline to keep prices just and reasonable and not unduly discriminatory. Case-by-case complaints remain available, for violations of the statutory "just, reasonable and non-discriminatory" requirement (as with wireless under *Orloff*), but not for the tariffing requirement.[13] There has been no judicial finding that the FCC, unlike FERC (as we will learn in this chapter), must monitor the market to ensure that prices remain just and reasonable.

Variation #3: Regulator removes price regulation on a seller-by-seller basis. FERC uses this approach for wholesale electric sales. It will occupy the remainder of this Chapter 7, after we address one more variation.

Variation #4: The federal statute preempts state rate regulation, with or without agency action. For wireless telephony, Congress has expressly preempted state regulation of entry and rates. States can continue to regulate "other terms and conditions," such as quality of service. States can escape preemption through two possible paths. The first is if the wireless services "are a substitute for land line telephone exchange service for a substantial portion of the communications within such State," provided the state's requirements are

---

9. *See* Orloff v. FCC, 352 F.3d 415, 420 (D.C. Cir. 2003) (upholding FCC's rejection of customer's complaint that by charging different prices to different customers, Verizon Wireless necessarily violated Section 202's prohibition against undue discrimination (quoting Orloff v. Vodafone AirTouch Licenses LLC, 17 FCC Rcd. 8987, 8997–98 (2002))).

10. Telecommunications Act of 1996 § 10, 47 U.S.C. § 160.

11. FCC has since classified wireless broadband as an "information service" not subject to Title II. *See* Appropriate Regulatory Treatment for Broadband Access to the Internet Over Wireless Networks, 22 FCC Rcd. 5901 (2007). To the extent wireless service is shifting to predominantly broadband service, wireless "telecommunication service" subject to FCC regulation is becoming less relevant.

12. As explained *supra* note 5, prior to the 1996 Act's addition of Section 10, 47 U.S.C. § 160, the FCC lacked authority to relieve Title II carriers of their obligation to file tariffs.

13. Policy & Rules Concerning the Interstate, Interchange Marketplace, 11 FCC Rcd. 20,730 (1996) (Second Report and Order), *on recon.*, 12 FCC Rcd. 15,014 (1997), *on second recon.*, 14 FCC Rcd. 6004 (1999), *petition for review denied sub nom.* MCI Worldcom, Inc. v. FCC, 209 F.3d 760 (D.C. Cir. 2000).

imposed "on all providers of telecommunications services necessary to ensure the universal availability of telecommunications service at affordable rates." The second is if the state demonstrates that "market conditions" are insufficient to protect consumers from unjust and unreasonable rates or undue discrimination. This latter exemption from preemption lasts only "for such periods of time, as the Commission deems necessary to ensure that such rates are just and reasonable and not unjustly or unreasonably discriminatory."[14]

More broadly, for any telecommunications carrier or telecommunications service (including but not limited to wireless), there is preemption of state regulation if the Commission has determined to forbear regulation under Section 10.[15]

7.A.2. Wholesale electricity: Seller-by-seller review

In wholesale electricity, the process of clearing sellers to price freely has taken a different route from telecommunications. The statutory "just and reasonable" standard remains in place; FERC cannot "forbear" from applying it. But FERC does remove itself from price-setting—not by exempting entire classes of sellers, but by screening individual sellers for market power. Recall that a seller has market power if it can "profitably . . . maintain prices above competitive levels for a significant period of time."[16] If a seller passes the market power screen, FERC allows it to price freely, on the assumption that market forces will discipline prices to "just and reasonable" levels.

What is the legal authority for trusting market forces to discipline prices? There are two sources. The first is *Hope Natural Gas*: What matters is not the methodology but the "end result." Cost-based pricing is only a methodology; it has no exclusive claim to justness and reasonableness.[17] The second source is economic theory: "[W]here neither buyer nor

---

14. 47 U.S.C. § 332(c)(3)(A). To date, the FCC has granted no state petition to regulate wireless service rates. *See* Tillman L. Lay, Taking Another Look at Federal/State Jurisdictional Relationships in the New Broadband World 30 n.98 (National Regulatory Research Institute 2011) (citing Termination of Stale or Moot Docketed Proceedings, 17 FCC Rcd. 1199, 1206 (2002)).

15. As already explained, Section 10(a) of the Telecommunications Act of 1996 (47 U.S.C. § 160(a)) authorizes the FCC to forbear. Section 10(e), 47 U.S.C. § 160(e), provides that "[a] State commission may not continue to apply or enforce any provision of this Act that the Commission has determined to forbear from applying under subsection (a)."

16. U.S. Dep't of Justice (DOJ) & Fed. Trade Comm'n (FTC), Horizontal Merger Guidelines (1997) [hereinafter *1997 Horizontal Merger Guidelines*], *available at* http://www.justice.gov/atr/public/guidelines/hmg.htm (these guidelines were issued in 1992 and revised in 1997); U.S. Dep't of Justice & Fed. Trade Comm'n, Horizontal Merger Guidelines (2010) [hereinafter *2010 Horizontal Merger Guidelines*], *available at* http://www.justice.gov/atr/public/guidelines/hmg-2010.pdf (revising 1997 guidelines). See also Chapter 4.A.3. FERC defines seller "market power" similarly, as the ability to "significantly influence price in the market by withholding service and excluding competitors for a significant period of time." Citizens Power & Light Corp., 48 FERC ¶ 61,210, at p. 61,777 (1989).
   Market power can be exercised by buyers also. *See* the *1997 Horizontal Merger Guidelines* § 0.1 (defining buyer market power as "the ability of a single buyer (a monopsonist), a coordinating group of buyers, or a single buyer, not a monopsonist, to depress the price paid for a product to a level that is below the competitive price and thereby depress output"). Since our discussion focuses on authorizing market prices for sellers, it will not address buyer market power.

17. Hope Natural Gas v. FPC, 320 U.S. 591 (1944), discussed in Chapter 6.B.2. *See also* Mont. Consumer

seller has significant market power, it is rational to assume that the terms of their voluntary exchange are reasonable, and specifically to infer that price is close to marginal cost,
such that the seller makes only a normal return on its investment."[18]

But FERC may not rely on theory alone, say the courts. Under the Federal Power Act
and the Natural Gas Act, a seller's market prices will be "just and reasonable" only if FERC
first screens the seller for market power, and then monitors the market continuously to
make sure the seller does not later gain market power. Explaining these two requirements,
and the techniques regulators use to satisfy them, will occupy the rest of this Chapter.

To reiterate: This seller-by-seller, screen-plus-monitor requirement applies only in the
FERC world. The courts have not required it of the FCC. As explained in Chapter 7.A,
the FCC has removed rate regulation from various service categories, based on findings
of competition, without any statutory obligation to monitor the markets or re-assess its
findings. Moreover, unlike FERC's situation, the courts have not required the FCC (outside of the unique context of RBOC in-region long-distance entry governed by 47 U.S.C.
§ 271, discussed in Chapter 3.A.3) to support its forbearance decisions with fact-intensive
findings in specific geographic areas. Applying *Chevron* deference, the courts have upheld
the FCC's "predictive judgments."[19]

Summarizing this overview: Under a statutory just and reasonable standard, there
are two main paths to price-setting. Chapter 6 described *cost-based rates*; Chapter 7
now discusses *market-based rates*. In both contexts, the "just and reasonable" standard
"guard[s] the consumer against excessive rates."[20] With embedded cost-based rates, regulators "guard the consumer" by disallowing imprudent costs, limiting the return on equity,
and assigning the risk of bad luck (Chapters 6.C and 6.D). With market-based rates,
regulators "guard the consumer" by screening sellers for market power, then relying on
market forces, monitored continuously, to discipline the prices.[21] The details on screening

---

Counsel v. FERC, 659 F.3d 910, 918 (9th Cir. 2011) (citing *Hope's* "end result" principle to reject consumer
arguments that the Federal Power Act allows only cost-based pricing and thus prohibits market-based
pricing); Cal. *ex rel.* Lockyer v. FERC, 383 F.3d 1006, 1013 (9th Cir. 2004) (finding that rates based on
market prices do not "*per se* violate" the just and reasonable standard).

18. Tejas Power Corp. v. FERC, 908 F.2d 998, 1004 (D.C. Cir. 1990). *See also* Cal. *ex rel.* Lockyer v. FERC,
383 F.3d at 1006 (agreeing with *Tejas*).

19. *See* Earthlink, Inc. v. FCC, 462 F.3d 1, 8, 12–13 (D.C. Cir. 2006) (finding that "the statute imposes no
particular mode of market analysis or level of geographic rigor," and that FCC is not required to conduct a "traditional market analysis (including market share, demand and supply elasticity, and other
factors)"; rather, "an agency's predictive judgments about areas that are within the agency's field of
discretion and expertise are entitled to *particularly deferential* review, as long as they are reasonable")
(citing other sources; emphasis in original). *But see* Cincinnati Bell Tel. Co. v. FCC, 69 F.3d 752, 760
(6th Cir. 1995) (rejecting FCC's request for deference to its "predictive judgment" where there was "little
common sense, . . . no statistical data or even a general economic theory, to support its argument" that
participation in Personal Communication Service by an entity owning 20 percent or more of a cellular
licensee would reduce the entity's incentive to compete; there must be "at least some support for [an
agency's] predictive conclusions").

20. Detroit v. FPC, 230 F.2d 810, 817 (D.C. Cir. 1955).

21. As explained in Chapter 6.E, somewhere between embedded cost rates and market-based rates is the

and monitoring come next. First we set forth the judicial requirements, then we describe how agencies have applied those requirements.

7.B. The courts speak: To prevent market power, regulators must screen and monitor

7.B.1. The obligation to screen

Two leading cases illustrate the requirement that FERC may grant a seller pricing discretion only after finding that competition will discipline the seller's prices.

FPC v. Texaco:[22] In the 1970s, prices charged by natural gas producers were set by the Federal Power Commission under the Natural Gas Act's "just and reasonable" standard.[23] To stimulate production, the FPC exempted small producers from "direct" price-setting. The small producers could charge any price, with no refund obligations for high prices. The prices would be set "indirectly," by capping the pipelines' (not the producers') cost recovery from LDCs. The FPC based the cap on "unreasonably high" gas costs. Those unreasonably high costs would, in turn, be determined by "comparison with the highest contract prices charged by large producers or the prevailing market price for intrastate sales in the same producing area." The FPC reasoned that these cost recovery caps would induce pipelines to "bargain prices down," resulting in small producer prices that were "just and reasonable."[24]

The Supreme Court found fault. The problem was not the experimental nature of the method, nor the absence of seller-specific rates. *Hope Natural Gas* (what counts is the "end result," not the methodology) allowed for experiments, and *Permian Basin* permitted "area rates" rather than seller-specific rates.[25] It was also reasonable for FPC to assume that pipelines' fear of non-recovery (if they paid to producer prices that were "unreasonably high") would cause them to "bargain prices down." The problem was the FPC's unsupported faith in the "standard of the marketplace," a faith that ignored Congress's concern that the marketplace itself was distorted:

> [T]he prevailing price in the marketplace cannot be the final measure of "just and reasonable" rates mandated by the Act. . . . Congress considered that the natural gas industry

---

price cap regime, where regulators establish a ceiling (usually having some connection to reasonable cost), then subject that ceiling to an annual change reflecting inflation (upwards) and productivity (downwards) factors.

22.   417 U.S. 380 (1974).

23.   As discussed in Chapter 3.A.2, Congress began removing producer price controls with the Natural Gas Policy Act of 1978, and eliminated them entirely in 1989.

24.   The Commission wanted to (a) increase small producers' "exploratory efforts which are so important to the discovery of new sources of gas," (b) ensure these producers that their contracts will not be "subject to regulatory change," and (c) relieve them of regulatory "expenses and burdens." Large producers, meanwhile, were subject to "direct" price ceilings. FPC v. Texaco, 417 U.S. at 383–85.

25.   Permian Basin Area Rate Cases, 390 U.S. 747 (1968), discussed in Chapter 6.B.2.a and 6.E.1.

was heavily concentrated and that monopolistic forces were distorting the market price for natural gas. . . .

This does not mean that the market price of gas would never, in an individual case, coincide with just and reasonable rates or not be a relevant consideration in the setting of area rates; it may certainly be taken into account along with other factors. It does require, however, the conclusion that Congress rejected the identity between the true and the actual market price.[26]

Farmers Union Central Exchange, Inc. v. FERC:[27] FERC again took a hit for its "undocumented reliance on market forces." Regulating oil pipeline transportation, FERC set price ceilings at levels intended to prevent "egregious exploitation," "gross abuse," "gross overreaching," and "unconscionable gouging" (FERC's language). Subject to these ceilings, rates would be disciplined by "competition" among oil pipelines. As FERC stated:

It is obvious that something has been holding these rates down. That something must be a marketplace force. The industry labels that force competition. . . . This is a rather soft kind of competition. It appears to be of a live and let-live kind. But this does not mean that it is not there. Nor does it necessarily negate a finding of considerable potency.[28]

Describing FERC's "evaluation of competition" as "not entirely clear" (likely a judicial euphemism), the court criticized FERC's—

virtually complete failure to make any express references to the extensive record compiled in this case. In fact, FERC pronounced that its 'massive record' in which 'experts discoursed on risk, on competition' was 'beside the point.' Such nonchalance cannot be countenanced when the Commission then goes on to rely on a factual finding as to competition in devising its ratemaking scheme.[29]

---

26. FPC v. Texaco, 417 U.S. at 388–91, 396–99. As a later court explained, the Commission decision reviewed in *Texaco* "had failed even to mention the just and reasonable standard; it appeared to apply only the standard of the marketplace in reviewing the reasonableness of a rate." Elizabethtown Gas Co. v. FERC, 10 F.3d 866, 870 (D.C. Cir. 1993) (quoting *Texaco*). *Texaco*'s principle, that regulators cannot rely blindly on market forces, was echoed by the Ninth Circuit in Montana Consumer Counsel v. FERC, 659 F.3d at 918–19:

   FERC's discretion is not without limit. FERC may not determine in advance that the prevailing market rate is by definition just and reasonable. . . . Comparisons of the rates charged by sellers to the rates charged by other sellers are insufficient—such comparisons tell FERC nothing about whether the rates are just and reasonable. FERC may not substitute prevailing market prices for its own judgment.

27. 734 F.2d 1486 (D.C. Cir. 1984).
28. Farmers Union Cent. Exch., Inc. v. FERC, 734 F.2d at 1494 (quoting FERC's opinion in Williams Pipe Line Co., 21 FERC ¶ 61,260, at p. 61,597 (1982)).
29. *Id.* at 1509.

More recent FERCs have gotten the message. The Commission allowed Transcontinental Gas Pipe Line Corp. (Transco) to sell gas at market prices, only after finding that (a) the pipeline was providing "comparable," cost-based transportation service to all producers, whether or not Transco-owned; and (b) there were "adequate divertible gas supplies" to give customers options and thus assure that Transco would price gas competitively. The court of appeals approved.[30] And in wholesale electric sales, FERC "collect[s] . . . empirical data on sellers' market power before authoriz[ing] the filing of market-based rates." Again the court approved FERC's approach.[31]

Is it sufficient to screen the applicant seller, or must the regulator also find the entire market competitive? Seller-screening is sufficient. The regulator need not "make a specific finding that a market is competitive in addition to screening for [a seller's] market power. . . . '[W]hat matters is whether an individual seller is able to exercise anti-competitive market power, not whether the market as a whole is structurally competitive.'"[32]

7.B.2. The obligation to monitor

A seller must lack market power at the time FERC grants it pricing discretion. But it can gain market power later—through mergers, acquisitions of assets, departures of competitors, transportation shortages, new entry barriers, predatory behavior, or luck. For the regulator to ignore this ongoing possibility is to place consumers at risk, unlawfully. That was FERC's error in *Farmers Union*: "[N]othing in the regulatory scheme itself acts as a monitor to see if [sufficient competition] occurs or to check rates if it does not. That is the fundamental flaw in the Commission's scheme."[33] Today's FERC therefore employs multiple monitoring techniques, detailed in Chapter 7.C.2.

7.C. The agencies act: Techniques and procedures for screening and monitoring

The combination of screening and monitoring has saved FERC from judicial reversal. "[T]he crucial difference between previous market-based regulatory policies rejected by the courts . . . and [FERC's current approach is] the dual requirement of an ex ante finding of the absence of market power and sufficient post-approval reporting requirements."[34] Absent the key steps of screening and monitoring, regulation would create "the false illusion that a government agency is keeping watch over rates, pursuant to the statute's

---

30. Elizabethtown Gas Co. v. FERC, 10 F.3d at 869, 870–71 (citing Tejas Power Corp. v. FERC, 908 F.2d 998).
31. Mont. Consumer Counsel v. FERC, 659 F.3d at 917.
32. *Id.* at 916 (quoting Blumenthal v. FERC, 552 F.3d 875, 882 (D.C. Cir. 2009)).
33. Farmers Union Cent. Exch., Inc. v. FERC, 734 F.2d at 1509.
34. Mont. Consumer Counsel v. FERC, 659 F.3d at 919–20 (quoting *Cal. ex rel. Lockyer v. FERC*, 383 F.3d at 1013).

mandate, when it is in fact doing no such thing."[35] How regulators carry out their duty to screen and monitor is discussed now.[36]

7.C.1. Screening sellers

When a prospective seller of wholesale electricity applies for pricing discretion, FERC tests for market power, entry barriers and affiliate abuse.

7.C.1.a. Market power screens: Horizontal and vertical

Market power is "the ability profitably to maintain prices above competitive levels for a significant period of time," along with the ability to "lessen competition on dimensions other than price, such as product quality, service, or innovation."[37] Market power causes multiple harms, including excessive prices, inefficient operations, diluted incentives for innovation, and "[c]ompromised system reliability in the long run resulting from distorted market signals and subsequent insufficient investment and system expansion."[38]

Market power is measured with reference to a particular "relevant market." A relevant market has a product dimension ("those commodities or services that are reasonably interchangeable by consumers for the same purposes") and a geographic dimension ("the area in which sellers of the relevant product effectively compete").[39] For a given product desired by a consumer, the relevant market is that group of substitute products, available in a geographic area accessible by the consumer, "such that a hypothetical profit-maximizing firm, . . . that was the only present and future producer or seller of those products in that area [i.e., a monopolist] likely would impose at least a 'small but significant and nontransitory' increase in price," that is, a price exceeding the level that would exist if the firm faced competition.[40]

FERC screens each market pricing applicant (and its affiliates) for both horizontal and vertical market power, in relevant market generation and transmission markets.[41] These concepts are discussed next.

---

35.   Farmers Union Cent. Exch., Inc. v. FERC, 734 F.2d at 1510 (quoting Texaco v. FPC, 474 F.2d 416, 422 (D.C. Cir. 1972), *vacated on other grounds*, 417 U.S. 380 (1974)).

36.   This subsection is only a summary of FERC practice, to illustrate how one agency carries out screening and monitoring. Anyone intending to participate or practice in this area should master the many details of the original sources cited in this section.

37.   *1997 Horizontal Merger Guidelines, supra* note 16; *2010 Horizontal Merger Guidelines, supra* note 16.

38.   Tabors Caramanis & Associates, Horizontal Market Power in Wisconsin Electricity Markets: A Report to The Public Service Commission of Wisconsin (2000), *available at* http://www.utilityregulation.com/content/reports/WImktstudy.pdf.

39.   Sunshine Cellular v. Vanguard Cellular Sys., 810 F. Supp. 486, 493 (S.D.N.Y. 1992).

40.   *1997 Horizontal Merger Guidelines, supra* note 16. Elaboration on this technical concept is beyond the scope of this legal text. Readers seeking mastery should refer to Market-Based Rates for Wholesale Sales of Electric Energy, Capacity & Ancillary Services by Public Utilities, FERC Order No. 697, 119 FERC ¶ 61,295, at pp. 215–334, as well as to the 1997 and 2010 versions of the Department of Justice's *Horizontal Merger Guidelines*.

41.   Market-Based Rates for Wholesale Sales of Electric Energy, Capacity & Ancillary Services by Public Utilities, FERC Order No. 697, 119 FERC ¶ 61,295, at p. 3 (codified at 18 C.F.R. pt. 35).

7.C.1.a.i. Horizontal market power

Horizontal market power arises when a firm or group of firms controls the supply of a particular good or service within a relevant market. To test for horizontal market power, FERC uses two screens: the *pivotal supplier* screen and the *wholesale market share* screen. The *pivotal supplier* screen assesses whether the seller, during periods of peak demand, can exercise market power unilaterally. A seller can exercise market power unilaterally if it is indispensable (also called "pivotal"). A seller is pivotal if it owns or controls an amount of available, uncommitted capacity that is necessary to keep the lights on. Capacity is necessary to keep the lights on if it exceeds the "supply margin," defined as the surplus of the market's available capacity over the market's annual peak demand.[42] If the seller controls more capacity than the supply margin, that seller is pivotal, because if it withholds its capacity from the market, supply will be insufficient to meet demand, leading to blackouts or other disruption. The seller's ability to withhold allows it to demand and sustain prices exceeding competitive levels. Even a small seller can be pivotal when demand is very high relative to capacity, such as on hot summer afternoons when air conditioner demand nears a market's capacity.

Here is a "stick figure" illustration of the pivotal supplier test, displayed in Figure 7.

1. Assume the market's annual peak demand during winter is 800 mW.
2. Assume the available capacity in the market is 1000 mW.
3. So the supply margin, that is, the excess of capacity over peak demand, is 200 mW.
4. The market's 1000 mW of capacity is distributed among six sellers as follows:
    A. 150 mW
    B. 150 mW
    C. 150 mW
    D. 150 mW
    E. 150 mW
    F. 250 mW
5. Assume all six sellers apply for permission to engage in market pricing, that is, to price at will.
6. Each of Applicants A-E will pass the test. Each has available capacity of 150 mW, less than the supply margin of 200 mW. If any one of them threatened to withhold its capacity to get a high price, customers could just ignore him and buy from someone else, because his withholding would leave us with 850 mW, more than the 800 mW of peak demand. None of Applicants A-E is indispensable. (Note that if two Applicants conspired to withhold, or merged and then threatened to

---

42. *Id.* at p. 45. Annual peak demand is the highest level electricity usage at a single point in a year. FERC uses this figure because it is "the most likely point in time that a seller will be a pivotal supplier."

withhold, we'd be at risk of losing 300 mW, bringing us down to 700 mW, below the peak demand of 800 mW. That problem of conspiracy is addressed by the "market share" test discussed shortly.)

7.   Now look at Applicant F. Its 250 mW exceeds the 200 mW supply margin. Applicant F is indispensable. If Applicant F withholds its 200 mW, total capacity will be only 750 mW, insufficient to meet the demand of 800 mW. To avoid blackout, customers will be willing to pay Applicant F above-market prices. So Applicant F has market power—the ability to sustain a price above competitive levels. FERC's pivotal supplier screen will detect Applicant F and prohibit it from setting his prices, unless he can "mitigate" his market power, perhaps by granting some other seller control over some of his capacity. Absent mitigation, FERC will cap his price at some level. That level could be based on Applicant F's own cost, or at some higher level that FERC finds lawful because it will attract more capacity to the market—thus reducing Applicant F's market power in the long run.

8.   Now move to the summer. Assume capacity remains the same (1000 mW) but demand is 900 mW because of air conditioning load. All the suppliers become pivotal (150 mW exceeds the supply margin of 100 mW); all have the ability to threaten to withhold; all have the ability to raise and sustain a price above competitive levels. For those high-demand hours, FERC could cap their prices.

Turning to the *wholesale market share screen*: This screen tests whether "a supplier may have a dominant position in the market, which is another indicator of potential unilateral market power and the ability of a seller to effect coordinated interaction with other sellers" to control prices and competitors' entry.[43] An applicant fails this screen if its market share of uncommitted capacity (meaning, capacity not committed to existing franchise or contract obligations) exceeds 20 percent for any season. The screen is run for each of four seasons, because shortages in some seasons will give the seller a higher market share. A seller that fails the screen will have a rebuttable presumption of market power. It can then present "historical evidence" to show an absence of market power.[44] If the applicant fails to persuade FERC, it can "mitigate" by granting some other seller control (or ownership) of enough capacity to bring the applicant below 20 percent; or it can agree to have its prices capped.

Why have two horizontal screens? Together they test for market power exercised unilaterally and through coordination. A pivotal supplier can act alone, while sellers with high market shares find it easier to coordinate their actions. As FERC explained: "Use of the two screens together enables the Commission to measure market power at both peak and off-peak times, and to examine the seller's ability to exercise market power unilaterally

43.   *Id.* at p. 65.
44.   *Id.* at pp. 34, 44.

Figure 7
FERC's Pivotal Supplier Test

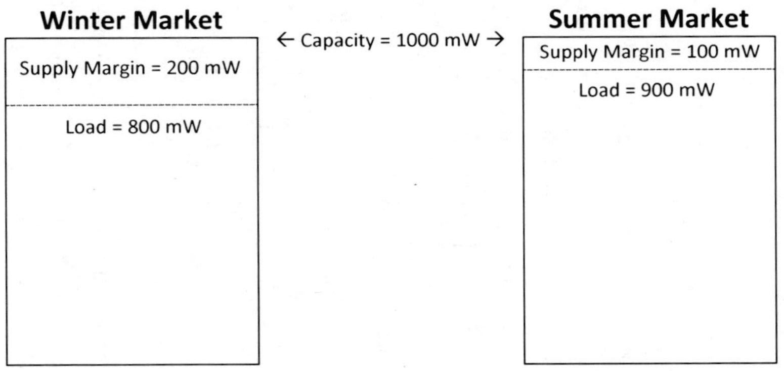

Winter Market

Supply Margin = 200 mW
Load = 800 mW

← Capacity = 1000 mW →

Summer Market

Supply Margin = 100 mW
Load = 900 mW

Will Applicant Receive Market Pricing Authority?
(Capacity ≤ Supply Margin)

	Applicant's Capacity		
A	150	Y	N
B	150	Y	N
C	150	Y	N
D	150	Y	N
E	150	Y	N
F	250	N	N

and in coordinated interaction with other sellers. Use of the two screens, therefore, provides a more complete picture of a seller's ability to exercise market power."[45]

7.C.1.a.ii. Vertical market power

Vertical market power exists when a firm or group of firms (a) competes in the "downstream" market for a particular good or service, and (b) owns or controls an "upstream" input essential to the production or delivery of the downstream good or service, where (c) that input is not economically duplicable by competitors.[46] In the telecommunications industry, a company can have vertical market power if it controls wholesale access services while serving retail customers, since access to the former is necessary to serve the latter. In the electric industry, a company can have vertical market power if it owns or controls both generation and transmission, or both generation and distribution, and can use its transmission or distribution facilities (assuming these facilities are not economically duplicable by others) to discriminate against competing generation sellers.

Where the market pricing applicant (or its affiliate) owns transmission, the applicant passes the vertical market power screen if it has on file a FERC-approved transmission tariff under Order No. 888 (which all transmission owners must do—see Chapter 4.B.3). If the transmission owner violates its tariff, FERC will revoke the applicant's market rate authority.[47]

7.C.1.b. Other entry barriers

A company exercises vertical market power by withholding or over-pricing an input essential to competitors. These actions can create an entry barrier—a difference in entry cost between incumbent and newcomer. To demonstrate the absence of vertical market power, the applicant for market pricing must describe its ownership or control of (or affiliation with an entity that owns or controls) any "intrastate natural gas transportation, intrastate natural gas storage or distribution facilities; sites for generation capacity development; and sources of coal supplies and the transportation of coal supplies such as barges and rail cars." Applicants need not provide, however, information on "natural gas supply, interstate natural gas transportation (which includes interstate natural gas storage), oil supply, and oil transportation." The reason is that open access transportation or common carrier obligations, imposed by other federal regulations, prevent the asset owner from using its control to create entry barriers to competitors.[48]

---

45. *Id.* at p. 36.
46. Bottleneck facilities, discussed in Chapter 4.B.2.b, are examples of such essential inputs that give rise to vertical market power.
47. Market-Based Rates for Wholesale Sales of Electric Energy, Capacity & Ancillary Services by Public Utilities, FERC Order No. 697, 119 FERC ¶ 61,295, at p. 21.
48. *Id.* at pp. 3, 441, 443–44. For more detail on entry barriers, especially in the context of retail competition, see Chapter 4.C.

7.C.1.c. Affiliate transactions

When an entity with market-based rate authority transacts with an affiliated franchised utility serving captive customers, special concerns arise because of the opportunity to overcharge customers who have no options. FERC therefore requires approval of each contract. Other protections appear in FERC's Code of Conduct (discussed in Chapter 4.B.5.c). A market pricer loses its market pricing authority if it (or an affiliate) violates the Code.[49]

* * *

A seller that passes FERC's screens receives permission to file a "market-based tariff." This tariff does not state a price; it merely signifies the seller's authority to charge any price.[50] A seller that fails a screen faces a rebuttable presumption of market power. The applicant can rebut the presumption with additional information and analysis. If the applicant still fails, it can sell power, but only at specific FERC-approved regulated rates or subject to a FERC-set cap, likely based on some measure of cost. Or it can propose to "mitigate" its market power by transferring control of some of its capacity to an independent entity.

7.C.2. Monitoring sellers and punishing violators

To gain permission to sell at market prices, the applicant must show facts. Over time, facts change. The seller without market power today can gain market power tomorrow. So the courts require the regulator to monitor. Monitoring ensures that competition continues to keep the seller's rates just and reasonable.[51] To meet the monitoring mandate, FERC requires market-based sellers to submit the following reports, among others:

1. a triennial update of the applicant's original market power analysis (certain sellers with less than 500 MW of power generation are exempt);
2. quarterly reports containing information on all contracts and transactions, including actual prices; and
3. a report within thirty days of any change in status or market conditions that affects the seller's market position, such as (a) changes in ownership or control of

---

49. *Id.* at p. 23.
50. As Chapter 9.E below will explain, this rate-silent tariff is a "filed rate" for purposes of the filed rate doctrine.
51. Farmers Union Cent. Exch., Inc. v. FERC, 734 F.2d at 1509. The courts have imposed no such requirement on the FCC. Once the FCC "forbears" from applying a regulation (based on a finding that continued regulation is not necessary to ensure justness and reasonableness or to protect consumers, and that the forbearance is in the public interest), the FCC has no obligation to revisit the question. *See* Telecommunications Act of 1996 § 10, 47 U.S.C. § 160. The FCC may revisit the issue *sua sponte*, or a party may petition the FCC to "undo" its forbearance decision based on new facts, but the FCC has no independent obligation to monitor a forbearance decision once made. In fact, under 47 U.S.C. § 160(c), a seller's forbearance petition is "deemed granted" if the FCC fails to act on it within a year (or a year plus 90 days if the FCC extends the one-year deadline).

generation, transmission assets or other inputs to electric power supply (including natural gas or oil supplies); (b) affiliation with an entity that owns such assets or inputs; or (c), long-term transmission outages (if they could reduce the size of the relevant geographic market, thereby increasing the seller's market share).[52]

These requirements satisfied the Ninth Circuit:

FERC has confirmed that it will monitor the data to ensure that the reported transactions are consistent with the data expected of a competitive, unmanipulated market. FERC is able to evaluate the reported data to determine whether the average prices charged by a seller are comparable to the average prices that would be charged in a competitive market where no sellers were able to exercise market power. If the data are consistent with a competitive market, FERC may properly assume that the charged rates fall within a zone of reasonableness.[53]

Monitoring works only if accompanied by enforcement. "[M]onitoring is not enough—FERC must have the tools to act when markets fail, and it must use those tools to ensure that customers pay only just and reasonable rates. Without enforcement, there is little reason to believe that sellers will police themselves."[54] FERC can punish violations of rules, orders or tariffs, or market manipulation, by revoking the seller's market-based rate authority, requiring disgorgement of profits and customer refunds, and imposing civil

---

52. Market-Based Rates for Wholesale Sales of Electric Energy, Capacity & Ancillary Services by Public Utilities, FERC Order No. 697, 119 FERC ¶ 61,295, at pp. 3, 1008–39. Again, this requirement applies only to electric utilities regulated under the Federal Power Act. Telecommunications companies who have gained pricing freedom have no such requirements. The FCC in theory could condition its grant of forbearance on the carrier providing periodic reports, but nothing requires the FCC to impose such a condition, and it has generally not done so. Section 10 of the Telecommunications Act (47 U.S.C. § 160) places no reporting obligation on the FCC with respect to the forbearance petitions it has granted. Under Section 11, 47 U.S.C. § 161, the FCC must review its regulations applicable to telecommunications service providers every two years to determine whether they are "no longer necessary," but *not* to determine whether re-institution of rules it has previously forborne is necessary.

53. *Mont. Consumer Counsel,* 659 F.3d at 918–19 (citing FERC's "broad discretion to establish effective reporting requirements"). *See also* Blumenthal v. FERC, 552 F.3d at 882–83 (rejecting state commission's attack on market rates, in part because "FERC reasonably relied on its continuing oversight of the market to guard against potential abuses of market power"; that oversight included required filings by the independent system operator of "quarterly and annual reports assessing the competitiveness of the market based on transactional data reflecting the behavior of each market participant").

54. *Mont. Consumer Counsel,* 659 F.3d at 920 n.5.

penalties.[55] And market-based rates are not unlawful merely because enforcement might fail, because those harmed by lax enforcement can seek judicial review.[56]

7.D. Are scarcity prices just and reasonable?

During shortages, prices rise. If they rise above levels normally considered "just and reasonable," are they unlawful? Not necessarily. That's what the Connecticut's Attorney General learned when challenging high prices charged by sellers with FERC-granted market rate authority. FERC declined to order price caps, and the court upheld the Commission:

> "[M]arket rates are expected and permitted to be higher than marginal costs during times of scarce supply. At the same time that they reflect existing scarcity, these high rates also serve a critical signaling function: encouraging new development that will increase supply. In fact, we recently vacated FERC's approval of a price-mitigation rule because it would have impaired this price-signaling function."[57]

The appellate court's reasoning recalls the Supreme Court's decision in *Mobil Oil Corp.*[58] Upholding certain production "incentives," the court found that the just and reasonable standard permitted the Commission to "employ price functionally in order to achieve relevant regulatory purposes."

---

55. Using new statutory authority added in 2005, FERC has created a multi-step methodology for penalizing actors who engage in manipulative or deceptive practices in FERC-jurisdictional energy markets. *See* Federal Power Act § 316A(a)–(b)), 16 U.S.C. § 825o-1(a)–(b) (2005); Natural Gas Act § 22, 15 U.S.C. § 717t(a) (2005); Enforcement of Statutes, Orders, Rules, and Regulations, 113 FERC ¶ 61,068 (2005) (2005 Policy Statement on Enforcement). *See also* Conrad Bolston, Improving FERC's Penalty Guidelines: A Comparative Analysis (electricitypolicy.com 2012), *available at* http://www.electricitypolicy.com/archives/4221-improving-fercs-penalty-guidelines-a-comparative-analysis.

   The FCC's penalty and restitution authority is not as broad as FERC's. The FCC does have authority to impose "forfeitures" (i.e., monetary fines) for violations of the Communications Act or FCC rules, *see* 47 U.S.C. §§ 501–505, but, as noted elsewhere in this chapter, once the FCC forbears from regulating prices under 47 U.S.C § 160, the FCC has no obligation to monitor, so there is nothing to penalize. Forbearance with respect to a particular obligation means that there is no longer an obligation for a carrier to violate, and thus for the FCC to enforce.

56. Mont. Consumer Counsel v. FERC, 659 F.3d at 917 n.2 ("We recognize the possibility that FERC in some cases may fail to detect market power due to lack of enforcement or ineffective screening protocols. In that event, parties may challenge FERC in court under existing law to force FERC to comply with its own orders.").

57. Blumenthal v. FERC, 552 F.3d at 883 (citing Edison Mission Energy, Inc. v. FERC, 394 F.3d 964, 968–69 (D.C. Cir. 2005) (noting that although the price-dampening rule might do some good, "the Commission gave no reason to suppose that it does not also wreak substantial harm—in curtailing price increments attributable to genuine scarcity that could be cured only by attracting new sources of supply")).

58. Mobil Oil Corp. v. FPC, 417 U.S. 283, 305–06 (1974), discussed in Chapter 6.F.

7.E. The future of market-based rates

Market-based rates can satisfy the just and reasonable standard, if the regulator screens sellers and monitors the markets. After multiple court decisions, these principles have become embedded in regulatory practice.

While this chapter has described market-based rates as a departure from cost-based rates, "cost" remains relevant to their lawfulness, for at least three reasons. First, a seller with market power can "mitigate" by accepting some cost-based cap. Second, to test whether a market pricing applicant faces sufficient competition to discipline its prices, FERC uses a "delivered price test" (DPT). The DPT determines whether the applicant has potential competitors, how many, and how much capacity they control. The test counts as competitors only those companies with cost structures sufficiently low to make them effective competitors of the applicant. Third, FERC requires market-pricing sellers to submit quarterly reports on prices charged, so that FERC can determine whether any sellers are able to sustain prices above the likely costs of ownership and production. The monitoring process thus checks not only market structure (market shares, seller indispensability, and entry barriers), but also the relationship of actual prices to benchmark industry costs. Cost remains relevant.[59]

FERC's market rates policy has not cleared the final legal threshold—the Supreme Court: "We reiterate that we do not address the lawfulness of FERC's market-based-rates policy, which assuredly has its critics."[60] But the Court's *Texaco* and *Permian Basin* decisions, stressing the methodological flexibility allowed by the "just and reasonable" standard and the Fifth Amendment, make reversal unlikely. The Court would have to reject the theory of markets—that competition, if effective, drives prices toward marginal cost.[61] Absent a statutory prohibition against market rates, any legal vulnerability in market rates policy would have to be in the regulator's execution, not in its theory.

---

59. *See* Market-Based Rates for Wholesale Sales of Electric Energy, Capacity & Ancillary Services by Public Utilities, FERC Order No. 697, 119 FERC ¶ 61,295, at pp. 25, 109, 717. With Order No. 697, FERC has traveled some distance from its less empirical treatment twenty years before. Then the D.C. Circuit criticized FERC for deeming a market rate lawful merely because (a) some customers agreed to it, (b) customers "would have substantial supply alternatives in the absence of the settlement," and (c) "many of Texas Eastern's customers are powerful economic entities and are not easily manipulated under any circumstances." *Tejas Power Corp.*, 908 F.2d at 1002 (remanding FERC approval because "[i]ts reliance upon the absence of significant pipeline market power is unsupported by substantial evidence" (quoting Texas Eastern Transmission Corp., 47 FERC ¶ 61,110, at p. 61,278 (1989))).

    To reiterate the contrast between the FERC and FCC worlds: Once the FCC decides to forbear from regulating prices under 47 U.S.C. § 160, it has no obligation to check market prices against cost, or even to collect cost data.

60. Morgan Stanley Capital Grp. Inc. v. Pub. Util. Dist. No. 1, 554 U.S. 527, 548 (2008). *Morgan Stanley* addressed the *Mobile-Sierra* doctrine; specifically, a buyer's ability to avoid rates it previously agreed to pay. The doctrine is the subject of Chapter 11.

61. "[W]here neither buyer nor seller has significant market power, it is rational to assume that the terms of their voluntary exchange are reasonable, and specifically to infer that price is close to marginal cost, such that the seller makes only a normal return on its investment." Tejas Power Corp. v. FERC, 908 F.2d at 1004. *See also* Cal. *ex rel.* Lockyer v. FERC, 383 F.3d at 1006.

A final thought on terminology: Casual discussants sometimes treat "competition" and "deregulation" as synonyms. It should be clear now that the term "deregulation" is a misnomer, because introducing competition requires detailed regulatory involvement. Where policymakers authorize competition but retain the statutory "just and reasonable" standard, regulation remains in place to ensure that competition works.[62]

---

62. Recognizing, again, the contrast between the FERC and FCC worlds. In the FERC world, regulatory involvement continues in the form of market monitoring and penalties. In the FCC world, once pricing flexibility is granted or forbearance occurs, regulatory involvement declines.

CHAPTER EIGHT
Discrimination
When Is Favoritism "Undue"?

Self-interest of the carrier may not override the requirement of equality in rates.[1]

Chapters 6 and 7 addressed the statutory requirement of justness and reasonableness, as applied to cost-based rates and market-based rates, respectively. Justness and reasonableness is necessary for lawfulness, but it is not sufficient. Regulatory statutes typically add that rates may not grant an undue preference:

> Every gas corporation, every electric corporation and every municipality shall furnish and provide such service, instrumentalities and facilities as shall be safe and adequate and in all respects just and reasonable. . . . No gas corporation, electric corporation or municipality shall make or grant any undue or unreasonable preference or advantage to any person.[2]

In the pricing context, discrimination can be lawful or unlawful, depending on whether it is "due" or "undue." This chapter illustrates the distinction with examples. Undue discrimination includes rate differences not justified by cost differences and rate differences with anti-competitive effect. Due discrimination includes rate differences based on customer profiles and load characteristics, rate differences arising from settlement strategies and contract histories, price discounting to retain customers, and rate differences arising from product differences. It then turns to a modern problem of discrimination: cost allocation on multi-utility systems.

8.A. Undue discrimination
8.A.1. Rate differences not justified by cost differences
The prohibition against undue discrimination distills to this golden rule: Treat similar customers similarly; dissimilar customers dissimilarly. Customers who cause similar costs should face similar cost-based rates.[3] Cost-causation underlies the common method for

---

1.   United States v. Ill. Cent. R.R., 263 U.S. 515 (1924).
2.   N.Y. PUB. SERV. § 65. *See also* D.C. CODE § 34-1101 ("The charge made by any public utility for a facility or service furnished, rendered, or to be furnished or rendered, shall be reasonable, just, and non-discriminatory."); KAN. STAT. ANN. § 66-101b ("Every unjust or unreasonably discriminatory or unduly preferential rule, regulation, classification, rate, charge or exaction is prohibited and is unlawful and void."). *See also* Section 205(b) of the Federal Power Act (FPA), 16 U.S.C. § 824d(b):

> No public utility shall, with respect to any transmission or sale subject to the jurisdiction of the Commission, (1) make or grant any undue preference or advantage to any person or subject any person to any undue prejudice or disadvantage, or (2) maintain any unreasonable difference in rates, charges, service, facilities, or in any other respect, either as between localities or as between classes of service.

3.   *See* Portland General Exchange, Inc., 51 FERC ¶ 61,108, at p. 61,245 n.62 (1990) ("[D]ifferences in rates must be based upon factual differences, for instance, in a utility's cost of service . . . .").

allocating the cost of capacity: Each customer group bears that share of the utility's total capacity cost equal to the group's proportional contribution to the peak demand, since peak demand is what drives the need for the capacity. To over-allocate cost to a group, relative to its contribution to peak demand, is unduly discriminatory.

Undue discrimination cannot be justified by self-interest. Illinois Central Railroad charged more to haul lumber from areas it served exclusively, compared to areas also served by competitors; yet the distance to destination lumber markets for the discounted areas was longer. Same freight, same destination market, same main route, different rates. The railroad defended the difference by arguing its business purpose: the lower rates would increase its traffic. The Interstate Commerce Commission found the discrimination undue, and the Supreme Court agreed: "Self-interest of the carrier may not override the requirement of equality in rates. . . . [T]he interests of the individual carrier must yield in many respects to the public need." That each rate itself was just and reasonable did not make the discrimination "due": "Both rates may lie within the zone of reasonableness and yet result in undue prejudice."[4]

Cost-based vs. market-based prices: Claims of undue discrimination usually arise where the seller is an incumbent utility with market power, charging cost-based prices. What if the regulator has authorized the seller to charge market-based rates—to price at will—because it lacks market power?[5] A seller lacks market power because its customers have alternatives. If customers have alternatives, a seller attempting undue price discrimination should fail because the customers will choose an alternative. What if the market-based seller is price-discriminating and succeeding (i.e., not losing sales)? There would be two possible reasons: (a) the seller lacks market power, so is pricing differentially based on cost differences or product differences (and therefore practicing due discrimination; *see* Chapter 8.B below); or (b) the seller has gained market power, and therefore should have its market rate authorization revoked.

Because market-pricing sellers are supposed to lack market power, FERC has authorized them to grant discounts. These sellers have no duty to post their discounts publicly or offer them to all similarly-situated buyers. FERC relies on the sellers' quarterly reporting requirements (discussed in Chapter 7.C.2 above) to monitor the discounts for evidence of market power, and invites potential victims of discrimination to file complaints.[6] Under this case-by-case regime, FERC has found undue discrimination arising from selective discounting, as illustrated by the *Portland General Exchange* case discussed next.

4. United States v. Ill. Cent. R.R., 263 U.S. 515, 524 (1924).
5. Cost-based prices and market-based prices were discussed in Chapters 6 and 7.
6. Market-Based Rates for Wholesale Sales of Electric Energy, Capacity & Ancillary Services by Public Utilities, 119 FERC ¶ 61,295, at pp. 718–19 (2007) ("[A]llegations of undue discrimination arising from selective discounting are best addressed on a case-by-case basis.").

8.A.2. Rate differences with anti-competitive effect

Portland General Electric (PGE) sold 30 mW of long-term power to its power marketing affiliate, Portland General Exchange (PGX), at rates below PGE's fully allocated cost.[7] PGX then resold 30 mW to two municipal wholesale customers at "market rates" that exceeded PGE's fully allocated cost. FERC ruled that PGE's sale to PGX was unduly preferential, based on three key facts: (a) PGE offered the discounted price to its affiliate, but not to the municipals; (b) there was no customer cost difference to justify the price difference, because PGE's service to PGX was similar to PGX's service to the municipals; and (c) PGE could not show that its discounted price to PGX was similar to other prices charged in the region. Nor could PGE show that it was forced to discount by its competitors' prices. (The need to meet a competitor's price can justify discrimination. *See* Chapter 8.B.3 below). FERC found that PGE's discounting undermined the very market forces that were the premise for PGX's market rate authority. And protecting those market forces required special attention to affiliate transactions: "Because the Commission is depending to a large degree upon the market to discipline prices in such circumstances, it is essential that affiliate transactions be above suspicion in order to ensure that the market is not distorted."[8]

Who has the burden of proof on anti-competitive effect? FERC will not presume that a rate disparity has anti-competitive effect; the complaining customer has the burden of proof.[9] But if the customer brings evidence of price squeeze (*see* Chapter 5.A.1, *supra*), the opposite rule applies: FERC presumes anti-competitive effect, which the utility has the burden of disproving.[10]

8.B. Due discrimination

8.B.1. Different customer profiles

To illustrate the golden rule (similar customers, similar rates; dissimilar customers, dissimilar rates) here are examples of discrimination that are "due" and "undue."

---

7.   "Fully allocated cost," sometimes called "fully distributed cost," refers to rates designed to recover all costs of production, both variable and fixed. *See* Associated Gas Distribs. v. FERC, 824 F.2d 981, 1007 (D.C. Cir. 1987) (citing FERC regulations stating that fully allocated cost is the rate that, "if the pipeline carries projected volume at the specified unit price, it should exactly recover all costs allocable to the relevant service for the period"). Fully allocated cost is distinguished from "incremental cost," which is the "added cost of (a small amount of incremental output). . . . It is synonymous with avoidable cost—the cost that would be saved by (slightly) reducing output." 1 ALFRED KAHN, THE ECONOMICS OF REGULATION: PRINCIPLES AND INSTITUTIONS 66 (1988).

8.   Portland General, 51 FERC ¶ 61,108, at p. 61,245 n.66, 6, 251 ("PGE's submittal is hereby rejected, without prejudice to PGE's resubmittal of rates meeting the requirements stated in the body of this order.").

9.   Cities of Bethany v. FERC, 727 F.2d 1131, 1140–41 (D.C. Cir. 1984) ("The general FERC rule . . . is that anti-competitive danger must be proved in order to invalidate an otherwise reasonable rate disparity.").

10.   *Id.* at 1141 ("When a utility competes with a wholesale customer in a retail market, FERC presumes anti-competitive effects from a rate disparity that burdens the customer-competitor.").

Different customer characteristics, different rate: Central Illinois Public Service Company priced its wholesale power differently as between municipal systems and rural cooperatives. The municipalities were "general service customers with heavy air conditioning loads." The rural cooperatives were, "by contrast, servicing mainly rural and farm customers." The discrimination was due discrimination, FERC found, because the different load profiles meant different costs to serve. While some rural cooperative customers were similar to some municipal customers, it was not unduly discriminatory to differentiate based on group characteristics.[11]

Different customer characteristics, same rate: Alabama Power Company proposed the same wholesale rate to its municipal and its rural cooperative customers. The cooperatives argued for a lower rate, on the grounds that the municipal customers caused higher costs. Charging both groups the same rate meant that the utility earned a higher return from the less costly cooperative customers. (The utility's returns from the cooperative and the municipal customers were 8.89 and 8.72, respectively.) FERC denied the cooperatives' request for an investigation, but the court of appeals reversed. FERC had to give the cooperatives a chance to prove undue discrimination. There is a limit, however, to the regulatory attention required:

> Although absolute equivalence of the overall rates of return yielded on revenues from customers or customer groups under a specific rate scheme may not be achievable in every case, it remains the standard. Any return disparity created by a rate scheme must therefore be as close to zero as the circumstances permit. . . . We have no doubt that there is a degree of disparity in rates of return under a uniformly-applied tariff within which the billing costs involved in attempting to conform charges to customer costs become so great as to outweigh the economic advantages which certain customers might enjoy if discrimination were completely eliminated. . . . The discrimination is, in effect, reasonable under those circumstances.[12]

8.B.2. Different settlement strategies and contract histories

Suppose a utility serving multiple customer groups proposes a general rate increase. Some groups settle and others litigate. The outcomes differ. Undue discrimination? Not necessarily,

---

11.   *Id.* at 1138 (upholding FERC's findings).
12.   Ala. Elec. Coop. v. FERC, 684 F.2d 20, 27–29 & n.38 (D.C. Cir. 1982). The context in *Alabama Electric Cooperative* was cost-based rates. If the context had been market-based rates, and if the seller lacked market power (meaning the buyer had alternatives), then the disfavored customer could have found a competing supplier willing to charge a lower price. If competition was effective, the possibility of losing the customer would pressure the original seller to reduce or eliminate the disparity in returns.

even if there are no cost differences between the groups: "[W]hen a temporary difference in rates between customer categories is the result of a settlement agreement that does not involve bad faith or improper conduct, the difference is lawful, provided that there is no evidence of actual competitive harm or undue burden to a customer group."[13]

This outcome rests on a principle embedded in the Federal Power Act and Natural Gas Act: Private agreements deserve deference.[14] A utility with two customer groups could legitimately enter into two different kinds of contracts: a "fixed rate" contract (which "does not permit a public utility to effect unilateral rate increases merely by filing them with the Commission"), and a "going rate" contract (which, while binding the utility to supply the customer for the contract term, makes the rate whatever the Commission authorizes, in response to requests of either party). At any point in time, these two contracts could produce different rates. To condemn any such difference as unduly discriminatory would make private negotiations impossible. As the court of appeals explained:

> "Business reality demands that natural gas companies should not be precluded by law from increasing the prices of their product whenever that is the economically necessary means of keeping the intake and outgo of their revenues in proper balance." (Citation omitted.) If a fixed rate contract with one of its customers were to prevent a public utility from changing the rates of its other customers, even though it had bargained in arm's length negotiations for the right to do so, this necessary flexibility would disappear.[15]

Another reason to tolerate rate differences arising from contract differences is to promote settlements. If differences due to settlements were inherently unduly discriminatory, "no utility company could afford to risk anything less than a full and complete settlement with all its customers. . . . Individual customers would have no incentive to settle."[16]

---

13.   *Cities of Bethany*, 727 F.2d at 1138–39 (finding no undue discrimination under the Federal Power Act). For an analogous case in the natural gas industry, *see* United Mun. Distribs. Grp. v. FERC, 732 F.2d 202, 212 (D.C. Cir. 1984) (finding "no sweetheart deal," and citing *Cities of Bethany* for the notion that "settlements would be severely discouraged if rate disparities arising out of settlements were considered unlawfully discriminatory"). *See also* City of Frankfort v. FERC, 678 F.2d 699 (7th Cir. 1982). The utility there discontinued its prior habit of offering fixed rate contracts, "in the interest of [its] financial stability." Frankfort, a wholesale customer of the utility, had failed to sign a fixed rate contract when it was available, so it signed a contract which allowed the utility to seek price increases. The resulting price disparity among customer groups was not unduly discriminatory. The court rejected the argument that rate disparity must always be justified by cost difference.

14.   We will address this principle in detail in Chapter 11, concerning the *Mobile-Sierra* doctrine.

15.   Boroughs of Chambersburg v. FERC, 580 F.2d 573, 577 (D.C. Cir. 1978) (quoting United Gas Pipe Line Co. v. Memphis Light, Gas and Water Div., 358 U.S. 103, 113 (1958). *Memphis*, a key case under the *Mobile-Sierra* doctrine, is discussed in Chapter 11.D.

16.   *Cities of Bethany*, 727 F.2d at 1139 & n.33 (quoting Delmarva Power & Light Co., 6 FERC ¶ 61,084, at p. 61,162 (1979)).

8.B.3. Price discounting to retain customers

The E.I. duPont Company was Carolina Power & Light's largest customer. It had a high load factor.[17] If duPont remained as a utility customer, its monthly rate payments would continue making a major contribution to the utility's fixed costs. But if duPont substituted self-generation for CP&L generation—which duPont was ready and willing to do—other customers might have to pick up those costs. Under these circumstances, a rate discount sufficient to retain duPont, while discriminatory, was not unduly discriminatory. The non-discounted customers would be better off with duPont staying, paying a rate that covered the incremental costs of serving duPont plus at least some contribution to CP&L's fixed costs.[18]

FERC authorized similar discounts during the natural gas industry transition.[19] Pipelines could price flexibly, subject to a maximum rate of fully allocated cost and a minimum rate of average variable cost. Each discounting pipeline had to report details to FERC within 15 days after a transaction. When customer interests attacked the discount programs as unduly discriminatory, the court disagreed. The discounts advanced both equity and efficiency:

> [FERC] saw substantial gains from such discounts: cheaper fuel supplies for the price-elastic customers receiving the discounts; reduced revenue short-falls for pipelines that would otherwise lose the business altogether; and protection for non-favored customers from rate increases that would ultimately occur if pipelines lost volume through inability to respond to competition. . . .
>
> The equitable argument in favor of such differentials is that they may benefit captive customers by making a contribution to fixed costs that otherwise would not be made at all. (The efficiency argument is that such differentials will raise total volume closer to the level it would attain if all sales were priced at marginal cost.)[20]

Two other points were important to FERC and to the court. First, the reporting requirement would enable FERC to distinguish between lawful and unlawful discounting. Second,

---

17. A customer's load factor is the ratio of its average load to its peak load, for a given time period. (Average load for a given period is the total consumption in the period divided by the number of hours in the period. A customer with a 100 percent load factor for a given period consumes at the same level for every hour in that period.) A utility builds its plant sufficient to cover peak load. Customers with low load factors leave the plant idle most of the time. Customers with high load factors use more of the plant over more hours, making them more desirable to the utility.

18. Carolina Power & Light Company, 151 P.U.R.4th 180 (N.C. Utils. Comm'n Apr. 26, 1994) (approving discount due to multiple factors: "the high load factor nature of duPont's load relative to the structure of CP&L's embedded plant; duPont's apparent intent, capability and economic incentive to self-generate; that the rate reduction appears to be commensurate with duPont's self-generation costs; that the proposed rate covers CP&L's incremental cost of providing service and makes a contribution to CP&L's fixed costs, including a return on common equity; and that the contract is subject to termination after the initial period subject to certain advance notice requirements being met").

19. *See supra* Chapter 3.A.2.

20. *Associated Gas Distribs.*, 824 F.2d at 1010–11.

upholding discounts carried out "Congress's intention in the NGA to allow a vital role for private contracting between the parties."[21]

8.B.4. Product differences

Customers who buy similar services should face similar prices.[22] There is, therefore, no undue discrimination when the price difference reflects a product difference. Citizens Utilities sold interruptible service to a snow-producing ski resort, at a rate discounted from the normal price for firm service. The discount tariff allowed the utility to interrupt service if by doing so the utility could avoid making new capacity purchases or incurring new transmission costs. The Vermont Public Service Board approved the discount because the service provided was of lower quality, and the rate at least covered the utility's short-run marginal cost.[23]

This example reveals an imprecision in terminology. Although practitioners often describe the *Citizens Utilities* situation as "due discrimination," technically it is not discrimination. True price discrimination occurs when there are different prices for the same product (or different products at the same price). Interruptible power and firm power are different products, just as a cab and a bus, or a Volkswagen and a Lexus, are different products. Consider also the difference between two airline fares, with and without refund rights. The passengers may sit on the same plane in adjacent seats, leaving at the same time and arriving at the same time, but they have purchased different products at two different prices. This is not discrimination.

8.C. Cost allocation within holding company systems

A subset of undue discrimination cases involves allocating costs among the utility subsidiaries of a holding company. The case law deals with two different situations. In one, the holding company plans, controls and operates all the system's assets centrally, for the mutual benefit of all the utility subsidiaries and their customers. The regulatory challenge is to allocate the costs of commonly used facilities among utility subsidiaries with different characteristics. The second type is a holding company system that has a mix of utility and non-utility activities. The regulatory challenge is to avoid allocating non-utility costs

---

21. *Id.* (citing United Gas Pipe Line Co. v. Mobile Gas Serv. Corp., 350 U.S. 332 (1956)—part of the *Mobile-Sierra* doctrine to be discussed in Chapter 11). Chapters 7.B.2 and 7.C.2 discussed the importance of monitoring in ensuring the lawfulness of market-based rates. *See also* Portland General, 51 FERC ¶ 61,108 (supporting the general policy allowing utilities to price off-system sales at below their fully allocated costs if "necessary to meet market competition. This practice benefits the off-system buyer and its customers and it provides for some revenues to be credited to customers of the seller.").

22. *See* St. Michaels Utils. Comm'n v. Fed. Power Comm'n, 377 F.2d 912, 915 (4th Cir. 1967) (The statutory provision's purpose is "to prevent favoritism by insuring equality of treatment on rates for substantially similar services."); Cities of Alexandria v. FPC, 555 F.2d 1020, 1027–28 (D.C. Cir. 1977).

23. Citizens Utilities Co., Docket No. 5625, 151 P.U.R.4th 238 (Vt. Pub. Serv. Bd. Mar. 28, 1994).

to the utility customers. (Today, many holding company systems have both characteristics, as we will see in the companion volume on corporate structure, mergers and acquisitions.)

In both types of holding company systems, decisions to allocate costs among the utility subsidiaries have caused legal controversy. These cases are relevant not only to the discrimination issues discussed in this chapter, but also to the federal–state jurisdictional issues discussed in Chapter 12. This dual importance, and the seminal role of the cases involved, justify a detailed discussion of the facts. The reader's patience will bear fruit. To assist, Figure 8 displays the structure of the two holding company systems—Middle South and Alcoa—discussed in this subchapter.

8.C.1. Systems that plan and operate utility assets centrally

Consider a holding company system with four electric utility subsidiaries, each owning generation, transmission, and distribution facilities and each having a retail obligation to serve. If the system wishes to exploit economies of scale in planning, construction and operation (so as to meet the combined companies' long-term needs at least feasible cost), then it must make asset decisions centrally. The autonomy typically enjoyed by each individual utility must give way to decisions made by the holding company. Those decisions include what resources to build or buy, and how to allocate their costs among the utility subsidiaries.

In this context, how does the prohibition against undue preference apply? If each utility subsidiary in the system had an identical set of assets, of identical vintage, all with identical original capital costs, depreciation rates and operating costs—and if for each utility the ratio of load to capacity was the same (e.g., each utility had surplus capacity of 15 percent above its peak load), then each utility would have exactly the same unit costs, that is, the same average capacity cost per kW of load and the same average operating cost per kWh of consumption. But if reality intrudes, if any one factor of any one utility varied from the others—if, for example, Subsidiary A had a shortage of capacity for a few years while Subsidiary B had a surplus, or if Subsidiary A's capacity costs were 20 percent higher than Subsidiary Y's capacity costs (because A's assets were newer so their book value was higher)—a differential would arise between the per-unit costs incurred by the two utilities. If both utilities were using each other's resources, effectively treating them as system resources, the prohibition against undue discrimination would require some cross-payments between the two subsidiaries. The cross-payments would ensure that subsidiaries enjoying similar benefits bear similar costs. That is how things work on most utility holding company systems: interaffiliate contracts allocate cost responsibility for separately owned resources that are jointly used, with the allocations designed to reduce cost differentials among the utility members.

This longstanding practice involved little controversy until the 1980s, when nuclear plant construction produced billions of dollars in unexpected costs. The textbook

Figure 8
Two Holding Company Systems

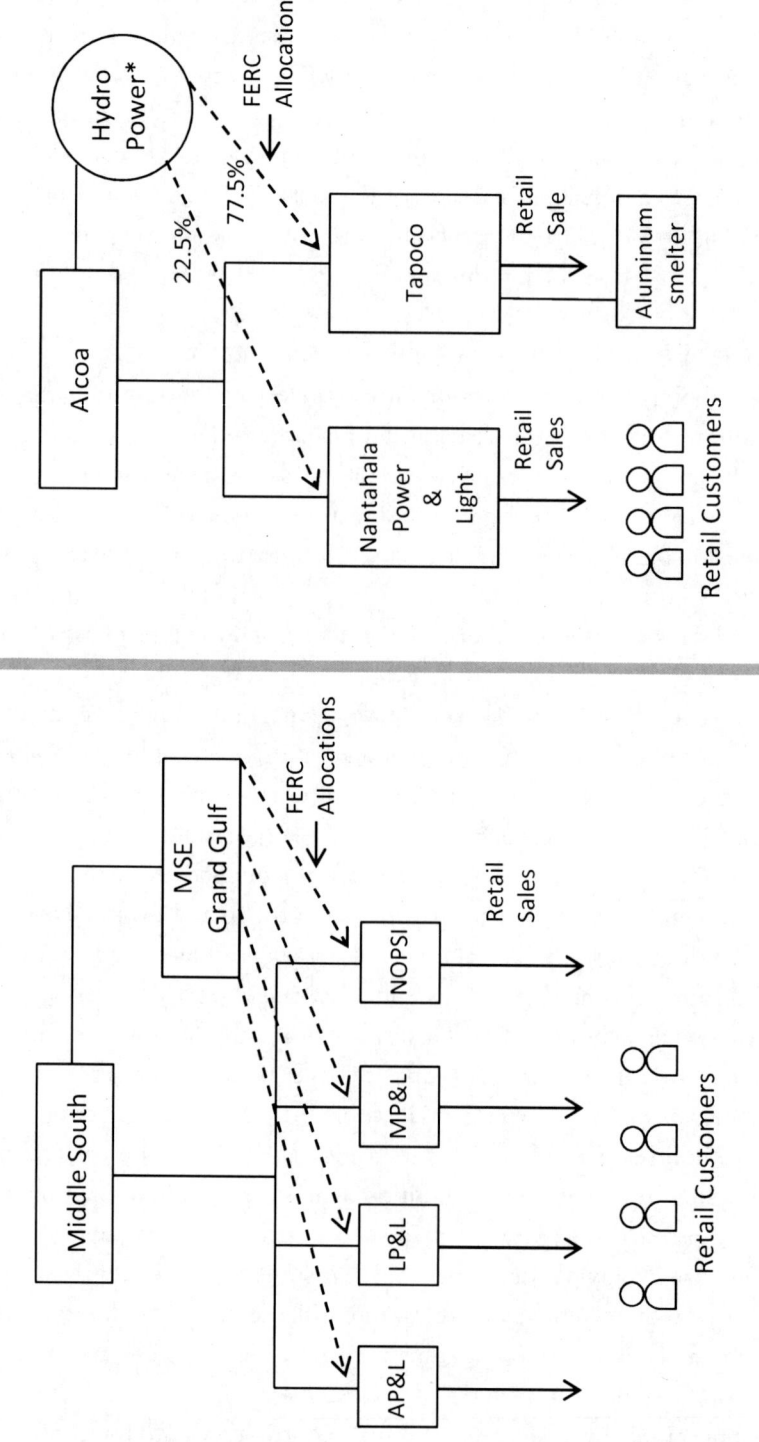

*The circle represents hydropower entitlement held by various members of the Alcoa system.

example, producing multiple federal and state appellate decisions and two U.S. Supreme Court decisions, is the Middle South (now called Entergy) system's experience with the Grand Gulf nuclear plant. Middle South was a centrally planned holding company system. Each retail utility subsidiary (sometimes called an "operating company") had its own board of directors, but all board members were selected by the holding company, the utilities' sole stockholder. The operating companies and the holding company were parties to a FERC-jurisdictional "System Agreement," whose purpose was

> to provide the contractual basis for the continued planning, construction, and operation of the electric generation . . . facilities of the Companies in such a manner as to achieve economies consistent with the highest practicable reliability of service. . . . This agreement also provides a basis for equalizing among the Companies any imbalance of cost associated with the construction, ownership and operation of such facilities as are used for the mutual benefit of all the Companies.

In short, the System Agreement aimed to "coordinate the addition of operating capacity by each individual operating company while achieving the greatest economies of scale."[24] A systemwide Operating Committee, representing all four utilities, coordinated the planning of generation and transmission capacity for each utility, and decided each utility's cost responsibility. These resulting cost allocations were effected through inter-utility payments for sales of energy and capacity. These inter-utility payments were approved by FERC because they involved the wholesale sale of electric power and the transmission of electric power.[25]

At any point in time, some subsidiaries owned more or less capacity than their proportionate share of the system's demand. The System Agreement therefore had formulas for sharing capacity costs. The "short" companies made payments to the "long" companies, based on proxy costs intended to make per-unit cost responsibility roughly equal among the utilities. Because responsibility for building and owning capacity rotated among the companies, and because the capacity costs of each new generating plant were roughly equal over time, this method of "rough equality" prevented undue discrimination.

Until the Grand Gulf Nuclear Plant. Grand Gulf's per-unit capacity cost was dramatically higher than the system's historical costs. To make a single utility responsible for Grand Gulf would upset the historic cost equality among the utility subsidiaries. The holding company therefore placed the plant in a wholesale subsidiary. That wholesale

---

24. Miss. Indus. v. FERC, 808 F.2d 1525, 1529 (D.C. Cir. 1987) (quoting the System Agreement).
25. See FPA § 201(b), 16 U.S.C. § 824(b) (vesting in FERC jurisdiction over the wholesale sale of electric energy in interstate commerce).

subsidiary and the four utility subsidiaries then entered into a Unit Power Sales Agreement (UPSA), which allocated the right to Grand Gulf capacity, and its costs, among the utilities. But the plant's costs ballooned, from an original estimate of $1.2 billion to a final cost of $3 billion (five times the cost of Middle South's most recently constructed nuclear plant). The ingredients were in place for a state-against-state battle over cost allocation, fought at FERC because the conduit for cost allocation was the FERC-jurisdictional UPSA.

Faced with these facts, FERC made the following findings and legal conclusions:

1. Middle South was an "integrated system," in which the "major critical decisions" for the entire system were made at the holding company level. The holding company's decisions bound the individual retail subsidiaries. They had no discretion to avoid the resulting costs.

2. Grand Gulf, like the system's previous generating units, was built to serve the needs of the whole system, including the need to diversify the system's fuel mix.

3. The plant's "unforeseen economic difficulties . . . disrupted the system's historic rough equalization of generation costs": The resulting "tremendous disparities in nuclear capacity costs . . . thus constitute undue discrimination under section 206 of the Federal Power Act."[26]

4. It was necessary to revise the UPSA, to allocate Grand Gulf's cost "so that each operating company would contribute proportionately to the system's investment in nuclear capacity. . . . The result of this [FERC-mandated] allocation of Grand Gulf is to give each operating company a share of the cost of nuclear capacity roughly proportionate to that company's relative share of system demand."[27]

The D.C. Circuit overturned FERC's reallocation because it still left the system with "vastly disparate" nuclear capacity costs. FERC had failed to explain why its allocation was not itself unduly discriminatory, or what criteria it used in determining what constituted undue discrimination.[28] On remand, FERC left its cost allocation decision unchanged, but provided an explanation that eventually satisfied the court. FERC stated that

principles of fairness in ratemaking support the concept that those who are responsible for the incurrence of costs be the ones who bear those cost burdens. Generating capacity

---

26. *Miss. Indus.*, 808 F.2d at 1537, 1557 (quoting lower decision Middle South Energy, Inc. Docket No. Er82-616-000, 31 FERC ¶ 61,305, at p. 61,646 (1985)).

27. *Id.* at 1538, 1558 (quoting lower decisions Middle South Energy, Inc., 26 FERC ¶ 63,044, at p. 65,109 (1984); *Middle South Energy*, 31 FERC ¶ 61,305, at p. 61,655).

28. Miss. Indus. v. FERC, 822 F.2d 1104 (D.C. Cir. 1987), *rev'g in part*, 808 F.2d 1525 (D.C. Cir. 1987) (adopting Judge Bork's dissent at 808 F.2d at 1568).

is built in order to meet demand. Therefore, the cost of capacity should be allocated throughout an electric utility system in proportion to demand. . . . A cost equalization approach that fails to consider demand would ignore the very determinant that controls the need for various levels of capacity.

FERC then described its criteria for determining undue discrimination within a centrally controlled holding company system as follows:

> [E]ach operating utility should contribute investments to meet the capacity needs of the system in the long term, and . . . each operating utility should share in the overall capacity costs of the system in rough proportion to the benefits it receives (*i.e.*, that its demand is met) from that system. . . . [A]n allocation scheme that would not achieve a rough equalization of production costs on a demand basis would be, in the absence of a rational explanation, unduly discriminatory because there would be no basis for disparity among similarly situated entities.[29]

This explanation accords with the simple principle that opened this chapter: similarly situated customers must pay similar rates, and the key to assessing similarity is cost causation.

What happens when multistate cost allocation occurs outside of federal jurisdiction? In the Middle South situation, undue discrimination within a multi-state utility system became a federal issue because the mechanism for allocating costs and benefits was a power supply contract subject to the Federal Power Act. What if there is cost allocation among states but no federal statute? Consider a utility making retail sales in multiple states, through a single corporation rather than through separate in-state subsidiaries. Whereas cost allocation among subsidiaries requires contracts, cost allocation among the divisions of a single corporation does not. In this context, it is possible for the states to use inconsistent cost allocation methods, each one legitimate under state law. Inconsistent cost allocations can place the company at risk of under-recovery, and the consumers at risk of over-recovery.[30] Some states

---

29. City of New Orleans v. FERC, 875 F.2d 903, 905 (D.C. Cir. 1989) (quoting System Energy Resources, Inc., 41 FERC ¶ 61,238, at p. 61,616 (1987), *aff'd*, 42 FERC ¶ 61,091 (1988)).

30. For years, PacifiCorp sold electric at retail in seven Western states through a single corporation. *See* Utah Power & Light Co., 45 FERC ¶ 61,095 at text accompanying nn.180–84 (1988) (describing how after the merger of PacifiCorp and Utah Power and Light into a single, multi-state company with divisions rather than subsidiaries, "[t]he seven affected states would be free to adopt different (and potentially inconsistent) cost allocation schemes," with the risk that "100 percent of the costs may not be recovered"). In contrast, the major telecommunications companies that provide state-jurisdictional sales (i.e., for intrastate service) in multiple states usually have a separate subsidiary and separate books and records for each state. Since physical facilities make up the bulk of the telecommunications' companies' costs, and physical facilities are obviously traceable to a particular state, those costs can be directly assigned to the appropriate subsidiaries; only central costs that are common to all the states would require allocation.

have created working committees aimed at reducing the potential for inconsistencies (i.e., both under-recovery and over-recovery), but they have no obligation to do so. This potential for inconsistency has not triggered federal court action, at least in the context of utility regulation.[31]

8.C.2. Systems that mix utility and non-utility businesses

When a holding company has interests in both utility and non-utility businesses, there is risk that the system will discriminate against customers of the utility. The well-known example involved Nantahala Power & Light, a small North Carolina utility; and its holding company owner Alcoa, the aluminum producer.

Simplifying the facts: Alcoa owned two electric subsidiaries—Nantahala, a traditional utility serving retail and wholesale loads in North Carolina; and Tapoco, a company that

---

This allocation of common costs associated with intrastate service did not involve federally jurisdictional contracts. Telecommunications companies of course raise a different cost allocation problem: between the interstate (FCC-jurisdictional) and intrastate (state-jurisdictional) services. We will visit this problem in Chapter 12, concerning federal–state jurisdictional relationships.

31. It has reached the courts in context of state taxation. Most states impose net income taxes on corporations doing business in their states. When the corporation is a multistate business, each state calculates the in-state net income by using an "apportionment formula." Most states use the same apportionment formula, consisting of the arithmetic average of three ratios: in-state payroll to total payroll, in-state property value to total property value, and in-state revenue to total revenue. The average of those three fractions is then multiplied by the company's total (all states) net income to arrive at the in-state net income subject to the state's corporate net income tax. While this three-factor formula is the one most commonly used, no federal law requires it. If states use inconsistent formulas, a company can end up paying state taxes on an amount of taxable income exceeding its total income.

That was the problem faced by the Moorman Manufacturing Company. Moorman produced animal feed in Illinois and sold it in Iowa. Illinois tax statutes used the standard three-factor apportionment formula. Iowa used a single-factor formula based on revenues only. Believing that the sum of the net income allocated by each of these states exceeded 100 percent of its net income, Moorman challenged Iowa's formula on Due Process and Commerce Clause grounds. The U.S. Supreme Court rejected both challenges. The Iowa formula did not violate the Due Process Clause because it produced an allocation of income to the state that was "rationally related to values connected with the taxing State." As for Moorman's Commerce Clause claim (based on the assertion that the same income was being taxed twice by the two states, rather than being allocated between the two states), the Court declared:

The only conceivable constitutional basis for invalidating the Iowa statute would be that the Commerce Clause prohibits any overlap in the computation of taxable income by the States. If the Constitution were read to mandate such precision in interstate taxation, the consequences would extend far beyond this particular case. For some risk of duplicative taxation exists whenever the States in which a corporation does business do not follow identical rules for the division of income. Accepting appellant's view of the Constitution, therefore, would require extensive judicial lawmaking. . . .

While the freedom of the States to formulate independent policy in this area may have to yield to an overriding national interest in uniformity, the content of any uniform rules to which they must subscribe should be determined only after due consideration is given to the interests of all affected States. It is clear that the legislative power granted to Congress by the Commerce Clause of the Constitution would amply justify the enactment of legislation requiring all States to adhere to uniform rules for the division of income. It is to that body, and not this Court, that the Constitution has committed such policy decisions.

Moorman Mfg. Company v. Bair, 437 U.S. 267, 277–80 (1978).

sold its entire electric output at retail to Alcoa's Tennessee aluminum smelting operations. (See Figure 8.) Through a series of FERC-jurisdictional agreements, Alcoa allocated between the two utilities the rights to low-cost hydroelectric power purchased by the holding company system from the Tennessee Valley Authority. Hydroelectric power being less expensive than alternative sources, the holding company system's natural incentive was to favor Tapoco (since Alcoa's aluminum operations competed in a worldwide market), and to disfavor Nantahala (since it had a monopoly over its retail and wholesale customers). As the court of appeals explained:

> [T]ransactions between the two subsidiaries cannot be presumed to be as fair as they would be if Nantahala and Tapoco were independent entities. . . . The opportunity for unfair treatment here is coupled with an incentive on the part of Alcoa to favor Tapoco in transactions between the two subsidiaries. Nantahala sells power to a public load; Tapoco sells power directly to Alcoa. As a consequence, any transaction between Nantahala and Tapoco that benefits Tapoco will also benefit Alcoa and at the same time work to the detriment of Nantahala's customers.

FERC found that the agreement allocated a "disproportionate share" of the low-cost TVA power to Tapoco. It then amended the contract in favor of Nantahala—but not as much as Nantahala's customers wanted. Specifically, FERC declined to allocate the TVA power to the two companies in proportion to their loads (a solution known as "roll-in"). Differences between the two companies, FERC found, in terms of history, purpose, location and electrical needs, justified some differential treatment. The court upheld FERC's decision.[32]

* * *

This chapter has discussed different types of discrimination. In distinguishing due from undue discrimination, commissions consider cost differences, product differences, competitive effects, customer profiles, settlement and contract histories, customer mobility and other factors.[33] The purpose is to prevent a company with market power from abusing that market power. When the seller does not have market power—when its customers

32. Nantahala Power & Light Co. v. FERC, 727 F.2d 1342, 1347 (4th Cir. 1984). Chapters 9.C and 12.B.2 will revisit this case, when exploring the filed rate doctrine and federal–state jurisdictional relationships, respectively.
33. A longer list includes "quantity of use, time of use, manner of service, and costs of rendering the two services, competitive conditions, consumption characteristics of the several classes, and the value of service to each class, which is indicated to some extent by the cost of alternate fuels available." Carolina Power & Light Company, *supra* note 18 (citing State *ex rel.* Utils. Comm'n v. Pub. Staff, 374 S.E.2d 361 (1988)); and State *ex rel.* Utils. Comm'n v. N.C. Textile Mfrs. Ass'n Inc., 328 S.E.2d 264 (1985).

have alternatives—FERC allows the market-price seller to discriminate, except when the discrimination favors an affiliate in a way that undermines the competitive forces that are the premise for market rates. Holding company systems present a special case, where the regulatory purpose is to achieve rough equality among the utility subsidiaries, and to prevent the unfair shifting of costs—or denial of benefits—between utility and non-utility affiliates.

CHAPTER NINE
Filed Rate Doctrine
The "Filed Rate" Is the Only Lawful Rate

Rate filings . . . are the essential characteristic of a rate-regulated industry.[1]

9.A. Filed rates: Purposes and principles

A railroad passenger buys a train ticket. The ticket agent misquotes the price at below the railroad's filed tariff rate. When the railroad catches the error, the passenger has to pay the difference. "[T]he rate of the carrier duly filed is the only lawful charge. . . . Ignorance or misquotation of rates is not an excuse for paying or charging either less or more than the rate filed."[2]

Welcome to the filed rate doctrine. Its legal source is mundane statutory language, like Missouri's:

> No corporation shall charge, demand, collect or receive a greater or less or different compensation for any service rendered or to be rendered than the rates and charges applicable to such services as specified in its schedule filed [with the Commission] and in effect at the time.[3]

Its message is simple: The only legal rate is the filed rate, the one in the commission's public files: "The legal rights of shipper as against carrier in respect to a rate are measured by the published tariff. Unless and until suspended or set aside [by the regulator], this rate is made, for all purposes, the legal rate."[4] Whether the commission has acted on the rate is irrelevant: "It is the filing of the tariffs, and not any affirmative approval or scrutiny by the agency, that triggers the filed rate doctrine."[5]

The doctrine's original goal was to prevent discrimination. Prior to the Interstate Commerce Act, "railroad companies often charged substantially higher rates on noncompetitive routes, granted secret discounts to preferred shippers, and overcharged competitors of

---

1. MCI Telecomms. Corp. v. AT&T Co., 512 U.S. 218, 231 (1994).
2. Louisville & Nashville R.R. Co. v. Maxwell, 237 U.S. 94, 97 (1915). While this agent's error appeared to be unintentional, that was not always the case:

   > Past experience shows that billing clerks and other agents of carriers might easily become experts in the making of errors and mistakes in the quotation of rates to favored shippers, while other shippers, less fortunate in their relations with carriers and whose traffic is less important, would be compelled to pay the higher published rates.

   Poor v. Chi., Burlington & Quincy Ry. Co., 12 I.C.C. 418, 421–22 (1907) (quoted in Maislin Indus., U.S., Inc. v. Primary Steel, Inc., 497 U.S. 116, 127–28 (1990)).
3. Mo. Rev. Stat. § 393.140(11).
4. Keogh v. Chi. & Nw. Ry. Co., 260 U.S. 156, 163 (1922).
5. Town of Norwood v. FERC, 202 F.3d 408, 419 (1st Cir. 2000).

preferred customers."[6] In passing the Act, Congress sought to "secure equality of rates as to all, and to destroy favoritism, these last being accomplished by requiring the publication of tariffs, and by prohibiting secret departures from such tariffs, and forbidding rebates, preferences and all other forms of undue discrimination."[7]

Over a century, the doctrine "has been extended across the spectrum of regulated utilities."[8] This extension has produced principles and applications that go beyond discrimination-prevention. This Chapter discusses seven:

- Courts must respect rates authorized by commissions.
- State commissions must respect rates authorized by federal commissions.
- Commissions must respect the rates they authorize.
- Courts cannot award antitrust damages to customers of utilities with filed rates.
- The doctrine applies to market-based (seller-set) rates.
- The doctrine applies to non-rate terms and conditions.
- Fraud does not block the filed rate defense.

9.B. Commission decisions constrain courts

Since the only legal rate is the commission-authorized rate, rates cannot be made or changed by courts. Two landmark cases apply this principle to federal and state courts, respectively.

9.B.1. Federal courts

Montana-Dakota Utilities Company and Northwestern Public Service Company were affiliates: They had common management, interlocking directorates, and joint officers. They also exchanged wholesale power, buying from and selling to each other at rates authorized by the Federal Power Commission under the Federal Power Act. Eventually they separated, disharmoniously. Montana-Dakota then sued Northwestern in federal district court, seeking compensation on grounds that Northwestern had overcharged and

---

6. Cal. *ex rel.* Lockyer v. FERC, 383 F.3d 1006, 1011 (9th Cir. 2004).
7. N.Y., New Haven & Hartford R.R. Co. v. Interstate Commerce Comm'n, 200 U.S. 361, 391 (1906); *see also Maislin*, 497 U.S. at 126 (citing the "close interplay" among the duty to file rates, the duty to adhere to those rates, the statutory filing requirement and the statutory prohibition against undue discrimination); Ariz. Grocery Co. v. Atchison, Topeka & Santa Fe Ry. Co., 284 U.S. 370, 384 (1932) ("In order to render rates definite and certain, and to prevent discrimination and other abuses, the statute require[s] the filing and publishing of tariffs specifying the rates adopted by the carrier, and makes these the legal rates, that is, those which must be charged to all shippers alike."); *Keogh*, 260 U.S. at 163 ("This stringent rule prevails, because otherwise the paramount purpose of Congress—prevention of unjust discrimination—might be defeated."); Tex. & Pac. R.R. Co. v. Abilene Cotton Oil Co., 204 U.S. 426, 440 (1907) ("[T]here is not only a relation, but an indissoluble unity between the provision for the establishment and maintenance of rates until corrected in accordance with the statute and the prohibitions against preferences and discrimination.").
8. Ark. La. Gas Co. v. Hall, 453 U.S. 571, 577 (1981). *See also MCI Telecomms. Corp.*, 512 U.S. at 220 ("The requirements of § 203 [of the Communications Act of 1934] that common carriers file their rates with the Commission and charge only the filed rate were the centerpiece of the Act's regulatory scheme.").

underpaid for wholesale power. Agreeing with Montana-Dakota, the trial court voided the contracts as fraudulent. The court then took two fatal steps: it found the previous wholesale rates unreasonable, and it awarded Montana-Dakota damages calculated to make it whole, based on the court's view of what were the reasonable rates.

The Supreme Court reversed. By awarding damages, the lower court had entered the Commission's exclusive domain. Here is the Court's famous language, as stated in *Montana-Dakota Utilities Co. v. Northwestern Public Service Co.*:

> [Montana-Dakota] cannot separate what Congress has joined together. It cannot litigate in a judicial forum its general right to a reasonable rate, ignoring the qualification that it shall be made specific only by exercise of the Commission's judgment. . . . It can claim no rate as a legal right that is other than the filed rate, whether fixed or merely accepted by the Commission, and *not even a court can authorize commerce in the commodity on other terms.*
>
> We hold that the right to a reasonable rate is the right to the rate which the Commission files or fixes, and that, except for review of the Commission's orders, *the court can assume no right to a different one* on the ground that, in its opinion, it is the only or the more reasonable one.

If Montana-Dakota wants recourse, it must visit the Commission, not a court, because the rate on file with the Commission, and only the Commission, can determine Montana-Dakota's rights.

The Court's phrase "except for review of the Commission's orders" bears emphasis. The doctrine prohibits the court from *setting* a rate (or awarding damages based on the court's view of the appropriate rate). But it does not prevent the court from *reversing* a regulator's rate decision if the decision is unlawful. In that instance, the court does not set the lawful rate; it remands the case to the commission to set the rate. The court and commission play distinct, non-overlapping roles. The commission issues the order setting the rate; the court determines the lawfulness of the commission's order.

9.B.2. State courts

A gas producer sued its pipeline customer for breach of contract, claiming underpayment for gas. The state court awarded contract damages, based on the court's view of what the payment should have been. Because the award was inconsistent with the rate set by the Federal Power Commission, the U.S. Supreme Court reversed, in *Ark. La. Gas Co. v. Hall.*[9] Here is a summary of this second landmark case.

9.　453 U.S. 571 (1981).

Natural gas producers had a contract to sell gas from the Sligo Gas Field to Arkansas Louisiana Gas Company (Arkla), a pipeline and gas reseller. The contract had a fixed price schedule and a "favored nations clause." The clause entitled the producers to receive from Arkla any higher price paid by Arkla to others for Sligo gas. The producers filed the contract with the Federal Power Commission, which authorized the sales at the contract-specified prices.

Arkla then bought Sligo Gas Field leases from the U.S. Government and began producing gas itself. Arkla's lease payments to the U.S. exceeded the producers' filed rate, but Arkla never told the producers. When the producers discovered the payments, they sued Arkla in state court for breach of contract. Arkla's lease payments triggered the favored nations clause, the producers argued: for each unit sold to Arkla, they were entitled to the excess of the lease payment rate over the filed rate.

The Louisiana Supreme Court agreed that Arkla had breached its contract. The court then took its fatal step: It calculated contract damages based on the difference between (a) the fixed price Arkla had been paying the producers, and (b) the rate that, in the Louisiana court's view, the Federal Power Commission would have approved had the producers sought relief there. The U.S. Supreme Court reversed:

> [Arkla argues that the state court's award] amounts to nothing less than the award of a retroactive rate increase based on speculation about what the Commission might have done had it been faced with the facts of this case. This, they contend, is precisely what the filed rate doctrine forbids. We agree. It would undermine the congressional scheme of uniform rate regulation to allow a state court to award as damages a rate never filed with the Commission and thus never found to be reasonable within the meaning of the Act. . . . Congress here has granted exclusive authority over rate regulation to the Commission. In so doing, Congress withheld the authority to grant retroactive rate increases or to permit collection of a rate other than the one on file. It would surely be inconsistent with this congressional purpose to permit a state court to do through a breach-of-contract action what the Commission itself may not do. . . . [T]he Louisiana Supreme Court's award of damages to respondents was necessarily supported by an assumption that the higher rate respondents might have filed with the Commission was reasonable. . . . But under the filed rate doctrine, the Commission alone is empowered to make that judgment, and until it has done so, no rate other than the one on file may be charged . . . . The court below . . . has consequently usurped a function that Congress has assigned to a federal regulatory body. This the Supremacy Clause will not permit.

Were the producers left with no remedy? Yes, because the Federal Power Commission in a separate proceeding declined to grant a rate increase retroactively. Arkla was off the hook, and the producers were stuck: "A finding that federal law provides a shield for the challenged conduct will almost always leave the state-law violation unredressed."[10]

9.C. Federal commission decisions constrain state commissions

We have just seen how the filed rate doctrine precludes rate-setting by federal and state courts. In the latter case, the filed rate doctrine combined with the Supremacy Clause to preempt the state court.[11] The same limitation applies to state commissions. The leading case is *Nantahala Power & Light v. Thornburg.*[12]

Chapter 8.C.2 (on undue discrimination) summarized the facts.[13] Here is a brief reminder. The holding company Alcoa owned two subsidiaries: Nantahala, a North Carolina utility with retail and wholesale customers; and Tapoco, an aluminum smelter in Tennessee. The holding company system had rights to low-cost hydroelectric power sold by the Tennessee Valley Authority. The hydroelectric power was attractive because it would displace other, more expensive sources. A set of wholesale contracts allocated the hydroelectric rights so as to favor Tapoco and disfavor Nantahala. FERC ordered changes to the contracts, increasing Nantahala's share from 20 percent to 22.5 percent.

FERC's adjustment was insufficient, said the North Carolina Utilities Commission (NCUC). In the subsequent retail rate case, the NCUC set Nantahala's retail rates as if Nantahala had purchased 24.5 percent of the available hydroelectric power, rather than the 22.5 percent authorized by FERC. (Because hydroelectricity displaces higher cost sources, the NCUC's treatment made Nantahala's retail rates lower than they would have been had the NCUC accepted the FERC allocation.)

---

10.   *Id.* at 578–84. *See also Keogh*, 260 U.S. at 163 ("The rights as defined by the tariff cannot be varied or enlarged by either contract or tort of the carrier."); Brown v. Cassens Transp. Co., 675 F.3d 946 (6th Cir. 2012) ("[W]ithout the filed-rate doctrine, victorious plaintiffs [in utility rate suits] would wind up paying less than non-suing ratepayers." (quoting Wegoland Ltd. v. NYNEX Corp., 27 F.3d 17, 21 (2d Cir. 1994))); Valdez v. State, 54 P.3d 71, 75 (N.M. 2002) ("The policy behind the filed rate doctrine is to prevent price discrimination[,] to preserve the role of agencies in approving rates and to keep courts out of the rate-making process.").

11.   The Supremacy Clause of the U.S. Constitution provides:

   This Constitution, and the Laws of the United States which shall be made in Pursuance thereof; and all Treaties made, or which shall be made, under the Authority of the United States, shall be the supreme Law of the Land; and the Judges in every State shall be bound thereby, any Thing in the Constitution or Laws of any State to the Contrary notwithstanding.

   U.S. CONST. art. VI, cl. 2. Chapter 12.B.2 will discuss the Supremacy Clause in detail, in the larger context of federal–state regulatory relations.

12.   476 U.S. 953 (1986).

13.   Recall that a dispute over rights to low-cost hydroelectric power produced an appeal of FERC's allocation to the Fourth Circuit, discussed in Chapter 8.C.2. That dispute was between Alcoa and municipal wholesale customers, who took service under a FERC-jurisdictional contract. Now we deal with the same fact situation but a different jurisdictional situation: the North Carolina Commission addressing how to treat FERC's allocation in retail rates.

The U.S. Supreme Court found the NCUC action preempted by the Federal Power Act. The Court began by articulating this principle: "[A] state utility commission setting retail prices must allow, as reasonable operating expenses, costs incurred [by a retail utility] as a result of paying a FERC-determined wholesale price . . . . [This requirement is] driven by the need to enforce the exclusive jurisdiction vested by Congress in FERC over the regulation of interstate wholesale utility rates . . . ." Applying this principle to the North Carolina facts, the Court explained that "FERC's [allocation] decision directly affects Nantahala's wholesale rates by determining the amount of low-cost power that it may obtain, and FERC required Nantahala's wholesale rate to be filed in accordance with that allocation." Once FERC ordered that allocation, Nantahala was limited to that amount. The NCUC had no power to treat Nantahala as having discretion to buy a larger amount:

> There is only NCUC's assertion that Nantahala should have obtained more of the low-cost, FERC-regulated power than Nantahala is in fact entitled to claim under FERC's order. Such a rationale runs directly counter to FERC's order, and therefore cannot withstand the pre-emptive force of FERC's decision.

By treating Nantahala as having more access to low-cost hydroelectric power than FERC allowed, the NCUC order resulted in "trapped cost." The Court's further explanation is crucial to understanding this oft-used phrase:

> FERC has ordered Nantahala to set its wholesale rates in light of an allocation of 22.5 percent of the entitlement power given jointly to Tapoco and Nantahala by TVA (and thus to calculate its overall rates as if it needed to purchase the remainder of its power at purchased-power rates). NCUC, in contrast, has ordered Nantahala to set its retail rates in light of an allocation of 24.5 percent of the entitlement power. Because purchased power is more expensive than entitlement power, NCUC's order prevents Nantahala from recovering the full costs of acquiring power under the FERC-approved scheme: Nantahala must under NCUC's order calculate its retail rates as if it received more entitlement power than it does under FERC's order, and as if it needed to procure less of the more expensive purchased power than under FERC's order. A portion of the costs incurred by Nantahala in procuring its power is therefore trapped.[14]

By trapping costs, the NCUC violated the filed rate doctrine. The doctrine requires, said the *Nantahala* Court, "that interstate power rates filed with FERC or fixed by FERC must be given binding effect by state utility commissions determining intrastate rates." So while *Montana-Dakota* and *Arkansas Louisiana* applied the doctrine to protect FERC's

---

14. *Nantahala*, 476 U.S. at 962–71.

310   *Chapter Nine*

jurisdiction from being "usurped" by federal and state courts, the *Nantahala* Court used the doctrine to prevent interference with FERC decisions by state commissions. The filed rate doctrine thus applies to state regulators, "as a matter of federal pre-emption through the Supremacy Clause."[15]

Crucial caveat: The filed rate doctrine does not mean that a state commission can never disallow a utility's cost incurred under a FERC-jurisdictional contract. We will discuss this matter in detail in Chapter 12.B.2.c, but here is a preview. Suppose a retail utility has a choice of purchasing from two wholesale sellers, High and Low. Assume that each seller offers a FERC-approved rate but High's rate is high and Low's rate is low. Describing this scenario, the *Nantahala* Court said:

> Without deciding this issue, we may assume that a particular quantity of power procured by a utility from a particular source could be deemed unreasonably excessive if lower cost power is available elsewhere, even though the higher cost power actually purchased is obtained at a FERC approved, and therefore reasonable, price.

But that was not the situation faced by Nantahala and the NCUC:

> Nantahala's procurement of purchased power is not unreasonably large given that Nantahala could not have treated itself as having access to any more low cost entitlement power than it is eligible to include under FERC's interpretation of what would be a fair allocation . . . . The North Carolina court's ruling that Nantahala had purchased an unreasonably large quantity of high cost power from TVA therefore conflicts with FERC's orders in the same manner as would a refusal to recognize a FERC approved price as a reasonable cost for purposes of retail ratemaking.[16]

* * *

Nantahala, along with *Mississippi Power & Light v. Mississippi ex rel. Moore*,[17] continues to influence federal–state jurisdictional relations in the area of power supply planning. We will address this practical subject in Chapter 12.B.2.c.

---

15. Entergy La., Inc. v. La. Pub. Serv. Comm'n, 539 U.S. 39, 47 (2003) (citing *Ark. La. Gas Co.*, 453 U.S. at 581–82).
16. *Nantahala*, 476 U.S. at 972–73.
17. 487 U.S. 354 (1988).

9.D. Commission must respect its own rates

Because the filed rate doctrine's roots are statutory (recall the Missouri provision quoted in Chapter 9.A), a commission cannot avoid it through rulemaking. Primary Steel, a shipper-customer of trucker Quinn Freight, learned this the hard way. Its story became the leading case of *Maislin Industries, U.S., Inc. v. Primary Steel, Inc.*[18]

The Interstate Commerce Commission issued a rule allowing parties to negotiate private rates below the filed rate. Primary Steel negotiated rates with Quinn Freight (a subsidiary of Maislin), then used Quinn for 1,081 shipments. When Maislin went bankrupt, the bankruptcy estate sued Primary Steel for $187,923 in undercharges—the difference between the negotiated rate and the filed rate. Primary Steel refused to pay—and lost. Like the unlucky train ticket purchaser, Primary Steel had to pay the filed rate: "The legal rights of shipper as against carrier in respect to a rate are measured by the published tariff. *Unless and until suspended or set aside*, this rate is made, for all purposes, the legal rate." Because the ICC never found the tariff rate unreasonable, Primary Steel had to pay the filed rate, notwithstanding the ICC's rule allowing negotiated rates. The Court then turned to the ICC: "By refusing to order collection of the filed rate solely because the parties had agreed to a lower rate, the ICC has permitted the very price discrimination that the Act by its terms seeks to prevent."[19]

The doctrine also prevents a commission from revising retroactively a rate it had established previously. This restriction enables customers to "know in advance the consequences of the purchasing decisions they make."[20] Recall the gas industry transition, discussed in

---

18. 497 U.S. 116 (1990).
19. *Id.* at 128–30. While the *Maislin* facts explain the filed rate doctrine's limits on agency rulemaking, trucker representatives will need to pause before citing the case to support claims for undercharge compensation. A provision in the Negotiated Rates Act of 1993 ("NRA"), Pub. L. No. 103-180, 107 Stat. 2044, 49 U.S.C. 10701(f), *repealed by* ICC Termination Act of 1995, Pub. L. No. 104-88, 109 Stat. 803, 809, had modified *Maislin*'s rule of complete recovery of undercharges. Further, the U.S. Supreme Court has held that "the 'filed rate' doctrine does not bar the ICC from enjoining a trustee from collecting liquidated damages found in a filed tariff when it is shown that the carrier violated the ICC's credit regulations." Friedman's Express v. Pa. Power & Light Co., 184 B.R. 229, 231, 1995 Bankr. LEXIS 1036 (Bankruptcy Ct. E.D. Pa. 1995) (citing ICC v. Transcon Lines, 513 U.S. 138 (1995)). And as we will see in Chapter 9.E below (applying the filed rate doctrine to market-based rates), privately negotiated rates can co-exist with the filed rate doctrine. In the FERC world, when the commission authorizes a seller to charge negotiated rates, that authorization itself becomes the "filed rate."

    The Interstate Commerce Commission no longer exists. Congress replaced it with the Surface Transportation Board in 1995.
20. Transwestern Pipeline Co. v. FERC, 897 F.2d 570, 577 (D.C. Cir. 1990). *See also* Columbia Gas Transmission Corp. v. FERC, 831 F.2d 1135, 1141 (D.C. Cir. 1987) ("wholesale purchasers of electricity cannot plan their activities unless they know the cost of what they are receiving, particularly if they are retailers, who must calculate their appropriate resale rates, . . . but also if they are large-scale purchaser-users"); San Diego Gas & Elec. Co. v. Sellers of Energy, 127 FERC ¶ 61,191, at p. 26 (2009) (explaining that the filed rate doctrine "forbids a regulated entity [from] charging rates for its services other than those properly filed with the appropriate regulatory authority" and that considerations include "preservation of the agency's primary jurisdiction over reasonableness of rates and the need to insure that regulated companies charge only those rates of which the agency has been made cognizant" (quoting November 2000 Order, 93 FERC ¶ 61,121, at p. 61,380 (2000))).

Chapter 3.A.2. A sequence of FERC orders (some of which did not survive judicial review) required pipelines to (a) unbundle gas sales from transportation service, and (b) offer their customers non-discriminatory transportation so they could shop for competing supplies. Pipelines had historically purchased gas for the formerly captive customers under take-or-pay contracts with producers. When these customers shopped elsewhere, the pipelines were left with large liabilities to the producers. The producers insisted on "buydowns" or "buyouts"—payments from the pipelines to settle the liabilities. One FERC solution was to allow pipelines to recover a portion of these take-or-pay costs from their wholesale customers through a "purchase deficiency" surcharge on prospective purchases:

> Customers' purchases of natural gas decreased sharply during the period from 1983 to 1986 and thereby exacerbated the pipelines' problems. FERC therefore proposed to base the charge upon the customer's "deficiency" of purchases during this period. This "purchase deficiency" was to be calculated by measuring the customer's purchases in the "deficiency period" (1983–86) against its purchases in a prior "base period" (1981–82).

FERC's deficiency period method violated the filed rate doctrine, because it caused a "retroactive change in rates without advance notice." In other words, FERC failed to honor its own previously approved rate:

> Predictability [is] the fundamental policy underlying the filed rate doctrine and the [deficiency method] contravenes that policy: Had Tennessee's customers known of these charges, they could have either purchased less gas from [the pipeline] during the base period or more gas during the deficiency period (or both) and could have thereby reduced their gas costs.[21]

* * *

The filed rate doctrine limits not only federal courts (*Montana-Dakota*), state courts (*Arkansas Louisiana*), and state commissions (*Nantahala*); it limits the rate-setting agency itself. Just as the federal court in *Montana-Dakota* and the state court in *Arkansas Louisiana* could not award state law damages that conflicted with the FERC-filed rate, and just as the state commission in *Nantahala* could not set retail rates that conflicted with the FERC-filed rate, FERC itself could not impose charges that conflicted with its own filed rate.

In *Associated Gas Distributors*, FERC imposed a retroactive charge. The general prohibition against retroactivity (albeit with multiple exceptions) is the subject of Chapter

---

21.   Associated Gas Distribs. v. FERC, 893 F.2d 349, 353–54 (D.C. Cir. 1989).

10. While we treat the filed rate doctrine and the retroactivity prohibition in separate chapters, the latter is actually a subset of the former. As FERC has written: "The rule against retroactive ratemaking is an outgrowth of the filed rate doctrine, and prohibits the Commission from adjusting current rates to make up for over- or under-collections of costs in prior periods."[22]

9.E. Application to market-based rates

As we learned from *Maislin* (see Chapter 9.D), no one—not seller, federal court, state court, or commission—may vary from the filed rate. What if there is no filed *rate*? What if the regulator has authorized the seller to sell at any possible rate? Recall market-based pricing (from Chapter 7): FERC authorizes sellers, if they pass the market power screens, to charge whatever rate they can negotiate. For these sellers, there is no specific "rate" on file at FERC. Does the filed rate doctrine still apply? Yes, say the courts. A market-based rate tariff, "instead of setting forth rate schedules or rate-fixing contracts, simply state[s] that the seller will enter into freely negotiated contracts with purchasers."[23] This tariff, which merely records the seller's FERC-granted right to price at will, is itself the "filed rate."

Because the market-based tariff is the filed rate, parties to market-based rate contracts are in the same position as the parties in *Montana-Dakota* and *Arkansas Louisiana*: The courts cannot grant them damages premised on some rate other than the filed rate. There is one exception: if the seller has violated a FERC condition on the authorization to charge market rates. We discuss each issue in turn.

9.E.1. Antitrust and contract damages unavailable

Gallo, a wine producer, was a retail gas customer of EnCana, an energy trader. EnCana had "blanket authority," granted by FERC, to sell gas at market-based rates. EnCana's standard contract pegged its rates to trade publication indices. Upset by the high prices it was paying mid-contract, Gallo sued EnCana for antitrust damages, arguing that EnCana had inflated the contract prices by manipulating the published indices.[24] The court paused, because of the filed rate doctrine: "A challenge to market-based natural gas rates established pursuant to FERC's blanket market certificate would require a court to reconsider natural gas rates that FERC had already determined to be reasonable." As was the case

---

22. San Diego Gas & Electric Co., 127 FERC ¶ 61,191, at n.20 (2009) (citing Associated Gas Distribs. v. FERC, 898 F.2d 809, 810 (D.C. Cir. 1990)).

23. Morgan Stanley Capital Grp. v. Pub. Util. Dist. No. 1 of Snohomish Cnty., 554 U.S. 527, 537 (2008). *See also* El Paso Electric Co., 108 FERC ¶ 61,071, at p. 19 n.29 (2004) ("Enron had a filed rate—its market-based rate tariff, which the Commission previously had accepted.").

24. Many FERC-jurisdictional (i.e., wholesale) contracts based their prices on published indices. Manipulation of these indices was widespread. Wholesalers misreported prices to the publications, inflated them further through "wash trades," then charged high prices under contracts that referenced the indices. *See* FERC, Final Report on Price Manipulation in Western Markets (Mar. 26, 2003), *available at* http://www.ferc.gov/legal/maj-ord-reg/land-docs/PART-I-3-26-03.pdf.

in *Montana-Dakota* and *Arkansas Louisiana*, a court has no authority to grant damages based on some rate other than the seller-selected, FERC-authorized, rate. The court allowed the lawsuit to proceed, however, because the defendant-seller had not shown "that all the transactions comprising the indices were FERC-approved transactions or otherwise shielded from challenge." Some of the index inputs might have been "misreported or wholly fictitious," as distinct from FERC-authorized rates. "[B]arring claims that such fictitious transactions damaged purchasers in the natural gas market would not further the purpose of the filed rate doctrine."[25]

A similar fate met electric customers seeking state law contract damages for allegedly unlawful prices arising from a "dysfunctional" wholesale market. During the California energy crisis, Grays Harbor, a wholesale customer, paid a very high $249 per mWh price for power. It agreed to that price, it said, only because it "believed that the rate was based on a properly functioning market, when in fact the price resulted from a dysfunctional, manipulated market." Grays Harbor sued Idaho Power, its market-pricing seller, under state contract law, seeking the difference between the $249 and a "price that reflects a fair price absent dysfunction, manipulation and the intentional withholding of electric power." The court had no jurisdiction to award damages, because doing so would require the court to determine the proper price, a matter within FERC's exclusive jurisdiction: "Even in the context of market-based rates, FERC actively regulates and oversees the setting of rates. . . . [W]hile market-based rates may not have historically been the type of rate envisioned by the filed rate doctrine, we conclude that they do not fall outside of the purview of the doctrine."[26]

9.E.2. "Retroactivity" allowed if seller has violated a market rate condition

We learned from *Associated Gas* (discussed in Chapter 9.D) that the filed rate doctrine bars a commission from setting rates retroactively. In that case, FERC violated the filed rate doctrine when it computed prospective charges based on a "deficiency" of purchases in a prior period. Retroactivity is allowed, however, if a market-based seller violates a regulatory condition. Here are two examples.

When Enron applied for market rates, it told FERC what assets it controlled. (FERC requires this information to determine if the market-pricing applicant has market power. See Chapter 7.C.2 on screening and monitoring.) FERC granted Enron's application, on condition that Enron report any control of additional assets. Enron then acquired control

---

25. E. & J. Gallo Winery v. EnCana Corp., 503 F.3d 1027, 1041–48 (9th Cir. 2007). The court also rejected the sellers' argument that the indices themselves were FERC-jurisdictional, FERC-authorized prices. FERC's authority under the Natural Gas Act covers gas, not indices.

26. Pub. Util. Dist. No. 1 of Grays Harbor Cnty. Wash. v. IDACORP Inc., 379 F.3d 641, 645–51 (9th Cir. 2004). The court of appeals allowed Grays Harbor to amend its complaint to argue that the contract itself was void due to "mutual mistake" or other theories that would not require the court to determine the appropriate rate.

of El Paso's assets without telling FERC. On discovering the deception, FERC ordered Enron to disgorge the profits earned from the El Paso facilities. The disgorgement, while "retroactive," did not violate the filed rate doctrine because Enron violated a condition of its authorization to charge the filed rate.[27]

Broadening this point, the Ninth Circuit has held that the "filed rate" includes all regulatory obligations accompanying the permission to charge market rates. Among FERC's requirements for electricity sellers are quarterly reports containing transaction-specific data. FERC uses this information for monitoring—to verify that market-pricing sellers are not charging rates above just and reasonable levels. During the California energy crisis, non-compliance with quarterly reporting was "rampant," because sellers were using aggregated data to mask their actual prices. Despite this noncompliance, FERC allowed the sales to continue, subjecting California consumers to high prices resulting from "a variety of market machinations, such as 'round trip trades' and 'hockey-stick bidding,' coupled with manipulative corporate strategies, such as those nicknamed 'FatBoy,' 'Get Shorty,' and 'Death Star.'" When California's Attorney General sought refunds, FERC resisted, asserting that the filed rate doctrine protected the rates from retroactive changes. The Ninth Circuit disagreed. The reporting requirements were an "integral part" of any market-based tariff. A seller's failure to heed them rendered its charges illegal, making disgorgement possible without violating the filed rate doctrine: "The power to order retroactive refunds when a company's non-compliance has been so egregious that it eviscerates the tariff is inherent in FERC's authority to approve a market-based tariff in the first instance."[28]

FERC's solution: Since 2001, FERC has applied the following language to sellers with existing authorization to charge market rates:

> As a condition of obtaining and retaining market based rate authority, the seller is prohibited from engaging in anti-competitive behavior or the exercise of market power. The seller's market-based rate authority is subject to refunds or other remedies as may be appropriate to address any anti-competitive behavior or exercise of market power.[29]

This condition is now part of every market-based seller's "filed rate." The doctrine's prohibition against retroactivity no longer prevents refunds of rates made excessive by "anti-competitive behavior or the exercise of market power."

---

27. El Paso Electric Co., 108 FERC ¶ 61,071 (2004).
28. Cal. *ex rel.* Lockyer v. FERC, 383 F.3d 1006, 1012–15 (9th Cir. 2004). See footnotes 6, 7, and 8 of the court's opinion for technical (and vivid) definitions of "FatBoy," "Get Shorty" and other terms.
29. Investigation of Terms and Conditions of Public Utility Market-Based Rate Authorizations, 97 FERC ¶ 61,220 (2001).

9.F. Application to antitrust law

What if a regulated seller behaves anti-competitively—that is, conspires to fix prices—and drives the market price above competitive levels? Outside of regulated industries, the plaintiff customer can sue for antitrust damages, measured by the excess of (a) the price inflated by anti-competitive behavior over (b) the price that would have emerged from effective competition. Inside regulated industries, the plaintiff confronts the filed rate doctrine, which prevents the courts from awarding money damages.

The leading case is *Keogh v. Chicago & Northwestern Railway Co.*[30] Keogh, a shipper, complained that the defendant railroad companies conspired to fix prices at levels higher than would have existed under fair competition. The railroads had filed their rates with the ICC, which approved them after a hearing in which Keogh participated. The shipper sought antitrust damages, based on the difference between the rates charged and rates that would have existed under effective competition. The Supreme Court dismissed the suit, reasoning that the shipper's legal rights under antitrust law were limited by the filed rate:

> Section 7 of the Anti-Trust Act gives a right of action to one who has been "injured in his business or property." Injury implies violation of a legal right. The legal rights of shipper as against carrier in respect to a rate are measured by the published tariff. Unless and until suspended or set aside, this rate is made, for all purposes, the legal rate, as between carrier and shipper. The rights as defined by the tariff cannot be varied or enlarged by either contract or tort of the carrier.

Allowing financial damages would have required a court to displace the ICC in determining the "just and reasonable rate," in violation of the filed rate doctrine. The Supreme Court added three other concerns: allowing individual antitrust courts to award damages would produce discriminatory outcomes, since individual courts would inevitably reach different results; proving the hypothetical competitive rate would be difficult; and damages would be speculative (the benefit of a lower rate might have accrued to Keogh's customers rather than retained by Keogh as profit). Damages were unavailable, but other remedies were possible. Since price-fixing "may be" illegal, the Court said, the Government could institute actions for injunction, forfeiture or criminal proceedings. Because these remedies did not involve ratemaking, they were not barred by the filed rate doctrine.[31]

---

30.   260 U.S. 156 (1922).
31.   *Id.* at 163. *See also* Square D Co. v. Niagara Frontier Tariff Bureau, 476 U.S. 409, 422 & n.28 (1986). (retaining possibility of injunctive relief); Carnation Co. v. Pac. Westbound Conference, 383 U.S. 213 (1966). The Court in *Carnation* allowed an antitrust suit to proceed because the shipper alleged that the transport companies (here, shipping companies) that conspired to set a price did not have the Federal Maritime Commission's permission to do so.

The intersection between antitrust damages and the filed rate doctrine returned sixty-four years later, in *Square D Co. v. Niagara Frontier Tariff Bureau*.[32] Shippers sued truckers under the Sherman Act for allegedly conspiring to fix rates for freight between Canada and the United States. The truckers were members of a bureau "organized to engage in collective ratemaking activities pursuant to an agreement filed with and approved by the ICC." The ICC's statute exempted collective ratemaking from the antitrust laws, as long as the rate-setting process complied with an ICC-approved agreement. The truckers had filed their rates with the ICC, which accepted them without a hearing. Arguing that the truckers' ratemaking procedures violated the ICC-approved agreement, the shippers sought antitrust damages, based on the difference between the rates they paid and the rates that would have prevailed in a non-price-fixed, competitive market. The U.S. Supreme Court dismissed the suit, citing *Keogh*. The absence of a hearing was irrelevant. Once rates are filed with and accepted by the agency, the filed rate doctrine deems them lawful.[33]

* * *

The *Keogh* and *Square D* decisions underscore the consumer-protective importance of FERC's 2001 rule, described above, that a "seller's market-based rate authority is subject to refunds or other remedies as may be appropriate to address any anti-competitive behavior or exercise of market power." While anti-competitive conduct by rate-regulated entities is not immune from the antitrust laws, private remedies are limited to injunctive relief; a court cannot award money damages.[34] In addition, the unilateral exercise of market power to extract high prices (as contrasted with collusive price fixing) is not, by itself, an antitrust violation.[35] Thus a tariff condition like FERC's rule, allowing refunds of charges arising from market power or collusion, is critical to customers who have no antitrust remedy.[36]

---

32. 476 U.S. 409 (1986).
33. *Id.* at 412, 423–24. The Court also rejected arguments, from the shipper and from the Solicitor General, that *Keogh* should be overruled. Given the many years during which courts have followed *Keogh*—"an established guidepost at the intersection of the antitrust and interstate commerce statutory regimes for some 6 1/2 decades"—the overruling should come not from the Court but from Congress. *Id.*
34. In addition to *Keogh* and *Square D*, *see* Town of Norwood v. FERC, 202 F.3d 408, 418–19 (1st Cir. 2000) (applying the *Keogh* doctrine to the electric industry, finding that the existence of a rate regulatory regime under the Federal Power Act may foreclose monetary damages for Sherman Act violations even where the regulated rate consisted of a market-based rate). *See also* City of Kirkwood v. Union Elec. Co., 671 F.2d 1173 (8th Cir. 1982).
35. United States v. Grinnell Corp., 384 U.S. 563, 571 (1966).
36. Tenneco Oil Co., 26 FERC ¶ 61,030, at p. 61,069 (1984); STEPHEN BREYER, REGULATION AND ITS REFORM 15–16 (1984) (protection from price-gouging is a traditional purpose of regulation).

9.G. Application to non-rate terms and conditions

The phrase "filed rate doctrine" is a slight misnomer, because the doctrine "is not limited to 'rates' per se."[37] It applies also to "the services, classifications, charges, and practices included in the rate filing."[38] In *Nantahala*, the "filed rate" was FERC's allocation of responsibility to purchase hydroelectric power. Here are three additional examples of non-rate features protected by the doctrine: gas production, rail service and long-distance telephone service.

Gas production: Northern Natural Gas, an interstate pipeline, had 125 contracts to buy gas from various Kansas producers. The contracts were subject to the Natural Gas Act. The largest contract required Northern to buy from Republic Natural Gas the full quantity that Republic was allowed (by state production regulations) to produce. Northern's contracts with other producers limited its purchase obligations to that portion of its needs not satisfied by its purchases from Republic. The Kansas Corporation Commission later issued a "ratable purchase" order that conflicted with Northern's FPC-approved contracts: pipelines purchasing from Kansas producers had to buy from each well the identical percentage of that well's allowable production. Kansas's order was preempted by the Natural Gas Act. While its order did not interfere with prices, it did interfere with a "comprehensive scheme of federal regulation of 'all wholesales of natural gas in interstate commerce, whether by a pipeline company or not and whether occurring before, during, or after transmission by an interstate pipeline company.'"[39]

Rail service: A railroad was weary of mudslides that damaged its tracks on a branch line. (On one occasion, "portions of the embankment wholly vanished under the waters of the Des Moines River.") So the railroad stopped using the line, then obtained permission from the Interstate Commerce Commission to abandon service on the line. A brick-making company that depended on the line sued the railroad in state court for violating (a) an Iowa statute, by breaching the railroad's "unqualified and unconditional duty to furnish car service and transportation to all persons who apply"; and (b) Iowa common law, by failing to maintain the roadbed and by tortiously interfering with the brick-maker's contracts. Deriding the lawsuit as "little more than an attempt by a disappointed shipper to gain from the Iowa courts the relief it was denied by the [Interstate Commerce] Commission," the Supreme Court found it preempted: "A system under which each State could, through its courts, impose on railroad carriers its own version of reasonable service requirements could hardly be more at odds with the uniformity contemplated by Congress in enacting the Interstate Commerce Act."[40]

---

37. *Nantahala Power & Light Co.*, 476 U.S. at 966.
38. *E. & J. Gallo Winery*, 503 F.3d at 1040 (quoting E. & J. Gallo Winery v. EnCana Energy Servs., No. 03-5412, 2005 U.S. Dist. LEXIS 24240, at *30 (E.D. Cal. Sept. 30, 2005)).
39. N. Natural Gas Co. v. Kan. Corp. Comm'n, 372 U.S. 84, 90–91 (1963) (quoting Phillips Petroleum Co. v. Wisconsin, 347 U.S. 672, 682 (1954)).
40. Chi. & N.W. Transportation Co. v. Kalo Brick & Tile Co., 450 U.S. 311, 324–26 (1981).

Long-distance telephone service: AT&T sold a package of wholesale discounted long-distance services to a "switchless reseller" of bundled telephone service. The parties' contract made the service subject to the rates, terms, and conditions of AT&T's FCC-filed tariff. Dissatisfied with service delays and billing inaccuracies, the reseller withdrew from the contract and sued AT&T in state court for contract breach, arguing that the contract included assurances by AT&T's salesperson and brochures of "faster provisioning, the allocation of charges through multilocation billing, and various matters relating to deposits, calling cards, and service support." Once again, the filed rate doctrine preempted the lawsuit. Section 203(a) of the Communications Act of 1934 required every common carrier to file schedules and tariffs "showing all charges" and "showing the classifications, practices, and regulations affecting such charges." The FCC-filed tariff comprised the exclusive terms and conditions. If the contract could be supplemented by myriad state law claims, the tariff uniformity envisioned by the Communications Act would be undermined. The Ninth Circuit had thought the doctrine did not apply because the dispute involved services and billing, not rates, but the Supreme Court disagreed:

> Rates . . . do not exist in isolation. They have meaning only when one knows the services to which they are attached. Any claim for excessive rates can be couched as a claim for inadequate services and vice versa. If "discrimination in charges" does not include non-price features, then the carrier could defeat the broad purpose of the statute by the simple expedient of providing an additional benefit at no additional charge . . . . An unreasonable "discrimination in charges," that is, can come in the form of a lower price for an equivalent service or in the form of an enhanced service for an equivalent price . . . . [A customer] can no more obtain unlawful preferences under the cloak of a tort claim than it can by contract.[41]

9.H. Fraud does not block the filed rate defense

In *Arkansas Louisiana*, the Supreme Court reserved the question whether the filed rate doctrine precludes a suit based on fraud.[42] But many years earlier, the Court had held that "[n]either the intentional nor accidental misstatement of the applicable published rate will bind the carrier or shipper."[43] And after *Arkansas Louisiana*, the Court has stated that the doctrine applies "even if a carrier intentionally misrepresents its rate and a customer relies on the misrepresentation . . . . The rights as defined by the tariff cannot be varied

---

41. AT&T v. Cent. Office Tel., Inc., 524 U.S. 214, 223–24, 226 (1998).
42. 453 U.S. at 583 n.13 ("We save for another day the question whether the filed rate doctrine applies in the face of fraudulent conduct.").
43. Louisville & Nashville R.R. Co., 237 U.S. at 98.

or enlarged by either contract or tort."[44] To award damages would require the court to determine what the rate would have been absent the fraudulent conduct—a role only the agency can play.

Consistent with this reasoning, courts have cited the doctrine to dismiss fraud suits in diverse cases.

1.   JMC sold international phone calling cards to the "maritime market" (foreign ships and their crew members, and cruise ships and their passengers). JMC retained AT&T to provide the actual service. But AT&T's service to the Philippines was poor, allegedly because AT&T used a Philippines company rather than providing the service exclusively as promised. Even if the promise was fraudulent, the doctrine barred damages.[45]

2.   Consumers sued New Mexico's Superintendent of Insurance, alleging that rates for title insurance were excessive because insurance companies bribed the Superintendent. The filed rate doctrine barred the claim, because resolution would require the court to set rates, an action exclusively the job of the Superintendent.[46]

3.   Cable customers alleged that Time Warner defrauded them by double-charging for network upgrades—once through an FCC tariff and again through a fee approved by the City of Minneapolis. Because a court-mandated award would require damages "measured by comparing the filed rate and the rate that might have been approved absent the conduct in issue," the filed rate doctrine barred the claim.[47]

4.   AT&T allegedly lured a reseller into a wholesale contract by promising to file a new FCC tariff with prices lower than its current filed tariff. AT&T never filed the discount tariff, instead billing the reseller at the higher filed rate. The filed rate doctrine barred the reseller's fraud suit.[48]

5.   Long-distance telephone customers sued AT&T for deceptive billing practices; specifically, rounding telephone calls up to the next higher full minute. (A conversation lasting 61 seconds was billed as two minutes.) The customers sought disgorgement of the excess revenues earned from the rounding. AT&T's practice

---

44.   *Cent. Office Tel.*, 524 U.S. at 222–27 (quoting *Keogh*, 260 U.S. at 163).
45.   AT&T Corp. v. JMC Telecom, 470 F.3d 525, 535 (3d Cir. 2006) ("enforcement of the duty of good faith and fair dealing would impermissibly enlarge the rights as defined by the tariff").
46.   Coll v. First Am. Title Ins. Co., 642 F.3d 876 (10th Cir. 2011).
47.   Crumley v. Time Warner Cable, 556 F.3d 879, 881–82 (8th Cir. 2009) ("[E]ven if a carrier intentionally misrepresents its rate and a customer relies on the misrepresentation, the carrier cannot be held to the promised rate if it conflicts with the published tariff" (quoting *Cent. Office Tel.*, 524 U.S. at 222)). *See also* Firstcom, Inc. v. Qwest Corp., 555 F.3d 669, 680–81 (8th Cir. 2009) ("[T]o the extent Firstcom seeks recovery for a price discount it was allegedly entitled to [under claims of promissory estoppel and fraud], its claims are barred by the filed rate doctrine.").
48.   Fax Telecommunicaciones v. AT&T, 138 F.3d 479, 489 (2d Cir. 1998) (finding that "[i]f this court were to enforce the promised rate and award damages on that basis, we would effectively be setting and applying a rate apart from that judged reasonable by the FCC, in violation of the . . . filed rate doctrine").

was not disclosed on its bills or its advertising, but was disclosed in its FCC tariffs. The filed rate doctrine protected AT&T; its application "in any particular case is not determined by the culpability of the defendant's conduct or the possibility of inequitable results." To excuse customers from paying a lawful tariff would "subvert the authority of [the FCC] and undermine the regulatory regime." Further, while successful plaintiffs would win a reduced rate, customers who did not join the suit would still face the higher rate, thus upsetting a central purpose of the doctrine—to prevent discrimination.[49]

6.   How about consumers who sued for violations of the Racketeer Influenced and Corrupt Organizations (RICO) Act? The plaintiff-consumers charged that Northwestern Bell bribed members of the Minnesota Public Utilities Commission to raise rates. They sought damages based on their excess payments. The requested damages "necessarily and plainly challenge the rates previously approved by the Commission . . . . [T]he underlying conduct does not control whether the filed rate doctrine applies. Rather, the focus for determining whether the filed rate doctrine applies is the impact the court's decision will have on agency procedures and rate determinations."[50]

Does the fraud victim have any recourse? Possibly. If the seller fraudulently induced the customer to enter a FERC-jurisdictional contract, at a rate that the seller then filed, a court could invalidate the contract under state law contract principles. "[S]etting aside the contracts . . . would not interfere with the [federal agency's] rate-making powers" (as opposed to awarding damages based on the rate level the court determined would have prevailed absent the fraud).[51]

---

49.   Marcus v. AT&T Corp., 138 F.3d 46, 58, 61 (2d Cir. 1998) (quoting Sun City Taxpayers' Ass'n. v. Citizens Utils. Co., 45 F.3d 58, 62 (2d Cir. 1995), and citing *Maislin*, 497 U.S. at 126; *Keogh*, 260 U.S. at 163).

50.   H.J., Inc. v. Nw. Bell Tel. Co., 954 F.2d 485, 489, 493 (8th Cir. 1992). *See also* Taffet v. S. Co., 930 F.2d 847, 856 (11th Cir. 1991), *vacated*, 958 F.2d 1514 (11th Cir. 1992), *vacation aff'd en banc*, 967 F.2d 1483 (11th Cir. 1992). Retail customers brought a RICO claim, charging that Alabama Power and Georgia Power conspired with the accounting firm Arthur Andersen to understate their net income in filings before their respective state commissions, and in so doing, obtained rate increases fraudulently. The trial court agreed with the defendants that the filed rate doctrine barred the suit. A panel of the 11th Circuit reversed the trial court, describing the doctrine's purpose as "preserv[ing] the regulating agency's authority over the setting of reasonable rates." The panel reasoned that "[t]he possibility of a RICO action against a utility which defrauds its [state commission] creates great incentive for that utility to present its [commission] with accurate and truthful information." Permitting the suit, therefore, would "enhance rather than infringe" on the commission's authority. The Court of Appeals *en banc* vacated the panel's decision and affirmed the trial court's dismissal of the lawsuit, due to the filed rate doctrine: "The rate-setting schemes in both Alabama and Georgia are incompatible with a rate-payer's cause of action to recover damages measured by the difference between the filed rate and the rate that would have been charged absent some alleged wrongdoing. Allowing consumers of the Utilities' services to recover damages for 'fraudulent' rates or otherwise 'erroneous' rates would disrupt greatly the states' regulatory schemes and, in the end, would cost consumers dearly." 967 F.2d at 1491.

51.   Gulf States Utils. Co. v. Ala. Power Co., 824 F.2d 1465, 1472 (5th Cir. 1987).

* * *

The filed rate doctrine establishes utilities' obligation to place their rates in a public file, and to charge only those filed rates. With rates publicly known, the chance for undue discrimination is reduced. The doctrine also has broader purposes: to protect a commission's exclusive ratesetting power from usurpation by courts or other commissions, and to ensure that a commission acts consistently with its own prior decisions. The doctrine applies in both the cost-based and market-based rate contexts, and to non-rate terms as well. These applications, and the relevant cases, are displayed in Figure 9.

Filed Rate Doctrine Applies to All Fora, All Types of Rates and All Types of Law

	Applies to:	Case	Type of Law
Forum	Federal courts	*Montana-Dakota*	Contract, tort
		Keogh	Antitrust
		Gallo	Antitrust
	State courts	*Arkansas Louisiana Gas*	Contract
	Federal commission	*Maislin*	Contract
		Transwestern Pipeline	Contract
	State commissions	*Nantahala*	Contract
Type of "Rate"	Cost-based rate	*Montana-Dakota*	Contract, tort
	Market-based rate	*Morgan Stanley*	Contract
		Gallo	Contract
		Enron Power	Contract
	Gas production	*Northern Natural Gas*	Contract
	Rail service	*Chicago & N. W. Transp.*	Duty to serve, tort
	Long-distance phone service	*AT&T v. Cent. Office Tel.*	Contract

CHAPTER TEN

Retroactive Ratemaking

The Prohibition and the Exceptions

The Commission may not disinter the past merely because experience has belied projections, whether the advantage went to customers or the utility; bygones are bygones.[1]

10.A. Three bases

In cost-based ratemaking, a commission sets rates for a future period (called the "rate year"). There are two major steps: (1) computing the utility's "annual revenue requirement" based on projections of reasonable costs, and (2) dividing that revenue requirement by the predicted volume of sales.[2] The revenue requirement includes an *authorized* return on equity. The utility's *actual* return on equity, when the rate year closes, will match its authorized return only if actual costs and sales exactly match the projections (or if positive and negative deviations balance out perfectly). In reality, that matching never occurs. As a result, the utility's actual return on equity typically varies from the authorized return. May the regulator "correct" this outcome, refunding to customers any excess or making them pay extra to cover any shortfall?

The general answer is no. "It is a fundamental rule that utility rates are exclusively prospective in nature."[3] The rule stems from ratemaking's legislative character: legislative activity is prospective,[4] and the legislature has delegated its ratemaking authority to the regulator. To "correct" a pre-existing rate based on end-of-year results, the commission would have to order a change to previously approved rates, then apply that change to a past period. That is the definition of retroactive ratemaking.[5]

The rule against retroactivity has roots in statutes, the Constitution and policy. These roots are discussed next.

10.A.1. Statutory basis

The statutory basis is, naturally, statutory language. Section 5(a) of the Natural Gas Act is typical. It requires the commission to "determine the just and reasonable rate to be *thereafter*

---

1. Associated Gas Distribs. v. FERC, 898 F.2d 809, 810 (D.C. Cir. 1990) (Williams, J., concurring in denial of rehearing and rehearing *en banc*).
2. Rate-setting is of course more complicated than this single sentence suggests. See Chapter 6 and its references for details.
3. Narragansett Elec. Co. v. Burke, 381 A.2d 1358, 1364 (R.I. 1977).
4. *See* Citizens Utils. Co. v. Ill. Commerce Comm'n, 529 N.E.2d 510, 515–17 (Ill. 1988) ("The rule prohibiting retroactive ratemaking is consistent with the prospective nature of legislative activity."); Mountain Water Co. v. Mont. Dep't of Pub. Serv., 835 P.2d 4, 5 (Mont. 1992) (citing State *ex rel.* Billings v. Billings Gas Co., 173 P. 799, 801 (Mont. 1918)) (holding that "[r]ate-making is a legislative activity and is therefore prospective only in its effect").
5. San Diego Gas & Elec. Co. v. Sellers of Energy, 127 FERC ¶ 61,191, at p. 9 (2009) (citing Associated Gas Distribs. v. FERC, 898 F.2d 809, 810 (D.C. Cir. 1990)) (holding that the Commission may not "adjust[] current rates to make up for over- or under-collections of costs in prior periods").

observed and in force" (emphasis added), the term "thereafter" signaling prospectivity only. Note that this prospectivity enforces the filed rate doctrine, itself a statutory principle. As explained in Chapter 9.A, once a commission has accepted a rate for filing (assuming that the acceptance is lawful), the accepted rate is the lawful rate—and the only lawful rate. That it produces an actual return different from the authorized return does not make the lawful rate an unlawful rate. To "correct" this difference by granting customer refunds or forcing customer paybacks would be to disregard a previously approved rate, just as FERC did in *Associated Gas Distributor*, when it violated the filed rate doctrine by approving a "purchase deficiency" surcharge. If the actual return varies from the authorized return, the regulator can change the rates, but only prospectively.

10.A.2. Constitutional basis

The constitutional basis of the rule against retroactivity is the Fifth Amendment's Takings Clause. Recall that the Clause's "just compensation" command requires regulators to honor "distinct, investment-backed expectations."[6] On approving a lawful rate, a commission creates a distinct expectation, relied on by investors, that the utility can collect that rate until it is changed prospectively. Refunds of overearnings would undermine those legitimate expectations. Conversely, denying a utility an opportunity to collect past shortfalls does not violate the Takings Clause, because the utility had no legitimate expectation of retroactive recovery. It understood its revenue requirement to include an authorized return, not a guaranteed return.[7]

10.A.3. Policy basis

The rule "ensures the predictability and stability of utility rates and generally prevents utility companies from recovering losses that stem from 'past company mismanagement or improper forecasting.'"[8] Its "equity lies in its steady application regardless of what party is seeking to reexamine the past."[9]

* * *

---

6. *See supra* Chapter 6.B.2.a (citing Penn Cent. Transp. Co. v. New York, 438 U.S. 104, 124 (1978) (requiring courts in Takings cases to consider, among other factors, "the extent to which the regulation has interfered with distinct investment-backed expectations").

7. Mountain Water Co. v. Mont. Dep't of Pub. Serv., 835 P.2d 4, 5 (Mont. 1992) (holding that the Montana Commission's refusal to allow utility to collect past shortfalls was not a denial of just compensation).

8. Archer Daniels Midland Co. v. Iowa, 485 N.W.2d 465, 467 (Iowa 1992) (quoting Office of Consumer Advocate v. Iowa State Commerce Comm'n, 428 N.W.2d 302, 306 (Iowa 1988)); Citizens Utils. Co. v. Ill. Commerce Comm'n, 529 N.E.2d 510, 515–17 (Ill. 1988) ("[B]ecause the rule prohibits refunds when rates are too high and surcharges when rates are too low, it serves to introduce stability into the ratemaking process.").

9. Pub. Utils. Comm'n of Cal. v. FERC, 894 F.2d 1382, 1384 (D.C. Cir. 1990).

This chapter next illustrates the rule against retroactivity with four common examples, then discusses seven exceptions.

10.B. Four illustrations

10.B.1. Tax payments lower than estimates

Over twenty-two years, a water utility paid lower taxes than the level assumed in the revenue requirement approved by the Illinois Commerce Commission. When the Commission found out, it ordered a rate reduction, retroactively. The Illinois Supreme Court reversed: "The tax benefits at issue here originated as expenses that the company was allowed to recover. . . . [T]here can be no retroactive adjustment in this case simply because the Commission has now decided to treat the tax benefits differently."[10]

10.B.2. Tax depreciation differences

A utility's revenue requirement includes depreciation expense. The effect is to charge customers for the annual amortization of an asset's original cost over its useful life. In federal tax law, depreciation is a deductible expense. El Paso Natural Gas, a FERC-regulated pipeline, charged cost-based rates that assumed federal tax costs based on straight-line depreciation. But the utility paid its taxes, lawfully, based on accelerated depreciation.[11] Having collected from ratepayers amounts exceeding its actual tax costs in the asset's early years, it recorded the excess in a deferred tax account, to be used for the pipeline's tax liabilities in the asset's later years, when the actual tax costs would exceed the level reflected in rates. But mid-stream, the pipeline changed its ratemaking method, from cost-based to a method that made its tax cost irrelevant to the rate level. What should happen to the $100 million in the deferred tax account, reflecting amounts previously collected from ratepayers? The Court held that FERC could not refund the money to customers:

> [A] [r]efund . . . would effectively force El Paso to return a portion of rates approved by FERC and collected by El Paso. This kind of post hoc tinkering would undermine the predictability which the [retroactivity] doctrine seeks to protect . . . . The rule against retroactive ratemaking also tends to make this highly regulated market approximate ordinary ones, where, for example, General Motors may not, after a sale, demand another $500 to cover its costs, and a buyer may not demand a refund because he just discovered that a competitor had been offering similar cars for less.[12]

---

10. Citizens Utils. Co. v. Ill. Commerce Comm'n, 529 N.E.2d 510, 517 (Ill. 1988).
11. Straight-line depreciation yields an equal depreciation expense each year. That is, for a $900 asset with a useful life of thirty years, straight line depreciation yields an annual depreciation expense of $30. In accelerated depreciation, often allowed by tax law, the business books a disproportionate share of depreciation expense in the asset's early years. Since depreciation expense is a deductible expense for tax purposes, accelerated depreciation lowers the business's tax bill in the asset's early years.
12. Pub. Utils. Comm'n of Cal. v. FERC, 894 F.2d 1372, 1383 (D.C. Cir. 1990).

10.B.3. "Direct billing" of gas production costs

The Natural Gas Policy Act of 1978 (NGPA) set ceiling prices for "first sales" (typically sales by gas producers to pipelines). It also allowed producers to charge pipelines for specified "production-related costs" (e.g., compressing, gathering and processing). FERC authorized producers to collect from pipelines, prospectively, certain production-related costs associated with past gas sales. Because the pipelines had advance notice of these costs before making their purchases, the producers' charges were not disputed.

What was disputed was the pipelines' recovery of these costs from their wholesale gas customers. The pipelines had a dual rate structure. One component was the "purchased gas adjustment" (PGA) clause, which recovered "through prospective sales, on the basis of reasonably current calculations, the fluctuating production-related costs they are required to reimburse producers." The second component was "direct billing," through which the pipelines recovered from the wholesale gas customers the retroactive, undisputed payments made to producers. The direct billing charge was recovered prospectively but it was calculated based on past purchases. This direct billing component constituted unlawful retroactive ratemaking, because it was a "surcharge, over and above the rates on file at the time of sale, for gas [customers] had already purchased." While FERC had given advance notice of the producers' charge to the pipelines, there had been no advance notice to the pipelines' wholesale customers.[13]

10.B.4. Someone else's cost

What if the past costs are not the utility's costs, but the costs of the utility's *supplier*? Recall the gas industry's "take-or-pay" problem. Pipelines had contracted to buy specified quantities from producers, which they had to pay for regardless of their customers' needs. As Chapter 3.C.3.c.iii explained, FERC authorized pipelines to recover a portion of past take-or-pay obligations from local gas distribution companies. Then Iowa-Illinois Electric & Gas Company, having paid its take-or-pay share to its pipeline, received permission from the Iowa Utilities Board to recover the cost through a surcharge on prospective retail purchases. Archer Daniels Midland, a large retail customer of the Iowa-Illinois, appealed, claiming retroactive ratemaking.

The Iowa Supreme Court upheld the Board. The ban on retroactive ratemaking prevents utilities from avoiding the consequences of "past company mismanagement or improper forecasting." But here, the past cost was not the local utility's past cost, because the utility was not a party to the producer-pipeline contract that created the take-or-pay obligation. The past cost was the pipeline's, not the local utility's. From the local utility's perspective,

---

13.   Columbia Gas Transmission Corp. v. FERC, 831 F. 2d 1135, 1138–40 (D.C. Cir. 1987).

the cost was a current expense, invoiced currently by the pipeline. There was nothing retroactive about it.[14]

10.C. Seven exceptions

Some commission orders have retroactive effect in a chronological, dictionary sense, but are not retroactive ratemaking in a legal sense. They fall into seven categories.

10.C.1. Regulatory "notice"

The rule against retroactivity lets parties "know the consequences of the purchasing decisions they make." Can a commission let customers know the *possible* consequences of their decisions, while preserving its ability to change a rate retroactively? Yes: by notifying customers of possible rate changes *before they purchase under the rate*. The notice "'changes what would be purely retroactive ratemaking into a functionally prospective process by placing the relevant audience on notice at the outset that the rates being promulgated are provisional only and subject to later revision.'"[15]

To give this advance notice, commissions can declare that the current rates (or rates newly proposed by a utility) will remain in (or go into) effect "subject to refund." The "subject to refund" phrase gives notice that, should the commission find the current rates (or rate increase) excessive, it will order the utility to refund the excess, back to the date of the notice. That refund decision would be retroactive in a dictionary sense but not in a legal sense, because everyone had notice of the possibility.[16]

What if the consumer intervenor files a complaint seeking a rate *decrease*? Since a complaint proceeding can take several months, some statutes again allow the commission to declare the rates being complained of (i.e., the current rates) "subject to refund" as of the date the complaint was filed. If the commission then grants the complaint and requires a

---

14. *Archer Daniels*, 485 N.W.2d at 467–68.
15. San Diego Gas & Electric Co. v. Sellers of Energy, 127 FERC ¶ 61,191, at p. 27 (2009) (quoting Pub. Utils. Comm'n of Cal. v. FERC, 988 F.2d 154, 164 (D.C. Cir. 1993)).
16. *See*, for example, Section 4c(e) of the Natural Gas Act, 15 U.S.C. § 717c(e), explained by the Court of Appeals as follows:

> When a natural gas company files new rates under § 4 of the Act, a limited form of retroactive rate collection may occur. The Commission may order the [proposed] rates suspended for up to five months. If it is unable to resolve their validity within that period, it must let them go into effect. Then, if it ultimately finds them unjust or unreasonable, it may order the company to make refunds to customers. [T]his exception to the rule against retroactive rate changes is simply a necessary compromise to accommodate delays in the approval process.

> Pub. Utils. Comm'n of Cal. v. FERC, 894 F.2d 1372, 1382 (D.C. Cir. 1990) (quoting E. Tenn. Natural Gas Co. v. FERC, 863 F.2d 932, 941 (D.C. Cir. 1988)); *see also* Ky. Utils. Co. v. FERC, 760 F.2d 1321, 1328 (D.C. Cir. 1985) ("If the newly filed rate is eventually determined to be excessive, the Commission enjoys authority, of course, to order the utility to refund the excess portion to its ratepayers.").

lower rate, there can be refunds back to the date of the complaint. Those refunds would not violate the ban on retroactivity, because there was notice.

The same approach applies when the commission itself thinks the current rates might be too high. Assume that the commission in 2010 had approved rates based on an authorized return on equity of 10.5 percent. It later learns that the utility in 2012 earned 13.0 percent. These are lawful earnings because they were earned under a lawful rate. But the commission can issue an order initiating an investigation, and declare the rates "interim subject to refund" as of the date of the order. That way, if the case takes eight more months to process before the commission lowers the rates, the customers can receive refunds for purchases made during those eight months. This sequence of events is displayed in Figure 10-A.

10.C.2. Utility "deferral" of expenses

As Chapter 6 explained, in cost-based ratemaking the regulators base prospective rates on a combination of embedded costs and predictions of future costs and future sales. The rule against retroactivity tells us that when actual experience varies from predictions, the changes can be prospective only. If the approved revenue requirement assumed $25 million in normal storm-restoration costs, but a once-in-a-century storm caused costs of $150 million, the rule against retroactivity bars the commission from making ratepayers pay the extra cost.

But there is an exception, called "deferral." The commission can allow the utility to record the actual storm costs on its books as a "deferred asset." This regulatory action does not itself promise cost recovery; it allows the utility to *argue* for recovery when it next seeks a rate increase. Without an express order allowing deferral, no later recovery would be possible, because of the rule against retroactivity. As the Idaho Commission explained: "When [Idaho Power Company] became aware the [environmental] cleanup costs would be substantial, the Company had the opportunity to request rate relief or deferral of these costs for future recovery. It did neither . . . . [W]e are without a means to provide recovery of this expense retroactively."[17] This concept of cost deferral is displayed in Figure 10-B. Note that commissions tend to restrict deferrals to expenditures that are both large and unexpected; otherwise, rate levels become unstable and unpredictable.

10.C.3. Affiliate transactions

Washington Natural Gas Company bought gas from its affiliate at a price the Commission found excessive. The utility argued that disallowing its already-incurred payment would be retroactive ratemaking. The state statute required that the commission (a) approve affiliate contracts in advance, and (b) exclude from the revenue requirement any unreasonable

---

17. Idaho Power Co., 161 P.U.R.4th 18 (Idaho Pub. Util. Comm'n Jan. 31, 1995).

Figure 10-A

Avoiding Retroactive Ratemaking: "Interim Rates Subject to Refund"

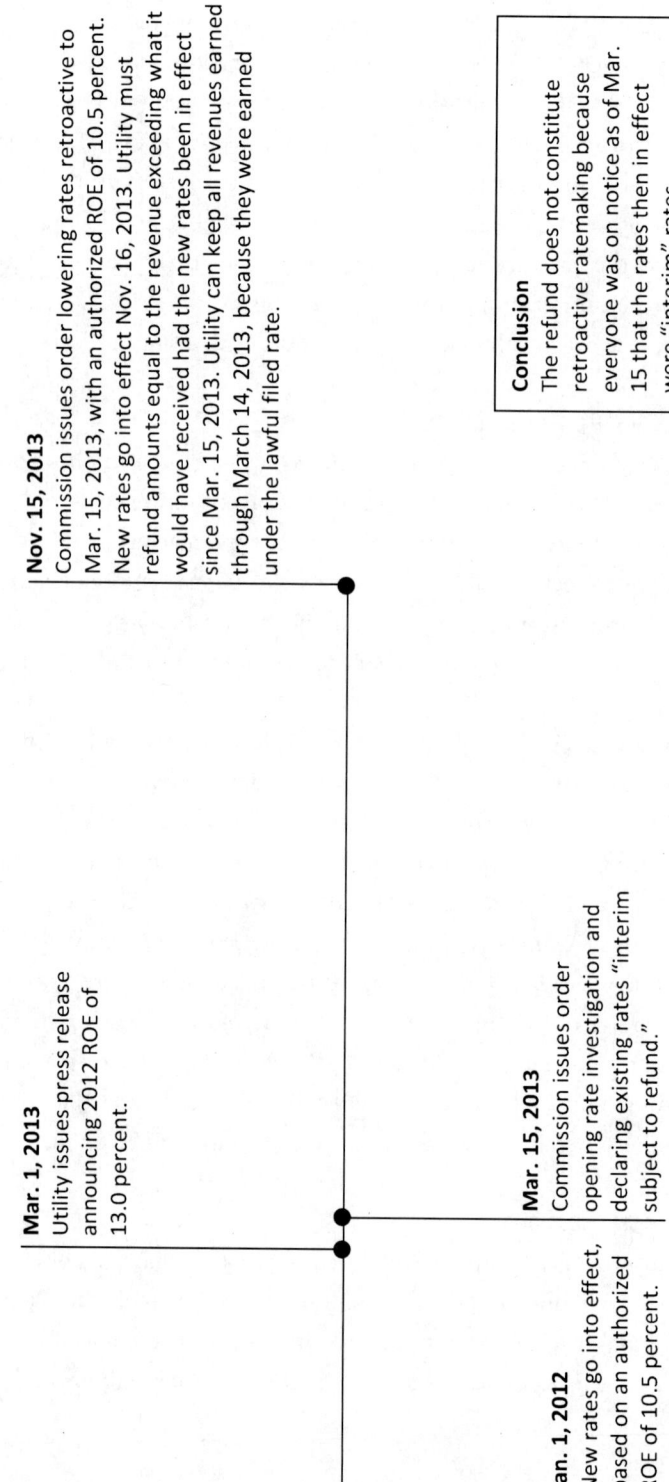

Mar. 1, 2013
Utility issues press release announcing 2012 ROE of 13.0 percent.

Jan. 1, 2012
New rates go into effect, based on an authorized ROE of 10.5 percent.

Mar. 15, 2013
Commission issues order opening rate investigation and declaring existing rates "interim subject to refund."

Nov. 15, 2013
Commission issues order lowering rates retroactive to Mar. 15, 2013, with an authorized ROE of 10.5 percent. New rates go into effect Nov. 16, 2013. Utility must refund amounts equal to the revenue exceeding what it would have received had the new rates been in effect since Mar. 15, 2013. Utility can keep all revenues earned through March 14, 2013, because they were earned under the lawful filed rate.

Conclusion
The refund does not constitute retroactive ratemaking because everyone was on notice as of Mar. 15 that the rates then in effect were "interim" rates.

Figure 10-B

Avoiding Retroactive Ratemaking: "Deferral" of Storm Costs

Jan. 1, 2012
New rates go into effect. Rates are based on a revenue requirement that assumes "normal" storm-restoration and repair costs of $25 million.

Apr. 15, 2012
Utility informs commission that restoration and repair costs will be at least $150 million. Utility requests permission to "defer" the costs for consideration in its next rate case.

Nov. 15, 2012
Utility files a request for rate increase, seeking, among other things, full recovery of $175 million in restoration and repair costs incurred in 2012 due to the Mar. 15, 2012, storm.

Mar. 15, 2012
"Once in a decade" storm occurs.

May 15, 2012
Commission grants utility's request to defer the costs and specifies the accounts on the utility's books where the costs are to be recorded. Commission states that its granting of a deferral does not constitute a commitment to allow later recovery.

June 15, 2013
Commission issues order granting rate increase. The order approves for recovery $90 million for the 2012 restoration and repair costs, the amount determined to be prudent, to be recovered over three years. Therefore, the annual revenue requirement includes $30 million in storm-restoration and repair costs.

Conclusion
The $30 million annual recovery is not retroactive ratemaking, even though the recovery is a "correction" of past rates, because Commission allowed the costs to be "deferred."

payments from utility to affiliate. Because the statute provided notice, the commission's disallowance was not retroactive ratemaking.[18]

10.C.4. Hard-to-predict costs

When a utility promises to cover the future medical costs of today's employees, it should recover those costs from today's customers, because they are the beneficiaries of these employees' efforts. What's the connection to retroactive ratemaking? Before the 1990s, utilities accounted for retiree medical benefits on a "cash basis." This meant that current rates reflected the current medical costs of today's retirees, but did not reflect the future medical costs of today's employees. In 1990, the Financial Accounting Standards Board required companies to switch to accrual accounting. Applied to ratemaking, this switch meant that utilities had to reflect, in today's rates, their estimates of today's employees' future medical costs.

The retroactivity problem arose because of the transition. As of the date of the switch, "the company will have already accumulated a significant future liability for the retirement medical benefits of existing employees that it has never accounted for in its books." When New England Power Company sought to recover this liability from ratepayers, amortized over a 20-year period, wholesale customers argued retroactive ratemaking. The court of appeals, upholding FERC, disagreed. The court acknowledged that the accumulated costs related to past service by past employees: "[C]harging current ratepayers for the transition obligation is unquestionably charging for costs incurred to provide service to other, earlier ratepayers." And the charges would be retroactive ratemaking if the utility had "shifted . . . costs that it tried but failed to collect in the past." Here, in contrast, the utility *had not tried to collect these costs in the past*. The utility "always planned to collect these costs from future ratepayers." The customers therefore had notice that they would end up bearing the costs. All the company did was "defer collection of certain charges until the point at which they become ascertainable." The Court carefully distinguished hard-to-predict future costs from past costs:

> [I]t is permissible for a company to defer collection of certain charges until the point at which they become ascertainable, so long as the ratepayers have notice that the charges will be collected in the future. It is not, however, permissible for a company to devise a formula intended to estimate actual charges—to serve as a proxy for actual charges—and then go back and collect any shortfall caused by imperfections in that proxy.[19]

---

18. Wash. Util. & Transp. Comm'n v. Wash. Natural Gas Co., 137 P.U.R.4th 335 (Wash. Utils. & Transp. Comm'n Sept. 28, 1992).

19. Town of Norwood v. FERC, 53 F.3d 377, 380–84 (D.C. Cir. 1995).

10.C.5. Commission self-correction

What if past regulatory decisions put the utility on a path toward overearning? A regulator can "correct" its past decisions without violating the ban, if its rate change is prospective only. Recall Chapter 6.E.2's prior discussion of "price caps." Under the FCC's approach, carriers selected a productivity "X-factor" and an associated price cap. The X-factor caused an annual reduction in the rate allowed by the cap, with the reduction reflecting the assumed increase in productivity. The lower the productivity X-factor, the lower the cap. After some experience, the FCC determined that the authorized X-factors were too low; the carriers were capable of achieving more productivity than the FCC had assumed. To retain these prior X-factors would embed the low productivity estimates in future rates. So the FCC adjusted the price cap downward, prospectively, to the level it would be at had the prior X-factor been higher. Bell Atlantic and others argued retroactive ratemaking, but the court disagreed:

> [T]he changes would affect future rates only and were not intended to reclaim revenues
> carriers had earned in previous years. The one-time adjustments brought the price cap
> indices to a level that—according to the Commission—accurately reflected the carriers'
> costs and productivity, and prevented past Commission mistakes from being embedded
> in future rates. As the Commission put it, the one-time adjustment merely ensures that,
> in the future, higher earnings must be attained through actual improvements in produc-
> tivity and will not continue to accrue as a result of administrative error. The adjustments
> therefore have no retroactive effect.

Even if there was a retroactive effect, the Commission had announced its intent to conduct such a "performance review" when it first set the price caps. The carriers therefore had "made all of their X-factor elections with that [possibility of change] in mind. Petitioners could not have reasonably assumed that the price cap index would not be altered."[20]

10.C.6. Judicial reversal of commission rate decisions

If a court finds a commission-approved rate increase unlawful, may the commission order refunds without violating the rule against retroactivity? The general answer is yes: "[A]n agency, like a court, can undo what is wrongfully done by virtue of its [prior] order."[21] But the application of this principle depends on the answers to two distinct questions: (1) Is the solution authorized by statute? (2) Is the solution blocked by the filed rate doctrine?

After the court of appeals found it had set a pipeline's rate too low, FERC imposed a corrective surcharge on the pipeline's customers. The surcharge was a lump sum based on

---

20.   Bell Atl. Tel. Cos. v. FCC, 79 F.3d 1195, 1205 (D.C. Cir. 1996).
21.   United Gas Improvement Co. v. Callery Props., 382 U.S. 223, 229 (1965) (interpreting Natural Gas Act).

each customer's total prior purchases made under the erroneous rate. The customers challenged the surcharge as retroactive ratemaking. The court of appeals disagreed. Finding the statute silent on the effect of judicial reversal, it held that an agency "can undo what was wrongfully done." Absent such remedial authority, "the pipeline's primary right under the NGA to propose and collect a justified rate would be drastically curtailed, . . . pipelines would be substantially and irreparably injured by FERC errors, and judicial review would be powerless to protect them from much of the losses so incurred." The Court then turned to the filed rate doctrine. In its initial rate filing, the pipeline obviously had given notice of the new, higher rate it sought to charge. When FERC ordered the rate lowered, the pipeline filed new tariff sheets expressly reserving the right to seek a later surcharge should the FERC order be reversed. These steps, the court said, gave customers sufficient notice, making the doctrine inapplicable: "The filed rate doctrine simply does not extend to cases in which buyers are on adequate notice that resolution of some specific issue may cause a later adjustment to the rate being collected at the time of service."[22]

But retail customers in Illinois had a different experience. When a reviewing court found a state commission-approved rate to be unlawfully high, consumers sought "restitution" of the excessive amounts paid during the entire period the rate was in effect. The Illinois Supreme Court rejected this position, citing the filed rate doctrine: the commission-approved rate is the lawful rate, which the utility is obligated to charge, even if a court later finds it excessive. The court also cited a state statute providing that a commission order "shall remain in effect during the pendency of an appeal, unless it is stayed or suspended." Since the rate was lawful until the courts found it unlawful, customers were entitled to a refund only from the date the court issued its order.[23]

10.C.7. Disgorgement of illegal gains

When a lawful rate produces results different from projections, the commission cannot change it retroactively. But if a seller charges a rate other than the lawful rate, the commission can order disgorgement. Disgorgement is not retroactive ratemaking because it does not change the outcome of a lawful rate; it eliminates unjust enrichment from an unlawful rate.

The prominent example is Enron. Discussing the intersection between market-based rates and the filed rate doctrine, Chapter 9.E described how Enron gained control of El Paso Electric's physical assets without telling FERC—a breach of Enron's market rate authorization, in which FERC required Enron to notify it of any later asset acquisition. Using El Paso's assets, Enron made sales worth millions of dollars. Enron's failure to inform "impeded the Commission's ability to ensure that utilities do not acquire market power and that rates remain just and reasonable." FERC ordered Enron to disgorge its El

---

22.   Natural Gas Clearinghouse v. FERC, 965 F.2d 1066, 1074–76 (D.C. Cir. 1992) (applying *Callery*, 382 U.S. 223, and citing other court and FERC decisions).

23.   Indep. Voters of Ill. v. Ill. Commerce Comm'n, 510 N.E.2d 850, 855–57 (Ill. 1987).

Paso-related profit. Although Enron had a "filed rate"—its market-based tariff—the disgorgement order was not retroactive ratemaking. It was a remedy for Enron's failure to obey conditions it accepted. By accepting those conditions, Enron had notice that its violation could produce disgorgement.[24]

* * *

The rule against retroactivity prevents ratemaking-by-ambush. Rates, like statutes, are prospective legislative acts. Prohibiting retroactivity aligns rates with legitimate expectations, thus satisfying the Constitution and making policies predictable. Look-backs are permissible, however, if preceded by notice. Finally, there is no protection for sellers who violate their tariffs, because the rights under those tariffs are conditioned on compliance.

---

24. El Paso Electric Company, 108 FERC ¶ 61,071, at p. 31 (2004). Enron was not the lone example of misbehavior producing disgorgement. *See, e.g.*, Transcon. Gas Pipe Line Corp. v. FERC, 998 F.2d 1313, 1320 (5th Cir. 1993) (upholding Commission denial of recovery of money lost when illegally selling gas, through affiliates, at unduly discriminatory prices below its filed rate; denial was "well within [the Commission's] equitable powers"); Dominion Resources, 108 FERC ¶ 61,110 (2004) (approving settlement requiring disgorgement of profit likely gained from violating FERC's Standards of Conduct by communicating non-public storage information to favored business partners); El Paso Electric Co., 105 FERC ¶ 61,131, at p. 35 (2003) (requiring refund of time value of revenues received from transmission service provided in violation of the filed rate doctrine, because the utility had failed to file the agreements at FERC; disgorgement was not a retroactive rate change but an "appropriate and proportionate remedy" for a violation of the Act).

    But see Coastal Oil & Gas Corp. v. FERC, 782 F.2d 1249, 1253 (5th Cir. 1986) (rejecting order to disgorge *revenues* as a "penalty" not authorized by statute because it deprived pipeline of all cost recovery for illegally sold gas and therefore "restores the status *quo ante*" of neither party; FERC could, however, order disgorgement of *profits* earned from the sale).

CHAPTER ELEVEN

Mobile-Sierra Doctrine

When Does Contract "Sanctity" Give Way to Government-Ordered Amendments?

[T]here is nothing in the structure or purpose of the Act from which we can infer the right, not otherwise possessed and nowhere expressly given by the Act, of natural gas companies unilaterally to change their contracts.[1]

In 1956, Dwight Eisenhower was reelected President, Don Larsen pitched baseball's only World Series perfect game,[2] and the U.S. Supreme Court established the *Mobile-Sierra* doctrine. The doctrine is "refreshingly simple: The contract between the parties governs the legality of the filing. Rate filings consistent with contractual obligations are valid; rate filings inconsistent with contractual obligations are invalid."[3] The question of how refreshing, and how simple, has occupied practitioners for more than 50 years.

11.A. Principle: The commission cannot let parties out of their contracts

1947: Pacific Gas & Electric had historically sold electricity to Sierra Pacific Power. Facing growing post-World War II demand growth, along with customer desires for lower rates, Sierra started negotiating with alternative suppliers. PG&E responded by offering Sierra Pacific a fifteen-year contract at a "special low rate." Sierra Pacific accepted. Five years into the contract, with Sierra's alternatives no longer available, PG&E filed at the Federal Power Commission (FPC) for a rate increase of 28 percent.

2000: California faced transmission and generation shortages, with power prices rising rapidly to unheard-of levels. Faced with a "dysfunctional market" and anxious about supply, Western retail utilities with an obligation to serve signed multi-year contracts to buy power at five times the historical prices. (The sellers had FERC-granted permission to charge these "market-based rates.") Several years later, the retail utilities filed complaints with FERC, asserting that the contract prices were not just and reasonable. They asked FERC to modify the contracts, prospectively and retroactively, to reduce the rates and order refunds.

In each of these situations, a contract signatory tried to escape the deal it signed. In the first example, the seller argued the price was unlawfully low; in the second example, the buyers argued the price was unlawfully high. How do regulators and courts respond? When can a regulator intervene in a private contract? That is the subject of the "venerable *Mobile-Sierra* doctrine," the Supreme Court's interpretation of the Natural Gas Act and the Federal Power Act. The doctrine was established for cost-based contracts in *United Gas Pipe Line Co. v. Mobile Gas Service Corp.* and *Federal Power Commission v. Sierra*

---

1. United Gas Pipe Line Co. v. Mobile Gas Serv. Corp., 350 U.S. 332, 343–44 (1956).
2. On October 8, 1956, the author's date of birth.
3. Richmond Power & Light v. FPC, 481 F.2d 490, 493 (D.C. Cir. 1973).

Pacific Power Co. and applied to modern, market-based transactions in *Morgan Stanley Capital Group Inc. v. Public Utility District No. 1.*[4]

The Mobile-Sierra doctrine distills to this principle: Under the Natural Gas Act (Mobile) and the Federal Power Act (Sierra), a party to a FERC-jurisdictional contract cannot unilaterally ask FERC to change the contract, unless the contract itself authorizes the change. "[T]here is nothing in the structure or purpose of the [Natural Gas] Act from which we can infer the right, not otherwise possessed and nowhere expressly given by the Act, of natural gas companies unilaterally to change their contracts." This restriction "fully promotes the purposes of the Act. By preserving the integrity of contracts, it permits the stability of supply arrangements which all agree is essential to the health of the natural gas industry."[5] Contract stability benefits consumers too: "[U]ncertainties regarding rate stability and contract sanctity can have a chilling effect on investments and a seller's willingness to enter into long-term contracts and this, in turn, can harm customers in the long run."[6]

To emphasize the statutory insistence on "contract sanctity," the Supreme Court has emphasized the "marked contrast" between the Natural Gas Act (which allows individual, bilateral contracts) and the Interstate Commerce Act (which precludes private contracts, allowing only uniform tariffs):

> The vast number of retail transactions of railroads made policing of individual transactions administratively impossible; effective regulation could be accomplished only by requiring compliance with a single schedule of rates applicable to all shippers. On the other hand, only a relatively few wholesale transactions are regulated by the Natural Gas Act and these typically require substantial investment in capacity and facilities for the service of a particular distributor. Recognizing the need these circumstances create for individualized arrangements between natural gas companies and distributors, the Natural Gas Act permits the relations between the parties to be established initially by contract, the protection of the public interest being afforded by supervision of the individual contracts, which to that end must be filed with the Commission and made public.[7]

---

4. United Gas Pipe Line Co. v. Mobile Gas Serv. Corp., 350 U.S. 332 (1956); Federal Power Comm'n v. Sierra Pac. Power Co., 350 U.S. 348 (1956); Morgan Stanley Capital Grp. Inc. v. Pub. Util. Dist. No. 1, 554 U.S. 527 (2008).
5. United Gas Pipe Line Co. v. Mobile Gas Serv. Corp., 350 U.S. at 343–45.
6. Morgan Stanley Capital Grp., Inc. v. Pub. Util. Dist. No. 1, 554 U.S. 527, 550–51 (2008) (quoting FERC's Order No. 697 on market-based rates, discussed in Chapter 7.C.1).
7. United Gas Pipe Line Co. v. Mobile Gas Serv. Corp., 350 U.S. at 338–39.

Having set forth the doctrine's principle and purposes, we turn to its complexities, in five subchapters:

- Chapter 11.B addresses the "public interest" exception: the "rare" circumstances in which FERC will modify an otherwise valid contract.
- Chapter 11.C describes the logical relationship between the general principle and the "public interest" exemption. The general principle becomes a rebuttable presumption that contracts entered into freely are inherently "just and reasonable." The presumption can be rebutted by facts that satisfy the public interest exception.
- Chapter 11.D explains that while the presumption protects contracts from regulatory involvement uninvited by the parties, it allows the parties to contract for regulatory involvement.
- Chapter 11.E describes how a party can escape (escape, not rebut) the presumption: by showing fraud, duress, or illegality in the contract's creation.
- Chapter 11.F shows how the courts have applied the presumption to market-based contracts, non-signatories, and tariffs.

11.B. The "public interest" exception

If a party cannot change a contract unilaterally, can the Commission? Yes, but not easily. In *Sierra Pacific*, the seller PG&E, under the contract it signed, was earning a return on equity less than half what the Federal Power Commission deemed "just and reasonable." The FPC granted the rate increase PG&E sought. The Supreme Court reversed. PG&E had to lie in the bed it made:

> [W]hile it may be that the Commission may not normally *impose* upon a public utility a rate which would produce less than a fair return, it does not follow that the public utility may not itself agree by contract to a rate affording less than a fair return or that, if it does so, it is entitled to be relieved of its improvident bargain. . . . [I]t is clear that a contract may not be said to be either "unjust" or "unreasonable" simply because it is unprofitable to the public utility.[8]

So when may, or must, the Commission modify a contract? Section 206(a) of the Federal Power Act says that the Commission "shall" modify any contract that is "unjust, unreasonable, unduly discriminatory or preferential." The Court had to reconcile this obligation to modify unreasonable contracts with the need to preserve "stability" of contracts. It did so by creating the "public interest" exception. The exception allows the Commission to change a contract whose language gives the parties no right to a change. The exception

---

8.   FPC v. Sierra Pac. Power Co., 350 U.S. 348, 355 (1956) (emphasis in original).

is available, however, only when the rates "seriously harm the *public interest*, not [when] they are unfair to one of the parties that voluntarily assented to the contract."[9] Harm so "serious" as to warrant regulatory intervention in private contracts will occur "only in circumstances of unequivocal public necessity."[10]

Same standard for sellers and buyers: In both *Mobile* and *Sierra*, the movants were sellers seeking higher rates. Sellers, therefore, were on the *Sierra* Court's mind when it established the three paths to the "public interest" exception: "where [a rate] [1] might impair the financial ability of the public utility to continue its service, [2] cast upon other consumers an excessive burden, or [3] be unduly discriminatory."[11] When the *Morgan Stanley* Court, in the wake of the California crisis, dealt with buyer complaints, it recognized that *Sierra*'s low-rate, seller-oriented factors are "not the exclusive components of the public interest," because they "are not all precisely applicable to the high-rate challenge of a purchaser . . . ." In the high-rate context, "the relevant question is not whether 'other customers' [of the utility] would be excessively burdened, but whether any customers of the purchaser would be . . . ." But the standard for buyers "must be the same, generally speaking, as the standard for a seller's challenge: The contract rate must seriously harm the public interest."[12]

11.C. One standard—with a rebuttable presumption

To clarify the relationship between (a) *Mobile-Sierra*'s prohibition on modifying contracts and (b) the "public interest" exception to the prohibition, the *Morgan Stanley* Court described the doctrine as a rebuttable presumption: "[FERC] must presume that the rate set out in a freely negotiated wholesale-energy contract meets the 'just and reasonable' requirement imposed by law." The basis for the presumption is the Court's belief in markets: "In wholesale markets, the party charging the rate and the party charged [are] often sophisticated businesses enjoying presumptively equal bargaining power, who could be expected to negotiate a 'just and reasonable' rate as between the two of them."[13] The public interest exception, then, is an exception to the presumption; it states the evidentiary mountain one must climb to rebut the presumption: "The presumption may be overcome only if FERC concludes that the contract seriously harms the public interest."[14]

---

9. Morgan Stanley Capital Grp., Inc. v. Pub. Util. Dist. No. 1, 527 U.S. at 546–47 (emphasis added).
10. Permian Basin Area Rate Cases, 390 U.S. 747, 822 (1968). This high threshold has been echoed by FERC: "[T]he public interest (as opposed to the private interest of the party seeking the rate increase) only rarely is served by making the requested [contract] change (that is, granting the requested increase), and a strict standard is appropriate." Northeast Utilities Service Co., 66 FERC ¶ 61,332 (1994).
11. FPC v. Sierra Pac. Power Co., 350 U. S. at 355.
12. Morgan Stanley Capital Grp., Inc. v. Pub. Util. Dist. No. 1, 527 U.S. at 548–49 (brackets in the original).
13. *Id.* at 530, 545 (quoting Verizon Commc'ns v. FCC, 535 U.S. 467, 479 (2002)).
14. *Id.* at 530–31. Before *Morgan Stanley*, discussions of the regulator's power to modify contracts commonly referred to two distinct burdens: the "normal" burden of proving that a contract is "unjust and unreasonable" and the heavier, "*Mobile-Sierra*," "unequivocal public necessity" burden of satisfying the "public interest" exception. *See id.* at 535 (citing FERC references to "two modes of review—one with

At what point in time does the presumption attach? It is triggered by the agreement's existence, regardless of whether or when FERC actually reviews and blesses the arrangement. The presumption then lasts as long as the contract lasts. Those seeking to challenge the contract, by offering evidence to support the presumption-ending "public interest" exception, may do so at any time in the contract's life.[15]

11.D. Three ways to preserve the regulator's role

While insisting that the Commission respect contracts, the doctrine does not tell the parties how to write their contracts. The parties can negotiate over the regulator's role. Here are the main options.

Party-initiated changes: Absent "serious harm" to the public, the *Mobile-Sierra* presumption prohibits the regulator from changing a contract. But the parties can write their contract to invite the regulator's involvement. They can "contract out of the *Mobile-Sierra* presumption by specifying in their contracts that a new rate filed with the Commission would supersede the contract rate."[16] How might the parties do so? Put another way: If "[t]he contract between the parties governs the legality of the filing [with the Commission],"[17] what words can parties write into their contract to preserve their rights to seek contract changes?

The answer is known as the "Memphis Clause." In *United Gas Pipe Line Co. v. Memphis Light, Gas & Water Division*, the pipeline's long-term contracts with its customers had this sentence: "All gas delivered hereunder shall be paid for by Buyer under Seller's

---

the *Mobile-Sierra* presumption and the other without—as the 'public interest standard' and the 'just and reasonable standard.'"). The Ninth Circuit clarified the situation:

> We do not find this way of viewing the statutory terrain useful. The FPA establishes a single, albeit general, standard for FERC's adjudication of contract challenges like the present one: whether the challenged contract is just and reasonable. 16 U.S.C. § 824e(a). The question therefore cannot be whether the *Mobile-Sierra* or the "just and reasonable" standard of review applies. Instead, we understand *Mobile-Sierra* to establish *presumptions* regarding whether certain electricity contracts meet the statutory standard, and hold that lack of profitability alone is not a basis for deeming a contract unreasonable when the seller has agreed to the rate that proves unprofitable.

Pub. Util. Dist. No. 1 of Snohomish Cnty. v. FERC, 471 F.3d 1053, 1060 n.7 (9th Cir. 2006) (emphasis added). The *Morgan Stanley* Court agreed with this reasoning (while reversing the Ninth Circuit on other grounds): "There is only one statutory standard for assessing wholesale electricity rates, whether set by contract or tariff—the just-and-reasonable standard." *Morgan Stanley*, 554 U.S. at 545. The "term 'public interest standard' refers to the differing *application* of that just-and-reasonable standard to contract rates." *Id.* at 535 (emphasis in original).

15.   Morgan Stanley Capital Grp., Inc. v. Pub. Util. Dist. No. 1, 554 U.S. at 545–46. The Supreme Court rejected the Ninth Circuit's view "that all initially filed contracts must be subject to review without the *Mobile-Sierra* presumption." The Court criticized the Ninth Circuit's reading of *Mobile-Sierra* "'as the equivalent of an estoppel doctrine,' whereby an initial Commission opportunity for review prevents the Commission from modifying the rates absent serious future harm to the public interest." *Id.* at 546 (quoting Ninth Circuit opinion).

16.   *Id.* at 534.

17.   Richmond Power & Light v. FPC, 481 F.2d at 493.

Rate Schedule (the appropriate rate schedule designation is inserted here), *or any effective superseding rate schedules*, on file with the Federal Power Commission."[18] Mid-contract term, the pipeline filed new, higher rates with the Commission. The Commission accepted the new rates as just and reasonable. The customers, citing *Mobile*, challenged the Commission's power to accept the new rates.

The Supreme Court upheld the Commission. The above-quoted clause "constitut[ed] undertakings by the purchasers to pay United's 'going' rates, as established from time to time in accordance with the procedures prescribed by the Natural Gas Act." The "procedures prescribed by the Natural Gas Act" allow a pipeline to file rate increases with the Commission. The contract thus was "vitally different" from the one in *Mobile*, which involved a rate *fixed by contract for the life of the contract*.[19] United had reserved the right to file changes in the rate; Mobile and Sierra had not. (Note that the generality of the clause's language—"or any effective superseding rate schedules"—made it possible for a buyer as well as the seller to seek a rate change. The statute provides for buyer complaints that could lead the Commission to impose a "superseding rate schedule" if it found the current rates not "just and reasonable.")

Commission-initiated changes, limited to the "serious harm" situation: A *Memphis* clause preserves the *contracting parties'* statutory rights to seek rate change, without having to show "serious harm" to "the public interest." What about the Commission—can it change a rate on its own? The answer is "yes." Recall that Section 206(a) states that the Commission "shall" change a rate that is "unjust, unreasonable, unduly discriminatory or preferential." The obligation implicit in the term "shall" is an "indefeasible right . . . to replace rates that are contrary to the public interest."[20] But that Commission "right" is itself hemmed in by the *Mobile-Sierra* presumption: Before ordering the change, the Commission must find "serious harm" to the public interest—unless, again, the contract itself authorizes the change. This means that the parties can contract to limit, or not limit, the Commission's involvement in their affairs. They cannot remove the Commission's "indefeasible right" to protect the public interest, but they can contract to limit the Commission's involvement to those situations.

Commission-ordered changes, not limited to "serious harm" situations: Consider a long-term term contract that fixed the rate for the first year, then allowed for rate changes. That was the situation in *Papago Tribal Utility Authority v. FERC*,[21] involving an electric sales contract between Arizona Public Service (seller) and Papago (buyer). Here is the key contract language:

---

18. United Gas Pipe Line Co. v. Memphis Light, Gas & Water Div., 358 U.S. 103, 105 (1958) (emphasis supplied by Court).
19. *Id.* at 108.
20. Papago Tribal Utility Auth. v. FERC, 723 F.2d 950, 953 (D.C. Cir. 1983).
21. *Id.*

The rates hereinabove set out . . . are to remain in effect for the initial one (1) year of the term of this contract and thereafter unless and until changed by the Federal Power Commission or other lawful regulatory authority, with either party hereto to be free unilaterally to take appropriate action before the Federal Power Commission or other lawful regulatory authority in connection with changes which may be desired by such party.

The court found that this language allowed the Commission, after the first year, to change the contract's rates if it found those rates unjust and unreasonable, without having to find a "public interest" exception. (During the first year the Commission would have had to make a "public interest" finding, because the rate was fixed by contract.)

* * *

The cases discussed here—*Mobile, Sierra, Memphis* and *Papago*—outline three paths for involving the Commission in their contract:

1. The parties can agree that one or both can unilaterally seek rate changes from the Commission without having to satisfy the "public interest" exception. (*Memphis*)
2. The parties can preclude each other, and the Commission, from seeking rate changes—except changes that the Commission finds are required by the "public interest," that is, to avoid "serious harm." (No contract can eliminate the Commission's "indefeasible right" to order changes necessitated by the "public interest.") (*Mobile* and *Sierra*)
3. The parties can preclude each other from seeking rate changes, but leave undisturbed the Commission's authority to change the rates upon a filing that the current rates are not just and reasonable. (*Papago*)

It all boils down to the "refreshingly simple" rule: Subject to the Commission's "indefeasible right" to protect the "public interest," both the Commission's power to change a contract and the parties' rights to trigger that power depend on the contract language. Absent contract language specifying such power and rights, "the *Mobile-Sierra* presumption remains the default rule."[22] That presumption can be overcome only when circumstances create the "unequivocal public necessity," the "serious harm" to the "public interest" that triggers the public interest exception.

---

22.   Morgan Stanley Capital Grp., Inc. v. Pub. Util. Dist. No. 1, 554 U.S. at 534.

11.E. Escape from the presumption: Fraud, duress, illegality

Morgan Stanley instructs that we must presume justness and reasonableness for contracts that are "freely negotiated." The presumption does not apply, therefore, if "there is unfair dealing at the contract formation stage—for instance, if [FERC] finds traditional grounds for the abrogation of the contract such as fraud or duress." Nor does the presumption apply if the rates become unjust and unreasonable because of a party's illegal behavior, such as a seller's market manipulation:

> [I]f it is clear that one party to a contract engaged in such extensive unlawful market manipulation as to alter the playing field for contract negotiations, the Commission should not presume that the contract is just and reasonable. Like fraud and duress, unlawful market activity that directly affects contract negotiations eliminates the premise on which the *Mobile-Sierra* presumption rests: that the contract rates are the product of fair, arm's-length negotiations.[23]

To clarify: A party citing fraud, duress or illegality as a reason to change the contract is not using the public interest exception to overcome the presumption; he is arguing that the presumption does not apply because the premise of "sophisticated parties" and "equal bargaining power" does not exist.

11.F. Special applications

11.F.1. Market-based contracts

Recall from Chapter 7.C.1 (market-based pricing) that wholesale electric sellers who pass FERC's screens for horizontal and vertical market power are free to sell at any price. Unlike cost-based sellers, they do not submit contracts to FERC for approval. In the market-based pricing context, FERC approves sellers, not contracts. This difference in regulatory review does not change the *Mobile-Sierra* presumption. Market-based contracts, like cost-based contracts, are presumed to be "just and reasonable," because the parties are "often sophisticated businesses enjoying presumptively equal bargaining power, who could be expected to negotiate a 'just and reasonable' rate." With the presumption in place, FERC can change a negotiated, market-based rate only if that rate "seriously harms the consuming public."[24]

The California crisis tested buyers' patience with these principles. In the middle of the price fly-ups and infrastructure shortages, Public Utility District No. 1 of Snohomish County, a retail utility, signed a nine-year contract to buy power from Morgan Stanley at $105/mWh. Prior to the crisis, prices in the Pacific Northwest averaged $24/mWh.

---

23. *Id.* at 547, 554.
24. *Id.* at 545 (quoting Verizon Commc'ns, Inc. v. FCC, 535 U.S. at 479).

The contract price was lower, however, than spot prices during the crisis, which reached $3,300/mWh.

Snohomish and other buyers later filed complaints at FERC, asserting that the contract prices were not "just and reasonable" and insisting that FERC order rate reductions. They made two distinct arguments. First, the *Mobile-Sierra* presumption should not apply because FERC had never approved the contracts. (In the market pricing context FERC approves sellers, not contracts.) Second, even if the presumption did apply, the prices were so high (due to a market that FERC investigations deemed "dysfunctional") as to trigger the "public interest" exception. FERC declined to revise the contracts, citing *Mobile-Sierra*. The Ninth Circuit reversed.[25] Sorting all this out, the Supreme Court in *Morgan Stanley* elaborated on its "presumption" analysis by addressing four questions.

1. Does the presumption apply even if the seller's prices are high because the market is "dysfunctional"? Yes. FERC has no obligation to evaluate the market's competitiveness before presuming a contract price to be reasonable. A market's dysfunction does not change the doctrine's premise that sophisticated parties bargain at arm's length:

> Markets are not perfect, and one of the reasons that parties enter into wholesale-power contracts is precisely to hedge against the volatility that market imperfections produce.
>
> [T]he mere fact that the market is imperfect, or even chaotic, is no reason to undermine the stabilizing force of contracts that the FPA embraced as an alternative to "purely tariff-based regulation." . . . We may add that evaluating market "dysfunction" is a very difficult and highly speculative task—not one that the FPA would likely require the agency to engage in before holding sophisticated parties to their bargains.[26]

This passage does not mean that market dysfunction is irrelevant to a contract's lawfulness. But protection from dysfunction must come not from modifying contracts on the buyer's request, but from screening sellers before granting market rate authority:

> [W]e do not address the lawfulness of FERC's market-based-rates scheme, which assuredly has its critics. But any needed revision in that scheme is properly addressed in a challenge to the scheme itself, not through a disfigurement of the venerable *Mobile-Sierra* doctrine. We hold only that FERC may abrogate a valid contract only if it harms the public interest.[27]

---

25.   Pub. Util. Dist. No. 1 of Snohomish Cnty. v. FERC, 471 F.3d at 1053.
26.   Morgan Stanley Capital Grp., Inc. v. Pub. Util. Dist. No. 1, 554 U.S. at 547–48 (quoting Verizon Commc'ns, Inc. v. FCC, 535 U.S. at 479).
27.   *Id.* at 548.

2. In applying the "public interest" exception, that is, in determining whether prices cause the public "serious harm," is FERC limited to assessing conditions only at the time the contract commenced? No. This was FERC's error. In finding that the utility buyers' high-cost burdens did not trigger the public interest exception, FERC compared the contract prices to the prices the buyers had been paying others at the time they entered into the contract. Based on that comparison, FERC concluded that the buyers would save about 20 percent over the contracts' lives; in other words, buying from Morgan Stanley was a good deal. Here, the court found fault. FERC had failed to consider

> the disparity between the contract rate and the rates consumers would have paid (but for the contracts) *further down the line, when the open market was no longer dysfunctional.* That disparity, past a certain point, could amount to an "excessive burden" [i.e., a burden sufficient to trigger the "public interest" exception]. . . . The "unequivocal public necessity" that justifies overriding the *Mobile-Sierra* presumption does not disappear as a factor once the contract enters into force.[28]

3. Does the presumption of justness and reasonableness disappear just because the contract price exceeds marginal cost? No. The Ninth Circuit had found that the standard for overcoming the *Mobile-Sierra* presumption was whether consumers' rates exceeded "marginal cost." The Supreme Court rejected this standard:

> A presumption of validity that disappears when the rate is above marginal cost is no presumption of validity at all, but a reinstitution of cost-based rather than contract-based regulation. We have said that, under the *Mobile-Sierra* presumption, setting aside a contract rate requires a finding of "unequivocal public necessity," . . . or "extraordinary circumstances," . . . In no way can these descriptions be thought to refer to the mere exceeding of marginal cost. . . . The "marginal cost" standard . . . would threaten to inject more volatility into the electricity market by undermining a key source of stability.[29]

4. What happens to the Mobile-Sierra *presumption if the seller has manipulated the market?* As explained in Chapter 11.E above, the presumption does not apply if the rates are illegal; if, for example, the seller's market manipulation drove the rate above

---

28. *Id.* at 552–53 (emphasis added, citations omitted). What if a contract is inconsistent with FERC's policies or rules? Would the doctrine preclude FERC from rejecting it, unless FERC found that the inconsistency caused "serious harm"? If the presumption means that a contract "need not conform to the FERC's view of the best way to implement a just and reasonable rate, term or condition," the result could be to "restrict the FERC's discretion precisely when it needs it most—when it wishes to impose policy in a case where parties have contractually provided otherwise." *See* John E. McCaffrey, Morgan Stanley Capital Group, Inc. v. Public Utility District No. 1 *Revisits the* Mobile-Sierra *Doctrine: Some Answers, More Questions,* 30 ENERGY L. J. 53 at text accompanying n.201 (2009).
29. Morgan Stanley Capital Grp., Inc. v. Pub. Util. Dist. No. 1, 554 U.S. at 550–51 (citations omitted).

non-manipulated levels. In the California dispute, a FERC Staff Report had determined that "abnormally high prices [from manipulation] in the spot market during the energy crisis influenced the terms of contracts in the forward market" (Supreme Court's paraphrase). But FERC rejected the buyers' challenges to the contracts because the prices were not high enough to overcome the *Mobile-Sierra* presumption, that is, to cause "serious harm." That was FERC's potential error, the court said. If seller manipulation caused the higher price, there was no presumption to overcome. The price would be illegal, period. The Court remanded for FERC to "amplify or clarify" its point.[30]

11.F.2. Non-signatories

Mobile-Sierra disputes usually involve the contracting parties: one party seeking a contract change, the other resisting. What if the contract challenger is a non-signatory? It makes no difference: the *Mobile-Sierra* presumption still applies. That was the result in *NRG Power Marketing, LLC v. Maine Public Utilities Commission*.[31]

After years of negotiations, most New England market participants reached agreement on regional tariffs designed to prevent chronic capacity shortages. The tariffs, filed at FERC by ISO New England, a regional transmission organization,[32] established capacity obligations for the region's load-serving entities, along with the prices they had to pay for capacity if they did not self-supply. The agreement also had language incorporating the *Mobile-Sierra* presumption: any future challenges to the tariff rates had to satisfy the "public interest" exception by showing serious harm. This burden would apply "whether the [price is challenged] by a Settling Party, a non-Settling Party, or [by] the FERC acting *sua sponte*." FERC accepted the settlement tariffs, including the *Mobile-Sierra* provision.

The Maine Public Utilities Commission and others challenged FERC's approval of the *Mobile-Sierra* provision. They won in the D.C. Circuit, which invalidated the agreement's *Mobile-Sierra* provision: "[W]hen a rate challenge is brought by a non-contracting third party, the *Mobile-Sierra* doctrine simply does not apply."[33] The U.S. Supreme Court reversed:

> The "venerable *Mobile-Sierra* doctrine" rests on "the stabilizing force of contracts." . . . To retain vitality, the doctrine must control FERC itself, and, we hold, challenges to contract rates brought by noncontracting as well as contracting parties. . . . A presumption applicable to contracting parties only, and inoperative as to everyone else—consumers,

---

30. *See id.* at 554–55 (requiring, to rebut the presumption, "a causal connection between unlawful activity and the contract rate"). FERC has stated that buyers "must demonstrate that a particular seller engaged in unlawful manipulation in the spot market and that such manipulation directly affected the particular contract or contracts to which the seller was a party." To be "unlawful" manipulation, the seller's acts must be illegal when committed. Nev. Power Co. and Sierra Pac. Power Co. v. Enron Power Mktg., Inc., 125 FERC ¶ 61,312, at pp. 25, 28 (2008).
31. 558 U.S. 165 (2010).
32. Regional transmission organizations were described in Chapters 3.A.1 and 4.B.5.d.
33. Me. Pub. Utils. Comm'n v. FERC, 520 F.3d 464, 478 (2008) (per curiam).

advocacy groups, state utility commissions, elected officials acting *parens patriae*—could scarcely provide the stability *Mobile-Sierra* aimed to secure.[34]

The upshot: non-signatories still may challenge contracts, but they face the same hurdle the parties face. They must satisfy the "public interest" exception—unless the contract says otherwise.

11.F.3. Application to tariffs

In each of the main cases—*Mobile, Sierra, Memphis, Papago, Morgan Stanley* and *NRG Power Marketing*, the reviewing courts emphasized *contract* stability. What if the disputed rates are not contract rates, but *tariff* rates—that is, rates not negotiated between and applicable to contracting parties, but rates of general applicability filed unilaterally by the seller and accepted by FERC? Does the *Mobile-Sierra* presumption and its difficult "public interest" exception still apply? The *NRG Power Marketing* Court did not resolve this question because it had not been addressed by the court of appeals.[35]

Here is the current state of play on the applicability of the doctrine to tariffs. Under the New England settlement that led to *NRG Power Marketing*, ISO New England filed with FERC a tariff providing that rates for capacity would be produced by a "reverse auction" (sometimes called a "descending clock" auction). This is not like an art auction where buyers bid, win and then pay the price they bid. In a reverse auction, the competitors are the sellers, not the buyers. The buyers state the quantity they wish to buy. The auctioneer then sets an "auction starting price." In response, competing sellers indicate the quantity they are willing to sell at that price. If the sellers offer more quantity than the buyers need, the auctioneer lowers the price to receive a new set of seller offers of quantity. This step is repeated until a price is reached at which the total quantity offered by sellers equals the quantity desired by buyers. That price becomes the market price paid by all buyers and received by all sellers. There are no buyer-seller negotiations. The price is set not by a buyer–seller contract but by a tariff-defined auction.

FERC found that the rates produced by the auction were not contract rates. The rates apply to all buyers in the New England market, not only those buyers who signed the settlement leading to the tariff. Further, the rates are determined unilaterally by the tariff-prescribed auction process, not by bargaining between buyers and sellers. They more resemble tariff rates, FERC said. Still, FERC held that it had discretion to apply the *Mobile-Sierra* presumption, even though the presumption originated in a contract context. So,

---

34. NRG Power Mktg. LCC v. Me. Pub. Utils. Comm'n, 558 U.S. at 166–70, 175–76 (quoting Morgan Stanley Capital Grp., Inc. v. Pub. Util. Dist. No. 1, 554 U.S. 527).

35. *Id.* at 176 ("Whether the rates at issue [in the New England tariffs] qualify as 'contract rates,' and, if not, whether FERC had discretion to treat them analogously are questions raised before, but not ruled upon, by the Court of Appeals. They remain open for that court's consideration on remand.").

FERC applied the presumption, accepting the tariff as filed, to "balance the need for rate stability with the requirement that rates be just and reasonable." Auction-produced rates, FERC said, "share with freely-negotiated contracts certain market-based features that tend to assure just and reasonable rates." Specifically, the auctions "provide a market-based mechanism to appropriately value capacity resources based on their location, satisfying cost-causation principles." Applying the *Mobile-Sierra* presumption to these rates

> would promote rate stability, [a feature] . . . particularly important in this case, which was initiated in part because of the unstable nature of capacity revenues and the effect that that instability has on generating units, particularly those critical to maintaining reliability.[36]

The D.C. Circuit upheld FERC. The court emphasized its *Chevron* obligation to defer to reasonable agency interpretations,[37] the breadth of the "just and reasonable" standard, and the fact that FERC is "not bound to any one ratemaking formula." FERC's decision to apply the *Mobile-Sierra* presumption to this particular tariff, thereby requiring challengers to meet the "public interest" standard, was based on "ample reasoning," including FERC's conclusions that the rates emerging from the capacity auction "provide a market-based mechanism to appropriately value capacity resources based on their location," and that "rates disciplined by a market are consistent with the FPA's requirements."[38]

FERC has cautioned that it is not mandating a *Mobile-Sierra* presumption in all non-contract rate situations: "[T]he Commission could find that a "public interest" standard of review that is tolerable in the context of the broader goals and purposes of the Settlement at issue here might be intolerable in the context of other circumstances."[39] In fact, the Commission has removed *Mobile-Sierra* provisions from tariff settlements where the facts "did not rise to the compelling level as those present" in the New England proceeding." An example was an "ordinary pipeline rate case of general applicability." There, the settlement was "not intended to correct serious deficiencies in the natural gas market, . . . and [there were] no demonstrable market forces that contributed to the derivation of the Settlement rates."[40]

36. Devon Power LLC, 134 FERC ¶ 61,208 (2011), *rehearing denied*, Devon Power LLC, 137 FERC ¶ 61,073 (2011).
37. Chevron, U.S.A. Inc. v. NRDC, Inc., 467 U.S. 837 (1984).
38. New England Power Generators Ass'n. v. FERC, 707 F.3d 364 (D.C. Cir. 2013) (quoting FERC's orders in *Devon Power*).
39. *Devon Power*, *supra* note 36, 134 FERC ¶ 61,208.
40. High Island Offshore System LLC, 135 FERC ¶ 61,105 (2011). Three authors argue that the discretion to decide which non-contract rates warrant the *Mobile-Sierra* presumption allows FERC to (a) shield rates from "future challenge in order to promote investment or to protect parties that reasonably relied on those rates;" (b) preserve settlements arrived at "after protracted bargaining," and, more generally, (c) "consider "the consequences of its orders for the character and future development of the industry." David G. Tewksbury, Stephanie S. Lim and Grace Su, *New Chapters in the* Mobile-Sierra *Story:*

* * *

The *Mobile-Sierra* doctrine limits the regulator's role in privately negotiated contracts. The doctrine rebuttably presumes that "freely negotiated" contracts are just and reasonable. To promote contract stability, the doctrine prohibits the Commission from changing these contracts, except in situations of "unequivocal public necessity." There must be "serious harm" to the public interest, as distinct from harm to a contracting party's private interest. Parties must live with their "improvident bargains."

The presumption of justness and reasonableness does not apply if the contract was formed through fraud, duress or other illegal action, such as market manipulation. The presumption does apply to market-based contracts and to non-signatories. FERC has applied it not only to contracts but also to tariffs, but not automatically.

In drafting their contracts, parties can define the boundaries of Commission involvement. They can "contract out" of the *Mobile-Sierra* presumption, using language that preserves their right to seek contract change and the Commission's power to order contract change. Or they can limit the Commission's powers, subject to its "indefeasible right" to order change when there is "serious harm" to the "public interest."

Each of these features, and the associated cases, are displayed in Figure 11.

Application of the Doctrine After NRG Power Marketing, LLC v. Maine Public Utilities Commission, 32 Energy L. J. 433 at text accompanying nn.114–16 (2011). The authors also suggest that FERC, to "preserve market expectations and promote stability," could apply the presumption to certain unilateral proposals, such as for transmission rate incentives granted under section 219 of the Federal Power Act, thereby protecting them from future rate challenges. *Id.* at text accompanying n.158.

Figure 11
Mobile-Sierra **Doctrine:**
When May FERC Change the Parties' Contract Terms?

Rebuttable presumption	The rate in a "freely negotiated contract" is "just and reasonable." FERC's power to modify is limited to the "public interest" exception.[a]
Applies to	Cost-based rates[b] Market-based rates[c] Non-signatories[d] Some tariffs[e]
Two paths for contracting out of the presumption	1. Contract allows each party to seek change unilaterally.[f] 2. Contract allows the FERC to change the contract if its terms are unjust or unreasonable.[g]
"Public interest" exception to the presumption	Movant must show "serious harm" to the "public interest," i.e., "unequivocable public necessity." A contract is not "'unjust' or 'unreasonable' simply because it is unprofitable to the public utility."[h]
Escape from the presumption	Movant must show that contract was obtained through fraud or duress or that rate became unjust or unreasonable due to seller's illegal act.[i]

Notes
a *Morgan Stanley*
b *Mobile, Sierra*
c *Morgan Stanley*
d *NRG Power Marketing*
e *Devon Power, High Island Offshore*
f *Memphis*
g *Papago*
h *Mobile, Sierra, Permian Basin*
i *Morgan Stanley*

PART THREE

Jurisdiction
State, Federal and Future

The power to regulate rests in both state and federal hands. Bounded by the Commerce Clause, the Tenth Amendment, and the Supremacy Clause, legislators enact statutes and regulators issue orders. How their actions interact—cooperatively, independently, indifferently, disagreeably—is the subject of Chapter 12.

Public utilities build and maintain the physical infrastructure that brings some stability to modern life. Yet regulation's legal infrastructure is anything but stable. Policymakers are rethinking the purposes of regulation, and the roles and responsibilities of regulators and legislators. Courts are rethinking Congress's powers under the Commerce Clause and government's relationship to property owners under the Takings Clause. What these uncertainties mean for regulation's future is the subject of Chapter 13.

CHAPTER TWELVE
The Federal–State Relationship

> *The concept [of federalism] does not mean blind deference to 'States' Rights' any more*
> *than it means centralization of control over every important issue in our National Gov-*
> *ernment and its courts. The Framers rejected both these courses. What the concept does*
> *represent is a system in which there is sensitivity to the legitimate interests of both State*
> *and National Governments, and in which the National Government, anxious though it*
> *may be to vindicate and protect federal rights and federal interests, always endeavors to*
> *do so in ways that will not unduly interfere with the legitimate activities of the States.*[1]

Our regulated industries live with two historical legacies: the Framers' 1789 decision to
have both federal and state governments, and Congress's 1930s decisions to allocate regulatory powers between those two levels. As a result, most utilities today face both federal
and state regulation. This bi-jurisdictional context produces three distinct perspectives:

1.   Federal regulators want state regulators to promote, or at least not conflict with,
     federal policies.
2.   State regulators want federal regulators to support, or least not preclude, state
     policies.
3.   Regulated utilities want to avoid getting caught in a federal–state conflict, where
     complying with a state requirement violates a federal requirement, or complying
     with a federal requirement violates a state requirement.

These wishes are not always granted, for at least four reasons. First, Congress and state
legislatures enact statutes at different times for different reasons. Unlike the House and
Senate in Congress, they are not legislative partners, enacting laws jointly. There are no
conference committees to work out federal–state differences before enactment. Second,
federal and state statutes drafted in the 1920s and 1930s allocated state and federal powers based on then-clear distinctions between national policies and local services. Those
distinctions have blurred: due to technology, physical interconnectedness and efforts to
encourage competition over multi-state territories, in-state actions have multi-state effects
and national decisions have in-state effects.[2] Third, the political process does not update
statutes continuously to adjust jurisdiction to new industry facts. Fourth, at any point in
time, state and federal regulators can hold different views on the relative roles and merits

---

1.   Younger v. Harris, 401 U.S. 37, 44 (1971).
2.   *See, e.g.,* New York v. FERC, 535 U.S. 1, 16 (2002) (explaining that "the landscape of the electric indus-
     try has changed since the enactment of the FPA, when the electricity universe was 'neatly divided into
     spheres of retail versus wholesale sales'" (quoting Transmission Access Policy Study Grp. v. FERC, 225
     F.3d 667, 691 (D.C. Cir. 2000))); MCI Telecomms. Corp. v. AT&T Co., 512 U.S. 218, 220–21 (1994)
     (describing structural changes wrought by technology and competition).

of regulation and competition as alternative means to induce industry performance, and on the techniques that can best advance those views.[3]

So we have disputes: cases going to court because one jurisdictional level is accused of interfering with the other. The federal–state relationship is unavoidably a struggle, but it is not a zero-sum game. This challenge of dual regulation—to embody "sensitivity to the legitimate interests of both State and National Governments"—is the subject of this chapter. It addresses two major questions:

What are the limits on federal and state actions? Our constitutional system has five possible trip wires—limits on regulatory action that, when violated, mean that one level has unlawfully diminished the powers of the other. (In this context, "regulatory action" means action by a commission or legislative body, since the wire can be tripped by either a commission order or a statute.) The first three are limits on federal power to protect state policies; the last two are limits on state power to protect federal policies:

1. The Commerce Clause authorizes Congress to regulate only those business activities that involve "commerce between the states."

2. The Tenth Amendment prohibits Congress from acting on matters reserved to the states.

3. A federal agency cannot act outside the authority granted by Congress.

4. The "dormant" Commerce Clause prohibits a state from discriminating against, or unduly burdening, interstate commerce.

5. The Supremacy Clause prohibits states from taking actions that undermine the goals of federal statutes.

For each of the five limits, we explain its constitutional source and provide illustrations from inside and outside utility regulation.

Within those five limits, how do federal and state regulators interact? There are six models of federal–state interaction: (1) bright line divisions, where each level operates within its assigned statutory domain; (2) federal regulator enlists the states in carrying out a federal program; (3) state regulators request the federal regulator's help carrying out a state program; (4) joint boards of federal and state regulators produce advice for the federal regulator; (5) regional compacts; and (6) concurrent jurisdiction, where both levels act on the same transaction independently of each other. For each of these six models, we provide statutory examples and explain their workings.

---

3. For additional discussion of the reasons for federal–state differences in regulatory policies, see the following essays by the author, all available at http://www.scottemplinglaw.com/essays: FEDERAL–STATE JURISDICTIONAL RELATIONS: PICK YOUR METAPHOR, COORDINATED REGULATION OR JURISDICTIONAL WRESTLING: WHICH WILL PRODUCE BETTER INDUSTRY PERFORMANCE?, JURISDICTIONAL PEACE REQUIRES JOINT PURPOSE, FEDERAL–STATE RELATIONS: A PLEA FOR CONSTITUTIONAL LITERACY.

Caveats: This chapter is not a substitute for mastering the jurisdictional details of any particular regulated industry. It does not purport to discuss every statute and case on federal–state conflict in regulated industries, although most of the leading cases make an appearance. The goal is to illustrate the limits, and the ways regulators can work together within those limits.

12.A. Limits on federal action

There are three limits on federal action. Congress's power is limited by the Constitution's Commerce Clause and the Tenth Amendment, while federal agencies are limited by the statutes Congress passes.

12.A.1. Commerce Clause

The Commerce Clause of the U.S. Constitution grants Congress the power "[t]o regulate Commerce . . . among the several States."[4] It allows Congress to—

1.   regulate "the use of the channels of interstate commerce";
2.   "protect the instrumentalities of interstate commerce, or persons or things in interstate commerce, even though the threat may come only from intrastate activities"; and
3.   regulate "those activities having a substantial relation to interstate commerce, i.e., those activities that substantially affect interstate commerce."[5] This category includes intrastate activities that "have such a close and substantial relation to interstate commerce that their control is essential or appropriate to protect that commerce from burdens and obstructions."[6]

Federal regulation of utility activities is permissible, therefore, if the activities affect, or are part of, interstate commerce. Whether Congress has exceeded its Commerce Clause powers is a question for courts."[7] Two centuries of judicial oversight have given us illustrations of congressional actions falling inside and outside its Commerce Clause power. Well-known examples follow.

---

4.   U.S. CONST., art. I, § 8, cl. 3.
5.   United States v. Lopez, 514 U.S. 549, 558–59 (1995) (describing the "three broad areas of activity" Congress is authorized to regulate) (citations omitted).
6.   NLRB v. Jones & Laughlin Steel Corp., 301 U.S. 1, 8, 37 (1937).
7.   Hodel v. Va. Surface Mining & Reclamation Ass'n, 452 U.S. 264, 311 (1981) (Rehnquist, J., concurring in the judgment) ("Simply because Congress may conclude that a particular activity substantially affects interstate commerce does not necessarily make it so."). *See also* Heart of Atlanta Motel, Inc. v. United States, 379 U.S. 241, 273 (Black, J., concurring) ("Whether particular operations affect interstate commerce sufficiently to come under the constitutional power of Congress to regulate them is ultimately a judicial rather than a legislative question, and can be settled finally only by this Court.").

12.A.1.a. Within Congress's Commerce power

Production and consumption of homegrown wheat: To increase the price of wheat, federal rules limited each farm's production. Farmer Filburn grew more wheat than his authorized allotment because he wanted leftovers for his family. When he was penalized by the federal government, he sued and lost. That his own effect on market demand was trivial was not "enough to remove him from the scope of federal regulation where, as here, his contribution, taken together with that of many others similarly situated, is far from trivial."[8]

Intrastate milk sales: The Commerce Clause allowed federal regulation of the price of milk sold intrastate because it competes with milk sold interstate.[9]

Racial discrimination by local restaurants and hotels: Ollie's Barbecue seated whites but restricted African Americans to take-out. The Supreme Court upheld the application of the Civil Rights Act of 1964 against Ollie's. Although interstate patrons were few, the restaurant spent $70,000 annually on food that had been in interstate commerce. Racial discrimination reduced spending and discouraged interstate travel, to the detriment of the interstate economy.[10]

Intrastate loan-sharking: A federal statute made it a federal crime to collect on intrastate loans using "violence or other criminal means" (in Perez's case, threats of broken legs and castration). The Supreme Court upheld a conviction for intrastate loan sharking. Intrastate loan shark operations finance organized crime. Organized crime, in turn, affects interstate commerce by funding bookmakers and narcotics dealers, and by enabling the criminal underworld to take control of legitimate businesses: "[L]oan sharking in its national setting is one way organized interstate crime holds its guns to the heads of the poor and the rich alike and siphons funds from numerous localities to finance its national operations."[11]

Intrastate coal mining: In the Surface Mining Control and Reclamation Act, Congress established a federal enforcement and inspection program for surface mining within each state. Upholding the program, the court cited congressional findings that (a) in-state surface mining adversely affects interstate commerce by "destroying or diminishing the utility of land for commercial, industrial, residential, recreational, agricultural, and forestry purposes, by causing erosion and landslides, by contributing to floods, . . . by destroying fish and wildlife habitats, by impairing natural beauty, . . . by creating hazards dangerous to life and property, . . . and by counteracting governmental programs and efforts to conserve soil, water, and other natural resources"; and that (b) federal standards are "essential . . . to insure that competition in interstate commerce among sellers of coal produced in different

---

8. Wickard v. Filburn, 317 U.S. 111, 127–28 (1942).
9. United States v. Wrightwood Dairy Co., 315 U.S. 110 (1942).
10. Katzenbach v. McClung, 379 U.S. 294 (1964). *See also* Heart of Atlanta Motel, Inc. v. United States, 379 U.S. at 252–53 (upholding statute's prohibition against refusal by hotel, located near interstate highways, to rent rooms to African Americans; citing congressional findings that such hotel restrictions reduced interstate travel and therefore adversely affected interstate commerce).
11. Perez v. United States, 402 U.S. 146, 148, 156, 157 (1971).

States will not be used to undermine the ability of the several States to improve and maintain adequate standards on coal mining operations within their borders."[12]

12.A.1.b. Outside Congress's Commerce power

Gun possession within a school zone: The Supreme Court struck a federal statute banning possession of a firearm within a school zone. The statute did not regulate a commercial activity, or require that the possession or possessor "have any concrete tie to" interstate commerce. Unlike Filburn's consumption of wheat, possessing a gun in a school zone is "in no sense an economic activity that might, through repetition elsewhere, substantially affect any sort of interstate commerce"; nor was the prohibition on possessing guns in a school zone "an essential part of a larger regulation of economic activity, in which the regulatory scheme could be undercut unless the intrastate activity were regulated."[13]

Individual obligation to purchase health insurance: A mandate that most citizens purchase "minimum essential" health insurance coverage fell outside Congress's interstate commerce power. "The power to *regulate* commerce presupposes the existence of commercial activity to be regulated." Congress cannot use that power to create commerce in order then to regulate it.[14]

* * *

Might the limits on Congress's Commerce power affect utility regulation? Not likely. "[I]it is difficult to conceive of a more basic element of interstate commerce than electric energy, a product used in virtually every home and every commercial or manufacturing facility. No State relies solely on its own resources in this respect."[15] Given the nation's dependence on infrastructural utilities, and their physical interconnectedness, it is not surprising that there are no modern cases striking a federal utility regulation for being outside Congress's Commerce Clause power.

12.A.2. Tenth Amendment

The Tenth Amendment provides: "The powers not delegated to the United States by the Constitution, nor prohibited by it to the States, are reserved to the States respectively, or to the people."[16] Together, the Commerce Clause and the Tenth Amendment establish the

---

12. Hodel v. Va. Surface Mining & Reclamation Ass'n, 452 U.S. at 277, 281–82 (1981) (quoting Congress's findings).
13. United States v. Lopez, 514 U.S. at 561, 567.
14. Nat'l Fed'n of Indep. Bus. v. Sebelius, 132 S. Ct. 2566, 2586 (2012) (Roberts, C.J.) (emphasis in original). The Court upheld the individual mandate upheld under Congress's taxing power.
15. FERC v. Mississippi, 456 U.S. 742, 757 (1982).
16. U.S. CONST. amend. X.

boundary between federal and state legislative powers. In determining that boundary, courts have taken two approaches. As the Supreme Court has explained:

> In some cases the Court has inquired whether an Act of Congress is authorized by one of the powers delegated to Congress in Article I of the Constitution. . . . In other cases the Court has sought to determine whether an Act of Congress invades the province of state sovereignty reserved by the Tenth Amendment. . . . In a case like these, involving the division of authority between federal and state governments, the two inquiries are mirror images of each other. If a power is delegated to Congress in the Constitution, the Tenth Amendment expressly disclaims any reservation of that power to the States; if a power is an attribute of state sovereignty reserved by the Tenth Amendment, it is necessarily a power the Constitution has not conferred on Congress.[17]

While federal utility regulatory statutes have not violated the Commerce Clause, several have set off Tenth Amendment alarms. Before presenting the two best-known opinions, it is necessary to clarify two Tenth Amendment principles.

Congress regulates individuals, not states: As explained in Chapter 1, regulators regulate nouns linked to verbs, entities performing actions. The Tenth Amendment is triggered when the federal statute regulates a state—not when it regulates a private entity.[18] Recall the Commerce Clause discussion of intrastate coal mining.[19] The federal Surface Mining Control and Reclamation Act required "steep-slope operators" to limit and repair land damage caused by their mining activities. Who would enforce compliance? The Act offered the job to the states; if a state didn't want the job, the federal government would take it on. The statute regulated private individuals (the coal mining companies); it required no action by the state. For that reason, the mining companies' Tenth Amendment challenge lost:

> [T]here can be no suggestion that the Act commandeers the legislative processes of the States by directly compelling them to enact and enforce a federal regulatory program. . . . The most that can be said is that the . . . Act establishes a program of cooperative federalism that *allows* the States, within limits established by federal minimum standards,

---

17. New York v. United States, 505 U.S. 144, 155–56 (1992) (citations omitted). *See also* United States v. Darby, 312 U.S. 100, 124 (1941) (Tenth Amendment states "but a truism that all is retained which has not been surrendered").

18. *See* New York v. United States, 505 U.S. at 162 ("While Congress has substantial powers to govern the Nation directly, including in areas of intimate concern to the States, the Constitution has never been understood to confer upon Congress the ability to require the States to govern according to Congress' instructions"); *id.* at 165 (describing how the Constitutional Convention "opted for a Constitution in which Congress would exercise its legislative authority directly over individuals rather than over States").

19. See Chapter 12.A.1, discussing Hodel v. Va. Surface Mining & Reclamation, 452 U.S. 264.

to enact and administer their own regulatory programs, structured to meet their own particular needs.[20]

Preempting is not invading: The Surface Mining Act barred the states from enacting a program less stringent than the federal standards. A state's choice was to implement the federal standards or have the federal government do the regulating. This restriction was not an invasion of the state's sovereign powers in violation of the Tenth Amendment. If the Commerce Clause authorized Congress's actions (it did, due to the interstate effects of intrastate mining), Congress could "displace or preempt state laws regulating private activity affecting interstate commerce when these laws conflict with federal law." What the Congress cannot do is "commandeer the legislative processes of the States by directly compelling them to enact and enforce a federal regulatory program."[21]

Whereas the Surface Mining Act imposes responsibilities on private entities, the two statutes discussed next regulate activities of states. The first survived Tenth Amendment attack, the second did not.

Using state administrative machinery to adjudicate federal rights (upheld): Seeking to reduce the nation's dependence on imported oil, Congress enacted the Public Utility Regulatory Policies Act of 1978 (PURPA).[22] Section 210 required utilities to purchase capacity and energy from "qualifying facilities" (QFs)—entities certified by FERC as owning "cogenerators" or "small power production facilities." So far, so good: PURPA imposed obligations on utilities, not states. But the statute assigned responsibilities to state commissions. They had to set the prices QF would receive, either by issuing general rules or by resolving utility–QF disputes case by case.[23]

The Supreme Court upheld the Act against Mississippi's Tenth Amendment challenge. The Court acknowledged that Congress was "us[ing] state regulatory machinery to advance federal goals," including "adjudicat[ing] disputes arising under the statute."[24] Using the state's regulatory machinery for federal purposes did not invade the state's sovereignty, however. Since the state commission already had jurisdiction to address state law disputes (such as utility–customer disputes), it "can satisfy section 210's requirements simply by opening its doors to [PURPA] claimants." Requiring states to resolve QF-utility disputes was no different from Congress's longstanding practice of entitling plaintiffs to have their federal claims heard in state courts. That practice is justified because federal law is "the

---

20. Hodel v. Va. Surface Mining & Reclamation, 452 U.S. at 288–89 (citations omitted) (emphasis added).
21. Hodel v. Va. Surface Mining & Reclamation Ass'n, 452 U.S. at 288, 290. We will discuss preemption in Chapter 12.B.2 below.
22. *See supra* Chapter 3.A.1 (describing PURPA as an example of changing the traditional monopoly market structure by authorizing new wholesale sellers).
23. PURPA § 210(f), 16 U.S.C. § 824a-3(f); 18 C.F.R. § 292.401(a). Congress also authorized funds to help states carry out their obligations.
24. FERC v. Mississippi, 456 U.S. at 759.

prevailing policy in every state," and "should be respected accordingly in the courts of the State. . . . Any other conclusion would allow the States to disregard . . . the preeminent position held by federal law throughout the Nation[,]" and would "fl[y] in the face of the fact that the States of the Union constitute a nation." Further, although PURPA required states to make available their existing regulatory machinery to carry out a federal program, there was nothing in PURPA "directly compelling" the States to enact a legislative program.[25]

Making states take title to nuclear waste (invalidated): The Low-Level Radioactive Waste Policy Amendments Act of 1985[26] gave each state a choice, with respect to radioactive waste generated within its boundaries: Either dispose of it consistently with federal rules, or take title and possession. If the state does not take possession timely, it "shall be liable for all damages directly or indirectly incurred by such generator or owner as a consequence of the failure of the State to take possession of the waste."[27] Unlike Section 210 of PURPA, this provision violated the Tenth Amendment:

> Because an instruction to state governments to take title to waste, standing alone, would be beyond the authority of Congress, and because a direct order to regulate, standing alone, would also be beyond the authority of Congress, it follows that Congress lacks the power to offer the States a choice between the two. . . . Congress has . . . held out the threat, should the States not regulate according to one federal instruction, of simply forcing the States to submit to another federal instruction. A choice between two unconstitutionally coercive regulatory techniques is no choice at all.[28]

Congress could have used its Commerce Clause authority to regulate the waste generators directly. Instead, it regulated the state: "[T]he Act commandeers the legislative processes of the States by directly compelling them to enact and enforce a federal regulatory program." Unlike the surface mining situation, where the state had a choice between enforcing federal standards or having the federal government do the enforcing, here the state's choice was to enact and enforce the federal program or become an involuntary owner of the waste. That was "no choice at all."[29]

12.A.3. Agency statutory authority

A legislature creates an agency to exercise powers delegated by the legislature, and those powers only. A party aggrieved by an agency's decision can therefore argue that the agency has exceeded its legislated authority.[30] When this argument arises under federal

---

25. *Id.* at 758–61, 765 (quoting Hodel v. Va. Surface Mining & Reclamation Ass'n, 452 U.S. at 288.
26. 42 U.S.C. §§ 2021b-2021j.
27. 42 U.S.C. § 2021e(d)(2)(C).
28. New York v. United States, 505 U.S. at 176.
29. *Id.* (quoting Hodel v. Va. Surface Mining & Reclamation Ass'n, 452 U.S. at 288).
30. *See, e.g.,* 5 U.S.C. § 706(2)(c) ("reviewing court shall . . . hold unlawful and set aside agency actions,

law, courts apply a special rule of interpretation, one that rests a thumb on the agency's side of the scale. If the statute does not bar the agency's action, that is, "if the statute is silent or ambiguous with respect to the specific issue, the question for the court is whether the agency's answer is based on a permissible construction of the statute." If the agency's interpretation is consistent with the statute, the court may not "simply impose its own construction on the statute." *Chevron U.S.A. Inc. v. Natural Res. Def. Council, Inc.*[31] Many parties lose their court challenges due to *Chevron* deference. (State courts vary in whether they apply *Chevron*-type deference to state agency decisions under state law.)

To understand this concept of agency exceeding authority, here are four examples of state challenges to federal actions. The first (and most dramatic) one succeeded, the other three failed.

Replacing corporate board: In 2003, FERC issued an order replacing the Board of Directors of the California Independent System Operator (CAISO).[32] The original state statute creating the CAISO mandated a Board with only California residents. FERC found that requirement unduly discriminatory, in violation of the Federal Power Act.[33] The legislature then passed a new law requiring that the CAISO Board be appointed by the Governor, who then appointed a new Board. FERC rejected this arrangement as inconsistent with its Order No. 2000, which required that regional transmission organization boards must be independent of "market participants." (The State of California was a major market participant because its state water agency bought and sold wholesale power.)

FERC's two rejections were not the problem. The problem was that FERC ran out of patience. Instead of just issuing a second rejection, FERC imposed a solution. FERC both ordered that the Governor-appointed Board be replaced and specified the process for replacement. There would be a seven-member board, its candidates located by an independent search firm. As support for its actions, FERC cited Section 206(a) of the Federal Power Act: the Board's composition was a "practice . . . affecting [a] rate," and Section 206(a) authorized FERC to "determine" the appropriate practice and "fix the same by order."

The court of appeals reversed. There would be no *Chevron* deference, because FERC's action was an "unprecedented invasion of internal corporate governance" at war with the statutory language. When Congress used the term "practice," it was not "intending to empower FERC to re-make the corporate governance of regulated utilities." When a word has many meanings, it must be understood "by the company it keeps," that is, by its context. Section 206(a) deals with *transactions involving the sale of electric energy*—rates, charges and classifications employed by public utilities. It does not deal with corporate

findings and conclusions found to be . . . in excess of statutory jurisdiction, authority, or limitations, or short of statutory right").
31. 467 U.S. 837, 843 (1984).
32. The CAISO would eventually become a "regional transmission organization" created under FERC's Order No. 2000. For an explanation of Order No. 2000, see Chapters 3.A.1 and 4.B.5.d.
33. For a discussion of discrimination, due and undue, see Chapter 8.

governance. FERC itself had long viewed the term "practice" in transactional terms—as a "consistent and predictable course of conduct of the supplier that affects [the utilities'] financial relationship with the consumer." Further, FERC's breach of statutory boundaries had no limits:

> If FERC can remove a board of directors and dictate the method of choosing a new one because the method of selecting the old one might have made it appear discriminatory, or have even given cause to fear future discrimination, then it would seem that FERC could also dictate the choice of CEO, COO, and the method of contracting for services, labor, office space, or whatever one might imagine, assuming FERC made the appropriate finding. However, we really need no such parade of horribles. The very act attempted by FERC in this case is quite enough to reveal the drastic implications of its overreaching.[34]

FERC had other alternatives. It could have rejected the proposal to create CAISO as inconsistent with the Act's prohibition on discrimination. It could have specified the conditions (including a seven-member board recruited by an independent search firm) under which it would approve CAISO's creation, leaving the final choice with CAISO's creators. What FERC could not do was accept the CAISO's creation but then unilaterally restructure the Board.

Transmission of retail power: FERC's Order No. 888 required all investor-owned transmission owners to offer "unbundled" transmission service non-discriminatorily. The obligation is to transmit wholesale power, and also retail power if the recipient's state has authorized retail electricity competition.[35] New York argued that FERC exceeded its Federal Power Act authority because Order No. 888 regulates a retail transaction. (Section 201(b)(1) Act denies FERC jurisdiction over the sale of electric energy at retail.) The Court disagreed. The Federal Power Act's jurisdictional provisions grant FERC two distinct powers: over (a) "transmission of electric energy in interstate commerce" and (b) "the sale of electric energy at wholesale in interstate commerce." Although Section 201(b) denies to FERC jurisdiction over the *sale* of retail electricity, the *transmission* of electricity is distinct from its sale, if the transmission service is an unbundled service. As the court explained, "There is no language . . . limiting FERC's *transmission* jurisdiction to the wholesale market, although the statute does limit FERC's *sale* jurisdiction to that at wholesale.[36]

---

34. Cal. Indep. Sys. Operator v. FERC, 372 F.3d 395 (D.C. Cir. 2004) (quoting other sources).

35. *See supra* Chapter 3.A.1. FERC declared that when a utility "unbundles" transmission service, that is, sells it separately from generation service, the utility is providing "transmission of electric energy in interstate commerce"—a service that is exclusively FERC's to regulate. *See* Federal Power Act § 201(b), 16 U.S.C. § 824(b).

36. New York v. FERC, 535 U.S. at 17 (emphasis in original). The Court cited its decision in *FPC v. Louisiana Power & Light Co.*, 406 U.S. 621, 636 (1972), finding that a similar provision in the Natural Gas Act, 15 U.S.C. § 717(b) signaled jurisdiction over "interstate 'transportation' regardless of whether the gas transported is ultimately sold retail or wholesale").

Ten-digit area codes: In the 1990s, the influx of faxes, modems, cell phones and pagers caused many areas to run out of phone numbers. The Telecommunications Act of 1996 directed FCC to "create or designate one or more impartial entities to administer telecommunications numbering and to make such numbers available on an equitable basis."[37] The FCC delegated some numbering authority to state commissions. There was a condition on the delegation: if a state used the "area code overlay" method for creating new area codes, it had to use 10-digit local dialing "between and within area codes in the area covered by the new code."[38]

New York argued that the FCC's 10-digit dialing rule exceeded its statutory authority because the rule would apply to intrastate service as well as interstate service. New York cited, among other things, the Communication Act's "state savings clause": "[N]othing in this Act shall be construed to apply or to give the Commission jurisdiction with respect to . . . intrastate communication service."[39] The Court upheld the Commission. First, the statutory language granting the FCC "exclusive jurisdiction" over numbering administration was "unambiguous and straightforward" evidence of Congress's intent to override the state savings clause. Congress therefore authorized the FCC to carry out numbering administration for intrastate service. Second, the Commission could reasonably interpret the phrase "administer telecommunications numbering" to include determining the number of digits for local calls.[40]

Dialing parity: The 1996 Act directed the FCC to issue rules on dialing parity. (Prior to these rules, the incumbent AT&T discriminated against customers of non-AT&T carriers, like MCI or Sprint, by requiring them to dial a long access code before connecting long-distance.)[41] The FCC applied its rules to all telephone service, whether interstate or intrastate. California, citing the "state savings clause" quoted above, challenged the rules' application to intrastate calls. The Eighth Circuit found that the FCC had exceeded its authority. Unlike numbering administration, the Act had no language granting the FCC "exclusive jurisdiction" over dialing parity. (Recall that in the numbering administration case, the explicit "exclusive jurisdiction" language overcame the state savings clause.) Without an "exclusive jurisdiction" clause, and without any other "clear grant of intrastate authority to the FCC, [the state savings clause] stands as a fortification against the Commission's intrusion into telecommunications matters that are intrastate in character."

---

37.   47 U.S.C. § 251(e)(1).
38.   47 C.F.R. § 52.19(c)(3)(ii). An area code overlay "occurs when a new area code is introduced to serve the same geographic area as an existing area code." 47 C.F.R. § 52.19(c)(3). It is one of three methods for injecting new area codes, the other two being (a) splitting a shortage area into two parts, each with a different area code; and (b) realigning boundaries between two adjacent area codes.
39.   47 U.S.C. § 152(b) (exceptions omitted).
40.   New York v. FCC, 267 F.3d 91, 101–105 (2d Cir. 2001) (citing Chevron U.S.A. Inc. v. Natural Res. Def. Council, Inc., 467 U.S. 837).
41.   *See* 47 U.S.C. § 153(15) (defining "dialing parity").

The U.S. Supreme Court reversed the Eighth Circuit, upholding the dialing parity rules as within the FCC's jurisdiction. The FCC had general authority, under Section 201(b) of the 1934 Act (as amended), to "prescribe such rules and regulations as may be necessary in the public interest to carry out the provisions of this [1934] Act." Those "provisions" include the 1996 provisions on dialing parity. Further, the FCC's general rulemaking authority is not confined to interstate matters; it applies to all matters delegated to the FCC unless specifically excepted. The general rulemaking authority therefore overcame the state savings clause. And whereas other provisions, such as those relating to whole-sale interconnection, assign roles explicitly to states, the dialing parity provision does not mention states.[42]

12.B. Limits on state action

The limits on states are the Constitution's "dormant" Commerce Clause and the Supremacy Clause.[43]

12.B.1. Dormant Commerce Clause

The Commerce Clause has two purposes. One is to empower Congress to regulate interstate commerce—the subject of Chapter 12.A.1 above. The other is to prevent states from impeding interstate commerce. This second purpose is called the "dormant Commerce Clause" because it is not explicit in the Constitution. But it permeates the nation's history:

> Our system, fostered by the Commerce Clause, is that every farmer and every craftsman shall be encouraged to produce by the certainty that he will have free access to every market in the Nation, that *no home embargoes will withhold his exports, and no foreign state will by customs duties or regulations exclude them*. Likewise, every consumer may look to the free competition from every producing area in the Nation to protect him from exploitation by any. Such was the vision of the Founders; such has been the doctrine of this Court which has given it reality.[44]

---

42. California v. FCC, 124 F.3d 934, 941 (8th Cir. 1997), *rev'd in part sub nom.* AT&T Corp. v. Iowa Utils. Bd., 525 U.S. 366, 379–85 (1999). In a separate opinion, reversed in the same Supreme Court order, the Eighth Circuit described the state savings clause as "hog tight, horse high, and bull strong, preventing the FCC from intruding on the states' intrastate turf." 120 F.3d 753, 800 (8th Cir. 1997).

43. Of course, state agencies are also limited by state statutes, but that limit does not grow out of the federal–state relationship, which is the subject of this Chapter.

44. H. P. Hood & Sons, Inc. v. Du Mond, 336 U.S. 525, 539 (1949) (emphasis added). *See also* Wyoming v. Oklahoma, 502 U.S. 437, 454 (1992) ("It is long established that, while a literal reading evinces a grant of power to Congress, the Commerce Clause also directly limits the power of the States to discriminate against interstate commerce."); Gen. Motors Corp. v. Tracy, 519 U.S. 278, 305–06 (1997) (the objective is to "preserve a national market for competition undisturbed by preferential advantages conferred by a State upon its residents or resident competitors").

A state regulatory program can violate the dormant Commerce Clause in two distinct ways: by discriminating against interstate commerce, and by burdening it excessively.

12.B.1.a. Discrimination

When states practice "economic protectionism—that is, regulatory measures designed to benefit in-state economic interests by burdening out-of-state competitors,"[45] courts apply a "virtually *per se* rule of invalidity."[46] Despite the rule's clarity, violations are frequent.

Prohibiting export of hydroelectric power: Acting under a state statute, the New Hampshire Commission prohibited New England Power Company from selling outside the state hydroelectricity generated inside the state. The U.S. Supreme Court struck the statute. The Commerce Clause "precludes a state from mandating that its residents be given a preferred right of access, over out-of-state consumers, to natural resources located within its borders or to the products derived therefrom."[47]

Limiting imports of out-of-state coal: An Oklahoma statute directed in-state coal-fired electric plants, if producing power for sale in the state, to burn at least 10 percent Oklahoma-mined coal. Wyoming, wanting to sell more of its coal to Oklahoma generators, challenged the statute as discriminatory. The Court invalidated the statute. Oklahoma had "reserved a segment of the Oklahoma coal market for Oklahoma-mined coal, to the exclusion of coal mined in other States." Oklahoma's defense: by sustaining its own coal-mining industry it reduced its reliance on a single source. (Before the statute, nearly all of Oklahoma-burned coal came from Wyoming.) The Court was unimpressed: "We have often examined a 'presumably legitimate goal,' only to find that the State attempted to achieve it by 'the illegitimate means of isolating the State from the national economy.'"[48]

Tax credits for ethanol: An Ohio statute gave gasoline dealers a tax credit for sales of ethanol (as a component of gasohol). But a seller of non-Ohio ethanol received credits only to the extent the state of origin provided its dealers a tax credit for Ohio-produced ethanol. The Court held that Ohio discriminated unconstitutionally, by "explicitly depriving certain products of generally available beneficial tax treatment because they are made in certain other States."[49] Ohio argued that its scheme *encouraged* trade by inducing other states to give Ohio ethanol reciprocal treatment. The Court didn't buy. It already had struck a

---

45. Wyoming v. Oklahoma, 502 U.S. at 454.
46. Philadelphia v. New Jersey, 437 U.S. 617, 624 (1978).
47. New England Power Co. v. New Hampshire, 455 U.S. 331, 338 (1982).
48. Wyoming v. Oklahoma, 502 U.S. at 455–57 (quoting Philadelphia v. New Jersey, 437 U.S. at 627). *See also* Alliance for Clean Coal v. Miller, 44 F.3d 591, 595–96 (7th Cir. 1995) (striking Illinois's "none-too-subtle" effort to protect in-state coal production; state statute required certain generators to install, and ensured rate recovery of, scrubbers, to "enable them to continue to burn Illinois coal," even if use of lower-sulfur, non-Illinois coal would be less expensive; and required state commission to consider the effect on Illinois employment of any utility plan to decrease use of Illinois coal by 10 percent; "even ingenious discrimination is forbidden by the Commerce Clause").
49. New Energy Co. of Ind. v. Limbaugh, 486 U.S. 269 (1988).

Mississippi statute blocking sales in Mississippi of non-Mississippi milk unless the other state accepted Mississippi milk. "Mississippi may not use the threat of economic isolation as a weapon to force sister States to enter into even a desirable reciprocity agreement."[50] Ohio also pleaded that its tax credit's effect was minor, involving only one in-state and one out-of-state manufacturer. But in discrimination, size doesn't matter: "Varying the strength of the bar against economic protectionism according to the size and number of in-state and out-of-state firms affected would serve no purpose except the creation of new uncertainties in an already complex field."[51]

It's not discrimination if the differentially treated companies are not competitors: Ohio imposed a 5 percent sales tax on all in-state sales of goods, including the sale of natural gas. Sales of gas by the retail local distribution companies (LDC) were exempted. So the tax applied to non-LDC sellers like producers, pipelines and independent marketers, but not to the utilities that had an obligation to serve. General Motors bought most of its gas from out-of-state marketers, and thus had to pay a "use" tax that was a substitute for the sales tax. General Motors challenged the tax as facially discriminatory: while the tax applied to all non-LDC sellers, Ohio and non-Ohio, it did not apply to LDC sales, all of which were in-state.

The Court upheld the tax. The difference in tax treatment between LDCs and non-LDCs was not unconstitutionally discriminatory because LDCs and non-LDCs were not "similarly situated." They competed in different markets because their products were different. LDCs served a "core market of small, captive users, typified by residential consumers who . . . are captive to the need for bundled benefits. These are buyers who live on sufficiently tight budgets to make the stability of rate important, and who cannot readily bear the risk of losing a fuel supply in harsh natural or economic weather." Non-LDCs served a different market: large customers like General Motors, who "have no need for bundled protection." Given this difference in markets, there is no unconstitutional discrimination. The purpose of the dormant Commerce Clause is to prevent states from distorting competition. If there is no "actual or prospective competition between the supposedly favored and disfavored entities in a single market[,] . . . competition would not be served by eliminating any tax differential as between sellers, and the dormant Commerce Clause has no job to do."[52]

---

50. *Id.* at 274–75 (quoting Great Atl. & Pac. Tea Co. v. Cottrell, 424 U.S. 366, 379 (1976)).

51. *Id.* at 276–77. *See also* Or. Waste Sys. v. Dep't of Envtl. Quality, 511 U.S. 93 (1994) (invalidating Oregon's surcharge on the disposal in Oregon of solid waste from out of state); West Lynn Creamery, Inc. v. Healy, 512 U.S. 186 (1994) (invalidating Massachusetts's tax on all milk sold in the state, where the proceeds are used to subsidize in-state producers).

52. Gen. Motors Corp. v. Tracy, 519 U.S. at 299–303. The Court acknowledged that while the LDC and the marketers were not competitors in the captive market, they could be competitors in the non-captive market, because General Motors had a choice between buying from the LDC or from non-LDCs. So in fact, the tax differential could affect competition in the non-LDC market. This possibility caused the Court to compare the consequences of upholding the tax differential or invalidating it. The Court chose to emphasize the captive market, thus upholding the tax differential. The Court "recogniz[ed] an obligation to proceed cautiously lest we imperil the delivery by regulated LDC's of bundled gas to the

Three ways to discriminate constitutionally: The dormant Commerce Clause limits, but does not prohibit, discrimination by states. The first way to discriminate lawfully is when the state, acting as regulator, demonstrates a purpose "unrelated to economic protectionism."[53] It must be "a legitimate local purpose . . . that could not be served as well by available non-discriminatory means."[54] A Maine statute made it a crime to "import[] into this State any live fish, including smelts, which are commonly used for bait fishing in inland waters."[55] The statute's discriminatory, trade-blocking effect was undisputed. But (a) imported bait carried a risk of parasites and non-native species; and (b) there were no less discriminatory ways to prevent this harm, because effective parasite-testing techniques did not yet exist. The Commerce Clause did not require Maine "'to sit idly by and wait until potentially irreversible environmental damage has occurred or until the scientific community agrees on what disease organisms are or are not dangerous before it acts to avoid such consequences.'"[56]

The second way to discriminate constitutionally is to act not as a regulator but as a seller. When the state acts not in its "distinctive governmental capacity, . . . [but] in the more general capacity of a market participant," the dormant Commerce Clause does not apply. In that situation, the state's "business methods, including those that favor its residents, are of no greater constitutional concern than those of a private business."[57] Maryland paid a bounty for abandoned, inoperable cars (to be turned into scrap). Out-of-state suppliers had to provide more exacting evidence of ownership than did in-state suppliers. This discrimination did not violate the Commerce Clause because Maryland was a market participant—a buyer of scrap metal.[58] Nor did South Dakota violate the Commerce Clause when its Cement Commission policy confined sales from the state-owned cement plant to in-state residents.[59]

---

noncompetitive captive market." Skeptical of its institutional capacity to analyze economic consequences, the Court concluded that any market adjustment would be better handled by Congress. *Id.* at 303.

53. Wyoming v. Oklahoma, 502 F.2d at 454.

54. Maine v. Taylor, 477 U.S. 131, 138 (1986) (quoting Hughes v. Oklahoma, 441 U.S. 322, 336 (1979)).

55. ME. REV. STAT. ANN., tit. 12, § 7613.

56. Maine v. Taylor, 477 U.S. 131, 148 (1986) (quoting United States v. Taylor, 585 F. Supp. 393 (D. Me. 1984) (district court opinion)). Note the opening sentences of the Supreme Court's majority and dissenting opinions. *Compare id.* at 132 (majority opinion) ("Once again, a little fish has caused a commotion."), *with id.* at 152 (Stevens, J., dissenting) ("There is something fishy about this case.").

57. New Energy Co. of Ind. v. Limbaugh, 486 U.S. at 277. *See also* Reeves, Inc. v. Stake, 447 U.S. 429, 437 (1980) (the Commerce Clause "responds principally to state taxes and regulatory measures impeding free private trade in the national marketplace").

58. Hughes v. Alexandria Scrap Corp., 426 U.S. 794, 806–10 (1976) ("Maryland has not sought to prohibit the flow of hulks, or to regulate the conditions under which it may occur. Instead, it has entered into the market itself to bid up their price. . . . Nothing in the purposes animating the Commerce Clause prohibits a State, in the absence of congressional action, from participating in the market and exercising the right to favor its own citizens over others").

59. Reeves, Inc. v. Stake, 447 U.S. at 438–39 (recognizing "considerations of state sovereignty," the "role of each State 'as guardian and trustee for its people,'" and "'the long recognized right of trader or manufacturer, engaged in an entirely private business, freely to exercise his own independent discretion as to parties with whom he will deal'") (quoting other sources). As for the political problems likely to arise

The third path for sustaining a facially discriminatory statute is for Congress to authorize it. That authorization must be "unmistakably clear."[60] A prominent example, directly relevant to public utility practitioners, is the decades-long decision by most states (at least until the late 1990s) to erect barriers to competition by granting monopolies over retail sales in electricity and gas (and before 1996, local telephone service). Congress has authorized this practice by "altogether exempting state regulation of in-state retail sales of natural gas from attack under the dormant Commerce Clause."[61] The Court analogized Section 1(b) of the Natural Gas Act[62] (exempting "local distribution of natural gas" from federal regulation) to the McCarran Act (the federal insurance statute that allows state discrimination against interstate commerce in that industry):

> The declaration [in the Natural Gas Act], though not identical in terms with the one made by the McCarran Act, . . . concerning continued state regulation of the insurance business, is in effect equally clear, in view of the [NGA's] historical setting, legislative history and objects, to show intention for the states to continue with regulation where Congress has not expressly taken over.[63]

Current controversy—Preferences for in-state renewable energy: Over two dozen states have statutes requiring their electric utilities to purchase specified percentages of their power supply needs from renewable sources. Known as "renewable portfolio" statutes, they often include an in-state preference: they either specify a percentage to be purchased from in-state sources or grant extra "renewable energy credits" (which can be sold in a

---

when states-as-market-participants discriminate against each other, they were for Congress to solve: because the "competing considerations in cases involving state proprietary action often will be subtle, complex, politically charged, and difficult to assess under traditional Commerce Clause analysis[,] . . . the adjustment of interests in this context is a task better suited for Congress than this Court." *Id.*

60. South-Central Timber Dev., Inc. v. Wunnicke, 467 U.S. 82, 91–92 (1984) (requiring "a clear expression of approval by Congress," to avoid "the risk that unrepresented interests will be adversely affected by restraints on commerce"). *See also* S. Pac. Co. v. Ariz. *ex rel.* Sullivan, 325 U.S. 761, 769 (1945) ("Congress has undoubted power to redefine the distribution of power over interstate commerce. It may either permit the states to regulate the commerce in a manner which would otherwise not be permissible, . . . or exclude state regulation even of matters of peculiarly local concern which nevertheless affect interstate commerce.").

61. Gen. Motors Corp. v. Tracy, 519 U.S. at 292.

62. 15 U.S.C. § 717(b).

63. Panhandle E. Pipe Line Co. v. Pub. Serv. Comm'n of Indiana, 332 U.S. 507, 521 (1947) (citing Prudential Ins. Co. v. Benjamin, 328 U.S. 408 (1946) (finding that McCarran Act authorized discriminatory state taxation of out-of-state insurance companies)). Note: *Panhandle Eastern* was not technically a discrimination case. Section 1(b) of the Natural Gas Act authorized states not to *discriminate* against interstate commerce but to *regulate* interstate commerce, specifically by regulating retail sales. In *Prudential Insurance*, however, there was discrimination. South Carolina had imposed on out-of-state insurance companies a tax that did not apply to their in-state competitors. The Court upheld the measure by interpreting the McCarran Act to permit "the continued regulation and taxation by the states of the business of insurance," including imposing taxes that are discriminatory. Prudential Ins. Co. v. Benjamin, 328 U.S. at 429.

credit market) for purchases from in-state sources. This type of facial discrimination has drawn Commerce Clause challenges.[64]

Efforts to justify in-state preferences have mixed results. A goal of incubating or saving in-state industries will not justify such discrimination.[65] A geographic restriction that is based on the need to produce a particular in-state benefit (such as reliability, pollution reduction or in-state peak load reduction) might survive challenge; a technology preference that is superficially neutral but that disguises in-state protectionism will not. A policy of favoring resources that are plentiful in-state, without excluding resources from out-of-state, will likely survive.[66] A state also could become a market participant,[67] as a purchaser of renewable energy or renewable energy credits.[68] No court has ruled on these options.[69]

---

64. For a description of a Commerce Clause challenge to the in-state location requirement in a Massachusetts statute, Mass. Gen Laws ch. 169, § 83, see the Appendix in Carolyn Elefant & Ed Holt, The Commerce Clause and Implications for State Renewable Portfolio Standard Programs (Clean Energy States Alliance, 2011), *available at* http://www.cleanenergystates.org/resource-library/resource/cesa-report-the-commerce-clause-and-implications-for-state-renewable-portfolio-standard-programs-pdf. The case settled when the state commission revised its regulations.

    Ontario has a variation on the state renewable preference problem. Any renewable generator seeking a guaranteed, long-term contract to sell its output to the Ontario Power Authority at the Ontario-fixed price must demonstrate that a specified portion of the equipment used in the generator was made in Ontario. A panel of the World Trade Organization has ruled this requirement a violation of the Agreement on Trade-Related Investment Measures (TRIMS). World Trade Organization, Canada—Certain Measures Affecting the Renewable Energy Generation Sector (2012); World Trade Organization, Canada—Measures relating to the Feed-In Tariff Program (2012). The generation facility also must be located in Ontario. The panel did not rule on that feature.

65. In Bacchus Imps. Ltd. v. Diaz, 468 U.S. 263, 272 (1984), a Hawaii statute imposed a 20 percent tax on wholesale sales of liquor but exempted two products: okolehao (a brandy made from an indigenous Hawaii plant) and fruit wine produced in the state. Because there was competition between the taxed and tax-exempt products, the discrimination violated the Commerce Clause. (Recall *General Motors*'s emphasis on competition.) The state sought to justify the statute as necessary "to subsidize nonexistent (pineapple wine) and financially troubled (okolehao) liquor industries peculiar to Hawaii." The Court rejected the argument: "[W] perceive no principle of *Commerce Clause* jurisprudence supporting a distinction between thriving and struggling enterprises under these circumstances, and the State cites no authority for its proposed distinction." *Id.* at 272 (emphasis in original).

66. Elefant & Holt, *supra* note 64, at 15–16. Maryland has a special "tier" for energy produced from chicken manure, and North Carolina has one for swine waste. *See* Md. Code Ann., Pub. Util. Cos. §§ 7-701 *et seq.*; N.C. Gen. Stat. § 62-133.8.

67. *See* Hughes v. Alexandria Scrap, 426 U.S. 794 (1976).

68. For example, the New York State Energy Research and Development Authority buys renewable credits. *See* Order Resolving Main Tier Issues, Case 03-E-0188 (N.Y. Pub. Serv. Comm'n Apr. 2, 2010), *available at* http://www.nyserda.ny.gov/Program-Planning/Renewable-Portfolio-Standard/History.aspx.

69. The author is not necessarily recommending any of these actions; they are mentioned for purposes of completeness. Any state blockage of interstate commerce, whether done through regulation or as a market participant, risks distorting the market, penalizing efficient producers, raising customer costs and inviting retaliation. *See* C. & A. Carbone v. Town of Clarkstown, 511 U.S. 383, 414 (1994) ("Laws that hoard for local businesses the right to serve local markets or develop local resources work to isolate States from each other and to incite retaliation, since no State would stand by while another advanced the economic interests of its own business classes at the expense of its neighbors.").

    For other sources on this topic of renewable energy purchases, *see* Kristin Engel, *The Dormant Commerce Clause Threat to Market Based Environmental Regulation: The Case of Energy Deregulation*, 26 Ecology L.Q. 243 (1999); Nancy Rader & Scott Hempling, The Renewables Portfolio Standard: A Practical Guide (National Association of Regulatory Utility Commissions, 2001), *available at* http://www.scotthemplinglaw.com/files/pdf/ppr_renewables_portfolio_standard_0201_0.pdf; Steven

12.B.1.b. Burden

While state regulations that *discriminate* against interstate commerce are "virtually *per se* invalid," those that *burden* interstate commerce evenhandedly are permitted, unless the burden is "clearly excessive in relation to the putative local benefits." *Pike v. Bruce Church, Inc.*[70] The Supreme Court described the *Pike* balancing test as follows:

> Where the statute regulates even-handedly to effectuate a legitimate local public interest, and its effects on interstate commerce are only incidental, it will be upheld unless the burden imposed on such commerce is clearly excessive in relation to the putative local benefits. . . . If a legitimate local purpose is found, then the question becomes one of degree. And the extent of the burden that will be tolerated will of course depend on the nature of the local interest involved, and on whether it could be promoted as well with a lesser impact on interstate activities.[71]

How does the *Pike* balancing test apply to the public utility regulation? Utility regulation is "one of the most important of the functions traditionally associated with the police power of the States."[72] Courts have recognized the states' need to "prevent, on the one

---

Ferrey, *Sustainable Energy, Environmental Policy and States' Rights: Discerning the Future of Energy Through The Eye of the Commerce Clause*, 12 N.Y.U. Envtl. L.J. 507, 604 (2004); Patrick R. Jacobi, *Renewable Portfolio Standard Generator Applicability Requirements: How States Can Stop Worrying and Learn to Love the Dormant Commerce Clause*, 30 Vt. L. Rev. 1079, 1132 (Summer 2006); Nathan E. Endrud, *State Renewable Portfolio Standards: Their Continued Validity and Relevance in Light of the Dormant Commerce Clause, the Supremacy Clause, and Possible Federal Legislation*, 45 Harv. J. on Legis. 259 (Winter 2008); Lincoln L. Davies, *State Renewable Portfolio Standards: Is There a "Race" and Is It "To the Top"?*, 3 San Diego J. Climate & Energy L. 3 (2011–2012).

70. 397 U.S. 137, 142 (1970).
71. *Id.* Ironically, in this leading case confirming states' authority to burden commerce, the state lost. Bruce Church grew cantaloupes in Arizona and sold them throughout the United States. Its cantaloupes were of higher quality than those grown elsewhere in Arizona. The company's packing sheds, centralized for efficiency, were in California. Its packages did not identify the fruit as coming from Arizona. The Arizona regulator ordered Bruce Church to process and package in Arizona. The Supreme Court found that the order was

> not for the purpose of keeping the reputation of its growers unsullied, but to enhance their reputation through the reflected good will of [Bruce Church's] superior produce. [Arizona], in other words, is not complaining because the company is putting the good name of Arizona on an inferior or deceptively packaged product, but because it is not putting that name on a product that is superior and well packaged.

Even assuming this state interest in in-state packaging was legitimate, said the Court, it was "tenuous"—too small to justify requiring Bruce Church to build a redundant operation in Arizona: "[The Commerce Clause] cannot permit a State to require a person to go into a local packing business solely for the sake of enhancing the reputation of other producers within its borders." *Id.* at 142–46.

   Note that while the case is usually cited for the "balancing" principle—that "evenhanded" burdens on commerce are permitted if supported by a legitimate and substantial state interest—it is also a discrimination case. The opinion balanced the state's reputation interest against the company's burdens, but also criticized Arizona's insistence that Bruce Church do its packaging in Arizona rather than California.
72. Ark. Elec. Coop. Corp. v. Ark. Pub. Serv. Comm'n, 461 U.S. 375, 377 (1983). *See also* New Orleans Pub.

hand, the evils of an unrestricted right of competition and, on the other hand, the abuses of monopoly."[73] This need is sufficient constitutional justification for state regulation of health and safety,[74] quality of service, rates, corporate structure, and measures to maintain the utility's financial viability.[75]

These state powers were tested when utilities challenged various provisions of the Wisconsin Holding Company Act. The Seventh Circuit's opinion calls on both prongs of the dormant Commerce Clause: its prohibition against discrimination and its accommodation of non-discriminatory burdens.[76]

State ban on out-of-state utility companies (upheld): Section 196.53 of the Wisconsin statute provided that only Wisconsin corporations may receive licenses to "own operate,

---

Serv., Inc. v. City of New Orleans, 798 F.2d 858, 862 (5th Cir. 1986) ("The regulation and adjustment of local utility rates is of paramount local concern and a matter which demands local administrative expertise."); Minn. Gas Co. v. Pub. Serv. Comm'n, Dep't of Pub. Serv. of Minn., 523 F.2d 581, 583 (8th Cir. 1975) (holding that "[r]egulation of public utility rates has long been held an area of public interest subject to State police power legislation. It is an implied condition of all private contracts in such areas of public interest that the agreement is subject to frustration by subsequent legitimate exercises of the State's police power. Thus, private parties cannot by contract insulate themselves from State rate regulations adopted thereafter.") (citations omitted); Am. Elec. Power Co. v. Ky. Pub. Serv. Comm'n, 787 F.2d 588 (1986) (noting that "[t]here is little question . . . that the regulation of consumer electric rates is an important state interest"); Otter Tail Power Co. v. N.D. Pub. Serv. Comm'n, 451 N.W.2d 95, 107 (N.D. 1990) ("A state's interest in public utility regulation in furtherance of the public good is substantial and ranks among the most important functions traditionally associated with the police power of the States.") (internal quotation marks omitted).

73. People *ex rel.* N.Y. Edison Co. v. Willcox, 100 N.E. 705, 207 N.Y. 86, 93 (1912). *See also* Gen. Motors Corp. v. Tracy, 519 U.S. at 288–94 (citations and footnotes omitted):

> [T]he States' . . . experiments with free market competition in the manufactured gas and electricity industries . . . dramatically underscored the need for comprehensive regulation of the local gas market. . . . [I]n the latter half of the 19th century . . . the States generally left any regulation of the industry to local governments. . . . The results were both predictable and disastrous, including an initial period of "wasteful competition," followed by massive consolidation and the threat of monopolistic pricing. The public suffered through essentially the same evolution in the electric industry. Thus, by the time natural gas became a widely marketable commodity, the States had learned from chastening experience that public streets could not be continually torn up to lay competitors' pipes, that investments in parallel delivery systems for different fractions of a local market would limit the value to consumers of any price competition, and that competition would simply give over to monopoly in due course. It seemed virtually an economic necessity for States to provide a single, local franchise with a business opportunity free of competition from any source, within or without the State, so long as the creation of exclusive franchises under state law could be balanced by regulation and the imposition of obligations to the consuming public upon the franchised retailers.

74. Gen. Motors Corp. v. Tracy, 519 U.S. at 305–06 (recognizing need to "avoid[] any jeopardy to service of the state-regulated captive market. . . . State regulation of natural gas sales to consumers serves important interests in health and safety in fairly obvious ways, in that requirements of dependable supply and extended credit assure that individual buyers of gas for domestic purposes are not frozen out of their houses in the cold months.").

75. Balt. Gas & Elec. Co. v. Heintz, 760 F.2d 1408, 1424 n.14 (4th Cir. 1985) (recognizing state's need to regulate utility's "financial practices, its relations with other public service companies, and mergers and other corporate changes").

76. Alliant Energy Co. v. Bie, 330 F.3d 904 (7th Cir. 2003). The author was an expert witness for the State of Wisconsin in the litigation before the U.S. District Court that led to the Seventh Circuit opinion.

manage or control" assets used for heat, light, water or power service in the state. The Wisconsin utilities challenged this provision as discriminating against interstate commerce. The Court disagreed. "The provision of public utilities that are generated, distributed, and consumed in Wisconsin is an inherently local and intrastate business." Even where a utility serves both Wisconsin and non-Wisconsin customers, it still must comply with intrastate regulations. Applying the Commerce Clause's balancing test announced in *Pike v. Bruce Church*, the Court assumed "that a local incorporation requirement has a minimal burden on interstate commerce and serves a legitimate and important state interest in regulating intrastate commerce."[77]

State ban on out-of-state holding companies (invalidated): Section 196.795(5)(L) required that a *holding company* owning a Wisconsin public utility be incorporated under Wisconsin law. The Court saw a "fundamental distinction" between the business activities of a public utility and those of a holding company: "The provision of public utilities within Wisconsin is intrastate commerce. An investment opportunity in a Wisconsin utility is, on the other hand, an article of interstate commerce." The business of a utility holding company's business is to own stock in a utility:

> If ownership of a Wisconsin utility company must lie with a Wisconsin Corporation, a potential article of interstate commerce, *i.e.*, the investment in the utility, is stopped at the border. . . . If every State adopted this rule there would be no interstate investment in public utilities at all. No holding company parent could own public utility companies in more than one State . . . .

The Court found the provision "clearly invalid" because there was no valid state purpose. A state can prohibit all holding companies. But once it allows them, it cannot prohibit their interstate ownership. The Court analogized to garbage: "States may choose not to zone land for dumping, but once the land is opened up for trash it must be opened up for all refuse, no matter where it originates."[78]

---

77. *Id.* at 915 (citing Eli Lilly & Co. v. Sav-On-Drugs, Inc., 366 U.S. 276, 279 (1961) (finding legitimate state interest served by requiring business certificate prior to selling in the state; Lilly could not escape state regulation merely because it is also engaged in interstate commerce).

78. *Id.* at 912 (footnote omitted) (citing Lewis v. BT Inv. Managers, Inc., 447 U.S. 27 (1980) (holding that Florida statute prohibiting out-of-state banks, trusts, and bank holding companies from providing investment advisory services within the state violated Commerce Clause); Or. Waste Sys., Inc. v. Dep't of Envtl. Quality of Oregon, 511 U.S. 93 (1994); and City of Phila. v. New Jersey, 437 U.S. 617 (1978)).

State regulation of holding company structure and finance (upheld): Wisconsin utilities challenged three other provisions regulating the holding company's financial transactions and business activities:

1. Section 196.795(3) required Commission review before a person could acquire 10 percent or more of a utility holding company's outstanding stock.
2. Section 196.795(6m)(b) limited the amount of a utility holding company's investments in nonutility businesses.
3. Sections 196.795(5)(a) and (7)(a), 201.01(2), and 201.03(1) authorized the commission to regulate a utility's securities issuances.

The Court upheld them all. Unlike the in-state incorporation requirement for holding companies, none of these provisions discriminated between in-state and out-of-state activities. The holding company acquisition provision applied no matter where the involved parties were located or incorporated; the asset cap applied to assets regardless of their location; and the securities regulation provisions applied whether the securities entered interstate commerce or remained in-state.

The three provisions did affect interstate commerce, but extraterritorial effect does not automatically invalidate a facially neutral statute. Constitutionality depends on balancing the effect on interstate commerce with the in-state benefit. While the provisions had "no small impact" on interstate commerce, the regulation of public utilities was "one of the most important of the functions traditionally associated with the police power of the States." The more complicated the corporate structure, the stronger the justification for state regulation:

> This [state] interest is served well by the structural provisions because they help to prevent such abuses as cross-subsidization and deceptive reporting of cost allocation. . . . The more products a firm is responsible for, the easier it is for the firm to misreport the allocation of its costs. This danger can be tempered by limiting the public utility holding company's involvement with and ownership of businesses and assets unrelated to providing the public utility [service].[79]

---

79. Alliant Energy Co. v. Bie, 330 F.3d at 916–17 (quoting Ark. Elec. Coop. Corp. v. Ark. Pub. Serv. Comm'n, 461 U.S. 375, 377 (1983) (citing S. Union Co. v. Mo. Pub. Serv. Comm'n, 289 F.3d 503, 507–08 (8th Cir. 2002) (upholding against Commerce Clause challenge Missouri's requirement that the state commission approve a utility's purchase of another utility, because "[a] public utility's investments in other companies can affect its regulated rate of return, if investment losses are allocated to the regulated business"); and Balt. Gas & Elec. Co v. Heintz, 760 F.2d at 1425 (upholding against Commerce Clause attack Maryland statute prohibiting non-utilities from acquiring more than 10 percent of a Maryland utility, because "a necessary adjunct to ensuring the protection of consumers is the authority to regulate the corporate structure of public utilities" given the possibility that holding companies will engage in "deceptive financing practices, non-disclosure of important corporate accounts, and the manipulation of various 'service charges,'" to the consumers' detriment))).

12.B.2. Supremacy Clause

Congress can preempt state laws. Preemption means "displac[ing] state regulation even though this serves to 'curtail or prohibit the States' prerogatives to make legislative choices respecting subjects the States may consider important.'"[80] The source of this congressional power is the Constitution's Supremacy Clause:

> This Constitution, and the Laws of the United States which shall be made in Pursuance thereof; and all Treaties made, or which shall be made, under the Authority of the United States, shall be the supreme Law of the Land; and the Judges in every State shall be bound thereby, any Thing in the Constitution or Laws of any State to the Contrary notwithstanding.[81]

The central role of congressional intent: The ultimate source of federal preemption is a federal statute. A federal statute can preempt state law directly, or it can authorize a federal agency to preempt.[82] Either preempting source—statute or agency—can act on state (and local) law in any of its forms: a state constitutional provision, a state statute, a state agency order, or a local ordinance or charter. Common to all preemption is Congress's intent to preempt.[83] Whether that intent exists, and its boundaries, is the core question in every preemption dispute. Congress's intent can reveal itself in one of three ways. The first is express language in the statute. The other two ways are implicit in the statute; they are known as "occupation of the field" preemption and "conflict" preemption. After explaining and illustrating these preemption paths, we discuss the court-made presumption against preemption.

12.B.2.a. Express preemption

Congress can preempt state law expressly (provided, of course, it is acting within its Commerce Clause powers). The Telecommunications Act of 1996 has two prominent examples. It expressly preempts (a) state laws preventing competition in telecommunications, and (b) state regulation of rates and entry for wireless telephony.[84]

---

80. FERC v. Mississippi, 456 U.S. at 759 (quoting Hodel v. Va. Surface Mining & Reclamation Ass'n, 452 U.S. at 290).

81. U.S. Const. art. VI, cl. 2. *See also* McCulloch v. Maryland, 17 U.S. (4 Wheat.) 316, 436 (1819) ("States have no power . . . to retard, impede, burden or in any manner control, the operations of the constitutional laws enacted by Congress to carry into execution the powers vested in the general government . . . .").

82. *See* La. Pub. Serv. Comm'n v. FCC, 476 U.S. 355, 368 (1986) ("Preemption may result not only from action taken by Congress itself; a federal agency acting within the scope of its congressionally delegated authority may pre-empt state regulation.").

83. *Id.* at 369 ("The critical question in any pre-emption analysis is always whether Congress intended that federal regulation supersede state law.").

84. *See* 47 U.S.C. § 253(a) ("No State or local statute or regulation, or other State or local legal requirement, may prohibit or have the effect of prohibiting the ability of any entity to provide any interstate or

12.B.2.b. Occupation of the field preemption

Absent explicit statutory language, Congress can demonstrate preemptive intent by crafting a "scheme of federal regulation . . . so pervasive as to make reasonable the inference that Congress left no room for the States to supplement it . . . ." This inference would be reasonable because either—

1. "the Act of Congress may touch a field in which the federal interest is so dominant that the federal system will be assumed to preclude enforcement of state laws on the same subject," or
2. "the object sought to be obtained by the federal law and the character of obligations imposed by it may reveal the same purpose."[85]

Field preemption felled a Michigan statute that required each "public utility" transporting gas within the state to get state commission approval before issuing securities. The Supreme Court viewed the federal field broadly, describing the Natural Gas Act as a "comprehensive scheme of federal regulation" that (a) granted FERC exclusive jurisdiction over the interstate transportation and sale of natural gas for resale and (b) gave FERC "a number of tools for examining and controlling the issuance of securities of natural gas companies in the exercise of its comprehensive authority." Those tools included ratemaking, accounting, issuances of certificates of public convenience and necessity, and authority to block self-dealing in a company's securities.

The state argued, accurately, that the Natural Gas Act gave FERC no express authority to regulate securities issuances. But the court found preemption anyway, by equating Michigan's review of securities with "regulation of . . . [pipelines'] rates and facilities," a task committed exclusively to FERC. The Court also saw a federal–state overlap in statutory purpose—to protect investors and consumers from "evils and injurious effects on the public of overcapitalization." State actions to prevent overcapitalization would affect the pipeline's rates—again FERC's exclusive domain. The state statute's other purpose—to allow for proper maintenance of pipeline facilities—is also exclusively FERC's. "In short, the things [the state statute] is directed at, the control of rates and facilities of natural gas companies, are precisely the things over which FERC has comprehensive authority . . . ."[86]

---

intrastate telecommunications service."); *see also* 47 U.S.C. § 332(c)(3)(A) ("[N]o State or local government shall have any authority to regulate the entry of or the rates charged by any commercial mobile service or any private mobile service . . . .").

85. Rice v. Santa Fe Elevator Corp., 331 U.S. 218, 230 (1947).
86. Schneidewind v. ANR Pipeline Co., 485 U.S. 293, 300–01, 308–10 (1988). The Court also saw potential for two types of conflict preemption (the subject of the next subsection): the state might deny a securities issuance necessary to finance a facility approved by FERC; and the state might order a change in the pipeline's capital structure, which would affect rates set by FERC.

The field preemption argument failed, however, when Pacific Gas & Electric challenged a 1976 California statute. The statute forbade the construction of additional nuclear plants unless the state found there were facilities and processes for storing and disposing of nuclear waste. The federal Atomic Energy Act did indeed occupy a field, the field of "radiological safety aspects involved in the construction and operation of a nuclear plant." But that field did not include the area of traditional state responsibility, specifically, "regulating electrical utilities for determining questions of need, reliability, cost, and other related state concerns." Applying the presumption that "the historic police powers of the States were not to be superseded by the Federal Act unless that was the clear and manifest purpose of Congress,"[87] the court found no such congressional purpose. Instead, Congress "has preserved the dual regulation of nuclear-powered electricity generation: the Federal Government maintains complete control of the safety and 'nuclear' aspects of energy generation; the States exercise their traditional authority over the need for additional generating capacity, the type of generating facilities to be licensed, land use, ratemaking, and the like."[88]

12.B.2.c. Conflict preemption

12.B.2.c.i. In general

Even if Congress has not occupied the field, a state law is preempted to the extent that it conflicts with federal law. A conflict arises when—

1. "compliance with both federal and state regulations is a physical impossibility,"[89] or

2. state law "stands as an obstacle to the accomplishment and execution of the full purposes and objectives of Congress."[90]

Congress can, but need not, specify subjects where conflict preemption will apply. Congress did so for electricity reliability. For most of the 20th century, the regulatory responsibility for electric reliability rested with state commissions applying quality of service principles.[91] In 2005 Congress created a federal regulatory role, by requiring FERC to certify an "electric reliability organization" with authority to set and enforce national and regional reliability standards subject to FERC review.[92] Congress did not want to preempt fully states' longstanding authority over service quality, but it did want consistent rules across

---

87. The presumption is discussed in Chapter 12.B.2.d below.
88. Pac. Gas & Elec. Co. v. State Energy Res. Conservation & Dev. Comm'n, 461 U.S. 190, 205–12 (1983).
89. Fla. Lime & Avocado Growers, Inc. v. Paul, 373 U.S. 132, 142–43 (1963).
90. Hines v. Davidowitz, 312 U.S. 52, 67 (1941).
91. See the discussion of quality of service in Chapter 2.D.
92. *See* Federal Power Act § 215, 16 U.S.C. § 824o. We detailed this federal reliability authority in Chapter 3.B.4, concerning quality of service.

the nation's interconnected electric system. The solution was a provision stating that the new statute did not "preempt any authority of any State to take action to ensure the safety, adequacy, and reliability of electric service within that State, as long as such action is not inconsistent with any [federal] reliability standard."[93]

Conflict preemption was also at issue when a Maryland state law prohibited a holding company from acquiring more than 10 percent of a utility's stock. This state law prohibited acquisitions that the federal Public Utility Holding Company Act permitted under certain circumstances. Baltimore Gas & Electric argued conflict preemption. The Fourth Circuit disagreed. The state law did not "frustrate" PUHCA's purpose. That purpose was not to facilitate the creation of utility holding companies (BGE's argument), but to restrain them. Given this purpose, Congress's decision not to ban all holding companies did not preempt states from banning so.[94]

12.B.2.c.ii. State review of retail utility purchases under FERC-jurisdictional contracts
No discussion of conflict preemption in utility regulation would be complete without addressing a long-controverted question: What happens when FERC and the state address different ends of the same wholesale transaction; specifically, when FERC approves a seller's wholesale contract with a retail utility as "just and reasonable," but the state commission disallows the retail utility's purchase cost under that contract as imprudent? In this long-controverted area, there are two lines of cases. One line is non-preemptive (i.e., the state is free to disallow the retail utility's costs) and the other line is preemptive (i.e., the state is preempted from disallowing the retail utility's costs). These two lines of cases are not themselves in conflict because they deal with two distinct fact patterns.

The non-preemptive line: In these cases, the retail-utility-as-wholesale-buyer, acting autonomously, purchases under a FERC-approved contract, but does so imprudently (e.g., the utility bought more than was prudent given that lower-priced alternatives were available). There is no preemption because the state's review of the utility's prudence is analytically distinct from FERC's approval of the seller's price. The leading case is *Kentucky West Virginia Gas Co. v. Pennsylvania Public Utilities Commission*.[95] The Pennsylvania Commission disallowed costs incurred by a retail gas utility purchasing under a FERC-approved contract. Rejecting the utility's preemption challenge, the court of appeals cited

---

93. *See* Federal Power Act § 215(i)(3). The provision adds this clause: "except that the State of New York may establish rules that result in greater reliability within that State, as long as such action does not result in lesser reliability outside the State than that provided by the reliability standards." If the reader will permit an opinion: This clause is best viewed as a superfluous result of one state's urging, because Congress could not have meant to prevent every state other than New York from establishing reliability rules that increase reliability above the federal standards.

94. Balt. Gas & Elec. Co. v. Heintz, 760 F.2d at 1416. The Public Utility Holding Company Act, which was repealed 2005, will be discussed in the companion volume on corporate structure, mergers and acquisitions.

95. 837 F.2d 600 (3d Cir. 1988).

the "long-standing notion that a State Commission may legitimately inquire into whether the retailer prudently chose to pay the FERC-approved wholesale rate of one source, as opposed to the lower rate of another source." The inquiry can occur "without impugning the reasonableness of the wholesale rate," because the state and FERC are doing different things:

> Since the question here of whether the retailer acted with economic prudence in purchasing from one wholesaler rather than another is never before FERC, the PUC is not regulating the same activity. Consequently we find no conflict between FERC's authority and that granted to the PUC [by the applicable state statute].[96]

FERC itself has made clear that determining the reasonableness of a retail utility's wholesale purchase decision is the job of the state commission, not FERC:

> The Commission's decisions and its longstanding practice in setting wholesale rates support the *Pike County* exception to the *Narragansett* doctrine. The Commission has consistently recognized that wholesale ratemaking does not, as a general matter, determine whether a purchaser has prudently chosen from among available supply options.[97]

FERC has made similar findings, in both electricity and gas cases, for more than thirty years.[98]

---

96. *Id.* at 609. Practitioners refer to this reasoning as the "*Pike County* doctrine," after *Pike County Light & Power Co. v. Pennsylvania Public Utility Commission*, 465 A.2d 735, 737–38 (Pa. Commw. Ct. 1983). This state court case, which preceded *Kentucky West Virginia*, applied the same reasoning in the context of a wholesale transaction between affiliates.

97. Central Vermont Public Service Corp., 84 FERC ¶ 61,194 (1998) (clarifying that FERC's approval of a wholesale rate schedule does not preclude the New Hampshire Commission from determining whether Connecticut Valley [the wholesale buyer and retail utility] acted imprudently purchasing from CVPS rather than using available lower-priced power). The "*Narragansett* doctrine" in FERC's passage refers to *Narragansett Electric Co. v. Burke*, 381 A.2d 1358 (R.I. 1977), a Rhode Island Supreme Court decision holding, unremarkably, that a state commission lacked authority to set a wholesale rate paid by its retail utility, because wholesale rates are exclusively FERC-jurisdictional.

98. *See, e.g.*, Philadelphia Electric Co., 15 FERC ¶ 61,264 (1981) (cautioning that "we did not mean by this order [accepting a wholesale contract] to prejudge, for our own purposes or those of the respective state commissions, a determination of the prudence of either party in entering into this transaction"); Southern Co. Services, Inc., 26 FERC ¶ 61,360 (1984) (the Commission "is not empowered to disapprove or modify a power sales agreement on the grounds that the buyer may not be making the best possible deal. . . . [T]he question of the prudence of a utility's power purchases is properly an issue in the buying utility's rate case where it seeks to pass the costs of its purchased power on to its ratepayers"); Southern Co. Services, Inc., 20 FERC ¶ 61,332 (1982) (same); Minnesota Power & Light Co., 43 FERC ¶ 61,104, at p. 61,342–43, *reh'g denied*, 43 FERC ¶ 61,502, *order denying reconsideration*, 44 FERC ¶ 61,302 (1988); Palisades Generating Co., 48 FERC ¶ 61,144, at p. 61,574 & n.10 (1989). In its Order No. 636 (relating to unbundling of pipeline transportation from gas commodity sales, as discussed in Chapter 3.A.2), FERC made clear that LDCs' actions in FERC-jurisdictional restructuring proceedings, including LDC agreements to absorb take-or-pay costs, could be subject to prudence challenges and disallowances in state commission proceedings. FERC Order No. 636, 57 Fed. Reg. 13,267, 13,308 & n.288 (Apr. 16,

Why is there no conflict when a state deems unreasonable a buyer's decision to purchase under a wholesale contract that FERC found reasonable? Because the retail-utility-as-wholesale-buyer had *autonomy*: the legal discretion to make the wholesale purchase that it made. The state commission is addressing whether the utility exercised that discretion prudently. There is no conflict with FERC authority because the question asked by FERC (Did the wholesale seller overcharge the wholesale buyer?) is different from the question asked by the state commission (Did the wholesale buyer buy imprudently?)[99]

The preemptive line: The preemptive line has a fact fundamentally different from the non-preemptive line: the buying utility's lack of discretion. Whereas in the non-preemptive line the buying utility had *autonomy* over its purchase decision (i.e., the legal discretion to choose among wholesale sources), in the preemptive line the buying utility *has no discretion* over the purchase decision (because its discretion was removed by a FERC order). If FERC has removed the utility's discretion over a decision, the utility cannot be found imprudent for making that decision. In these situations, state commissions that found (or were asked by interevenors to find) imprudence were preempted because their actions conflicted with the FERC-imposed constraints. The two leading cases are *Nantahala Power & Light Co. v. Thornburg* and *Mississippi Power & Light Co. v. Mississippi ex rel. Moore*.[100] Because the full factual picture was presented in prior chapters, a sketch here will suffice.[101]

In *Nantahala*, FERC modified a wholesale contract that allocated low-cost hydro-electric power between Alcoa's two subsidiaries, Nantahala (a retail utility) and Tapoco (an aluminum manufacturer). FERC allocated to Nantahala a 22.5 percent share. The North Carolina Commission then set Nantahala's retail rates as if FERC had allocated Nantahala a 24.5 percent share. Hydroelectric power being lower cost than Nantahala's other sources, the state commission's decision lowered the utility's retail rates (and thus

---

1992) (codified at 18 C.F.R. pt. 284) (citing Ky. W. Va. Gas Co. v. Pa. Pub. Utils. Comm'n, 837 F.2d 600, and Pike Cnty. Light & Power Co. v. Pa. Pub. Util. Comm'n, 465 A.2d 735).

99. The novice reader might be confused by one point: If the retail utility, when buying at wholesale, acted imprudently in choosing a higher-priced seller, there must have been available a lower-priced wholesale seller of comparable quality. If both those wholesale sellers are selling at prices regulated by FERC, how could FERC have found both prices "just and reasonable" for Federal Power Act purposes? The answer is that two different wholesale seller's prices can vary widely for multiple good reasons. Recall that under embedded cost-based ratemaking (Chapter 6), the rate base reflects the book value of the utility's plant. Book value is original cost less depreciation. Two generating plants, one five years old and one 25 years old, could produce power of equal quality, but the book value of the 25-year-old plant will have been reduced by 25 years of depreciation expense, so its associated embedded cost rate will be much lower. The prudent utility would choose the lower-priced source, not the higher-priced source, but both sources could have cost-based prices deemed just and reasonable by FERC.

100. Nantahala Power & Light Co. v. Thornburg, 476 U.S. 953 (1986); Miss. Power & Light Co. v. Miss. *ex rel.* Moore, 487 U.S. 354 (1988).

101. The *Nantahala* facts were detailed in Chapter 8.C.2 and 9.C (concerning discrimination and filed rate doctrine, respectively). The *Mississippi Power & Light* facts were detailed in Chapter 8.C.1, concerning discrimination in cost allocation on the Middle South multi-state holding company system. (The case discussed there was the D.C. Circuit decision in *Mississippi Industries*, but the U.S. Supreme Court in *Mississippi Power & Light* dealt with the same factual context.) In the *Mississippi Power & Light* case, the author filed an *amicus* brief with the Supreme Court on the side of the state.

the utility's cost recovery) below what they would have been had the North Carolina Commission honored FERC's allocation.

That was the state commission's error: it treated Nantahala as having the *discretion to buy* more hydroelectric power than the FERC-modified contract allowed. As the U.S. Supreme Court explained: "The fact that NCUC is setting retail rates does not give it license to ignore the limitations that FERC has placed upon Nantahala's available sources of low-cost power." By treating Nantahala as having more access to low-cost hydroelectric power than FERC allowed, the NCUC order resulted in "trapped cost":

> Because purchased power is more expensive than entitlement [hydroelectric] power, NCUC's order prevents Nantahala from recovering the full costs of acquiring power under the FERC-approved scheme: Nantahala must, under NCUC's order, calculate its retail rates as if it received more entitlement power than it does under FERC's order, and as if it needed to procure less of the more expensive purchased power than under FERC's order. A portion of the costs incurred by Nantahala in procuring its power is therefore trapped.[102]

As explained in Chapter 8.C.2, the state commission's failure to honor the FERC-ordered allocation violated the filed rate doctrine, which applies to the states through the Supremacy Clause. The state was preempted.

Mississippi Power & Light presented a high-cost version of the buyer-without-discretion situation. Mississippi Power & Light was one of four retail utility subsidiaries in the Middle South holding company system. For several decades, the system had conducted joint, centralized planning among the subsidiaries. ("Joint" meant that the object was to minimize power supply costs for system as a whole; "centralized" meant that final decisions on power supply and cost responsibility were made by the holding company, not the retail utilities.) The utility subsidiaries shared the costs of all system assets, under a System Agreement. For the Grand Gulf nuclear plant, the method for cost-sharing involved creating a wholesale generating company, Middle South Energy (MSE), which would own Grand Gulf. MSE would sell Grand Gulf's capacity and energy to each retail utility subsidiary, each one a wholesale buyer from MSE, under a FERC-jurisdictional contract. That contract allocated percentages of cost responsibility (along with rights to capacity and energy) among the four utilities.[103]

Middle South's history of central planning, long approved by FERC, necessarily eliminated the decisional autonomy of the retail utility subsidiaries. Their sole shareholder,

---

102.   Nantahala Power & Light Co. v. Thornburg, 476 U.S. 953, 970–71 (1986).
103.   The multi-state dispute over these percentages was the subject of the *Mississippi Industries* case discussed in Chapter 8.C.1, relating to undue discrimination. Grand Gulf thus left two distinct legal tracks: one on undue discrimination and the other on preemption.

the holding company, directed them to sign the agreement with MSE. Meanwhile, Grand Gulf's construction cost rose from an original estimate of $1.2 billion to an actual $3 billion. The Mississippi Attorney General, representing retail customers and upset by MP&L's large share of a large cost, asked the state commission to investigate MP&L's prudence in buying its share of Grand Gulf power. The state commission declined, citing preemption. When Mississippi Supreme Court reversed the state commission,[104] matters moved to the U.S. Supreme Court.

The U.S. Supreme Court reversed. It described Mississippi Power & Light as having been "ordered [by FERC] to . . . purchase" its FERC-designated share of Grand Gulf.[105] Having been "ordered" by FERC to purchase its share, MP&L had no choice but to do so. From this fact, the court reasoned that Mississippi Commission was preempted from investigating MP&L's prudence in purchasing its share. Any state disallowance for impru-dence would put MP&L in an impossible situation: being penalized by the state for doing what it was "ordered" to do by FERC. As with *Nantahala*, the state disallowance would conflict with the FERC-approved contract, in violation of the filed rate doctrine, a federal legal principle applied to the states through the Supremacy Clause.

The Supreme Court's reasoning in the preemptive case line can be capsulized this way:

1.   FERC has exclusive authority over wholesale rates, including the allocation of wholesale power.

2.   FERC used that authority to allocate entitlement to low-cost hydroelectric power *(Nantahala)* and responsibility for high-cost Grand Gulf nuclear power *(Missis-sippi Power and Light)*.

3.   The filed rate doctrine (explained in Chapter 9) entitles a seller to charge and receive the rate on file. That filed rate constrains courts and agencies, federal and state. The doctrine is a federal rule applicable to states through the Supremacy Clause.

4.   State ratemaking that disregards the FERC-approved rate on file conflicts with the federal decision, and therefore is preempted.[106]

---

104.   The Mississippi Supreme Court described MP&L as insisting that the Supremacy Clause "forces its unneeded power down the throats of Mississippi ratepayers." Mississippi v. Miss. Pub. Serv. Comm'n, 506 So. 2d 978 (1987), *rev'd*, Miss. Power & Light Co. v. Miss. *ex rel.* Moore, 487 U.S. 354 (1988).

105.   Miss. Power & Light Co. v. Miss. *ex rel.* Moore, 487 U.S. at 372–74. The word "ordered" requires some explanation. The Federal Power Act does not authorize FERC to "order" buyers to do anything. Under the relevant sections of the Act, sections 205 and 206, FERC regulates the actions of sellers, not buyers. I believe the Court used the term "ordered" to reflect the key fact: that MP&L's membership in a FERC-approved holding company system that used FERC-approved centralized planning techniques had no discretion to choose its power sources. Given MP&L's lack of discretion, the FERC decision to allocate a Grand Gulf share to MP&L is the logical and practical equivalent of "ordering" MP&L to take that share.

106.   *See* Miss. Power & Light Co. v. Miss. *ex rel.* Moore, 487 U.S. at 371–72 (citing Nantahala Power & Light Co. v. Thornburg, 476 U.S. at 963–66).

Uncertainties: This discussion has made clear that federal and state courts (*Kentucky West Virginia* and *Pike County*) and FERC (in *Central Vermont* and the other cited cases) see the two lines of cases as distinct and consistent. The U.S. Supreme Court, however, has not affirmed the reasoning underlying the non-preemption line, as evidenced by this passage from *Nantahala*:

> Without deciding this issue [i.e., whether states can disallow from a retail utility's rates costs that the utility incurs under a contract approved by FERC], we may assume that a particular *quantity* of power procured by a utility from a particular source could be deemed [by the state commission] unreasonably excessive if lower cost power is available elsewhere, even though the higher cost power actually purchased is obtained at a FERC-approved, and therefore reasonable, *price*.

But that assumption was inapplicable to Nantahala's situation:

> The North Carolina Supreme Court apparently felt that Nantahala procured an unreasonably large amount of purchased power in light of the availability of lower cost entitlement power. But Nantahala's procurement of purchased power is *not* unreasonably large given that Nantahala could not have treated itself as having access to any more low cost entitlement power than it is eligible to include under FERC's interpretation of what would be a fair allocation.[107]

12.B.2.d. The presumption against preemption

Overlaid on the three preemption paths (express, occupation of the field and conflict) is a principle with heavy relevance to utility regulation. Where the state law addresses a subject "traditionally occupied by the States 'we start with the assumption that the historic police powers of the States were not to be superseded by the Federal Act unless that was the clear and manifest purpose of Congress.'"[108] Congress frequently bolsters this presumption by including anti-preemption language, known as "state savings clauses." In this chapter we have already encountered several, such as Section 2(b) of the Communications Act of 1934, 47 U.S.C. § 152(b) (precluding FCC from regulating "intrastate communication service"), and Section 215(i)(3) of the Federal Power Act (preserving state authority over electricity reliability, to the extent "not inconsistent" with federal standards).

Two cautions about section 2(b): Recall that section 2(b) prevented the FCC from requiring state commissions to use FCC-prescribed depreciation practices when they set rates for

---

107. Nantahala Power & Light Co. v. Thornburg, 476 U.S. at 972–73 (emphasis in original).
108. Hillsborough Cnty. v. Automated Med. Labs., Inc., 471 U.S. 707, 715 (1985) (quoting Jones v. Rath Packing Co., 430 U.S. 519, 525 (1977)).

intrastate communications services.[109] But the provision has limits. First, section 2(b) does not limit the FCC when it is not possible to separate the interstate and intrastate components of a communication service. In the early 1970s, the FCC issued an order exercising jurisdiction over, and authorizing, "the connection and use of customer-provided terminal equipment with telephone company facilities for long-distance message communication." The order "unavoidably affect[ed] intrastate as well as interstate communication" because "[u]sually it is not feasible, as a matter of economics and practicality of operation, to limit the use of such equipment to either interstate or intrastate transmissions." As the FCC explained, "exchange plant, particularly subscriber stations and lines, is used in common and indivisibly for all local and long-distance telephone calls." In conflict with the FCC order, the North Carolina Commission proposed a rule prohibiting customer-provided equipment "except for use exclusively with facilities separate from those used in intrastate communication." The state commission then challenged the FCC's order as inconsistent with Section 2(b). The Fourth Circuit upheld the FCC. The court acknowledged that the savings clause ousts FCC jurisdiction over services, facilities and disputes "which in their nature and effect are separable from and do not substantially affect the conduct or development of interstate communications." But where the FCC has reasonably found that separability is not feasible, the savings clause must give way to the FCC's authority. There cannot be two conflicting rules governing the same equipment.[110]

Second, section 2(b)'s scope was narrowed by the 1996 amendments, which both (a) pre-empted state laws precluding competition in local telephone service; and (b) authorized the FCC to establish rules for promoting that competition. The FCC now has authority to (i) establish preemptive methodologies for pricing of unbundled services,[111] and (ii) preempt and "act for" a state commission that "fails to act to carry out its responsibilities concerning interconnection agreements."[112]

---

109.   La. Pub. Serv. Comm'n v. FCC, 476 U.S. at 373, 377 (finding, among other things, that: (1) section 2(b) contains both a "substantive jurisdictional limitation on the FCC's power, and a rule of statutory construction; and (2) the phrase in section 2(b)—"*nothing* in this chapter shall be construed to apply or to give the Commission jurisdiction" over intrastate service—overrides the specific grant to the FCC, in 47 U.S.C. § 220, of authority over depreciation.

110.   N.C. Utils. Comm'n v. FCC, 537 F.2d 787 (4th Cir. 1976). *See also* N.C. Utils. Comm'n v. FCC, 552 F.2d 1036 (4th Cir. 1977) (upholding the FCC's registration program implementing its policy authorizing customer-provided equipment); Computer & Commc'ns Indus. Ass'n v. FCC, 693 F.2d 198, 214–15 (D.C. Cir. 1982) (agreeing with Fourth Circuit and upholding FCC preemption of state regulation of intrastate customer premises equipment, including state-authorized bundling of CPE costs with charges for intrastate service, such state regulation being inconsistent with FCC policy of fostering competition in CPE markets).

111.   See the discussion of TELRIC in Chapter 4.B.4.b.

112.   47 U.S.C. § 252(e)(5). *See also* AT&T Corp. v. Iowa Utils. Bd., 525 U.S. at 385 (While the 1996 Act assigns states the job of reviewing and approving interconnection agreements, it does "not logically preclude the Commission's issuance of rules to guide the state-commission judgments."); *see id.* at 381 n.8 ("After the 1996 Act, § 152(b) may have less practical effect. But that is because Congress, by extending the Communications Act into local competition, has removed a significant area from the States' exclusive control.").

Caution: The presumption against preemption does not apply when the issue is the federal agency's authority to act: The presumption against preemption applies, naturally, when there is a preemption issue—that is, when the question is whether "a given state authority conflicts with, and thus has been displaced by, the existence of Federal Government authority." The presumption does not apply when the question is not preemption, but is instead whether the federal agency is acting within its statutory authority. New York cited the presumption in arguing that FERC did not have authority, in Order No. 888, to apply the non-discriminatory access requirement to unbundled transmission of retail sales. The Court rejected the argument as inapplicable.[113]

* * *

The federal–state jurisdictional relationship is guided by five legal sources: the positive Commerce Clause, dormant Commerce Clause, Tenth Amendment, Supremacy Clause and the agency's enabling statute. Figure 12 organizes the main cases discussed in this Chapter, according to the legal source that determined the outcome, and that outcome.

12.C. Regulating within the limits: Six models of federal–state interaction

The federal–state regulatory relationship is a statutory relationship bounded by constitutional principles. It is a statutory relationship because regulators, whether federal or state, can take only those actions authorized by statutes (except that some state commissions also draw some powers from their state constitutions). That statutory relationship then is bounded by federal constitutional principles because the U.S. Constitution limits the powers of both the federal and state governments, including each level's power to affect the other.

Within these limits, federal and state commissions interact in different ways, reflecting different congressional visions. The cases and statutes we have discussed reveal five categories of interaction: "bright line" divisions, federal regulator enlists state help, state regulator enlists federal help, joint boards, and regional bodies. A final category of federal–state relationship is that of no interaction; but rather, overlapping, non-cooperating jurisdiction.

12.C.1. Bright line divisions

In bright line divisions, the federal and state levels regulate different transactions (or the actions of different parties to the same transaction). Most of these bright lines are bright in words only; their practical blurriness has required agency and judicial

113. New York v. FERC, 535 U.S. at 18 (explaining that the presumption against preemption applies most often "when a controversy concerned not the scope of the Federal Government's authority to displace state action, but rather whether a given state authority conflicts with, and thus has been displaced by, the existence of Federal Government authority"). We discussed this case in Chapter 12.A.3.

Figure 12
The Federal–State Relationship: Powers and Limits

Congress's Commerce Powers

Federal Wins–State Loses	Federal Loses–State Wins
Federal regulation of farmers' in-state wheat production is permissible where such production, combined with all others similarly situated, has non-trivial effect on interstate commerce. (*Wickard v. Filburn*)	Federal ban on possessing gun in school zone is outside of Congress's Commerce powers because mere possession is not commerce. (*Lopez*)
Federal regulation of intrastate milk sales is permissible if they compete with interstate milk sales. (*Wrightwood Dairy*)	Federal mandate that individuals purchase health insurance is outside of Congress's Commerce powers because inactivity (non-purchase of insurance) is not commerce. (*National Federation of Independent Businesses*)
Federal regulation of small restaurants' racial discrimination is permissible where restaurant bought products in interstate commerce. (*McClung*)	
Federal regulation of in-state surface mining is permissible because (a) mining's environmental effects are interstate and (b) interstate competition among mining companies can undermine individual state efforts to improve coal mining standards. (*Virginia Surface Mining*)	
Congress can regulate intrastate loan sharking because it finances interstate organized crime. (*Perez*)	

Dormant Commerce Clause

State may not require in-state incorporation of utility holding company. (*Alliant v. Bie*)	State may require in-state incorporation of public utility serving in the state; burden is nondiscriminatory and justified by in-state benefit. (*Alliant v. Bie*)
State may not ban the export of hydropower produced in the state. (*New England Power v. New Hampshire*)	State may regulate non-utility investments by the corporate family of public utility serving in the state; burden is nondiscriminatory and justified by in-state benefit. (*Alliant v. Bie*)
State may not limit coal imports by requiring coal-burning utilities to use at least 10 percent in-state coal. (*Wyoming v. Okla*)	Exemption of LDCs from state sales tax on gas marketers is not unconstitutionally discriminatory because LDCs and marketers do not compete in the same market. (*General Motors v. Tracy*)
Ohio may not condition tax credits for sale of non-Ohio ethanol on whether the other state grants tax credits for sale of Ohio ethanol. (*New Energy Co. of Indiana*)	State may block import of bait if there is risk of irreversible harm from parasites, and there is no less discriminatory way to prevent the harm. (*Maine v. Taylor*)
Desire to incubate new industry or save struggling companies does not justify state tax scheme discriminating in favor of in-state product. (*Bacchus Imports*)	State may discriminate against interstate commerce when acting as a "market participant." (*Hughes v. Alexander Scrap; Reeves v. Stake*)
Requirement that fruit grower erect packaging operation in-state is not justified by states' interest in having its reputation enhanced by grower's high quality product. (*Pike v. Bruce Church*)	

Tenth Amendment

Federal Wins-State Loses

Congress may require state commissions to establish prices and adjudicate disputes under federal rules concerning utility obligations to buy electricity from federally certified "qualifying facilities." (*FERC v. Mississippi*)

Federal law preempting states from establishing mining standards less stringent than federal standards does not invade state prerogatives. (*Virginia Surface Mining*)

Federal Loses-State Wins

Congress may not force states to (a) regulate disposal of nuclear waste according to federal criteria or, (b) take title to the waste. (*New York v. U.S.*)

Supremacy Clause

Federal Wins-State Loses

Where FERC requires wholesale buyer to accept specified cost allocation, state is preempted from setting retail rates as if buyer had discretion to accept a different cost allocation. (*Nantahala, Mississippi Power & Light*)

Natural Gas Act preempts states from regulating securities issuances of gas pipelines; Congress has occupied the field. (*Schneidewind*)

Congress authorized FCC to establish the methods by which states must price unbundled services. (*AT&T v. Iowa Utils. Bd.*)

FCC has power to preempt state rules on customer premises equipment. (*NCUC v. FCC*)

Federal Loses-State Wins

FERC's decision that seller's wholesale price is "just and reasonable" does not preempt state commission from finding that retail utility's purchase from that seller was imprudent. There is no conflict preemption because the FERC and states are regulating different actions. (*Kentucky West Virginia; Pike County*)

State may ban corporate structures that the federal statute (PUHCA, now repealed) allowed. There is no conflict preemption because Congress intended to restrict, not encourage, holding company structures. (*BG&E v. Heintz*)

State law prohibiting construction of nuclear plants, until state agency found that facilities and processes for storing waste were sufficient, was not preempted by the Atomic Energy Act. The federal Act addressed safety; the state law addressed economics. (*Pacific Gas & Electric v. State Energy Resources*)

Due to federal statute's state savings clause, states were not required to use FCC-prescribed depreciation practices when setting rates for intrastate communications services. (*Louisiana Public Serv. Comm'n v. FCC*)

Federal Agency's Statutory Powers

Federal Wins-State Loses

FERC has power to regulate unbundled transmission service in interstate commerce. (*New York v. FERC*)

FCC has power to set rules for dialing parity in local phone service; FCC's general rulemaking authority overcame statute's state savings clause. (*AT&T v. Iowa Utils. Bd.*)

FCC has exclusive jurisdiction to set rules for area codes, notwithstanding federal statute's state savings clause. (*Calif. v. FCC*)

Federal Loses-State Wins

FERC has no power to change RTO's Board of Directors. (*Calif. Indep. Sys. Op.*)

clarification. Three examples of such divisions are interstate–intrastate, retail–wholesale and bundled–unbundled.

12.C.1.a. Interstate–intrastate

As we have seen, the Communications Act of 1934 grants comprehensive regulatory powers to the FCC, but through 47 U.S.C. § 152(b)(1) denies the FCC jurisdiction over "intrastate communication service." This boundary is not always clear-cut, as demonstrated by the previously discussed cases on dialing parity, numbering administration, customer premises equipment and local telephone service. When interstate and intrastate services are not separable (e.g., customer premises equipment), or when Congress has explicitly granted FCC authority affecting intrastate service (e.g., numbering administration, oversight of development of local competition), the bright line goes away.

Both the Federal Power Act and the Natural Gas Act grant FERC jurisdiction over transactions in "interstate commerce" but deny jurisdiction over intrastate transactions. Thus section 201(b)(1) of the FPA provides:

> The provisions of this Part shall apply to the transmission of electric energy in interstate commerce and to the sale of electric energy at wholesale in interstate commerce . . . . The Commission shall have jurisdiction over all facilities for such transmission or sale of electric energy, but shall not have jurisdiction . . . over facilities used in local distribution or only for the transmission of electric energy in intrastate commerce, or over facilities for the transmission of electric energy consumed wholly by the transmitter."[114]

Similarly, the Natural Gas Act grants FERC exclusive jurisdiction over

> the transportation of natural gas in interstate commerce, to the sale in interstate commerce of natural gas for resale for ultimate public consumption for domestic, commercial, industrial, or any other use, and to natural-gas companies engaged in such transportation or sale, but [FERC's jurisdiction] shall not apply to any other transportation or sale of natural gas or to the local distribution of natural gas or to the facilities used for such distribution or to the production or gathering of natural gas.[115]

---

114. 16 U.S.C. § 824(b)(1).
115. *See* 15 U.S.C § 717(b). The Natural Gas Act then expressly exempts from FERC jurisdiction "any person engaged in or legally authorized to engage in the transportation in interstate commerce or the sale in interstate commerce for resale, of natural gas received by such person from another person within or at the boundary of a State if all the natural gas so received is ultimately consumed within such State, or to any facilities used by such person for such transportation or sale, provided that the rates and service of such person and facilities be subject to regulation by a State commission." 15 U.S.C. § 717(c). This exclusion of intrastate transactions has led to the label "Hinshaw pipeline," referring to a natural gas pipeline that "receives all of its out-of-state gas from persons 'within or at the boundary of a [s]tate if all the natural gas so received is ultimately consumed' within the state in which it is received.'"

The Federal Power Act's distinction between "interstate" and "intrastate" regularly confuses the newcomer. The accepted view today is that any transmission or sale of electric energy within the interconnected United States is in "interstate commerce," even if the transaction's contractual origin and destination are within a single state.[116] The jurisdictional effect is that all wholesale sales and unbundled transmission service are subject to the Federal Power Act—unless they occur within Alaska, Hawaii, or the majority of Texas that is not interconnected with other states.[117]

12.C.1.b. Retail–wholesale

The Federal Power Act assigns to FERC jurisdiction over the "sale of electric energy at wholesale" (in interstate commerce), while denying FERC jurisdiction over "any other sale" of electric energy.[118] The effect is to leave retail sales to the states. Similarly, the Natural Gas Act grants FERC authority over "the sale in interstate commerce of natural gas for resale for ultimate public consumption" (as well as the "transportation of natural gas in interstate commerce").[119]

Consumers Energy Co. v. FERC, 226 F.3d 777 (6th Cir. 2000) (quoting 15 U.S.C. § 717(c)). Sales by Hinshaw pipelines are regulated by state commissions, not by FERC. But these pipelines become subject to FERC jurisdiction if they "engage in activities that go beyond the intrastate transport of gas." Pub. Utils. Comm'n of Cal. v. FERC, 143 F.3d 610, 615 (D.C. Cir. 1998).

116. *See* FPC v. Fla. Power & Light Co., 404 U.S. 453 (1972). Florida Power and Light Company and Florida Power Corporation were members of the Florida Power Pool. Florida Power Corp. connected with Georgia Power Company (Georgia Power) at a "bus" south of the Georgia-Florida border. (A "bus" is a connector or group of connectors that serves as a common connection for two or more circuits.) Florida Power Corp. regularly exchanged power with Georgia Power. Based on these facts, the Federal Power Commission had found that FP&L transmitted power to FPC's "bus," and that this power was simultaneously transferred from the "bus" to a Georgia utility. The Commission thus found that the transactions between the two Florida utilities were in "interstate commerce" for purposes of the Federal Power Act. The Supreme Court affirmed. Because electrons, commingled in the bus, moved across state lines, Florida Power & Light engaged in transmission in interstate commerce. As a result, Commission jurisdiction attached to the contractual transactions within Florida. *See also* New York v. FERC, 535 U.S. at 16 ("transmissions on the interconnected national grids constitute transmissions in interstate commerce") (citing FPC v. Fla. Power & Light Co.).

117. The Texas story, well-known to industry insiders, would take many paragraphs to explain. For a glimpse, read the "midnight wiring" case, *West Texas Utilities Co. and Central Power and Light Co. v. Texas Electric Service Company and Houston Lighting and Power Company*, 470 F. Supp. 798 (N.D. Tex. 1979). This one-of-a-kind opinion describes TESCO's and HLP's efforts to "ensure freedom from federal regulation." Their only option was "not to operate interconnected with any facility used for the transmission or sale of electricity in interstate commerce." West Texas Utilities was desperate to interconnect with its Oklahoma affiliate, to avoid SEC-ordered divestiture due to its holding company's decades-long failure to obey the Public Utility Holding Company Act's command to operate as a single "integrated public-utility system." (Subsidiaries can't operate as a single integrated public utility system if they are not interconnected with each other.) WTU executed a "secret and clandestine maneuver," in the darkness of May 4, 1976, to "perform[] a midnight wiring of electrical circuits charged with 69,000 volts of electricity" between WTU and its Oklahoma affiliate. The effect was to plunge most of Texas (and its utilities) into interstate commerce. With this action, WTU "maliciously and willfully violated its long standing agreement" with other Texas utilities by "forc[ing them] into interstate operations without [their] voluntary consent."

118. 16 U.S.C. § 824(b)(1).

119. 15 U.S.C. § 717(b).

In earlier times, the courts had viewed wholesale–retail and interstate–intrastate distinctions as synonymous for Commerce Clause purposes. This view meant that a state could not regulate wholesale transactions because they were necessarily interstate, and thus denied to states by the Commerce Clause. This view left a gap in regulation because the Federal Power Act exempts wholesale sales by government-owned systems and certain rural cooperatives. The Supreme Court fixed this problem when the Arkansas Commission sought to regulate a rural cooperative's in-state wholesale sales. Applying the dormant Commerce Clause's balancing test, the Court focused on "'the nature of the state regulation involved, the objective of the state, and the effect of the regulation upon the national interest in the commerce,'" to find that the state's interest in regulating wholesale rates within their borders justified the burdens on commerce.[120]

The bright line wholesale–retail division can result in FERC and state addressing the same factual issue but reaching different results. Consider an electric utility serving both retail and wholesale customers, where retail customers comprise 90 percent of the company's load and wholesale customers 10 percent. Suppose the company builds a nuclear plant whose capacity will serve both sets of customers. It will seek retail rate recovery of 90 percent of the plant's costs from its retail regulators and 10 percent from FERC. The state could find that the company's construction decisions were imprudent, leading to $100 million in total excess costs, while FERC finds no imprudence. The state would disallow $90 million (90 percent of $100 million) from retail rates, while FERC would disallow no dollars. There is no preemption because the state is acting within its exclusive retail jurisdiction. While the factual issue is the same, the transactions are different: FERC is regulating the wholesale sale; the state is regulating the retail sale. (Contrast the discussion of concurrent jurisdiction (Chapter 12.C.6 below), where the two regulatory levels address the same corporate restructuring transaction.)

12.C.1.c. Bundled–unbundled

In the electric industry, transmission facilities carry electric current. When that transportation function is bundled with retail power (meaning that the retail customer buys electric service—the coffee and the coffee cup together), the transmission cost is a component of the retail revenue requirement, all of which is subject to state jurisdiction exclusively. But recall Order No. 888, from Chapter 3.A.1. It required transmission owners to provide transmission service unbundled (meaning, available for sale separately) from electric energy. That unbundling obligation applies to the transmission of wholesale electricity

---

120.   Ark. Elec. Coop. Corp. v. Ark. Pub. Serv. Comm'n, 461 U.S. at 390–91, 394–95 (quoting Ill. Natural Gas Co. v. Cent. Ill. Pub. Serv. Co., 314 U.S. 498, 505 (1942)). Another necessary result of the Court's decision to render the wholesale–retail distinction irrelevant to the Commerce Clause is to subject state regulation to the Commerce Clause. *See* Gen. Motors Corp. v. Tracy, 519 U.S. at 291 (finding that "state regulation of retail sales is not, as a constitutional matter, immune from our ordinary Commerce Clause jurisprudence").

and retail electricity (the latter only if the state has authorized competition in retail electricity). FERC then found, in Order No. 888, that this unbundled transmission service is a FERC-jurisdictional service, even when the transmission is of retail power. That was the finding upheld by the Supreme Court in *New York v. FERC*.[121]

12.C.1.d. Transmission–distribution

The Federal Power Act grants FERC exclusive authority over the "transmission of electric energy in interstate commerce," but not over "facilities used in local distribution."[122] The line between "transmission" and "local distribution" is bright in terms of legal language but required some pencil-sharpening for purposes of industry practice. To add the necessary clarity, FERC's Order No. 888 developed a seven-factor test to distinguish "transmission" from "local distribution."[123]

Notice the word "local" in the statutory phrase "local distribution." Since every statutory word counts,[124] if there is "local distribution" there must be non-local distribution. And there is. FERC has stated that the transportation of wholesale power, over lines which would otherwise be labeled "distribution," is subject to FERC jurisdiction. Thus a particular "distribution" facility can play two jurisdictional roles: when it carries bundled retail power, it is "local distribution" excluded from FERC's jurisdiction; when it carries wholesale power, it is "non-local" distribution that is subject to FERC's jurisdiction.[125]

---

121.   535 U.S. 1 (2002). The case is discussed in Chapter 12.B.2.d.

122.   Federal Power Act § 201(b)(1), 16 U.S.C. § 824(b)(1).

123.   The seven factors are

   1. Local distribution facilities are normally in close proximity to retail customers.
   2. Local distribution facilities are primarily radial in character.
   3. Power flows into local distribution systems; it rarely, if ever, flows out.
   4. When power enters a local distribution system, it is not reconsigned or transported on to some other market.
   5. Power entering a local distribution system is consumed in a comparatively restricted geographical area.
   6. Meters are based at the transmission/local distribution interface to measure flows into the local distribution system.
   7. Local distribution systems will be of reduced voltage.

   FERC Order No. 888, 61 Fed. Reg. 21,540, at text accompanying n.517 (May 10, 1996) (codified at 18 C.F.R. pts. 35 & 385).

124.   Bailey v. United States, 516 U.S. 137, 146 (1995) ("[W]e assume that Congress used two terms because it intended each term to have a particular, nonsuperfluous meaning."); Montclair v. Ramsdell, 107 U.S. 147, 152 (1883) (courts should "give effect, if possible, to every clause and word of a statute, avoiding . . . any construction which implies that the legislature was ignorant of the meaning of the language it employed").

125.   *See* California Pacific Electric Co., 133 FERC ¶ 61,018, at p. 40 (2010) ("when a local distribution facility is used in a wholesale transaction, we have jurisdiction over that [distribution] transaction") (citing FERC Order No. 2003, 104 FERC ¶ 61,103, at p. 804 (2004)).

12.C.1.e. Local distribution and bulk power system

Yet another bright line distinction involves facilities subject to federal reliability standards. Section 215 of the Federal Power Act established federal regulation over actions that affect the reliability of the "bulk power system." The statutory definition lacked a bright line.[126] FERC now has created one. It has placed within the bulk power system category all facilities operated at or above 100 kV, and created a process for case-by-case exceptions.[127]

12.C.2. Federal enlists state

Our discussion of the Tenth Amendment (Chapter 12.A.2) showed that Congress may, consistent with the Tenth Amendment, enlist states' adjudicatory machinery to carry out a federal policy. Recall that section 210 of the Public Utility Regulatory Policies Act of 1978 (PURPA) requires states to administer the process by which utilities make mandatory purchases from "qualifying facilities," including establishing the rates for those sales.[128] The Telecommunications Act of 1996 required states to oversee the arbitrations that set the terms and conditions by which CLECs accessed the ILEC-owned bottleneck facilities and services necessary to compete in local telephone markets.[129]

Another state-helps-federal situation, one not rooted in an explicit statutory provision, is where a state decision becomes an input to a federal decision. When FERC approved the proposed vertical merger between San Diego Gas & Electric and Enova Energy, it included a condition requiring the merged company's compliance with the California Commission's rules on affiliate relations.[130] And FERC has stated that the normal presumption of prudence accorded a utility disappears, shifting the burden of going forward to the utility, if a state commission has found imprudence.[131]

---

126.   Section 215(a)(1) provides:

> (1) The term "bulk-power system" means—
> (A) facilities and control systems necessary for operating an interconnected electric energy transmission network (or any portion thereof); and
> (B) electric energy from generation facilities needed to maintain transmission system reliability.
> The term does not include facilities used in the local distribution of electric energy.

Federal Power Act § 215(a)(1). More discussion of FERC's reliability jurisdiction appears in Chapter 3.B.4.
127.   Revisions to Electric Reliability Organization Definition of Bulk Electric System and Rules of Procedure, 141 FERC ¶ 61,236 (2012).
128.   See the discussion of PURPA in Chapter 3.A.1. *See also* FERC v. Mississippi, 456 U.S. 742, discussed in Chapter 12.A.2.
129.   *See supra* Chapter 3.A.3. *See also* 47 U.S.C. § 251; Verizon Commc'ns, Inc. v. FCC, 535 U.S. 467 (2002).
130.   San Diego Gas & Electric Co. & Enova Energy, Inc., 79 FERC ¶ 61,372 (1997), *order denying reh'g*, 85 FERC ¶ 61,037 (1998).
131.   *See supra* Chapter 6.C.5, and Southern California Edison Co., 8 FERC ¶ 61,198, at p. 61,680 (1980) (shifting burden of going forward to utility, due to state commission's finding of imprudence; utility had offered FERC only "vague generalizations about the problems inherent in all building projects"), *aff'd sub nom.* Anaheim v. FERC, 669 F.2d 799 (D.C. Cir. 1981).

There is a difference, however, between (a) using a state finding as input to a federal decision, and (b) delegating a federal responsibility to a state agency. The 1996 Act provides that in "determining" which ILEC elements must be unbundled and provided to CLECs, the FCC must "consider, at a minimum, whether . . . the failure to provide access to such network elements would *impair the ability* of the telecommunications carrier seeking access to provide the services that it seeks to offer."[132] After several court-reversed attempts to complete this task,[133] the FCC said it would make nationwide findings on "impairment" based on such factors as "specific services, specific geographic locations, the different types and capacities of facilities, and customer and business considerations." It also authorized states to create exclusions from the FCC's nationwide findings. The court of appeals declared this authorization to the states to be unlawful, because the Act did not authorize subdelegation. Subdelegation to a subordinate within the agency enjoys a presumption of lawfulness absent contrary congressional intent, but subdelegation to a third party requires affirmative congressional authorization. The problem is one of accountability: "When an agency delegates authority to its subordinate, responsibility—and thus accountability—clearly remain with the federal agency. But when an agency delegates power to outside parties, lines of accountability may blur, undermining an important democratic check on government decision-making."[134]

12.C.3. State enlists federal

In some unusual situations, a state commission can enlist federal help. An example is FERC's merger policy. When processing electricity merger requests, FERC's competition review focuses on wholesale markets only, but it will address the merger's effect on retail competition if a "state lacks authority under state law and asks us to do so."[135]

A complex variant on the state-enlists-federal relationship, unique to the Federal Power Act, is the question of whether a state can order a utility to make a filing with FERC. In the one case addressing this subject, the court of appeals found the state preempted. Western Massachusetts Electric Company (WMECO) was one of three retail utility subsidiaries of Northeast Utilities. Two subsidiaries served in Massachusetts and one in Connecticut. A FERC-jurisdictional, wholesale power supply agreement, signed by all three subsidiaries, allocated power supply costs among them.[136] The Massachusetts Commission, dissatis-

---

132. 47 U.S.C. § 251(d)(2) (emphasis added).
133. A partial history of these attempts appears in *United States Telecom Ass'n v. FCC*, 359 F.3d 554 (D.C. Cir. 2004).
134. *Id.* at 565.
135. FERC Order No. 642, 65 Fed. Reg. 70,984, at text accompanying nn.33 & 34 (Nov. 28, 2000). *See also id.* at text accompanying n.94 (FERC does not "intend to address regulatory evasion concerns that affect retail electricity prices unless a state lacks adequate authority to consider such matters and requests us to do so.").
136. We saw other examples of interaffiliate power supply allocations in the *Mississippi Power & Light* and *Nantahala* cases, discussed at Chapter 12.B.2.c.ii.

fied with how the agreement charged costs to WMECO (who recovered those costs from Massachusetts retail customers), directed the utility to file a rate change at FERC under section 205 of the Federal Power Act. The court found the state action preempted, because the Federal Power Act envisions only voluntary filings:

> Like most traditional regulatory schemes, the two provisions together [referring to sections 205 and 206] allow the utility the choice among various reasonable rate practices. Unless the Commission can prove that an existing rate practice is unreasonable, the utility's previously filed rate practice may remain in effect. Similarly, the utility may change any rate practice so long as it can prove that the proposed change is reasonable. To accept Massachusetts' claim that [§] 205 includes "regulator-compelled" utility-proposed changes would prevent the utility from choosing among reasonable rate-practice alternatives.

The problem was that the filing would allocate costs from Massachusetts to other states. The court worried that reading the statute to allow such state-directed actions "threatens confusion, possibly chaos":

> What is to prevent each state in a multistate service area from requiring the utility to file a different set of "reasonable" rate practices with FERC? Neither law nor economics can identify one unique set of rates or practices as reasonable, . . . and each state would prefer a rate structure that benefitted its residents to the detriment of its neighbors. . . . FERC perhaps could sort out consequent confusions, but requiring it to do so has a procedural cost; in addition, the accompanying uncertainty could raise capital costs to the detriment of the very consumer whom the regulatory statute seeks to protect.[137]

Given the preempting statute's idiosyncrasies (in particular the relationship between sections 205 and 206 referred to in the court's opinion), it is unclear whether there is a more general principle against a state ordering its utility to make federal filings, at least where the purpose and effect is not to shift costs to other states.

States can avoid Massachusetts's preemptive fate if the utility agrees to make the state-sought filing. (WMECO made the Massachusetts-directed filing at FERC under protest.[138]) The Southwest Power Pool (SPP) (a regional transmission organization that is a "public utility" under the Federal Power Act[139]) has agreed to make filings at FERC as directed by its "Regional State Committee," an organization consisting of commissions from the states whose utilities are members of SPP. The SPP reserves its Federal Power Act right to

---

137. Massachusetts v. United States, 729 F.2d 886, 887–88 (1st Cir. 1984) (opinion by Judge, now Justice, Breyer).
138. *See* Western Massachusetts Electric Co., 23 FERC ¶ 61,025 (1983).
139. *See* Chapters 2.F.5 and 3.A.1 for a discussion of regional transmission organizations.

make its own filings, thus setting up the possibility that FERC could receive two compet-ing filings from the same utility.[140]

Another example is the Vermont Public Service Board's state statutory authority to arbi-trate transmission disputes (which are exclusively FERC-jurisdictional, because Vermont is part of the interconnected U.S.—*see* Chapter 12.C.1.a), *if* the transmission owner's tariff provides for that arbitration.[141] In other words, a FERC-jurisdictional entity can commit to file at FERC the result of a state-run arbitration. FERC would not be bound by the Vermont Board's decision, however, because a federal agency cannot delegate its authority to a third party absent clear congressional intent.[142]

12.C.4. Joint boards

The Communications Act, the Federal Power Act and the Natural Gas Act all provide for joint federal–state boards.

The FCC can refer to a Federal–State Joint Board "any matter arising in the adminis-tration" of the Communications Act."[143] The Board has the powers of a hearing examiner, meaning it can make recommendations to the Commission but cannot bind it. Its mem-bers are appointed by the FCC and include commissioners from the FCC and the states. In addition to authorizing discretionary use of a Joint Board, the Act requires the FCC to form a Board, and take into account its recommendations, when—

1. defining the parameters of universal service (in which case the Joint Board also includes a consumer advocate);[144] or

2. addressing the "separation" of common carrier property and expenses between interstate and intrastate service.[145]

---

140. Section 7.2 of the SPP's Bylaws (which are part of its FERC-approved transmission tariff), authorizes the creation of a "Regional State Committee." The provision describes the RSC's responsibility for develop-ing proposals on transmission pricing and cost recovery, including the allocation of costs among users and among states. The tariff then states:

    As the RSC reaches decisions on the methodology that will be used to address any of these issues, SPP will file this methodology pursuant to Section 205 of the Federal Power Act. However, noth-ing in this section prohibits SPP from filing its own related proposal(s) pursuant to Section 205 of the Federal Power Act.

    SOUTHWEST POWER POOL, GOVERNING DOCUMENTS TARIFF 76, *available at* http://www.spp.org/publica-tions/2010-11-30_Bylaws%20and%20Membership%20Agreement%20Tariff.pdf. SPP thus has agreed, with FERC's approval, to make filings as directed by this group of states.

141. *See* VT. STAT. ANN. tit. 30, § 214(b) ("The board shall have authority to arbitrate disputes between or among users or prospective users of transmission facilities located within the state, where such disputes arise under any agreement or under any state or federal tariff relating to the provision of or entitlements to transmission services and providing for arbitration by the board . . . .").

142. *See* U.S. Telecom Ass'n v. FCC, 359 F.3d at 565, and the discussion at Chapter 12.C.2 above.

143. 47 U.S.C. § 410(a).

144. 47 U.S.C. § 254(a)(1).

145. 47 U.S.C. § 410(c).

Besides these specific Joint Board obligations, the FCC has created and convened a Federal–State Joint Conference on Advanced Services.[146]

The Federal Power Act also provides for a joint board. Section 209(a) authorizes FERC to refer "any matter" arising under Part II of the Act (16 U.S.C. §§ 824 et seq.) to a board consisting of members from affected states. The members would be appointed by FERC from persons nominated by state commissions or their governors. The board would not have FERC's full decisionmaking powers; it "shall be vested with the same power and be subject to the same duties and liabilities as in the case of a member of the Commission when designated by the Commission to hold any hearings."[147] Unlike the FCC, FERC has not used a section 209 joint board in modern times.[148]

12.C.5. Regional compacts

An interstate compact can be approved by Congress under the Constitution's Compact Clause.[149] Despite the nation's many multi-state utility systems and markets, and the resulting overlaps between federal and state regulation, use of compacts has been limited.

One compact in continuous use is that among Idaho, Montana, Oregon and Washington. It was authorized by the Pacific Northwest Electric Power Planning and Conservation Act of 1980.[150] The Act's purposes include encouraging "conservation and efficiency in the use of electric power" and "the development of renewable resources within the Pacific Northwest," so as to assure "the Pacific Northwest of an adequate, efficient, economical, and reliable power supply" and to "protect, mitigate, and enhance fish and wildlife." The Act authorized the four states to form the Pacific Northwest Electric Power and Conservation Planning Council, consisting of two representatives from each state appointed by their governors. The Council is obligated to adopt a "regional energy conservation and electric power plan" for meeting the region's electricity needs cost-effectively. The Plan must give highest priority to energy conservation, then renewable sources, then "generating resources utilizing waste heat or generating resources of high fuel conversion efficiency"; and then, to "all other resources." The Council adopted its first plan in 1983. Its "Sixth

---

146.   *See* FED. COMMC'NS COMM'N, FCC ENCYCLOPEDIA, FEDERAL–STATE JOINT CONFERENCE ON ADVANCED TELECOMMUNICATIONS SERVICES, *available at* http://www.fcc.gov/encyclopedia/federal-state-joint-conference-advanced-telecommunications-services. This Joint Conference is "part of the Commission's ongoing efforts to ensure that advanced services are deployed as rapidly as possible to all Americans. It serves as a forum for an ongoing dialogue among the Commission, state regulators, and local and regional entities regarding the deployment of advanced telecommunications capabilities." *Id.*

147.   A similar provision appears in the Natural Gas Act, 15 U.S.C. § 717p.

148.   *But see* State-Federal Regional RTO Panels, RTO Informational Filings, 97 FERC ¶ 61,182 (Nov. 9, 2001) (authorizing "State-Federal regional panels" to discuss issues related to regional transmission organizations).

149.   The U.S. Constitution provides: "No State shall, without the consent of Congress, . . . enter into any Agreement or Compact with another State . . . ." U.S. CONST. art. I, § 10, cl. 3.

150.   Pacific Northwest Electric Power Planning and Conservation Act of 1980, Pub. L. No. 96-501, 94 Stat. 2697 (codified at 16 U.S.C. §§ 839–839h).

Northwest Conservation and Electric Power Plan" was issued in February 2010.[151] Unlike the joint boards under the Communications Act, the Natural Gas Act, and the Federal Power Act (which can make only non-binding recommendations), the Northwest Council has substantive power, in this sense: All actions of the Bonneville Power Administration (an agency of the U.S. Government and the region's largest power supplier and transmission owner) must be consistent with the plan (subject to certain exceptions).[152]

Another existing compact possibility, not yet used, relates to the siting of electric transmission facilities. In 2005, Congress was concerned that individual states could block transmission projects that traversed their boundaries but had regional or national benefits. The result was section 216 of the Federal Power Act. It provides a path by which FERC can issue to a project developer a permit to use eminent domain authority, preemptive of state law. The permit is available only for transmission in an area designated by the Department of Energy as a "national interest electric transmission corridor," and only after FERC has made a series of public interest findings. The Applicant also must show that a state has (a) "withheld approval" for more than a year, (b) lacks authority to act, (c) or has conditioned its approval such that "the proposed construction or modification will not significantly reduce transmission congestion in interstate commerce or is not economically feasible."[153]

States can preclude a preemptive permit by creating a compact under Section 216(i). To qualify, three or more contiguous states must establish a "regional transmission siting agency" to "(A) facilitate siting of future electric energy transmission facilities within those States; and (B) carry out the electric energy transmission siting responsibilities of those States." If such a compact exists, FERC "shall have no authority to issue a permit for the construction or modification of an electric transmission facility within a State that is a party to a compact, unless (a) the members of the compact are in disagreement" and (b) the Department of Energy makes the finding described in section 216(b)(1)(C) (relating to a state lacking authority or withholding approval for a year or excessively conditioning approval). No transmission applicant has yet sought a FERC permit, and thus no states have formed an interstate transmission siting agency.

---

151. *See* Northwest Power & Conservation Council, Sixth Northwest Power and Conservation Plan (2010), *available at* http://www.nwcouncil.org/energy/powerplan/6/final/SixthPowerPlan.pdf.

152. 16 U.S.C. § 839b(a)–(d). For thoughts on applying the regional planning concept to other regions, see Robert Marritz, The Case for Regional Power Planning Councils (ElectricityPolicy.com, Sept. 2010), *available at* http://www.electricitypolicy.com/archives/2527-the-case-for-regional-power-planning-councils.

153. *See* Federal Power Act § 216(b), 16 U.S.C. § 824p. The details of section 216 are discussed in Chapter 2.E, relating to eminent domain. As explained there, the Fourth Circuit has interpreted the phrase "withheld approval" to mean failing to act only; it rejected the FERC view that "withheld approval" includes rejecting an application. The result of the Fourth Circuit decision is that if a state rejects an application within the twelve-month period, FERC has no authority to issue a preemptive permit.

12.C.6. Overlapping jurisdiction

The previous five subsections addressed jurisdictional relationships in which the federal and state levels play distinct roles, either (a) in the same market (such as states administering PURPA pursuant to FERC rules, or states resolving interconnection arbitrations pursuant to FCC rules); or (b) in the same transaction (such as states addressing the retail rate recovery of a utility's wholesale purchase while FERC addresses the wholesale rate charged for that purchase).

Mergers and acquisitions present a sixth category. When these reorganizations trigger both state and federal jurisdictions, both levels examine the same transaction. Their jurisdictions overlap, and there is no preemption. No statutory language in the Communications Act, the Federal Power Act or the Natural Gas Act suggests preemption, and no court has ever found preemption. A merger applicant seeking approval from FERC and seven states must get a "yes" from all eight fora.[154]

* * *

Our utility industries face two levels of regulation because our Founders created two levels of government. Each level has enacted substantive statutes dealing with the same industries. The interactions between these two levels are guided and constrained by the Commerce Clause, the Tenth Amendment and the Supremacy Clause. Regulatory policy thus emerges from multiple intersections of federal and state constitutions, statutes, court orders and commission decisions.

These intersections can cause tension when technology, market structure, transactional practices and policy preferences change more rapidly than statutory authority. Much of the litigation and appellate reversals occur in the context of applying old statutes to modern contexts. Still, federal and state regulatory statutes, and the agencies implementing them, have a series of working models for state–federal interactions, including bright lines, federal policy enlisting states, state agencies enlisting federal support, joint boards, regional compacts and concurrent jurisdiction. As the concluding chapter will discuss, much work lies ahead to shape new policies, through legislation and commission orders, that bring out the best from these legal relationships.

---

154.   *Cf.* Wisconsin Electric Power Co., 79 FERC ¶ 61,158, at text accompanying n.425 (1997) ("We will not revisit our decision not to set the issue of the potential impairment of state regulation for hearing. We believe that the most appropriate fora for the parties, including the Wisconsin Commission, to consider the proposed merger's effect on state regulation is in proceedings before the state commissions themselves."). The companion volume on corporate structure, mergers and acquisitions will address in detail how both state and federal agencies address these transactions.

Federal and state utility commissions are of course not the only stops merger applicants need to make. The Federal Trade Commission and U.S. Department of Justice, as well as their state counterparts, will usually play a role.

CHAPTER THIRTEEN
Jurisdiction's Future

Since regulatory law's beginnings a century ago, much about utility service has changed. Market structures, products and services, sellers and buyers, regulatory techniques and federal–state relations—all are in motion. Yet regulation's foundational legal principles remain in force. The statutory "just and reasonable" standard guards against monopoly markets' tendencies toward exploitation, inefficiency and indifference while protecting shareholders from regulatory capriciousness. The statutory prohibition against "undue preference" is still the small entrants' slingshot in their battle for access to incumbent-controlled bottlenecks. The Constitution's Takings and Due Process Clauses continue to protect shareholders and landowners from regulatory confiscation. The Supremacy Clause allows Congress to adjust federal–state jurisdictional relationships, subject to the state-protective limits in the Commerce Clause and Tenth Amendment. There is nothing "old world" about the law of public utility performance. It continues to allocate powers and protections among legislators, regulators, sellers, buyers, landowners and others affected by our infrastructural industries. Utility law's past is very much a part of the present.

These legal principles also provide stability for an uncertain future. Thirty years ago, utilities' obligations and activities were well-defined. Utilities issued debt and equity, built infrastructure, sold utility service and charged regulated rates. Regulators' roles were comparably clear: They approved financings, authorized and sited infrastructure, established quality of service standards and set rates. The utility's job was to provide its customers defined services at reasonable rates while earning a fair return for shareholders. The commission's job was to protect customers from monopoly abuse while keeping the utilities healthy.

Regulatory life is no longer so simple. Today's commissions design programs, make markets, collect and disburse funds, oversee construction projects, protect the environment, promote economic development, stimulate renewable energy and energy efficiency, host interest group gatherings and broker compromises. These activities are bumping up against statutory boundaries—exposing mismatches between expanding public needs and traditional regulatory powers and inviting the aggrieved to accuse commissions of exceeding their authority. When these disputes reach the courts, judges focus on three questions:

1. Is the commission pursuing an authorized *goal?* The traditional goals are adequate service, reasonable rates and reasonable returns. The expanded goals include diverse energy sources, increased access to telecommunications technology, economic development and environmental protection.

2. Is the commission performing an authorized *role?* The traditional roles are setting rates, establishing and enforcing standards, and controlling market entry. The expanded roles include changing customer behavior; restructuring markets; and administering programs for energy conservation, renewable energy and consumer education.

3. Assuming the commission is performing an authorized role to achieve an authorized goal, is the commission basing its decisions on authorized *criteria*? Traditional criteria were cost and need. Expanded criteria include environmental effects, aesthetic values, market competitiveness, labor–management peace, economic growth, and respect for historic and indigenous sites.[1]

These three dimensions—goals, roles and criteria—define how legislatures delegate authority. So when commission aspirations exceed legislative clarity, courts push back. The risk of judicial reversal

increases when regulators (1) pursue state goals without a clear statutory basis; (2) play a new role without sufficiently delegated authority; (3) make decisions based on criteria that are not aligned with explicit goals, or (4) balance criteria without a statutory preference or balancing test.[2]

As the regulatory profession continues to search for the best mix of incumbents and newcomers, of monopoly services and competitive services, of legislative roles and commission roles, this risk is a constant. There will always be friction between new policy aspirations and existing statutory boundaries. But the process of change will be smoother if decisionmakers and practitioners identify the uncertainties before they become conflicts. This concluding chapter therefore raises, for each of this volume's Parts, key questions that deserve our attention.

13.A. Market structure

13.A.1. Evaluating alternative arrangements

Part 1, on market structure, described our four-decade experiment in converting monopoly markets to competitive markets. To evaluate this effort, policymakers are asking these questions:

1. For each product and service provided by markets in which a utility is a participant: Is the market performing to its full potential, in terms of cost, quality, innovation and responsiveness to consumers?

2. If not, what feature(s) of the market structure must change to improve performance? Is it, for example, the array of sellers, their market shares, their incentives (both positive and negative), the costs of entry and exit, or the actions or inactions of regulators?

3. To induce improvement, should regulators focus on the performance of a particular company, the performance of the market as a whole, or both? Each focus produces a

---

1. The goal-role-criteria analysis was introduced in a seminal paper, ERIC FILIPINK, SERVING THE "PUBLIC INTEREST": TRADITIONAL VS. EXPANSIVE UTILITY REGULATION (National Regulatory Research Institute 2009), *available at* http://www.nrri.org/pubs/multiutility/NRRI_filipink_public_interest_jan10-02.pdf.
2. *Id.* at 5–6.

different trajectory of questions. For example, when a utility proposes a merger so it can be "more competitive," is the appropriate regulatory focus on that single utility or the entire market? This year's market or the next decade's market? Or: When a new competitor seeks entry into a historically monopolistic market, should regulators encourage the entry because it increases diversity, innovation and the pressure to perform; or discourage the entry because it may reduce economies of scale or put the incumbent at risk?

4. Is broadband a natural monopoly that requires a certified, exclusive franchise accompanied by regulatory oversight? If so, through what process should that franchise be awarded? First-come-first-awarded, or competition based on merits? Or is broadband a potentially competitive product and, if so, what steps are necessary to eliminate unearned incumbent advantages and attract multiple competitors? Is the bundling of content and delivery pro-competitive packaging or anti-competitive tying; or is it somewhere in between, where antitrust law tolerates it but alert regulation can guide it? Which of the separation options discussed in Chapter 4.B.5—functional unbundling, corporate unbundling, independent operation, divestiture—are appropriate?

5. Smart grid is a goal, not a product. What are the specific products and services necessary to make a grid "smart"? What are the metrics for measuring benefits and costs? Over what time span and for which segments of the population? Which of these products and services are natural monopolies and which are potentially competitive services? Should the provider of the monopoly features be allowed also to provide competitive features, or does the risk of favoritism and undue discrimination exceed the consumer benefit of vertical economies? The preceding paragraph's questions about broadband apply also.

6. For customers seeking to "go off the grid" (e.g., substituting cell phones for wireline, solar panels for utility delivery, neighborhood microgrids for traditional distribution systems, inside-the-fence generators for utility-owned generation), what is their responsibility to help maintain the embedded infrastructure that (a) was built for them long before these options emerged, and (b) stands ready to back them up when their own equipment fails to satisfy their full needs? Is there a societal risk that the better-informed and better-off can "leave the system" while the less-endowed have to stay and pay for it?

7. What is the incumbent's appropriate tenure? Ten years, fifty years, permanent, or indefinite? The choice between supplier monopoly and supplier diversity is a choice between customer convenience and customer choice, supply certainty and supply risk, price predictability and price uncertainty, concentrated political power and multiple political voices. By what process should we weigh these values? In decisions about market structure, how do we reduce the influence of inertia? Which decisions belong in the legislatures and which in the commissions?

13.A.2. Defining obligatory service

1. The purpose of regulation is performance—of the market, of individual sellers and of consumers. When we judge a utility's performance, we ask: How well does it carry out its obligation to serve? Answering that question requires one to define the service that is the utility's obligation to provide. Is it the bundle of activities consumers have always received, or is it only that portion of the traditional bundle that remains strictly a natural monopoly? What roles should regulation play in redefining the obligatory service?

2. A current example of the question: Four states (Hawaii, Maine, Oregon, Vermont) have transferred all or part of the energy efficiency role to a non-utility franchisee or contractor. In those states, the incumbent utility's obligation is to procure and deliver the power necessary to meet the demand that remains after energy efficiency has done its work. This service obligation is an obligation to produce (or procure) and deliver. In the other 46 states, the utility's obligation includes both the production and delivery job and the energy efficiency job. The utility must rank its options, then exploit the lowest cost options until some other lower cost option displaces them. If energy conservation is lower cost than energy production, the prudence standard requires the utility to pursue energy conservation. If action is prudent, then inaction is imprudent. Is the commission ready to apply this logic, by calibrating compensation to performance? Will compensation be sufficient inducement, or is market structure change—such as transferring the utility's energy efficiency role to others—a more reliable, less expensive solution? What facts must we gather from these experiments to know the answer?

13.A.3. Universal service

1. For which aspects of traditional utility service should there remain a government-sanctioned, last resort provider? Should the terms of service be convenient and predictable, out of sympathy for the non-choosing and choiceless; or inconvenient and uncertain, to induce citizens to shop and thereby help competition develop?

2. Is the decision to preserve the last resort option a political choice, whose cost should be borne by taxpayers? Or is it a regulatory policy decision, whose cost should be borne by utility customers? What are the criteria for drawing that line?

13.A.4. Other features

1. Incumbent utilities have enjoyed a unique power (the power of eminent domain) and a unique protection (insulation from liability for ordinary negligence).[3] When we open formerly monopolistic markets to competition, how should we weigh the trade-offs between (a) making these powers and protections generally available to all competitors, and (b) making competition uneven by granting these powers and protections only to the incumbent?

---

3. *See* Chapters 2.E (eminent domain) and 2.F (negligence liability).

2. Regulators establish standards for service quality. What constitutes quality—download speed, supplier responsiveness, diversity of offerings, customer opportunity to combine services from multiple suppliers? By what process should we make these decisions? Which aspects of these decisions belong with legislatures and which with commissions?

13.B. Pricing

Historically, utility pricing focused on satisfying the "revenue requirement": allocating to every customer slivers of the utility's total fixed and variable costs, so that the sum of all customer payments equals the utility's revenue requirement, then raising or lowering the rates prospectively as actual costs and sales vary from predictions. The revenue requirement was central to regulation because the utility's financial strength was central to customer service.

When setting prices today, regulators have two additional purposes: induce efficient consumer behavior, and condition utility compensation on performance. Performance consists not only of efficient, cost-effective hourly and daily operations, but also preparedness for storms, terrorism, environmental regulation and universal broadband access. These new concerns have spawned, in some states, two types of pricing changes: (a) changes in price-setting, such as peak and off-peak pricing (sometimes even hourly pricing) so that prices track actual operating cost, as well as congestion, rather than merely allocate shares of total annual cost; and (b) changes in revenue requirement procedure, where surcharges and riders reduce the risk of non-recovery while they channel dollars toward specified actions.

1. Do these changes still produce the revenue stability necessary for the utility's financial health? Is there a conflict between (a) keeping the utility financially healthy and (b) holding it accountable for its performance? If so, what are the ways to escape or reduce the conflict?

2. Does targeted compensation (i.e., riders and surcharges) produce in the utility full-throated commitment to the public interest, or only narrow pursuit of reward-through-compliance?[4]

3. Commissions have allowed imprudent costs in rates when disallowance of the imprudent amount would leave the incumbent unable to serve. While possibly rational in the short term, is this policy wise for the long term, or does it invite suboptimal performance by entities that are "too big to fail"? Concern with the incumbent's ability to serve exists only when there is no alternative to the incumbent. When there are alternatives, the commission is free to impose consequences commensurate with poor performance. When is the right time to consider and create alternatives—before or after the next bet-the-company action?

---

4. As embodied by "The rat must smell the cheese," the oft-repeated, oft-quoted creed of John Rowe, outgoing CEO of Exelon Corp. *See, e.g., Outline for John Rowe's Keynote Speech at American Council for an Energy Efficient Economy*, 1 (Sept. 28, 2009), http://www.exeloncorp.com/assets/newsroom/speeches/docs/spch_Rowe_ACEE.pdf.

4. Prudence review has most often focused on actions: infrastructure built unnecessarily or too expensively. What about inactions? Inaction on climate change exposes companies and customers to large environmental compliance costs later. Failure to set prices that discourage over-consumption, and failure to educate consumers about conservation, lead to unnecessary construction later. When there is an immediate need for capacity, conservation options take a back seat because they won't bear fruit in time. How can the regulator use these occasions to prevent repetition, to ensure that alternatives to capacity become part of the plan before the capacity is needed? What are the ways to hold utilities accountable for past inactions that leave commissions with lousy options?

13.C. Federal–state jurisdictional relationships
13.C.1. Interdependencies

Water, telecommunications and gas need electricity to operate; electricity and gas need telecommunications and water to operate; electricity and water need gas; everyone needs transportation. While interdependence implies vulnerability, it also offers opportunity; in particular, the opportunity to create new services that empower more customers. The prominent example is smart grid, whose infrastructure combines inputs from both telecommunications and electricity, helping customers to shape their demands and stimulating new competitors to satisfy those demands. This infrastructural intertwining requires us to revisit jurisdictional boundaries drawn decades ago. At the federal level, energy regulation and telecommunications regulation reside in different agencies. At the state level, they usually sit in the same commission, but often subject to different statutes. To produce the best regulatory decisions, we will need to revisit these regulatory boundaries. As I explained in a prior paper:

> Decisionmakers face the challenge of determining whether, where, how, and when to integrate broadband networks to support smart grid connectivity, for individual utilities and across the nation's three interconnected electric power systems, and how to do so cost-effectively. This effort will require not only billions in investment dollars, but also clear guidance from policymakers: guidance about performance expectations and about the roles, responsibilities, and rights of incumbent electric utilities, alternative power suppliers, telecommunications companies, and other service providers. Since policymaking guidance comes from statutes and regulatory actions, guidance clarity will require jurisdictional clarity. Producing that jurisdictional clarity presents a challenge, given the many decisionmakers involved. There must be consistent decisionmaking among four national entities (Federal Communications Commission (FCC), Federal Energy Regulatory Commission (FERC), National Institute of Standards and Technology (NIST), and Congress) and at least 104 state entities (52 state and local regulatory agencies and, potentially, 52 state and local legislative bodies). The success of this endeavor will depend on each

of these entities' answering—explicitly, consistently, and in advance of major expenditures—at least seven distinct questions:

1.   Do they share the same mission, and if not, are the differences compatible?
2.   Can each of the policymakers and the industries they oversee carry out a multi-discipline initiative under existing single discipline statutes?
3.   Can the parties execute a coherent national policy within a diverse regulatory system in which the broadest authority resides at the state level?
4.   Will policymakers authorize recovery of and returns on investment sufficient to induce long-term capital investments during an era when customers insist on keeping rates low?
5.   How do the regulators or legislators induce utility innovation—or penalize its absence?
6.   How do policymakers ensure that incumbent utilities plan and operate evenhandedly, where the utility has incentive and opportunity to exploit its special status?
7.   How can decisionmakers achieve industry-wide acceptance of the smart grid's public interest prerequisites?[5]

13.C.2. Obligation to serve

Our utilities' obligation to serve has been rooted historically in state law. With growing interconnectedness and new interdependencies, do we need to revisit this decision? Is there a national interest in guaranteed service for electricity, gas, water and telecommunications? Do the "network effects" (the benefit to all of connecting to all) justify making the service affordable? When states repeal the incumbent's obligation to serve, as some have for traditional telephone service, should the nation be indifferent or should it step in? If so, for what levels and types of services?

13.C.3. Infrastructure readiness

We depend on our utilities to (a) maintain their existing plant, (b) expand that plant to meet new needs and goals (like population growth, educational objectives, business development and remote delivery of medical services), and (c) protect it from bad weather and terrorist attack. Where the utilities' obligation to serve is rooted in state law, it is state law that regulates readiness. But there is risk of state underinvestment due to the classic problem of externalities: the benefits of one state's investment will accrue in part to other states, and the harm from one state's underinvestment will land in part on other states.

---

5.   Scott Hempling, *Broadband's Role in Smart Grid's Success: Seven Jurisdictional Challenges, in* BROADBAND NETWORKS, SMART GRIDS AND CLIMATE CHANGE 75 (Eli Noam, Lorenzo Maria Pupillo & Johann Kranz eds., 2012).

Alfred Kahn explained the externality concept well. His example of negative externality: "Your very presence on this planet takes up space that could otherwise be empty, blocks my view and, through your demand for food, induces farmers to use just a little more insecticide that helps pollute my lakes." His example of positive externality: "It is in *my* interest to have you use water freely—perhaps more freely than you would if you had to pay the marginal cost of supplying it to you—especially if I ride on the subway next to you."[6]

The risk of state underinvestment led Congress in 2005 to create a national regulatory structure for electricity reliability, one that preempted inconsistent state standards.[7] In what other areas should we adopt new federal policies, whether framed as guidance to states or mandates to utilities, to ensure that infrastructure modernization meets national standards?

13.D. Corporate structure and changes in control

In the 20th century, the corporate structure of electric and gas utilities passed through several stages: from (a) local ownership of vertically integrated utilities, to (b) holding company empires of scattered utility properties mixed with non-utility businesses, built by leveraging the local utilities' market power and milking their customers, to (c) the break-ups required by the Public Utility Holding Company Act of 1935, to (d) PUHCA's 2005 repeal, allowing any company to acquire any utility asset anywhere. Similar corporate structure change has occurred in telecommunications, from the Bell System's longstanding monopoly to the 1984 breakup to today's reconsolidations authorized by the 1996 Act.

Since the 1980s, utilities have been merging and reorganizing without predictable, consistent regulatory guidance. Antitrust remains available to block anti-competitive actions. But because its principles are largely court-made, its practical influence varies with plaintiff litigation resources, Attorney General priorities and trial court outcomes. Further, antitrust law prevents only anti-competitive actions; it does not inject and nurture competition. Regulatory law, at the federal and state levels, also yields varied results. Some commissions interpret their corporate reorganization statutes to require "no harm" while other commissions require some benefits. Few commissions have articulated a vision that guides corporate structure planners toward couplings that place the public interest first.

Although there have been dozens of mergers since the mid-1980s, there are dozens more to go before we reach humorist Art Buchwald's prediction of just two remaining conglomerates, when "every company west of the Mississippi will have merged into one giant corporation known as Samson Securities[, and] [e]very company east of the Mississippi

---

6. 1 ALFRED KAHN, THE ECONOMICS OF REGULATION: PRINCIPLES AND INSTITUTIONS 193–94 (1970; 1988) (emphasis in original).
7. *See* Chapters 3.B.4 and 12.C.1.e.

will have merged under an umbrella corporation known as the Delilah Company."[8] There is, therefore, still time to ask and answer the questions necessary to create policies that give the necessary guidance. Those questions include the following:

1. Are the markets that are producing utility mergers and acquisitions disciplined by effective competition? Or is effective competition impossible because the merging parties are entities with state-granted monopolies and captive customers, supported by a regulatory infrastructure committed to keeping them healthy?

2. Even in markets where there is no longer a government-granted monopoly, such as long-distance, wireless and some local telephone markets, does the century-long history of government influence make market forces an unreliable source of benefit–cost discipline in merger transactions?

3. For "no harm" statutes, does "harm" mean only "making customers worse off relative to the pre-merger status quo"? Or does it mean "failure to produce the customer benefits that the best-performing company would provide"? That is, does "harm" occur when a merger focuses on its promoters' market-growing goals rather than the customers' need for the best performers?

4. Also emerging is a trend opposite to consolidation: the decentralization and diversification of supply. As discussed in Chapter 2.A.2, technology now allows some customers to self-generate, form neighborhood "microgrids," and create other ways to reduce dependence on the traditional utility. Meanwhile, independent entrants are breaking into the generation and even transmission sectors. Is this decentralizing potential consistent with economies of scale and scope? If so, what are the risks that incumbents will use consolidations to gain first-mover advantage in immature markets, thereby reducing entry by newcomers?

This last subsection, on corporate structure, mergers and acquisitions, will be the focus of the companion volume to the current book. I hope it stimulates reader comments that contribute to that volume.

* * *

The questions in all four of these areas—market structure, pricing, jurisdiction and corporate structure—are far from complete. I leave it to readers to raise more, and provide answers, as they pursue careers in the regulation of public utility performance.

---

8.   Art Buchwald, *Samson Marries Delilah*, THE VICTORIA ADVOCATE (July 27, 1985), http://news.google.com/newspapers?id=Wy1JAAAAIBAJ&sjid=q38MAAAAIBAJ&pg=6037%2C1089581 (republishing column from 1966).

SELECTED BIBLIOGRAPHY

Books

ABA Section of Antitrust Law. *Antitrust Law Developments (Seventh)*. 2012.

Areeda, Phillip E., and Herbert Hovenkamp. *Antitrust Law: An Analysis of Antitrust Principles and Their Application*. 3d ed. 2006. Supp. 2012.

Astrachan, James B., et al. *The Law of Advertising*. 2012.

Baumol, William J., John C. Panzar, and Robert D. Willig. *Contestable Markets and the Theory of Industry Structure*. 1982.

Benjamin, Stuart Minor, et al. *Telecommunications Law and Policy*. 3d ed. 2012.

Berresford, John W. "Amendments to Section 332—Mobile Radio." In *The Communications Act: A Legislative History of the Major Amendments, 1934-1996*, ed. Max D. Paglin. 1999.

Bosselman, Fred, et al. *Energy Economics and the Environment*. 2000.

Bressman, Lisa, Edward Rubin, and Kevin Stack. *The Regulatory State*. 2010.

Breyer, Stephen G., and Richard B. Stewart. *Administrative Law and Regulatory Policy*. 1979.

Brotman, Stuart N. *Communications Law and Practice*. 2012.

Byrnes, William. "Telecommunications Regulation: Something Old and Something New." In *The Communications Act: A Legislative History of the Major Amendments, 1934-1996*, ed. Max D. Paglin. 1999.

Frankena, Mark, and Bruce Owen. *Electric Utility Mergers: Principles of Antitrust Analysis*. 1994.

Hempling, Scott. "Broadband's Role in Smart Grid's Success: Seven Jurisdictional Challenges." In *Broadband Networks, Smart Grids and Climate Change*, eds. Eli Noam, Lorenzo Maria Pupillo & Johann Kranz. 2012.

Hempling, Scott. *Preside Or Lead? The Attributes and Actions of Effective Regulators*. 2d ed. 2013.

Hovencamp, Herbert. *Federal Antitrust Policy: The Law of Competition and Its Practice*. 3d ed. 2005.

Huber, Peter W., and Michael K. Kellog. *Federal Telecommunications Law*. 2d ed. Supp. 2012.

Kahn, Alfred E. *The Economics of Regulation: Principles and Institutions*. 1988.

Keeton, W. Page, et al. *Prosser and Keeton on Torts*. 5th ed. 1984.

Kutler, Stanley I. *Privilege and Creative Destruction: The Charles River Bridge Case*. 1971.

Mogel, William A., ed. *Regulation of the Gas Industry*. 2012.

Mogel, William A., and David J. Muchow, eds. *Energy Law and Transactions*. 2012.

Noam, Eli. *Telecommunications Regulation Today and Tomorrow*. 1983.

Pierce, Richard J., and Ernest Gellhorn. *Regulated Industries in a Nutshell*. 4th ed. 1999.

Rotunda, Ronald D., and John E. Nowak. *Treatise on Constitutional Law: Substance and Procedure*. 2d ed. 1989.

Scherer, Frederick M., and David Ross. *Industrial Market Structure and Economic Performance*. 1990.

Schwartz, Bernard, ed. *The Economic Regulation of Business and Industry: A Legislative History of U.S. Regulatory Agencies*. 1973.

Shapiro, Sidney A., and Joseph P. Tomain. *Regulatory Law and Policy: Cases and Materials*. 2003.

Sidak, J. Gregory, and Daniel F. Spulber. *Deregulatory Takings and the Regulatory Contract: The Competitive Transformation of Network Industries in the United States*. 1997.

Tomain, Joseph P., and Richard D. Cudahy. *Energy Law in a Nutshell*. 2d ed. 2011.

Viscusi, W. Kip, Joseph E. Harrington, and John M. Vernon. *Economics of Regulation and Antitrust*. 4th ed. 2005.

Articles

"Management Invaded"—A Real or False Defense? 5 Stan. L. Rev. 110 (1952).

Areeda, Phillip. *Essential Facilities: An Epithet in Need of Limiting Principles*. 58 Antitrust L.J. 841 (1989).

Brennan, Timothy J., and James Boyd. *Stranded Costs, Takings, and the Law and Economics of Implicit Contracts*. 11 J. Reg. Econ 41 (1997).

Bronin, Sara C. *Curbing Energy Sprawl with Microgrids*. 43 Conn. L. Rev. 547 (2010).

Buchwald, Art. "Samson Marries Delilah." *The Victoria Advocate* (July 27, 1985).

Bush, Darren, and Carrie Mayne. *In (Reluctant) Defense of Enron: Why Bad Regulation Is to Blame for California's Power Woes (or Why Antitrust Law Fails to Protect Against Market Power When the Market Rules Encourage Its Use)*. 83 Or. L. Rev. 207 (2007).

Davies, Lincoln L. *State Renewable Portfolio Standards: Is There a "Race" and Is It "To the Top"?* 3 San Diego Journal of Climate & Energy Law 3 (2011-2012).

Dowling, Thomas R. *Attacks on Executives: Revival of the Invasion of Management Defense and Public Utility Autonomy.* 50 St. Louis L.J. 629 (2006).

Endrud, Nathan E. *State Renewable Portfolio Standards: Their Continued Validity and Relevance in Light of the Dormant Commerce Clause, the Supremacy Clause and Possible Federal Legislation.* 45 Harv. J. on Legis. 259 (Winter 2008).

Engel, Kristin. *The Dormant Commerce Clause Threat to Market Based Environmental Regulation: The Case of Energy Deregulation.* 26 Ecology L.Q. 243 (1999).

Ferrey, Steven. *Sustainable Energy, Environmental Policy, and States' Rights: Discerning the Future of Energy Through the Eye of the Commerce Clause.* 12 N.Y.U. Envtl. L.J. 507 (2004).

Frattaroli, Sarita. *Dodging the Bullet Again: Microsoft III's Reformulation of the Foremost Technological Tying Doctrine.* 90 B.U.L. Rev. 1909 (2010).

Jacobi, Patrick R. *Renewable Portfolio Standard Generator Applicability Requirements: How States Can Stop Worrying and Learn to Love the Dormant Commerce Clause.* 30 Vt. L. Rev. 1079 (Summer 2006).

Johnson, Regina R., and Bruce W. Radford. *Rating the Consumer Education Campaigns.* 138 Pub. Util. Fortnightly 38 (2000).

Jones, G. E. *Origins of the Certificate of Public Convenience and Necessity: Developments in the States, 1870-1920.* 79 Colum. Law Rev. 426 (1979).

Kessler, Barry J. *State Action Antitrust Exemption as Applied to Public Utility Regulation: Borough of Ellwood City v. Pennsylvania Power Co.* 20 Urb. L. Ann. 289 (1980).

Kwoka, John. *Vertical Economies in Electric Power: Evidence on Integration and Its Alternatives.* 20 Int'l J. Industrial Org. 653 (2002).

Kwoka, John, Michael Pollitt, and Sanem Sergici. *Divestiture Policy and Operating Efficiency in U.S. Electric Power Distribution.* 38 J. Reg. Econ. 86 (2010).

Lavey, Warren *The Public Policies That Changed the Telephone Industry into Regulated Monopolies: Lessons from Around 1915.* 39 Fed. Com. L. J. 171 (1987).

Littlechild, Stephen C. *The Nature of Competition and the Regulatory Process,* in "Effective Competition" in Telecommunications, Rail and Energy Markets. *Intereconomics*, Volume 46, Number 1, January/February (2011). doi: 10.1007/s10272-011-0362-y

Marritz, Robert. *The Case for Regional Power Planning Councils.* ElectricityPolicy. com (2010).

McCaffre, John E. Morgan Stanley Capital Group Inc. v. Public Utility District No. 1 *Revisits the* Mobile-Sierra *Doctrine: Some Answers, More Questions.* 30 Energy L. J. 53 (2009).

Meeks, James E. *Concentration in the Electric Power Industry: The Impact of Antitrust Policy.* 72 Colum. L. Rev. 64 (1972).

Pierce, Richard J. *Reconstituting the Natural Gas Industry from Wellhead to Burnertip.* 25 Energy L.J. 57 (2004).

Pierce, Richard J. *The State of the Transition to Competitive Markets in Natural Gas and Electricity.* 15 Energy L.J. 323 (1994).

Posner, Richard A. *Natural Monopoly & Its Regulation.* 21 Stan. L. Rev. 548 (1999).

Reiter, Harvey. *Competition and Access to the Bottleneck: The Scope of Contract Carrier Regulation under the Federal Power and Natural Gas Acts.* 18 Land & Water L. Rev. 1 (1983).

Reiter, Harvey. *The Contrasting Policies of the FCC and FERC Regarding the Importance of Open Transmission Networks in Downstream Competitive Markets.* 57 Fed. Comm. L.J. 243 (2005).

Renda, Andrea. *Catch Me If You Can! The Microsoft Saga and the Sorrows of Old Antitrust.* 1 Erasmus L. and Econ. Rev. 1 (2004).

Renda, Andrea. *Competition-Regulation Interface in Telecommunications: What's Left of the Essential Facility Doctrine.* 34 Telecomm. Policy 23 (2010).

Richards, Eric L. *Exploring the Far Reaches of the State Action Exemption: Implications for Federalism.* 57 St. John's L. Rev. 274 (1983).

Selwyn, Lee, and Helen Golding. *Revisiting the Regulatory Status of Broadband Internet Access: A Policy Framework for Net Neutrality and an Open Competitive Internet.* 63 Fed. Com. L.J. 9194 (2010).

Sheldrew, Judy. *Shutting the Barn Door before the Horse is Stolen: How and Why State Public Utility Commissions Should Regulate Transactions between a Public Utility and Its Affiliates.* 4 Nev. L.J. 164, 167 (2003).

Stine, Aaron C., and Eric D. Gorman. *Putting a Lid on State-Sanctioned Cartels: Why the State Action Doctrine in its Current Form Should Become a Remnant of the Past.* 66 U. Miami L. Rev. 123 (2011).

Trujillo, Elizabeth . *State Action Antitrust Exemption Collides with Deregulation: Rehabilitating the Foreseeability Doctrine.* 11 Fordham J. Corp. & Fin. L. 349 (2006).

Twaite, Kari. *Monopoly Money: Reaping the Economic and Environmental Benefits of Microgrids in Exclusive Utility Service Territories.* 34 Vt. Law Rev. 975 (2010).

Reports and Papers

Barnes, Justin. *Renewable Portfolio Standards Update: 2012's Compliance Modifications, Progress and Prognostications.* The Renewable Energy Markets Association (2012).

Bluhm, Peter, and Phyllis Bernt. *Carriers of Last Resort: Updating a Traditional Doctrine.* National Regulatory Research Institute (2009).

Bluhm, Peter, and Sherry Lichtenberg. *Fundamentals of Telecommunications Regulation: Markets, Jurisdiction, and Challenges.* National Regulatory Research Institute (2011).

Brockway, Nancy. *Advanced Metering Infrastructure: What Regulators Need to Know About Its Value to Residential Customers.* National Regulatory Research Institute (2008).

Congressional Budget Office. *Electric Utilities: Deregulation and Stranded Costs* (1998).

Elefant, Carolyn, and Ed Holt. *The Commerce Clause and Implications for State Renewable Portfolio Standard Programs.* Clean Energy States Alliance (2011).

European Regulators' Group for Electricity and Gas (ERGEG). *Smart Metering with a Focus on Electricity Regulation.* E07-RMF-04-03 (2007).

Federal Communications Commission. *Connecting America: The National Broadband Plan* (2010).

Federal Energy Regulatory Commission. *Final Report on Price Manipulation in Western Markets, Fact-Finding Investigation of Potential Manipulation of Electric and Natural Gas Prices.* Docket No. PA02-2-000 (2003).

Federal Energy Regulatory Commission. *Survey on Demand Response, Time-Based Rate Programs/Tariffs and Advanced Metering Infrastructure—Glossary* (2008).

Filipink, Eric. *Serving the "Public Interest": Traditional vs. Expansive Utility Regulation.* National Regulatory Research Institute (2009).

Gaynor, Daniel E. *Technological Tying.* FTC Bureau of Economics. Working Paper No. 284 (2006).

Golkar, Masoud Aliakbar. *Power Quality in Electric Networks: Monitoring, and Standards.* International Conference on Renewable Energies and Power Quality (2007). http://www.icrepq.com/icrepq07/273_aliakbar.pdf (accessed July 22, 2013).

Hempling, Scott. *Riders, Trackers, Surcharges, Pre-Approvals and Decoupling: How Do They Affect the Cost of Equity?* ElectricityPolicy.com (2012).

Hempling, Scott, and Scott Strauss. *Pre-Approval Commitments: When and Under What Conditions Should Regulators Commit Ratepayer Dollars to Utility-Proposed Capital Projects?* National Regulatory Research Institute (2008).

Hom, S., and C. Pittiglio. *Standard Review Plan on Transfer and Amendment of Antitrust License Conditions and Antitrust Enforcement.* U.S. Nuclear Regulatory Commission, NUREG-1574, Rev. 2 (2007).

Kranz, Johann J., and Arnold Picot. *Toward an End-to-End Smart Grid: Overcoming Bottlenecks to Facilitate Competition and Innovation in Smart Grids.* National Regulatory Research Institute (2011).

Lay, Tillman L. *Taking Another Look at Federal/State Jurisdictional Relationships in the New Broadband World.* National Regulatory Research Institute (2011).

Morris, Derek. *Dominant Firm Behaviour under UK Competition Law.* Paper presented to Fordham Corporate Law Institute, Thirtieth Annual Conference on International Antitrust Law and Policy, October 23-24 (2003).

O'Connor, Phillip R. *Retail Electric Choice: Proven, Growing, Sustainable.* COMPETE Coalition (2012).

Rader, Nancy, and Scott Hempling. *The Renewables Portfolio Standard: A Practical Guide.* National Association of Regulatory Utility Commissions (2001).

Stumberg, Robert. *Management Prerogatives in Utility Regulation: Guidance for State Regulators.* Unpublished Paper (on file with author).

Tabors Caramanis and Associates. *Horizontal Market Power in Wisconsin Electricity Markets: A Report to the Public Service Commission of Wisconsin* (2000).

The Regulatory Assistance Project. *Revenue Regulation and Decoupling: A Guide to Theory and Application* (2011).

Tierney, Susan F. *ERCOT Texas's Competitive Power Experience: A View from the Outside Looking In.* Analysis Group (2008).

U.S. Department of Justice and Federal Trade Commission. *Horizontal Merger Guidelines* (1992, rev. 1997).

TABLE OF AUTHORITIES

Court Cases

Principal cases appear in boldface. Agency issuances are listed in a separate section.

Louisiana Energy & Power Auth. v. FERC, 141 F.3d 364 (D.C. Cir. 1998), 149n87

Louisiana Power & Light Co., FPC v., 406 U.S. 621 (1972), 367n36

Louisiana Pub. Serv. Comm'n v. FCC, 476 U.S. 355 (1986), 217n3, 379nn82–83, 388n109

Louisville & Nashville R.R. Co. v. Maxwell, 237 U.S. 94 (1915), 304n2, 319n43

M

MacDonald v. FPC, 505 F.2d 355 (D.C. Cir. 1974), 262n177

Maine v. Taylor, 477 U.S. 131 (1986), 372n54, 372n56

Maine Pub. Utils. Comm'n v. FERC, 520 F.3d 464 (2008), 350n33

Maislin Indus., U.S., Inc. v. Primary Steel, Inc., 497 U.S. 116 (1990), 305n7, 311, 311nn18–19, 321n49

Marcus v. AT&T Corp., 138 F.3d 46 (2d Cir. 1998), 321n49

Marine Bancorp., United States v., 418 U.S. 602 (1974), 130n36

Market Street Ry. Co. v. Railroad Comm'n of Cal., 324 U.S. 548 (1945), 105, 105n124, 106nn125–126, 108, 228n41, 252n142

Maryland v. United States, 460 U.S. 1001 (1983), 172n154, 207nn45–46

Massachusetts v. United States, 729 F.2d 886 (1st Cir. 1984), 398n137

Massena, Town of v. Niagara Mohawk Power Corp., No. 79-CV-163, 1980 U.S. Dist. LEXIS 9382 (N.D.N.Y. 1980), 26n33

Matsushita Elec. Indus. Co. v. Zenith Radio Corp., 475 U.S. 574 (1986), 198n14

McCulloch v. Maryland, 17 U.S. (4 Wheat.) 316 (1819), 379n81

MCI Commc'ns Corp. v. AT&T, 708 F.2d 1081 (7th Cir. 1983), 81n47, 130n36, 135n51

MCI Commc'ns Corp. v. AT&T, 462 F. Supp. 1072 (N.D. Ill. 1978), 81n47

MCI Telecomms. Corp. v. AT&T Co., 512 U.S. 218 (1994), 79n36, 269n5, 304n1, 305n8, 358n2

MCI Telecomms. Corp. v. FCC, 580 F.2d 590 (D.C. Cir. 1978), 79n37

MCI Telecomms. Corp. v. FCC, 765 F.2d 1186 (D.C. Cir. 1985), 269nn4–5

MCI Worldcom, Inc. v. FCC, 209 F.3d 760 (D.C. Cir. 2000), 270n13

McPhee & McGinnity Co. v. Union Pac. R.R. Co., 158 F. 5 (8th Cir. 1907), 14n2

Microsoft Corp., United States v., 253 F.3d 34 (D.C. Cir. 2001), 200n25, 203n35, 203nn38–39

Midwestern Gas Transmission Co. v. East Tenn. Natural Gas Co., 36 FPC 61 (1966), *aff'd sub nom.* Midwestern Gas Transmission Co. v. FPC, 388 F.2d 444 (7th Cir. 1968), 235n75, 236n82, 243n114

Milwaukee & Suburban Transp. Corp. v. Public Serv. Comm'n of Wis., 108 N.W.2d 729 (Wis. 1961), 255n151

N

O

R

Agency Issuances

Decisions that start with an administrative opinion and then move into the courts are included here with the court action.

Transcontinental Gas Pipe Line Corp., 58 F.P.C. 2038 (1977), *aff'd & remanded sub nom.* Tennessee Gas Pipeline Co. v. FERC, 606 F.2d 1094 (D.C. Cir. 1979), 253n145

Transmission Planning and Cost Allocation by Transmission Owning and Operating Pub. Util., Order No. 1000, 136 FERC ¶ 61,051 (2011), *order on reh'g*, Order No. 1000-A, 139 FERC ¶ 61,132, *order on reh'g*, Order No. 1000-B, 141 FERC ¶ 61,044 (2012), *petition for review docketed,* 75n23, 93n97

Trunkline Gas Co., 95 FERC ¶ 61,337 (2001), 111n146

U

Use of Recording Devices in Connection with Tel. Servs., In the Matter of, 11 F.C.C. 1033 (1947), 169n146

Utah Associated Mun. Power Sys. v. PacifiCorp, 87 FERC ¶ 61,044 (1999), 162n128

Utah Power & Light Co., 45 FERC ¶ 61,095 (1988), 299n30

Utility Workers Union of Am. v. West Va.-Am. Water Co., Case No. 11-0740-W-C, 289 P.U.R.4th 507, 2011 W. Va. PUC LEXIS 1258 (W. Va. Pub. Serv. Comm'n May 31, 2011), 55n122

V

Verizon Commc'ns, Inc., Memorandum Opinion and Order, 20 FCC Rcd. 18,433 (2005), 83n64

Verizon New England Inc., 2004 Vt. PUC LEXIS 161 (Vt. Pub. Serv. Bd. Sept. 20, 2004), 50n107

Version 4 Critical Infrastructure Prot. Reliability Standards, Order No. 761, 139 FERC ¶ 61,058 (2012), 93n94

Virginia Elec. Power Co., 11 FERC ¶ 63,028 (1980), *aff'd*, 15 FERC ¶ 61,052 (1981), 236n84, 239n101, 248n127

W

Washington Util. & Transp. Comm'n v. Washington Natural Gas Co., 137 P.U.R.4th 335 (Wash. Utils. & Transp. Comm'n Sept. 28, 1992), 334n18

Washington Water Power Co., 83 FERC ¶ 61,097, *further order*, 83 FERC ¶ 61,282 (1998), 162n128

Weber v. Union Light, Heat and Power Co., Case No. 2000-066 2000 Ky. PUC LEXIS 1342 (Ky. Pub. Serv. Comm'n Aug. 4, 2000), 5n12

Western. Mass. Elec. Co., D.P.U. 95-86, 165 P.U.R.4th 70 (Mass. Dep't Pub. Util. 1995), 53nn115–116

Western Mass. Elec. Co., 23 FERC ¶ 61,025 (1983), 398n138

West Va.-Am. Water Co., Case No. 10-0920-W-42T (W. Va. Pub. Serv. Comm'n Apr. 18, 2011), 55n123

Federal Acts

Racketeer Influenced and Corrupt
Organizations (RICO) Act, 321

Securities Exchange Act of 1934,
135n47

Sherman Antitrust Act
generally, 26n35, 131n37, 132, 135,
138–139, 144, 196, 200, 317,
317n34
§ 2, 127–128, 127n27, 129,
147n76
§ 7, 316

Surface Mining and Control and
Reclamation Act, 361, 363–364

Telecommunications Act of 1996, codified
in scattered provisions of 47
U.S.C. §§ 151–714
generally, 80n44, 82–83, 82n53, 85,
86, 112, 122n18, 124n22, 125,
132, 146–147n76, 147, 152, 153,
155, 156, 156n112, 199n21, 201,
207, 209, 231, 281n51, 368, 379,
388n112, 396, 397
§ 601(b)(1), 134n46

State Acts

Connecticut Unfair Trade Practices Act,
90n85

Illinois Public Utilities Act, 209n53

Indiana Environmental Compliance Plan
Pre-Approval Act, 255

Mississippi Baseload Act, 256

New Jersey Electric Discount and Energy
Competition Act of 1999,
164n134, 191n3

Wisconsin Holding Company Act, 376

United States Code

5 U.S.C. § 706(2)(c), 365n30
15 U.S.C. § 2, 127n27
15 U.S.C. § 18, 179n173
15 U.S.C. § 79 *et seq.*, 164n132
15 U.S.C. § 717(b), 367n36, 373n62,
392n115, 393n119
15 U.S.C. § 717(c), 392n115, 393n115
15 U.S.C. § 717c(b), 149n85
15 U.S.C. § 717c(b)(1), 123n21
15 U.S.C. § 717c(e), 220n7, 330n16

15 U.S.C. § 717d(a), 149n85,
220n7
15 U.S.C. § 717f(h), 59n137
15 U.S.C. § 717p, 400n147
15 U.S.C. § 717t(1), 283n55
15 U.S.C. §§ 3301 *et seq.*, 77
16 U.S.C. § 152(b)(1), 392
16 U.S.C. § 796(18)(A), 73n10
16 U.S.C. §§ 824 *et seq.*, 400
16 U.S.C. § 824(b), 297n25, 367n35

INDEX

G

Gas utilities
bundled product, 76
city gate, 76
direct billing of gas production costs, 329
historical background, 76–77
local distribution companies (LDCs), 76, 78, 78n30, 111–112, 395
marketing data, 168–169
merchant function, 76, 93
non-rate features protected by filed rate doctrine, 318
pipeline companies, 77, 110–111, 144, 328
purchased gas adjustment (PGA), 329
retail gas, 124, 151–152
stranded investment, 98
sufficient competition, 208
technical quality, 45
vertically integrated, 76, 76n24
wellhead gas, 78
wholesale gas, 98, 124, 148
"Going off the grid," 406
Gross negligence, 65–66
Group self-service, 20–22
Gun possession within school zone, 362

H

Hawaii
bankruptcy orders, 49–50
energy efficiency contractor, 25–26
exclusive franchisee for specific service, 25, 33, 407
protection of in-state business, 374, 374n65
Health insurance, individual obligation to purchase, 362

Heating, ventilation, and air conditioning, 183
Holding companies
acquiring utilities, 40–41
cost allocation within, 294–295
state ban on out-of-state holding companies, 377–378
state regulation of structure and finance, 378
Home security, 184
Hydroelectric power, 143, 300–302, 308–309, 318, 370, 384–385, 386, 387

I

ILECs. *See* Incumbent local exchange carriers
Illinois
return-on-equity reductions, 51
statutory law, 48, 51
virtual monopoly, 41–42
Imprudence, 235
burdens of proof, 246–248
disallowance defense, 246
failure to heed official criticisms, 242–243
failure to oversee contractors and employees, 239–240
failure to secure remedies against erring supplier, 242–243
failure to use reasonable management practices, 239
financial consequences of cost disallowance, 250
imprudent action, 238–239
imprudent inaction, 243
imputing unearned revenues, 243–244
management prerogative, 246

P

Pacific Northwest Electric Power and Conservation Planning Council, 400

Pacific Northwest Electric Power Planning and Conservation Act of 1980, 400

Pennsylvania
eminent domain, 94
exclusive franchise, 86–88
retail competition, 88, 88n77

Perfect competition, 11

Performance failures. *See* Imprudence

Pole Attachments Act, 232, 232n60

Power quality, 19, 19n12

Predatory pricing, 197–198

Preemption. *See also* Supremacy Clause
Atomic Energy Act challenge, 381
Communications Act challenge, 392
conflict preemption, 381–382
express preemption, 379–380
Federal Power Act challenge, 384
field preemption, 380
Natural Gas Act challenge, 380–381
overview, 8
presumption against, 387–389

Price caps, 258

Pricing, 213–214. *See also* Anti-competitive pricing
cost-based rates, 213, 216. *See also* Cost-based rates
discriminatory. *See* Discrimination
future trends, 408–409
just and reasonable. *See* Just and reasonable prices
market-based rates, 213
overview, 7
retroactive ratemaking, 214

Privity, 64

Product promotion advantages, 179–180

Prudence principles, 235–236. *See also* Imprudence
burdens of proof, 246–248
cost recovery, 252
deference to utility expertise, 248–250
fact-intensive analysis, 237
facts known at time of decision, 237
future trends, 409
reasonable behavior based on industry norms, 236–237
rebuttable presumption of prudence, 246–248
uneconomic outcome but prudent actions, 251–252
unique role and duties of utility, 237

Public–private overlap, 43, 58–59

Public Utility Holding Company Act of 1935 (PUHCA), 72, 72n5, 75, 76, 76n24, 208, 382, 393, 393n117, 411

Public Utility Regulatory Policies Act of 1978 (PURPA), 73, 84, 208, 208n50, 364, 396

Q

Quality of service, 44–45, 70, 91–93
components of quality, 45–46
customer relations, 46
future trends, 408
meter accuracy, 46
reliability, 46
safety, 46
statutory bases, 44–45
technical quality, 45

R

Racial discrimination, 361